# Electric and Hybrid Vehicles

# Electric and Hybrid Vehicles
## Design Fundamentals

## Third Edition

Iqbal Husain

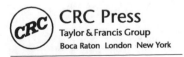

CRC Press
Taylor & Francis Group
Boca Raton London New York

CRC Press is an imprint of the
Taylor & Francis Group, an **informa** business

Third edition published 2021
by CRC Press
6000 Broken Sound Parkway NW, Suite 300, Boca Raton, FL 33487-2742

and by CRC Press
2 Park Square, Milton Park, Abingdon, Oxon, OX14 4RN

© 2021 Taylor & Francis Group, LLC

First edition published by CRC Press 2003
Second edition published by Routledge 2010
Third edition published by CRC Press 2021

CRC Press is an imprint of Taylor & Francis Group, LLC

ISBN: 978-1-138-59058-8 (hbk)
ISBN: 978-0-367-69393-0 (pbk)
ISBN: 978-0-429-49092-7 (ebk)

Typeset in Times
by codeMantra

# Contents

# Preface to the Third Edition

Automobile engineers of multiple disciplines collaborate to make the complex and intriguing technologies of a vehicle. The vehicle itself serves as an excellent and exciting system to educate students about electrical, mechanical and chemical engineering. The purpose of this textbook is to describe and present the vehicle from a systems engineering perspective in the context of modern electric and hybrid vehicles. Over the past decade, electric road transport technologies have advanced significantly that made it essential to include more of the evolving technologies and design elements of electric powertrain components in the third edition of this book.

The global sale of electric vehicles that include both battery electric vehicles (BEVs) and plug-in hybrid vehicles (PHEVs) exceeded the 5 million mark in 2019 with the ratio between BEVs and PHEVs tilting more toward the former. The adoption rate has been steadily increasing, taking only 6 months for 1 million BEVs to be sold as opposed to the 5 years it took for the first million BEVs to be sold. Environmental concerns and energy challenges prompted the societal demand for clean, efficient and sustainable vehicles for urban transportation. The market drivers are technology improvements and cost reduction in battery and powertrain components, tightening emission standards around the world, and investments in new business opportunities. Traditional original equipment manufacturers (OEMs) as well as new generation manufacturers are responding to the demand with many models of varying range and features.

This book will present a comprehensive systems-level perspective of electric and hybrid electric vehicles with emphasis on technical aspects, mathematical relationships and basic design guidelines. Additions in the third edition include analysis and design guidelines for electric powertrain components, particularly that of traction inverters, electric machines and motor drives. The technology trend to incorporate WBG power electronics and reduced rare-earth permanent magnet electric machines in the powertrain components has been highlighted. Charging stations are a critical component for the electric vehicle infrastructure, and hence, a chapter on vehicle interactions with the power grid has been added. Autonomous driving is another emerging technology which will become an integral part of modern vehicles equipped with either electric or internal combustion engines. A chapter on autonomous driving system architecture and the hardware and software needs for such systems has been included in this edition of the book. The platform has been set for systems-level simulations to develop models using various softwares used in academia and industry, such as MATLAB/Simulink, PLECS, PSIM, Motor-CAD and Altair Flux. Examples and simulation results are provided in this edition using these software tools. Contact information for obtaining these software products are provided for the users.

This book will provide the educational materials on electric and hybrid vehicles for classroom use and may also serve as a reference for the design and development of electric and hybrid vehicles and their components to a working engineer. Discussion on most topics has been limited to fundamentals only, considering the wide spectrum of technical aspects related to electric and hybrid vehicle systems. Appropriate references are given to direct the readers toward details on topics for further reading. The intent of the book is to provide the students and engineers with the necessary background for starting the design process and evaluating the relevant technologies.

The book, similar to the earlier editions, starts with a systems-level introduction to electric and hybrid vehicles along with the historical background of these vehicles in Chapter 1. The laws of physics that govern vehicle motion and roadway fundamentals are presented in Chapter 2. The design guidelines for the power and energy requirements based on force-velocity characteristics of ground vehicles are established in this chapter. The electric and hybrid vehicle architectures and powertrain component sizing requirements are addressed in Chapter 3. The autonomous vehicle architecture, and its hardware and software components are presented in Chapter 4.

Chapters 5 and 6 discuss the energy sources and energy storage systems for electric and hybrid vehicles. The electrochemical fundamentals of energy storage devices such as batteries, fuel cells, ultracapacitors, compressed air and flywheel are given in these chapters. Several battery models based on the fundamentals are presented, which will be useful for system simulation and prediction of terminal voltage-current characteristics.

Chapters 7 through 10 cover the powertrain electrical components. The various types of electric machines and their basic operating principles are discussed in Chapter 7, while the controls for AC electric motors are described in Chapter 8. The power electronic components required for static power conversion, charging station and for electric motor drives are presented in Chapter 9. The electric motor drives for both DC and AC types are presented in Chapter 10.

In-vehicle communication system design is an essential element for a modern vehicle. CAN communication network and protocols are described in Chapter 11. The chapter also discusses the controller implementations for different powertrain electronic control units. Vehicle interactions with the grid through fast chargers and charging stations are covered in Chapter 12.

Chapters 13 and 14 cover the mechanical components. The internal combustion engines suitable for hybrid vehicles are discussed in one chapter, while the power transmission components, brakes, and cooling systems are presented in the other chapter. Chapter 15 focuses on hybrid control strategies where several example strategies are given with emphasis on increased fuel economy and reduced emissions.

The book is intended to be used as a textbook for an undergraduate/beginning graduate-level course on electric and hybrid vehicles. The materials in this book are multidisciplinary enough to teach electrical, mechanical and chemical engineers all in one course utilizing the systems approach. The 15 chapters of the book can be covered in a three-credit, one-semester or in a four-credit, one-quarter course with emphasis on the systems rather than the components. In this case, Chapters 1 through 5, Chapter 11, Chapter 12 and Chapter 15 could be covered in depth, while the remaining chapters should be used lightly to introduce the electrical and mechanical components. This type of course will certainly mimic the real situation existing in many industries where multidisciplinary engineers work together to device a system and develop a product. Alternatively, the book can be used in a three-credit, one-semester or a four-credit, one-quarter course for electrical or mechanical engineering students with emphasis on either the electrical or the mechanical components.

For software products and tools useful for simulation analysis, please contact
*MATLAB and Simulink*:
The MathWorks, Inc.
E-mail: info@mathworks.com
Web: www.mathworks.com
*PLECS*:
Plexim, Inc.
E-mail: info@plexim.com
Web: www.plexim.com
*PSIM*:
Powersim, Inc.
E-mail: support@powersimtech.com
Web: www.powersimtech.com
*Motor-CAD*:
E-mail: info@ motor-design.com
Web: www.motor-design.com
*Altair Flux*:
Altair
Email at: www.altair.com/contact-us/
Web: www.altair.com/

# Acknowledgments

I would like to express my sincere gratitude to all those who helped me devotedly to complete the book. I am thankful to my current and former graduate students who helped me complete the third edition in several ways including contributing to materials on different topics, reviewing chapters and drawing figures for the book. I am thankful to Adam Stevens for contributions to the chapter on autonomous vehicles, to Dr. Md Sariful Islam for contributions to the chapter on electric machines, to Dr. M. A. Awal for contributions to the chapter on grid interaction of electric vehicles and to Yukun Luo for reviewing the chapter on vehicle controllers and communications. I am thankful to Dhrubo Rahman and Ritvik Chattopadhyay for creating many of the simulation example problems in the book. I am also thankful to Dr. Rajib Mikail, Dr. Ashfanoor Kabir, Dr. Li Yang, Dr. Siddharth Mehta, Sodiq Agoro and Taohid Latif who helped in different aspects of the book. I also thank Rawshan Ara Mowri for helping with the indexing of the book.

   The acceptance of the book as a text in several universities nationally and internationally provided the incentive to improve and complete the third edition. I offer my sincere gratitude to the many users of the first and second editions of the book, many of whom provided useful suggestions that helped enhance the book materials. I am particularly thankful to Professor Roydon Fraser of University of Waterloo, Professor Annette von Jouanne of Baylor University and Dr. Ir. G. Maarten Bonnema of University of Twente, The Netherlands for their very helpful suggestions for the third edition. I am especially thankful to Nora Konopka of Taylor and Francis Group for encouraging me to undertake the project on the book's third edition. Finally, my sincere apologies and heartfelt gratitude to my mother Mamataz, my wife, Salina, and my children Inan, Imon and Rushan who patiently stood by me with grave understanding and continuous support while I was preoccupied with the project.

**Iqbal Husain**
*Raleigh, NC*

# Author

**Dr. Iqbal Husain** is the ABB Distinguished Professor in the Department of Electrical & Computer Engineering at North Carolina State University, Raleigh, NC. He is also the Director of the FREEDM NSF Engineering Research Center and the Director of Power Electronics for the PowerAmerica Institute at North Carolina State University. Prior to joining NC State, he was at the University of Akron where he built a successful power electronics and motor drives program. He was a visiting Professor at Oregon State University, Corvallis, OR, in 2001. He worked as a summer researcher for Wright Patterson AFB Laboratories in 1996 and 1997. Professor Husain received his PhD in electrical engineering from Texas A&M University in 1993.

Professor Husain's research interests are in the areas of control and modeling of electrical drives, design of electric machines, systems controls for power conditioning circuits, electric and hybrid vehicles, and renewable energy systems. He has worked extensively with switched reluctance and permanent magnet motor drives in the areas of design optimizations, sensorless and high-performance controls, acoustic noise prediction and parameter identification methods. In the FREEDM center, his research is focused on power electronics integration into power systems. The primary applications of his work are in the transportation, automotive, aerospace and power industries. Professor Husain first developed a course on electric and hybrid vehicles in 1996 at the University of Akron prior to these cars gaining their popularity. He was the lead faculty advisor for the Department of Energy and General Motors sponsored *Challenge X: Crossover to Sustainable Mobility* competition between 2004 and 2008.

Professor Husain, along with his graduate students, received many prize paper and best paper awards in IEEE conferences, IEEE Transactions and other symposiums over the years. He received the 2006 SAE Vincent Bendix Automotive Electronics Engineering Award, the 2004 College of Engineering Outstanding Researcher Award, the 2000 IEEE Third Millennium Medal and the 1998 IEEE-IAS Outstanding Young Member Award. He is the recipient of the National Science Foundation CAREER Award in 1997. He became an IEEE Fellow in 2009. He was the Distinguished Lecturer of IEEE Industry Applications Society for 2012–2013. He served as the Editor-in-Chief of the IEEE Electrification Magazine from 2015 to 2019.

# 1 Introduction to Electric and Hybrid Vehicles

The transition to electric road transport technologies has gained significant momentum over the past decade aided by both the technological advancements over the years and the growing interest among consumers. Electric vehicles (EVs) are now being offered with improved performances and capabilities such as increased acceleration, extended range and fast charging options. The global sale of EVs that include both battery electric vehicles (BEVs) and plug-in hybrid vehicles (PHEVs) exceeded the 5 million mark in 2019 with the ratio between BEVs and PHEVs titling more towards the former. Whereas it took 5 years for the first million EVs to be sold, it took only 6 months for the next million and the rate of adoption has been ever increasing. The compelling impetus to develop clean, efficient and sustainable vehicles for urban transportation stems from both environmental and economic considerations. Passenger vehicles constitute an integral part of our everyday life, yet the exhaust emissions of the conventional internal combustion engine vehicles (ICEVs) are to blame for the major source of urban pollution that causes the greenhouse effect leading to global warming [1]. The dependence on oil as the sole source of energy for passenger vehicles has economical and political implications, and the crisis will inevitably become acute as the oil reserve of the world diminishes. The number of automobiles in our planet exceeds 1.4 billion according to some estimates, and the increasing number of automobiles being introduced on the road every year is only adding to the pollution problem. There is also an economic factor that is inherent in the poor energy conversion efficiency of the internal combustion (IC) engines. When efficiency is evaluated on the basis of conversion from crude oil to traction effort at the wheels, the number for the alternative EVs is not significantly higher; however, it does make a difference. The emission due to power generation at localized plants is much easier to regulate than those emanating from ICEVs that are individually maintained and scattered all over the places. The people dwelling in cities are not exposed to power plant-related emissions, since these are mostly located outside urban areas. Furthermore, electric power can be generated using renewable sources such as hydro, wind and solar, which would provide the most environmentally friendly approach. The EVs enabled by high-efficiency electric motors and controllers, and powered from alternative energy sources provide the means for a clean, efficient and environmentally friendly urban transportation system. EVs are the only zero-emission vehicles (ZEVs) possible which provide the opportunity to curb the pollution problem in an efficient way.

EVs made their way into public use as early as in the middle of the 19th century, even before the introduction of gasoline-powered vehicles [2]. In 1900, 4,200 automobiles were sold, of which 40% were steam powered, 38% were electric powered and 22% were gasoline powered. However, the invention of the starter motor, improvements in mass production technology of gas-powered vehicles and inconvenience in battery charging led to the disappearance of EVs in the early 1900s. However, the environmental issues and the unpleasant dependence on oil led to the resurgence of interest in EVs in the 1960s. The growth in the enabling technologies over the next several decades and environmental and economic concerns renewed the interest in research and development for EVs.

The interest and research in EVs soared in the 1990s with the major automobile manufacturers embarking on plans for introducing their own EVs or hybrid electric vehicles (HEVs). General Motors introduced the first EV *Saturn EV1* for public usage in 1995, although to a limited market in California and Arizona. The vehicle has since been discontinued, but the event is undoubtedly a milestone in modern vehicle history. The consumer market is more interested in vehicles that can travel long distances on one full charge of the battery-pack. Another feature that the society desires is the reduction of the battery-pack charging time to a level comparable to that of filling up a gas tank.

The limited range of the battery-powered EVs led researchers and auto industries to search for alternatives in the 1990s. The aggressive efforts by the industry led to the rapid development of HEVs. Toyota led the way among the industries introducing the first production hybrid vehicle *Toyota Prius* in the late 1990s. Many other industries have since introduced hybrids for the consumers addressing the concerns about environmental pollution and excessive dependence on fossil fuels. The HEVs or simply hybrid vehicles use both electric machines and an IC engine for delivering the propulsion power; these vehicles have lower emissions compared to a similarly sized conventional ICEV resulting in less environmental pollution. The IC engine used in a hybrid vehicle is, of course, downsized compared to an equivalent ICEV. The IC engine in combination with the electric motor and an energy storage unit provides the extended range and curve down the pollution. The hybrid vehicle serves as a compromise for the environmental pollution problem and the limited range capabiltiy of a BEV. The hybrids are looked upon by many as a shorter-term solution until the range limitation and infrastucture problems of zero-emission EVs are solved.

After about a decade of reign of HEVs in the passenger road vehicle electrification sector, EVs started reappearing with battery-powered vehicles from pioneering companies like Tesla and Nissan. Although Tesla has started offering BEVs since 2008, those vehicles were targeted for a niche market in the domain of luxury vehicles. In 2011, Nissan offered the more affordable Nissan Leaf, which was soon followed by Ford with Ford Focus Electric. With rapid expansion of the global sales together with innovations in the electric powertrain, EVs are well on their way to sustainable mass-production market. Currently, traditional vehicle manufacturers and new generation EV manufacturers are all offering various types of EVs. In addition, charging stations are being installed in various urban and highway locations with many providing fast charging options. Several companies are offering wireless power chargers.

As the number of EVs plugging in into the power grid for charging the vehicle batteries is rising, the burden on the utility to deliver the electricity is also increasing. Along with the supply of electricity come the infrastructure needs where extensive charging outlets and stations are required to meet the needs of the growing EV market. As the number of EVs increase, a large number of vehicles will be connected to the power grid simultaneously, which may cause a significant threat to the quality and stability of the overall grid. Even connecting and charging a large number of EVs at the household level will significantly increase the power system's electricity demand. With increasing introduction of fast charging stations and superchargers, the electricity supply issue will need to be addressed by either the charging station owner or the utility since these EV charging requires a burst of power over a short period of time. The utility industry views the growth in EV as a business opportunity but is also cautious about asset expansion planning and reconfiguration planning of the power distribution infrastructure.

The limited range problem of BEVs can be overcome by adding a fuel cell engine that will generate electricity for the electric motors as long as fuel is available. The fuel cell is an electrochemical energy converter but has much higher efficiencies compared to a heat engine such as the IC engine. The fuel for these engines is hydrogen or gases from which hydrogen can be extracted. This concept has led to the development of fuel cell electric vehicles (FCEVs) and to the discussions on hydrogen economy. The fuel cells are currently available in very limited quantities as fuel cell vehicles failed to gain momentum despite attempts by Honda and few other OEMs to establish the commercial value of FCEVs. Another factor for the decline in FCEV production is the technological improvements and cost reduction of Li-ion batteries used in BEVs.

The vast improvement in vehicle electrification in recent years has coincided with a radical transformation of society's understanding of transportation where autonomous driving and ride-sharing services have opened the door to freedom of movement. While autonomous driving systems can be deployed either in conventional ICEVs or in EVs, there is a power demand from the powertrain requirement on the vehicles. Connectivity within the vehicle and with the infrastructure for both autonomous and shared vehicles is likely to be easier for implementation with EVs.

The trend in using alternative vehicles is increasing today with EVs serving as ZEVs and hybrid vehicles filling in for ultra-low-emission vehicles. The core technologies for these alternative vehicles beyond the energy storage system are quite the same. The primary objective of this book is to introduce the system of alternative vehicle and the core enabling technologies embedded in that system. Chapters have also been dedicated for introducing autonomous vehicle technologies and power system charging infrastructure in this book.

## 1.1 ELECTRIC VEHICLES

An *electric vehicle* is a vehicle having the two features: (i) The energy source is portable and electrochemical or electromechanical in nature, and (ii) traction effort is supplied only by an electric motor. Figure 1.1 shows the block diagram of an EV system driven by a portable energy source. The electromechanical energy conversion linkage system between the vehicle energy source and the wheels is the powertrain of the vehicle. The powertrain has electrical as well as mechanical components. More will be discussed on the components for EVs in a later section.

The fuel for EVs is stored in an energy storage device, such as a battery-pack, for energy delivery upon demand. The primary source of energy for electricity generation for these vehicles is varied ranging from fossil fuels to solar energy. The BEV requires fuel delivered in electrical form to the vehicle through the electric power transmission system. Solar EVs use solar panels and a power converter to charge the batteries on the vehicle. The special feature of these EVs is that these are ZEVs as far as pollution within the vehicle is concerned. The FCEV can also be ZEVs if pure hydrogen is used as fuel on board the vehicle.

## 1.2 HYBRID ELECTRIC VEHICLES

The terms *hybrid electric vehicle* and *hybrid vehicle* generally refer to vehicles that use an IC engine in conjunction with one or more electric machines for propulsion. A hybrid road vehicle is one in which the propulsion energy during specified operational missions is available from two or more kinds or types of energy stores, sources or converters, of which at least one store or converter must be on board. The definition of hybrid road vehicle is proposed by the technical committee 69 of Electric Road Vehicles of the International Electrotechnical Commission.

The definition of hybrid vehicles can be extended to vehicles that have engines different from IC engines. The vehicle in which energy from fuel cells and battery-packs is utilized to deliver propulsion power through an electric motor is also a hybrid vehicle. The fuel cell is essentially an engine where stored chemical energy in the fuel is converted into electrical energy directly without the involvement of any combustion process. Triple hybrids are also possible where a fuel cell engine, electric machine and IC engine are all used to provide propulsion power. The traction electric motors can operate independently or in association with the IC engine to power the wheels of the vehicle depending on the type of vehicle architecture. The blending of the power from two or

**FIGURE 1.1** An EV system.

more devices can be achieved through an electrical or a mechanical device. The power flow control and blending of the mechanical and electrical transmission paths are internal and transparent to the user; the driver in a hybrid vehicle interfaces with the vehicle in the same way as he does with a present-day conventional ICEV.

The vehicle design complexity increases significantly with hybrid vehicles, since controls and support systems are needed for both the IC engine and the electric machine in addition to the components needed for controlled blending of power coming from the two sources. The power transmission paths of the HEV consist of different mechanical and electrical subsystems. The high performance and high efficiency of the electric power transmission path reduce the run time of the IC engine, thereby reducing emissions and increasing fuel efficiency.

The components and the power transmission paths for the electric and hybrid vehicles are discussed in the following section. The hybrid vehicle architectures will be addressed in Chapter 3 after vehicle kinetics are presented in Chapter 2.

## 1.3   ELECTRIC AND HYBRID VEHICLE COMPONENTS

The automobile is a complex system made of numerous hardware components and software algorithms interconnected through mechanical links and electrical communications network. The design of the automobile extends from systems-level design to intricate details of a subsystem or component design. The system design fundamentals are in the physics of motion, energy and power, and in the principles of energy conversion from one form to another, the forms being chemical, electrical and mechanical. The primary hardware components in the automobile are the energy conversion and power transmission devices; many secondary components are necessary for the functioning of the primary components. This book addresses the system-level design fundamentals, the primary hardware components and the connectivity among these components. The secondary components will be discussed as and when appropriate. A chapter is dedicated to discuss the various cooling systems required in a modern automobile.

The primary energy conversion devices in an electric or hybrid vehicle are the *IC engine*, the *electric machine* and the *energy storage device*. The IC engine is a heat engine that converts chemical energy to mechanical energy. The electric machine can be used either as a *motor* or as a *generator* to convert mechanical power to electrical power or vice versa, respectively. In FCEVs, the *fuel cell* is the engine that converts chemical energy to electrical form. The *transmission* in the vehicle is a key component for power transfer from the IC engine to the wheels.

With the introduction of electric machines for power and energy transfer in electric and hybrid vehicles, energy storage devices and electrical-to-electrical power/energy conversion devices become essential. A high-energy capacity *battery-pack* is the most common energy storage device in these vehicles. An *ultracapacitor-bank* can also be used for energy storage in hybrid vehicles. *Flywheels* have also been used in prototype research hybrid vehicles for energy storage in mechanical form.

The electric machines require an *electric drive* to control the machine and deliver the required power based on requested demands and feedback signals. The electric drives are made of *power electronic devices* and *electronic controllers*. The drives are electrical-to-electrical energy conversion device that converts steady voltages with fixed frequency into a variable voltage supply for the electric machine. The drives can also process electrical power in the other direction assisting the electric machine to convert mechanical power into electrical power when the electric machine operates as a generator. The *DC/DC converter* is another electrical power management device used for DC power conversion from high to low voltage levels or vice versa. The converter is made of power electronic devices and energy storage inductors; this device can be bidirectional as well. The DC/DC converter is a key component for the fuel cell interface with the electric motor drive.

The energy flow in a vehicle starts from the source of energy and ends at the wheels with the delivery of propulsion power; the path for this power and energy flow is known as the *powertrain* of the vehicle. The energy source within the vehicle could be the diesel or gasoline for the IC engines or the stored energy in batteries for electric motors.

The flow of power and energy in the powertrain is controlled by a set of electronic controllers. In addition to the *electronic controller units* (*ECUs*) for each of the energy conversion and power transmission devices in the powertrain, there is a master controller for coordinating the system-level functions of the vehicle. This controller is termed as the *vehicle supervisory controller* (*VSC*). The supervisory controller is a key component in hybrid vehicles since it has to coordinate the energy conversion of multiple devices and power transmission through both the electrical and mechanical paths. The supervisory controller is like the brain of the vehicle designed to generate the control commands for the individual powertrain component ECUs. The supervisory controller interacts with the components of the vehicle through a communication network, which is based on a *controller area network* (*CAN*) protocol. The CAN protocols are presented in Chapter 11, while the hybrid vehicle control strategies are discussed in Chapter 15.

The primary powertrain components in a conventional ICEV are the engine and the transmission. These components deliver power to the wheels through the driveshaft and other coupling devices. The coupling devices include the differential and final drive in most cases. This mechanical power transmission path (MPTP) is shown in Figure 1.2. The power transmission path in an electric vehicle is mostly electrical except for the coupling devices between the electric propulsion motor and the wheels. This power transfer path will be referred to as the electrical power transmission path (EPTP). This transmission path is shown in Figure 1.3. The coupling device can simply be a gear to match electric machine speeds to vehicle speeds. The coupling can even be direct without any gearing in wheel-mounted motors, which are known as *hub motors*. The striking difference in this path from that in an ICEV is that power and energy flow can be bidirectional. In EVs, kinetic energy of the vehicle can be processed back to the energy storage device through the electric machine when the vehicle brakes to slow down or stop.

Both the electrical and mechanical transmission paths exist in the powertrain of a hybrid vehicle. The architecture and components of the powertrain of an HEV is varied depending on the type of hybrid vehicle. A generic configuration for a charge sustaining hybrid is shown in Figure 1.4. The *charge sustaining hybrids* are those that never need to be plugged in for recharging the energy storage system. The only energy source within the vehicle is the stored fuel for the IC engine. All of the propulsion energy gets processed through the engine regardless of whether the power transmission path is electrical or mechanical. The propulsion power comes from one or more electric motors and the IC engine. The propulsion power is transmitted to the wheels through either the MPTP or

**FIGURE 1.2**   Power transmission path in a conventional ICE vehicle.

**FIGURE 1.3**   Power transmission path in an EV.

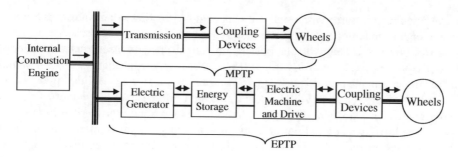

**FIGURE 1.4** An HEV powertrain.

the EPTP, or the combination of the two. The MPTP is associated with an IC engine and transmission, whereas the EPTP consists of the energy storage system, a generator, a propulsion motor and transmission. The combination of electric machines and IC engine and the arrangements of the power transmission paths give rise to a variety of architectures for HEVs. The energy sources and the power conversion devices can be arranged in series, parallel or a series–parallel combination giving rise to these various hybrid architectures. The hybrid vehicle architectures are discussed in Chapter 3.

The arrangement of the electrical components of the generic hybrid vehicle is shown in Figure 1.5. The electric generator shown in the hybrid configuration of Figure 1.5 is coupled to the engine and can be operated either as a generator or as a motor. During generation, the power through the generator can be used to charge the energy storage using a bidirectional inverter, or to deliver energy directly to the propulsion motor through the DC bus. The generator can also be operated as a motor during engine starting and torque boosting to meet driver peak acceleration demands. The energy storage system will absorb or deliver power depending on the system state of charge and driving conditions. Another bidirectional inverter conditions the power flow for the propulsion motor, which delivers torque to the wheels. The propulsion motor can also capture regenerative energy during vehicle braking. The energy storage devices used in hybrid vehicles are presented in Chapters 5 and 6. The starter-generator and propulsion motor in the EPTP use high-power electric machines. These electric machines need to have motoring and generating capability, high power density, high efficiency and high starting torque over a wide speed range to meet the performance specifications.

The different types of electric machines are discussed in Chapter 7, while the machine controller methods and the electric drives are presented in Chapters 8 and 10, respectively. The power

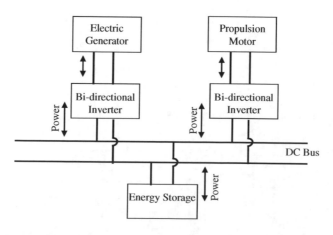

**FIGURE 1.5** Electrical components of an HEV.

electronic components for the electric motor drives and the DC/DC converters are presented in Chapter 9. The different types of IC engines and their fundamentals are presented in Chapter 13. The power transmission components, brakes and cooling system are discussed in Chapter 14.

## 1.4   VEHICLE MASS AND PERFORMANCE

The several vehicle mass definitions used in this book are common to those used in the automotive industry. The *vehicle curb mass* $m_v$ is the total mass of a vehicle with all standard equipment, components, lubricants, full tank of gas but without any passenger or cargo. The *gross vehicle mass* $m_{gv}$ of a vehicle is the curb mass plus the passengers and cargo. The *maximum gross vehicle mass* is the curb mass plus the maximum number of passengers and the maximum mass of the cargo that the vehicle is designed for. Often the term weight is generally used for vehicles instead of mass, although it is the mass of the vehicle that is being referred. The mass defines the intrinsic physical property of the vehicle, whereas weight is the force of the vehicle due to the gravitational pull. The scientifically correct term mass will be used in this book for the calculations and analysis.

The vehicle curb mass is distinguished between *sprung mass* and *unsprung mass* in relation to the location of the components with respect to the vehicle suspension system. The spring mass is the fraction of the vehicle curb mass that is supported by suspension including suspension members that are in motion. The unsprung mass is the remaining fraction of vehicle curb mass that is carried by the wheels and moving with it.

The front-to-rear mass distribution is critical for balance and good ride performance of a vehicle. The mass distribution can be defined in terms of axle-to-axle lengths. Let

$l$ = axle-to-axle length,
$a$ = front axle to vehicle center of gravity, known as front longitudinal length,
$b$ = rear axle to vehicle center of gravity, known as rear longitudinal length.

The front vehicle mass is

$$m_{vf} = \frac{b}{l} m_v.$$

And the rear vehicle mass is

$$m_{vr} = \frac{a}{l} m_v.$$

The packaging of components for good balance and ride performance is very important, especially for hybrid vehicles that have more powertrain components than a conventional vehicle. The EVs and hybrids with large energy capacity have significant battery mass requiring efficient packaging within the vehicle. The dynamic effects of braking cause a dynamic mass shift; the front brakes are responsible for about 70% of vehicle braking. A 60:40 or less ratio of front-to-rear vehicle mass distribution is required considering balance, ride performance and dynamic braking.

The ratio of sprung-to-unsprung mass also has to be carefully evaluated during the vehicle packaging and layout design. A 10:1 ratio of sprung-to-unsprung mass is a desirable target, although a slightly lower ratio can be used for hybrid vehicles that may have more unsprung components. The electric motors mounted on the hub or disk brakes along with the entire caliper assembly add to the unsprung mass of the vehicle.

An equivalent vehicle mass in terms of the curb mass and the number of passengers is used in sizing the powertrain components. The equivalent mass to be used in the design calculations is given by

$$m_{eq} = k_m m_v + N_p m_p$$

where $k_m$ is mass factor related to the translational equivalent of all rotating inertias, $N_p$ is the number of persons in the vehicle and $m_p$ is the average mass of the persons. $k_m$ is a dimensionless mass factor that accounts for the inertia of all the rotating components such as wheels, driveline components, engine with ancillaries and hybrid electric machines. The mass factor is given by [3]

$$k_m = 1 + \frac{4J_w}{m_v r_{wh}^2} + \frac{J_{eng}\xi_{eng}^2\xi_{FD}^2}{m_v r_{wh}^2} + \frac{J_{em}\xi_{em}^2\xi_{FD}^2}{m_{cv} r_{wh}^2}$$

where $\xi_{eng/em}$ and $\xi_{FD}$ are the engine/electric machine transmission and final drive gear ratios.

The steering performance of a vehicle is measured in terms of the steering angles, which is the average of the left and right wheel angles [4]. Right to left vehicle mass balance is also needed for good steering performance. Packaging the hybrid components above the vehicle center of gravity will result in a good steering performance and handling of the vehicle.

## 1.5 ELECTRIC MOTOR AND ENGINE RATINGS

The strengths of electric motors and IC engines are typically described with kilowatt (kW) or horsepower (HP) ratings, although a comparison between electric motors and IC engines in terms of power units only is not fair. The power that an electric motor can continuously deliver without overheating is its rated power, which is typically a derated figure. For short periods of time, the motor can deliver two to three times the rated power. Therefore, higher torque and power is available from an electric motor for acceleration, and the motor torque can be the maximum under stall conditions, i.e., at zero speed. The motor type determines whether maximum torque is available at zero speed or not. On the contrary, an IC engine is rated at a specific r/min level for maximum torque and maximum power. The IC engine maximum torque and power ratings are typically derived under idealized laboratory conditions. In practical situations, it is impossible to achieve the rated power; the maximum power available from an IC engine is always smaller than the rated power.

The torque characteristics of motors are shown in Figure 1.6 along with torque characteristics of IC engines. The characteristics of specific motors and IC engines will differ somewhat from these generalized curves. For electric motors, a high torque is available at starting, which is the rated torque of the motor. The peak or rated power from a motor is obtained at base speed ($\omega_b$) when the motor characteristics enter the constant power region from constant torque region once the voltage limit of the power supply is reached. The motor rated speed ($\omega_{rated}$) is at the end of the constant power region. The IC engine peak power and torque occur at the same speed. At this stage, it will be helpful to review the power and torque relation, which is as follows:

FIGURE 1.6   Electric motor and IC engine torque characteristics.

$$\text{Power (W)} = \text{Torque (N m)} \times \text{Speed (rad/s)}. \tag{1.1}$$

The power–torque relation in HP and ft · lbs is

$$\text{HP} = \frac{\text{Torque (ft · lbs)} \times \text{rpm}}{5,252}.$$

Figure 1.6 depicts that the IC engine does not produce any torque below a certain speed. A transmission is essential for an IC engine to match the vehicle speed with the narrow high-power speed range of the engine. On the other hand, the electric motor produces high torque even at zero speed and typically has constant power characteristics over a wide speed range. Therefore, the electric motor can be attached directly to the drive wheels with a single-gear transmission to accelerate the vehicle from zero speed all the way up to the top speed. The fixed gear ratio is appropriately sized based on the operating speed range of the motor and the top speed of the vehicle. Single-stage transmission gears are designed to match the higher speed of the electric motor with the lower speed of the wheels, typically in the range of 10–15:1. Typical maximum electric motor speeds are 15,000 rev/m for wheel speeds around 1,000 rev/m.

The power and torque densities of electric machines are typically much higher than that of a comparable-sized IC engine. The power and torque densities improve as the rated speed of the electric machine increases. Electric machines are designed for high-speed operation to minimize size and weight. The power and torque densities also depend on the type of electric machine used. The motor and, hence, the vehicle speed are controlled directly through the power electronic converter feeding the current into the motor.

The electric motor is the sole propulsion unit in EVs, while in HEVs, the electric motor and the IC engine together in a series or parallel combination provide the propulsion power. The electric motor for propulsion in the EV/HEV is desired to have a high starting torque to meet acceleration requirements, high power density to reduce the weight, and high efficiency to extend the battery range. The ideal candidate motor drive should also have a wide operating speed range to facilitate a single-gear transmission stage. The important characteristics of an electric or hybrid vehicle motor include flexible drive control, fault tolerance, high efficiency and low acoustic noise. The motor drive must be capable of handling voltage fluctuations from the source. The requirements of an electric or hybrid vehicle motor, not necessarily in order of importance, are summarized in the following:

- Ruggedness.
- High torque-to-inertia ratio $\left(\dfrac{T_e}{J}\right)$. Large $\dfrac{T_e}{J}$ results in "good" acceleration capabilities.
- Peak torque capability of about 200%–300% of continuous torque rating.
- High power-to-weight ratio $\left(\dfrac{P_e}{w}\right)$.
- Capability to operate with varying DC bus voltage.
- Low acoustic noise, low EMI, low maintenance and low cost.
- Extended constant power region of operation.

## 1.6 ELECTRIC AND HYBRID VEHICLE HISTORY

The history of EVs is quite interesting. It includes the insurgence of EVs following the discovery of electricity and the means of electromechanical energy conversion, and later being overtaken by gasoline-powered vehicles [5]. The people digressed from a potential environmentally friendlier mode of transportation due to the lack of enabling technologies in the early years but are now revisiting that prospect aided with significant technical developments over the years [6].

### 1.6.1 The Early Years

Prior to the 1830s, the means of transportation was only through steam power, since the laws of electromagnetic induction, and consequently electric motors and generators, were yet to be discovered. Faraday demonstrated the principle of electric motor as early as in 1820 through a wire rod carrying electric current and a magnet, but it was in 1831 when he discovered the laws of electromagnetic induction that enabled the development and demonstration of electric motors and generators that is essential for electric transportation. The history of EVs in those early years up to its peak period in the early 1900s is summarized below:

- Pre 1830 – Steam-powered transportation.
- 1831 – Faraday's law, and shortly thereafter, invention of DC motor.
- 1834 – Non-rechargeable battery-powered electric car used on a short track.
- 1851 – Non-rechargeable 19-mph electric car.
- 1859 – Development of lead storage battery.
- 1874 – Battery-powered carriage.
- Early 1870s – Electricity produced by dynamo-generators.
- 1885 – Gasoline-powered tricycle car.
- 1900 – 4,200 automobiles sold:

    40% steam powered
    38% electric powered
    22% gasoline powered

The specifications of some of the early EVs are given below:

- 1897 – French Krieger Co. EV: Weight – 2,230 lbs, Top Speed – 15 mi/h, Range – 50 miles/charge.
- 1900 – French B.G.S. Co. EV: Top Speed – 40 mph, Range – 100 miles/charge.
- 1915 – Woods EV: Top Speed – 40 mph, Range – 100 miles/charge.
- 1915 – Lansden EV: Weight – 2,460 lbs, 93 miles/charge, 1 ton payload capacity.
- 1912 – 34,000 EVs registered; *EVs outnumber gas-powered vehicles 2-to-1*.
- 1920s – EVs disappear and ICEVs become predominant.

The factors that led to the disappearance of EV after its short period of success are as follows:

1. Invention of starter motor in 1911 that made gas vehicles easier to start.
2. Improvements in mass production of Henry Ford's Model T (gas-powered) vehicles, which sold for $260 in 1925 compared to $850 in 1909. EVs were more expensive.
3. Rural areas had very limited access to electricity to charge batteries, whereas gasoline could be sold in those areas.

### 1.6.2  1960s

EVs started to resurge in the 1960s primarily due to the environmental hazards caused by the emissions of ICEVs. The major ICEV manufacturers, General Motors and Ford, became involved in EV research and development. The General Motors started a 15 million dollar program that culminated in the vehicles called Electrovair and Electrovan. The components and specifications of the two Electrovair vehicles are given below.

**Electrovair I (1964) and Electrovair II (1966) by GM**
- Systems and characteristics:

Motor – Three-phase induction motor, 115 HP, 13,000 rev/m
Battery – Silver–zinc (Ag–Zn), 512 V, 680 lbs.
Motor drive – DC-to-AC inverter using silicon-controlled rectifier (SCR)
Top speed – 80 mi/h
Range – 40–80 miles
Acceleration – 0–60 mi/h in 15.6 s
Vehicle weight – 3,400 lbs

The Electrovair utilized Chevy Corvair body and chassis. Among the positive features was the acceleration performance that was comparable to ICEV Corvair. The major disadvantage of the vehicle was the silver–zinc (Ag–Zn) battery-pack that was too expensive and heavy with short cycle life and requiring a long recharge time.

An additional factor in the 1960s that provided the impetus for EV development includes the 'The Great Electric Car Race' cross-country competition (3,300 miles) between an EV from Caltech and another one from MIT in August 1968. The race generated great public interest in EVs and provided an extensive road test of the technology. However, the 1960s technology was not mature enough to produce a commercially viable EV.

### 1.6.3   1970s

The scenario turned in favor of EV in the early 1970s as gasoline prices increased dramatically due to energy crisis. The Arab oil embargo of 1973 increased demands for alternate energy sources, which led to an immense interest in EVs. It became highly desirable to be less dependent on foreign oil as a nation. In 1975, 352 electric vans were delivered to US postal service for testing. In 1976, Congress enacted the Public Law 94-413, the *Electric and Hybrid Vehicle Research, Development and Demonstration Act of 1976*. This act authorizes a federal program to promote electric and hybrid vehicle technologies and to demonstrate the commercial feasibility of EVs. The Department of Energy (DOE) standardized the EV performance, which is summarized in Table 1.1.

The case study of a GM EV of the 1970s is as follows:

* System and characteristics:

  Motor – Separately excited DC, 34 HP, 2,400 rev/m
  Battery-pack – Ni–Zn, 120 V, 735 lbs
  Auxiliary battery – Ni–Zn, 14 V

**TABLE 1.1**
**EV Performance Standardization of 1976**

| Category | | Personal Use | Commercial Use |
|---|---|---|---|
| Acceleration from 0 to 50 kph | | <15 s | <15 s |
| Gradability at 25 kph | | 10% | 10% |
| Gradability at 20 kph | | 20% | 20% |
| Forward speed for 5 min | | 80 kph | 70 kph |
| Range | Electric | 50 km, C cycle | 50 km, B cycle |
| | Hybrid | 200 km, C cycle | 200 km, B cycle |
| Nonelectrical energy consumption in hybrid vehicles (consumption of nonelectrical energy must be less than 75% of the total energy consumed) | | <1.3 MJ/km | <9.8 MJ/km |
| Recharge time from 80% discharge | | <10 h | <10 h |

Motor drive – Armature DC chopper using SCRs; field DC chopper using BJTs.
Top speed: 60 mi/h
Range – 60–80 miles
Acceleration – 0–55 mi/h in 27 s.

The vehicle utilized a modified Chevy Chevette chassis and body. This EV was used mainly as a testbed for Ni–Zn batteries. Over 35,500 miles of on-road testing proved that this EV is sufficiently road worthy.

## 1.6.4   1980s AND 1990s

The 1980s and 1990s saw tremendous developments of high-power, high-frequency semiconductor switches, along with the microprocessor revolution, which led to improved power converter design to drive the electric motors efficiently. The period also contributed to the development of magnetic bearings used in flywheel energy storage systems, although these are not utilized in the mainstream EVs development projects.

In the last two decades, legislative mandates pushed the cause for ZEVs. Legislation passed by the California Air Resources Board in the 1990 stated that by 1998, 2% of vehicles should be ZEVs for each automotive company selling more than 35,000 vehicles. The percentage was to increase to 5% by 2001 and to 10% by 2003. The legislation provided a tremendous impetus to develop EVs by the major automotive manufacturers. The legislation was relaxed somewhat later due to practical limitations and the inability of the manufacturers to meet the 1998 and 2001 requirements. The mandate further relaxed to stand as 4% of all vehicles sold should be ZEV by 2003 and an additional 6% of the sales must be made up of ZEVs and partial ZEVs, which would have required General Motors to sell about 14,000 EVs in California.

Motivated by the pollution concern and potential energy crisis, the government agencies, federal laboratories and the major automotive manufactures launched a number of initiatives to push for the ZEVs. The partnership for next-generation vehicles (PNGV) is such an initiative established in 1993, which is a partnership of federal laboratories and automotive industries to promote and develop EVs and HEVs. A later initiative by the DOE and the automotive industries is the Freedom CAR initiative.

The trends in EV developments in recent years can be attributed to the following:

- High level of activity at the major automotive manufacturers.
- New independent manufacturers bring vigor.
- New prototypes are even better.
- High levels of activity overseas.
- High levels of hybrid vehicle activity.
- A boom in individual or small company ICEV to EV conversions.

The case studies of two GM EVs of the 1990s are given in the following.

### 1.6.4.1   GM Impact 3 (1993 Completed)
- Based on 1990 Impact displayed at the Los Angeles auto show.
- Two-passenger, two-door coupe, street legal and safe.
- Twelve built initially for testing, 50 built by 1995 to be evaluated by 1,000 potential customers.
- System and characteristics:

Motor – One, three-phase induction motor, 137 HP, 12,000 rev/m
Battery-pack – Lead–acid (26), 12 V batteries connected in series (312 V), 869 lbs.

Motor drive – DC-to-AC inverter using IGBTs.
Top speed – 75 mi/h
Range – 90 miles on highway.
Acceleration – 0–60 miles in 8.5 s.
Vehicle weight – 2,900 lbs.

The vehicle was used as a testbed for mass production of EVs.

### 1.6.4.2  Saturn EV1

- Commercially available EV made by GM in 1995.
- Leased in California and Arizona for a total cost of about $30,000.
- System and characteristics:

Motor – One, three-phase induction motor
Battery-pack – Lead–acid batteries
Motor Drive – DC-to-AC inverter using IGBTs.
Top Speed – 75 mi/h
Range – 90 miles in highway, 70 miles in city.
Acceleration – 0–60 miles in 8.5 s.
- Power consumption:

30 kWh/100 miles in city, 25 kWh/100 miles in highway.

This vehicle was also used as a testbed for mass production of EVs.

### 1.6.5  RECENT EVS AND HEVS

The manufacturers of EVs in the 1990s faced a stiff challenge as their significant research and development efforts on ZEV technologies have been hindered by unsuitable battery technologies. A number of auto industries started developing hybrid vehicles to overcome the battery and range problem of battery-powered EVs. The Japanese auto industries led this trend with Toyota and Honda entering the market from the late 1990s with their Prius and Insight model hybrids. The Honda Insight using a mild parallel hybrid system and the Toyota Prius with a series–parallel hybrid architecture typify the two modern schools of thought regarding passenger hybrid vehicles. The Insight utilizes a simple lightweight parallel powertrain featuring a single electric machine and a high-voltage battery-pack. The electric machine is an integrated starter/generator serving as a starter motor, generator and assist traction motor. The hybrid systems in the Honda Civic Hybrid are similar to that of the Insight. The vehicle has high parts interchangeability with their conventional sibling and delivers the benefits of hybridization without introducing high costs. The powertrain systems in the Ford Escape Hybrid and the GM Two-Mode hybrids are similar to that of the Prius with relatively complex and expensive power-split systems. The systems have one IC engine and two electric machines. These systems get the most benefit possible from a hybrid system, and therefore, offer the greatest increase in fuel efficiency, but are also more expensive to produce than a mild hybrid. The HEVs use both an electric motor and an IC engine, but all of the propulsion energy ultimately comes from the gasoline fuel. Currently, a number of production hybrid vehicle models are available from almost all the major automotive industries around the world. In 2020, 76 different models of HEVs are available from 13 different manufacturers. Six of these HEVs from six different manufacturers with the best fuel economy are given in Table 1.2 [7].

HEVs have penetrated the market at an extraordinary rate in the first decade of the 21st century, but EVs did not fall too far behind. BEVs started making their way back in the later part of the decade due to the niche market demand, advances in battery technology and pioneering efforts by

**TABLE 1.2**

**Model Year 2020 Hybrid Electric Vehicle Examples**

| Make and Model | Vehicle Type | Engine Size/Cylinders | Fuel Economy (miles/g) (City/Combined/Highway) |
|---|---|---|---|
| Toyota Prius Eco | Sedan/Wagon | 1.8 L, I4 | 58/56/53 |
| Hyundai Ioniq Blue | Sedan/Wagon | 1.6 L, I4 | 57/58/59 |
| Honda Insight | Sedan/Wagon | 1.5 L, I4 | 55/53/49 |
| Kia Niro FE | Sedan/Wagon | 1.6 L, I4 | 52/50/49 |
| Hyundai Sonata Blue | Sedan/Wagon | 2.0 L, I4 | 51/52/54 |
| Toyota Camry Hybrid LE | Sedan/Wagon | 25 L, I4 | 51/52/53 |

a few companies. In 2008, Tesla motors delivered the Tesla Roadster, which is the first production vehicle to use Li-ion battery technology and the first BEV to travel more than 200 miles on a single charge. The Tesla Roadster was designed for performance with an acceleration rating of 0–60 mph in 3.9 s. The vehicle was produced between 2008 and 2012, and about 2,450 vehicles were sold during that period in over 30 countries. The vehicle's components and specifications are as follows:

- Battery pack: 375 V, 53 kWh capacity made of 6,831 Li-ion cells.
- Nominal range: 244 miles/charge.
- Vehicle curb mass: 1,238 kg; battery-pack mass 450 kg.
- Electric motor: 215 kW, 400 N m peak three-phase AC induction motor; peak speed 14,000 rpm; base speed 5,133 rpm.
- Transmission gear ratio: 8.28 to 1 in forward motion and 3.12 to 1 in reverse.

Tesla Roadster is slated to return in 2021 with an improved performance of 0–60 mph in 1.9 s and a top speed of 250 mph.

The EV production changed significantly within the last decade, and almost all of the major automotive manufacturers including both traditional and emerging OEMs have vehicles to offer for sale or lease to the general public. The available selection is wide with varying performance and cost as the vehicle manufacturers come with their variations to gain their share in this emerging market. In 2020, there are 27 different models of BEVs available from 11 different manufacturers. The top five BEVs with the highest all electric range from five different manufacturers from the 2020 vehicles are listed in Table 1.3 [7]. The most popular EV in the market in terms of the number of sales is the Tesla Model 3, which sold more than 300,000 vehicles in 2019. Beijing Senova D50 from BAIC (Beijing Auto Works) and the Nissan Leaf came in second and third with 111,147 and 69,870 vehicles, respectively, sold in 2019. For the powertrain, most of the EV manufacturers use PM synchronous motors. AC induction motor is the other machine type used by some vehicle manufacturers who see the value of using these machines due to the cost of PM machines.

While BEVs made their entry into the market, few auto manufacturers started developing and offering the PHEVs. The most notable among these is the Chevy Volt from General which was available for several years starting from 2010. Chevy Volt is a PHEV40 with a range of 40 miles. Toyota also started offering a PHEV version of their most successful Toyota Prius hybrid soon after the introduction of Chevy Volt. For model year 2020, there are 35 types of PHEVs available offered by 17 different manufacturers. Seven PHEVs from 2020 with the highest all electric range are listed in Table 1.4 [7].

The FCEV is a viable alternative to BEVs to serve as a ZEV without the range problem provided a hydrogen dispensing infrastructure can be established. Daimler-Chrysler built a prototype electric van called NECAR1 in 1994 using a 50 kW Ballard proton exchange membrane

**TABLE 1.3**

**Model Year 2020 Battery Electric Vehicle Examples**

| Make and Model | Vehicle Type | Powertrain: Electric Motor/Battery-Pack | Fuel Economy (miles/gge) (City/Combined/Highway) | All Electric Range (miles) |
|---|---|---|---|---|
| Tesla Model 3 long range | Sedan/Wagon | 211 kW electric motor; 230 Ah battery | 136/130/123 | 373 |
| Chevrolet Bolt EV | Sedan/Wagon | 150 kW electric motor; 188 Ah battery | 127/118/108 | 259 |
| Hyundai Kona Electric | SUV | 150 kW electric motor; 180 Ah battery | 132/120/108 | 258 |
| Kia Soul | Sedan/Wagon | 201 kW electric motor; 180 Ah battery | 127/114/101 | 243 |
| Jaguar I-PACE | SUV | 201 kW electric motor; 223 Ah battery | 80/76/72 | 234 |

**TABLE 1.4**

**Model Year 2020 Plug-in Hybrid Electric Vehicle Examples**

| Make and Model | Vehicle Type | Powertrain: Electric Motor/Engine Size | Fuel Economy (miles/gge), Gasoline; (City/Combined/Highway) | Fuel Economy, Combined (miles/gge) | All Electric Range (miles) |
|---|---|---|---|---|---|
| Karma Revero GT | Sedan/Wagon; series hybrid | 175 kW electric motor; 1.5 L, I3 | 27/26/25 | N/A | 61 |
| Honda Clarity PHEV | Sedan/Wagon; parallel hybrid | 135 kW electric motor; 1.5 L, I4 | 44/42/40 | 110 | 48 |
| Chrysler Pacifica Hybrid | Van; parallel hybrid | 89 kW electric motor; 3.6 L, V6 | 29/30/30 | N/A | 32 |
| Hyundai Ioniq Plug-in | Sedan/Wagon; parallel hybrid | 32 kW electric motor; 1.6 L, I4 | 53/52/52 | 119 | 29 |
| Kia Optima Plug-in | Sedan/Wagon; parallel hybrid | 50 kW electric motor; 2.0 L, I4 | 39/41/40 | 101 | 28 |
| Ford Fusion Energi Plug-in | Sedan/Wagon; parallel hybrid | 68 kW electric motor; 2.0 L, I4 | 43/42/40 | 103 | 26 |
| Toyota Prius Prime | Sedan/Wagon; series–parallel hybrid | 23 & 53 kW electric motor; 1.8 L, I4 | 55/53/54 | 133 | 25 |

(PEM) fuel cell. Toyota built a prototype fuel cell vehicle in 1994 based on RAV4 sports utility vehicle (SUV) using a 20 kW PEM fuel cell. The range of NECAR1 was 81 miles, while the range for the Toyota vehicle, called FCHV, was 155 miles. In December 2002, the city of Los Angeles began leasing one of the five Honda FCX vehicles, which is the first fuel cell vehicle authorized for commercial use which had an 85 kW PEM fuel cell and a range of 185 miles. Between 2008 and 2014, Honda produced the Honda FCX Clarity, which is a fuel cell/battery hybrid using a 100 kW PEM fuel cell and a 288 V Li-ion battery-pack. The vehicle is powered by a 100 kW, 255 N m peak rated PM synchronous motor for propulsion. The vehicle has a 72 miles/kg fuel usage which is equivalent to 74 miles/gge ('gge' stands for gasoline gallon equivalent). Honda reintroduced the vehicle in 2017 as Honda Clarity Fuel Cell but with expansion of the brand to include the Honda Clarity Electric and the Honda Clarity Plug-in Hybrid. In 2020, four FCEVs are available which are given in Table 1.5 [7].

**TABLE 1.5**

**Model Year 2020 Fuel Cell Electric Vehicles**

| Make and Model | Vehicle Type | Powertrain: Electric Motor/Battery-Pack | Fuel Economy (miles/gge) (City/Combined/Highway) |
|---|---|---|---|
| Honda Clarity | Sedan/Wagon | 130 kW electric motor; 346 V Li-ion battery | 68/68/67 |
| Hyundai Nexo | SUV | 120 kW electric motor; 240 V Li-ion battery | 59/57/54 |
| Hyundai Nexo Blues | SUV | 120 kW electric motor; 240 V Li-ion battery | 65/61/58 |
| Toyota Mirai | Sedan/Wagon | 113 kW electric motor; 245 V NiMH battery | 67/67/67 |

## 1.7 WELL-TO-WHEEL ANALYSIS

The well-to-wheel (WTW) efficiency is the measure of the overall efficiency of a vehicle starting from the extraction of raw fuel to the wheels including the efficiencies of energy conversion, transport and delivery at each stage. The fuel can be extracted from the earth or sea or derived from a renewable source; the transportation can be through the land or sea or electrically through the transmission lines; and the energy conversion can be through the heat engines, electric machines or electrochemical devices. The energy transport and conversion path can be divided into two segments of well-to-tank (WTT) and tank-to-wheel (TTW). The fuels for transportation are produced from energy feedstock in the wells through different fuel production pathways. The fuel stored in a vehicle is processed to deliver propulsion power at the wheels. The WTT segment comprises feedstock-related stages (recovery, processing, transportation and storage) and fuel-related stages (production, transportation, storage and distribution). The TTW segment comprises the energy conversion and delivery stages from the tank to the wheels of a vehicle. This WTW efficiency is consequently the product of the WTT and TTW efficiencies. Figure 1.7 represents the processes involved in evaluating the WTW efficiency. The WTW efficiency is an important factor for evaluating the overall impact, long-term feasibility and environmental effects of the alternative vehicles such as the EVs, HEVs, PHEVs and FCEVs. The suitable energy paths can be identified and selected using WTW analysis to formulate energy strategies and energy policies. The WTW analysis also provides a level ground for comparing the alternative vehicles with the conventional ICEVs. The fundamental laws of physics and chemistry with a common base for input parameters, numerical procedures, technology standards and user behavior must be used for these analyses [8].

**FIGURE 1.7**    Processes involved in WTW efficiency calculation.

**TABLE 1.6**

**Energy Consumption, Efficiency and Emissions for Passenger Cars Using GREET**

| | SI ICEV (Baseline CG and RFG) | Plug-in SI HEV (Gasoline and Electricity) | BEV (Electricity) |
|---|---|---|---|
| Total energy (Wh) | 257,551 | 526,261 | 1,632,131 |
| WTT efficiency | 79.5% | 66.5% | 38.0% |
| TTW efficiency | 21.9% | 23% | 48.51% |
| WTW efficiency | 17.41% | 15.29% | 18.43% |
| $CO_2$ (g/million BTU) | 17,495 | 57,024 | 219,704 |
| $CH_4$ (g/million BTU) | 109.120 | 145.658 | 296.031 |
| $N_2O$ (g/million BTU) | 1.152 | 1.535 | 3.111 |
| VOC: total (g/million BTU) | 27.077 | 25.630 | 19.679 |
| CO: total (g/million BTU) | 15.074 | 23.553 | 58.448 |
| $NO_x$: total (g/million BTU) | 50.052 | 87.100 | 239.571 |

The TTW efficiency for conventional ICEVs is inherently low (around 25%), because of the low efficiency of the gasoline or diesel engine and the losses in the powertrain components. In the case of HEVs, the engine is downsized and controlled to operate at higher-efficiency regions most of the time, which results in lower fuel consumption. The TTW efficiency of HEVs is higher than that of an ICEV and is estimated to be around 50% [9]. The efficiency of an electric powertrain is around 80%–90%. The TTW efficiency in BEVs is high due to their large-capacity batteries and electric-only mode of operation. However, when WTT efficiencies are included in the comparisons, the overall WTW efficiencies are not significantly different for any type of the vehicles. The WTW efficiencies of HEVS and EVs are similar to ICEVs because of the lower WTT efficiencies. The WTT efficiency for the PHEV depends on the proportions of the grid energy and the gasoline energy used during a drive cycle.

The WTW efficiencies and emission impacts can be evaluated for a comparison using the GREET model developed at the Argonne National Laboratory [10]. GREET model is essentially a multidimensional spreadsheet model available for public use for analyzing fuel cycles from the source to wheel for a vehicle. GREET is the acronym for *Greenhouse Gases, Regulated Emissions, and Energy Use in Transportation*. The model has more than 100 fuel production pathways and more than 70 vehicle systems.

Table 1.6 shows the WTW efficiencies and emissions for conventional ICEV, BEV and PHEV analyzed for a typical mid-size sedan using the GREET model [9,11]. The CG and RFG represents conventional gasoline and reformulated gasoline vehicles. The WTT efficiency was found to be 66.5% for PHEVs (grid-connected hybrids) using 33% grid energy and 67% gasoline for operation. On the other hand, the WTT efficiency for conventional and regular hybrid vehicles is 79.5%. The reason for low efficiency of PHEV is due to the fact that electricity is mostly generated from conventional energy sources that have very low efficiency.

The greenhouse gas ($CO_2$, $CH_4$, $N_2O$, CO, VOC and $NO_x$) emissions are also found to be higher in PHEVs than in conventional gasoline vehicles according to the results in Table 1.6. The TTW efficiency for the plug-in hybrid is not significantly different from the baseline vehicle since the IC engine usage is still quite high. Poor efficiencies in both WTW and TTW result in an overall low WTW efficiency for plug-in hybrids. More on efficiency calculation is presented in the next section.

## 1.8 EV/ICEV COMPARISON

The relative advantages and disadvantages of alternative vehicles over conventional ICEVs can be better appreciated from a comparison of the two on the basis of efficiency, pollution, cost and dependence on oil.

## 1.8.1 Efficiency Comparison

In order to evaluate the efficiencies of different types of vehicles on a level ground, the complete process in both systems starting from crude oil to power available at the wheels must be considered, i.e., the analysis must be carried out based on WTW efficiencies. The EV process starts not at the vehicles but at the source of raw power whose conversion efficiency must be considered to calculate the overall efficiency of EVs. The power input $P_{IN}$ to any vehicle ultimately comes from a primary energy source even before it is stored in a vehicle tank. The power extracted from a piece of coal by burning it is an example of primary power obtained from a primary energy source. The power that is available in a vehicle from an energy storage tank or device is applied power obtained from a secondary source of energy. The applied or secondary power is obtained indirectly from raw materials. The electricity generated from crude oil and delivered to an electric car for battery charging is an example of secondary power. The raw or primary power is labeled as $P_{IN\ RAW}$, while the secondary power is designated as $P_{IN\ PROCESS}$.

An example efficiency comparison is presented here based on the complete WTW processes involved in an EV and an ICEV. The complete EV process can be broken down into its constituent stages involving power generation, transmission and usage as shown in Figure 1.8. The primary power from the source is fed to the system only at the first stage, although the secondary power can be added in each stage. Each stage has its efficiency based on total input to that stage and output delivered to the following stage. The efficiency of each stage must be calculated from input–output power considerations, although the efficiency may vary widely depending on the technology being used. Finally, the overall efficiency can be calculated by multiplying the efficiencies of all the individual stages. The overall efficiency of the EV system shown in Figure 1.8 is as follows:

$$\eta_{EV} = \frac{P_0}{P_{IN}} = \frac{P_0}{P_0 + \sum_{i=1}^{7} P_{LOSSi}} = \frac{P_0}{P_6}\frac{P_6}{P_5}\frac{P_5}{P_4}\frac{P_4}{P_3}\frac{P_3}{P_2}\frac{P_2}{P_1}\frac{P_1}{P_{IN}} = \eta_1\eta_2\eta_3\eta_4\eta_5\eta_6\eta_7$$

The ICEV process details are illustrated in Figure 1.9. The process starts from the conversion of crude oil to fuel oil in the refinery, and then includes the transmission of fuel oil from refinery to gas stations, power conversion in the IC engine of the vehicle and power transfer from the engine to the wheels through the transmission. The efficiency of the ICEV process is the product of the efficiencies of the individual stages indicated in Figure 1.10 and is given by

$$\eta_{ICEV} = \eta_1\eta_2\eta_3\eta_4$$

**FIGURE 1.8**   The complete EV process from crude oil to power at wheels.

**FIGURE 1.9**   The complete ICEV process from crude oil to power at the wheels.

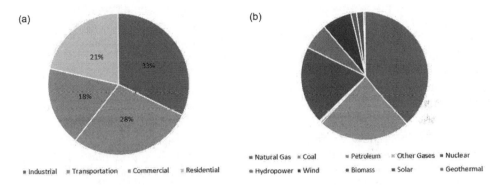

**FIGURE 1.10**   2019 US energy usage and generation: (a) energy consumption by end-use sector and (b) electricity generation by source.

**TABLE 1.7**
**Battery Electric and IC Engine Vehicle WTW Efficiencies**

|  | Battery EV Efficiency (%) | | ICEV Efficiency (%) | |
| --- | --- | --- | --- | --- |
|  | **High** | **High** | **Low** | **Low** |
| Refinery (petroleum) | 97 | 90 | 85 | 95 |
| Distribution to fuel tank |  | 99 | 95 |  |
| Engine |  | 22 | 20 |  |
| Electricity generation | 40 |  |  | 33 |
| Transmission to wall outlet | 92 |  |  | 90 |
| Battery charger | 90 |  |  | 85 |
| Battery (lead/acid) | 75 |  |  | 75 |
| Motor/controller | 85 |  |  | 80 |
| FC fuel processor |  |  |  |  |
| PEM fuel cell |  |  |  |  |
| Plug-in grid/gasoline ratio |  |  |  |  |
| Transmission/axle | 98 | 98 | 95 | 95 |
| Well-to-wheel | 20 | 19 | 15 | 14 |

A sample comparison of EV and ICEV process efficiencies based on the diagrams of Figure 1.8 and 1.9 is given in Table 1.7. Representative numbers have been used for the energy conversion stages to convey a general idea about the efficiencies of the two systems. Table 1.7 shows that the overall efficiency of an EV is comparable to the overall efficiency of ICEV.

### 1.8.2 Pollution Comparison

The transportation accounts for about one-third of all energy usage, making it the leading cause of environmental pollution through carbon emissions. The transportation sector includes vehicles that transport people or goods, such as cars, trucks, buses, motorcycles, trains, aircraft, boats, barges and ships. From the pie chart in Figure 1.10a, we can see that 28% of energy usage in the United States is in the transportation sector [12]. It has been projected that if 10% of automobiles nationwide were ZEVs, regulated air pollutants would be cut by 1 million tons per year and 60 million tons of greenhouse carbon dioxide gas would be eliminated [13]. With 100% electrification, i.e., every ICEV replaced by EV, the following has been claimed:

- Carbon dioxide in air, which is linked to global warming, would be cut in half.
- Nitrogen oxides (a greenhouse gas causing global warming) would be cut slightly depending on government regulated utility emission standards.
- Sulfur dioxide, which is linked to acid rain, would increase slightly.
- Waste oil dumping would decrease, since EVs do not require crankcase oil.
- EVs reduce noise pollution since they are quieter than ICEVs.
- Thermal pollution by large power plants would increase with increased EV usage.

The EVs will considerably reduce the major causes of smog, substantially eliminate ozone depletion and reduce greenhouse gases. With stricter $SO_2$ power plant emission standards, EVs would have little impact on $SO_2$ levels. Pollution reduction is the driving force behind EV usage. Pollution can be cut drastically when EV batteries are charged from electricity produced from renewable sources. The energy sources for electricity generation in 2019 are shown in the pie chart of Figure 1.10b [12], which shows that a significant percent of electricity is still being produced through non-renewable sources. In 2019, 7% of electricity generation has come from hydropower, 7% from wind and 4% from other renewable sources. On the other hand, 39% of electricity came from natural gas, while 24% was produced from coal and 20% from nuclear fuel. For reference, the total U.S. electricity generation in 2019 has been 100.2 quadrillion BTUs.

### 1.8.3 Capital and Operating Cost Comparison

The initial EV capital costs are higher than ICEV capital cost primarily due to the expensive battery-packs and lack of mass production opportunities. The power electronics stages are also expensive, although not at the same level as batteries. EV capital costs are expected to decrease as the volume increases. Capital costs of EVs easily exceed capital costs of ICEVs, but the EV costs are expected to decrease as the volume increases. Total life cycle cost of an EV is projected to be less than that of a comparable ICEV. The EVs are more reliable and will require less maintenance making it favorable over ICEV as far as the operating cost is concerned.

### 1.8.4 US Dependence on Foreign Oil

The importance of search for alternative energy sources cannot be overemphasized, and sooner or later there will be an energy crisis if we, the people of the planet, do not reduce our dependence on fossil fuels. Today's industries, particularly the transportation industry, are heavily dependent on oil, the reserve of which will eventually deplete in the not-so-distant future. An average ICEV in its lifetime uses 94 barrels of oil based on 28 miles/gallon fuel consumption. On the other hand, an average EV uses about two barrels of oil in its lifetime based on 4 miles/kWh and the percentage of oil used in the EV process for electricity generation.

## 1.9 ELECTRIC VEHICLE MARKET

The electric powertrain found its commercial value in HEVs towards the end of the last century and has been maintaining its presence with modest growth over the last two decades. The growth momentum shifted towards EVs with both traditional and new generation manufacturers making a push for commercializing BEVs. Motivated by the growing concern about global pollution and the success of electric motor-driven transportation in various sectors, the interest is ever increasing for sedan and light-duty truck EVs that can deliver the range and performance of its ICEV counterparts. In the last few years, the global EV sales growth has been around 60% with the total sales exceeding 2 million units globally from 2018 [14]. The leader in EV sales is China where government subsidy, regulatory pressure and micro-EVs helped develop a healthy market. The adoption of EVs and HEVs is affected by technology, regulations, incentives and regional needs. While technology itself drives a niche market, regulation and incentives are big drivers for market entry of new technology. In the United States, the regulatory requirements have been the primary motivator, while in China the major increase in BEV growth has been due to the incentives. In Europe, the strict $CO_2$ emission restrictions have prompted the auto manufacturers to focus on PHEVs, particularly on the 48 V micro-HEVs.

We typically discuss about EVs for passenger and public transportation but tend to forget about their use as off-road vehicles in specialty applications where the range is not an issue. The EVs have penetrated the off-road vehicles market successfully over the years for cleaner technology as well as for cost advantages. The examples of such applications are airport vehicles for passenger and ground support; recreational vehicles as in golf carts and theme parks, plant operation vehicles like fork lifts, loader trucks; vehicles for disabled persons; utility vehicles for ground transportation in closed but large compounds; etc. There are also EVs that run on tracks for material haulage in mines. EVs have also been introduced for construction vehicles and other off-road vehicles. The locomotives that run on tracks with electricity supplied from transmission lines are no different from other EVs, the major difference being in the way energy is supplied for the propulsion motors.

The impediments for the mass acceptance of EVs by the general public have been the limited EV range and the lack of EV infrastructure. The solution of the range problem is evolving from extensive research and development in batteries and installation of fast charger units. Many customers are also aware that they typically drive less than 50 miles a day for which a lower range EV is readily available. The issues related to infrastructure are as follows:

- Battery charging facilities. Residential and public charging facilities/stations.
- Standardization of EV plugs, cords, outlets and safety issues.
- Sales and distribution.
- Service and technical support.
- Parts supply.

The current initial cost of an EV is also a big disadvantage for the EV market. The replacement of the batteries even for EVs is quite expensive added to which is the limited life issue of these batteries.

The increasing use and sales of EVs and for transportation electrification in general have created extensive job opportunities for electrical, mechanical and chemical engineers on the technical side. The job opportunities related to EV are emerging in the following areas:

- Power electronics and motor drives: Design and development of the electrical systems of an EV.
- Power generation: Additional resources required for increased utility demand due to EV usage.

- Packaging and cooling: Design of components and systems for thermal management of electric powertrain components.
- Battery-pack design and development: Engineers and scientists needed for design and development of batter-packs as well as for research on next-generation batteries.
- EV infrastructure: Design and development of battery charging stations, hydrogen generation, and storage and distribution systems.

## PROBLEMS

1. Search through reference materials and write a report on the following topics:
    i. Commercial and research electric and hybrid vehicle programs around the world over the last 5 years describing the various programs, goals, power range, motor used, type of IC engine, battery source, etc.
    ii. Case study of a recent electric and hybrid vehicles.
    iii. State and/or Federal legislations and standardizations.
2. Using the GREET model (available from the Argonne National Laboratory website https://greet.es.anl.gov/, find the total energy usage and WTT, TTW, and WTW efficiencies of a BEV, an ICEV and a FCEV.

## REFERENCES

1. A. Venkatram and N. Schulte, *Urban Transportation and Air Pollution*, Elsevier Press, Amsterdam, Netherlands, June, 2018.
2. E.H. Wakefield, *History of Electric Automobile*, SAE International, Warrendale, PA, 1994.
3. T.D. Gillespie, *Fundamentals of Vehicle Dynamics*, SAE International, Warrendale, PA, 1992.
4. J.M. Miller, *Propulsions Systems for Hybrid Vehicles*, Institute of Electrical Engineers, London, 2004.
5. M.H. Westbrook, *The Electric Car*, The Institute of Electrical Engineers, London and Society of automotive Engineers, Warrendale, PA, 2001.
6. R. Hodkinson and J. Fenton, *Lightweight Electric/Hybrid Vehicle Design*, Society of Automotive Engineers, Warrendale, PA, 2001.
7. "Model Year 2020 Vehicles," Department of Energy Alternative Fuels Data Center. Online https://afdc.energy.gov/vehicles/search/, accessed April 9, 2020.
8. Ulf Bossel, "Well-to-Wheel Studies, Heating Values, and the Energy Conservation Principle," European Fuel Cell Forum. Online www.efcf.com/reports (E10), accessed October 22, 2003.
9. F. Kreith, R.E. West and B.E. Isler, "Efficiency of advanced ground transportation technologies," Transactions of the ASME, Journal of Energy Resources Technology, 124, 173–179, September 2002.
10. Online https://greet.es.anl.gov/, accessed June 24, 2020.
11. S. Chanda, *Powertrain Sizing and Energy Usage Adaptation Strategy for Plug-in Hybrid Electric Vehicles*, M.S. Thesis, University of Akron, Akron, OH, 2008.
12. Online https://www.eia.gov/energyexplained/electricity/, accessed June 24, 2020.
13. J. DeCicco, F. An and M. Ross, "Technical options for improving the fuel economy of U.S. cars and light trucks by 2010-2015," The Energy Foundation Report, April 2001. Online https://www.yumpu.com/en/document/view/6776991/, accessed October 16, 2020.
14. P. Hertzke, N. Müller, S. Schenk and T. Wu, "The Global Electric-vehicle Market is Amped Up and on the Rise," McKinsey & Company, May 2018. Online https://www.mckinsey.com/industries/automotive-and-assembly/our-insights, accessed October 16, 2020.

# 2 Vehicle Mechanics

The fundamentals of a vehicle design are embedded in the basic mechanics of physics, particularly in Newton's second law of motion relating force and acceleration. Newton's second law states that *the acceleration of an object is proportional to the net force exerted on it.* The object accelerates when the net force is non-zero, where the term net force refers to the resultant of the forces acting on the object. In the vehicle system, several forces act on it with the resultant or net force dictating the motion according to Newton's second law. A vehicle propels forward with the aid of the force delivered by the propulsion unit overcoming the resisting forces due to gravity, air and tire resistance. The acceleration and speed of the vehicle depend on the power available from the traction unit and the existing road and aerodynamic conditions. The acceleration also depends on the composite mass of the vehicle including the propulsion unit, all mechanical and electrical components and the batteries.

A vehicle is designed based on certain given specifications and requirements. Furthermore, the electric and hybrid vehicle system is large and complex involving multidisciplinary knowledge. The key to designing such a large system is to divide and conquer. The system-level perspective helps in mastering the design skills for a complex system where the broad requirements are first determined and then system components are designed with a more focused guidelines. For example, first the power and energy requirement from the propulsion unit is determined from a given set of vehicle cruising and acceleration specifications. The component-level design begins in the second stage where the propulsion unit, the energy source and other auxiliary units are specified and designed. In this stage, the electrical and mechanical engineers start designing the electric motor for electric vehicles (EVs) or the combination of electric motor and internal combustion engine for hybrid EVs. The power electronics engineers design the power conversion unit which links the energy source with the electric motor. The controls engineer works in conjunction with the power electronics engineer to develop the propulsion control system. The chemists and the chemical engineers have the primary responsibility of designing the energy source based on the energy requirement and guidelines of the vehicle manufacturer. Many of the component designs proceed in an iterative manner, where various designers have to interact with each other to insure that the design goals are met.

The design is an iterative process, which starts with some known factors and other educated guesses or assumptions to be followed by scientific analysis in order to verify that the requirements are met. In this chapter, we will develop the tools for scientific analysis of vehicle mechanics based on Newton's second law of motion. After defining and describing a roadway, the vehicle kinetics issues will be addressed. The roadway and kinetics will be linked to establish the equation for the force required from the propulsion unit. The force from the propulsion unit, which can be an electric motor or an internal combustion engine or a combination of the two, is known as the *tractive force*. Once force requirement is defined, one would proceed to calculate the power and energy required for a vehicle under consideration. The emphasis of study in this book is on the broad design goals, such as finding the power and energy requirement and predicting the range for a given energy source, thereby maintaining a top-level perspective. The design details of a subsystem are beyond the scope of this book, and the readers are referred to the literature of the respective areas for further details.

## 2.1 ROADWAY FUNDAMENTALS

A vehicle moves on a level road and also up and down the slope of a roadway. We can simplify our description of the roadway by considering a straight roadway, since the horizontal maneuvering has minimal impact on the force and power requirement from the propulsion unit. Furthermore, we will define a tangential co-ordinate system that moves along with the vehicle with respect to a fixed two-dimensional system. The roadway description will be utilized to calculate the distance traversed by a vehicle along the roadway.

The fixed co-ordinate system is attached to the earth such that the force of gravity is perpendicular to the unit vector $\bar{i}_F$. Let us consider a straight roadway, i.e., the steering wheel is locked straight along the $x_F$-direction. The roadway is then on the $x_F y_F$ plane of the fixed co-ordinate system (Figure 2.1).

The two-dimensional roadway can be described as $y_F = f(x_F)$. The *roadway position vector* $\bar{r}(x_F)$ between two points $a$ and $b$ along the horizontal direction is

$$\bar{r}(x_F) = x_F \bar{i}_F + f(x_F) \bar{j}_F \quad \text{for} \quad a \le x_F \le b.$$

The direction of motion and distance traversed by the vehicle is easier to express in terms of the *tangent vector* of the roadway position vector given as

$$\bar{T}(x_F) = \frac{d\bar{r}}{dx_F} = \bar{i}_F + \frac{df}{dx_F} \bar{j}_F$$

The distance norm of the tangent vector $\left\| \bar{T}(x_F) \right\|$ is

$$\left\| \bar{T}(x_F) \right\| = \sqrt{1 + \left[ \frac{df}{dx_F} \right]^2}$$

The *tangential roadway length s* is the distance traversed along the roadway. Mathematically, $s$ is the arc length of $y_F = f(x_F)$ over $a \le x_F \le b$. Therefore,

$$s = \int_a^b \left\| \bar{T}(x_F) \right\| dx_F.$$

The roadway percent grade can be described as a function of the roadway as

$$\beta(x_F) = \tan^{-1} \left[ \frac{df(x_F)}{dx_F} \right].$$

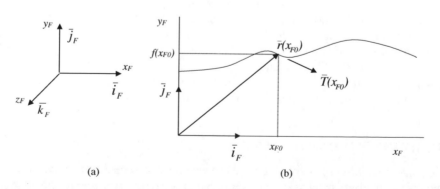

(a)                                                  (b)

**FIGURE 2.1**   (a) Fixed co-ordinate system. (b) Roadway on the fixed co-ordinate system.

**FIGURE 2.2**   Grade of the roadway.

The *average roadway percent grade* is the vertical rise per 100 horizontal distance of roadway with both distances expressed in the same unit. The angle $\beta$ of the roadway associated with the slope or grade is the angle between the tangent vector and the horizontal axis $x_F$ as shown in Figure 2.2. If $\Delta y$ is the vertical rise in meters, then

$$\% \text{ grade} = \frac{\Delta y}{100 \text{ m}} 100\% = \Delta y\%.$$

The tangent of the slope angle is, $\tan \beta = \dfrac{\Delta y}{100 \text{ m}}$.

The percent grade or $\beta$ is greater than zero when the vehicle is on an upward slope and is less than zero when the vehicle is going downhill.

### Exercise 2.1

A straight roadway has a profile in the $x_F y_F$ plane given by $f(x_F) = 3.9\sqrt{x_F}$ for $0 \le x_F \le 2$ miles. $x_F$ and $y_F$ are given in feet.

(a) Plot the roadway, (b) find $\beta(x_F)$, (c) find the percent grade at $x_F = 1$ mile and (d) find the tangential road length between 0 and 2 miles.

Ans. (b) $\tan^{-1} \dfrac{1.95}{\sqrt{x_F}}$; (c) 2.68% and (d) 10,580 ft.

## 2.2   LAWS OF MOTION

Newton's second law of motion can be expressed in equation form as

$$\sum_i \bar{F}_i = m\bar{a}$$

where $\sum_i \bar{F}_i$ is the net force, $m$ is the mass and $\bar{a}$ is the acceleration. The law is applied to the vehicle by considering a number of objects located at the several points of contact of the vehicle with the outside world on which the individual forces act. Examples of such points of contact are the front and rear wheels touching the roadway surface, the frontal area that meets the force from the air resistance, etc. We shall simplify the problem by merging all these points of contact into one location at the center of gravity (cg) of the vehicle, which is justified since the extent of the object is immaterial. For all the force calculations to follow, we shall consider the vehicle to be a particle mass located at the cg of the vehicle. The cg can be considered to be within the vehicle as shown in Figure 2.3.

The particle motion is described by the particle velocity and acceleration characteristics. For the position vector $\bar{r}$ for the particle mass on which several forces are working as shown in Figure 2.4, the velocity $v$ and acceleration $a$ are

**FIGURE 2.3**   Center of gravity (cg) of a vehicle.

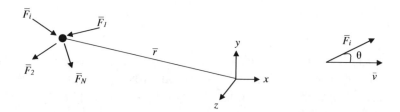

**FIGURE 2.4**   Forces on a particle.

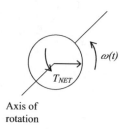

**FIGURE 2.5**   Rigid body rotation.

$$\bar{v} = \frac{d\bar{r}}{dt} \text{ and } \bar{a} = \frac{d\bar{v}}{dt}.$$

The power input to the particle for the $i$th force is

$$P_i = \bar{F}_i \cdot \bar{v} = \left|\bar{F}_i\right|\left|\bar{v}\right|\cos\theta$$

where $\theta$ is the angle between $F_i$ and the resultant velocity $v$.

For a rigid body rotating about a fixed axis, the equivalent terms relating motion and power are torque, angular velocity and angular acceleration. Let there be a number of independent torques acting on a rigid body causing it to rotate about one of its central principal axes of inertia as shown in Figure 2.5. If $J$ (unit: kg-m$^2$) is the polar moment of inertia of the rigid body, then the rotational form of Newton's second law of motion in the scalar form is

$$\sum_i T_i = T_{NET} = J\alpha$$

where

$\omega$ = angular speed (rads/s) and
$\alpha = \frac{d\omega}{dt} = \frac{d^2\theta}{dt^2}$ = angular acceleration (rads/s$^2$).

The power input for the $i$th torque is $P_i = T_i\omega$.

## 2.3   VEHICLE KINETICS

The tangential direction of forward motion of a vehicle changes with the slope of the roadway. In order to simplify the equations, a tangential co-ordinate system is defined below so that the forces acting on the vehicle can be defined through a one-dimensional equation. Let $\bar{u}_T(x_F)$ be the *unit tangent vector* in the fixed co-ordinate system pointing in the direction of increasing $x_F$. Therefore,

$$\bar{u}_T(x_F) = \frac{\bar{T}_F(x_F)}{\left\|\bar{T}_F(x_F)\right\|} = \frac{\bar{i}_F + \dfrac{df}{dx_F}\,\bar{j}_F}{\sqrt{1+\left[\dfrac{df}{dx_F}\right]^2}}.$$

The tangential co-ordinate system shown in Figure 2.6 has the same origin as the fixed co-ordinate system. The $z$-direction unit vector is the same as in the fixed co-ordinate system, but the $x$- and $y$-direction vectors are constantly changing with the slope of the roadway.

Newton's second law of motion can now be applied to the cg of EV in the tangential co-ordinate system as

$$\sum \bar{F}_T = m\bar{a}_T = m\frac{d\,\bar{v}_T}{dt}$$

where $m$ is the total vehicle mass. In terms of the components of the co-ordinate system,

$$\sum \bar{F}_{xT} = m\frac{d\,\bar{v}_{xT}}{dt} \text{ (compoment tangent to the road)},$$

$$\sum \bar{F}_{yT} = m\frac{d\,\bar{v}_{yT}}{dt} \text{ (component normal to the road)},$$

$$\sum F_{zT} = m\frac{d\,\bar{v}_{zT}}{dt} = 0 \text{ (since motion is assumed confined to the } x\text{–}y \text{ plane)}.$$

$v_{xT}$ is the vehicle tangential velocity. The gravitational force in the normal direction is balanced by the road reaction force, and hence, there will be no motion in the $y_T$ normal direction. In other words, the tire always remains in contact with the road. Therefore, the normal velocity $v_{yT}$ is zero. The vehicle motion has been assumed confined to the $x_F y_F$ or $x_T y_T$ plane, and hence, there is neither force nor velocity acting in the $z$-direction. These justified simplifications allow us to use a one-directional analysis for vehicle propulsion in the $x_T$-direction. It is shown in the following that the

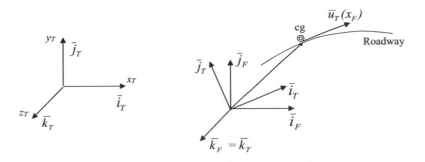

**FIGURE 2.6**   Tangential co-ordinate system and the unit tangent vector on a roadway.

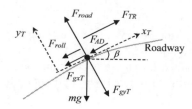

**FIGURE 2.7**   Forces acting on a vehicle.

vehicle tractive force and the opposing forces are all in the $x_T$-direction, and hence, the vector sign '-' will not be used in the symbols for simplicity.

The propulsion unit of the vehicle exerts the *tractive force* $F_{TR}$ to propel the vehicle forward at a desired velocity. The tractive force must overcome the opposing forces, which are summed together and labeled as the *road load force* $F_{RL}$. The road load force consists of the gravitational force, rolling resistance of the tires and the aerodynamic drag force. The road load force is

$$F_{RL} = F_{gxT} + F_{roll} + F_{AD} \tag{2.1}$$

where $x_T$ is the tangential direction along the roadway. The forces acting on the vehicle are shown in Figure 2.7.

The gravitational force depends on the slope of the roadway. The force is positive when climbing a grade and is negative when descending a downslope roadway. The gravitational force to be overcome by the vehicle moving forward is

$$F_{gxT} = mg \sin \beta \tag{2.2}$$

where $m$ is the total mass of the vehicle, $g$ is the gravitational acceleration constant and $\beta$ is the grade angle with respect to the horizon.

The rolling resistance is produced by the flattening of the tire at the contact surface with the roadway. In a perfectly round tire, the normal force to the road balances the distributed weight borne by the wheel at the point of contact along the vertical line beneath the axle. When the tire flattens, the instantaneous center of rotation at the wheel moves forward from beneath the axle towards the direction of motion of the vehicle as shown in Figure 2.8. The weight on the wheel and the road normal force are misaligned due to the flattening of the tire and form a couple that exerts a retarding torque on the wheel. The *rolling resistance force* $F_{roll}$ is the force due to the couple, which opposes the motion of the wheel. The force $F_{roll}$ is tangential to the roadway and always assists in braking or retarding the motion of the vehicle. The tractive force $F_{TR}$ must overcome this force $F_{roll}$ along with the gravitational force and the aerodynamic drag force. The rolling resistance can be minimized by keeping the tires as much inflated as possible. The ratio of the retarding force due to rolling

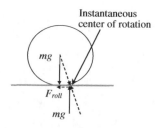

**FIGURE 2.8**   Rolling resistance force of wheels.

resistance and the vertical load on the wheel is known as the *coefficient of rolling resistance* $C_0$. The rolling resistance force on a roadway of slope $\beta$ is

$$F_{roll} = \begin{cases} \text{sgn}[v_{xT}]mg\cos\beta\left(C_0 + C_1 v_{xT}^2\right) & \text{if } v_{xT} \neq 0 \\ (F_{TR} - F_{gxT}) & \text{if } v_{xT} = 0 \text{ and } \left|F_{TR} - F_{gxT}\right| \leq C_0 mg\cos\beta \\ \text{sgn}[F_{TR} - F_{gxT}](C_0 mg\cos\beta) & \text{if } v_{xT} = 0 \text{ and } \left|F_{TR} - F_{gxT}\right| > C_0 mg\cos\beta \end{cases} \quad (2.3)$$

Typically $0.004 < C_0 < 0.02$ (unitless) and $C_1 \ll C_0$ (s²/m²). $C_0 mg$ is the maximum rolling resistance at standstill. The $\text{sgn}[v_{xT}]$ is the signum function given as

$$\text{sgn}[v_{xT}] = \begin{cases} 1 & \text{if } v_{xT} \geq 0 \\ -1 & \text{if } v_{xT} < 0 \end{cases}.$$

The aerodynamic drag force is the viscous resistance of the air working against the motion of the vehicle. The force is given by

$$F_{AD} = \text{sgn}[v_{xT}]\{0.5\rho C_D A_F (v_{xT} + v_0)^2\} \quad (2.4)$$

where $\rho$ is the air density in kg/m³, $C_D$ is the aerodynamic drag coefficient (dimensionless and typically is $0.2 < C_D < 0.4$), $A_F$ is the equivalent frontal area of the vehicle and $v_0$ is the head-wind velocity.

## 2.4 DYNAMICS OF VEHICLE MOTION

The tractive force is the force supplied by the electric motor in an EV and by the combination of electric motor and internal combustion engine in a HEV to overcome the road load. The dynamic equation of motion in the tangential direction is given by

$$k_m m \frac{dv_{xT}}{dt} = F_{TR} - F_{RL} \quad (2.5)$$

where $k_m$ is the rotational inertia coefficient to compensate for the apparent increase in the vehicle's mass due to the on-board rotating mass. Typical value of $k_m$ is between 1.08 and 1.1, and it is dimensionless. Additional explanation on rotational inertia appears in Section 2.7.4. $\frac{dv_{xT}}{dt}$ is the acceleration of the vehicle.

The dynamic equations can be represented in the state space format for simulation of an EV or a HEV system. The motion described by Equation 2.5 is the fundamental relationship required for dynamic simulation of the vehicle system. $v_{xT}$ is one of the state variables of the vehicle dynamical system. The second equation needed for modeling and simulation is the velocity equation where either $s$ or $x_F$ can be used as the state variable. The slope of the roadway $\beta$ will be an input to the simulation model, which may be given in terms of the tangential roadway distance $s$ as $\beta = \beta(s)$ or in terms of the horizontal distance as $\beta = \beta(x_F)$. If $\beta$ is given in terms of $s$, then the second state variable equation is

$$\frac{ds}{dt} = v_{xT}. \quad (2.6)$$

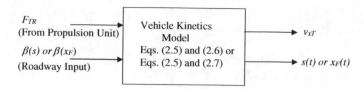

**FIGURE 2.9**   Modeling of vehicle kinetics and roadway.

If $\beta$ is given in terms of $x_F$, then the second state variable equation is

$$\frac{dx_F}{dt} = \frac{v_{xT}}{\sqrt{1 + \left[\dfrac{df}{dx_F}\right]^2}}. \qquad (2.7)$$

The input–output relational diagram for simulating the vehicle kinetics is shown in Figure 2.9.

## 2.5   PROPULSION POWER

The desired power rating of the electric motor or the power required from the combination of electric motor and internal combustion engine (i.e. the propulsion unit) can be calculated from the above equations based on the system constraints of starting acceleration, vehicle rated and maximum velocity and vehicle gradability. The torque at the wheels of the vehicle can be obtained from the power relation

$$\text{Power} = T_{TR} \cdot \omega_{wh} = F_{TR} \cdot v_{xT} \ [\text{W}] \qquad (2.8)$$

where $T_{TR}$ is the tractive torque in Nm and $\omega_{wh}$ is the angular velocity of the wheel in rads/s. $F_{TR}$ is in $N$ and $v_{xT}$ is in m/s. The angular velocity and the vehicle speed is related by

$$v_{xT} = \omega_{wh} \cdot r_{wh} \qquad (2.9)$$

where $r_{wh}$ is the radius of the wheel in meters. The losses between the propulsion unit and wheels in the transmission and the differential have to be appropriately accounted for while specifying the power requirement of the propulsion unit.

A big advantage of an electrically driven propulsion system is the elimination of multiple gears to match the vehicle speed and the engine speed. The wide speed range operation of electric motors enabled by power electronics control makes it possible to use a single gear-ratio transmission for instantaneous matching of the available motor torque $T_{motor}$ with the desired tractive torque $T_{TR}$. The gear ratio and the size depend on the maximum motor speed, the maximum vehicle speed and the wheel radius. A higher motor speed relative to the vehicle speed means a higher gear ratio, larger size and higher cost. However, higher motor speed is also desired in order to increase the power density of the motor. Therefore, a compromise is necessary between the maximum motor speed and the gear ratio to optimize the cost. Planetary gears are typically used for EVs with the gear ratio rarely exceeding 10.

### 2.5.1   Force–Velocity Characteristics

Having identified the fundamental forces and the associated dynamics for EV and HEVs, let us now attempt to relate these equations to a vehicle design specification and requirements. For an efficient design of the propulsion unit, the designer must know the force required to accelerate the vehicle to a cruising speed within a certain time and then to propel the vehicle forward at the rated steady-state

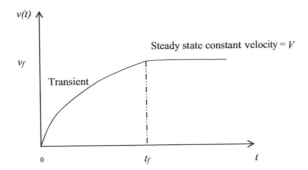

**FIGURE 2.10** Plot of velocity profile.

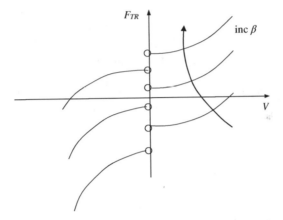

**FIGURE 2.11** Tractive force versus steady-state velocity characteristics.

cruising speed and at the maximum speed on a specified slope. The useful design information is contained in the vehicle speed versus time and the steady-state tractive force versus constant velocity characteristics, illustrated in Figures 2.10 and 2.11. In the sections to follow and in the remainder of this book, we will always assume the velocity to be in the tangential direction and denote it by $v$ instead of $v_{xT}$ for simplicity. The steady-state constant velocity will be denoted by the upper case $V$.

The tractive force versus steady-state velocity characteristics can be obtained from the equation of motion (Equation 2.5). When steady-state velocity is reached, $\dfrac{dv}{dt} = 0$; and hence, $\Sigma F = 0$. Therefore, we have

$$F_{TR} - F_{AD} - F_{ROLL} - F_{gxT} = 0$$

$$\Rightarrow F_{TR} = mg\left[\sin\beta + C_0\,\mathrm{sgn}(V)\right] + \mathrm{sgn}(V)\left[mgC_1 + \frac{\rho}{2}C_D A_F\right]V^2.$$

Note that

1. $\dfrac{dF_{TR}}{dV} = 2V\,\mathrm{sgn}(V)\left(\dfrac{\rho C_D A_F}{2} + mgC_1\right) > 0 \;\; \forall\, V$ and

2. $\lim\limits_{V \to 0^+} F_{TR} \neq \lim\limits_{V \to 0^-} F_{TR}.$

The first equation reveals that the slope of $F_{TR}$ versus $V$ is always positive, meaning that the force requirement increases more than the velocity increase as the vehicle speed increases, which is due

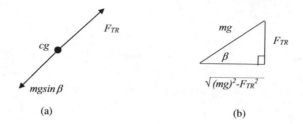

**FIGURE 2.12** (a) Force diagram to determine maximum gradability. (b) Tractive force and $mg$ with respect to the grade.

to the aerodynamic drag force opposing the vehicle motion. Also, the discontinuity of the curves at zero velocity is due to the rolling resistance force.

## 2.5.2 Maximum Gradability

The maximum grade that a vehicle will be able to overcome with the maximum force available from the propulsion unit is an important design criterion as well as performance measure. The vehicle is expected to move forward very slowly when climbing a steep slope, and hence, we can make the following assumptions for maximum gradability:

1. The vehicle moves very slowly $\Rightarrow v \cong 0$.
2. $F_{AD}$ and $F_{roll}$ are negligible.
3. The vehicle is not accelerating, i.e., $dv/dt = 0$.
4. $F_{TR}$ is the maximum tractive force delivered by motor (or motors) at near zero speed.

At near stall condition, under the above assumptions,

$$\Sigma F = 0 \Rightarrow F_{TR} - F_{gxT} = 0 \Rightarrow F_{TR} = mg \sin \beta.$$

Therefore, $\sin \beta = \dfrac{F_{TR}}{mg}$. The maximum percent grade is

$$\text{Max.\% grade} = 100 \tan \beta$$

$$\Rightarrow \text{Max.\% grade} = \frac{100 F_{TR}}{\sqrt{(mg)^2 - F_{TR}^2}} \tag{2.10}$$

The force diagram for the maximum gradability condition is shown in Figure 2.12.

## 2.6 VELOCITY AND ACCELERATION

The energy required from the propulsion unit depends on the desired acceleration and the road load force that the vehicle has to overcome. The maximum acceleration is limited by the maximum tractive power available and the roadway condition at the time of vehicle operation. Although the road load force is unknown in a real-world roadway, significant insight about the vehcile velocity profile and energy requirement can be obtained through studies of assumed scenarios. The vehicles are typically designed with a certain objective, such as maximum acceleration on a given roadway slope on a typical weather condition. Two simplified scenarios that will set forth the stage for designing electric and hybrid EVs are discussed in the following.

## 2.6.1 CONSTANT $F_{TR}$, LEVEL ROAD

In the first case, we will assume a level road condition where the propulsion unit for an EV exerts a constant tractive force. The level road condition implies that $\beta(s) = 0$. We will assume that the EV is initially at rest, which implies $v(0) = 0$. The free body diagram at $t = 0$ is shown in Figure 2.13a.

Assume $F_{TR}(0) = F_{TR} > C_o mg$, i.e., the initial tractive force is capable of overcoming the initial rolling resistance. Therefore,

$$\Sigma F(0) = ma(0) = m\frac{dv(0)}{dt}$$

$$\Rightarrow F_{TR} - C_0 mg = m\frac{dv(0)}{dt}.$$

Since $F_{TR}(0) > C_0 mg$, $\dfrac{dv(0)}{dt} > 0$ and the velocity $v$ increases. Once the vehicle starts to move, the forces acting on it changes. At $t > 0$,

$$\Sigma F = m\frac{dv}{dt} \Rightarrow F_{TR} - F_{AD} - F_{roll} = m\frac{dv}{dt}$$

$$\Rightarrow F_{TR} - \text{sgn}\,[v(t)]\frac{\rho}{2}C_D A_F v^2(t) - \text{sgn}[v(t)]mg\left(C_0 + C_1 v^2(t)\right) = m\frac{dv}{dt}$$

Assuming $v(t) > 0$ for $t > 0$ and solving for $\dfrac{dv}{dt}$,

$$\frac{dv}{dt} = \left(\frac{F_{TR}}{m} - gC_0\right) - \left[\frac{\rho}{2m}C_D A_F + gC_1\right]v^2$$

Let us define the following constants for a constant $F_{TR}$ acceleration

$$K_1 = \frac{F_{TR}}{m} - gC_0 > 0$$

$$K_2 = \frac{\rho}{2m}C_D A_F + gC_1 > 0$$

which gives $\dfrac{dv}{dt} = K_1 - K_2 v^2$.

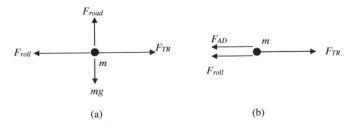

(a)     (b)

FIGURE 2.13 Forces acting on the vehicle on a level road: (a) free body diagram at $t = 0$ and (b) forces on the vehicle at $t > 0$.

### 2.6.1.1  Velocity Profile

The velocity profile for the constant $F_{TR}$, level road case can be obtained from solving for $v$ from the $\dfrac{dv}{dt}$ equation above, which gives (see Figure 2.14)

$$v(t) = \sqrt{\frac{K_1}{K_2}} \tanh\left(\sqrt{K_1 K_2}\, t\right) \qquad (2.11)$$

The terminal velocity can be obtained by taking the limit of the velocity profile as time approaches infinity. The terminal velocity is

$$V_T = \lim_{t \to \infty} v(t) = \sqrt{\frac{K_1}{K_2}} \;\Rightarrow\; \sqrt{K_1 K_2} = K_2 V_T.$$

### 2.6.1.2  Distance Traversed

The distance traversed by the vehicle can be obtained from the following relation:

$$\frac{ds(t)}{dt} = v(t) = V_T \tanh(K_2 V_T t)$$

The distance as a function of time is obtained by integrating the above equation:

$$s(t) = \frac{1}{K_2} \ln\left[\cosh(K_2 V_T t)\right] \qquad (2.12)$$

The starting acceleration is often specified as 0 to $v_f$ m/s in $t_f$ s, where $v_f$ is the desired velocity at the end of the specified time $t_f$ s. The time to reach the desired velocity and distance traversed during that time is given by

$$t_f = \frac{1}{K_2 V_T} \cosh^{-1}\left[e^{(K_2 s_f)}\right] \text{ and} \qquad (2.13)$$

$$s_f = \frac{1}{K_2} \ln\left[\cosh(K_2 V_T t_f)\right], \text{ respectively.} \qquad (2.14)$$

The desired time can also be expressed as

$$t_f = \frac{1}{\sqrt{K_1 K_2}} \tanh^{-1}\left(\sqrt{\frac{K_2}{K_1}}\, v_f\right) \qquad (2.15)$$

where $v_f$ is the velocity after time $t_f$.

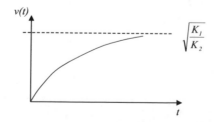

**FIGURE 2.14**  Velocity profile for a constant $F_{TR}$ on a level road.

For example, let $t_{V_T}$ = time to reach 98% of the terminal velocity $V_T$. Therefore,

$$t_{V_T} = \frac{1}{\sqrt{K_1 K_2}} \tanh^{-1}\left(\frac{0.98 V_T}{V_T}\right) \text{or}$$

$$t_{V_T} = \frac{2.3}{\sqrt{K_1 K_2}} \text{ or } \frac{2.3}{K_2 V_T}. \tag{2.16}$$

### 2.6.1.3  Tractive Power

The instantaneous tractive power delivered by the propulsion unit is

$$P_{TR}(t) = F_{TR} v(t).$$

Substituting for $v(t)$,

$$P_{TR}(t) = F_{TR} V_T \tanh(K_2 V_T t).$$

$$\Rightarrow P_{TR}(t) = F_{TR} V_T \tanh\left(\sqrt{K_1 K_2} t\right) = P_T \tanh\left(\sqrt{K_1 K_2} t\right). \tag{2.17}$$

The terminal power can be expressed as $P_T = F_{TR} V_T$. The tractive power required to reach the desired velocity $v_f$ over the acceleration interval $\Delta t$ (refer to Figure 2.15) is

$$P_{TRpk} = P_T \tanh\left(\sqrt{K_1 K_2} t_f\right). \tag{2.18}$$

The mean tractive power over the acceleration interval $\Delta t$ is

$$\overline{P_{TR}} = \frac{1}{t_f} \int_0^{t_f} P_{TR}(t)\, dt$$

$$\Rightarrow \overline{P_{TR}} = \frac{P_T}{t_f} \frac{1}{\sqrt{K_1 K_2}} \ln\left[\cosh\left(\sqrt{K_1 K_2} t_f\right)\right] \tag{2.19}$$

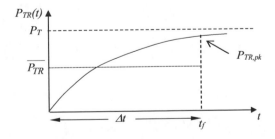

**FIGURE 2.15**   Acceleration interval $\Delta t = t_f - 0$.

#### 2.6.1.4 Energy Required

The energy requirement for a given acceleration and constant steady-state velocity is necessary for the design and selection of the energy source or batteries to cover a certain distance. The rate of change of energy is the tractive power given as

$$P_{TR}(t) = \frac{de_{TR}}{dt}$$

where $e_{TR}$ is the instantaneous tractive energy. The energy required or energy change during an interval of the vehicle can be obtained from the integration of the instantaneous power equation as

$$\int_{e_{TR}(0)}^{e_{TR}(t_f)} de_{TR} = \int_{t=0}^{t_f} P_{TR}\, dt \tag{2.20}$$

$$\Rightarrow \Delta e_{TR} = t_f \overline{P_{TR}}$$

### Example 2.1

An EV has the following parameter values:

$$m = 800 \text{ kg}, C_D = 0.2, A_F = 2.2 \text{ m}^2, C_0 = 0.008, C_1 = 1.6*10^{-6} \text{ s}^2/\text{m}^2,$$

Also, take density of air $\rho = 1.18 \text{ kg/m}^3$, and acceleration due to gravity $g = 9.81 \text{ m/s}^2$.

The vehicle is on level road. It accelerates from 0 to 65 mi/h in 10 s such that its velocity profile is given by

$$v(t) = 0.29055t^2 \text{ for } 0 \le t \le 10 \text{ s}.$$

a. Calculate $F_{TR}(t)$ for $0 \le t \le 10$ s.
b. Calculate $P_{TR}(t)$ for $0 \le t \le 10$ s.
c. Calculate the energy loss due to nonconservative forces $E_{loss}$.
d. Calculate $\Delta e_{TR}$.

#### Solution

a.

From the force balance equation,

$$F_{TR} - F_{AD} - F_{roll} = m\frac{dv}{dt}$$

$$\Rightarrow F_{TR}(t) = m\frac{dv}{dt} + \frac{\rho}{2}C_D A_F v^2 + mg(C_0 + C_1 v^2)$$

$$= 464.88t + 0.02192t^4 + 62.78 \text{ N}.$$

b.

The instantaneous power is

$$P_{TR}(t) = F_{TR}(t) \times v(t)$$

$$= 135.07t^3 + 0.00637t^6 + 18.24t^2 \text{ W}.$$

c.

The energy lost due to nonconservative forces

$$E_{loss} = \int_0^{10} v(F_{AD} + F_{roll})\,dt = \int_0^{10} 0.29055t^2(0.0219t^4 + 62.78)\,dt$$

$$= 15{,}180 \text{ J}.$$

d.

The kinetic energy of the vehicle is

$$\Delta KE = \frac{1}{2}m\left[v(10)^2 - v(0)^2\right] = 337{,}677 \text{ J}$$

Therefore, the change in tractive energy is

$$\Delta e_{TR} = 15{,}180 + 337{,}677$$

$$= 352{,}857 \text{ J}.$$

## Exercise 2.2

An EV has the following parameter values $\rho = 1.16\,\text{kg/m}^3$, $m = 692\,\text{kg}$, $C_D = 0.2$, $A_F = 2\,\text{m}^2$, $g = 9.81\,\text{m/s}^2$, $C_0 = 0.009$ and $C_1 = 1.75 \times 10^{-6}\text{s}^2/\text{m}^2$. The EV undergoes constant $F_{TR}$ acceleration on a level road starting from rest at $t = 0$. The maximum continuous $F_{TR}$ that the electric motor is capable of delivering to the wheels is $1{,}548\,\text{N}$.

a. Find $V_T(F_{TR})$ and plot it.
b. If $F_{TR} = 350\,\text{N}$, (i) find $V_T$, (ii) plot $v(t)$ for $t \geq 0$, (iii) find $t_{VT}$, (iv) calculate the time required to accelerate from 0 to 60 mph and (v) calculate $P_{TRpk}$, $\overline{P_{TR}}$, $\Delta e_{TR}$ corresponding to acceleration to $0.98\,V_T$.

Ans. (a) $V_T(F_{TR}) = 53.2\sqrt{1.45\times10^{-3}F_{TR} - 0.0883}$ m/s, (b) (i) 34.4 m/s, (ii) $v(t) = 34.4\tanh(1.22\times10^{-2}t)$ m/s, (iii) 189 s, (iv) 85.6 s and (v) $P_{TRpk} = 11.8\,\text{kW}$, $\overline{P_{TR}} = 8.46\,\text{kW}$, $\Delta e_{TR} = 1.61$ MJ.

## 2.6.2 Non-constant $F_{TR}$, General Acceleration

In the general case, with a non-constant $F_{TR}$ and an arbitrary velocity profile as shown in Figure 2.16, the force can be calculated as

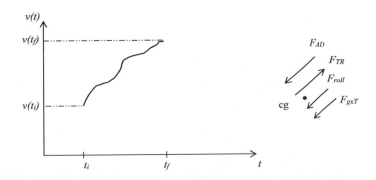

**FIGURE 2.16** Arbitrary velocity profile.

$$\Sigma F = m\frac{dv}{dt}$$

$$\Rightarrow F_{TR} - F_{AD} - F_{roll} - F_{gxT} = m\frac{dv}{dt}$$

$$\Rightarrow F_{TR} = m\frac{dv}{dt} + mg\sin\beta + F_{AD} + F_{roll}$$

$$= m\frac{dv}{dt} + mg\sin\beta + \left[ mgC_1 + \frac{\rho}{2}A_FC_D \right]v^2 + mgC_0. \qquad (2.21)$$

The instantaneous tractive power $P_{TR}(t)$ is

$$P_{TR}(t) = F_{TR}(t)v(t)$$

$$= mv\frac{dv}{dt} + v\left( F_{gxT} + F_{AD} + F_{roll} \right). \qquad (2.22)$$

The change in tractive energy $\Delta e_{TR}$ is

$$\Delta e_{TR} = \int_{t_i}^{t_f} P_{TR}(t)dt$$

$$= m\int_{v(t_i)}^{v(t_f)} v\,dv + \int_{t_i}^{t_f} (v)F_{gxT}\,dt + \int_{t_i}^{t_f} (v)\left( F_{AD} + F_{roll} \right)dt \qquad (2.23)$$

The energy supplied by the propulsion unit is converted into various forms of energy, some of which are stored in the vehicle system, while others are lost due to the non-constructive forces. It is interesting to note the type of energy associated with each term in Equation 2.23. Let us consider the first term on the right side of Equation 2.23

$$m\int_{v(t_i)}^{v(t_f)} v\,dv = \frac{1}{2}m\left[ v^2(t_f) - v^2(t_i) \right] = \Delta \text{ (kinetic energy)}$$

Also,

$$\int_{t_i}^{t_f} (v)F_{gxT}\,dt = mg\int_{t_i}^{t_f} v\sin\beta\,dt = mg\int_{s(t_i)}^{s(t_f)} \sin\beta\,ds = mg\int_{f(t_i)}^{f(t_f)} df$$

$$= mg\left[ f(t_f) - f(t_i) \right]$$

$$= \Delta \text{ (potential energy)}$$

The above term represents change in vertical displacement multiplied by $mg$, which is the change in potential energy.

The third and fourth terms on the right side of Equation 2.23 represent the energy required to overcome the non-constructive forces that include the rolling resistance and the aerodynamic drag force. The energy represented in these terms is essentially the loss term. Therefore,

$$\int_{t_i}^{t_f} (v)(F_{AD} + F_{roll})\,dt = E_{loss}.$$

Let $K_3 = mgC_0$, $K_4 = mgC_1 + \dfrac{\rho}{2}C_D A_F$. For, $v(t) > 0$, $t_i \leq t \leq t_f$,

$$E_{loss} = K_3 \int_{t_i}^{t_f} \frac{ds}{dt}\,dt + K_4 \int_{t_i}^{t_f} v^3\,dt;$$

$$= K_3 \Delta s + K_4 \int_{t_i}^{t_f} v^3\,dt.$$

In summary, we can write

$$\Delta e_{TR} = \frac{1}{2}m\left[v^2(t_f) - v^2(t_i)\right] + mg\left[f(t_f) - f(t_i)\right] + \int_{t_i}^{t_f}(v)(F_{AD} + F_{roll})\,dt \text{ or}$$

$$\Delta e_{TR} = \Delta \text{ (kinteic energy)} + \Delta \text{ (potential energy)} + E_{loss}$$

### Exercise 2.3

The vehicle with parameters given in Exercise 2.2 accelerates from 0 to 60 mph in 13.0 s for the following two acceleration types: (i) constant $F_{TR}$ and (ii) uniform acceleration.

  a. Plot on the same graph, the velocity profile of each acceleration type.
  b. Calculate and compare the tractive energy required for the two types of acceleration.

$$F_{TR} = \text{const.} = 1,548 \text{ N}.$$

Ans. (b) $\Delta e_{TR} = 0.2752$ MJ for constant $F_{TR}$ and $\Delta e_{TR} = 0.2744$ MJ for uniform acceleration.

## 2.7   TIRE–ROAD FORCE MECHANICS

A number of forces including the traction force act at the tire-ground contact plane of a moving vehicle. The traction torque from the propulsion system is converted into a traction force through an interaction of the pneumatic tire and the road surface at the tire–road interface. The pneumatic tire is designed to perform several functions of a ground vehicle including support of the vehicle weight and provide traction for driving and braking. The performance potential of a vehicle depends not only on the characteristics of the propulsion system and transmission but also on the maximum traction (or braking) force that can be sustained at the tire–road interface. The maximum friction force sustainable is determined by the friction coefficient of the pneumatic tire which depends on its road adhesion characteristics and the normal load on the drive axle or axles. The smaller of the propulsion system traction (or braking) force and the maximum sustainable friction force determines the overall behavior of the vehicle. The traction properties at the tire–road interface are fundamental in evaluating the dynamic behavior of a vehicle. The study of tire mechanics helps understand the mechanism of force transmission between the axle and the road. The subject is complex, and several theories have been proposed to provide the understanding of the process involved [1–3]; a basic overview is presented in this book.

## 2.7.1   Slip

The friction forces that are fundamental to vehicle traction depend on the difference between the tire rolling speed and its linear speed of travel. The tire rolling speed is related to the wheel angular speed and is given by

$$v_{tire} = \omega_{wh} r_{wh}$$

where $\omega_{wh}$ is the wheel speed and $r_{wh}$ is the driven wheel radius. The wheel speed of travel is equivalent to the vehicle translatory speed $v$. Vehicle linear velocity $v$ and the tire speed $v_{tire}$ differ in magnitude and direction as shown in Figure 2.17. The angle between the tire velocity and the vehicle velocity is known as slip angle $\alpha$, shown in Figure 2.17 with exaggeration. The difference in speed itself is generated due to the tire properties and the interaction of forces at the tire–road interface. The tire forces do not act through a point but are distributed over the contact patch area of the tire with the road surface. Furthermore, the forces are not uniform along the contact patch in either longitudinal or lateral directions. The vehicle traction force $F_{TR}$ works in the longitudinal direction. Longitudinal and lateral forces will be discussed further later; first, let us discuss the vehicle slip in the longitudinal direction.

The tire treads gradually enter the contact patch of a moving vehicle when traction torque is applied to the driven wheel. The tire treads in front end of the contact patch undergo high levels of compression compared to the rear end due to the traction torque applied at the axle. The rolling of the wheels and the traction torque also causes a shift in instantaneous center of rotation. The sidewall of the tire simultaneously goes through shear deformation. The distance that the tire travels when subject to propulsion torque will be less than that in a free rolling tire due to the compression. This results in a difference between the wheel angular speed and vehicle speed, which is known as *longitudinal slip* or simply *slip*. Slip is defined as the ratio of linear vehicle velocity and the spin velocity of the wheel. Mathematically, slip $s$ of a vehicle is given as

$$s = \left(1 - \frac{v}{\omega_{wh} r_{wh}}\right) \tag{2.24}$$

where $v$ is the vehicle velocity. Since vehicle velocity $v$ is smaller than wheel angular velocity converted to linear velocity $\omega_{wh} r_{wh}$, the slip is a positive number between 0 and 1.0 for propulsion. Slip is often expressed as a percentage.

**FIGURE 2.17**   Speed and forces in the tire–road contact patch area.

The vehicle velocity is then given by

$$v = \omega_{wh} r_{wh} (1-s)$$

During vehicle braking, the tire is subject to similar compression due to the applied braking torque, and a difference in vehicle speed and wheel angular speed occurs enabling the vehicle stop. The slip during braking is given as

$$s = \left(1 - \frac{\omega_{wh} r_{wh}}{v}\right) \tag{2.25}$$

## 2.7.2 TRACTION FORCE AT TIRE–ROAD INTERFACE

The rotary motion of the axles is converted to linear motion of the vehicle at the tire–road interface to enable vehicle motion. When a torque is applied at a driven wheel through the axle of a vehicle, friction forces proportional to the traction torque are developed at the tire–road interface. The forces on the tire are not localized at a point as mentioned previously but are the resultant of the normal and shear stresses exerted by each element of the tire tread distributed in the contact patch. The stress under the tire is distributed non-uniformly in the $x$- and $z$-directions along the two-dimensional contact patch at the tire–road interface; this two-dimensional stress distribution gives rise to both longitudinal and lateral forces. The longitudinal and lateral forces can be obtained by integrating the shear stress in the contact patch over the contact area. The longitudinal force is the traction force responsible for the forward velocity of the vehicle. We will focus our discussion on the longitudinal force; this force has been referred to as traction force $F_{TR}$ earlier in the chapter.

The forces on a wheel and the stress distribution at the tire–road interface are shown in Figure 2.18. The stress distribution and the resultant forces are shown in relation with the contact patch area at the tire–road interface. The traction torque $T_{TR}$ working around the axis of rotation of the wheel results in the wheel angular velocity $\omega_{wh}$; this traction torque is primarily responsible for the distributed pressure or stress at the tire–road interface. The longitudinal stress distribution

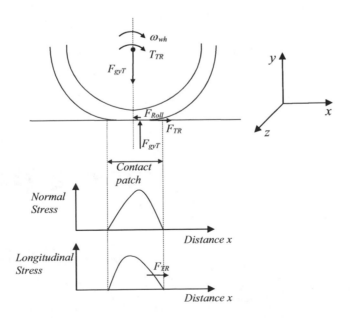

**FIGURE 2.18** Forces on the wheel and stress distribution at the tire–road interface.

over the contact patch is shown to have generated the traction force. In addition, there is normal stress due the weight borne at the axle of wheel which works in the vertical *y*-direction. The vertical or normal pressure shifts forward due to the deformation of the tire at the tire–road interface. Consequently, the centroid of the normal road reaction force is shifted forward and is not aligned with the spin axis of the wheel. This results in the rolling resistance force $F_{roll}$. Figure 2.18 also shows the normal stress distribution over the contact patch area of the rolling tire. The normal stress distribution integrated over the contact patch area results in the normal road reaction force $F_{gyT}$. The normal force $F_{gyT}$ plays a strong role in determining the traction force limit, which is addressed later in the section.

### 2.7.3  FORCE TRANSMISSION AT TIRE–ROAD INTERFACE

The tire–road interface can be thought of a gear mechanism responsible for the generation of the traction force. The conversion of rotary motion of the wheels to linear motion of the vehicle can be compared to the ball-screw arrangement shown in Figure 2.19, which is a gear mechanism used for force transmission along with conversion of rotary motion to linear motion. Let us consider that power is being transmitted from the rotary gear to the linear gear with the latter held stationary. The rotary gear is driven along its spin axis by a rotary motor, which enables the rotary system of motor and gear to move along the linear gear train. In this system, when torque is applied by the rotary motor friction force is developed in the gear train that helps the rotary system move forward or backward. This type of friction force enables vehicle propulsion along the road surface except that a pneumatic tire and a paved surface is used for developing the friction force which has been labeled as traction force $F_{TR}$.

Two mechanisms contribute to the friction coupling at the tire–road interface in a vehicle; these are *adhesion* and *hysteresis* [3]. Adhesion and hysteresis friction forces generated at the tire–road interface due to the vehicle propulsion torque are shown in Figure 2.20. Adhesion to the road results

**FIGURE 2.19**  Ball-screw gear arrangement for converting rotary motion to linear motion.

**FIGURE 2.20**  Forces at tire–road interface on a rolling tire.

from the intermolecular bonds between the rubber and road surface aggregates. In the microscopic level, the road surface is not smooth but has the peaks and valley of the surface aggregates as shown in Figure 2.20. The adhesion friction dominates in dry pavements, but the contribution decreases under wet conditions. The hysteresis is the deformation of the rubber when it is sliding over the road aggregates; the friction component comes from the energy loss due to hysteresis. Water does not affect hysteresis friction significantly; tires with improved wet traction are designed with high-hysteresis rubber in the tread.

The friction forces of adhesion and hysteresis depend heavily on the deformation of the tire at the tire–road interface due to the tire properties and the interaction of forces. This tire deformation results in the vehicle longitudinal slip, and the vehicle slip itself is fundamental to vehicle traction. The slip determines the traction force that the tire–road interface can support. Therefore, some slip is essential for vehicle traction, but too much slippage reduces the traction force limit.

### 2.7.4 QUARTER CAR MODEL

The study of the laws of motion often starts from the consideration of a quarter car, i.e., one quarter of the vehicle. The quarter car model is shown in Figure 2.21. The quarter car model allows analyzing separately the behavior of driving (powered) wheels and trailing (unpowered) wheels. Moreover, as the chassis and wheel dynamics are treated separately, this model is especially useful to study suspension dynamics if vertical components of forces are taken into account.

Using the same assumptions as in Section 2.3, the $x$-component of Newton's second law of motion applied to the chassis is

$$F_{Rw} - F_{AD} - F_{gxT} - F_{Rr} = m\frac{dv}{dt} \tag{2.26}$$

where $F_{Rw}$ is the reaction force exchanged between the wheel and the chassis, $m$ is the mass of a quarter of the chassis and $F_{Rr}$ is the reaction force between the front and the rear portions of the car, as shown in Figure 2.22. The components on the $y$-axis are omitted as suspension dynamics will not be analyzed here.

**FIGURE 2.21**   Quarter car model.

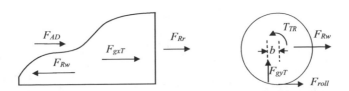

**FIGURE 2.22**   $x$-Axis force components of chassis and forces and torques of wheels in the quarter car model.

The wheel dynamics can be achieved from the balance of forces and torques as

$$-F_{Rw} - F_{roll} = m_w \frac{dv}{dt}$$                                        (2.27)

$$T_{TR} - F_{gyT}b + F_{roll}r_{wh} = J_w \frac{d\omega_{wh}}{dt}$$              (2.28)

where $T_{TR}$ is the driving or tractive torque, $m_w$ is the mass of the wheel and $r_{wh}$ is the wheel radius. $T_{TR}$ is zero for the trailing wheel. The tractive force is the force supplied by the electric motor in an EV and by the combination of electric motor and IC engine in a HEV to overcome the road load.

Substituting Equations 2.27 and 2.28 in Equation 2.26, we can write

$$\frac{T_{TR}}{r_{wh}} - F_{gyT}\frac{b}{r_{wh}} - F_{AD} - F_{gxT} - F_{Rr} = (m + m_w)\frac{dv}{dt} + \frac{J_w}{r_{wh}}\frac{d\omega_{wh}}{dt}$$                          (2.29)

It can be easily concluded that the road load force of Equation 2.29 has the same components as that of Equation 2.1 and that the term $T_{TR}/r_{wh}$ plays the role of the traction force. To accelerate the vehicle, the traction force has to overcome rolling resistance, aerodynamic load, weight component and the equivalent force of the rear portion of the car. The right-hand side of Equation 2.29 can be written in simplified form as

$$(m + m_w)\frac{dv}{dt} + \frac{J_w}{r_{wh}}\frac{d\omega_{wh}}{dt} = k_m m \frac{dv}{dt}$$                          (2.30)

The term $k_m m \dfrac{dv}{dt}$ is an equivalent force of inertia accounting for the translating mass of the quarter car plus the inertia of the rotating masses. Finally, the general form of the dynamic equation of motion in the tangential direction assumes the same form as Equation 2.5:

$$k_m m \frac{dv}{dt} = F_{TR} - F_{RL} - F_{Rr}$$                                (2.31)

where $k_m$ is the rotational inertia coefficient. In Equation 2.30, the tangential speed of the wheel can also differ from the spin velocity of the wheel, according to the value of the slip.

## 2.7.5  TRACTION LIMIT AND CONTROL

The maximum rolling resistance force that can be sustained at the tire–road interface depends on the amount of vehicle slip and the vertical load on the wheel. A slip-dependent friction coefficient $\mu(s)$ and the vertical load define the rolling resistance on the wheel as

$$F_{roll}(s) = \mu(s)F_{gyT}$$

where $F_{gyT}$ is the normal force on the wheel.

Accordingly, wheel equations can be rewritten as

$$-F_{Rw} - F_{roll}(s) = m_w \frac{dv}{dt}$$

$$T_{TR} - F_{gyT}b + F_{roll}(s)r_{wh} = J_w \frac{d\omega_{wh}}{dt}$$

Typical friction coefficients for both longitudinal and lateral forces as a function of slip for a fixed slip angle are shown in Figure 2.23. The traction force limit in the contact patch increases almost linearly with slip at the beginning as the majority of tire tread elements are worked most effectively without significant slip. The traction force limit reaches its peak at around 20% of the slip. The relationship between traction effort limit and slip becomes nonlinear beyond the peak; when the slip reaches 100%, the vehicle is sliding only without any linear velocity.

On a dry pavement, the traction force limit peak is about 80%–90% of the vertical load. Peak friction coefficient $\mu_p$ defines this limit. The friction coefficient when the slip reaches 100% is known as sliding coefficient $\mu_s$. The friction coefficients vary depending on the road condition, although the shape of the curves remains the same. The nominal peak and sliding friction coefficients for several ground conditions are given in Table 2.1. The peak and sliding friction coefficients of an icy road will be much smaller than that of a dry pavement meaning the wheel will slip much more easily for the same traction torque from the propulsion system. In wheel slippage conditions, the tire–road interface cannot develop the traction force due to the lower friction force limits even though there is traction torque at the wheels. The location of where the peak will appear depends on the slip angle. For smaller slip angles, the peak appears at smaller slip values.

Traction control system (TCS) is incorporated in today's vehicles for controlling both longitudinal and lateral forces. The longitudinal control algorithm limits the traction force to prevent slippage. The lateral control is achieved by keeping the yaw motion to zero. This can be achieved, for example, by controlling the steering angle. The independent slippage prevention on each wheel of a four-wheel-drive vehicle greatly improves the lateral stability. The dynamics of traction systems are highly nonlinear and time-variant; consequently, the design of model-based TCS is also nonlinear and time-varying. The major difficulty for designing such systems is the real-time estimation of friction coefficient versus slip characteristics for different tires and road surfaces.

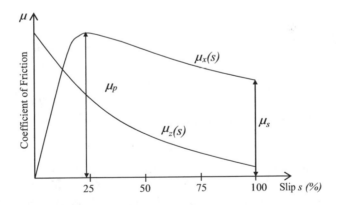

**FIGURE 2.23** Longitudinal and lateral traction force coefficient variation.

**TABLE 2.1**
**Nominal Longitudinal Peak and Sliding Friction Coefficients**

| Surface | Peak Coefficient, $\mu_p$ | Sliding Coefficient, $\mu_s$ |
|---|---|---|
| Asphalt and concrete (dry) | 0.9 | 0.75 |
| Concrete (wet) | 0.8 | 0.7 |
| Asphalt (wet) | 0.6 | 0.5 |
| Gravel | 0.6 | 0.55 |
| Snow | 0.2 | 0.15 |
| Ice | 0.1 | 0.07 |

## 2.8  PROPULSION SYSTEM DESIGN

The steady-state maximum velocity, maximum gradability and the velocity equations can be used in the design stage to specify the power requirement of a particular vehicle.

Let us consider the tractive power requirement for initial acceleration, which plays a significant role in determining the rated power of the propulsion unit. The initial acceleration is specified as 0 to $v_f$ in $t_f$ s. The design problem is to solve for $F_{TR}$ starting with a set of variables including vehicle mass, rolling resistance, aerodynamic drag coefficient, percent grade, wheel radius, etc., some of which are known, while others have to be assumed. The acceleration of the vehicle in terms of these variables is given by

$$a = \frac{dv}{dt} = \frac{F_{TR} - F_{RL}}{m} \tag{2.32}$$

The tractive force output of the electric motor for an EV or the combination of electric motor and internal combustion engine for a HEV will be a function of the vehicle velocity. Furthermore, the road load characteristics are also function of velocity resulting in a transcendental equation to be solved to determine the desired tractive power from the propulsion unit. The other design requirements also play a significant role in determining the tractive power. The problem is best handled by a computer simulation where the various equations of Sections 2.5 and 2.6 can be used iteratively to calculate the tractive force and power requirements from the propulsion unit for the given set of specifications.

The insight gained from the scenarios discussed in this chapter will be used later to specify the power ratings of the electric motor and internal combustion engines for electric and hybrid vehicles in the next chapter.

## PROBLEMS

### 2.1

A length of road is straight and it has a profile in the $x$–$y$ plane described by

$$f(x) = 200 \ln\left[7.06 * 10^{-4}(x + 1,416)\right].$$

where $0 \le x \le 3$ mile $= 15,840$ ft.; $f(x)$ and $x$ are in feet.

a. Plot the road profile in the $x$–$y$ plane for $0 \le x \le 15,840$ ft.
b. Derive an expression for $\beta(x)$. Calculate $\beta$ (500 ft.).
c. Derive an expression for *percent grade* $(x)$. Calculate *percent grade* (500 ft.).
d. Derive an expression for tangential road length $s(x)$, such that $s(0) = 0$. Calculate $s$ (500 ft.)
e. Can you find an expression for $x(s)$, i.e., can you express $x$ as a function of $s$? Show some steps in your attempt.

### 2.2

A straight roadway has a profile in the $x$–$y$ plane given by

$$f(x_f) = 4.1\overline{)x_f} \quad \text{for } 0 \le x_f \le 2 \text{ mile} = 10,560 \text{ ft.}$$

$f(x_f)$ and $x_f$ are in ft.

a. Derive an expression for $\beta(x_f)$. Calculate $\beta$ (1 mile).
b. Calculate the tangential road length, $s$ from 0 to 2 miles.

## 2.3

An EV has the following parameter values:

$m = 692\,\text{kg}$, $C_D = 0.2$, $A_F = 2\,\text{m}^2$, $C_0 = 0.009$, $C_1 = 1.75*10^{-6}\text{s}^2/\text{m}^2$.
Also, take $\rho = 1.16\,\text{kg/m}^3$, $g = 9.81\,\text{m/s}^2$,

a. *EV at rest* The EV is stopped at a stop sign at a point in the road where the grade is +15%. The tractive force of the vehicle is supplied by the vehicle brakes.
   i. Calculate the tractive force necessary for zero rolling resistance (the vehicle is at rest).
   ii. Calculate the minimum tractive force required from the brakes to keep the EV from rolling down the grade.

b. *EV at constant velocity* The EV is moving at a constant velocity along a road that has a constant grade of −12%.

   i. Plot, on the same graph, the magnitudes of the tangential gravitational force ($F_{gxT}$), the aerodynamic drag force ($F_{AD}$) and the rolling resistance force ($F_{roll}$) versus velocity for $0 < V \leq 180$ mph. Over that range of velocity, does $F_{gxT}$ dominate? When does $F_{AD}$ dominate? When does $F_{roll}$ dominate? Label these regions on the graph.
   ii. Derive an expression for the tractive force as a function of velocity. Plot this expression on its own graph. Is the tractive force always in the same direction?

## 2.4

Showing all steps, derive and plot the velocity profile (i.e., $v(t)$) for constant $F_{TR}$-constant grade acceleration. (Constant grade means that $\beta$ is constant but not necessarily zero.) Given:

1. The EV starts from rest at $t = 0$.
2. Resultant of $F_{gxT}$ and $F_{TR}$ is enough to overcome the rolling resistance to get the EV moving.
3. $v(t) \geq 0$ for $t \geq 0$.

What effect does gravity have on the velocity profile?

## 2.5

A vehicle accelerates from 0 to 60 mi/h in 10 s with the velocity profile given by

$$v(t) = 20\ln(0.282t + 1)\ \text{m/s}\ \ \text{for}\ 0 \leq t \leq 10\,\text{s}.$$

The vehicle is on level road. For the problem use the parameters given in Problem 2.3.
   (a) Calculate and plot $F_{TR}(t)$ and $P_{TR}(t)$ for $0 \leq t \leq 10$ s. (b) Calculate $\Delta e_{TR}$. How much of $\Delta e_{TR}$ is $\Delta KE$? How much is $E_{loss}$?

## 2.6

Using the vehicle parameters given in Problem 2.3, calculate and plot, on the same graph, steady-state $F_{TR}$ versus $V$ characteristics for $\beta = \pm 4°$ and $-60 \leq V \leq 60$ mi/h, but $V \neq 0$.

## 2.7

An EV racer will attempt to jump five city buses as shown in the Figure P2.7. The vehicle will start at rest at a position 100 m from the beginning of the take-off ramp. The vehicle will accelerate uniformly until it reaches the end of the take-off ramp at which time it will be traveling at 100 mi/h (miles per hour). The vehicle has the following parameter values:

**FIGURE P2.7**

$$m = 692 \text{ kg}, C_D = 0.2, A_F = 2 \text{ m}^2, C_0 = 0.009, C_1 = 1.75 * 10^{-6} \text{ s}^2/\text{m}^2.$$

Also, take density of air $\rho = 1.16 \text{ kg/m}^3$, and acceleration due to gravity $g = 9.81 \text{ m/s}^2$.

a. Sketch and label the velocity profile of the vehicle from the time it starts to the time it reaches the end of the take-off ramp. How much time does the vehicle take to reach the end of the take-off ramp?

b. Calculate the change in gravitational potential energy, from start to the end of take-off ramp.

c. Calculate energy loss, $E_{loss}$ from start to the end of take-off ramp, if $\Delta e_{TR} = 8.28 \times 10^5$ J during that period.

## 2.8

The parameters of a vehicle are given below:

Vehicle mass = 2,000 kg
Driver/one passenger = 80 kg
Rolling resistance coefficient, $C_0 = 0.01$
Wheel radius, $r_{wh} = 0.3305$ m
Aerodynamic drag coefficient, $C_{AD} = 0.45$
Frontal area, $A_F = 2.5 \text{ m}^2$

The vehicle accelerates from 0 velocity to 21 m/s in 5 s on a 0.5% roadway grade when it reaches the maximum power limit of the propulsion unit. The vehicle then accelerates in the constant power mode for another 7 s. The maximum power limit is 145kW.

a. Write the *dv/dt* equation for constant power acceleration for the given conditions.

b. What is the velocity after a total time of 10 s?

c. What is the velocity at 12 s if the roadway grade changes to 4% at 10 s?

**2.9**

    a. Find the wheel speed of the vehicle given in Problem 2.8 when the vehicle velocity is 60 mph and the wheel slip is 15%.

    b. The coefficient of friction as a function of wheel slip is given by

$$\mu(s) = \mu_{pk}\left[a(1 - e^{-bs}) - cs\right]$$

The parameters for the coefficient of friction on a dry pavement are as follows:

$$\mu_{pk} = 0.85, \, a = 1.1, \, b = 20, \, \text{and} \, c = 0.0035$$

Calculate the traction force limit for slip = 15% on a 1% slope with a driver and a passenger for the vehicle in Problem 2.8.

## REFERENCES

1. J.Y. Wong, *Theory of Ground Vehicles*, John Wiley & Sons, Inc., Hoboken, NJ, 2008.
2. W.E. Meyer and H. W. Kummer, "Mechanism of Force Transmission Between Tire and Road," SAE Publication No. 490A, National Automobile Week, March 1962.
3. T.D. Gillespie, *Fundamentals of Vehicle Dynamics*, SAE International, Warrendale, PA, 1992.

# 3 Vehicle Architectures and Design

The propulsion component that is common in advanced vehicle technologies alternative to the conventional internal combustion engine vehicles (ICEVs) is the electric powertrain. Electric vehicles (EVs), hybrid electric vehicles (HEVs), plug-in hybrid vehicles (PHEV) and fuel cell electric vehicles (FCEV) all have an electric powertrain component whether or not they have another engine-equipped mechanical powertrain component. The placement of the different powertrain components in the EVs and hybrid vehicles with respect to each other is referred to as the architecture of the vehicle. The motivation for exploring and developing new configurations is higher carbon emission reduction and enhanced driver experience benefits.

The configuration of a battery electric vehicle (BEV) has the simplest architecture with the powertrain consisting of an electric machine, a power electronics converter and a gearbox. In HEVs, there is an additional powertrain, and at least two fuel sources feeding into their respective energy converters. Consequently, HEVs offer the possibility of various different types of powertrain architectures. This chapter presents the architectures and design of these alternative vehicle technologies. This chapter starts with the components used and their sizing in EVs. The classification of hybrid architectures and component sizing of HEVs are discussed. The features of PHEV and FCEV are also included in this chapter. Further details of fuel cells and fuel cell vehicles appear in Chapter 6.

The fuels in alternative vehicles can be derived from sources alternative to the fossil fuels. Many of these vehicles also use a combination of alternative fuels and conventional fuels. The EVs may appear to be operating solely on alternative fuels by the use of modern battery technology, but the ultimate source may be the conventional fossil fuels depending on how the electricity to recharge the batteries was generated. EVs with batteries charged from renewable energy sources, such as wind, solar and hydro, provide the best scenario of alternative energy transportation.

## 3.1 ELECTRIC VEHICLES

EVs, as defined in Chapter 1, have portable energy source and the tractive effort comes solely from one or more electric machines. The BEV powered by only one or more electric machines has the most straightforward architecture without the need for power blending. The detailed structure of an EV system along with the interaction among its various components is shown in Figure 3.1. The primary components of an EV system are the motor, controller, power source and transmission.

**FIGURE 3.1**  Major electrical components and choices for an EV system.

Electrochemical batteries have been the traditional source of energy in EVs. Lead/acid batteries were used in the first commercially available EV Saturn EV1 in 1996, but since then, the technology has progressed towards NiMH and Li-ion batteries. The batteries need a charger to restore the stored energy level once its available energy is near depletion due to usage. The limited range problem of battery-driven EVs prompted the search for alternative energy sources, such as fuel cells and flywheels. Prototypes, limited number of models and fleet vehicles have been developed with fuel cells over the last two decades, but at the same time battery technology have also progressed significantly. Several different types of Li-ion battery chemistry have emerged that are being used in both EVs and HEVs.

The EVs developed in recent years are based on induction machines or permanent magnet machines. In the early developmental stages of EVs, DC machines were used, but their many disadvantages turned EV developers to look into various types of AC machines. The rare-earth material-free, maintenance-free and low-cost nature of induction machines is appealing to some developers. High-speed operation of induction machines comes with a penalty in size and weight, although recent studies on re-rating of induction motors for EVs are opening new perspectives even in the high-speed range. The high efficiency together with high power density features of permanent magnet machines makes them an attractive solution for EV applications, although the cost of permanent magnets can become prohibitive in the future unless low-cost options for high-energy permanent magnets are developed. The high power density and potentially low production cost of switched reluctance machines make it ideally suitable for EV applications. However, the acoustic noise problem has so far been the deterrent for the use of switched reluctance machines in EVs. The electric motor design includes not only the electromagnetic aspects of the machine but also the thermal and structural considerations. The motor design tasks of today are supported by the finite element studies and various computer-aided design tools making the design process highly efficient.

The electric motor is driven by a power electronics-based power processing unit that converts the fixed DC voltage available from the source into a variable voltage, variable frequency source controlled to maintain the desired operating point of the vehicle. The power electronics circuit comprises power semiconductor devices that saw a tremendous development over the past three decades. The enabling technology of power electronics is a key driving force in developing efficient and high-performance powertrain unit for EVs. The advances in power solid-state devices and VLSI (very large-scale integration) technology are responsible for the development of efficient and compact power electronics circuits and electronic control units. High-power devices in compact packaging are available today enabling the development of lightweight and efficient power processing units known as power electronic motor drives. The developments in high-speed digital signal processors or microprocessors enable complex control algorithm implementation with high degree of accuracy. The controller includes algorithms for both the motor drive in the inner loop as well as system-level control in the outer loop.

## 3.2  HYBRID ELECTRIC VEHICLES

The term "hybrid vehicles" in general usage refers to vehicles with two or three different types of sources delivering power to the wheels for propulsion. The most common hybrid vehicles have an IC engine and one or more electric machines for vehicle propulsion. The IC engine can be used to generate electric energy 'on-board' to power the electric machines. An energy storage device buffers the electrical energy flow between the electric machine operated as a generator and the electric machine operated as a motor. An electric machine can be operated both as a motor and as a generator. Vehicles architectures with only one electric machine use it both for electric power generation and for vehicle propulsion power; the constraint being that electric power generation and power delivery through electric propulsion are not possible simultaneously. In hybrid vehicles, the traction electric motors can operate independently or in association with the IC engine to power the wheels depending on the type of vehicle architecture. The subject of treatment in this section is the basic architectures of HEVs.

There are several ways of classifying hybrid vehicles; the most common approach is based on the path of energy flow from its store to the wheels through the power transmission paths. In a HEV, the propulsion power is transmitted to the wheels through either the mechanical power transmission path or the electric power transmission path or the combination of the two. The mechanical path is made of an IC engine and a transmission, whereas the electrical path consists of an energy storage system, a generator, a propulsion motor and a transmission. The vehicle powertrain is designed to meet the vehicle base load requirements as well as the peak load requirements during acceleration and starting. The arrangement of the hybrid powertrain components in the power transmission path gives rise to the architecture-based hybrids known as *series*, *parallel* and *series–parallel* hybrids.

The hybrid vehicles can also be classified based on the degree of hybridization into *mild*, *power* and *energy* hybrids. This classification is based on the powertrain size deviation from a conventional vehicle. The progression from mild to energy hybrids is related to the degree of downsizing the engine and upsizing the electrical and energy storage components.

The hybrid vehicles are also classified as *charge-depleting* or *charge-sustaining* hybrids depending on whether or not the energy storage device needs to be charged from an external source or is self-sustaining with its on-board electricity generation capability. The BEVs are an extreme example of charge-depleting vehicle, which does not have any on-board electricity generation capability. PHEVs are also examples of charge-depleting hybrids; these vehicles operate in the battery-only electric mode for certain distances and then as HEV for longer distances. The PHEVs are essentially HEVs but with a large-enough energy storage system that will get depleted of its charge and will need to be plugged in to restore operation in the electric-only mode. The charge-sustaining vehicles, such as the hybrids available commercially, have a smaller capacity energy storage system; the on-board IC engine and electric generator are sufficient to restore the charge in its energy storage device. The charge-sustaining hybrids never need to be plugged in.

### 3.2.1 Hybrids Based on Architecture

#### 3.2.1.1 Series and Parallel Hybrids
The HEVs evolved out of two basic configurations: Series and parallel. A series hybrid is one in which only one energy converter can provide propulsion power. The IC engine acts as a prime mover in this configuration to drive an electric generator that delivers power to the battery or energy storage link and the propulsion motor. The components' arrangement of a series HEV is shown in Figure 3.2.

A parallel hybrid is one in which more than one energy conversion device can deliver propulsion power to the wheels. The IC engine and the electric motor are configured in parallel with a mechanical coupling that blends the torque coming from the two sources. The components' arrangement of a parallel hybrid is shown in Figure 3.3.

FIGURE 3.2   Series HEV powertrain.

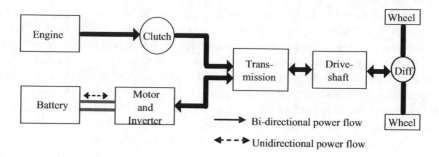

**FIGURE 3.3**    Parallel HEV powertrain.

Series HEV is the simpler type where only the electric motor provides all the propulsion power to the wheels. A downsized IC engine drives a generator, which supplements the batteries and can charge them when they fall below a certain state of charge (SoC). The power required to propel the vehicle is provided solely by the electric motor. Beyond the IC engine and the generator, the propulsion system is exactly the same as that in an EV; the electric motor power requirements are exactly the same as that in an EV.

The drawback of the series configuration is the size of the electrical traction motor, which has to be rated for the maximum power requirement of the vehicle. The drawback can be removed if the engine is used in parallel with the electric machine to supply power to the wheels. This is called a parallel architecture where both the IC engine and the electric motor are connected to the driveshaft through transmission and clutch. In the parallel HEV, the power requirements of the electric motor in the parallel hybrid are lower than that of an EV or series hybrid, since the IC engine complements for the total power demand of the vehicle. The propulsion power may be supplied by the IC engine alone, by the battery-motor set, or by the two systems in combination.

Both series and parallel hybrids come in a variety of types. The mission of the vehicle and the optimum design for that mission dictates the choice. If the HEV is to be basically an EV with an IC engine assist for achieving acceptable range, then the choice could be series hybrids with the IC engine ensuring that the batteries remian charged all the time. On the other hand, if the hybrid vehicle is to be basically a vehicle with almost all the performance characteristics and comforts of an IC engine vehicle but with lower emission and fuel usage standards, then the choice could be a parallel configuration. Parallel HEVs have been built with performance that is equal, in all aspects of normal operation, to a conventional car. However, some series hybrid vehicles have also been built that perform as well as the IC engine vehicles.

The advantages of a series hybrid architecture can be summarized as follows:

- Flexibility of location of engine-generator set.
- Simplicity of drivetrain.
- Suitable for short trips with stop and go traffic.

The disadvantages of a series hybrid architecture are as follows:

- It needs three propulsion components: IC engine, generator and motor.
- The motor must be designed for the maximum sustained power that the vehicle may require, such as when climbing a high grade. However, the vehicle operates below the maximum power for most of the time.
- All three drivetrain components need to be sized for maximum power for long-distance sustained, high-speed driving. This is required since the batteries will exhaust fairly quickly leaving IC engine to supply all the power through the generator.

The advantages of a parallel hybrid architecture are as follows:

- It only needs two propulsion components: IC engine and motor/generator. In parallel HEV, motor can be used as generator and vice versa.
- A smaller engine and a smaller motor can be used to get the same performance, until batteries are depleted. For short-trip missions, both can be rated at half the maximum power to provide the total power, assuming that the batteries are never depleted. For long-distance trips, engine may be rated for the maximum power, while the motor/generator may still be rated to half the maximum power or even smaller.

The disadvantages of a parallel hybrid architecture are as follows:

- The control complexity increases significantly, since power flow has to be regulated and blended from two parallel sources.
- The power blending from the IC engine and the motor necessitates a complex mechanical device.

A simpler architecture with reduced components capable of delivering good acceleration performance is the 'through-the-road' parallel architecture. This architecture has one engine powering the front wheels and one electric machine powering the rear wheels. The engine is the primary propulsion unit of the vehicle, while the electric machine is used for load leveling supplying the propulsion power during acceleration and capturing vehicle kinetic energy through regeneration during deceleration. When the charge in the energy storage device falls below a set level, the engine is commanded to deliver torque in excess of what is required to meet the driver demand. The additional energy supplied by the engine is used to charge the energy storage device by operating the rear electric machine as a generator. Power is transferred from the engine to the electric machine through the road, and hence the name *through-the-road* parallel. This charge-sustaining mechanism may not be that efficient, but the architedture offers great simplicity without the need for a coupling device to blend the torque from the engine and the electric motor. The vehicle can deliver good acceleration performance using the parallel operation of two propulsion units; the fuel efficiency can also be improved by about 20%–30% compared to a similarly sized IC engine vehicle. Additionally, the architecture gives four-wheel drive capability.

### 3.2.1.2  Series–Parallel Hybrid

The parallel hybrid architecture is better suited to passenger vehicles where the electric motor and IC engine can be operated in parallel to deliver high performance when higher power is required [1]. On the other hand, the series hybrid architecture is equipped with a small output engine that can always be operated in its most efficient operating region to generate electrical power. The output electric power can be used directly to drive the propulsion motor or charge the energy storage system. Series hybrid vehicles tend to be heavy and typically have difficulty meeting acceleration requirements since the powertrain components need to be sized for the maximum continuous output power for charge-sustaining operation.

The advanced hybrids combine the benefits of series and parallel architectures into a series–parallel hybrid architecture with charge-sustaining capability [1,2]. In these combination hybrids, the IC engine is also used to charge the battery. The architecture is relatively more complicated, involving additional mechanical links and controls compared to the series hybrid, and an additional generator compared to the parallel hybrid. The vehicle is primarily a parallel HEV but with a small series element added to the architecture. The small series element ensures that the battery charge is sustained in prolonged wait periods such as in traffic lights or in a traffic jam. The controller for the series–parallel architectures effectively utilizes the IC engine and electric motors to deliver up to their maximum capabilities through flexible adaptation with driving conditions.

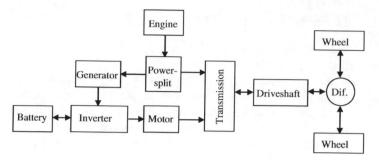

**FIGURE 3.4**   Series–parallel combination HEV.

The series–parallel architecture is the one that has been used in the first ever commercially available hybrid vehicle, the Toyota Prius. The vehicle architecture uses a mechanical power-split device that was developed by the Japanese researchers from Equos Research [3,4]. The compact transaxle design in the powertrain integrates two electric motors to simplify the manufacture of both conventional vehicles and hybrid vehicles in the same production plant without significant alteration of the same assembly line. Most of the series–parallel passenger hybrid vehicles available in the market today have three power plants (the engine and two electric machines) mounted in the front transaxle. The power-split device divides the output from the engine into mechanical and electrical transmission paths using a planetary gearset. The components' arrangement in the series–parallel architecture based on the Toyota Prius hybrid design is shown in Figure 3.4. The power-split device allocates power from the IC engine to the front wheels through the driveshaft and the electric generator depending on the driving condition. The power through the generator is used to recharge the batteries. The electric motor can also deliver power to the front wheels in parallel to the IC engine. The inverter is bidirectional and is used to either charge the batteries from the generator or to condition the power for the electric motor. For short bursts of acceleration, power can be delivered to the driveshaft from both the internal combustion engine and the electric motor. A central control unit regulates the power flow for the system using multiple feedback signals from the various sensors.

The series–parallel hybrids are capable of providing continuous high output power compared to either a series or a parallel hybrid for similarly sized powertrain components. The series–parallel vehicle can operate in all three modes of series, parallel and power-split mode. There is significantly greater flexibility in the control strategy design for a series–parallel hybrid vehicle that leads to better fuel economy and lower emissions.

### 3.2.1.3   Series–Parallel 2 × 2 Hybrid

A series–parallel 2 × 2 vehicle architecture with two electric machines, one IC engine and a battery energy storage system is shown in Figure 3.5. The architecture offers the same attractive features of series–parallel architecture described in the previous section but with an inherent four-wheel drive capability. The engine is coupled to one set of wheels, typically the front wheels, through a transmission. One electric machine is coupled to the engine mechanically while the other electric machine is coupled to the other set of wheels, typically the rear wheels. The front-mounted electric machine or generator is mostly used for generation and starting. The rear-mounted motor is used for regenerative braking and traction. The engine is used for traction and also for supplying power to the generator. During acceleration, the engine powers the front wheels while the rear-mounted electric machine powers the rear wheels. However, during peak acceleration demand, the front electric machine can be operated as a motor to add torque at the front axle. The torque blending between the front axle and rear axles is through electronic controls and does not require any mechanical power-split device like that in the Prius series–parallel architecture. The downside to the series–parallel 2 × 2 is the complexity of the control algorithm and the mounting requirements of powertrain components in both the front and rear axles.

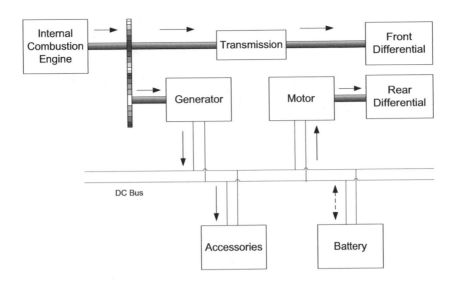

**FIGURE 3.5**   Series parallel 2 × 2 vehicle architecture.

### 3.2.2   HYBRIDS BASED ON TRANSMISSION ASSEMBLY

#### 3.2.2.1   Pre- and Post-transmission Hybrids

HEVs can be classified as pre- and post-transmission hybrids depending on the location of the mechanical transmission with respect to the electric drive. In the pre-transmission configuration, the output shafts of the electric motor and the IC engine are connected through a mechanical coupling before the mechanical transmission gearbox. The transmission matches the combined output of the electric drive and IC engine with the vehicle speed. The parallel hybrid architecture shown in Figure 3.3 is a pre-transmission configuration. The series–parallel architecture shown in Figure 3.4 is also a pre-transmission configuration. Figure 3.6 shows the series–parallel architecture using the epicyclic or planetary gearset; 'R', 'P' and 'S' denote the 'ring', 'planet' and 'sun' gears of the gearset to which the three powertrain components are connected. The planetary gearset output shaft delivers power to the wheels through the driveshaft and the final drive. The mechanical transmission component including the gearbox is located in between the final drive and the propulsion components of IC engine, electric motor and generator, which makes the architecture a pre-transmission hybrid configuration. This non-shifting, clutchless, pre-transmission configuration with planetary gearset is the most popular passenger hybrid configuration. The planetary gearset torque–speed relationships will be presented later in Chapter 14.

In the post-transmission hybrid configuration, the electric motor drive is coupled to the output shaft of the transmission. A gearbox may be used to match the transmission output speed which varies over the entire vehicle speed range as shown in Figure 3.7. The electric motor drive can be operated at higher speeds compared to the vehicle speed with the gear coupling, but electric motor drive must span the entire speed range of the vehicle. Consequently, motor drives for post-transmission configurations are required to have a wide constant power speed region (CPSR), preferably with 4:1 or higher ratio between top speed and base speed. The configuration poses packaging challenges and connection issues with the final drive; continuous engagement with the wheel results in no-load spin losses with certain types of electric machines. HEVs with wheel or hub motors are of similar post-transmission configuration. High-torque, low-speed motors are required for hub motors which are directly mounted on the wheels without any matching transmission or gear. Hub motor results in higher unsprung mass; the motors are subjected to higher levels of vibration and temperature and are also prone to environmental effects such as water, sand, dust, salt and gravel.

**FIGURE 3.6**  Power-split pre-transmission hybrid configuration.

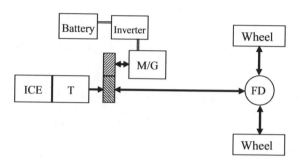

**FIGURE 3.7**  Parallel post-transmission hybrid configuration.

### 3.2.2.2   P0–P4 Hybrid Architectures

The electric machine within the electric drive is the link between the electrical system and the vehicle system with the pre- and post-transmission arrangements broadly defining the location of the electric drive with respect to the transmission. The pre- and post-transmission arrangements are further classified by the industry as P0, P1, P2, P3 and P4 architectures based on the type of the connection between the electric machine and the powertrain such as belt, integrated or gear mesh. The P0, P1 and P2 architectures are pre-transmission type, while P3 and P4 architectures are the post-transmission type. The four connection type-based architectures are described below with their configurations shown graphically in Figure 3.8.

> P0 – The electric machine is connected with the internal combustion engine through a belt at the front end serving as the replacement of the traditional alternator with higher power rating and regeneration capability. This electric machine is also known as the belt starter generator (BSG).
>
> P1 – The electric machine is connected on the crankshaft side of the IC engine through a gearset. This is an integrated starter generator (ISG) arrangement. Neither P0 nor P1 architectures allow the mechanical disconnection of the electric machine from the IC engine.
>
> P2 – The electric machine is side-attached to the transmission through a belt or gearset and is decoupled from the IC engine through a clutch rotating at IC engine speed or geared to rotate at a multiple of IC engine speed. The pre-transmission hybrids with planetary gear-set connections are of P1 or P2 type.
>
> P3 – The P3 is a post-transmission configuration with the electric machine connected with the transmission through a gear mesh. The electric machine is decoupled from the IC engine and rotates at a multiple of wheel speed.

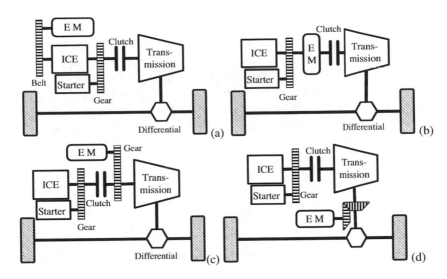

**FIGURE 3.8** HEV P0 to P4 architectures: (a) P0 architecture with belt-starter generator; (b) P1 architecture ISG; (c) P2 architecture and (d) P3 or P4 architecture.

P4 – The P4 architecture is also a post-transmission configuration with the electric machine connected through a gear mesh on the rear axle of the vehicle or in the wheels hub. Similar to P3 architecture, the electric machine is decoupled from the IC engine and rotates at a multiple of wheel speed. In P2, P3 or P4 configurations, the electric machine is disconnected from the IC engine through a clutch.

Each of the four configurations has their advantages and disadvantages in terms of functionality, cost, fuel economy improvement and drivability. The fuel economy improvement comes from the brake regeneration operation where the size and capacity of the electric machine matters and the engine on/off operation particularly on stop and go traffic in urban areas. The improvement comes from electric-only modes reducing inefficient engine operation times at light load conditions. For example, a 20% fuel economy improvement is expected using P0 architecture compared with the baseline vehicle that has a conventional alternator. A combination architecture may also be used to improve fuel economy and driver experience; for example, adopting a P0P4 architecture more than 30% fuel economy improvement is expected with increased driver experience.

### 3.2.2.3  48 V Hybrid Architectures

An increasing number of HEV architectures are evolving around 48 V system serving as a low-cost hybrid alternative in the category of mild hybrids. The 48 V architectures are a less disruptive approach of vehicle electrification for increasing fuel economy and reducing carbon emissions with a 48 V powertrain electrification. European Union has 95 g/km $CO_2$ emission requirement to be met by vehicle manufacturers by 2021, which cannot be achieved by improvements in ICEVs alone; this is driving the micro-hybrid demand and market in Europe with lower voltage electrified powertrain. Lower voltage and higher power battery-packs can be utilized for start–stop operation, electric propulsion assist, regenerative energy capture, and supplying the ever-growing vehicle load demands. With 15–25 kW electrification, 48 V hybrids can deliver fuel economy improvements, handle higher power auxiliaries and provide improved handling, drivability and comfort compared to ICEVs. The safety features are also well managed with 48 V systems compared to higher voltage systems. These mild hybrids bridge the gap to full hybrids and BEVs where consumers have historically been reluctant to purchase due to the high cost.

### 3.2.3 Hybrids Based on Degree of Hybridization

The classification based on the degree of hybridization corresponds to the mission that the vehicle is designed to achieve [5]. This is a more consumer-oriented classification method used by the automotive industry. There are three 'mission-based' classes: mild hybrids, power hybrids and energy hybrids. The 'mild' hybrids have the lowest degree of hybridization with a moderate effect on fuel economy and emissions. Typical electrical rating of a mild hybrid would be in the range of 5–10 kW, with energy capacity in the range of 1–3 kWh. The 'power' hybrids have a larger electric propulsion component, with an electrical rating as high as 40 kW; these hybrids allow significant amount of power transfer between battery and motor drive system, although the battery storage is designed with relatively low energy capacity (3–4 kWh). The power hybrids have a greater potential to provide fuel economy improvements. These also have better engine-out emissions due to a more focused engine duty schedule. Power hybrids, like the mild hybrids, are charge-sustaining type receiving all motive energy from the on-board combustion of the fossil fuel. The 'energy' hybrid employs a high-energy battery system capable of propelling the vehicle for a significant range without engine operation. The electrical rating and battery capacity are typically in the ranges of 70–100 kW and 15–20 kWh. A zero emission range of 50 miles would meet the daily commute range of the majority of population based on average driving habits of about 12,000 miles/year in the United States. The energy hybrids are obviously charge-depleting type with provisions to recharge the batteries at home electrically. These vehicles are the subject of treatment in the following section.

## 3.3 PLUG-IN HYBRID ELECTRIC VEHICLE

The PHEVs are similar to the charge-sustaining hybrids except that they have a higher capacity energy storage system with a power electronic interface for connection to the grid. The energy storage system in a PHEV can be charged on-board and also from an electrical outlet. The vehicle can operate in a battery-only mode for a much longer period than the charge-sustaining hybrid vehicles. The PHEV is intended to operate as a pure BEV for the design-specified distances during the daily commute. The IC engine is used to provide additional power and range for long-distance driving. This type of vehicle is also sometimes known as a 'range extender'. The energy obtained from the external power grid in the PHEV displaces the energy that would otherwise be obtained by burning fuel in the vehicle's IC engine. This has the potential of higher usage of alternative fuels in comparison to other hybrid vehicles where all of the energy comes from the fossil fuel.

The architectural choices for PHEVs are the same as those charge-sustaining hybrids. The series architecture is the simplest architecture and is highly suitable for PHEVs. The IC engine and electric generator need not be sized to match the peak rating of the traction electric motor due to the availability of high-energy capacity battery-pack. An on-board power electronic interface similar to that of a BEV is necessary for grid connection. The architecture of the series PHEV is shown in Figure 3.9. Parallel and series–parallel architectures similar to the regular hybrids but with the grid connectivity are also possible with PHEVs.

A plug-in hybrid is generally rated based on the zero-emission distance traveled; it is designated as PHEV'X' where 'X' is the distance traveled in miles using off-board electrical energy. This range of travel where the IC engine is not used is known as the zero-emission vehicle (ZEV) range. A PHEV40 is a plug-in hybrid with a useable energy storage capacity equivalent to 40 miles of driving energy on a reference driving cycle. The PHEV40 can displace petroleum energy equivalent to 40 miles of driving on the reference cycle with off-board electricity.

The PHEV uses the battery-pack storage energy for most of its driving, thereby reducing the vehicle emissions, and air and noise pollution. The maintenance cost of a PHEV is low since the vehicle is primarily electric. A PHEV can also be used to even out electricity demands during peak load demand on the grid. Excess battery charge from the plug-in hybrid can be used to send power

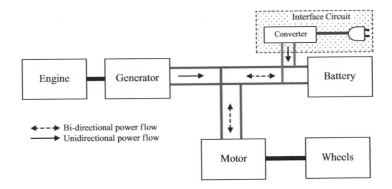

**FIGURE 3.9**   Block diagram of a series PHEV.

back to the grid during peak periods. The concept is known as 'Vehicle-to-Grid' power or V2G. The vehicle can be recharged again during off-peak periods.

The major drawback of the PHEV is the poor well-to-wheel (WTW) efficiency compared to conventional gasoline and regular hybrid vehicles. This is because the PHEV has the poor efficiency segments of both the IC engine vehicle and the EVs in the WTW energy conversion pathway. However, the PHEV has the potential to be both more efficient and environmentally friendlier if the electricity to recharge the batteries can be obtained from renewable sources.

The higher capacity battery in the PHEV increases the mass of the vehicle. The added mass affects the performance; components have to be sized for higher power rating to achieve good performance. The batteries are also quite expensive, and as a result, the cost of the vehicle is also high.

The zero-emission range of the PHEV depends on the way the vehicle is used. The batteries used in the vehicle must be charged using grid electrical power to achieve maximum efficiency and cost reductions. The benefits of the PHEV decrease if the recharging capability through plug-in is unavailable. The use of the engine to charge the batteries should be minimized to maximize efficiency. Energy is always lost during charging and discharging of the battery-pack. The desired mode of operation when the IC engine has to be used is the series mode.

## 3.4   ELECTRIC VEHICLES: SKATEBOARD CHASSIS

The BEVs with its high acceleration performance, quiet and smooth power, wide torque range, lower operating costs and minimal maintenance are not only getting widespread customer acceptance but also enabling numerous new manufacturers challenge the traditional vehicle manufacturers. The emergence of many new manufacturers can be attributed to the simplicity and flexibility in packaging the electric powertrain within the chassis of the vehicle. In an EV, the only propulsion components is the electric motor although there can be multiples of those powering one or more axles or mounted on the wheel hub. The equivalent architecture of the different motor, inverter and gearbox arrangements in a vehicle can be simplified to the block diagram shown in Figure 3.10. The electric motor and inverter ratings of the electric powertrain determine the propulsion capability of the vehicle. The energy storage or battery capacity determines the range of the vehicle on a full charge.

The most popular electric powertrain component is emerging to be the combined unit of an electric motor, inverter and gearbox, referred to as the e-powertrain, which is to be placed in an axle of a vehicle known as the e-axle. The e-powertrain simplicity has also led the industry move towards a skateboard chassis where the energy source and e-powertrain for the vehicle are enclosed within the chassis. This type of design thinking allows for greater flexibility and customization for different types of vehicles within the same chassis. The design was originally envisioned and implemented by General Motors in 2002 in AUTOnomy chassis on top of which the Hy-Wire concept vehicle was built later that year. The skateboard concept has been adopted more recently by Tesla, Rivian and

**FIGURE 3.10**   EV equivalent powertrain architecture.

**FIGURE 3.11**   Skateboard chassis layout for EVs.

other EV manufacturers. A skateboard chassis layout for EVs is shown in Figure 3.11. The skateboard design provides greater vehicle design freedom, more usable passenger space and a modular platform to increase production scale. With an e-powertrain concept, it is possible to design heavier vehicles with more than e-axles.

## 3.5   POWERTRAIN COMPONENT SIZING

The complete design of a vehicle is complex involving numerous variables, constraints, considerations and understanding of the systems interactions. The interactions are typically interdisciplinary and require multi-physics analysis and simulations. The full treatment of a vehicle design is beyond the scope of this book, but from the roadway fundamentals, the vehicle dynamics and the architectures presented thus far, we can address the fundamental calculations involved in sizing of the powertrain components. The calculations provide the design data for starting computer modeling and simulation for detailed analysis of a complex EV and HEV systems. The computer modeling and simulation continues with design iterations and subsystem resizing and controller updates until simulation results meet the specifications. The basic equations and principles that lay the foundation for the design of electric and hybrid vehicles are presented next. Design considerations will be highlighted when appropriate.

The primary design specifications related to powertrain sizing are: (i) the initial acceleration, (ii) rated velocity on a given slope, (iii) maximum % grade and (iv) maximum steady-state velocity. The zero-emission range is the most important specification for sizing the capacity of the battery-pack. The energy required for a given acceleration and constant steady-state velocity can be used for the sizing of the energy system.

This section first presents the sizing of the propulsion component for an EV. Then, the sizing of powertrain components for a hybrid vehicle is presented followed by a design example.

## 3.5.1  EV Powertrain Sizing

The major components in the powertrain of an EV are the electric motor and the energy storage system. The sizing of the electric motor involves finding the power rating of the motor and the operating speed range. The voltage rating and the dimensional packaging constraints must also be specified at the system-level design stage. The design of the machine itself is handled by the electric machine designed to meet the requirements set at the system level. The discussion below addresses the power rating of the electric machine to meet vehicle performance requirements. The sizing of the energy storage device will be addressed later in the hybrid vehicle design section.

Electric motors have three major segments in its torque–speed characteristics: (i) Constant torque region, (ii) constant power region and (iii) natural mode region. The envelop of the electric motor torque–speed characteristics is shown in Figure 3.12. The motor delivers rated torque up to the base speed or rated speed of the motor when it reaches its rated power condition. The motor rated speed is defined as the speed at which the motor can deliver rated torque at rated power. The motor operates in a constant power mode beyond the rated speed where torque falls off steadily at a rate that is inversely proportional to speed. Electric motor can operate at speeds higher than rated using field weakening in the constant power region. There is a third natural mode region for very high motor speeds where the torque falls off rapidly being inversely proportional to the square of the speed. The natural characteristic region can be an important part of the overall torque speed curve of certain motors that can be used to reduce the power rating of the motor. However, in most cases, the vehicle's maximum speed is considered to be at the end of the constant power region. Note that the curves in Figure 3.12 show the envelope, i.e., the operating torque and speed limits in different regions. The electric motor can operate at any point within the envelope through the feed from a power electronics-based motor drive component. The salient feature of wide-operating speed range characteristics of an electric motor makes it possible to eliminate multiple gear ratios and the clutch in EV and other applications. A single-gear ratio transmission is sufficient for linking the electric motor with the driveshaft. Electric motors with extended constant power region characteristics are needed to minimize the gear size in EVs.

The size of an electric motor depends on the maximum torque required from the machine. The higher the maximum torque required, the larger will be the size of the motor. In order to minimize the size and weight, electric motors are designed for high-speed operation for a given power rating. Gears are used to match the higher speed of the electric motor with the lower speed of the wheels. Typical motor speeds can be in the vicinity of 15,000 rev/m for typical wheel speeds of around

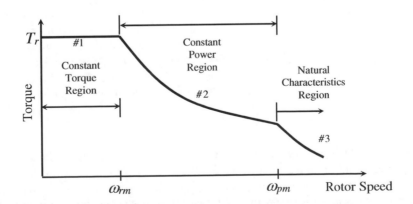

**FIGURE 3.12**  Electric motor torque–speed envelope.

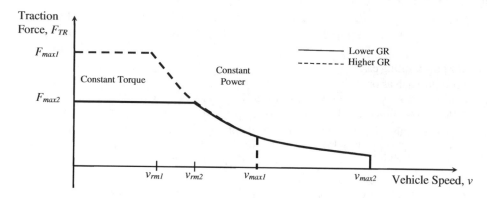

**FIGURE 3.13** Electric motor torque–speed characteristics in terms of traction force and vehicle speed for two gear ratios.

1,000 rev/m for lightweight passenger vehicles. The transmission gear achieves this speed reduction in the range of ~10–15:1 typically in two stages of 3–4:1 of speed reduction. The gear sizing depends on whether the low- or the high-speed performance of the EV is more important based on the power rating determined for the EV.

The tractive force versus speed characteristics of the propulsion system can be widely different for two gear ratios as shown in Figure 3.13. Note that the rated speeds shown are for the drivetrain unit comprising of the electric motor and transmission system, and that the electric motor rated speed is different from these values. The electric motor speed can first be converted into drivetrain unit speed or vehicle wheel speed using the gear ratio as shown earlier. The motor rated speed at the wheel $\omega_{rm,wh}$ in rad/s can be converted to linear vehicle speed using $v_{rm} = \omega_{rm,wh} \cdot r_{wh}$, where $r_{wh}$ is the radius of the wheel. The symbol $v_{rm}$ is referred to here as the equivalent electric motor linear speed after accounting for the transmission gear and the wheel radius. A higher wheel speed or vehicle speed can be attained with a smaller gear ratio, but the peak traction force that the drivetrain can deliver will be smaller. The smaller traction force will limit the initial acceleration and maximum gradability capabilities of the vehicle. On the other hand, if a high gear ratio is used in the transmission for the same electric motor, the peak traction force available at the wheels will be higher, but the maximum vehicle speed $v_{max}$ will be limited. Therefore, we can conclude that the gear ratio depends on the motor rated speed, vehicle rated speed, vehicle maximum speed, wheel radius and maximum gradability. It must be observed that a higher gear ratio entails a larger gear size. Therefore, the gear ratio and the electric motor rated speed must be selected simultaneously to optimize the overall size and performance requirements.

In the following, the design of the electric motor will be discussed in view of the specified requirements of the initial acceleration, the rated velocity on a given slope, the maximum steady-state velocity and the maximum gradability. In the process, the following parameters will be used: rated motor power $P_m$, rated motor speed $\omega_{rm}$, rated wheel speed $\omega_{fwh}$, rated vehicle speed $v_f$, vehicle total mass $m$, vehicle frontal area $A_F$, rolling resistance coefficients $C_0$ and $C_1$, and aerodynamic drag coefficient $C_D$. The design process starts with a set of known parameters and some educated guess, and ends with the final design values that meet the requirements after several iterations.

### 3.5.1.1 Initial Acceleration

The initial acceleration is specified as 0 to $v_f$ in $t_f$ s. $v_f$ is the vehicle rated speed obtained from $v_f = \omega_{fwh} \cdot r_{wh}$. The design problem is to solve for $F_{TR}$ starting with a set of parameters including vehicle mass, rolling resistance, aerodynamic drag coefficient, percent grade, wheel radius, etc., some of which are known, while others have to be assumed. The acceleration of the vehicle in terms of these variables is given by Equation 2.32, repeated here for convenience

$$a = \frac{dv}{dt} = \frac{F_{TR} - F_{RL}}{m}$$

The motor power rating can be obtained by solving the above differential equation for a given force–velocity profile, such as one of the two shown in Figure 3.13, and the following boundary conditions:

At $t=0$, vehicle velocity $v=0$.
At $t=t_f$, vehicle velocity $v=v_f$.

Integrating the differential equation within the interval $t=0$ to $t=t_f$ for velocities 0 to $v_f$

$$m \int_0^{v_f} \frac{dv}{F_{TR} - F_{RL}(v)} = \int_0^{t_f} dt$$

The vehicle rated velocity is higher than the motor rated velocity and lies in the constant power region of motor torque–speed characteristics. Splitting the integral on the left side into two velocity regions of $0$–$v_{rm}$ for the constant torque mode and of $v_{rm}$–$v_f$ for the constant power mode, one can write

$$m \int_0^{v_{rm}} \frac{dv}{\dfrac{P_m}{v_{rm}} - F_{RL}(v)} + m \int_{v_{rm}}^{v_f} \frac{dv}{\dfrac{P_m}{v} - F_{RL}(v)} = t_f \tag{3.1}$$

The road-load resistance force $F_{RL}$ can be expressed as a function of velocity as shown in Chapter 2 for given values of rolling resistance, aerodynamic drag force and roadway slope. Equation 3.1 can then be solved for motor power rating $P_m$ for specified vehicle rated velocity $v_f$ and rated motor speed. Note that Equation 3.1 is a transcendental equation with $F_{RL}$ being a function of velocity and can be solved numerically to find the motor power rating $P_m$. In fact, extensive computer computation and simulation aids a practical design to derive the required motor power rating and gear ratio of the powertrain.

An interesting analysis has been presented in [6] to stress the importance of extended constant power region of motor torque–speed characteristics. It has been shown that for $F_{RL}=0$, the motor power rating is

$$P_m = \frac{m}{2t_f} \left( v_{rm}^2 + v_f^2 \right) \tag{3.2}$$

Equation 3.2 shows that the motor power rating will be minimum when $v_{rm}=0$, which means that the electric motor that operates entirely in the constant power mode is the smallest motor to satisfy the requirements. In the other extreme case, the motor power will be the double that of the smallest case if the motor operates entirely in the constant torque mode with $v_{rm}=v_f$. Of course, eliminating the constant torque region and operating entirely in the constant power region is not practically realizable. In a practical setting, the electric motor should be designed with a low base speed or rated speed and a wide constant power region.

### 3.5.1.2 Rated Vehicle Velocity
The drivetrain designed to accelerate the vehicle from 0 to rated velocity will always have the sufficient power to cruise the vehicle at rated speed, provided the roadway slope specified for initial acceleration has not been raised for rated velocity cruising condition.

### 3.5.1.3 Maximum Velocity
The traction power required to cruise the vehicle at maximum vehicle velocity $v_{max}$ is

$$P_{TR,max} = mgv_{max}\sin\beta + \left[mgC_1 + \frac{\rho}{2}A_FC_D\right]v_{max}^3 + mgv_{max}C_0 \qquad (3.3)$$

The dominant resistance force at high speeds is the aerodynamic drag force with the power requirement to overcome it increasing at a cubic rate. For vehicles designed with fast acceleration characteristics, $P_m$ is likely to be greater than $P_{TR,max}$. If $P_{TR,max} > P_m$ derived earlier to meet the initial acceleration requirement, then $P_{TR,max}$ will define the electric motor power rating. The natural mode region of electric motors can be used to meet very high maximum vehicle velocity requirements to minimize the motor size.

#### 3.5.1.4   Maximum Gradability

The maximum gradability of a vehicle for a given motor and gear ratio can be derived from

$$\text{Max.\% grade} = \frac{100F_{TR}}{\sqrt{(mg)^2 - F_{TR}^2}}.$$

The maximum traction force $F_{TR}$ available from the preliminary motor design can be plugged into the above equation to check whether the vehicle maximum gradability conditions are met or not. If the maximum electric motor power derived for acceleration or maximum vehicle velocity is not enough to meet the maximum gradability requirement of the vehicle, then either the motor power rating or the gear ratio has to be increased. Care must be taken not to violate the maximum vehicle velocity requirement when increasing the gear ratio. The gear ratio and motor power is decided in a coordinated manner to meet both the requirements, while maintaining a reasonable size for both the electric motor and the gear.

### 3.5.2   HEV Powertrain Sizing

The HEV powertrain architecture and control technique depends on the desired requirements including, but not limited to, performance, range and emission. The performance requirements of initial acceleration, cruising velocity, maximum velocity and gradability dictate the power requirements of the IC engine and motor. The power requirements can also be specified in terms of multiple driving schedules that have the worst-case demands embedded in them. The energy required by the drivetrain to meet the range specification dictates the design of the energy storage system, which can be a battery-pack or a combination of battery and ultracapacitors. Meeting the emission standard depends solely on the IC engine emission characteristics, since the electric motor has zero emission.

The power required in a hybrid vehicle comes from a combination of the electric motor and IC engine outputs. The mission of the vehicle plays a big role in apportioning the power requirement between the electric motor and heat engine. A hybrid vehicle designed for urban commute-type transportation will have a different combination of drivetrain subsystems than a family sedan designed for both urban and highway travel. The power requirement of the electric motor and the IC engine for an urban commute vehicle will definitely be lower than that required for cars designed for highway travel. For urban vehicles that are used solely for daily commutes of less than 100 miles, the designer must consider the BEV instead of a PHEV. The design engineer evaluates the design trade-offs based on the mission and specifications and selects one of the series or parallel configurations discussed earlier. The subsystems of the drivetrain have their individual control units and the components are coordinated through a supervisory control unit. The mission of the vehicle also dictates the type of control to be employed for the vehicle. For example, the highway vehicles require a control strategy designed to maximize the fuel economy. The designed system must be capable of handling all real-world situations within the limits of the design requirements. Appropriate safety measures must also be incorporated in the controller to handle situations when certain subsystems fail or underperform.

The sizing of the components of both the electrical system and the mechanical system starts once the drivetrain architecture is laid out based on the mission of the vehicle. In a series hybrid vehicle, the electrical system design is the same as that of an EV. The IC engine size is specified for keeping the batteries charged. The sizing of the components of a parallel hybrid vehicle is much more complex. If the vehicle is designed with heavier biasing on the IC engine, then the batteries can be downsized and reconfigured for maximum specific power instead of maximum specific energy. The battery and the motor serve to supply peak power demands during acceleration and overtaking without being completely discharged. The battery also acts as a reservoir for the regenerative braking energy. Ultracapacitors can be used instead of batteries provided they meet the requirements during peak power demands. If the vehicle is to be more battery biased, then the system is configured such that the battery energy is depleted as much as about 80% from its fully charged capacity at the end of the longest trip. Once the power requirements of the electrical and mechanical system are apportioned for the parallel hybrid vehicle, the electrical components are designed based on the power designated for the electrical system using the same design philosophy as that used for the EV components. A philosophy parallel to that used for EV can be used to design the mechanical system, where the components are sized based on initial acceleration, rated cruising velocity, maximum velocity and maximum gradability [7]. The gear ratio between the IC engine and the wheel shaft of a parallel hybrid vehicle can be obtained by matching the maximum speed of the IC engine to the maximum speed of the driveshaft. A single-gear transmission is desired to minimize complexity. The sizing of the components of a parallel hybrid vehicle is discussed below.

### 3.5.2.1 Rated Vehicle Velocity

In a hybrid vehicle, the electric motor primarily serves to meet the acceleration requirements, while the IC engine delivers the power for cruising at rated velocity assuming that the battery energy is not sufficient to provide the required power throughout the desired range. Therefore, the IC engine size is determined by the vehicle cruising power requirement at its rated velocity independent of the electric motor power capacity. Thus, the IC engine size should be determined first in the case of HEV; its size can be used to reduce the power requirement of the electric motor responsible for vehicle acceleration characteristics.

The road-load characteristics developed in Chapter 2 and the force–velocity characteristics of the IC engine (derived from the torque speed characteristics of an IC engine) are useful in sizing the IC engine. Figure 3.14 shows example curves of IC engine characteristics with engine displacement as a parameter along with the road-load characteristics for an assumed grade and vehicle parameters. The correct IC engine size is determined from the intersection of the worst-case road-load characteristics with the IC engine force–velocity profile at rated velocity, plus allowing a nominal

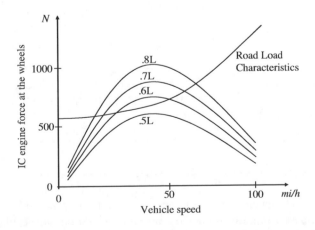

**FIGURE 3.14** Typical IC engine force–velocity characteristics and road–load characteristics.

**FIGURE 3.15** Electric power requirement as a function of vehicle speed at which IC engine is added.

10% margin for the battery-pack recharging [7]. The exact amount of margin needed is the subject of a more complicated analysis, involving vehicle driving cycles, battery capacity, battery charge/discharge characteristics and generator characteristics.

### 3.5.2.2 Initial Acceleration

The electric motor with its higher peak power capabilities is more heavily used during initial acceleration. The mechanical power available from the IC engine can be blended with the electric motor power for acceleration, thereby reducing the power requirement of the electric motor. The power required from the motor depends on the velocity at which torque blending from the two propulsion units starts. Figure 3.15 shows the effect of torque blending on the electric motor-rated power requirement during initial acceleration with a single-gear transmission for the IC engine. The figure shows that there will be very little power contribution from the engine until a minimum critical velocity $v_{cr}$ mph of the vehicle is reached due to its poor low-speed torque capability. Therefore, torque blending should start after the vehicle has attained the critical velocity with single-gear transmission avoiding the use of engine for initial acceleration as much as possible without significantly increasing the rating of the electric motor. The power requirement from the electric motor increases nonlinearly with speed if IC engine torque blending is delayed beyond $v_{cr}$ mph. The qualitative figure shows two curves with the extent of the constant power region as a parameter, $x$ being an integer number. The lower curve has much wider constant power region than the upper curve. The curves emphasize once again the need for extended constant power region of operation of the electric motor to minimize its size. The power requirement of the IC engine determined from rated vehicle velocity condition would typically be enough to provide the initial acceleration in combination with the electric motor.

### 3.5.2.3 Maximum Velocity

The power requirement from the propulsion system at maximum velocity is $F_{TR} \cdot v_{max}$, which is supplied by a combination of the engine and the electric motor. This requirement is given by

$$P_{TR,max} = F_{TR} \cdot v_{max} = mgv_{max}\sin\beta + \left[mgC_1 + \frac{\rho}{2}A_FC_D\right]v_{max}{}^3 + mgv_{max}C_0$$

The electric motor power required to meet the maximum velocity conditions can be uniquely defined by subtracting the engine power determined for cruising at rated velocity from the maximum velocity power requirement. The electric motor power requirement calculated in this step would, in general, be less than the power requirement for the initial acceleration, unless the maximum velocity requirements are very stringent, such as very high speed on a steep grade.

### 3.5.2.4 Maximum Gradability

The maximum gradability condition must be checked once the sizing of the IC engine and the electric motor is done from the previous three requirements. The maximum gradability of a vehicle is given by

$$\text{Max.\% grade} = \frac{100 F_{TR}}{\sqrt{(mg)^2 - F_{TR}^2}}$$

If the condition is not met, then the size of either the engine or the motor or both must be increased or the gear ratio must be changed to meet the gradability requirements.

Although the design philosophy outlined above states that the IC engine sizing primary comes from the rated cruising velocity and the electric motor sizing comes from the initial acceleration, the practical design involves extensive computer simulation using various drive cycles, parameters of the vehicle and characteristics of chosen battery, motor, generator and IC engine. As in all systems cases, the sizing and design of the components of electric and hybrid vehicles is an iterative process that ends when all the design requirements are met. The discussions presented provide the theoretical basis for initial estimates avoiding unnecessary oversizing of components.

### 3.5.3 HEV Powertrain Sizing Example

An HEV powertrain sizing example is presented below for a series–parallel 2 × 2 hybrid vehicle. The vehicle was re-engineered from a 2005 Chevrolet Equinox for the national collegiate student vehicle design competition called Challenge X. This vehicle is termed as Akron hybrid vehicle in this book. The vehicle parameters and performance requirements for the design are given in Table 3.1. The overall design goal for the vehicle is increased fuel economy and reduced emissions without sacrificing customer amenities. The gains in fuel economy with vehicle hybridization can be achieved on the basis of downsizing the engine, reduction in engine idling operation, recovery of braking energy losses and flexibility in choosing engine operating point to enhance energy efficiency. These considerations form the basis of component sizing and selection and control strategy development for the Akron hybrid vehicle.

The design considers initial acceleration without the trailer but includes the mass of the driver. The vehicle cruising speed is 75 mph on a 3% grade and against a 20 mph headwind at high-engine fuel efficiency as well as high-electric drive efficiency. The Akron hybrid vehicle architecture is the same as that shown in Figure 3.5. The vehicle components have been sized to meet the initial acceleration demand through a combination of power delivered by the electric motor and the IC

**TABLE 3.1**
**Akron Hybrid Vehicle Parameters and Requirements**

| Description | Requirements |
|---|---|
| Vehicle mass | 4,400 lbs./1,995 kg |
| Driver/one passenger | 176 lbs./80 kg |
| Trailering capacity | 2,500 lbs./1,133 kg |
| Rolling resistance coefficient, $C_0$ | 0.009 |
| Wheel radius, $r_{wh}$ | 0.3305 m |
| Aerodynamic drag coefficient, $C_{AD}$ | 0.45 |
| Frontal area, $A_F$ | 2.686 m² |
| 0–60 mph | 9.0 s |
| 50–70 mph | 6.8 s |

engine, and to maintain charge sustaining operation at rated cruising velocity with the IC engine only. The electric motor, with its higher peak power capabilities, will be more heavily used during initial acceleration. The battery will be sized for peak power-handling only and not for continuous electric-only mode of operation. The IC engine and electric motor will be operated in the series mode for urban driving conditions. The electric generator will be sized to generate sufficient power with continuous operation during urban driving.

### 3.5.3.1 Total Power Required: Initial Acceleration

Power required during acceleration is usually sufficient to meet the maximum velocity and towing requirements. Therefore, the acceleration power which comes from the combined efforts of electric drive motor and IC engine is calculated first, but later it has to be verified that the other power requirements are met by the two drive components.

The initial acceleration requirements are met by operating the IC engine and electric motor at their peak torque capabilities until the power limit of the two is reached. Therefore, the drivetrain can be assumed to be opearting with constant torque (i.e., constant force $F_{TR}$) acceleration initially, and then with constant power acceleration.

In order to estimate the contant force required initially and the peak power requirement, three velocity profiles are considered and analyzed. These velocity profiles are with constant force $F_{TR}$ acceleration, unifrom acceleration and a third one termed smooth acceleration.

The velocity profile with constant force $F_{TR}$ acceleration is given by

$$v(t) = \sqrt{\frac{K_1}{K_2}} \tanh\left(\sqrt{K_1 K_2}\, t\right) \tag{3.4}$$

where

$$K_1 = \frac{F_{TR}}{m} - gC_0 - mg\sin\beta > 0$$

$$K_2 = \frac{\rho}{2m} C_D A_F + gC_1 > 0$$

The velocity profile for constant acceleration is

$$v(t) = at \tag{3.5}$$

where $a$ is the constant acceleration. For 0–60 mph in 9 s, the constant acceleration is

$$a = 2.98 \text{ m/s}^2$$

The velocity profile for smooth acceleration is [8]

$$v(t) = v_f \left(\frac{t}{t_f}\right)^x \tag{3.6}$$

The range of the exponent $x$ is between 0.47 and 0.53 with lower values used for slow accelerating vehicles and higher values used for fast accelerating vehicles. We will take $x = 0.5$ for our initial analysis.

The 0–60 mph velocity profiles for the three types of acceleration are shown in Figure 3.16. A force of $F_{TR} = 6,000$ N has been assumed for the constant force acceleration. The velocity profile

**FIGURE 3.16**   Velocity profile for the three types of initial acceleration.

**TABLE 3.2**
**Final Numbers Following Initial Sizing**

| $F_{TR,peak}$ | $P_{TR,peak}$ | Time and Velocity of Mode Transition | Time for 0–60 mph | Time for 50–70 mph |
|---|---|---|---|---|
| 7,500 N | 120 kW | 4.6s/16 m/s | 9 s | 5 s |

of Equation 3.6 requires siginifantly large force or torque initially, while the constant acceleration profile requires high power at the end of the initial acceleration period. The power and force required with constant acceleration at $t=9$ s are 6,899 N and 184 kW. The practical approach will be to accelerate faster than the constant acceleration profile, but less than the smooth acceleration profile, and transition to constant power acceleration approximately midway through the initial acceleration. The constant force for initial acceleration up to about 4 s obviously needs to be greater than 6,000 N.

The total power required to meet the acceleration requirements prior to accounting for the drivetrain losses is calculated through design iterations using computer simulation. The numbers given in Table 3.2 are arrived at after a few design iterations with different peak tractive force, peak tractive power and the time for transition of the control algorithm from constant force mode to constant power mode. The tractive force of 7,500 N is supplied by the combination of the electric motor and the IC engine. Furthermore, there will be a gear between the electric motor and the drivetrain, which will bring the torque requirements of electric motor but increase its speed requirement. The $F_{TR}$ versus velocity profile of Figure 3.17 matches well with the torque speed characteristics achievable from electric motors. The velocity ratio of the force characteristics between the peak vehicle velocity (60 m/s) to the onset of the constant power mode (16 m/s) is approximately 4:1, which can be obtained from well-designed electric motor drives. Therefore, assuming the drivetrain efficiency to be about 90%, the minimum combined power required is 132 kW.

### 3.5.3.2   IC Engine Power: Cruising Speed

Once the initial acceleration power requirements are calculated, the sizes of the IC engine and the electric traction motor can be determined. The IC engine size can be determined by the vehicle cruising power requirement at its rated velocity independent of the electric motor power capacity.

**FIGURE 3.17** Tractive power and force requirements with a combination of constant force and constant power modes of acceleration.

With this approach, the IC engine size should be determined first for the Akron hybrid vehicle, and then the remainder of the 130 kW power required can be met by an electric motor.

The IC engine power can be calculated from

$$P_{TR}(t) = V\left( mg\sin\beta + \left[ mgC_1 + \frac{\rho}{2} A_F C_D \right] V^2 + mgC_0 \right) \tag{3.7}$$

where $V$ is the rated velocity or cruising speed.

The HEV IC engine can be sized for the engine power required to maintain a steady expressway velocity of $x$ mi/h (say 75 mi/h), up an $y\%$ grade (say 3%), and against an $z$ mi/h (say 20) headwind at high-engine fuel efficiency. The engine power at highway speeds should also have good fuel efficiency; an IC engine's best fuel efficiency operating point is not necessarily at its maximum power capability point. Therefore, the IC engine can be selected with highway power capability less than the engine's maximum power rating for acceptable fuel efficiency.

### 3.5.3.3 Maximum Velocity

The power requirement from the propulsion system at maximum velocity is $F_{TR} \cdot v_{max}$, which is supplied by a combination of the IC engine and the electric motor. The power requirement for maximum velocity is

$$P_{TR,max} = F_{TR} \cdot v_{max} = mgv_{max}\sin\beta + \left[ mgC_1 + \frac{\rho}{2} A_F C_D \right] v_{max}^3 + mgv_{max}C_0 \tag{3.8}$$

With the IC engine and electric motor sized to meet the acceleration and cruising speed requirements, it has to be verified that the combination of the two can meet the vehicle maximum velocity requirements. If the combined power is less than the power required for maximum velocity, then one of the power plants size should be increased.

**TABLE 3.3**
**Battery Energy Requirements and Mass Estimates**

| Battery Type | Peak Acceleration and 10-mile ZEV Range at 40 mph Urban Driving | | | Peak Acceleration and 5-mile ZEV Range at 40 mph Urban Driving | | |
|---|---|---|---|---|---|---|
| | Energy (kWh) | Mass (kg) | Capacity (Ah) | Energy (kWh) | Mass (kg) | Capacity (Ah) |
| Lead acid | 3.5 | 94.3 | 11 | 2 | 47.2 | 5.5 |
| NiMH | 3.5 | 51.2 | 11 | 2 | 25.6 | 5.5 |
| Li-ion | 3.5 | 36.8 | 11 | 2 | 18.2 | 5.5 |

### 3.5.3.4 Generator Sizing

The generator is sized to maintain series operation of the vehicle for typical urban driving conditions. The calculations showed that cruising at constant velocity of 40 mph with a driver and a passenger on a 1% grade and 10% drivetrain losses requires 12 kW. Allowing for power to recharge the batteries, the generator can be sized to be 20 kW for the Akron hybrid vehicle.

### 3.5.3.5 Battery Sizing

The energy required by the electric motor for initial acceleration and a minimum zero emission range with constant velocity can be used to estimate the size of the battery. The energy for initial acceleration, calculated by integrating the power required for acceleration between 0 and 9 s, is 1.62 MJ or 450 Wh. The energy required for cruising at a constant velocity of 40 mph with a driver and a passenger on a 1% grade and 10% drivetrain losses is 3 kWh for a 10-mile (15 min) battery-only range or 1.5 kWh for a 5-mile (7.5 min) battery-only range. For a 300 V battery-pack, this requires a 10 Ah or 5 Ah battery-pack, respectively. Adding 10% margin, battery-packs with 11 Ah or 5.5 Ah can be used for 10- or 5-mile ZEV range, respectively. The estimated masses for three types of battery chemistry to meet these requirements are given in Table 3.3 based on nominal energy densities. The battery-pack voltage is considered to be 300 V DC.

## 3.6 MASS ANALYSIS AND PACKAGING

Vehicle mass budget must be evaluated during the design of a hybrid vehicle whether it is made from ground up or re-engineered from an IC engine vehicle. The vehicle fuel economy and emissions will improve as vehicle mass decreases. Hybrids tend to be a little heavier compared to a similarly sized IC engine vehicle due to the use of both electrical and mechanical components in the powertrain. However, a good design can yield comparable masses for similarly rated hybrids and IC engine vehicles. The downsized engine in the hybrid vehicle can more than make up for the masses added due to hybridization, which includes masses for electric machines, their controllers and cooling systems and traction battery and its accessories. Mass advantages are also to be gained in hybrids by reducing fuel system sizes and removing the 12 V battery.

A mass comparison of crossover vehicles between the Chevrolet Equinox and the converted Akron hybrid is given in Table 3.4. The engine downsizing from a 3.6 L V6 gasoline engine to a 1.9 L diesel engine did not give significant mass advantage since diesel engines tend be larger and heavier than gasoline engines for comparable sizes. The exhaust system mass increased due to the addition of diesel after treatment components. The fuel tank size was reduced by 50% that provided some mass savings for the hybrid. The masses of the electrical machines, controllers, traction battery and thermal management systems depend on the components chosen. The removal of the alternator and downsizing the 12 V accessories battery provided small mass savings. The cabin climate control system mass is somewhat higher for the hybrid due to the switching to an electric

## TABLE 3.4
## Mass Analysis of ICEV and HEV

| Component | ICE Vehicle Mass, kg | Hybrid Vehicle Mass, kg |
|---|---|---|
| Engine and transmission | 147 | 125 |
| Exhaust system | 40 | 50 |
| Fuel system (tank and lines) | 13 | 9 |
| Fuel mass | 38 | 15 |
| Electric drive motor | | 108 |
| Starter/generator | 6 | 22 |
| Starter/generator controller | | 26 |
| Electrical thermal management | | 15 |
| Traction battery | | 75 |
| Battery hardware, cooling | | 28 |
| 12V battery | 14 | 6 |
| Alternator | 5 | |
| **Total powertrain** | 263 | 479 |
| **Climate control and accessory** | 26 | 30 |
| **Glider with chassis subsystems** | 1,445 | 1,449 |
| **Total curb mass** | 1,734 | 1,954 |

**FIGURE 3.18**  Component packaging in a hybrid vehicle.

motor-driven compressor pump. The example analysis in Table 3.4 shows an increase of 82% in the powertrain mass for the Akron hybrid vehicle. The mass budget could have been restricted significantly had a downsized gasoline engine been used, although that would have adversely affected fuel economy.

Packaging of components also has to be carefully evaluated during the design of a hybrid vehicle. A component packaging diagram must be developed to ensure that all the system components fit in the vehicle without compromise to safety and customer amenities. A simplified layout diagram based on the Akron hybrid is shown in Figure 3.18; the fuel lines and exhaust piping are not shown here for keeping the figure simple. The packaging of the fuel and exhaust components can become cumbersome, especially when an IC engine vehicle is being re-engineered into a hybrid vehicle.

Adequate spaces under the vehicle must be available for routing the fuel lines and the exhaust piping. A high-voltage electrical circuit diagram has to be developed alongside fuel line and exhaust system drawing. While analyzing the packaging and mounting of the hybrid components, front-to-rear weight ratios must be maintained at 60:40 or less for acceptable drivability, ride performance and dynamic braking.

In conclusion, the mass savings in engine and fuel system downsizing in a hybrid vehicle will more or less be consumed by the additional components added; and the packaging issues are much more complicated for re-engineered vehicles. It would always be advantageous to design a hybrid from ground up rather than retrofit and re-engineer an existing IC engine vehicle.

## 3.7   MISSION-BASED DESIGN WITH VEHICLE SIMULATION

The vehicle design is driven by the customer which in turn sets the mission profile for the vehicle system and its powertrain. Vehicle acceleration, maximum speed, all-electric range, fuel economy and passenger and loading capacity are the choice factors that a customer cares about either in part or fully in selecting a passenger vehicle, which is essential to be considered during the vehicle design process. The considerations for the critical parameters resulting from the choice factors are widely different when designing a delivery truck as compared to that of designing a passenger sedan. In recent years, there has been an uptake in the interest and sales in EVs where the customers are willing to pay comparatively more than an equivalent IC engine vehicle due to a variety of reasons including high-acceleration performance, environmental consciousness, new technology appeal, quiet operation and convenience of fueling/charging at home and at work. The mission is set by the customer which necessitates simulation and analysis tools that incorporate the customer requirements. A simplified approach of incorporating the customer requirements in vehicle design and component sizing is to use the various standardized drive cycles used for evaluating vehicle performance in different driving scenarios. The various drive cycles available reflect the customer driving preferences and mission of the vehicle [9].

In this section, we will evaluate the vehicle system requirements and then utilize the one-dimensional vehicle system model developed earlier in Chapter 2 to build a system simulation model for the analysis, simulation and design of a vehicle using the standardized drive cycles. Although more complex design and analysis tools are used in the automotive industry, fast and easy-to-use design and simulation tool helps us develop an understanding of vehicle system and its components, evaluate different design topologies and identify the important system interactions.

### 3.7.1   VEHICLE SIMULATION MODEL

The simulation model of a vehicle system is an essential tool for the design and performance evaluation of the vehicle. With numerous choices available for electric and hybrid architectures, and on powertrain component technologies, simulation saves time and cost in predicting tank-to-wheel energy usage as well as in-depth vehicle performance outputs. The simulation models can be developed with varying degrees of sophistication as required by the user. At the vehicle level, a simulation model can predict fuel economy, emissions or wheel torque for a regulated drive cycle; at the subsystem level, component parameters such as electric machine or IC engine torque are available. The objectives of a simulation analysis are varied which can be summarized as follows:

- Vehicle performance prediction – Various vehicle-level performance parameters such as fuel economy, vehicle range and acceleration and load carrying capacities can be predicted for a given vehicle with specified powertrain components under different driving scenarios. The simulation model can be used to optimize and tune the supervisory control system of an electric or hybrid vehicle.

- Component sizing – Estimating the power and energy requirements of powertrain components such as electric machine power rating, inverter kVA requirement and battery capacity.
- Component testing – Powertrain and other auxiliary components can be tested with regards to their capacity and constraints including loss estimations under different driving scenarios. The loss estimations of the powertrain components are particularly useful in design the thermal systems for those such as electric machines, power electronics and battery systems.

For vehicle simulation, a forward-looking model is desired where a vehicle model responds to driver input commands to develop and deliver torque to the wheels similar to what it is in a real-world scenario. A modular structure of the simulation model is highly desirable so that components and configurations can be easily added or removed without having to start from scratch. This facilitates comparisons among different component technologies or components of different ratings. The performance comparison of alternative hybrid architectures is also easily accomplished with the modular structure.

The models are developed using both physical principles and empirical data. The vehicle dynamics and roadway fundamentals presented in Chapter 2 are the physical principles based on which the vehicle model can be developed. The driver behavior is modeled using various drive cycles, which are standardized speed and road grade profiles used to evaluate a vehicle's performance. For the components, either simplified models or look-up tables based on empirical data are used in the simulation. Detailed dynamic behavior of the components is often not required, since the time responses of many of the subsystems (such as the electric machine) are much faster than the vehicle dynamics. Simpler models of subsystems minimize the simulation time, since otherwise it would be significant for such a highly complex vehicle system. With this approach, it is possible to run a large number of simulations in order to tune the control strategy to perform well under a wide range of driving conditions. Because there are both mechanical and electrical dynamics, a variable-step stiff system solver is required.

The simulation block diagram of a vehicle system showing the interactions among the driver, the supervisory controller, the subsystems and the vehicle model is shown in Figure 3.19. The driver is modeled with a drive cycle and a PI regulator designed to minimize the error between the drive cycle velocity profile and the actual vehicle velocity. The speed profile of the drive cycle is assumed to be the vehicle speed desired by the driver. The PI regulator output creates a pedal position which is interpreted as either the accelerator pedal position or the brake pedal position. It is assumed that both pedals cannot be depressed simultaneously. The pedal position is read into the control strategy (located in the SCM or supervisory control module) to generate the subsystem commands. The powertrain, modeled in the subsystem block, produces the tractive torque $T_{TR}$, which is sent to the vehicle model. The brake pedal position input is passed through directly into the brake subsystem model to address safety concerns; however, the brake pedal position is also required by the supervisor controller to determine the magnitude of the powertrain regeneration command.

**FIGURE 3.19**   Vehicle simulation block diagram.

### 3.7.2 STANDARD DRIVE CYCLES

The standard drive cycles are used by the governmental agencies and automotive industry for performance evaluation of a vehicle, which includes certification of vehicle fuel economy. A drive cycle may have both speed and road grade components, although typically one is held constant while the other is varied.

Two commonly used standard drive cycles are the urban dynamometer driving schedule (UDDS) and the highway fuel economy test (HWFET), simulating urban and highway driving, respectively. The two drive cycles are shown in Figures 3.20 and 3.21. The UDDS drive cycle runs a distance of 7.5 miles in 1,369 s with frequent stops and has an average speed of 19.6 mph. The HWFET drive cycle runs a distance of 10.26 miles in 765 s and has an average speed of 48.3 mph.

Another standard drive cycle is the US06 drive cycle, which is used to test the effectiveness of the vehicle control strategy under extreme driving conditions. The drive cycle is shown in Figure 3.22. The US06 drive cycle is the most aggressive of the three drive cycles shown so far. It features rapid acceleration and hard braking, and has top speeds just over 80 mph. The Japanese technical standard drive cycle J1015, shown in Figure 3.23, is also useful in simulating urban driving with frequent stops.

The section will conclude describing the standard J227a driving cycle recommended by the Society of Automotive Engineers (SAE) to evaluate the performance of EVs and energy sources followed by an example EV simulation. This short drive cycle is useful for hand calculations needed to develop the concepts of electric and hybrid vehicle fundamentals. The SAE J227a has three schedules designed to simulate the typical driving patterns of fixed-route urban, variable-route urban and variable-route suburban travels. These three patterns are the SAE J227a driving schedules B, C and D, respectively. Each schedule has five segments in the total driving period: (i) acceleration time $t_a$ to reach the maximum velocity from start-up; (ii) cruise time $t_{cr}$ at a constant speed; (iii) coast time $t_{co}$ when no energy is drawn from the source; (iv) brake time $t_b$ to bring the vehicle to stop and (v)

**FIGURE 3.20**  Urban dynamometer driving schedule (UDDS).

**FIGURE 3.21**   Highway fuel economy driving schedule (HWFET).

**FIGURE 3.22**   US06 standard drive cycle.

**FIGURE 3.23**  Japan1015 Japanese standard drive cycle.

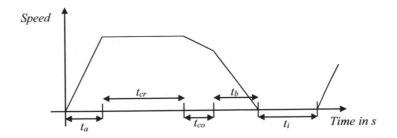

**FIGURE 3.24**  SAE J227a standard driving cycle.

idle time $t_i$ prior to the completion of the period. The driving cycle for J227a is shown in Figure 3.24 with the recommended times for each of the schedules given in Table 3.5. The figure drawn is slightly modified from the pattern recommended by the SAE. The J227a procedures specify only the cruise velocity and the time of transition from one mode to the other. The velocity profile at segments other than the cruising part is not fixed, and hence, the distance traversed during these other periods is also variable. In reality, the distances would depend on the acceleration capability of the vehicle under consideration. For simplicity, straight-line approximations have been assumed for these schedules in this book.

## TABLE 3.5
### SAE J227a Standard Driving Schedules

| Test Parameter | SAE J227a Schedules | | |
|---|---|---|---|
| | B | C | D |
| Max. speed, kph (mph) | 32 | 48 | 72 |
| Acceleration time, $t_a$ s | 19 | 18 | 28 |
| Cruise time, $t_{cr}$ s | 19 | 20 | 50 |
| Coast time, $t_{co}$ s | 4 | 8 | 10 |
| Brake time, $t_{br}$ s | 5 | 9 | 9 |
| Idle time, $t_i$ s | 25 | 25 | 25 |
| Total time, s | 72 | 80 | 122 |
| Approximate number of cycles per mile | 4–5 | 3 | 1 |

### Example 3.1

The vehicle parameters for the 2011 Nissan Leaf are: vehicle mass=1,521 kg; wheel radius=0.4 m; frontal area=2.16 m² and wheelbase=2.7 m. The electric motor parameters are: $L_d = 1.52$ mH, $L_q = 1.54$ mH, $R_{ph} = 0.046\,\Omega$, motor torque constant $K_e = 0.46$ (phase, peak) and $\lambda_m = 0.115\dfrac{Vs}{rad}$ (phase, peak). The battery is rated at 40 kWh with a nominal DC bus voltage of 360 V.

   i. Develop a simulation model of the vehicle and generate the plots for (a) motor torque, (b) motor power, (c) battery energy consumption and (d) battery state-of-charge (SoC) as a function of time using the UDDS standard drive cycle.

   ii. Calculate the energy required for 50 and 70 miles of drive the Nissan Leaf based on the energy consumption for one UDDS cycle.

### Solution

   i. The simulation model is developed using the software tool MATLAB-Simulink®. The block diagram of the simulation model is shown in Figure 3.25. The vehicle system is modeled based on the models developed in Chapter 2. The battery and motor components use models that will be discussed later in Chapters 5 and 7, respectively.

**FIGURE 3.25** EV simulation model built for PSIM for Examples 3.1 and 3.2.

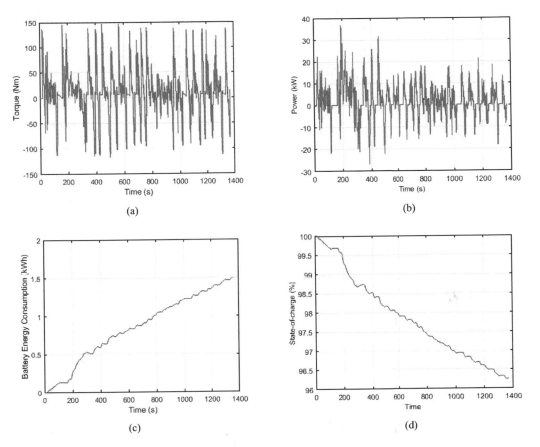

**FIGURE 3.26** Nissan Leaf electric motor and battery simulation results for one UDDS cycle: (a) motor torque, (b) motor power, (c) battery energy consumption and (d) battery SoC.

    The simulations were run for the UDDS drive cycle or the Nissan Leaf using sinusoidal voltages as input to the motor. The motor torque, motor power, battery energy consumption and battery SoC for one UDDS cycle is given in Figure 3.26.

ii. The total miles traveled in one UDDS cycle is 7.49 miles, and the energy consumed is 1.46 kWh, which results in a MPGGE of 172.9. The energy consumed for 50-mile distance is 9.75 kWh and that for 70-mile distance is 13.65 kWh. The energy consumption calculation neglects the mechanical transmission losses and electric power converter losses. The miles/gge is on the higher side since these and other stray losses have not been included in this calculation. Also, UDDS cycle has many falling slopes where regeneration takes place, where we have assumed regeneration at 30% to recover some of the kinetic energy. In UDDS, at lower speeds there will be much lower loss due to less aerodynamic drag (which varies as $v^2$). The official number for Nissan Leaf is 124 miles/gge in city.

## Example 3.2

The vehicle parameters for the Tesla Model 3 are: vehicle mass = 1,611 kg; wheel radius = 0.447 m; frontal area = 2.16 m$^2$ and wheelbase = 2.7 m. The electric motor parameters are: $L_d = 0.42$ mH, $L_q = 0.52$ mH, $R_{ph} = 0.028\ \Omega$, motor torque constant $K_e = 0.24$ (phase, peak) and $\lambda_m = 0.06\ \dfrac{\text{Vs}}{\text{rad}}$ (phase, peak). The battery is rated at 75 kWh with a nominal DC bus voltage of 375 V.

i. Develop a simulation model of the vehicle and generate the plots for (a) motor torque, (b) motor power, (c) battery energy consumption and (d) battery SoC as a function of time using the HWFET standard drive cycle.
ii. Calculate the energy required for 50 and 70 miles of drive the Nissan Leaf based on the energy consumption for one HWFET cycle.
iii. Calculate the energy required in the UDDS drive cycle in terms of battery SoC. Then, estimate how many miles the vehicle will go for SoC to go from 100% to 0%. Finally, calculate fuel economy in terms of miles/charge.

### Solution

i. The simulation model shown in Figure 3.25 is used after updating the parameters with the Tesla Model 3 vehicle. The simulations were run for the HWFET drive cycle using sinusoidal voltages as input to the motor. The motor torque, motor power, battery energy consumption and battery SoC for one HWFET cycle is given in Figure 3.27.
ii. The total miles traveled in one HWFET cycle is 10.3 miles and the energy consumed is 2.24 kWh, which results in a miles/gge of 155. The energy consumed for 50-mile distance is 10.87 kWh and that for 70-mile distance is 15.22 kWh. The energy consumption calculations neglect the mechanical transmission losses and electric power converter losses. The calculated miles/gge is higher than the official figures since these and other stray losses have not been accounted for in this simulation. The official number for Tesla Model 3 is 132 miles/gge in highway.

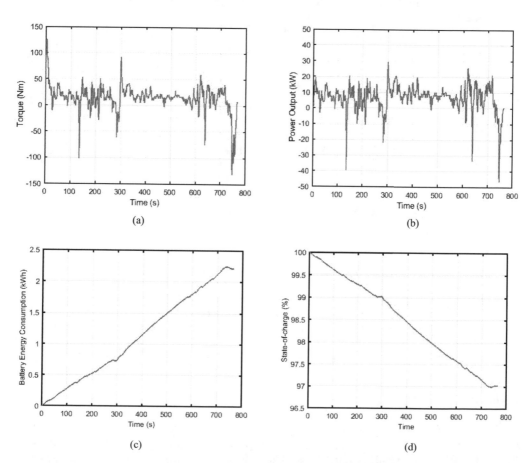

**FIGURE 3.27**    Tesla Model 3 electric motor and battery simulation results for one UDDS cycle: (a) motor torque, (b) motor power, (c) battery energy consumption and (d) battery SoC.

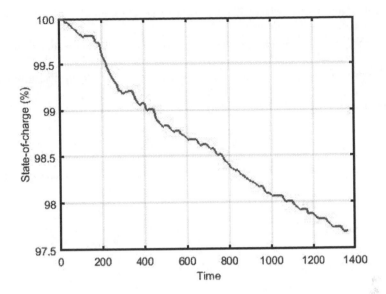

**FIGURE 3.28**  Tesla Model 3 battery SoC simulation for one UDDS cycle.

iii. The battery capacity of the Tesla battery is 75 kWh and the battery voltage is 375 V. The simulation is started with the battery at full charge (100% SoC).

As seen from Figure 3.28, the SoC drops 2.3% from 100% to 97.7% during the UDDS drive cycle. This corresponds to an energy consumption of 1.73 kWh. The distance traveled during the UDDS cycle is 7.49 miles. Therefore, the distance that can be traveled in one full charge of the battery can be calculated as follows:

$$\text{Range} = \frac{100}{\Delta \text{SoC}_{UDDS}} \times \text{Distance}_{UDDS}$$

On substituting, we get

$$\text{Range} = \frac{100}{2.3} \times 7.49 = 325 \text{ mi}$$

This calculation neglects mechanical losses in the motor and transmission and losses in the inverter.

## PROBLEMS

### 3.1

The parameters of a parallel HEV are as follows:

| Description | Parameters |
| --- | --- |
| Vehicle mass | 1,800 kg |
| Driver/one passenger | 80 kg |
| Rolling resistance coefficient: $C_0$, $C_1$ | 0.01, 0 |
| Aerodynamic drag coefficient, $C_{AD}$ | 0.4 |
| Frontal Area, $A_F$ | 2.6 m² |

The vehicle is to accelerate uniformly (i.e., constant acceleration) from 0 to 60 mph in 10 s.

    a. Find an expression for traction force as a function of time $F_{TR}(t)$ for this initial acceleration period.

    b. Find an expression for traction power as a function of time $P_{TR}(t)$ for the initial acceleration period.

    c. Find the energy $\Delta e_{TR}$ required for initial acceleration between 0 and 10 s.

## 3.2

The vehicle parameters and performance requirements of the vehicle are used for sizing calculations:

| Description | Requirements |
|---|---|
| Vehicle mass | 1,800 kg |
| Driver/one passenger | 176 lbs./80 kg |
| Trailering capacity | 1,000 kg |
| Rolling resistance coefficients: $C_0$, $C_1$ | 0.01, 0 |
| Wheel radius, $r_{wh}$ | 0.3305 m |
| Aerodynamic drag coefficient, $C_{AD}$ | 0.45 |
| Frontal area, $A_F$ | 2.5 m$^2$ |
| 0–60 mph | 8.0 s |
| 50–70 mph | 6.3 s |
| Sustained cruising speed (with trailer) | 55 mph at 7% grade |
| Sustained cruising speed (without trailer) | 70 mph at 0.5% grade |
| Zero emission range (without trailer) | 5 miles at 40 mph |

The initial acceleration requirement is without the trailer, but the total mass must account for the driver and one passenger.

    a. Calculate the velocity and power at the end of 5 s for a constant force initial acceleration. The constant force is 7,600 N.

    b. The vehicle accelerates in the constant power mode after the initial constant force acceleration period of part (a) with a constant power of 140 kW. Write the $dv/dt$ equation for constant power acceleration for the given conditions. What is the velocity after a total time of 8 s. (You can solve the equation numerically.)

    c. Calculate the power required for a steady-state velocity of 55 mph at 7% with trailer.

## REFERENCES

1. C.C. Chan and K.T. Chau, *Modern Electric Vehicle Technology*, Oxford University Press, Oxford, UK, 2001.
2. R. Hodkinson and J. Fentos, *Lightweight Electric/Hybrid Vehicle Design*, SAE International, Warrendale, PA, 2001.
3. R. K. Jurgen (editor), *Electric and Hybrid Electric Vehicles*, PT-85, SAE International, Warrendale, PA, 2002.
4. A. Nagasaka, M. Nada, H. Hamada, S. Hiramatsu, Y. Kikuchi, and H. Kato., "Development of Hybrid/ Battery ECU for the Toyota Hybrid System, Technology for Electric and Hybrid Vehicles," SAE Publication, SP-1331, SAE International, Warrendale, PA, 1998.
5. J.F. Ronning and G.L. Grant, "Global Hybrid Electric Vehicle Markets and Missions," Electric and Hybrid Electric Vehicles and Fuel Cell Technology, SAE Publication, SP-1466, SAE International, Warrendale, PA, 1999.

6. M. Ehsani, K.M. Rahman and H.A. Toliyat, "Propulsion system design for electric and hybrid vehicles," *IEEE Transactions on Industrial Electronics*, 44(1), 19–27, February 1997.

7. J.R. Howell and R.O. Buckius, *Fundamentals of Engineering Thermodynamics*, second edition, McGraw-Hill, New York, NY, 1992.

8. H.K. Ng, A.D. Vyas and D.J. Santini, "The prospects for Hybrid Electric Vehicles, 2000–2005: Results of a Delphi Study," Electric and Hybrid Electric Vehicles and Fuel Cell Technology, SAE Publication SP-1466, pp. 95–106, SAE International, Warrendale, PA, 1999.

9. T.J. Barlow, S. Latham, I.S. McCrae and P.G. Boulter, "A Reference Book of Driving Cycles for Measurement of Road Vehicle Emissions," Published Project Report PPR354, TRL Limited, 2009.

# 4 Autonomous Vehicles

With a rapid increase in the types, production and sales of battery electric vehicles, the transportation sector has gone through a major transformation over the past decade. This technical growth in vehicle electrification coincided with a radical transformation of society's need and understanding of mobility. The tremendous increase in the use of shared vehicles signifies a trend to move away from personal car ownership to an era where transportation is seen as a service. Self-driving vehicles appear to be on the horizon with companies testing driverless vehicles in geofenced areas. The future of mobility is likely to involve the convergence of these three technological areas: electric drivetrains, self-driving vehicles and ride sharing services. While significant benefits can be realized from each of these technologies independently, the convergence of these technologies has the potential to improve our current transportation by being cheaper, more convenient, safer, allow higher productivity for workers, be better for the environment and make better use of our infrastructure.

According to an analysis by former GM vice president Lawrence Burns and Columbia University economist Jefferey Sachs, a shared, electric, autonomous transportation service would be more than 70% cheaper for a citizen of a city like Ann Arbor, MI, and about 80% fewer vehicles would be needed than personally owned vehicles to provide the same mobility [1]. Traditional owned vehicles are overbuilt, able to travel at speeds more than 120 mph and carry five or more passengers. With ride sharing services, vehicles could be tailored for a specific trip allowing for most vehicles to be significantly reduced in size and weight. Not only would such a service provide lower personal costs, but the environmental costs would be significantly reduced as well. Emissions from cars and trucks amount to one fifth of the greenhouse gases released in the United States [2]. With electric drivetrains, the energy required to propel the vehicle can be produced from cleaner sources such as solar, wind, hydro-electric and nuclear power plants. The combination of self-driving taxis and electric vehicles allows for the vehicles to self-charge, a safer task than the autonomous refueling of a gasoline-powered vehicle. Self-driving vehicles would also eliminate the need for vast expanses of valuable real estate to be covered with asphalt for parking. In addition to the environmental and cost savings of self-driving, electric, shared vehicles, they will also be safer than traditional vehicles. According to the National Highway Traffic Safety Administration, 36,560 people were killed in motor vehicle traffic crashes on US roadways in 2018 [3]. It is expected that the development of self-driving vehicles will greatly reduce this number.

While autonomous vehicles have been discussed almost since the invention of the automobile itself, it was not until the convergence of computational processing, sensor technology and the advances in probabilistic robotics that the possibility of self-driving cars was technically possible. In 2004, the Defense Advanced Research Projects Agency (DARPA) held a competition that would award the first team to autonomously complete a 150-mile course in the Mojave desert a one million dollar prize. None of the 15 teams that qualified for the final race finished the course and no one claimed the prize. The Carnegie Melon Red Team went the farthest completing 7.32 miles. DARPA held the competition again in 2005 this time awarding a $2 million prize to the Sebastian Thrun-led team with their entry "Stanley" from Stanford University [4]. In total, five vehicles completed the 130-mile race. The methods used in the 2005 race were published here [5]. The successful autonomous navigation of 130 miles of desert road opened a new error of autonomous mobility. The DARPA challenge was again held in 2007 in an urban setting to see if the vehicles could learn to navigate city streets dealing with other cars and objects. A team from Carnegie Mellon and GM known as Tartan Racing claimed the $2 million prize with their entry named "Boss" [6]. The methods used were published here [7]. The DARPA Grand Challenges were significant in that it opened a new era of innovation, design and development of autonomous vehicles. However, immediately following the competition, only a few companies recognized the potential of this technology, and it took several years to spark the interest among the major automotive companies. Currently, automobile companies such as GM, Ford, Tesla, Mercedes-Benz, Audi, BMW and IT companies, such as Waymo, Uber and Baidu, are developing and testing autonomous vehicles for market entry. These companies are working to overcome several challenges including safety, affordability and regulatory hurdles. The safety of self-driving cars is intimately linked to the perception and decision-making aspects that rely heavily on artificial intelligence. In order to insure the profitability of self-driving vehicles and services, the additional cost of sensors and computational processing hardware should not significantly increase the cost in comparison to conventional vehicles. While many automobile manufacturers offer vehicles with automated braking, lane keeping, blind spot detection, adaptive cruise, etc., the ultimate goal is to enable passengers to be able to totally disengage from the navigation of the vehicle once the destination has been set.

Electric vehicles provide an enhanced opportunity to move towards autonomous driving since the powertrain simplicity offers the scope and space to add communication and computation resources needed for advanced vehicle features. The current battery technology of electric vehicles requires them to be recharged more frequently than IC engines need to be refueled, and hence, self-driving capabilities will enhance the usability of electric vehicles. In addition, since the safe automated refueling of an IC engine is significantly more challenging than the automated safe recharging of an electric vehicle, the combination of electric vehicles and self-driving vehicles creates a mutually beneficial symbiosis.

The degrees of autonomy in advanced vehicles range from some basic safety maneuvers such as automated braking to fully autonomous vehicles where there is no need for a driver to engage for any reason. Many vehicles on the road today have some level of autonomy such as adaptive cruise, lane keeping or safety breaking. Completely autonomous vehicles are still in the research and development stage; however, testing is currently underway for vehicles that can operate without driver intervention in geofenced locations.

## 4.1   FIVE LEVELS OF AUTONOMOUS DRIVING

Autonomous driving has been progressing through increased levels of driver assistance over the past decade with fully automated or self-driving cars being evaluated in constrained environments. In 2013, the US Department of Transportation's National Highway Traffic Safety Administration (NHTSA) defined five different levels of autonomous driving and updated the policy in 2016 to reflect that they have officially adopted the levels of autonomy outlined in the SAE International's J3016 document. The degree of automation is formally recognized in the autonomous driving system (ADS) through these five levels of driver assistance whose definitions are given below:

*Level 0*: This is the basic level which is the same as what we are used to with conventional vehicles, i.e., the driver (human) controls everything: steering, throttle, acceleration and brakes.

*Level 1*: This is a driver assistance level where a special function such as steering or accelerating can be done automatically by the vehicle controller, but most functions of driving are still under the control of the driver.

*Level 2*: From level 2, the autonomy moves into a different level where at least one driver assistance system, such as speed control and lane-centering, is automated using information about the driving environment. The driver is disengaged from physically operating the vehicle by having his or her hands off the steering wheel and foot off the acceleration pedal at the same time but must always be ready to take control of the vehicle when needed.

*Level 3*: In level 3, the vehicle ADS can perform the safety critical functions of cruising and steering under certain traffic or environmental conditions, although drivers are still necessary in a stand-by mode. The driver is, however, not required to monitor the driving conditions as in the previous levels. The technical challenge associated in this level is the transfer of control from vehicle to human when needed.

*Level 4*: This level is when the driving is fully autonomous and vehicles' ADS are designed to maneuver through the roadway and perform all safety critical driving functions within the operational design domain of the vehicle. The design domain does not cover every driving scenario.

*Level 5*: This ADS in level 5 requires a fully autonomous system where the vehicle self-driving performance is to equal or exceed that of a human driver in every driving scenario including extreme environments such as dirt roads.

## 4.2   AUTONOMOUS VEHICLE FUNCTIONAL ARCHITECTURE

The autonomous vehicle architecture is built around the technologies of sensors, signal processing, perception and planning algorithms, controls and actuators. The autonomous vehicle's functional architecture defines and identifies the system functionalities, its components' functions and their interactions to achieve the mission goal of autonomous driving. An example autonomous vehicle architecture is shown in Figure 4.1. The architecture includes hardware and software segments with data exchange between them. The hardware components include sensors, actuators and processors

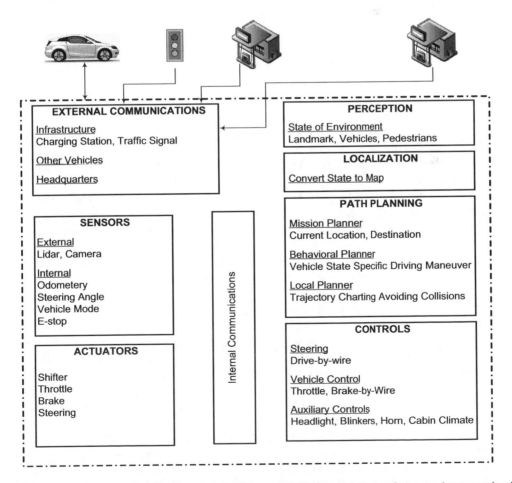

**FIGURE 4.1**   Autonomous vehicle's functional architecture with the hardware, software and communication components.

to host the software. The software components include perception, localization, path planning and control algorithms to generate the commands for actuation.

In the autonomous vehicle, the sensing and communication components provide the necessary information to enable the perception and mapping tasks such as object detection and vehicle trajectory tracking. The software processes start with the hardware sensors some of which may depend on external communications. Advanced signal processing techniques play a key role in the software processes of perception, localization and path planning. In this section, we will discuss the hardware sensors and external communications, while the next section will cover the software stacks.

## 4.2.1 Sensors

The sensors for the ADS system are components built and designed to communicate externally to capture information about the environment such as state of the vehicle or relative position of nearby objects. The sensors in an autonomous vehicle may include camera, lidar, radar, ultrasonic sensor, global positioning system (GPS) or inertial measurement unit (IMU). The different types of sensors differ from each other in many aspects and have their own advantages and disadvantages. A suitable sensor selection and placement planning will balance function, range and cost, and overcome the adverse effects of weather, visibility and blind spot detection. Cameras are the most common type of sensors used to capture visual encoded information to provide situational awareness. A multi-camera system is used for debugging signs and markers, detection and tracking of cars, bikes and pedestrians. Sensing quality for cameras strongly depends on the environmental conditions such as weather and light reflection. Radar is another type of sensor that sends out radio waves and measures the time for the wave to reflect back as well as the direction of arrival (DoA). Radars have the longest range, and depending on the sophistication, the range estimation can be between 10 and 250 m. The drawback of radar is its low resolution and inability to identify small objects. Radar can be used for cross-traffic set-ups, blind spots and rear collisions. Long-range radar is most commonly used for adaptive cruise control (ACC). Mid-range radar systems with range from about 40 to 150 m are used in emergency braking and supporting automated overtaking processes. Another sensor used in autonomous driving is lidar which measures distance to a target by illuminating it with pulsed laser light and measuring the time it takes for the reflected light to return to the sensor. Lidar is often used to create dense 3D maps of the environment. Lidar has enhanced discrimination due to a smaller wavelength and is good for capturing information in various types of ambient light, whether day or night. Ultrasonic sensors, which have an operating range of about 2 m, have been used in automobiles for many years now for parking assistant-type functions. The range and angular span of the abovementioned sensor technologies used in autonomous vehicles are shown in Figure 4.2. A qualitative comparison of different sensing technologies is given in Table 4.1. The number and type of sensors are selected according to their range and performance for the mission of the vehicle.

Autonomous vehicles combine readings of multiple sensor types for redundancy and to compensate for the weaknesses of various sensors. A suitable sensor plan balances function, range and cost. The process of combining information from multiple sensors is known as *sensor fusion*. Sensor fusion is often done by some form of Kalman filtering. With nonlinear process and measurement model, a nonlinear version of the Kalman filter must be used. Either the Extended Kalman filter, Unscented Kalman filter, or Cubature Kalman filter can be used for fusing measurements and process models of nonlinear systems [8].

Internal sensors of the vehicle are critical in completing the functions of autonomous driving which include physical sensors as well as signals from the ADS. Examples of these sensors are speed sensor, operating mode and E-stop. Operating mode signal identifies the driving pattern such as sports mode, normal mode and emergency mode, which is based on the driver input, battery state-of-charge and charging station distance.

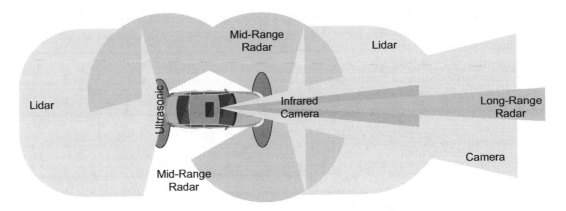

**FIGURE 4.2**   Sensor technologies for object detection and environment mapping.

**TABLE 4.1**
**Comparison of Different Sensor Technologies for Autonomous Vehicles**

|           | Range     | Range Resolution | Angle Resolution | Bright Light Performance | Low Light Performance | Radial Velocity | Weather Robustness | Material Cost |
|-----------|-----------|------------------|------------------|--------------------------|-----------------------|-----------------|--------------------|---------------|
| Radar     | Very good | Good             | Average          | Very good                | Very good             | Very good       | Very good          | Medium        |
| Lidar     | Good      | Very good        | Very good        | Good                     | Very good             | Average         | Average            | High          |
| Camera    | Very good | Average          | Good             | Good                     | Poor                  | Poor            | Poor               | Low           |
| Ultrasonic| Poor      | Poor             | Poor             | Good                     | Good                  | Poor            | Good               | Low           |

### 4.2.2   EXTERNAL COMMUNICATIONS

The sensing and communication components provide the necessary information in an autonomous vehicle to enable the vehicle for its perception tasks such as object detection and vehicle direction tracking. Additional information such as 3D maps, GPS data, traffic situations, road conditions and weather situations may be brought in through external communications for the software processes of autonomous driving. The additional features of a connected vehicle are enabled by vehicle-to-vehicle (V2V) and vehicle-to-infrastructure (V2I) communications which allows the vehicle to receive and/or transmit information to other agents in the environment. V2V connects cars to each other for sharing data about route and speed; for example, one vehicle can send information to nearby vehicles to avoid collisions. V2I communications allow vehicles to receive information transmitted from various infrastructure or transmits signals such as traffic light, parking meters, parking garages and charging stations to enhance both safety and efficiency of driving. For example, switch off street lights map if no drivers are on a given road or which charging station should be targeted based on the electric vehicle's range and locations of charging stations.

While many self-driving car companies are attempting to achieve full autonomy without V2V and V2I communication, this technology has the potential to greatly enhance the performance of these vehicles providing a means for optimized traffic flow. Autonomous driving systems require incredible data handling and processing capabilities and speeds to be compatible with the timing of human reflexes. The various sensors in an autonomous vehicle generate unprecedented amount of data which requires a much faster network than the existing 4G technology. It is expected that the 5G mm wave wireless technology will be used in autonomous vehicles having a fast, reliable and fully responsive network.

The information provided by the various sensors constitute large data sources that are processed by the software stack for generating useful information that ultimately determine actuation commands. There are three metrics based on which the data processing in the distribution system of the autonomous vehicle is evaluated, which are throughput ratio, transmission latency and packet loss. *Throughput ratio* determines the maximum amount of data that can be processed by CPUs, irrespective of how efficient or accurate the intelligent algorithms are. *Transmission latency* is measured by time elapsed between sending and receiving of data. An increase in latency will affect every module resulting in degraded performance since the autonomous vehicle is a real-time system. *Packet loss* refers to the loss of data during transmission which inevitably exists due to the uncertainty of physical links whether for wired or wireless units.

## 4.3 SOFTWARE STACK: PERCEPTION, LOCALIZATION, PATH PLANNING AND CONTROL

Advanced signal processing, communications and learning algorithms for sensing, environment mapping, self-positioning and planning play a key role in the autonomous driving of vehicles. While a standard software methodology does not yet exist for accomplishing all the required tasks of autonomous driving, all strategies would include at least these four elements: perception, localization, path planning and vehicle control. The output of the path planning goes into the vehicle controller for decision-making which then sends commands to the actuators. The work flow for the software stack is shown in Figure 4.3. The controller uses optimization algorithms based on sensor signal inputs and driver path requests to generate the commands for the actuators to follow the trajectory. The actuators are the electric drive or engine, brake and steering systems.

### 4.3.1 PERCEPTION

The task of perception involves taking measurements from external sensors such as cameras, radar, lidar and ultrasonic sensors and converting this sensory input into meaningful information that can ultimately be used by the localization, path planning and vehicle control modules of the system. Tasks included in the perception module are as follows:

- Detecting locations and trajectories of vehicles, bicycles and pedestrians
- Detecting road signs
- Detecting the state of traffic lights
- Detecting drivable area
- Detecting lane markings
- Detecting cross walks
- Localizing the vehicle within a global map
- Localizing the vehicle within a lane.

**FIGURE 4.3** Work flow for the software stack.

The perception algorithms used in the DARPA challenges were based on traditional computer vision algorithms. However, deep learning tools are now applied in perception especially for object detection and tracking to increase accuracy of position, orientation and size. A new era in computer vision began in 2012 with the successful application of deep learning to image classification when Alex Krizhevsky et al. applied a deep convolutional neural network (CNN) to develop AlexNet that achieved a top-five classification error rate of 15.5%; a more than 10.8% improvement to the runner up algorithm in the ImageNet Large-Scale Vision Recognition Challenge (ILSVRC) [9]. The matrix multiplication operations that comprise deep learning algorithms are very similar to the operations used in processing graphics of video games. The advances in Graphics Processing Units (GPUs) were instrumental in the success of deep learning. The 2012 ImageNet winning algorithm was the first application of training a CNN on GPUs. Training a CNN on a GPU can decrease the learning time by a factor of 100 or more from training on a CPU. The main provider of GPUs for use in deep learning is NVIDIA; this is due to hardware capabilities and the wide-spread use of NVIDIA's CUDA software by the deep learning community. CUDA serves as the interface between a high-level programming language like Python and the GPU hardware. Tesla, Inc., in partnership with Samsung, began to produce its own chips dedicated for autonomous driving. The chip production started in 2017 and Tesla began shipping vehicles with the new hardware in 2019. Tesla claims their chips offer 21 times the performance of the NVIDIA chips used previously. The higher performance is likely due to the chips being purpose-built specifically for autonomous driving.

Semantic segmentation is a deep learning algorithm that classifies each pixel with a certain label. In autonomous driving, semantic segmentation is used to determine the location of the drivable area among other things. Combining the semantic segmentation of the drivable area with a lidar point cloud provides a straight-forward way to distinguish lidar points hitting the roadway from lidar points hitting objects or sidewalks. Semantic segmentation can also be done with lidar point clouds themselves and can serve as a means of localizing the vehicle.

One of the reasons deep learning has spread so fast is that the community has a culture of being highly open source. State-of-the-art algorithms are often available for free download upon release. Top AI researchers have dedicated significant amounts of their careers to educating people about deep learning. Andrew Ng is an AI researcher and founder of Coursera who offers deep learning specialization courses through Deeplearing.ai with many Python code exercises using Google's Tensorflow API. Jeremy Howard is another data scientist who has built a state-of-the-art library based in Python that builds upon the Facebook maintained PyTorch API and offers this library as well as free educational resources through his company Fast.ai.

One important task of the perception module is to track the location and trajectory of other vehicles. This is done by mapping the pixel location of a vehicle in each image frame to real-world coordinates and estimating the future trajectory of the vehicle using a state space model of the vehicle [10]. A common vehicle model when the steering angle is not known such as when tracking another vehicle is the so-called coordinated turn model; this is also known as the constant velocity turn rate (CVTR) model. The CVTR assumes the longitudinal velocity and yaw rate are constant from one time step to the next. Acceleration changes are modeled as disturbance noise. The CVTR model is given as follows:

$$
\begin{bmatrix} \dot{x}(t) \\ \dot{y}(t) \\ \dot{v}(t) \\ \dot{\phi}(t) \\ \dot{\omega}(t) \end{bmatrix} = \begin{bmatrix} v(t)\cos(\phi(t)) \\ v(t)\sin(\phi(t)) \\ 0 \\ \omega(t) \\ 0 \end{bmatrix} + \begin{bmatrix} 0 & 0 \\ 0 & 0 \\ 1 & 0 \\ 0 & 0 \\ 0 & 1 \end{bmatrix} \begin{bmatrix} q_c^v(t) \\ q_c^\omega(t) \end{bmatrix}
$$

where $x(t)$ and $y(t)$ are the global 2D position coordinates, $v(t)$ is the estimated velocity, $\phi(t)$ is the yaw angle, $w(t)$ is the change in yaw angle, and $q_c^v(t)$ and $q_c^\omega(t)$ are used to model translational and rotational acceleration as process noise. This continuous-time model is converted to a discrete-time model with the Euler method:

$$
\begin{bmatrix} x_k \\ y_k \\ v_k \\ \phi_k \\ \omega_k \end{bmatrix} = \begin{bmatrix} x_{k-1} + \dfrac{2v_{k-1}}{\omega_{k-1}}\sin\left(\dfrac{\omega_{k-1}T}{2}\right)\cos\left(\phi_{k-1}+\dfrac{\omega_{k-1}T}{2}\right) \\ y_{k-1} + \dfrac{2v_{k-1}}{\omega_{k-1}}\sin\left(\dfrac{\omega_{k-1}T}{2}\right)\sin\left(\phi_{k-1}+\dfrac{\omega_{k-1}T}{2}\right) \\ v_{k-1} \\ \phi_{k-1} + T\omega_{k-1} \\ \omega_{k-1} \end{bmatrix} + \begin{bmatrix} 0 & 0 \\ 0 & 0 \\ 1 & 0 \\ 0 & 0 \\ 0 & 1 \end{bmatrix} \begin{bmatrix} q_{k-1}^v \\ q_{k-1}^\omega \end{bmatrix}
$$

where $T$ is the sampling time. To avoid a divide by zero in the case that the turn rate $\omega_{k-1}$ is zero, the $x$ and $y$ location predictions can be calculated considering the vehicle is going in a straight line.

The model of the vehicle is combined with the model of the sensors in a process known as sensor fusion. The models of sensors are called measurement models. For example, a radar gives measurements of distance and heading angle of an object. The measurement model of a radar is described as follows:

$$
\begin{bmatrix} d_k \\ \varphi_k \end{bmatrix} = \begin{bmatrix} \sqrt{\left(p_k^1\right)^2 + \left(p_k^2\right)^2} \\ \arctan\left(\dfrac{p_k^2}{p_k^1}\right) \end{bmatrix} + \begin{bmatrix} r_k^1 \\ r_k^2 \end{bmatrix}
$$

where $p_k^1$ and $p_k^2$ are the distances of the target vehicle in the $x$- and $y$-directions, $r_k^1$ and $r_k^2$ are the measurement noise parameters, $d_k$ is the distance of the target vehicle and $\varphi_k$ is the angle of the target vehicle.

## 4.3.2 LOCALIZATION

The goal of the localization system is to identify the location of the vehicle on a global coordinate system. An autonomous vehicle builds a global map of their current environment and uses this map to navigate or deduce its location at any point in time. On-board sensor data are used for positioning of the vehicle. One approach is to use GPS-IMU fusion where the IMU measures changes in position and orientation and the GPS readings are used to correct the accumulated errors of the IMU. However, this type of sensor-based positioning is not accurate enough in urban scenarios. In the future smart vehicles will be able to use the 5G network mm wave MIMO receivers to obtain much better accuracy than GPS-based positioning. The positioning accuracy depends on the coverage of the communication system which is expected to be high in urban areas.

Dense 3D maps aid in the localization of the vehicle and provide locations of nearby stationary objects. Google Street View is one such dense 3D map that has served as the ground truth for Google's self-driving car project. The maps contain locations of stationary objects as well as traffic signs and traffic signals. Knowing the precise location of traffic signals greatly simplifies the classification of the state of the signal by allowing the computer vision algorithm to ignore potential false-positive traffic signal detections such as bus lights [2]. The dense 3D maps are also used for localizing the vehicle. This can be accomplished by matching 3D point clouds of lidar scans with the dense 3D maps using particle filters. Other works have matched semantically segmented images with the dense 3D maps for localizing with a camera [11].

The final estimate for the location of the vehicle will involve fusing all the location sensor measurements with the motion model of the vehicle. Sensors that may be combined to localize the vehicle are cameras, lidar, GPS, IMU, radar and ultrasonic. The process model in the case of localizing the self-driving vehicle, as opposed to an outside vehicle, will include the steering angle and acceleration. The kinematic bicycle model has been shown to offer a sufficient level of accuracy and is widely used [12].

### 4.3.3 PATH PLANNING

Path planning refers to the task of determining a trajectory the vehicle is expected to follow. It includes high-level decisions such as what roads to take; intermediate decisions such as driving maneuvers, i.e., change lanes, slow to stop, follow lead car, etc., and low-level decisions such as determining the actual trajectory waypoints that the vehicle will follow. The planning algorithm utilizes maps of the environment and takes inputs from the perception and localization modules. The planning algorithm utilizes policies that have either been learned through training on driving data or directly input by engineers.

Path planning for autonomous driving can be divided into three hierarchical problems [13].

- *Mission planning*: What roads to take to navigate from point A to point B
- *Behavioral planning*: How to ensure acceptable driving practices are maintained
- *Local planning*: How to determine the desired position and velocity trajectories.

#### 4.3.3.1 Mission Planning

The highest level of planning is the mission planning. Mission planning focuses on traffic and road connections. All possible routes are weighted based on time of travel or some other criteria and the shortest path to the final destination can be solved with Dijkstra's algorithm or the A* algorithm [14]. Mission planning is similar to the output of common GPS mapping services used by human drivers.

#### 4.3.3.2 Behavioral Planning

Behavioral planning must take in all the information about the roadway and the surrounding vehicles to calculate what maneuver to execute. The advances in behavioral planning are critical for the success of level-4 and level-5 autonomous driving. Behavior planning sets the high-level driving actions or maneuvers. The behavior must be safe and efficient. The behavioral planning module must be able to handle noisy and inaccurate inputs such as false positives. The output of the behavioral planning module goes to the local planner for determining the path and velocity trajectories. Some examples of driving maneuvers output by the behavioral planning module are as follows:

- Track current speed limit
- Track the speed of the leading vehicle and maintain a safe distance
- Decelerate to stop at intersection
- Stop and remain stopped in the current position
- Switch or merge onto a connected drive lane.

Lanelet maps are an elegant mapping data structure developed in 2014 that provide valuable information for autonomous vehicles [15]. Lanelets are represented as nodes on a directed graph and store the following information:

- Left and right boundaries of a given lane
- Regulatory elements at the end of the lanelet
- Regulatory attributes such as the speed limit
- Connectivity to other lanelets to allow traversal to other lanelets
- Each lanelet has four possible connecting lanelets: before, after, to the left and to the right
- Lanelets are represented as nodes on a graph.

A growing area of research in autonomous driving is in the use of reinforcement learning for behavioral planning. A reinforcement learning agent learns a policy that gives an action that it expects will receive the highest reward. Feedback from the environment provides the reward for actions and the agent adjusts its policy accordingly. In autonomous driving, the reward function could be determined by the actions given by human drivers in certain situations. The reinforcement learning agent is given sensory input from the environment such as camera inputs and vehicle state and outputs a desired maneuver. If the agent's maneuver matches closely with that of the human drivers then the policy gets reinforced. If the human drivers did something different, the policy is updated so that it will be closer to the human driver's action the next time it sees similar inputs. Reinforcement learning is often done in simulation environments and training can be quite computationally expensive. Reinforcement learning can also be done with level-1 or level-2 autonomous vehicles or by having a test driver. If the driver must intervene during a certain maneuver, the policy is penalized so that it adjusts its behavior. Another closely related area of research is inverse reinforcement learning. This involves taking the inputs and the actions generated by an expert and learning the reward function.

There are several drawbacks to the reinforcement learning approach. One, reinforcement learning algorithms require large amounts of data and are relatively computationally expensive even compared to other deep learning methods. Second, and perhaps more important, it is difficult to ensure the safety of the learned system as the neural networks used for inference are like black boxes. Without fully understanding the causal relationships of the policy generated by the reinforcement learning agent, one cannot guarantee specific behavior in new situations. Due to the large variety of scenarios a vehicle might encounter, a direct reinforcement learning approach is unlikely to succeed. However, hierarchical reinforcement learning approaches, where maneuvers are considered low-level policies under the umbrella of different driving scenarios help to narrow down the training task.

Making deep learning generally, and reinforcement learning more specifically, more interpretable is an active area of research. Many researchers in AI feel reinforcement learning is a path to general artificial intelligence as it closely mimics one of the ways in which humans learn. Without understanding the causal relationships behind the agents' policies, it will be difficult to control the agents in a way in which we can guarantee they will be able to solve complex tasks in a safe manner.

### 4.3.3.3 Local Planning

Local planning involves taking a given maneuver and outputting the position and velocity trajectories. For instance, the behavioral planning module may indicate a lane change maneuver. Lane change requires different shapes for different situations. The shape of the trajectory depends on speed and acceleration limitations as well as the time horizon of the execution. For comfort it is desired that the lateral acceleration is minimized as much as possible while still achieving the objective within the time window. The lateral acceleration is dependent upon both the velocity as well as the curvature of the path.

If the behavioral planner indicates to follow a lane at the speed limit, the local planner must monitor the velocity of the vehicle in front such that a certain time-to-collision and distance-to-collision buffer is maintained. Turning onto a road requires calculating a window of opportunity in the presence of oncoming traffic, and this requires the estimation of current location as well as predictions of the future trajectory of the oncoming vehicles. Time-to-collision provides a measure of safety and is used to assess potential maneuvers. Time-to-collision is calculated by calculating a point in which the vehicles will collide in the future given likely trajectories and then predict the amount of time for the vehicles to arrive at that collision point.

Predicting the future trajectory of dynamic obstacles is not a trivial task. Maneuver-based assumptions can be used to predict the trajectory. For example, one assumption is that a car will likely follow its lane. Another assumption is that a vehicle will slow down if trying to merge or make a turn. Also changing lanes often involves applying a turn indicator. It must be taken into consideration that often agents violate these rules so a multi-modal hypothesis for collision checking is important.

Typically, a swath- or circle-based estimation of the vehicle's future position is used for collision checking. To compute a swath, a conservative estimate of the car's footprint is moved along points of a given trajectory. With conservative size estimates, collisions may be falsely reported along a path even if a collision would not occur; however, if a collision will occur it is never missed. One limitation of conservative collision estimates is that paths through narrow openings might be eliminated causing a planner to get stuck. Using the circle-based representation, some number of overlapping circles with a given radius is used to encompass the footprint of the car as shown in Figure 4.4. Knowing the trajectory of the given circles, it is efficient to compute a collision by checking if an object's trajectory footprint is within the circles radius.

In addition to avoiding dynamic objects, static objects are also considered in the collision avoidance task by using an occupancy grid map. Occupancy grids are grid maps that indicate whether a grid cell is occupied or not. In addition to static objects, all non-drivable area is considered occupied such as lawns and sidewalks. The sensors give a probability of a square being occupied. If the probability is over some threshold, the square is marked as occupied. If an occupancy grid is implemented in a way that each cell stores the distance to the closest object, the collision detection can be done using a simple lookup in an array.

The trajectories generated by the local planner are constrained by vehicle kinematics, the position of static and dynamic obstacles and regulatory elements such as lane and speed constraints. In addition, soft constraints such as maintaining a certain distance from lead car and comfort constraints relating to both longitudinal and lateral acceleration must also be taken into consideration.

Due to a limited turning angle, there is a maximum curvature or minimum radius that a vehicle can follow. Curvature is one over the radius of a circle tangent to a given point on the path. In order to maintain vehicle stability, frictional forces on the tires must be kept below levels that would cause the tires to lose traction. The longitudinal velocity at any point along the trajectory is constrained by the maximum allowed lateral acceleration and the curvature at that point and is given by

$$v^2 \leq \frac{\max a_{lat}}{\kappa}$$

**FIGURE 4.4**   Circle-based estimate of vehicle footprint.

The curvature along a 2D path has a closed form solution as

$$\kappa = \frac{x'y'' - y'x''}{(x'^2 + y'^2)^{\frac{3}{2}}}$$

With these objectives and constraints, the position and velocity trajectories are determined by solving a constrained optimization problem. The optimization goal for a given a start position heading and curvature is to find the path to an end position heading and curvature that minimizes a cost function and satisfies the constraints. The starting and end values serve as the boundary conditions. The constraints include the motion model of the vehicle and the longitudinal and lateral acceleration constraints. The curvature is often desired to be spread evenly throughout the path. This is done by minimizing the bending energy or the integral of squared curvature.

There are two common methods for assigning the trajectories, quintic splines and cubic spirals [16,17]. Both give a parametric representation of the path and allow for a relatively fast optimization. A quintic spline is a 5th-order polynomial and has 12 parameters to optimize: six parameters for the path in $x$ and six for the path in $y$. The limitation of splines is that it is difficult to constrain the curvature due to potential discontinuities in the curvature or its derivatives.

$$x(u) = \alpha_5 u^5 + \alpha_4 u^4 + \alpha_3 u^3 + \alpha_2 u^4 + \alpha_1 u + \alpha_0$$

$$y(u) = \beta_5 u^5 + \beta_4 u^4 + \beta_3 u^3 + \beta_2 u^4 + \beta_1 u + \alpha_0$$

$$u \in [0,1]$$

Spirals are parameterized by the curvature as a function of arc length. Spirals assure a smooth curvature variation along the trajectory, but $x$ and $y$ positions do not have a closed-form solution.

$$\kappa(s) = a_3 s^3 + a_2 s^2 + a_1 s + a_0$$

$$\theta(s) = \theta_0 + a_3 \frac{s^4}{4} + a_2 \frac{s^3}{3} + a_1 \frac{s^2}{2} + a_0 s$$

$$x(s) = x_0 + \int_0^s \cos(\theta(s'))ds'$$

$$y(s) = y_0 + \int_0^s \sin(\theta(s'))ds'$$

The heading angle $\theta$ has closed-form solution from the curvature spiral. $\theta$ can then be used with Simpson's rule to numerically approximate the $x(s)$ and $y(s)$ positions along the spiral [17]. Simpson's rule provides a more precise numerical estimate of the integral because it uses quadratic interpolations as opposed to linear interpolations that are used by the trapezoid or midpoint rule.

### 4.3.4 MOTION CONTROLS

The control system of the autonomous vehicle converts the intentions and goals of the planning unit into actions and generates command signals for the actuators.

The behavioral planner may give a value for final velocity based on the selected maneuver. A stop at stop light would be a zero-velocity reference. Velocity reference could also be the speed limit of a straight road. If the maneuver is to follow a lead vehicle, the speed of the lead vehicle regulates the speed. In this case, the speed profile is determined so as to keep a certain time-to-collision as well as to maintain a space buffer between the vehicles. In addition, it must be insured that our velocity at each point does not exceed the lateral acceleration constraint.

If the velocity and position trajectories were determined with the vehicle constraints in mind, then a proportional-integral (PI) or proportional-integral-differential (PID) controller can be used to track the given reference. Another approach would be to use model predictive control (MPC) which can include additional constraints. The limitation to MPC is the additional computation time required to solve the constrained optimization problem.

## 4.4  AUTOPILOT AND ACTUATORS

The autopilot in an autonomous driving vehicle is the device that enables a vehicle to automatically turn, shift, accelerate and decelerate. The main components of the autopilot are: Steering wheel, accelerator/brake pedals, gear activator and vehicle drive controller. The actuators are the execution capable hardware devices that receive commands from the vehicle controller and enable the vehicle's motion in the desired direction. The autopilot is commonly referred to as the *drive-by-wire* system where electronic control systems using electromechanical actuators and human–machine interfaces are used for the vehicle's motion. The substitution of mechanical and hydraulic components with electronic components and electromechanical actuators in general is known as *by-wire* technology. In a conventional vehicle, human–machine interfaces such as pedal and steering feel emulators are used for transferring the driver's control signals to the vehicle driving components. This is similar to the fly-by-wire systems used widely in the aviation industry. The benefits of applying electronic technology are improved performance, safety and reliability with reduced manufacturing, operating and maintenance costs. By-wire technologies also open the opportunities for vehicle weight reduction and packaging flexibility. Examples of by-wire technologies that are being introduced in modern automobiles are steer-by-wire, throttle-by-wire and brake-by-wire. In an autonomous vehicle, these by-wire technologies are combined with replacing the driver and the driving system becomes a drive-by-wire system.

### 4.4.1  THROTTLE-BY-WIRE

Throttle position in a modern vehicle with IC engines is set by the fuel controller based on the throttle position obtained from a throttle sensor; the throttle itself is typically activated by a physical cable linked to the gas pedal by the driver. In a throttle-by-wire system, the engine throttles are operated by electromechanical actuator responding to an electronic signal from the engine controller unit instead of a physical cable operating it. For throttle-by-wire, there is no physical connection between the gas pedal and the throttle, but the gas pedal sends a signal through the vehicle communication network.

### 4.4.2  STEER-BY-WIRE

A typical electric power steering system (EPS) topology is as outlined in Figure 4.5. When the driver generates the input torque $T_d$ at the steering wheel, it is transmitted through the upper steering column to the torsion bar that twists with an angle $q$. An elastic torque, proportional to the torsion bar twist, opposes the input torque. The EPS controller calculates the assisting torque needed based on the steering torque applied by the driver to the steering wheel, the steering wheel position and the vehicle's speed. The EPS motor is the electromechanical actuator that rotates the steering gear with an applied force to reduce the torque required from the driver to maneuver the steering wheel. The torque assistance level required varies depending on the driving conditions and is determined by the wheel speed sensors and the torque sensor, which measures the torque applied to the steering wheel

**FIGURE 4.5**  Electronic power steering system with rack and pinion arrangement.

by the driver. The EPS has an electric machine, a motor controller and a gear reduction that takes the assist torque input and controls the motor current. The resulting shaft torque ultimately turns the wheels through the gear mechanism and the rack. The motor controller uses a high-precision motor shaft position sensor to feed back the rotor position and phase current information to the motor controller for controlling the motor output torque. Permanent magnet machines are typically used in EPS systems with both surface permanent magnet (SPM) and interior permanent magnet (IPM)-type motors being used. The EPS motor has the strictest torque ripple requirements since any ripple at the output shaft of the motor will be transmitted to the driver through the steering column and wheel.

In a steer-by-wire technology, the mechanical steering connection between the hand wheels and road wheels, which include steering shaft, column and gear reduction mechanism, are replaced with algorithms, electronics and actuators. In such a unit, there is no physical connection between the steering wheel and the tires. In fact, the steer-by-wire unit does not need to use steering wheels at all; when a steering wheel is used, some type of steering feel emulator is used to provide the driver with feedback. In an autonomous driving system, the required torque as calculated by the autonomous driving controller can be applied directly to the electric motor actuator to turn the vehicle in the desired direction by the steer-by-wire unit.

### 4.4.3 Brake-by-Wire

Brake-by-wire is the ability to engage vehicle brakes through electronic controls and electromechanical actuators. Brake-by-wire is in fact a spectrum of technologies that can use either electrohydraulic to electromechanical actuators designed with safety features and fail-safe operation of a vehicle in conjunction with other control units such as stability control, traction control and automatic braking unit. The anti-lock brake system (ABS) is the precursor to brake-by-wire which allows the vehicle to brake automatically without any driver input. The brake-by-wire technology goes one step further where the brake engagement is through electronic signals only without any mechanical linkage or hydraulics even if there is a driver involved; the brake pedal in a brake-by-wire system is replaced by a pedal feel emulator. Electric park brake which is now widely used in vehicles is also part of the brake-by-wire system.

Brake-by-wire can support all the functionalities of the conventional hydraulic brakes and in addition provide faster dynamic response, smooth control, improved packaging and easier assembly. It is easier to incorporate safety and stability-related functionalities, and there is room for improvement in fuel economy due to less drag. Elimination of the hydraulic pumps and brake fluid is a reliability and maintenance advantage. In a brake-by-wire system, a force sensor is used to estimate the brake clamping force and the force feedback is used to generate the electric motor torque command for the electromechanical actuator. The electric motor has its own rotor position and current sensors that provide the feedback signals to the motor controller which is controlled in a torque-controlled mode as shown in Figure 14.23 of Chapter 14. The electric machines used in electromechanical brake systems are permanent magnet motors, although switched reluctance motors can also be used. In fact, switched reluctance motors are particularly advantageous for electromechanical brakes since they are much more fault tolerant and do not have the temperature-sensitive permanent magnets in the rotors. The environment for the electric motor in the brake system is harsh where temperature could increase rapidly due to the friction in the brake pads and brake rotors.

Brake-by-wire technology has been widely commercialized with the introduction of battery electric vehicles and hybrid vehicles as the technology is particularly compatible with regenerative braking where part of the vehicle kinetic energy can be captured, converted and used to recharge the batteries instead of wasting it through friction in the brake pads.

## 4.5 SAFETY ENHANCEMENTS WITH LEVEL 1 AUTONOMOUS DRIVING

Driver assists are being added in modern vehicles primarily for safety enhancements even if the vehicle is not fully autonomous. The three most common and useful driver assists work in protecting the vehicle occupants from the front, side and rear. The driver assist that protects the occupants from the front is ACC and collision avoiding automatic braking; the assist that protects from the side is lane control, while blind spot detection protects from the rear. The safety features are part of a more comprehensive system where many of them work in conjunction with each other. The controller for these various types of driver assists depends heavily on several sensors such as cameras, radar, lidar and GPS which are the same ones discussed earlier in the autonomous driving sections. Similar to the autonomous driving systems, sensor signal processing and control algorithms are also an integral part of the driver assist systems. Several of these driver assist systems are the beginnings of self-driving such as the lane centering assist and ACC.

### 4.5.1 CRUISE CONTROL

Cruise control is a servomechanism of a vehicle controller that automatically sets the vehicle speed at a set point commanded by the driver. Vehicle speed feedback is used in a closed-loop speed controller with its output setting the throttle command for fuel injection. The cruise controller is designed with safety concerns in mind where the driver is still engaged in driving with steering control and brake control. The cruise controls are deactivated when the driver presses the brake pedal. Cruise control can reduce driver fatigue during long-distance driving.

The ACC is an improved cruise control version where automatic braking or dynamic set-speed type controls are incorporated in the cruise control mechanism. Vehicles with ACC are considered a level 1 autonomous car. The automatic braking feature uses a single or a fusion of sensors, such as radar, lidar and camera to slow down or speed up to match the speed of the car in front of them. Some systems use forward collision warning which warns the driver if the vehicle in front gets too close given the speed of the two vehicles. Depending on the implementation, the ACC can be designed for a complete stop for safety purpose. The dynamic set-speed type ACC uses the GPS position of speed limit signs from a database to automatically adjust the cruise controller speed set-point.

### 4.5.2 LANE CONTROL

Lane control of a vehicle is another level 1 autonomous driving feature that maintains the vehicle within its lane as it begins to move out of its lane. Lane control is part of a lane departure warning and control system of a vehicle that can have varying degrees of driver assist depending on the implementation when a vehicle is veering out of its lane. The types of technology available range from a warning to the driver to one that reacts and proactively keeps the vehicle centered in the lane. The first assist type is *Lane Departure Warning* which warns the driver if the vehicle is leaving its lane with visual, audible and/or vibration warnings. The second type is *Lane Keep Assist* which automatically takes the step to steer the vehicle within the lane if the driver lets the vehicle drift too far. The most advanced type is the *Lane Centering Assist* which always tries to keep the vehicle centered in the current lane; the system will ask the driver to take over in challenging situations.

The type of sensors used in lane departure warning and control system are video sensors, laser sensors and infrared sensors. Camera is the most common visual sensor used which is mounted in the windshield near the rear mirror. Laser sensors when used are mounted on the front of the vehicle, while infrared sensors are mounted either behind the windshield or under the vehicle. Lane control system works through continuous sensing of the striped and solid lane markings of the road ahead. The system does not work in if the road has no lane markings or if the lane markings are faded. Lane marking dots are also sometimes difficult to track; cameras may also have difficulty sensing the lane markers if it is raining or snowing.

### 4.5.3 TRACTION CONTROL

The traction control system of a vehicle monitors wheel slippage that results in loss of road grip and will activate ABS to prevent slippage which compromises steering control and vehicle stability because of the difference in traction of the driven wheels. Difference in wheel slip may occur due to turning of a vehicle or varying road conditions. The amount of friction force available in wet, icy, uneven or soft surfaces between the road surface and the tires is much lower compared to a dry paved surface where one or more wheels will grip on the surface or in other words lose traction. In vehicles equipped with traction control system, control action is automatically started when the sensors detect loss of traction at any of the wheels.

The primary hardware for traction control and ABS are mostly the same. Sensors used for traction control are wheel speed sensors which sense changes in its speed due to loss of traction. When the traction control system detects that one or more driven wheels are spinning significantly faster than another, it activates the ABS to apply brake to the wheels that are spinning with reduced traction. This braking action on slipping wheels will cause power transfer to the wheels with traction due to the mechanical action of the differential to restore vehicle stability.

### 4.5.4 AUTOMATIC BRAKING

Automatic braking is a safety technology that automatically activates the vehicle's brake system when necessary. Sensors used for automatic braking are cameras and lidar. Cameras can be mounted at the top of the windshield which scans the road in front looking for contrast in the vertical surfaces. When a lidar is used, it would send out a signal that pings off objects in front of it to determine distance and speed. A radar can be installed in the bumper to overcome the range limitation of lidar. The software is programmed to recognize different types of images such as rear end of vehicles, motorcycles, bicycles and pedestrians.

## REFERENCES

1. L.D. Burns, "Sustainable mobility: A vision of our transport future," *Nature*, 497(7448), 181, 2013.
2. L.D. Burns and S. Christopher, *Autonomy: The Quest to Build the Driverless Car-and How It Will Reshape Our World*, ECCO, HarperCollins Publishers, New York, NY, 2018.
3. National Highway Traffic Safety Administration, "2018 Motor Vehicle Crashes: Overview," *Traffic Safety Facts Research Note, 2019*, pp. 1–10, 2019.
4. M. Montemerlo, S. Thrun, H. Dahlkamp, D. Stavens, and S. Strohband, "Winning the DARPA Grand Challenge with an AI robot," *Proceedings of the AAAI National Conference on Artificial Intelligence*, Boston, MA, 2006.
5. M. Buehler, K. Iagnemma and S. Singh (Eds.), *The 2005 DARPA Grand Challenge: The Great Robot Race*, vol. 36, Springer, New York, NY, 2007.
6. C. Urmson et al., "Autonomous driving in urban environments: Boss and the urban challenge," *Journal of Field Robotics*, 25(8), 425–466, 2008.
7. M. Buehler, K. Iagnemma and S. Singh (Eds.), *The DARPA Urban Challenge: Autonomous Vehicles in City Traffic*, 56, Springer, New York, NY, 2009.
8. I. Arasaratnam and S. Haykin. "Cubature Kalman filters," *IEEE Transactions on Automatic Control*, 54(6), 1254–1269, 2009.
9. A. Krizhevsky, I. Sutskever and G.E. Hinton, "Imagenet classification with deep convolutional neural networks," *Advances in Neural Information Processing Systems*, Lake Tahoe, NV, 2012.
10. L. Hammarstrand, edX MOOC Course by Chalmers University, "Sensor Fusion and Non-linear Filtering for Automotive Systems." Online https://www.edx.org/course/sensor-fusion-and-non-linear-filtering-for-automot, accessed June 15, 2020.
11. E. Stenborg, C. Toft and L. Hammarstrand, "Long-term visual localization using semantically segmented images," *2018 IEEE International Conference on Robotics and Automation (ICRA)*, IEEE, Brisbane, Australia, 2018.
12. P. Polack et al., "The kinematic bicycle model: A consistent model for planning feasible trajectories for autonomous vehicles," *2017 IEEE Intelligent Vehicles Symposium (IV)*, IEEE, Redondo Beach, CA, 2017.
13. S. Waslander and J. Kelley, Coursera MOOC Course by University of Toronto, "Motion Planning for Self-Driving Cars." Online https://www.coursera.org/learn/motion-planning-self-driving-cars#instructors, accessed June 15, 2020.
14. S. Russell and P. Norvig, *Artificial Intelligence: A Modern Approach*, Pearson Education Limited, Essex, 2014.
15. P. Bender, J. Ziegler and C. Stiller, "Lanelets: Efficient map representation for autonomous driving," *2014 IEEE Intelligent Vehicles Symposium Proceedings*, Dearborn, MI, 2014.
16. A. Piazzi and C. Guarino Lo Bianco, "Quintic G/sup 2/-splines for trajectory planning of autonomous vehicles," *Proceedings of the IEEE Intelligent Vehicles Symposium 2000 (Cat. No. 00TH8511)*, Dearborn, MI, 2000.
17. A. Kelly and B. Nagy, "Reactive nonholonomic trajectory generation via parametric optimal control," *The International Journal of Robotics Research*, 22(7–8), 583–601, 2003.

# 5 Battery Energy Storage

Energy as available in nature for conversion and usage by the society is known as primary energy. The sources of primary energy are in the oil wells or in other natural environments such as in the wind or in the sun. Examples of primary energy sources are: fossil fuels, wind, solar, hydro, wave, tidal nuclear, geothermal and biomass. Energy is extracted from the primary source either by burning it or by transforming the source energy through an energy conversion system. When primary energy is transformed by one or more energy conversion processes and/or devices, it is known as secondary energy; additional energy conversion devices use the secondary energy to deliver useful work. Several stages of energy conversion are necessary first for processing of the primary energy, and then for delivering it to the end user. Inefficiencies at varying degrees are associated in each of these conversion stages.

Primary sources have energy stored in them in chemical, heat, kinetic or some other alternative form. For example, energy is stored in fossil fuels in chemical form; energy is extracted from it in an IC engine vehicle by burning it in a heat engine. Wind energy is available in kinetic form which can be converted to electrical energy using a wind turbine. Electrical energy is an example of secondary energy that can be converted to mechanical work by an electric machine. Electrical energy can be obtained from the primary source by burning fossil fuels in thermal power plants, or from renewable primary sources of water, wind, solar or other primary sources. Electrochemical devices also produce electrical energy from chemical energy.

Energy derived from sources other than the burning of fossil fuels is known as alternative energy. Ideally, converters used for the processing of alternative energy must avoid the usage of fossil fuels during any stage of the energy conversion process. For example, the ideal solution for recharging batteries in electric vehicles is to use electricity derived from renewable energy sources such as wind or solar. If electricity from coal-fired power plants is used for recharging, then the environmental problems are only being shifted from one location to another.

Energy content of various raw fuels or materials refers to the energy that can be extracted from it for useful work. The parameter for energy content evaluation is *specific energy* or *energy density*. Specific energy is the energy per unit mass of the energy source, and its unit is Wh/kg. For fossil fuels, the energy content refers to the calorific or thermal energy that can be extracted from it by burning. Energy content for other materials is similarly evaluated in terms of specific energy for a level comparison. Specific energies of several energy sources are given in Table 5.1.

**TABLE 5.1**
**Nominal Energy Density of Sources**

| Energy Source | Nominal Specific Energy (Wh/kg) |
|---|---|
| Gasoline | 12,500 |
| Diesel | 12,000 |
| Bio-diesel | 10,900 |
| Natural gas | 9,350 |
| Ethanol | 8,300 |
| Methanol | 6,050 |
| Hydrogen | 33,000 |
| Coal (bituminous) | 8,200 |
| Lead acid battery | 35 |
| Lithium-polymer battery | 200 |
| Flywheel (carbon fiber) | 200 |

The specific energies are shown without taking containment into consideration. Specific energy of hydrogen and natural gas would be significantly lower than that of gasoline when containment is considered.

One of the challenges of energy is to store it in a convenient form so that it can be utilized when needed. In terms of storage, fossil fuels have the biggest advantage since these can be conveniently stored in a container. On the other hand, electrical energy is very useful in delivering work on demand using a highly efficient electromechanical device; however, energy storage in electrical form is not simple.

The mechanism for energy delivery must also be considered for the system under consideration. The energy transportation system has to be secure, efficient and environmentally friendly. Energy transportation over long distances using electrical transmission and distribution systems is highly efficient. Once an infrastructure is in place, energy converted to electrical form at one end (which is the generation side) can be delivered to industrial and residential units through the transmission and distribution system. On the other hand, fossil fuels are transported long distances using pipelines, ocean liners and land transportation before being finally dispersed at the gas stations.

The electrochemical devices are the most promising alternative technologies to the conventional fossil fuel burning power plants both in a vehicle and utility power stations. The electrochemical energy conversion processes have the advantages of high conversion efficiency, large enough power output and the availability of a wide selection of fuels. Batteries and fuel cells are energy storage and power generating devices that are suitable for both portable and stationary applications. The topics covered in this chapter include the fundamentals of battery structure and operation, cell chemistries of some of the promising battery technologies for electric and hybrid vehicles, and battery-pack designs. The presentations will help a design engineer size the energy storage system, and then select the appropriate battery technology for an application. Additional alternative energy storage devices are covered in the next chapter.

## 5.1   BATTERIES IN ELECTRIC AND HYBRID VEHICLES

The basic requirement for purely electric vehicles is a portable supply of electrical energy, which is converted to mechanical energy in the electric motor for vehicle propulsion. The electrical energy is typically obtained through conversion of chemical energy stored in devices such as batteries and fuel cells. The portable electrical energy storage power and energy density limitations led to range anxiety for the customers that delayed the commercialization of electric vehicles. Among the available choice of portable energy sources, batteries have been the most popular choice of energy source for electric vehicles since the beginning of research and development programs in these vehicles. The electric vehicles and hybrid electric vehicles that are available commercially today use batteries as the electrical energy source. The desirable features of batteries for electric and hybrid electric vehicle applications are high specific power, high specific energy, high charge acceptance rate for both recharging and regenerative braking and long calendar and cycle lifes. BEVs and PHEVs require high specific energy (Wh/kg) than that of charge sustaining HEVs which resulted in the universal adoption of Li-ion battery technology ever since the start of mass marketing of such vehicles from around 2010. The early mass marketed electric vehicles had a range of about 100 miles or less. Among those early entries, the first-generation Nissan Leaf with a Li-ion battery-pack of 25 kWh had an EPA range of 73 miles. The Chevrolet Bolt launched in 2017 has an EPA range of 238 miles with a 60 kWh Li-ion battery-pack. Vehicles with range in excess of 300 miles are considered luxury brands and require battery-packs around 100 kWh. In addition to the power and energy densities, battery packaging cell balancing, accurate state-of-charge measurement and recycling facilities for battery components are important considerations. Above all, the cost of batteries must be reasonable for electric and hybrid vehicles to be competitive with ICEVs.

There are two basic types of batteries: a primary battery and a secondary battery. Batteries that cannot be recharged and are designed for a single discharge are known as primary battery. Examples of these are the lithium batteries used in watches, calculators, cameras, etc., and the manganese dioxide batteries used to power toys, radios, flashlights, etc. Batteries that can be recharged by flowing current in the direction opposite to that during discharge are known as secondary batteries. The chemical reaction process during cell charge operation when electrical energy is converted into chemical energy is the reverse of that during discharge. The batteries needed and used for electric and hybrid vehicles are all secondary batteries, since they all are recharged either during that mode of vehicle operation or during the recharging cycle in the stopped condition using a charger. All the batteries discussed in this book are examples of secondary batteries.

The lead acid type of battery has the longest development history of all battery technology particularly for their need and heavy use in the industrial electric vehicles, such as golf cars in sports, passenger cars in airports, fork lifts in storage facilities and super markets. The power and energy densities of lead acid battery are lower compared to several other battery technologies. The research and development for alternative batteries picked up momentum following the resurgence of interest in electric vehicles and hybrid vehicles in the late 1960s and early 1970s. The sodium-sulfur batteries showed great promise in the 1980s with high energy and power densities, but safety and manufacturing difficulties led to the abandoning of the technology. The development of battery technology for low-power applications, such as cell phones and calculators opened the possibilities of scaling the energy and power of nickel-cadmium and lithium-ion type batteries for electric and hybrid vehicle applications. The major types of rechargeable batteries used or being considered for electric and hybrid vehicle applications are as follows:

- Nickel-metal-hydride (NiMH)
- Lithium-ion (Li-ion)
- Lithium-polymer (Li-poly)
- Sodium-sulfur.

The Li-ion battery technology is the most promising among the four battery chemistries mentioned above. There are several different types of Li-ion battery-pack chemistry available including Li-iron phosphate, Li-titanate, Li-manganese and Li-cobalt. The choice for the particular lithium type depends on the type of BEV.

The development of batteries is directed toward overcoming the significant practical and manufacturing difficulties. The theoretical predictions are difficult to match in manufactured products due to practical limitations. The theoretical and practical specific energies of several batteries are given in Table 5.2 for comparison.

Extensive research and interest in alternative vehicles have resulted in several promising battery technologies over the years. Pure electric vehicles are available commercially, but the cost is relatively higher since these require large capacity battery-packs. Hybrid electric vehicles minimize the battery capacity through using the combination of IC engine and electric machines. Even though the hybrid technology is much more complex than either a conventional or electric vehicle alone, the advantages gained in fuel economy through the addition of a smaller electric powertrain component are significant. The choice for a BEV becomes easier if consumers can accept vehicles with a range of 100 miles instead of 300 miles. This is certainly possible since the average daily commute is 32.8 miles/day in the United States assuming that an average vehicle is driven 12,000 miles/year. The average number of miles driven per day is much less in other countries of the world.

In the following section, battery cell structure and cell chemical reactions are discussed with examples of some of the common chemistries. This will enable us to define the parameters of a battery, which are needed for the macroscopic point of view. We will then dig deeper into the theoretical aspects of a battery cell. This will enable us to model, analyze and evaluate different types of batteries.

**TABLE 5.2**

**Specific Energy of Batteries**

| Battery | Specific Energy (Wh/kg) | |
|---|---|---|
| | Theoretical | Practical |
| Lead acid | 108 | 50 |
| Nickel-cadmium | | 20–30 |
| Nickel-zinc | | 90 |
| Nickel-iron | | 60 |
| Zinc-chlorine | | 90 |
| Zinc-bromide | | 70 |
| Silver-zinc | 500 | 100 |
| Sodium-sulfur | 770 | 150–300 |
| Aluminum-air | | 300 |
| Nickel metal hydride | | 70 |
| Li ion | | 150 |

## 5.2 BATTERY BASICS

The batteries are made of unit cells containing the stored chemical energy that can be converted to electrical energy. One or more of these electrochemical cells are connected in series to form one battery. The grouped cells are enclosed in a casing to form a battery module. A battery pack is a collection of these individual battery modules connected in a series and/or parallel combination to deliver the desired voltage and energy to the power electronic drive system.

### 5.2.1 BATTERY CELL STRUCTURE

The energy stored in a battery is the difference in free energy between chemical components in the charged and discharged states. This available chemical energy in a cell is converted into electrical energy only on demand using the basic components of a unit cell; these components are the positive and negative electrodes, the separators and the electrolytes. The electrochemically active ingredient of the positive or negative electrode is called the active material. Chemical reactions take place at the two electrodes, one of which releases electrons, while the other consumes those. The electrodes must be electronically conducting and are located at different sites separated from each other by a separator as shown in Figure 5.1. The connection points between the electrodes and the external circuit are called the battery terminals. The external circuit ensures that stored chemical energy is released only on demand and utilized as electrical energy.

The components of the battery cell are described in the following:

1. Positive Electrode: The positive electrode is an oxide or sulfide or some other compound that is capable of being reduced during cell discharge. This electrode consumes electrons from the external circuit during cell discharge. Examples of positive electrodes are lead oxide ($PbO_2$) and nickel oxyhydroxide (NiOOH). The electrode materials are in the solid state.
2. Negative Electrode: The negative electrode is a metal or an alloy that is capable of being oxidized during cell discharge. This electrode releases electrons to the external circuit during cell discharge. Examples of negative electrodes are lead (Pb) and cadmium (Cd). The negative electrode materials are in the solid state within the battery cell.
3. Electrolyte: The electrolyte is the medium that permits ionic conduction between positive and negative electrodes of a cell. The electrolyte must have high and selective conductivity

Negative Electrode

(a)

(b)

**FIGURE 5.1**    Components of a battery cell: (a) cell circuit symbol and (b) cell cross-section.

for the ions that take part in electrode reactions, but must be a non-conductor for electrons in order to avoid self-discharge of batteries. The electrolyte may be liquid, gel or solid material. Also, the electrolyte can be acidic or alkaline depending on the type of battery. Traditional batteries such as lead acid and nickel cadmium use liquid electrolytes. In lead acid batteries, the electrolyte is the aqueous solution of sulfuric acid ($H_2SO_4$(aq)). Advanced batteries for electric vehicles, such as sealed lead acid, nickel-metal-hydride (NiMH) and lithium-ion batteries use an electrolyte that is gel, paste or resin. Lithium-polymer batteries use a solid electrolyte.

4. Separator: The separator is the electrically insulating layer of material, which physically separates electrodes of opposite polarity. Separators must be permeable to the ions of the electrolyte and may also have the function of storing or immobilizing the electrolyte. Present day separators are made from synthetic polymers.

### 5.2.2  CHEMICAL REACTIONS

During battery operation, chemical reactions at each of the electrodes are sustainable only if electrons generated at the electrodes are able to flow through an external electrical circuit that connects the two electrodes. When a passive electrical circuit element is connected to the electrode terminals of a battery, electrons are released from the negative electrode and consumed at the positive electrode resulting in current flow into the external circuit. In this process, the battery gets discharged. The supply of electrons is due to the chemical reactions at the electrode surfaces inside the battery cell, which are collectively known as reduction and oxidation (redox) reactions. During battery discharge, the positive electrode gets chemically reduced as it absorbs electrons from the external circuit; the negative electrode gets oxidized as it releases electrons to the external circuit. For battery charging, a source with voltage higher than the battery terminal voltage has to be applied so that current can flow into the battery in the opposite direction. During charging, electrons are released at the positive electrode and consumed at the negative electrode; consequently, the positive electrode is oxidized and negative electrode is reduced.

Regardless of the battery cell chemistry, redox reactions take place at the electrodes during both cell charging and discharging for the release and absorption of electrons at the terminals. The generalized redox reactions are given by [1]

$$aA \underset{\text{Discharge}}{\overset{\text{Charge}}{\rightleftharpoons}} cC + nE^+ + ne^- \tag{5.1}$$

for the positive electrode, and

$$bB + nE^+ + ne^- \underset{\text{Discharge}}{\overset{\text{Charge}}{\rightleftharpoons}} dD \tag{5.2}$$

for the negative electrode. The combined chemical reaction is

$$aA + bB \underset{\text{Discharge}}{\overset{\text{Charge}}{\rightleftharpoons}} cC + dD \tag{5.3}$$

Chemical reactions 5.1 and 5.2 illustrate that electrons are released and absorbed during any redox reaction. The positive electrode Reaction 5.1 shows that during cell charging species A within the electrode is oxidized and becomes energized species C releasing electron(s) into the external circuit and positive ion(s) into the electrolyte. Similarly, the negative electrode Reaction 5.2 shows that the species B at the electrode combines with positive ion(s) from the electrolyte and electron(s) from the external circuit to form energized species D. The converse is true at the two electrodes during cell discharging. The coefficients $a$, $b$, $c$ and $d$ represent the numbers of moles associated with the species in the reactions; the coefficient $n$ represent the number of electrons and ions involved in the redox reactions.

In electric traction applications, battery cell operation is that of cell discharging when the energy is supplied from the battery to the electric motor for propulsion power and of cell charging when energy is supplied from an external source to store energy in the battery. In conventional vehicles, battery cells supply power to electrical accessories while discharging, and accept energy from an external device to replenish the stored energy during charging. We will next review the redox reactions during cell charging and discharging in a few battery chemistries starting with the lead acid battery cell. Lead acid is still the battery choice for powering electrical accessories in conventional, electric and hybrid electric vehicles.

Figure 5.2 shows the cell discharge operation of a lead acid battery cell into a passive resistive element. The positive electrode made of lead-oxide ($PbO_2$) is reduced by consuming electrons and ions. The electron supply is through the external circuit which originates at the negative electrode.

**FIGURE 5.2**   Lead acid battery: cell discharge operation.

The current flow is therefore out of the positive electrode into the electrical load with the battery acting as the source. The positive electrode reaction is given by

$$PbO_2(s) + 4H^+(aq) + SO_4^{2-}(aq) + 2e^- \rightarrow PbSO_4 + 2H_2O(l).$$

A highly porous structure is used for the positive electrode to increase $PbO_2(s)$/electrolyte contact area. A porous electrode structure results in higher current densities since $PbO_2$ is converted to $PbSO_4(s)$ during cell discharge. As discharge proceeds, the internal resistance of the cell rises due to $PbSO_4$ formation and decreases the electrolyte conductivity as $H_2SO_4$ is consumed. $PbSO_4(s)$ deposited on either electrode in a dense, fine-grain form can lead to sulfation. The discharge reaction is largely inhibited by the buildup of $PbSO_4$, which reduces cell capacity significantly from the theoretical capacity.

The negative electrode is made of solid lead (Pb); during cell discharge, lead is oxidized releasing electrons into the external circuit. The negative electrode reaction during cell discharge is

$$Pb(s) + SO_4^{2-}(aq) \rightarrow PbSO_4 + 2e^-.$$

Production of $PbSO_4(s)$ can degrade battery performance by making the negative electrode more passive.

The overall cell discharge chemical reaction is

$$Pb(s) + PbO_2(s) + 2H_2SO_4(aq) \rightarrow 2PbSO_4 + 2H_2O(l).$$

The cell charge operation is the reverse of the cell discharge operation. An external electrical source supplies current into the battery to reverse the chemical reactions as shown in Figure 5.3. During cell charging, the lead sulfate is converted back to the reactant states of lead and lead oxide. The electrons are consumed from the external source at the negative electrode, while the positive electrode produces the electrons. The current flows into the positive electrode from the external source thereby delivering electrical energy into the cell where it gets converted into chemical energy. The positive electrode is oxidized releasing electrons during cell charging as follows

$$PbSO_4(s) + 2H_2O(l) \rightarrow PbO_2(s) + 4H^+(aq) + SO_4^{2-}(aq) + 2e^-.$$

The negative electrode is reduced during cell charging absorbing electrons, and the chemical reaction is

$$PbSO_4(s) + 2e^- \rightarrow Pb(s) + SO_4^{2-}(aq).$$

**FIGURE 5.3**   Lead acid battery: cell charge operation.

The overall chemical reaction during cell charging is

$$2PbSO_4(s) + 2H_2O(l) \rightarrow Pb(s) + PbO_2(s) + 2H_2SO_4(aq).$$

The nickel-cadmium (NiCd) and nickel-metal-hydride (NiMH) batteries are examples of alkaline batteries where electrical energy is derived from the chemical reaction of a metal with oxygen in an alkaline electrolyte medium. The specific energy of alkaline batteries is lowered due to the mass addition of the carrier metal. The NiCd battery employs a nickel oxide positive electrode and a metallic cadmium negative electrode. The reactions take place in the presence of potassium hydroxide (KOH) electrolyte. The positive electrode chemical reaction is

$$NiOOH + H_2O + e^- \underset{\text{Charge}}{\overset{\text{Discharge}}{\rightleftharpoons}} Ni(OH)_2 + OH^-$$

The negative electrode chemical reaction is

$$Cd + 2OH^- \underset{\text{Charge}}{\overset{\text{Discharge}}{\rightleftharpoons}} Cd(OH)_2 + 2e^-$$

The overall chemical reaction is

$$Cd + 2NiOOH + 2H_2O \underset{\text{Charge}}{\overset{\text{Discharge}}{\rightleftharpoons}} 2Ni(OH)_2 + Cd(OH)_2$$

In NiMH batteries, the positive electrode is a nickel oxide similar to that used in a NiCd battery, while the negative electrode has been replaced by a metal hydride which stores hydrogen atoms. The concept of NiMH batteries is based on the fact that fine particles of certain metallic alloys when exposed to hydrogen at certain pressures and temperatures absorb large quantities of the gas to form the metal hydride compounds. Furthermore, the metal hydrides are able to absorb and release hydrogen many times without deterioration. The two electrode chemical reactions in a NiMH battery are as follows:

At the positive electrode,

$$NiOOH + H_2O + e^- \underset{\text{Charge}}{\overset{\text{Discharge}}{\rightleftharpoons}} Ni(OH)_2 + OH^-.$$

At the negative electrode,

$$MH_x + OH^- \underset{\text{Charge}}{\overset{\text{Discharge}}{\rightleftharpoons}} MH_{x-1} + H_2O + e^-.$$

M stands for metallic alloy, which takes up hydrogen at ambient temperature to form the metal hydride $MH_x$; $x$ is the number of hydrogen atoms absorbed. The overall chemical reaction is

$$NiOOH + MH_x \underset{\text{Charge}}{\overset{\text{Discharge}}{\rightleftharpoons}} Ni(OH)_2 + MH_{x-1}$$

## 5.3   BATTERY PARAMETERS

In this section, the various battery parameters including capacity and state of charge (SoC) are defined. The parameters mostly relate to the terminal characteristics of the battery that have the practical implications for use in an application.

### 5.3.1   BATTERY CAPACITY

The amount of charge released by the energized material at an electrode associated with complete discharge of a battery is called the *battery capacity*. The capacity is measured in Ah (1 Ah = 3,600 C or Coulomb, where 1 C is the charge transferred in 1 s by 1 A current in the SI unit of charge).

The theoretical capacity of a battery can be obtained Faraday's law of electrolysis which states that the mass of the elemental material altered at an electrode is directly proportional to the element's equivalent weight for a given quantity of electrical charge. The equivalent weight of the elemental material is given by the molar mass divided by the number of electrons transferred per ion for the reaction undergone by the material. This number is known as the valency number of ions for the substance. Mathematically, Faraday's law can be written as

$$m_R = \frac{Q}{F} \frac{M_m}{n} \qquad (5.4)$$

where $m_R$ is the mass of the limiting reactant material altered at an electrode, $Q$ is the total amount of electric charge passing through the material, $F$ is the Faraday number or Faraday constant, $M_m$ is the molar mass and $n$ is the number of electrons per ion produced at an electrode. $\frac{M_m}{n}$ is the equivalent weight of the reactant substance. The Faraday number is given by the amount of electric charge carried by one mole of electrons. The number of molecules or atoms in a mole is given by the Avogadro number $N_A$ which is equal to $6.022045 \times 10^{23}$ mol$^{-1}$. The amount of charge in one electron which is the elemental charge is equal to $e_0 = 1.6021892 \times 10^{-19}$ C. Therefore, the Faraday number is equal to $F = N_A e_0 = 96,485$ C/mol. The number of Faradays required to produce one mole of substance at an electrode depends on the way in which the substance is oxidized or reduced.

Therefore, the theoretical capacity of a battery (in Coulomb) can be obtained from Equation 5.4 as

$$Q_T = xnF \text{ C} \qquad (5.5)$$

where $x$ is the number of moles of limiting reactant associated with complete discharge of battery, and is given by

$$x = \frac{m_R}{M_m}.$$

Here $m_R$ is the mass of the reactant material in kg and $M_m$ is the molar mass of that material in g/mol.

The theoretical capacity in Ah is

$$Q_T = 0.278F \frac{m_R n}{M_m} \text{ Ah} \qquad (5.6)$$

The cells in a battery are connected in series and the capacity of the battery is dictated by the smallest cell capacity. Therefore, $Q_{Tbattery} = Q_{Tcell}$. Six battery cells connected in series to form a battery are shown in Figure 5.4.

### 5.3.2 Open-Circuit Voltage

The battery in its simplest form can be represented by an internal voltage $E_v$ and a series resistance $R_i$ as shown in Figure 5.5a. More representative but complex battery models are discussed later in the chapter. The battery internal voltage appears at the battery terminals as open-circuit voltage when

**FIGURE 5.4** Battery cells connected in series.

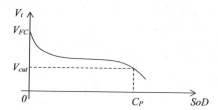

**FIGURE 5.5**   (a) Steady-state battery equivalent circuit and (b) battery open-circuit voltage characteristics.

**FIGURE 5.6**   Battery terminal voltage.

there is no load connected to it. The internal voltage or the open-circuit voltage (OCV) depends on the state of charge of the battery, temperature and past discharge/charge history (memory effects) among other factors. The open-circuit voltage characteristics are shown in Figure 5.5b. As the battery is gradually discharged, the internal voltage decreases, while the internal resistance increases. The open-circuit voltage characteristics have a fairly extended plateau of linear characteristics with a slope close to zero. The open-circuit voltage is not a good indicator of the state of charge; state of charge of a battery pack needs to be calculated considering discharge current characteristics, battery chemistry, temperature effects and number of charge/discharge cycles. Once the battery is completely discharged, the open-circuit voltage decreases sharply with more discharge.

### 5.3.3   TERMINAL VOLTAGE

Battery terminal voltage $V_t$ is the voltage available at the terminals when a load is connected to the battery. The terminal voltage is at its full charge voltage $V_{FC}$ when the battery is fully charged. For example, with lead acid battery it means that there is no more $PbSO_4$ available to react with $H_2O$ to produce active material. $V_{cut}$ is the battery cut-off voltage, where discharge of the battery must be terminated. The battery terminal voltage characteristic in relationship with the *SOD* is shown in Figure 5.6.

### 5.3.4   PRACTICAL CAPACITY

The *practical capacity* $Q_P$ of a battery is the actual charge released by the energized material at an electrode associated with complete discharge of the battery. The practical capacity is always much lower compared to the theoretical capacity $Q_T$ due to practical limitations. The practical capacity of a battery is given as

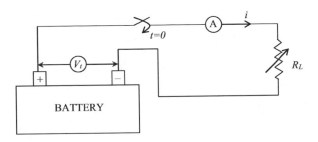

**FIGURE 5.7**   Battery capacity measurement.

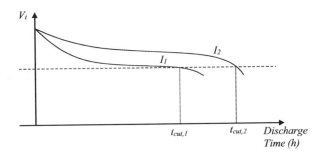

**FIGURE 5.8**   Constant current discharge curves.

$$Q_P = \int_{t_0}^{t_{cut}} i(t)\,dt \qquad\qquad (5.7)$$

where $t_o$ is the time at which battery is fully charged and $t_{cut}$ is the time at which battery terminal voltage is at $V_{cut}$. Therefore, $V_t(t_{cut}) = V_{cut}$.

The practical capacity of a battery is defined in the industry by a convenient and approximate approach of Ah instead of Coulomb (i.e., A-s) under constant discharge current characteristics, i.e., at a specified discharge rate (commonly referred to as C-rate) from 100% capacity to the cut-off voltage. Let us consider the experiment shown in Figure 5.7, where the battery is discharged at constant current starting from time $t = 0$. The ammeters and voltmeters measure the discharge current and the battery terminal voltage. The current is maintained constant by varying the load resistance $R_L$ until the terminal voltage reaches the cut-off voltage $V_{cut}$. The qualitative graphs of two constant current discharge characteristics at two different current levels are shown in Figure 5.8. The following data is obtained from the experiment:

$I = 80A$: Capacity $Q_{80A} = (80\ A)t_{cut} = 80\times1.8 = 144$ Ah
$I = 50A$: Capacity $Q_{50A} = (50\ A)t_{cut} = 50\times3.1 = 155$ Ah
$I = 30A$: Capacity $Q_{30A} = (30\ A)t_{cut} = 30\times5.7 = 171$ Ah

The results show that the capacity depends on the magnitude of discharge current. The smaller the magnitude of the discharge current, the higher the capacity of the battery is. To be accurate, when the capacity of a battery is stated, the constant discharge current magnitude must also be specified.

### 5.3.5   DISCHARGE RATE

The *discharge rate* is the current at which a battery is discharged under constant current characteristics. The rate is also known as C-rate which is expressed as $Q_P/h$-rate, where $Q_P$ is rated battery capacity and $h$ is discharge time in hours. For a battery that has a capacity of $Q_P$ Ah and is discharged over $\Delta t$ h, the discharge rate is $\dfrac{Q_P}{\Delta t}$.

*Example*: Let the capacity of a battery be 100 Ah. Therefore,

$$\text{C/5-rate or 0.2C-rate is } \frac{100\ \text{Ah}}{5\ \text{h}} = 20\ \text{A and}$$

$$\text{2C rate is } \frac{100\ \text{Ah}}{0.5\ \text{h}} = 200\ \text{A}.$$

Typically, the nominal capacity of a battery is given at a 1C-rate, and it decreases with increasing C-rate.

## 5.3.6 State of Charge

The *state of charge* (SoC) represents the present capacity of the battery. It is the amount of capacity that remains after discharge from a top-of-charge condition. The current is the rate of change of charge given by

$$i(t) = \frac{dq}{dt}$$

where $q$ is the charge moving through the circuit. The instantaneous theoretical state of charge $SoC_T(t)$ is the amount of equivalent charge remaining at the positive electrode and ready to be released by the energized material. If the state of charge is $Q_T$ at the initial time $t_o$, then $SoC_T(t_o) = Q_T$. For a time interval $dt$,

$$dSoC_T = -dq$$

$$= -i(t)dt$$

Integrating from the initial time $t_o$ to the final time $t$, the expression for instantaneous state of charge is obtained as

$$SoC_T(t) = Q_T - \int_{t_o}^{t} i(\tau)d\tau \tag{5.8}$$

The state of charge is often expressed as a percentage of the capacity of the battery as follows:

$$SoC_T(t) = \frac{Q_T - \displaystyle\int_{t_o}^{t} i(\tau)d\tau}{Q_T} \times 100\%$$

The state of charge will be increasing when a battery is being charged. If the state of charge is zero initially at $t = 0$, the state of charge at time $t$ expressed in percentage form is given by

$$SoC_T(t) = \frac{\displaystyle\int_{0}^{t} i(\tau)d\tau}{Q_T} \times 100\%$$

### 5.3.7 STATE OF DISCHARGE

The *state of discharge* (SoD) is a measure of the charge that has been drawn from a battery during discharge. Mathematically, state of discharge is given as

$$SoD_T(t) = \Delta q = \int_{t_0}^{t} i(\tau)d\tau \tag{5.9}$$

$$\Rightarrow SoC_T(t) = Q_T - SoD_T(t).$$

### 5.3.8 DEPTH OF DISCHARGE

The *depth of discharge* (DoD) is the percentage of battery rated capacity to which a battery is discharged. The depth of discharge is given by

$$DoD(t) = \frac{Q_T - SoC_T(t)}{Q_T} \times 100\%$$

$$= \frac{\int_{t_0}^{t} i(\tau)d\tau}{Q_T} \times 100\% \tag{5.10}$$

The withdrawal of at least 80% of battery (rated) capacity is referred to as deep discharge.

### 5.3.9 BATTERY ENERGY

Energy of a battery is measured in terms of the capacity and the discharge voltage. To calculate the energy, the capacity of the battery must be expressed in coulombs. 1 Ah is equivalent to $3,600\,C$, while $1\,V$ refers to $1\,J$ (J for joule) of work required to move $1\,C$ charge from the negative to positive electrode. Therefore, the stored electrical potential energy in a $12\,V$, $100\,Ah$ battery is $(12)(3.6 \times 10^5)\,J = 5.32\,MJ$. In general, the theoretical stored energy

$$E_T = V_{bat}Q_T$$

where $V_{bat}$ is the nominal no load terminal voltage and $Q_T$ is the theoretical capacity in C units. Therefore, using Equation 5.6, the theoretical energy is

$$E_T = \left[\frac{1,000\,Fn}{M_m}\,m_R\right]V_{bat} = 9.65 \times 10^7 \frac{nm_R}{M_m}V_{batt}\ \text{J} \tag{5.11}$$

The practical available energy is

$$E_p = \int_{t_0}^{t_{cut}} v(t)i(t)dt\ \text{Wh} \tag{5.12}$$

where $t_o$ is the time at which battery is fully charged, $t_{cut}$ is the time in hours at which battery terminal voltage is at $V_{cut}$, $v$ is the battery terminal voltage and $i$ is the battery discharge current. $E_p$ is dependent on the manner in which the battery is discharged. Practical energy in Watt-hours (Wh) multiplied by 3,600 gives the energy in J, i.e., W-s.

## 5.3.10  SPECIFIC ENERGY

The *specific energy* of a battery in terms of discharge energy related to complete discharge from fully charged condition is given by

$$SE = \frac{\text{Discharge Energy}}{\text{Total Battery Mass}} = \frac{E}{M_B}$$

The unit for specific energy is Wh/kg. The theoretical specific energy of a battery using Equation 5.9 is

$$SE_T = 9.65 \times 10^7 \times \frac{nV_{bat}}{M_m} \frac{m_R}{m_B} \text{ Wh/kg} \qquad (5.13)$$

If the mass of the battery $M_B$ is proportional to the mass of the limiting reactant of the battery $m_R$, then $SE_T$ is independent of mass. The specific energy of lead acid battery is 35–50 Wh/kg at C/3 rate. Since practical energy $E_P$ varies with discharge rate, the practical specific energy $SE_P$ is also variable.

The term 'energy density' is also used in the literature to quantify the quality of a battery or other energy sources. The term energy density refers to the energy per unit volume of a battery. The unit for energy density is Wh/L.

## 5.3.11  BATTERY POWER

The instantaneous battery terminal power is

$$p(t) = V_{bat}i \qquad (5.14)$$

where $V_{bat}$ is the battery terminal voltage and $i$ is the battery discharge current. Using Kirchhoff's voltage law for the battery equivalent circuit of Figure 5.5a, with $V_{bat} = V_t$

$$V_t = E_v - R_i i \qquad (5.15)$$

Substituting Equation (5.15) into Equation (5.14) yields

$$p(t) = E_v i - R_i i^2 \qquad (5.16)$$

Power versus current characteristic is shown in Figure 5.9.

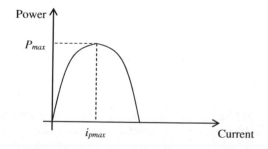

**FIGURE 5.9**  Battery power characteristics.

Using the maximum power transfer theorem in electric circuits, the battery can deliver maximum power to a DC load when the load impedance matches the battery internal impedance. The maximum power is

$$P_{max} = \frac{E_v^2}{4R_i} \tag{5.17}$$

Since $E_v$ and $R_i$ vary with the state of charge, $P_{max}$ also varies accordingly.

Maximum power output is needed from the battery in fast discharge conditions in vehicle applications, which occur when the electric motor is heavily loaded. Acceleration on a slope is such a condition, when the motor draws a lot of current to deliver maximum power required for traction.

The performance of batteries to meet acceleration and hill climbing requirements can be evaluated with the help of rated power specifications, which are based on the ability of the battery to dissipate heat. The *rated continuous power* is the maximum power that the battery can deliver over prolonged discharge intervals without damage to the battery. These do not necessarily correspond to $P_{max}$ on p-i curve of battery characteristics. The *rated instantaneous power* is the maximum power that the battery can deliver over a very short discharge interval without damage to the battery.

### 5.3.12  SPECIFIC POWER

The *specific power* of a battery is

$$SP = \frac{P}{M_B} \text{ (units: W/kg)} \tag{5.18}$$

where $P$ is the power delivered by battery and $M_B$ is the mass of battery. Typically, lead acid battery's maximum specific power is around 280 W/kg (which corresponds to $P_{max}$) at DoD = 80%. Similar to specific energy and energy density, the term power density is used to refer to the power of the battery per unit volume with units of W/L.

### 5.3.13  RAGONE PLOTS

In electrochemical batteries, there is a decrease in charge capacity (excluding voltage effects) with increasing currents. This is often referred to as the *Ragone* relationship and is described by *Ragone plots*. Ragone plots are usually obtained from constant power discharge tests or constant current discharge plots. Let us consider the experiment of Figure 5.6 again, but this time the current $i$ is adjusted by varying $R_L$ such that the power output at the battery terminals is kept constant. The experiment stops when the battery terminal voltage reaches the cut-off voltage, i.e., $V_t = V_{cut}$. We assume that the battery is fully charged at $t = 0$. The experiment is performed at several power levels and the following data is recorded: (i) power $p(t) = V_t i = P$, (ii) time to cut-off voltage $t_{cut}$ and (iii) practical energy $E_P = P t_{cut}$. The plot of $SP$ versus $SE$ on a log–log scale is known as the Ragone plot. The Ragone plots of several batteries along with alternative energy sources and IC engines are given in Figure 5.10 to give an idea about the relative power and energy capacities of these different devices.

## 5.4  ELECTROCHEMICAL CELL FUNDAMENTALS

The *electrochemical cells* use the oxidation and reduction reactions for the flow of electric currents that are known as faradaic currents. These cells form the basis of batteries and fuel cells that supply electrical energy from stored chemical energy using the electrochemical reactions. The electrochemical cells can be classified as either *galvanic cells* or *electrolytic cells*. The galvanic cells are

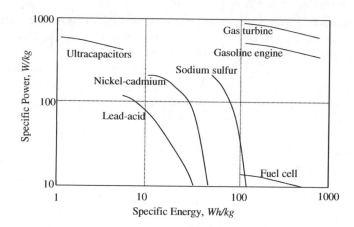

**FIGURE 5.10** Specific power versus specific energy (Ragone plots) of several batteries, a gasoline engine and a fuel cell.

those where the substances react spontaneously when an external electrical load is connected to the cell. In the galvanic cell, electrons flow through the external circuit and ions transfer from one electrode to another within the cell resulting in work done. The galvanic cells are also known as voltaic cells since volts or potentials are established due to the spontaneous chemical reactions. The electrolytic cells are those in which reactions are non-spontaneous, and effected by the imposition of external voltage greater than the open-circuit voltage of the cell. Electrical energy is expended by the external source and work is done on the electrochemical cell. When a battery cell is being charged to restore chemical energy within, it functions as an electrolytic cell. The battery cells will be referred to as electrochemical cells in general, since both discharging and charging are associated with the secondary battery cells used in electric and hybrid vehicles.

The fundamentals of a battery cell, or for that matter, of any other electrochemical cell, is in the physics and chemistry involved in the energy conversion process. In this section, we will analyze the fundamentals to gain sufficient understanding of the process so that electrochemical cell models can be developed. The models are useful not only for analyzing the electrochemical cells, but also for evaluating systems that include the electrochemical cell-based components for energy storage.

The fundamentals governing the principles and operation of an electrochemical cell are chemical thermodynamics, electrochemical reaction rates, electrode kinetics and mass transport [1–7]. Each one of these mechanisms influences the energy conversion from stored chemical energy into electrical energy in an electrochemical cell. The mechanisms are treated in detail in this section.

### 5.4.1 THERMODYNAMIC VOLTAGE

Electrochemical thermodynamics determine the electrical potential difference between the electrode and the electrolyte of an electrochemical cell even in the absence of any external electrical connection to the electrodes when there is no external electric current flow. The thermodynamic physics of the electrochemical cell explains the mechanism of electric potential build-up at an electrode and establishes the theoretical limits of work, conversion efficiency and potential of the cell.

The First Law of Thermodynamics states that energy is conserved during any process; energy can be transferred from a system to its surroundings or vice versa, but it cannot be created or destroyed. In chemical processes, system refers to the chemical species involved and the associated reactions; the container where the reaction takes place serves as the boundary of the chemical reaction. The three forms of energy for chemical processes are the internal energy of each substance, work done due to changes in pressure and volume or due to electrical current flow, and the heat transfer with the surroundings. In all chemical reactions, heat is either absorbed from or released to the surroundings. The amount of heat absorbed or released by the chemical reaction is equal to the change in internal energy only if there is no work done on or by the surroundings. However, if work done is not kept zero, some of the heat energy will be converted to work, and the total of heat absorbed or released is no longer equal to the change in internal energy. To represent the combined activity due to heat absorption or release, the term enthalpy representing the heat content of a substance or system has been introduced for convenience. By thermodynamic definition, enthalpy $H$ is given by

$$H = U + pV$$

where $U$ is the internal energy, $p$ is the pressure and $V$ is the volume of the system. The product of pressure and volume ($pV$) is related to the work of expansion.

In galvanic devices, stable substances react spontaneously to form new substances, which mean that the reaction can only go from a higher energy state to a lower one according to the First Law of Thermodynamics. The lower energy state that the substances will assume depends on another measure known as the entropy of a substance. *Entropy* is a measure of the disorder level for the particles (molecules, atoms, etc.) that make up a substance. Entropy is a property that is specified for every equilibrium state of a substance. Since entropy is a property, the change in entropy in going from one state to another is the same for all processes. The SI unit for entropy is J/K.

The Second Law of Thermodynamics states that a spontaneous reaction in a closed environment proceeds until the maximum entropy is reached for the substances involved. Based on the two Laws of Thermodynamics part of the enthalpy change has to be reflected in the form of entropy change ($T\Delta S$), where $T$ is the temperature in Kelvin and $\Delta S$ is the change of entropy. Therefore, the maximum available work from a chemical reaction or any process is [8,9]

$$\Delta G = \Delta H - T\Delta S.$$

In chemical reactions, $G$ is the Gibbs free energy, which determines the relative importance between the enthalpy and entropy terms driving a particular reaction. A chemical reaction is favorable or spontaneous if $\Delta H < 0$, and unfavorable or non-spontaneous if $\Delta H > 0$. Again, a reaction is spontaneous if $\Delta S > 0$, and non-spontaneous if $\Delta S < 0$. The Gibbs free energy of a system provides the net result when enthalpy and entropy forces of a reaction drive the system in opposite directions. A reaction is spontaneous if $\Delta G < 0$, and non-spontaneous if $\Delta G > 0$.

Gibbs free energy can be calculated from the enthalpy and entropy changes between the products and reactants of the chemical reaction as

$$\Delta G = \Delta H^o - T\Delta S^o \qquad (5.19)$$

where

$$\Delta H^o = \sum H_f^o(\text{products}) - \sum H_f^o(\text{reactants})$$

$$\Delta S^o = \sum S^o(\text{products}) - \sum S^o(\text{reactants})$$

The superscript '$o$' denotes standard-state conditions of 25°C and one atmospheric pressure, while the subscript '$f$' denotes the standard state free energies of formation. Standard enthalpies of formation and standard entropies are given in thermodynamic tables. The standard enthalpy of formation of an element is defined as zero.

Alternatively, when the free energies of formation for each substance involved in a chemical reaction are known, the Gibbs free energy change of reaction is

$$\Delta G = \Delta G_f^o(\text{products}) - \Delta G_f^o(\text{reactants})$$

Similar to the definition of enthalpies of formation, the standard free energy of formation of an element is defined as zero.

Let us consider the chemical reaction involved in silver-zinc battery to illustrate the concept of energy available in an electrochemical cell. The chemical reaction is [8]:

$$Zn + 2AgCl \rightarrow Zn^{++} + 2Ag + 2Cl^-$$

The amount of heat content liberated from the chemical reaction between metallic zinc and silver chloride solution when mixed at standard state conditions is $-233$ kJ/mol of Zn reacted, i.e., $\Delta H^o = -233$ kJ/mol. For the chemical reaction, $T\Delta S = -43$ kJ/mol. The Gibbs free energy in this example is

$$\Delta G = \Delta H - T\Delta S = -233 + 43 = -190 \text{ kJ/mole.}$$

The example illustrates that all of the enthalpy change cannot be converted to work; a minimum amount of energy has to be consumed by the entropy change which is usually reflected in the generated heat during chemical reactions.

Gibbs free energy is also useful in determining the maximum thermodynamic conversion efficiency of a galvanic cell, which is given by the ratio of Gibbs free energy and the total enthalpy change.

$$\eta_{EC} = \frac{\Delta G}{\Delta H} = 1 - \frac{T\Delta S}{\Delta H}. \tag{5.20}$$

For the given example of silver-zinc battery cell, $\eta_{EC} = 81.5\%$. The inherent high conversion efficiency compared to the thermodynamic upper limit of efficiencies in heat engines is an advantage of galvanic devices. However, just like the heat engines, the practical efficiency of galvanic devices during normal operation is much lower than the theoretical efficiency. The decrease in efficiency is directly related to the practical currents required in practical systems.

Gibbs free energy released in the chemical process of the electrochemical cell imposes the theoretical limit on the maximum work that can be done by the cell. This work is the charge transferred per mole under the force of the open-circuit voltage (OCV) of the cell. With $E$ being the electrode potential difference at equilibrium, the work done by the cell can be expressed as:

$$\Delta G = \text{Charge transferred per mole} \times \text{OCV}$$
$$= -nFE^o \tag{5.21}$$

The theoretical upper limit of a galvanic cell potential can be obtained from the above as

$$E^o = -\frac{\Delta G}{nF} \tag{5.22}$$

We will use the chemical reaction in a nickel-cadmium (NiCd) battery cell to calculate the equilibrium cell potential. The chemical reaction in a NiCd battery cell is given by

$$Cd + 2NiOOH \rightarrow Cd(OH)_2 + 2Ni(OH)_2$$

The Gibbs free energy change for the NiCd cell is

$$\Delta G = \Delta G_f^o(\text{products}) - \Delta G_f^o(\text{reactants})$$
$$= \left[(-470.25) + 2(-452.7)\right] - \left[0 + 2(-541.3)\right]$$
$$= -293.05 \text{ kJ/mole}$$

For the NiCd battery cell, two electrons are involved in the chemical reaction. The theoretical cell potential is thus

$$E^o = -\frac{-293{,}050}{2 \times 96{,}485} = 1.52 \text{ V}$$

The theoretical cell potential is never achievable in practice due to various electrochemical phenomena in the cell, which are described in the Sections 5.4.3–5.4.7. The nominal practical cell voltage in a NiCd cell is 1.3 V. This is true for all electrochemical cells. The thermodynamic cell potential only gives the theoretical upper value of cell potential for a battery chemistry.

The potential of an electrode is the potential difference between the electrode and the electrolyte that it is in contact with. The electrode potential is determined with respect to a reference electrode, since an absolute potential value cannot be obtained. Both chemical and electrical processes contribute to the electrode potential difference [6]. The environment at the vicinity of an electrode is changed due to chemical activities between the electrode and the electrolyte regardless of the electric potential difference at the solid-liquid phase boundary. The measure of the work done to bring a particle to its assumed potential is the chemical potential. Again, regardless of the changes in the chemical environment the transfer across the electric potential is accomplished by electric work done in its original sense. Although one cannot separate these two components for single species experimentally, the differences in the scales of the two environments make it possible to separate them mathematically [7,8]. The resultant potential for these two kinds of energy change is the electrochemical potential or simply the electric potential.

### 5.4.2 ELECTROLYSIS AND FARADAIC CURRENT

The process of *electrolysis* is the transfer of electrons between an electrode and a chemical species in solution resulting in an oxidation or a reduction reaction. An external electrical circuit is necessary for the redox reactions at the electrodes of the electrochemical cell. In order to understand the electrochemical phenomenon in a cell, and subsequently utilize that knowledge to develop simple models for these cells we must evaluate the nature of current and potential in the cell [8]. This section describes how current controls the reaction using Faraday's law of electrolysis and the relationship between charge and current.

The chemical reactions in 5.1 and 5.2 represent both a chemical process and an electrical process. The reaction rates can be completely determined using the electrical process by seeing that the chemical conversion can only occur if electrons are either arriving or leaving at the electrodes. Therefore, the chemical conversion rates are controlled or measured by the electrical current passing through a given electrode. Faraday's law of electrolysis relates the mass of a substance altered at an electrode to the quantity of electrical charge transferred at that electrode. The electrolysis rate in terms of moles electrolyzed is given by Faraday's law as (see Equation 5.5)

$$x = \frac{Q}{nF} \tag{5.23}$$

As was defined previously, $n$ is the number of electrons per ion released at an electrode, $F$ is the Faraday constant and $x$ is the number of moles electrolyzed. Again, by definition, electric current is the number of coulombs of electric charge flowing per second, i.e.,

$$i = \frac{dQ}{dt} \tag{5.24}$$

Equations 5.23 and 5.24 relate the faradaic current in an electrochemical cell with the reaction rate. Combining the two equations, we can write the reaction rate as

$$\frac{dx}{dt} = \frac{i}{nF} \text{ mole/s}$$

The reaction rate is typically expressed in mol/s per unit area since electrode reactions are a heterogeneous process occurring only at the electrode-electrolyte interface. The heterogeneous reaction rate depends on the mass transfer to the electrodes and various surface effects in addition to the electrode kinetics. The reaction rate per unit area is given by

$$\frac{dx}{dt} = \frac{i}{nFA} = \frac{j}{nF} \text{ mole/s-cm}^2 \tag{5.25}$$

where $A$ is the area in cm$^2$ and $j$ is the current density in A/cm$^2$.

### 5.4.3  ELECTRODE KINETICS

The study electrode kinetics includes the processes that govern the electrode reaction rates or the faradaic currents flowing in an electrochemical cell. A number of process rates dictate the electrode kinetics of which the two most common ones are:

1. The rate of electron transfer at the electrode surface between the electrodes and species in solution.
2. Mass transport of the active materials from the bulk solution to the electrode interface.

The rate of electron transfer at the electrode surface is governed by Faraday's law of electrolysis presented in the previous section. In this section, additional fundamental principles of electrode kinetics are described to establish the terminal voltage-current relationship in an electrochemical cell. The mass transport is another fundamental mechanism for the continuity of electrochemical reactions and will be addressed in the next section. It must be mentioned that the study of electrochemistry is vast and a detailed treatment is beyond the scope of this book. Only an overview of the fundamental theory for electrode kinetics is given here. The readers are referred to Refs. [8–10] for further details on this topic of electrochemistry.

When a redox couple is present at each electrode and there are no contributions from liquid junctions then the open-circuit potential is also the equilibrium potential. However, in general there is always ongoing activity at the electrode-electrolyte interface for many electrochemical cells. The critical potential at which the electrode reactions occur is known as standard potential $E^0$ for the specified chemical substances in the system. The electrode potential deviates from its so-called equilibrium state when there is external electric current flow. The relationship between the energy flow and the current is more complicated in the electrochemical cell than that for the conduction in a solid, since the current flow and chemical reactions are heterogeneous processes. Consequently, the relationships are non-linear, and approximations are often used to arrive at simpler mathematical expressions.

The electrode voltage-current relationship can be obtained using the forward and reverse reactions between the electrode and electrolytes. These currents can be obtained by relating reaction rates to the rate constants and the concentration of the reactants. Let us consider a general case where $n$ electrons are transferred between two species (reactant O) and (product R) at an electrode-electrolyte interface. The general electrode reaction is

$$O + ne^- \underset{k_r}{\overset{k_f}{\rightleftarrows}} R$$

where $k_f$ and $k_r$ are the forward and reverse rate constants, respectively. The rate constants are the proportionality factors linking the concentration of the species to the reaction rates. The concentration of species undergoing oxidation at a distance $x$ from the surface and at time $t$ will be denoted as $C_O(x, t)$; hence, the surface concentration is $C_O(0, t)$. Similarly, the surface concentration for the species undergoing reduction is $C_R(0, t)$.

The reaction rate obtained from the product of rate constant and species concentration can be equated to the reaction rate given by Equation 5.25 to establish the relationship between the species concentrations and faradaic current. Therefore, for the forward and reverse currents, we have

$$k_f C_O(0,t) = \frac{i_f}{nFA} \text{ and}$$

$$k_r C_R(0,t) = \frac{i_r}{nFA}$$

The net current flow at the electrode is the difference between the forward and reverse currents

$$i = i_f - i_r = nFA\left[k_f C_O(0,t) - k_r C_R(0,t)\right] \tag{5.26}$$

For the sake of simplicity in analyzing the electrode process, we will assume a single electron transfer (i.e., $n = 1$) at the electrode-electrolyte interface. In this case, the rate constants can be related to the electrical potential across the electrode-electrolyte interface using free energy considerations [8]. For the standard potential $E^0$, the forward and reverse rate constants are equal; this constant is known as the standard rate constant and is given the symbol $k^0$. The rate constants at other potentials are given in terms of the standard rate constant as

$$k_f = k^0 e^{(F/RT)(-\alpha)(E-E^0)}$$

$$k_r = k^0 e^{(F/RT)(1-\alpha)(E-E^0)}$$

Inserting these relations into Equation 5.26 gives the complete current-voltage characteristics at the electrode-electrolyte interface

$$i = FAk^0 \left(C_O(0,t)e^{(F/RT)(-\alpha)(E-E^0)} - C_R(0,t)e^{(F/RT)(1-\alpha)(E-E^0)}\right) \tag{5.27}$$

The approach used is referred to as the Butler-Volmer approach for analyzing electrode kinetics [8].

Although this equation describes the electrode kinetics quite accurately, it is generally impossible to express voltage in terms of current which would be the more useful form for modeling electrochemical cells. One approach is the Nernst solution which assumes that the current is so small that it can be neglected. The Nernst equation is given by

$$E = E^o + \frac{RT}{nF}\ln\frac{C_O(0,t)}{C_R(0,t)} \tag{5.28}$$

Although Nernst defined the equation independently, it can be derived from the Butler-Volmer equation assuming that the system is in equilibrium and the net current is zero. At equilibrium, the electrodes adopt a potential based on the bulk concentrations as dictated by Nernst and the bulk concentrations of O and R are also found at the surface. Using $i(t) = 0$ and $E = E_{eq}$ in Equation 5.27, we have

$$C_O(0,t)e^{(F/RT)(-\alpha)(E_{eq}-E^0)} = C_R(0,t)e^{(F/RT)(1-\alpha)(E_{eq}-E^0)}$$

This equation takes the Nernst relation form as

$$E_{eq} = E^o + \frac{RT}{F} \ln \frac{C_O^*}{C_R^*} \qquad (5.29)$$

where $E_{eq}$ is the equilibrium potential, and $C_O^*$ and $C_R^*$ are the bulk concentrations of the oxidation and reduction reactants, respectively.

Another approach for estimating the terminal potential is the Tafel solution which assumes that the current is large in one direction or the other. The approximation means that one of the two exponential terms in the Butler-Volmer expression of Equation 5.27 is negligible. The Tafel solution is given by

$$E(t) = E^0 + \frac{RT}{\alpha n F} \ln(i_0) - \frac{RT}{\alpha n F} \ln(i(t)) \qquad (5.30)$$

where $i_0$ is the exchange current obtained from the equilibrium condition. Although the net current is zero at equilibrium there is balanced faradic activity with equal forward and reverse currents. The exchange current is equal to these faradaic currents and is given by

$$i_0 = i_f = i_r = FAk^0 C_0^* e^{-\alpha(F/RT)(1-\alpha)(E_{eq}-E^0)} \qquad (5.31)$$

Although the Tafel relationship was originally derived from experimental data, it can also be deduced from the Butler-Volmer expression.

The reactant activities at the electrode-electrolyte interface cause the open-circuit voltage $E$ to deviate from the standard state voltage $E^0$. The electrode voltage difference between that at the equilibrium condition and when there is current flow due to charge transfer at the electrode-electrolyte interface is often referred to as the activation or charge transfer polarization overpotential. The charge transfer polarization is reflected as a voltage drop from the equilibrium position during cell discharge and will be denoted by $E_{ct}$.

### 5.4.4 Mass Transport

A complete electrochemical cell is formed when two electrodes are immersed in the same electrolyte. When an electrical circuit is completed by connecting an external load to the two electrodes, current flows through the external circuit. Electrode reactions and mass transport are two mechanisms for supporting continuous current flow. Current flow is maintained inside the cell through the mass transport of ions in the electrolyte. The dominant process for mass transport is the diffusion process where molecules transfer from a location with higher concentration to one with lower concentration. The mass transport can also occur through convection and migration. Convection is the mechanical movement of particles, which does not occur in a battery cell. In fuel cells, the pressure of fuel supply does cause some mass transport due to the convection effect. Migration is ion movement under the influence of an electric field where positively charged ions will migrate toward the negative electrode, while the negatively charged ions will move toward the positive electrode. The ion movement due to migration may be in the same direction as that due to the diffusion process or in the opposite direction. Since the diffusion process dominates over the convection and migration process only the diffusion process is addressed below.

The diffusion process for an active species in an electrochemical cell can be described by Fick's second law as

$$\frac{\partial C(x,t)}{\partial t} = D \frac{\partial^2 C(x,t)}{\partial x^2}$$

where $C(x, t)$ is the active species concentration, $D$ is the diffusion co-efficient of the electrochemical cell, and $x$ and $t$ are the space and time variables, respectively.

Let the species concentration at the electrode responsible for chemical reactions to maintain current flow is $C_d$. This concentration is less than the bulk concentration of the electrolyte $C_{bulk}$. A linear relationship for the diffusing current derived from Fick's law is given as [6]

$$C_d(t) = C_{bulk} - \frac{\delta}{nFAD} i(t) \qquad (5.32)$$

where $\delta$ is the diffusion layer thickness and $A$ is the surface area.

Porous electrodes are almost invariably used in electrochemical cells to decrease the activation potential. The active materials penetrate into the pores of the electrode to reach the reaction site. The increased surface area due to the pores results in parallel diffusion processes which is termed as branched diffusion process. The pores and increased surface area complicate the analysis of the diffusion process. The behavior of the branched diffusion has been shown to follow the pattern described by the constant phase element (CPE) instead of Fick's second law [10]. For a CPE, the phase angle of the frequency response remains the same for all frequencies. The CPE transfer function used to represent the overall diffusion process is given by

$$H(s) = \frac{C_d(s)}{i(s)} = \frac{K}{s^q}, \quad 0 < q < 1.$$

The time response of the CPE is easier to solve for simpler operations such as constant current discharge. That time response is

$$C_d(t) = C_{bulk} - Kit^q. \qquad (5.33)$$

The diffusion process described serves the purpose of representing both the energy storage and the impedance. The energy within a battery is stored or spatially distributed in the electrolyte in terms of the concentration of the active material. The movement of active material during cell reactions is controlled by the inherent impedance of the electrolyte. Both mechanisms have been represented by the diffusion process and are represented as a coupled mechanism from the electrical perspective. However, for certain analysis, it is desirable to separate the source and impedance. This separation is desirable for certain applications. For example, the fuel cell-type electrochemical device does not store any energy; the materials for chemical reactions in a fuel cell are supplied from external fuel. The electrochemical process is more accurately modeled by separated energy source (the fuel) and the impedance to the source. Another important need is for the prediction of how much energy is left in the battery, which is essentially calculating the SoC of the battery.

The separation of energy storage and impedance enables improved modeling of pulsed discharge characteristics of batteries which is essentially what takes place in electric and hybrid vehicles. For the complicated discharge currents in such applications, it is difficult to obtain analytical solutions of the CPE, and often one has to resort to numerical solutions.

### 5.4.5 ELECTRICAL DOUBLE LAYER

The electrical potential difference between the electrode and the electrolyte is due to the excess charges residing at the electrode-electrolyte interface. The excess charges at the electrode surface have to be counterbalanced by the charges of opposite polarity in the electrolyte. The two parallel layers formed with charged particles have a structure similar to that of a capacitor. This electrode interface layer is called electrical double layer or simply a double layer.

The electrical double layer has a thin but finite thickness in the range of a few Angstroms where all the excess charges reside. There is a strong electrostatic field at the surface, since there is no dielectric material other than the charged particles in the electrical double layer. The important properties of the electrical double layer are its capacitance, and the variation of electric potential and ion concentrations. Experimental results showed that the behavior of the capacitance is nonlinear depending on the interface potential [8].

In the electrochemical models, this double-layer capacitive behavior can be represented by an equivalent nonlinear capacitor $C_{dbl}$. In batteries, the double-layer capacitor does not a play a significant role in energy storage and can be neglected in simpler equivalent circuit models. However, this electrical double-layer concept forms the basis of making non-faradaic electrochemical devices known as supercapacitors or ultracapacitors. The ultracapacitors are discussed in Chapter 6.

### 5.4.6 Ohmic Resistance

The voltage drop due to migration in the electrochemical cell is caused by the ohmic resistance of the electrolyte. The electrical resistance of the electrode materials, bulk electrolyte and the electrode-electrolyte contact areas contribute to the ohmic voltage drop. The contact resistance gradually increases as the cell is being discharged during the formation of non-conducting film during cell reactions. A linear resistance is typically added in equivalent circuit models to represent the ohmic voltage drop.

A secondary electrolyte, known as supporting electrolyte or inert electrolyte, is often added in an electrochemical cell to reduce the ohmic voltage drop due to migration. The supporting electrolyte increases the conductivity of ions in the electrolyte. Additionally, the electrolyte reduces the electric field substantially which reduces the migration of the active species. The current conduction due to diffusion or migration reduces significantly with the addition of the supporting electrolyte. The inert ions in the cell are primarily responsible for the current conduction within the cell. The diffusion process still remains the dominant mechanism of supplying reactant materials to the electrodes.

### 5.4.7 Concentration Polarization

In an electrochemical cell, there are species that do not participate in the chemical reactions at the electrode, but contribute to the conduction of current. These species may be the ions from the supporting electrolyte or from the composition of the primary electrolyte. These species has to accumulate near the electrodes to aid in the flow of current, but do not react with the electrodes. Positive ions accumulate near the negative electrode, while the negative ions gather around the positive electrode. The result of this accumulation is a voltage drop caused by the electric field formed by the accumulation of the unreacted but charged particles. This is known as concentration polarization. This polarization follows a Nernst equation like relationship using the concentration of the inert ions [5]

$$E_C = \frac{RT}{nF} \ln \frac{C_{electrode,i}}{C_{bulk,i}} \tag{5.34}$$

where $C_{electrode,i}$ and $C_{bulk,i}$ are the concentrations of the inert ions at the electrode and the bulk solution. Polarization, regardless of its origin, is reflected at cell terminals as a voltage reduction from the open-circuit voltage.

## 5.5 BATTERY MODELING

Batteries and other electrochemical cells can be modeled at various levels depending on the use of the model. Battery models are useful for battery design, performance evaluation and system simulation at the application level. Modeling aids research on device design, construction and materials through understanding the factors that affect the energy conversion process. Models also help research on the performance of the device in an application, which can be utilized for improved design and better utilization.

At the most complex level, the fundamental physics and chemistry-based theories are used to develop *theoretical models* of electrochemical cells. These models reflect material properties and design factors on the device performance. The fundamental mechanisms of electrical power generation are characterized in these models in terms of both macroscopic behavior (terminal voltage and current characteristics) and microscopic (internal material and reactant behavioral processes) information. The models are very useful for the design and performance evaluation of a particular type of battery. The strength of these models is in the information obtained on the effect of design variables on performance during the design stage. These models characterize the physical and chemical relationships applied to each element of the device [5–8]. Numerical simulation techniques such as finite element analysis or computational fluid dynamics are also sometimes used to develop the analytical models. The drawbacks of the theoretical models are their complexity; often the models cannot be used to represent the device as a component of a larger system. Device parameters are not always available to the end user. The models could be specific for a particular chemistry and design. Dynamic response such as that of the battery SoC is difficult, if not impossible to analyze with most of these models.

Battery models that emphasize the macroscopic behavior are more useful for the performance evaluation at a system level (such as the electric or hybrid vehicle systems) and for the design of these systems. For example, a simplified battery model can be used for the dynamic simulation of a hybrid vehicle to predict the powertrain characteristics as well as the range on electric only operating mode. Depending on the simulation objective, the models can be represented by a set of electrical circuit components or by a simple empirical relationship of two parameters. These two types of models are the *electric circuit models* and *empirical models*, which are presented in this section. The electric circuit-based models are somewhat more complex than the empirical models, but are extremely useful for vehicle system level analysis. On the other hand, the empirical models allow a quick evaluation on the range of a vehicle based on the capacity or energy density.

The energy storage device models presented in this section are useful not just for electric and hybrid vehicle applications, but also for utility power system applications. Distributed power systems require energy storage devices with similar features as those required for electric and hybrid vehicles.

### 5.5.1 Electric Circuit Models

The equivalent electrical circuit-based models use lumped parameters that make them suitable for integration in the simulation model of a larger system. The models use a combination of circuit elements (resistors, capacitors and inductors) and dependent sources to give a circuit representation of the behavior and the functionality of the electrochemical cell. The model parameters are extracted from response data of the device eliminating the need to know the chemical processes and the design details. The electric circuit models range from a simple linear resistive model to a fairly complex one that characterizes the chemical processes in terms of lumped parameters. The accuracy of these models is in between those of the theoretical models and the empirical models; yet the circuit models are very useful for both simulation and design of a system. The application aspects of the battery can be evaluated effectively with insights into operation of the device as well as that of the system. Some of the more complex circuit models can be used to study the dynamic response such as the effect of pulse discharge which is a characteristic of hybrid and electric vehicles [7].

The primary electrochemical activities in the electrochemical cell are governed by two fundamental relationships: (i) Butler-Volmer relationship characterizing the electron exchange at the electrode-electrolyte interface and (ii) Faraday's law of electrolysis which states that current controls the reaction. Relating these relationships with the stored charge and the diffusing charge in the electrochemical cell enables us to develop an electric circuit model whose parameters can be obtained from experimental data.

In developing the battery models, it is more convenient to consider the stored and diffusion charges at a surface rather than the effective species concentration or surface activities. Let $q_s(t)$ and $q_d(t)$ be the instantaneous stored charge and the instantaneous diffusion charge in the vicinity of the electrode representing surface activities. If $Q$ is the total capacity of a cell, then the charge in the non-energized species can be represented as $Q - q_s(t)$.

As was mentioned previously, the difficulty is in finding an inverse for the Butler-Volmer equation so that terminal voltage can be represented in terms of electrode current. The Nernst and Tafel equations are approximations with limitations on the terminal current. One simplified approximation is the Unnewehr universal model [11] given by

$$E(t) = E_0 + R_\Omega i(t) + k_1 q_s(t)$$

where $E_0$ is the initial voltage of the cell, $R_\Omega$ is the series resistance and $k_1$ is a constant parameter. A generalized form to represent the solution to the Butler-Volmer equation is presented by Hartley and Jannette [12]:

$$E(t) = E_0 + R_\Omega i(t) + k_1 \ln\left(1 + |i|\right)\mathrm{sgn}(i) + k_2 \ln\left(1 + |q_d|\right)\mathrm{sgn}(i) + k_3 \ln(1 - q_s)$$

The constants $E_0$, $R_\Omega$, $k_1$, $k_2$ and $k_3$ depend on the properties of the electrochemical cell and can be determined from experimental data. While the Hartley model gives a mathematical representation of the terminal voltage, it is often convenient to find an equivalent electric circuit model for simulation and analysis of a battery cell. In the following, several such electric circuit models representing an electrochemical cell is given starting with a basic model derived from the Hartley model.

### 5.5.1.1 Basic Battery Model

Let us begin with a simple electrical equivalent circuit model that incorporates the fundamental principles, yet simple enough for characterization based on cell discharge data is shown in Figure 5.11. One of the key dynamics that has to be modeled is the diffusion process. While complex representations using a CPE or Warburg impedance can be used, an approximate solution to the change in diffusing charge has the same form as that of a voltage across an $RC$ circuit element. Therefore, the effect on the terminal voltage due to diffusion charge will be represented by the following first-order differential equation.

$$\frac{dv_d(t)}{dt} = \frac{1}{C_d} i(t) - \frac{1}{C_d R_d} v_d(t)$$

where $v_d(t)$ is the voltage dropped across the $R_d C_d$ parallel circuit that is proportional to the diffusion charge $q_d(t)$. Additional $RC$ circuit elements can be added to represent the diffusion charge, but we will keep it as a single $RC$ time constant for our simple model shown in Figure 5.11.

Another key cell dynamic that needs to be modeled is the effect of state of charge on the terminal voltage of the cell. Figure 5.6 showed how the battery terminal voltage decreases as the cell is being discharged. In the middle of the characteristics, the terminal voltage decrease is approximately linear which can be modeled by a series capacitor $C_s$ to represent the stored charge in the cell. The voltage across this storage capacitor $C_s$ is proportional to the stored charge $q_s(t)$. As the state of charge of the cell increases or decreases during charging or discharging, the voltage across the capacitor will increase or decrease, respectively. Additionally, an electrochemical cell losses charge while it is at rest. A resistor can be added in parallel to the storage capacitor to account for this loss of charge. This resistor $R_{sd}$ represents the self-discharge of the cell. The $C_s R_{sd}$ circuit elements representing the storage capacitor and self-discharge resistor is shown in Figure 5.11 in series with the diffusion parameters. The mathematical representation of this segment of the circuit model in relation to the terminal current is

$$\frac{dq_s(t)}{dt} = i(t) - \frac{1}{R_{sd}} q_s(t)$$

The two other parameters that need to be added to complete the electrochemical cell equivalent circuit is a voltage source in series with a resistor representing the ohmic resistance drop described in Section 5.5.6. The voltage source is taken to be the open-circuit voltage of the cell $E_0$, and $R_\Omega$ is the ohmic resistance both of which are shown in Figure 5.11 in series with the storage and diffusion parameters. This completes the simple equivalent circuit model of an electrochemical cell. The values of these circuit elements can be determined experimentally by applying a step change in battery current. The procedure for obtaining the parameters of this cell is given in Example 5.1.

## Example 5.1

A step discharge current of 15 A is applied to a three-cell generic battery to calculate its parameters for the model shown in Figure 5.11. The data collected from the experiment is shown graphically in Figure 5.12. The step command of 15 A constant current discharge is applied at 3,150 s and removed at 4,370 s. After the discharge, the battery terminal voltage settles to a lower voltage level of 5.873 V compared to its initial no-load voltage due to the reduction in the state of charge. $\Delta V_d$, $\Delta V_{Cs}$, $\Delta V_{R\Omega}$ are the voltage differences that need to be calculated from the test data to obtain the diffusion, storage and series resistance parameters, respectively. The time to reach 63% of $\Delta V_d$ is 100 s. Neglecting the self-discharge of the cells, calculate the battery equivalent circuit parameters.

**FIGURE 5.11**   Electric equivalent circuit battery model.

**FIGURE 5.12**   Test data for a battery to calculate equivalent circuit parameters.

*Solution*

Let us first calculate the equivalent series resistance of the battery. The voltage drop for the series resistance shows up in the output voltage characteristics as an instantaneous increase or decrease of the terminal voltage due to the step change in current. The voltage increase due to the 15 A step change in current is $\Delta V_{R\Omega} = 5.775 - 5.58 = 0.195$ V. Therefore, the series resistance value is

$$R_\Omega = \frac{\Delta V_{R\Omega}}{\Delta I} = \frac{0.195}{15} = 0.013\ \Omega$$

The resistance for the diffusion component $R_d$ is

$$R_d = \frac{\Delta V_d}{\Delta I} = \frac{0.098}{15} = 0.00653\ \Omega$$

The $RC$ time constant for the diffusion parameters is 100 s. Therefore, the diffusion capacitor $C_d$ can be calculated as

$$C_d = \frac{100}{0.00653} = 15,306\ \text{F}$$

The storage capacitor $C_s$ can be calculated from the voltage change due to the constant current discharge $\Delta V_{Cs}$ and the change in stored charge. This is calculated as follows:

$$C_s = \frac{\Delta Q}{\Delta V_{Cs}} = \frac{15(4,370 - 3,150)}{5.894 - 5.873} = 871,428.6\ \text{F}$$

### 5.5.1.2 Run-Time Battery Model

The Thevenin-type circuit model shown in Figure 5.11 with a constant open-circuit voltage does not allow prediction of the battery terminal voltage $V_t$ variations (i.e., DC response) and runtime information. Prediction of SoC, transient response, terminal voltage, run-time and temperature effects is possible with run-time models. A run-time model capable of predicting the capacity of battery has been developed by Chen and Rincon-Mora [13]. The circuit model, shown in Figure 5.13, has dependent current and voltage sources in addition to several passive components. The terminal voltage-current characteristics segment of the model is similar to that of Figure 5.11 except that the open-circuit voltage depends on the capacity or SoC of the battery.

The capacitor $C_{capacity}$ and a current-controlled current source model the capacity, SoC and run-time of the battery. The two $RC$ networks simulate the voltage-current transient response characteristics. The SoC is calculated based on the current drawn out of the cell and the initial capacity in the run-time segment of the model. The value of the capacitor $C_{capacity}$ is given by

$$C_{capacity} = 3,600 \cdot Q_C \cdot k_1 \cdot k_2$$

where $Q_c$ is the battery capacity in Ah, and $k_1$ an $k_2$ are cycle number and temperature-dependent correction parameters, respectively. The initial voltage across $C_{capacity}$ is set to 1 or lower depending

**FIGURE 5.13** Run-time battery model proposed by Chen and Rincon-Mora [13].

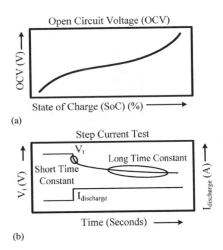

(a)

(b)

**FIGURE 5.14** Example experimental curves to obtain run-time model parameters: (a) SoC versus open-circuit voltage characteristics and (b) discharge plot for calculating $RC$ time constants.

**FIGURE 5.15** Impedance-based equivalent electric circuit battery model.

on whether the battery is initially fully charged or not. A value of '1' represents 100% SoC. Similarly, a value of '0' would indicate that the battery is fully discharged, i.e., SoC is 0%

SoC is bridged to the open-circuit voltage through a voltage-controlled voltage source. The relationship between SoC and open-circuit voltage is non-linear and has to be represented from experimentally obtained data for this model. However, the collection of the open-circuit voltage versus SoC data is extremely time consuming [14]. An example SoC versus open-circuit voltage characteristic and the discharge profile to calculate the $RC$ time constants are shown in Figure 5.14.

### 5.5.1.3 Impedance-Based Model

Another type of battery equivalent circuit-based model is the *impedance model*. Electrochemical impedance spectroscopy is applied to develop equivalent AC impedance-based circuit representation of the battery characteristics. The battery model based on impedance spectroscopy is shown in Figure 5.15. Impedance-based models are less intuitive, and are applicable only for a fixed SoC and temperature; prediction of DC response and run-time of a battery is difficult with these models.

### 5.5.1.4 First Principle Model

An interesting equivalent circuit model based on the fundamental electrochemical principles has been developed by Lei Xia [7]; the model is called the *first principle model*. While this is not one of the simpler electric equivalent circuit models, it isolates and relates the physical and chemical fundamentals of an electrochemical cell to an equivalent circuit parameter. The model has discrete, lumped parameter representation of all the electrochemical processes within the cell. The first principle model, shown in Figure 5.16, incorporates the following phenomenon within an electrochemical cell:

- Electrochemical energy conversion
- Diffusion process

**FIGURE 5.16**   First principle battery model with constant current source [7].

- – Charge transfer polarization
- – Concentration polarization
- – Electrical double layer
- – Ohmic resistance
- – Self-discharge.

In the equivalent circuit, the diffusion process has been described by a general CPE; open-circuit voltage and concentration polarization have been represented by the Nernst equations; charge transfer polarization has been represented by the Tafel equation; ohmic voltage drop has been represented by resistance $R_\Omega$; electric double layer has been represented by capacitance $C_{dbl}$; and resistance $R_{sd}$ represents self-discharge of the cell.

The first principle model is construction and chemistry independent. Parameters of the model can be derived from experimental response data of the device, which eliminates the need for the knowledge of electrochemical properties and the design details. The model is based on the fact that before the discharge of any current, the internal voltage $E_0$, the double-layer capacitor voltage $V_1$ and the terminal voltage $V_t$ (the variables are shown in Figure 5.16) are all the same. The charge transfer potential and the concentration polarization potential are zeroes for this condition. When a load is connected to the terminals, initially the discharge current is almost entirely supplied by the double-layer capacitor. As the double-layer capacitor discharges and the $V_1$ decreases, the charge transfer potential is established and the faradaic current $i_f$ starts to increase. When current $i_f$ increases to a point where $E_{ct}$ does not change appreciably, $i_d$ becomes minimal. In this situation, the faradaic current $i_f$ supplies the majority of the load current. The potential drop in this region is primarily due to the ohmic resistance.

As an example, the parameters for a generic battery cell are given below [7]:

Bulk electrolyte concentration: $C_0 = 2.616$ (dimensionless, but represents numerical value of the concentration)

Diffusion process parameters: $C_d(t) = C_0 - Ki_f(t)t^q$; $K = \dfrac{1}{227.5}$; $q = 0.68$

Open-circuit voltage (Nernst equation): $E(t) = 1.95 + 0.052 \ln C_d(t)$

Charge transfer polarization (Tafel equation): $E_{ct} = 0.118 + 0.28 \ln(i_f)$

Ohmic resistance: $R_\Omega = 0.05 \, \Omega$

Double-layer capacitor: $C_{dbl} = 50 \, \text{F}$

Concentration polarization: $E_c(t) = 0.04 \ln \dfrac{C_d(t)}{C_0}$

## 5.5.2  Empirical Models

The empirical models are the simplest of all models developed primarily for simple input-output relationships of the electrochemical devices. These models describe the performance of the device using arbitrary mathematical relationships matched with experimental or theoretical model data.

The mathematical or empirical relationships are established by curve fitting with experimental data. The physical reasons for the behavior are not as important as the terminal relationship between certain parameters of the device. The physical basis for device functionalities is non-existent in these models. Effects of design variations are impossible to analyze with the empirical models. Often only a subset of behaviors of the device is described such as the constant current discharge characteristics of a battery. The models do not provide the terminal $i$-$v$ characteristics of the device which is necessary in circuit simulation and analysis for hybrid and electric vehicles. However, the empirical models are very useful for a quick estimation of the range of an electric vehicle for a particular type of battery pack.

One of the widely used empirical battery model is based on the Peukert's equation relating discharge current with the battery capacity. The model is based on constant current discharge characteristics of the battery. A series of constant current discharge experiments give the $I$ versus $t_{cut}$ data for different constant current levels; $t_{cut}$ is the time when the terminal voltage reaches the cut-off voltage limit $V_{cut}$ during constant current discharge. The data obtained is used to fit Peukert's equation to develop the model as

$$I^n t_{cut} = \lambda \tag{5.35}$$

where $I$ is the constant discharge current, and $n$ and $\lambda$ are curve fitting constants of a particular battery. $n$ is a number between 1 and 2 with the value approaching 1 for smaller currents, but tends toward 2 for larger currents. The model does not specify the initial capacity, nor does it model the voltage variation or temperature, and aging factors. Peukert's model does not give any terminal $i$-$v$ information.

### Example 5.2

Find the curve fitting constants $n$ and $\lambda$ for Peukert's equation for the two measurements available from a constant current discharge experiment of a battery:
  (i) $(t_1, I_1) = (10, 18)$ and (ii) $(t_2, I_2) = (1, 110)$.

### *Solution*

Equation 5.35 is Peukert's empirical formula using the constant current discharge approach. Taking logarithm of both sides of Equation 5.35

$$log_{10}(I^n \times t_{cut}) = log_{10}(\lambda)$$

$$\Rightarrow log_{10}(I) = -\frac{1}{n}log_{10}(t_{cut}) + \frac{1}{n}log_{10}(\lambda)$$

Comparing with the equation for a straight line, $y = mx + b$, $I$ versus $t_{cut}$ curve is linear on a log-log plot as shown in Figure 5.17.
The slope of the straight line is

$$m = \frac{\Delta y}{\Delta x} = \frac{log(I_1) - log(I_2)}{log(t_1) - log(t_2)} = \frac{log\left(\dfrac{I_1}{I_2}\right)}{log\left(\dfrac{t_1}{t_2}\right)}$$

Therefore, $n = -\dfrac{log\left(\dfrac{t_1}{t_2}\right)}{log\left(\dfrac{I_1}{I_2}\right)}$.

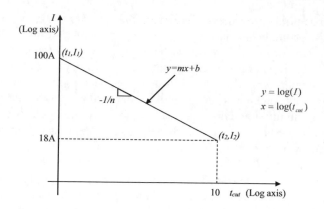

**FIGURE 5.17**  Plot of Peukert's equation using constant current discharge.

For the graph shown, $n = \dfrac{-1}{18/110} = 1.27 \; [\because t_1 = 10t_2]$

The other constant can now be calculated from Peukert's equation:

$$\lambda = 110^{1.27} * 1 = 391.4 \text{ Ah or}$$

$$\lambda = 18^{1.27} * 10 = 392.8 \text{ Ah.}$$

Another well-known and more general empirical model of a battery is based on the Shepherd equation [15]. The simplest form of the Shepherd model is

$$E = E_0 - iR - \left(\frac{\lambda}{\lambda - it}\right)Ki$$

where $E$ is the battery voltage, $i$ is the current and $t$ is the time. The parameters of the model are $E_0$, $R$, $K$ and $\lambda$ representing battery reference voltage, internal resistance, polarization constant and reference capacity. The model parameters have some physical meaning and relate the electrochemical behavior with the terminal $i$-$v$ characteristics of the battery. The output response is expressed as a function of time in this model; however, the model is difficult to use for discharge patterns other than constant current discharge.

### 5.5.2.1  Range Prediction with Constant Current Discharge

Peukert's equation with constant current discharge characteristics can be used to develop a *fractional depletion model* (FDM) of batteries. FDM of a battery can be used to predict the range of an electric vehicle. Using Peukert's equation, we can establish the relationship between $Q$ and $I$. The practical capacity of a battery is

$$Q = I \times t_{cut}$$

$$\Rightarrow t_{cut} = \frac{Q}{I}$$

Substituting into Peukert's equation

$$I^n\left(\frac{Q}{I}\right) = \lambda$$

$$\Rightarrow Q = \frac{\lambda}{I^{n-1}}$$

Since $0 < n-1 < 1$, for $I > 1$, $Q$ decreases as $I$ increases.

From Section 5.3.7, we know that

$$SoD = \int i(\tau)\,d\tau$$

$$\text{and } DoD = \frac{SoD}{Q(i)}.$$

SoD is the amount of charge that the battery generates to the circuit. Assume that at $t = t_0$, the battery is fully charged. Let us consider a small interval of time $dt$. Therefore,

$$d(DoD) = \frac{d(SoD)}{Q(i)}, \text{ where } d(SoD) = i(t)\,dt$$

We know that $Q = \dfrac{\lambda}{I^{n-1}}$ for constant current discharge. Let $Q = \dfrac{\lambda}{i^{n-1}}$ for time varying current as well, for the lack of anything better.

Therefore, $d(DoD) = \dfrac{i\,dt}{\lambda/i^{n-1}} = \dfrac{i^n}{\lambda}\,dt.$

Integrating, we obtain $\displaystyle\int_{t_0}^{t} d(DoD) = \int_{t_0}^{t} \frac{i^n}{\lambda}\,dt.$

$$\Rightarrow DoD(t) - DoD(t_0) = \int_{t_0}^{t} \frac{i^n}{\lambda}\,dt.$$

$DoD(t_0) = 0$, if the battery is fully charged at $t = t_0$.

The *fractional depletion model* is thus obtained as

$$DoD(t) = \left[\int_{t_0}^{t} \frac{i^n}{\lambda}\,dt\right] \times 100\% \tag{5.36}$$

The FDM based on current discharge requires knowledge of the discharge current $i(t)$. Therefore, this model to predict the electric vehicle range should be used when $i(t)$ is known.

### Example 5.3

The constant current discharge characteristics of the battery pack used in an electric vehicle is

$$\ln I = 4.787 - 0.74\ln t_{cut} - 0.0482(\ln t_{cut})^2$$

The current drawn from the battery during test drives of the electric vehicle for the SAE schedule J227a has the profile shown in Figure 5.18. The current magnitudes for the three SAE schedules are given in Table 5.3.

Find the range of the electric vehicle for each of the three schedules.

### Solution

Apply the FDM (Equation 5.36) to find the number of driving cycles for DoD = 100%.

**FIGURE 5.18** Pattern of current drawn from the battery.

**TABLE 5.3**
**Current Data for the Driving Schedules**

| Schedule J227a | $I_a$ (A) | $I_b$ (A) |
|---|---|---|
| B | 100 | 35 |
| C | 216 | 55.6 |
| D | 375 | 88.7 |

From FDM,

$$1 = \int_{t_0}^{t_{100\%}} \frac{i^n}{\lambda} dt.$$

First, we need to determine $\lambda$ and $n$ from the given battery characteristics

$$\frac{-1}{n} = -0.74 \Rightarrow n = 1.35$$

$$\frac{1}{n}\ln(\lambda) = 4.787 \Rightarrow \lambda = 645 \times 3{,}600 \text{ A-s}$$

Therefore,

$$1 = \int_0^{t_{100\%}} \frac{i^{1.35}}{645 \times 3{,}600} dt$$

For schedule B, fraction depleted over 1 cycle

$$\text{DoD for 1 cycle} \Rightarrow f_{cyc} = \int_0^{72} \frac{i^{1.35}}{645 \times 3{,}600} dt$$

$$\Rightarrow f_{cyc} = \int_0^{72} \frac{i^{1.35}}{645 \times 3{,}600} dt = 4.31 \times 10^{-7} \left[ \int_0^{19} \left( \frac{100t}{19} \right)^{1.35} dt + \int_{19}^{38} (35)^{1.35} dt \right]$$

$$= 4.31 \times 10^{-7} \left[ 9.41 \left( \frac{1}{2.35} \right) 19^{2.35} + 121.5(38 - 19) \right]$$

$$\Rightarrow f_{cyc} = 2.74 \times 10^{-3}$$

Let $N$ = # of cycles required for 100% DoD,

$$\therefore 1 = N \times f_{cyc} \Rightarrow N = \frac{1}{f_{cyc}}$$

$$\therefore N = \frac{1}{2.74 \times 10^{-3}} = 365 \text{ cycles}$$

From Table 3.5, the EV goes 1 mile in about 4 cycles for schedule B
   Therefore,

$$\boxed{\text{EV Range} = \frac{365}{4} = 91 \text{ miles for schedule B}}$$

Measured $N = 369 \Rightarrow$ Error $= 1.08\%$.
J 227a schedule C: From FDM, $N = 152$; EV Range $= 152/3 = 51$ miles.
Measured, $N = 184 \Rightarrow$ Error $= 17.4\%$
J 227a schedule D: FDM, $N = 41$; EV Range $= 41/1 = 41$ miles.
Measured, $N = 49 \Rightarrow$ Error $= 16.3\%$.

### 5.5.2.2 Range Prediction with Power Density Approach

An alternative approach of using Peukert's equation to develop a battery model is through the use of its Ragone relationship which is the specific power versus specific energy characteristics. Ragone relationship and the corresponding plots are linear on the log-log scale to a first-order approximation. Battery model in terms of specific power and specific energy is

$$(SP)^n (SE) = \lambda \tag{5.37}$$

where $n$ and $\lambda$ are curve fitting constants.

### Example 5.4

The data given in Table 5.4 is collected from an experiment on a battery with mass 15 kg. The data is used to draw the Ragone plot shown in Figure 5.19. Using the data points (8,110) and (67.5,10), calculate the constants of Peukert's equation $n$ and $\lambda$.

*Solution*
$n = 0.8894$ and $\lambda = 523.24$ Ah

Given a battery terminal power profile $p(t)$, the specific power $SP(t)$ profile can be obtained by dividing the power profile $p(t)$ by the total vehicle mass $m_V$ (Figure 5.20). The battery is assumed to be fully charged at $t = 0$.
   Let, $f_r(t)$ = fraction of available energy provided by battery from 0 to $t$, where $f_r(0) = 0$, since $SoD(0) = 0$. Now, consider the time interval $dt$ over which a fraction of available energy $df_r$ is provided by the battery

### TABLE 5.4
### Data from Constant Power Discharge Test

| $P$ (W) (Measured) | $t_{cut}$ (h) (Measured) | $E_P$ (Wh) (Calculated) | $SP$ (W/kg) (Calculated) | $SE$ (Wh/kg) (Calculated) |
|---|---|---|---|---|
| 150 | 6.75 | $(150)(6.75) = 1{,}013$ | $150/15 = 10$ | $1{,}013/15 = 67.5$ |
| 450 | 0.85 | 381 | 30 | 25.4 |
| 900 | 0.23 | 206 | 60 | 13.7 |
| 1,650 | 0.073 | 120 | 110 | 8 |

**FIGURE 5.19**   Ragone plot for Example 5.4.

**FIGURE 5.20**   Power and specific power.

$$df_r = \frac{dE}{E_{avail}} = \frac{\dfrac{dE}{m_V}}{\dfrac{dE_{avail}}{m_V}} = \frac{d(SE)}{SE_{avail}}.$$

If $dE$ is the energy provided by battery to the electrical circuit over $dt$ and $E_{avail}$ is the total available energy, then

$$dE = pdt.$$

Now $E_{avail}$ is a function of instantaneous power and we know that

$$d(SE) = (SP)dt.$$

Therefore,

$$SE_{avail} = f(SP).$$

We will use Peukert's equation to relate specific power and specific energy as follows:

$$(SP)^n \times SE_{avail} = \lambda.$$

Therefore, $df_r = \dfrac{SP}{\dfrac{\lambda}{(SP)^n}} dt = \dfrac{(SP)^{n+1}}{\lambda} dt.$

Integrating, $\displaystyle\int_{f_r(0)}^{f_r(t)} df_r = \int_0^t \frac{(SP)^{n+1}}{\lambda} d\tau.$

$$\Rightarrow f_r(t) = \int_0^t \frac{(SP)^{n+1}}{\lambda} d\tau. \tag{5.38}$$

Equation 5.38 is the FDM using power density approach. If $t$ = time at which $x\%$ of available energy has been used, then

$$\frac{x}{100} = \int_0^t \frac{(SP)^{n+1}}{\lambda} d\tau.$$

Note that, $1 = \int_0^{t_{100\%}} \frac{(SP)^{n+1}}{\lambda} d\tau.$

At $t_{100\%}$, 100%, i.e., all the available energy has been used by the system.

## 5.6  TRACTION BATTERIES

Lead acid batteries that have served the automotive industry over the past 100 years for powering electrical accessories in conventional IC engine vehicles does not have the power and energy density required in electric vehicles and hybrid vehicles. The push for zero-emission vehicles led to numerous research and development efforts on advanced batteries activities in the United States, Europe and Japan. Desirable features sought after in alternative battery technologies are high power and energy density, faster charge time and long cycle life. The research and development progressed slowly until recent years due to the lack of market penetration of electric vehicles. In the meantime, the growth in the electronics industry over the past several decades has led to tremendous advancements in alternative batteries, such as nickel-cadmium (NiCd), nickel-metal-hydride (NiMH) and Li-based batteries technologies. The rechargeable Li-ion battery is the technology of choice for cell phones and laptop computers. Further research on scaling of these battery technologies led to the development of several battery technologies for electric and hybrid vehicle applications. NiMH battery-packs are currently used in commercially available hybrid electric vehicles, while the Li-ion battery pack is used in the electric vehicle Tesla roadster. Emerging plug-in hybrid vehicles are also likely to use the Li-ion battery technology. While the NiMH and Li-ion batteries are the frontrunners today for electric and hybrid electric vehicles applications, several other battery technologies have been used in various prototype vehicles. In this section, we will review not only the promising battery technologies, but also those have been tried in various prototype electric vehicles.

The future of the battery technologies for electric and hybrid vehicle applications depend on factors including system cost, availability of raw materials, mass production capabilities and lifecycle characteristics. One must note that the electric and hybrid vehicles industry covers a wide spectrum and is not just limited to road vehicles. Some technologies may be more suitable for certain applications for various reasons. Representative properties of the promising batteries technologies along with that of lead acid battery are summarized below in Table 5.5 with information obtained from various literatures. The chemistry and additional information on the alternative battery technologies will then be presented in this chapter.

### 5.6.1  LEAD ACID BATTERY

The lead acid batteries have been the most popular choice of batteries for electric vehicles during the initial development stages. The lead acid battery has a long history that dates back to the middle of the 19th century and is currently a very mature technology. The first lead acid battery was produced as early as in 1859. In the early 1980s, over 100 million lead acid batteries were produced per year. The long existence of the lead acid battery is due to

- relatively low cost,
- easy availability of raw materials (lead, sulfur),
- ease of manufacture,
- favorable electromechanical characteristics.

**TABLE 5.5**

**Properties of Electric and Hybrid Electric Vehicles Batteries**

| Battery Type | Specific Energy, Wh/kg | Specific Power, W/kg | Energy Efficiency, % | Cycle Life |
|---|---|---|---|---|
| Lead acid | 35–50 | 150–400 | 80 | 500–1,000 |
| Nickel-cadmium | 30–50 | 100–150 | 75 | 1,000–2,000 |
| Nickel-metal hydride | 60–80 | 200–400 | 70 | 1,000 |
| Aluminum-air | 200–300 | 100 | <50 | Not available |
| Zinc-air | 100–220 | 30–80 | 60 | 500 |
| Sodium-sulfur | 150–240 | 230 | 85 | 1,000 |
| Sodium-nickel chloride | 90–120 | 130–160 | 80 | 1,000 |
| Lithium-polymer | 150–200 | 350 | Not available | 1,000 |
| Lithium ion | 90–160 | 200–350 | >90 | >1,000 |

**FIGURE 5.21**   Schematic diagram of lead acid battery showing through-partition connection.

Lead acid batteries can be designed to be of high power and are inexpensive, safe, and reliable. A recycling infrastructure is in place for them. However, low specific energy, poor cold temperature performance, and short calendar and cycle life are among the obstacles to their use in electric vehicles and hybrid electric vehicles.

Conventionally, lead acid batteries are of flooded-electrolyte cells, where free acid covers all the plates. This imposes the constraint of maintaining an upright position for the battery, which is difficult in certain portable situations. Efforts in developing hermetically sealed batteries faced the problem of build-up of an explosive mixture of hydrogen and oxygen on approaching the top-of-charge or over-charge condition during cell recharging. The problem is addressed in the valve-regulated lead acid (VRLA) batteries by providing a path for the oxygen, liberated at the positive electrode, to reach the negative electrode where it recombines to form lead-sulfate. There are two mechanisms of making the sealed VRLA batteries, the gel battery and the AGM (absorptive glass micro-fiber) battery. Both types are based on immobilizing the sulfuric acid electrolyte in the separator and the active materials leaving sufficient porosity for the oxygen to diffuse through the separator to the negative plate [16].

The construction of a typical battery consists of positive and negative electrode groups (elements) interleaved to form a cell. The through partition connection in the battery is illustrated in Figure 5.21. The positive plate is made of stiff paste of the active material on a lattice-type grid, which is shown in Figure 5.22. The grid made of a suitably selected lead alloy is the framework of a portable battery to hold the active material. The positive plates can be configured as flat pasted or in tubular fashion. The negative plates are always manufactured as pasted types.

### 5.6.2   NICKEL-CADMIUM BATTERY

The advantages of NiCd batteries are superior low-temperature performance compared to the lead acid battery, flat discharge voltage, long life and excellent reliability. The maintenance requirements

**FIGURE 5.22**   A lead acid battery grid.

of the batteries are also low. The lower practical cell voltage between 1.2 and 1.3 V means that more cells have to be connected in series to get the desired voltage. The specific energy of NiCd batteries is 30–50 Wh/kg, which is similar to that of lead acid batteries.

The biggest drawbacks of NiCd batteries are the high cost and the toxicity contained in cadmium. The environmental concerns may be overcome in the long run through efficient recycling, but the insufficient power delivered by the NiCd batteries is another important reason for not considering these batteries for electric and hybrid electric vehicles applications. The drawbacks of the NiCd batteries led to the rapid development of NiMH batteries, which are deemed more suitable for electric and hybrid electric vehicle applications.

### 5.6.3   NICKEL-METAL-HYDRIDE (NiMH) BATTERY

The nickel-metal-hydride is a successor to the nickel hydrogen battery, and is already in use in production hybrid electric vehicles. The positive electrode in a NiMH battery cell is nickel hydroxide ($Ni(OH)_2$) and the negative electrode is metal hydride. The chemical reactions of the NiMH battery cell have already been presented in Section 5.2. The negative electrode consists of a compressed mass of fine metal particles. The metallic alloy can absorb large number of hydrogen molecules under certain temperature and pressure to form the metal hydride. This can be thought of as an alternative approach of storing hydrogen. The proprietary alloy formulations used in NiMH are known as $AB_5$ and $AB_2$ alloys. In the $AB_5$ alloy, A is the mixture of rare earth elements and B is partially substituted nickel. In the $AB_2$ alloy, A is titanium and/or zirconium and B is again partially substituted nickel. The $AB_2$ alloy has higher capacity for hydrogen storage and less costly. The nominal cell voltage in a NiMH battery is 1.2 V, which is the same as that of NiCd; NiMH cells also have flat discharge characteristics. The capacity of the NiMH is significantly higher than that of NiCd with specific energy ranging from 60 to 80 Wh/kg. The specific power of NiMH batteries can be as high as 250 W/kg.

NiMH battery packs have the capability to operate in intermediate SoC conditions and deliver thousands of shallow discharge cycles with a 1%–2% swing of SoC. This feature is particularly suitable for charge sustaining HEVs, where it is necessary for the battery packs to survive more than 100,000 vehicle miles driven over 10 years. The cost advantages for NiMH battery packs are also favorable for battery-packs designed for high power density, but not so when designed for high specific energy required in EVs. Thus, the NiMH battery packs became the enabling technology for charge sustaining HEVs.

The components of NiMH are recyclable, but a recycling infrastructure is not yet in place. NiMH batteries have a much longer life cycle than lead acid batteries and are safe and abuse-tolerant. The disadvantages of NiMH batteries are the relatively high cost, higher self-discharge rate compared to NiCd, poor charge acceptance capability at elevated temperatures and low cell efficiency. NiMH is likely to survive as the leading rechargeable battery in the future for traction applications with strong challenge coming only from lithium-ion batteries.

### 5.6.4 Li-Ion Battery

The lithium metal has high electrochemical reduction potential relative to that of hydrogen (3.045 V) and the lowest atomic mass (6.94), which shows promise for a battery of 3 V cell potential when combined with a suitable positive electrode. The interest in secondary lithium cells soared soon after the advent of lithium primary cells in the 1970s, but the major difficulty was the highly reactive nature of the lithium metal with moisture that restricted the use of liquid electrolytes. The discovery in the late 1970s by researchers at Oxford University that lithium can be intercalated (absorbed) into the crystal lattice of cobalt or nickel to form $LiCoO_2$ or $LiNiO_2$ paved the way toward the development of lithium-ion batteries [17]. The use of metallic-Li is bypassed in Li-ion batteries by using lithium intercalated (absorbed) carbons ($Li_xC$) in the form of graphite or coke as the negative electrode along with the lithium metallic oxides as the positive electrode. The graphite is capable of hosting lithium up to a composition of $LiC_6$. The majority of the Li-ion batteries use either a layered oxide or iron phosphates of lithium as the positive electrode. Layered positive electrodes of cobalt oxide are expensive, but proved to be the most satisfactory. Nickel oxide, which costs less can also be used, but is structurally more complex. The performance is similar to that of cobalt oxide electrodes. The manganese oxide-based positive electrodes are also used since manganese is cheaper, widely available and less toxic. Alternative positive electrode material is the lithium iron phosphate ($LiFePO_4$) which can deliver stable and good performance at lower costs.

The cell discharge operation in a lithium-ion cell using $LiCoO_2$ is illustrated in Figure 5.23. During cell discharge, lithium ions ($Li^+$) are released from the negative electrode that travel through an organic electrolyte toward the positive electrode. In the positive electrode, the lithium ions are quickly incorporated into the lithium compound material. The process is completely reversible. The chemical reactions at the electrodes are as follows:

At the negative electrode,

$$Li_xC_6 \underset{\text{Charge}}{\overset{\text{Discharge}}{\rightleftharpoons}} 6C + xLi^+ + xe^- \text{ where } 0 < x < 1.$$

**FIGURE 5.23**  Lithium-ion cell. (By courtesy of Research Studies Press Ltd.)

At the positive electrode,

$$xLi^+ + xe^- + Li_{(1-x)}CoO_2 \underset{\text{Charge}}{\overset{\text{Discharge}}{\rightleftharpoons}} LiCoO_2.$$

During cell charge operation, the lithium ions move in the opposite direction from the positive electrode to the negative electrode. The nominal cell voltage for a Li-ion battery is 3.6 V, which is equivalent to 3 NiMH or NiCd battery cells.

The components of Li-ion batteries are also recyclable, but a recycling infrastructure is yet to be developed. The cost of Li-ion battery cells is now lower to that of comparable NiMH battery cells which suffer from higher material costs. Some Li-ion battery chemistries involve relatively inexpensive materials. The lower material cost does not reflect directly on the battery packs cost since more expensive management systems are necessary in Li-ion packs to address the safety concerns.

The main drawback of Li-ion batteries is that these are very sensitive to over-voltages and over-discharges. Over-voltage of Li-ion cell positive electrode results in solvent oxidation, and exothermic decomposition of the active material. Overvoltage and over-discharge can result in irreversible cell damage possibly accompanied by cell ignition [18].

The automotive industry has essentially settled on Li-ion cells using a layered cathode and a graphite anode for all types of electric and hybrid vehicles. The specific Li-ion pack chemistry varies depending on the type of BEV with the choices from $LiNiCoMnO_2$ (NMC), $LiNiCoAlO_2$ (NCA), $Li_2TiO_3$ (LTO) and $LiFePO_4$ (LFP). For BEVs, the Li-ion types of choice are the NMC and NCA ones which have the highest volumetric mass energy densities, long life and acceptable abuse tolerance, because of which they are universally used in passenger BEVs. Their cell voltages are at 3.6 V with capacity of 150–200 mAh/g. The LFPs have found applications in all-electric buses due to their lower cost although they have lower cell voltages at 3.2 V with a capacity of 150 mAh/g.

### 5.6.5 LI-POLYMER BATTERY

The Li-polymer evolved out of the development of solid state electrolytes, i.e., solids capable of conducting ions but are electron insulators. The solid state electrolytes resulted from the research in the 1970s on ionic conduction in polymers. These batteries are considered solid-state batteries, since their electrolytes are solids. The most common polymer electrolyte is the polyethylene oxide compounded with an appropriate electrolyte salt.

The most promising positive electrode material for Li-polymer batteries is the vanadium oxide $V_6O_{13}$ [16]. This oxide interlaces up to eight lithium atoms per oxide molecule with the following positive electrode reaction:

$$Li_x + V_6O_{13} + xe^- \underset{\text{Charge}}{\overset{\text{Discharge}}{\rightleftharpoons}} Li_x V_6O_{13} \text{ where } 0 < x < 8.$$

The Li-polymer batteries have the potentials for the highest specific energy and power. The solid polymers, replacing the more flammable liquid electrolytes in other type of batteries, can conduct ions at temperatures above 60°C. The use of solid polymers also has a great safety advantage in case of electric and hybrid electric vehicles accidents. Since the lithium is intercalated into carbon electrodes, the lithium is in ionic form and is less reactive than pure lithium metal. The thin Li-polymer cell gives the added advantage of forming a battery of any size or shape to suit the available space within the electric and hybrid electric vehicles chassis. The main disadvantage of the Li-polymer battery is the need to operate the battery cell in the temperature range of 80°C–120°C. Li-polymer batteries with high specific energy, initially developed for electric vehicle applications, also have the potential to provide high specific power for hybrid electric vehicle applications. The other key characteristics of the Li-polymer are good cycle and calendar life.

## 5.6.6 ZINC-AIR BATTERY

The zinc-air batteries have a gaseous positive electrode of oxygen and a sacrificial negative electrode of metallic zinc. The practical zinc-air battery is only mechanically rechargeable by replacing the discharged product, zinc hydroxide with fresh zinc electrodes. The discharged electrode and the potassium hydroxide electrolyte are sent to a recycling facility. In a way, the zinc-air battery is analogous to fuel cell with the fuel being the zinc metal. A module of zinc air batteries tested in German Mercedes Benz postal vans had a specific energy of 200 Wh/kg, but only a modest specific power of 100 W/kg at 80% depth-of-discharge (see Sections 3.4 and 3.5 for definition of depth-of-discharge and specific power). With the present day technology the range of zinc-air batteries can be between 300 and 600 km between recharges.

Other metal air systems have also been investigated but the work has been discontinued due to severe drawbacks in the technologies. These batteries include iron-air and aluminum-air batteries where iron and aluminum are, respectively, used as the mechanically recyclable negative electrode.

The practical metal-air batteries have two very attractive positive features: (i) the positive electrode can be optimized for discharge characteristics, since the batteries are recharged outside the battery, and (ii) the recharging time is rapid with a suitable infrastructure.

## 5.6.7 SODIUM-SULFUR BATTERY

Sodium, similar to the lithium, has a high electrochemical reduction potential (2.71 V) and low atomic mass (23.0) making it an attractive negative electrode element for batteries. Moreover, sodium is abundant in nature available at a very low cost. Sulfur, which is a possible choice for the positive electrode is also a readily available and another low-cost material. The use of aqueous electrolytes is not possible due to the highly reactive nature of sodium and solid polymers like those used for lithium batteries are not known. The solution of electrolyte came from the discovery of beta-alumina by scientists in Ford Motor company in 1966. Beta-alumina is a sodium aluminum oxide with a complex crystal structure.

Despite the several attractive features of NaS batteries, there are several practical limitations. The cell operating temperature in NaS batteries is around 300°C, which requires adequate insulation as well as a thermal control unit. The requirement forces a certain minimum size of the battery limiting the development of the battery for only electric vehicles, a market for which is not yet established. Another disadvantage of NaS batteries is in the absence of an overcharge mechanism. At the top-of-charge one or more cells can develop a high resistance, which pulls down the entire voltage of the series connected battery cells. Yet another major concern is the safety issue, since the chemical reaction between molten sodium and sulfur can cause excessive heat or explosion in the case of accident. The safety issues were addressed through efficient design, and manufactured NaS batteries have been shown to be safe.

The practical limitations and manufacturing difficulty of NaS batteries have led to the discontinuation of its development programs, especially when the simpler concept of sodium-metal chloride batteries was developed.

## 5.6.8 SODIUM-METAL-CHLORIDE BATTERY

The sodium-metal chloride battery is a derivative of sodium-sulfur battery with intrinsic provisions of overcharge and overdischarge. The construction is similar to that of NaS battery, but the positive sulfur electrode is replaced by nickel chloride ($NiCl_2$) or a mixture of nickel chloride and ferrous chloride ($FeCl_2$). The negative electrode and the electrolyte are the same as in NaS battery. The schematic diagram of a $NaNiCl_2$ cell is shown in Figure 5.24. In order to provide good ionic contact between the positive electrode and the electrolyte, both of which are solids, a second electrolyte of sodium chloraluminate ($NaAlCl_4$) is introduced in a layer between $NiCl_2$ and

**FIGURE 5.24** A sodium-nickel-chloride cell.

beta-alumina. The $NaAlCl_4$ electrolyte is a vital component of the battery, although it reduces the specific energy of the battery by about 10% [17]. The operating temperature is again high, similar to that of NaS battery. The basic cell reactions for the nickel chloride and ferrous chloride positive electrodes are

$$NiCl_2 + 2Na \underset{\text{Charge}}{\overset{\text{Discharge}}{\rightleftharpoons}} Ni + 2NaCl \ (2.58 \text{ V})$$

$$FeCl_2 + 2Na \underset{\text{Charge}}{\overset{\text{Discharge}}{\rightleftharpoons}} Fe + 2NaCl \ (2.35 \text{ V})$$

The cells in a sodium-metal chloride battery are assembled in a discharged state. The positive electrode is pre-fabricated from a mixture of Ni or Fe powder and NaCl (common salt). On charging after assembly, the positive electrode compartment is formed of the respective metal and the negative electrode compartment is formed of sodium. This procedure has two significant advantages, (i) pure sodium is manufactured *in situ* through diffusion in beta-alumina and (ii) the raw materials for the battery (common salt and metal powder) are inexpensive. Although iron is cheaper than nickel, the latter is more attractive as the metallic component because of fewer complications and wider operating temperature range.

The sodium chloride batteries are commonly known as the ZEBRA batteries, which originally resulted from a research collaboration between scientists from United Kingdom and South Africa in the early 1980s. The ZEBRA batteries have been shown to be safe under all conditions of use. The ZEBRA batteries have high potentials for being used as batteries for electric vehicles and hybrid electric vehicles. There are several test programs with the ZEBRA batteries.

### 5.6.9 Research and Development for Advanced Batteries

The battery research and development activities are focused on both improving the Li-ion battery technology and exploring novel chemistries that have strong potentials. The research efforts with Li-ion batteries are twofold: one is more efficient electrode design with, minimized inactive materials while the other is improved packaging to achieve higher volumetric energy density (kWh/L). The potential candidates for the next generation batteries beyond Li-ion are Li-air, Li-sulfur and solid-state batteries. The common element of these potential technologies is the replacement of the graphite with metallic Li anode that provides the highest energy density of all electrochemical couples. Research approaches include the development of higher-voltage cathode materials, higher specific capacity cathodes and anodes. The main issue that remains to be solved is the formation of dendrites during the cycling of Li.

On the commercialization front, General Motors introduced the new Ultium batteries in March 2020 for its electric vehicle platforms which features LG Chem's new chemistry NCMA (nickel-cobalt-manganese-aluminum) cathode [19]. The Ultium battery-pack layout is shown in Figure 5.25. The cell chemistry with large-format, pouch-style cells can be stacked vertically or horizontally inside the battery pack which will allow engineers to optimize battery energy storage and layout for each vehicle design. The energy capacity of Ultium options are between 50 and 200 kWh, which could enable range up to 400 miles on a full charge. The nickel-rich chemistry with up to 90% Ni requires 70% less cobalt than the current generation NCM (nickel-cobalt-manganese) cells. NCMA is more energy dense than the NCM, making for lighter and less-expensive batteries. This would enable the industry to get closer to the target of $100/kWh. GM is also developing zero-cobalt and zero-nickel anodes to reduce dependence on precious and semi-precious elements.

The battery research and development is guided by the goals established by the by US Advanced Battery Consortium (USABC) which is within the United States Council of Automotive Research (USCAR), an umbrella organization of US auto manufacturers formed in 1992 to strengthen the automotive technology base through collaborative research and development. USABC promotes the development of high energy density and high power density energy storage technologies setting the goals to support electric, hybrid and fuel cell vehicles. Goals are set for long-term development as well as long-term commercialization. The purpose of the commercialization goals is to develop batteries with a reasonable goal, while the long-term criteria was set to develop batteries for electric vehicles, which would be directly competitive with the IC engine vehicles. The specific power and specific energy long-term goals have been set aggressively at 400 W/kg and 200 Wh/kg to promote research and development. A subset of the goals set by USABC for advanced electric vehicle batteries is listed in Table 5.6. The calendar life for these batteries is targeted for 10 years, while cycle life has been set for 1,000 cycles at 80% DoD for both commercialization and long term goals.

**FIGURE 5.25**   Ultium battery-pack layout in a skateboard chassis. (Photo courtesy of General Motors.)

**TABLE 5.6**
**USABC Objectives for EV Advanced Battery Packs**

| Parameter | Minimum Goals for Long-Term Commercialization | Long-Term Goals |
|---|---|---|
| Specific energy (Wh/kg) (C/3 discharge rate) | 150 | 200 |
| Specific power (W/kg) (80% *DoD* per 30s) | 300 | 400 |
| Specific power (W/kg), Regen. (20% *DoD* per 10s) | 150 | 200 |
| Recharge time, h (20% → 100% *SoC*) | 4–6 | 3–6 |
| Cost, US $/kWh | 150 | 100 |

**TABLE 5.7**
**USABC Goals for HEV Advanced Energy Storage Systems**

| Parameter | Power Assist (Minimum) | Power Assist (Maximum) |
|---|---|---|
| Pulse discharge power, 10 s (kW) | 25 | 40 |
| Peak regenerative pulse power, 10 s (kW) | 20 | 35 |
| Total available energy (kWh) | 0.3 at C/1 rate | 0.5 at C/1 rate |
| Maximum weight (kg) | 40 | 60 |
| Maximum volume (L) | 32 | 45 |
| Cost, @1000,000 units/year (US $) | 500 | 800 |

**TABLE 5.8**
**USABC Goals for PHEV Energy Storage Systems**

| Parameter | PHEV-10 | PHEV-40 |
|---|---|---|
| Pulse discharge power, 10 s (kW) | 45 | 38 |
| Peak regenerative pulse power, 10 s (kW) | 30 | 25 |
| Available energy for charge depleting mode (kWh) | 3.4 | 11.6 |
| Available energy for charge sustaining mode (kWh) | 0.3 | 0.5 |
| Charge depleting life/discharge throughput (cycles/MWh) | 5,000/17 | 5,000/58 |
| Charge sustaining life cycle (cycles) | 300,000 | 300,000 |
| Maximum weight (kg) | 60 | 120 |
| Maximum volume (L) | 40 | 80 |
| Cost, @100,000 units/year (US $) | 1,700 | 3,400 |

The USABC has also set goals for hybrid electric vehicles at two levels of power-assist, one at the 25 kW level and the other for the 40 kW level. A subset of the goals set by USABC for power-assist hybrid electric vehicle energy storage system is listed in Table 5.7. The calendar life for these batteries is targeted for 15 years, while cycle life has been set for 300,000 cycles for specified SoC increments. The roundtrip energy efficiency has been set to 90% for both 25 and 40 kW power-assist hybrid electric vehicles.

The USABC has also specified goals for two main PHEV battery types: a high power/energy ratio battery providing 10 miles of all-electric range (PHEV-10) and a low power/energy ratio battery providing 40 miles of all-electric range (PHEV-40). PHEV-10 goals are set for a 'crossover utility vehicle' weighing 1,950 kg and the PHEV-40 goals are set for a midsize sedan weighing 1,600 kg. Few of these important goals set for PHEV development are listed in Table 5.8. The calendar life for these batteries is also targeted for 15 years, and roundtrip energy efficiency has been set to 90% for both PHEV-10 and PHEV-40. All the specified goals for energy storage systems for electric and hybrid electric vehicles are listed in the USABC website under USCAR at www.uscar.org.

## 5.7 BATTERY PACK MANAGEMENT

Batteries can be configured in series or in parallel or in a combination thereof. The battery pack, i.e., the energy storage device in an electric and hybrid vehicle, consists of a number of individual electrochemical cells connected in a series string to deliver the required voltage. Strings of series connected cells can be connected in parallel to increase the capacity of the storage system. The battery pack also includes electronics, which is typically located outside the battery pack. The electronic circuit of a battery pack controls charging, discharging and balanced utilization of the battery cells.

The electronic circuit along with its controller hardware and software algorithms is responsible for managing the battery pack and protecting the cells within the pack. The primary function of the battery management system is to protect the cells from operating outside the safe region. This ensures longer life of the battery and minimizes replacement costs.

The battery pack management techniques are general and suitable for any energy storage-based system, such as electric and hybrid vehicles, distributed power generation units and portable consumer electronics. Of all the applications, the most rigorous usage of energy storage systems is in hybrid vehicles where it goes through pulsed charge/discharge cycles. Hence, battery pack management is required to be of the most advanced type. The essentials of battery management systems, SoC measurement techniques, cell balancing methods and battery charging methods are covered in the Sections 5.7.1–5.7.4.

The battery management systems and methods of cell balancing presented are equally applicable to an ultracapacitor bank replicating an energy storage device. The ultracapacitor cells are also electrochemical cells, which are connected in a series string to form the energy storage system to supply power at the desired voltage level.

## 5.7.1 Battery Management System

The battery management system (BMS) consists of a set of algorithms based on voltage, current and temperature measurements to calculate essential battery parameters and determine charge/discharge power limits at a given time. Depending on the level of sophistication in the BMS, measurements can be from individual cells or group of cells or from the entire pack. The BMS is also responsible for generating command signals for cell equalization circuits if used in a battery pack. BMS ensures reliability and protection against overcharge, overdischarge, short circuits and thermal abuse. The BMS for an energy storage system are designed to have all or some of the following features:

- State of charge (SoC) estimation
- State of health (SoH) monitoring for cell and pack protection
- Temperature control
- Charge/discharge power control
- Cell equalization
- Data logging.

The measurements, parameter estimations and outputs generated in a BMS are shown in Figure 5.26 [20]. The BMS initializes once the system is powered, which happens when with key on in a hybrid electric vehicle. The only function during initialization is to record the self-discharge during the system off period. If the self-discharge is excessive, then it is reported to the SoH monitoring algorithm. The other parameters for battery management are estimated during each measurement cycle while the pack is on.

SoC provides information on the available capacity of a battery. This is necessary not only for the protection of the battery pack, but also for vehicle powertrain controls. The SoC should also be maintained within a certain band to enhance the life of the battery. In sophisticated management

**FIGURE 5.26**  Parameter estimations and pack management in a BMS.

systems, SoC of individual cells or group of cells in a pack are determined to verify the uniform distribution of SoC among the cells. The SoC is typically expressed as a percentage of the rated capacity instead of the maximum available capacity which could be less due to aging and environmental effects. However, the SoC could also be calculated based on the maximum available capacity. This SoC calculation can be used for cell equalization, since all cells in the series-string generally experience the same environment.

SoH is the working condition of the pack and measures the pack's ability to deliver power compared to a new pack. The fading of a cell capacity and power compared to other cells in the pack with aging indicates the deteriorating health of the cell. The cell capacity and other parameters are used in an algorithm to estimate the state of health (SoH) of a battery pack. The SoH information is useful for battery safety and for delivering power up to its maximum capability. The SoH estimation algorithms are based on comparing measured and estimated cell parameters with references or neighboring cells. The voltages and SoC anomalies of one cell compared to the nearby cells is indicative of poor health of that cell. Similarly, excessive self-discharge of the pack raises a flag, and is compared with preset limits to estimate the pack SoH. The SoH information can be used to replace damaged cells in a pack instead of replacing the entire pack.

The temperature is the primary environmental factor that affects the SoC of an energy storage system. Imbalances in temperature among the various cells in a pack will result in imbalances in the SoC. Additionally, temperature affects the self-discharge rates. The thermal management in a pack is part of the cooling system design for the pack, but the temperature information of the cells should be effectively utilized for protection and health monitoring of the cells.

The maximum power available from the battery at a given time is calculated in the BMS based on the SoC and terminal voltages ensuring that operating voltage, current, SoC and other design limits are not violated. The BMS sets the power limits during charging and discharging for battery protection. Batteries could get severely damaged due to inappropriate charging. The limits are reported to the supervisory controller for powertrain controls in electric and hybrid vehicles.

There are three levels of management systems: pack level management, modular-pack level management and cell level management. Pack level management is the most basic one where overall pack voltage and SoC is monitored, whereas the most complete cell equalization and balancing is possible when individual cell parameters of voltage, current and temperature are monitored. The charging and discharging power managements at the pack level leaves individual cells vulnerable to damage. In modular-pack level management, groups of cells are treated as a module for cell balancing and equalization; the BMS algorithms depend on group voltage, current and temperature measurements rather than pack or individual cell measurements. For packs employing cell equalizer circuits, the BMS generates command signals for cell voltage equalization based on its measurements and estimations. The circuits act on these signals to balance the cells or groups of cells.

Data logging is another important function of the energy storage management system. The data for voltage, current, temperature, SoC, and number of charge-discharge cycles could be stored as a function of time for SoH monitoring, diagnostics and fault analysis.

### 5.7.2 SoC Measurement

The SoC of the energy storage system is calculated using measurements of a physical parameter that varies with the SoC. The SoC varies with voltage, charge/discharge rate, self-discharge rate, temperature and aging. Depending on the parameters monitored, the SoC calculation can be either a voltage-based method or a current-based method. The more accurate SoC calculations use both voltage and current measurements in an observer-based method.

The voltage-based SoC measurement is applicable to cell chemistries where the voltages are directly related to the SoC. The relation between open-circuit voltage and SoC must be known a priori for a good estimation of the SoC. The voltage-based measurement is not at all suitable for lithium-ion cells, since the voltage for these cells is fairly steady over most of the charge-discharge cycle.

**FIGURE 5.27** Battery *SoC* measurement.

In current-based estimation, the SoC is obtained from the integration of current using the fundamental definition of charge $q = \int_0^t i(t)\,dt$. A simple SoC measurement diagram is shown in Figure 5.26. The charge and discharge currents out of and in to the storage device are measured directly using a current sensor. The integration of measured current gives the SoD when the initial condition is the fully charged condition of the battery. Knowing the initial capacity $C_p$ of the battery, SoC is calculated from

$$SoC(t) = C_P - SoD(t)$$

The method is also known as Coulomb counting. The method tends to accumulate errors if it is solely based on current information. A method of improving the SoC estimation is to incorporate the directly measurable parameters (voltage and current) into a mathematical model of the storage system to implement an observer-based SoC estimation method. This is a closed loop Coulomb counting method as opposed to the open-loop method of Figure 5.27. The closed loop method is based on feedbacks that can be empirically designed or generated using Kalman filters [20].

### 5.7.3 Battery Cell Balancing

The individual cells in the connected string of the battery pack are the unit battery cells. The available energy stored in a battery is cell is $E_{avail} = qV$, which states that both charge and voltage need to be balanced in a series string to maximize the output of a pack. When a series-string of electrochemical cells is charged as a pack, slight parameter mismatches in individual cells and temperature differences result in charge and voltage imbalances. The imbalances adversely affect the vehicle performance by reducing the throughput of the battery pack.

The chemical reactions in an electrochemical cell depend on the temperature and pressure. The temperature differences among the cells change the self-discharge rates causing imbalances in the charge of the cells. A low cell temperature reduces chemical activity which increases the cell's internal impedance. The increased internal resistance reduces the terminal voltage, and thus, the cell capacity. In addition, manufacturing differences and different aging characteristics result in parameter mismatches among individual cells, which cause voltage and capacity imbalances [21,22].

The charge imbalance also shows up as voltage differences. The imbalances tend to grow as the pack goes through repeated charge/discharge cycles. The weaker cells tend to charge slower and the stronger cells charge faster. The process shortens the pack life and reduces its utilization. The number of charge-discharge cycles affects some battery chemistry more than the others. For example, Li-ion batteries are highly sensitive to overvoltages and undervoltages. Li-ion batteries are recommended to limit the charge-discharge rates to no more than 2C, and also to keep the cells charged to at least 40% SoC to minimize aging.

The maximum throughput of the pack can be ensured by balancing the voltage and charge of individual cells. The cell balancing methods utilize electronic circuits and control to even out the voltages and SoC of a series string of electrochemical cells. The simplest strategy adopted for charging a series-string of cells is to monitor the cell voltages and discontinue charging when one of the cells (strongest cell) reaches the voltage limit for individual cells. Extended charging is another option where charging is continued even after the strongest cell has reached its capacity to bring the weaker cells up to capacity. When charging continues to bring the weaker cells to the maximum voltage, overvoltage results in the stronger cells. Overcharging is not at all an option with certain battery chemistry, while in others the process vents hydrogen gas (known as *gassing*) and removes water from the overcharged cells. Increased gassing in the cell at elevated temperatures shortens the cell life.

The overcharging in the stronger cells can be avoided if there is a path to shunt the charging currents once they reach the voltage limit. Similarly, the simplest protection during discharging of a pack is to shut down when the first cell reaches the minimum voltage limit. This cell is consequently the weakest cell in the series-string and is limiting the capacity of the pack. If discharging is continued to extract energy from the stronger cells, then the weaker cell voltage will fall below the minimum voltage level possibly causing damage to the cells.

The simple cell balancing strategies result in underutilization of the battery pack. Improved cell balancing circuits provide a path to bypass the weaker cells once they reach the minimum voltage provided the pack voltage level is still above the minimum voltage level of the system. Power electronic converter circuits are used to divert charging currents to boost the weaker cells or deplete charge from stronger cells for cell voltage equalization. The circuit topologies for cell balancing are presented in Chapter 9 after the power electronic devices and concepts are introduced.

### 5.7.4 BATTERY CHARGING

The charging of secondary batteries is accomplished in several phases using different charging currents. The phases are structured based on the battery chemistry to minimize the damage on the cells. The initial charging phase is the *bulk charging phase* when the cells are charged with the maximum current to replenish most of the charge lost during discharge. The last few percentages of SoC are replenished with the *absorption charging phase*. The charging current in this phase is kept low to prevent any damage to the cells. An *equalization phase* can also be used to fully charge and balance all the cells in the battery pack. The *float charge phase* starts once the battery is fully charged to compensate for energy lost over time due to self-discharge. Microprocessor controllers are used to set the charging profile based on an algorithm to tune the charging for a particular type of battery chemistry.

The battery charging circuits can apply either a constant current or a constant voltage or any combination of the two to design the charge profile. In the constant current charging method, known as I-charging, a current regulator in the battery charger maintains the set current level. The charging current levels are adjusted by the current regulator for the different phases of charging. The charging current can also be applied in the form of pulses by pulse-width modulation (PWM) control of the output voltage. The charging rate is controlled by adjusting the pulse width. The short durations between the pulses allows the chemical reactions within the cells to stabilize. Excessive chemical reactions that could lead to gassing are avoided by using pulse charging. An example multi-step charging profile with I-charging and PWM control is shown in Figure 5.28 [23].

For constant voltage charging, a voltage greater than the battery upper limit voltage is applied by the charger for bulk charging. A constant voltage charge is also usually applied during the absorption charging phase. During the float charging phase, the charger applies a DC voltage slightly lower than the battery upper limit voltage across the battery. A slight drop in the battery voltage results in charge being replenished in the battery. This form of charging is also known as trickle charging used to compensate for self-discharge in the cells.

**FIGURE 5.28**   Multi-step I-charging with PWM control.

## PROBLEMS

### 5.1

Estimate the weight of a 12 V, 100 Ah lead acid battery. Do this by calculating the reactant masses participating in the overall chemical reaction. Also, assume that the mass of $H_2O$ in the electrolyte is twice the mass of $H_2SO_4$. Neglect battery casing mass, electrode grid mass, separator mass and current bus mass. (Note that $n = 2$ for Pb and $PbO_2$ and $n = 1$ for $H_2SO_4$.)

### 5.2

In the nickel-cadmium cell, nickel oxyhydroxide, NiOOH is the active material in the charged positive plate. During discharge it reduces to the lower valence state, nickel hydroxide $Ni(OH)_2$, by accepting electrons from the external circuit:

$$2NiOOH + 2H_2O + 2e^- \underset{\text{charge}}{\overset{\text{Discharge}}{\rightleftarrows}} 2Ni(OH)_2 + 2OH^- \text{ (0.49 V)}$$

Cadmium metal is the active material in the charged negative plate. During discharge, it oxidizes to cadmium hydroxide, $Cd(OH)_2$, and releases electrons to the external circuit:

$$Cd + 2OH^- \underset{\text{charge}}{\overset{\text{Discharge}}{\rightleftarrows}} Cd(OH)_2 + 2e^- \text{ (0.809 V)}$$

The net reaction occurring in the potassium hydroxide (KOH) electrolyte is:

$$Cd + 2NiOOH + 2H_2O \underset{\text{charge}}{\overset{\text{Discharge}}{\rightleftarrows}} 2Ni(OH)_2 + Cd(OH)_2^- \text{ (1.299 V)}$$

Estimate the weight of an 11.7 V, 100 Ah Ni-Cd battery. Neglect the mass KOH component of the electrolyte.

### 5.3

A 12 V battery is connected to a series RL load as shown in Figure P5.3. The battery has a rated capacity of 80 Ah. At $t = 0$, the switch is closed and the battery begins to discharge.

**FIGURE P5.3**

   a. Calculate and plot the battery discharge current, $i(t)$, if the steady-state discharge rate is C/2. Neglect battery voltage drop.
   b. Calculate and plot $SoD(t)$ in Ah for $0 < t < 2$ h.
   c. Calculate and plot $SoC(t)$ assuming that at $t = 0$ the battery is charged to rated capacity. Assume also that the rated capacity is the practical capacity.
   d. Calculate the time corresponding to 80% DoD.

## 5.4

Given below are constant power discharge characteristics of a 12 V lead acid battery:

| SP (W/kg) | SE (Wh/kg) |
|-----------|------------|
| 10 | 67.5 |
| 110 | 8 |

   The battery characteristics are to be expressed in terms of Peukert's equation, which has the following form:

$$(SP)^n(SE) = \lambda \ (n \text{ and } \lambda \text{ are curve fitting constants})$$

   a. Derive the constants $n$ and $\lambda$, assuming a linear relationship between $\log(SP)$ and $\log(SE)$.
   b. Find the capacity $Q_T$ of the battery if the theoretical energy density is $SE_T = 67.5$ Wh/kg, given that battery mass of 15 kg.

## 5.5

An EV battery pack consists of four parallel sets of six series connected 12 V, 100 Ah lead acid batteries. One steady-state motoring (discharge) cycle of battery current is shown in Figure P5.5a. The steady-state regenerative braking (charge) cycle of battery is shown in Figure P5.5b.

(a)

(b)

**FIGURE P5.5**

   a. Suppose no regenerative braking is employed. How much time does it take to reach 80% DoD?
   b. If regenerative braking is employed such that for every 50 motoring cycles there is 1 regenerative braking cycle, how much time does it take to reach 80% DoD?

(Note: In this problem, neglect variation of capacity with discharge rate. Assume that the practical capacity is equal to the rated capacity.)

## 5.6

Given a lead acid battery having the following empirical characteristics:

$$(SP)^{0.9}(SE) = 216E4$$

where $SP$ = specific power and $SE$ = specific energy. The EV parameters are as follows:
$m = 700\,\text{kg}$, $M_B = 150\,\text{kg}$, $C_D = 0.2$, $A_F = 2\,\text{m}^2$, $C_0 = 0.009$, $C_1 = 0$.

Also, take $\rho = 1.16\,\text{kg/m}^3$ and $g = 9.81\,\text{m/s}^2$.

a. Derive and plot $F_{TR}(t)$ versus $t$. (Assume level road.)
b. Derive and plot $P_{TR}(t)$ versus $t$.
c. Calculate the EV range based on SAE J227a schedule B driving cycle using the power density approach of fractional depletion model (FDM). The SAE J227a driving cycle and the current profile of the EV are given in Figures P5.6a and P5.6b. (Assume no regenerative braking.)

(a)

(b)

**FIGURE P5.6**

## REFERENCES

1. D. Linden, Handbook of Batteries, 2nd edition, McGraw-Hills Inc., New York, NY, 1995.
2. C. Mantell, *Batteries and Energy Systems*, McGraw-Hills Inc., New York, NY, 1983.
3. K. Kordesch and G. Simadar, *Fuel Cells and their Applications,* John Wiley & Sons Inc., Chichester, 1996.
4. J. O'M Bockris, *Fuel Cells: Their Electrochemistry*, McGraw-Hills Inc., New York, NY, 1969.
5. J.S. Newman, *Electrochemical Systems*, Prentice Hall, Englewood Cliffs, NJ, 1991.
6. T. Erdey-Gruz, *Kinetics of Electrode Process,* John Wiley & Sons Inc., New York, NY, 1972.
7. L. Xia, *Behavioral Modeling and Analysis of Galvanic Devices*, PhD dissertation, University of Akron, Akron, OH, 2000.
8. A.J. Bard and L.R. Faulkner, *Electrochemical Methods: Fundamentals and Applications*, John Wiley & Sons Inc., New York, NY, 1996.
9. J.R. Elliott and C.T. Lira, *Introductory Chemical Engineering Thermodynamics*, Prentice Hall, Upper Saddle River, NJ, 1999.
10. T. T. Hartley and C. F. Lorenzo, "Insights into the fractional order initial value problem via semi-infinite systems," *Critical Reviews in Biomedical Engineering*, 36(1.20), 1–21, 2008.
11. R.L. Hartman II, *An Aging Model for Lithium-ion Cells*, PhD dissertation, University of Akron, Akron, OH, 2008.
12. T.T. Hartley and A.G. Jannette, "A first principles model for nickel-hydrogen batteries," *3rd International Energy Conversion Engineering Conference*, AIAA (American Institute of Aeronautics and Astronautics), San Francisco, CA, August 2005.

13. M. Chen and G.A. Rincon-Mora, "Accurate electrical battery model capable of predicting runtime and I-V performance," *IEEE Transactions on Energy Conversion*, 21(2), 504–511, June 2006.

14. S. Abu-Sharkh and D. Doerffel, "Rapid test and non-linear model characterization of solid-state lithium-ion batteries," *Journal of Power Sources*, 130, 266–274, 2005.

15. C.M. Shephard, "Design of primary and secondary cells," *Journal of the Electrochemical Society*, 112, 657–664, July 1965.

16. D.A.J. Rand, R. Woods and R.M. Dell, *Batteries for Electric Vehicles*, John Wiley & Sons Inc., New York, NY, 1998.

17. R.M. Dell and D.A.J. Rand, *Understanding Batteries*, Royal Society of Chemistry, London, 2001.

18. M.J. Isaacson, R.P. Hollandsworth, P.J. Giampaoli, F.A. Linkowsky, A. Salim and V.L. Teofilo, "Advanced lithium ion battery charger," *The Fifteenth Annual IEEE Battery Conference on Applications and Advances*, pp. 193–198, Long Beach, CA, January 2000.

19. Online https://media.gm.com/media/us/en/gm/home.html, accessed March 4, 2020.

20. G.L. Plett, "Extended Kalman filtering for battery managements systems of LiPB-based HEV battery packs: Part 1. Background," *Journal of Power Sources*, 134, 252–261, 2005.

21. W.F. Bentley, "Cell balancing considerations for lithium-ion battery systems," *Twelfth Annual IEEE Battery Conference on Applications and Advances*, pp. 223–226, New York, NY, January 1997.

22. R. Manfred Laidig and W. Job Wurst, "Technology implementation of stationary battery failure prediction," *Proceedings of the Ninth Annual IEEE Battery Conference on Applications and Advances*, pp. 168–172, Long Beach, CA, January 1995.

23. N.H. Kutkut and M. Deepak Divan, "Dynamic equalization techniques for series battery stacks," *IEEE Telecommunications Energy Conference*, pp. 514–521, Boston, MA, October 1996.

# 6 Alternative Energy Storage

Alternatives to batteries as the portable energy storage device for electric and hybrid electric vehicles are the fuel cells, ultracapacitors, compressed air tanks and flywheels. Many of these energy storage devices are equally useful for stationary power generation. The alternatives are to be evaluated based on the technological challenges, energy conversion efficiencies and fuel sources. Fuel cell is powered by hydrogen that has to be derived from primary energy sources. Electricity produced by the fuel cell using hydrogen as the fuel propels the electric powertrain of a fuel cell electric vehicle (FCEV). Hydrogen fuel delivery method needs to be in place in addition to the development of FCEVs. One possible infrastructure is to establish hydrogen filling stations where hydrogen will be produced and stored in tanks using electricity supplied through the transmission grid. The alternative to this is to produce hydrogen on-board using the reformer technology.

Ultracapacitor, similar to battery, is another electrochemical device where energy can be stored and used on demand by an electric powertrain. The ultracapacitor technology has advanced tremendously in the recent years, although it is unlikely to achieve specific energy levels high enough to serve as the sole energy storage device of a vehicle. However, ultracapacitors in conjunction with a battery or fuel cell has the possibility of providing an excellent portable energy storage system with sufficient specific energy and specific power for the next-generation vehicles.

Compressed air presents another type of energy storage concept that has been utilized to develop compressed air vehicles. The compressed air vehicles are recently gaining attention since the well-to-wheel efficiencies are comparable to those of FCEVs, but with a much simpler fuel chain. The fuel infrastructure requirement for compressed air vehicle is similar to that of a fuel cell vehicles; electricity from the grid would be used to compress air at local filling stations which would be dispensed to the air tanks of compressed air vehicles.

Flywheel is another storage device where energy is stored in mechanical form as kinetic energy. The energy is stored in a rotating disk and released on demand. Once again, electrical energy is the source for storing energy. Flywheel technology is not yet competitive enough with the alternatives discussed.

Technological challenges have to be overcome for the alternative energy storage devices before they can supply energy to mass produced alternative vehicles; some of the device technologies are well advanced compared to others. For all of the alternative energy storage devices, the energy source is electricity which is secondary in nature and has to be derived from either unsustainable or renewable sources. Again on the end user side, the powertrain is electric for all the alternative vehicles except for the compressed air vehicles.

The alternative energy storage devices and the source of their fuels are covered in this chapter. Principles of operation and modeling of the fuel cell and the ultracapacitor devices are the focus of this chapter; compressed air and flywheels will be covered in brief.

## 6.1 FUEL CELLS

A fuel cell is an electrochemical device that produces electricity by means of a chemical reaction, much like a battery. The major difference between batteries and fuel cells is that the latter can produce electricity as long as fuel is supplied, while batteries produce electricity from stored chemical energy and hence require frequent recharging.

The basic structure of a fuel cell (see Figure 6.1) consists of an anode and a cathode similar to a battery. The fuel that is supplied to the cell is hydrogen and oxygen. The concept of fuel cell is the opposite of electrolysis of water where hydrogen and oxygen are combined to form electricity

**FIGURE 6.1**   Basic fuel cell structure.

and water. The hydrogen fuel supplied to the fuel cell consists of two hydrogen atoms per molecule chemically bonded together in the form $H_2$. This molecule includes two separate nuclei, each containing one proton, while sharing two electrons. The fuel cell breaks apart these hydrogen molecules to produce electricity. The exact nature of accomplishing the task depends on the fuel cell type, although what remains the same for all fuel cells is that this reaction takes place at the anode. The hydrogen molecule breaks into four parts at the anode due to the chemical reaction releasing hydrogen ions and electrons. A catalyst speeds the reaction and an electrolyte allows the two hydrogen ions, which essentially are two single protons, to move to the cathode through the electrolyte placed between the two electrodes. The flow of electrons from the anode to the cathode through the external circuit is what produces electricity. For the overall cell reaction to complete, oxygen or air must be passed over the cathode. The cathode reaction takes place in two stages. First, the bond between the two oxygen atoms in the molecule breaks and then each ionized oxygen atom grabs two electrons coming from the anode through the external circuit to become negatively charged. The negatively charged oxygen atoms are balanced by the positively charged hydrogen atoms at the cathode and the combination produces $H_2O$ commonly known as water. The chemical reaction taking place in a fuel cell is

$$\text{Anode: } H_2 \rightarrow 2H^+ + 2e^-$$

$$\text{Cathode: } 2e^- + 2H^+ + \frac{1}{2}(O_2) \rightarrow H_2O$$

$$\text{Cell: } H_2 + \frac{1}{2}O_2 \rightarrow H_2O$$

The first rudimentary version of a fuel cell was built by Sir William Robert Grove in 1846. Fuel cell found its first application in space when NASA developed the device for an alternative power source. The source was first used in a moon buggy and is still used in NASA's space shuttles. There has been a tremendous interest on fuel cells in recent years for applications in other areas, such as electric vehicles and stationary power systems. The research sponsored by several U.S. research agencies and corporations has attempted to improve cell performance with two primary goals: the desire for higher power cells, which can be achieved through higher rates of reaction, and the desire for fuel cells that can internally reform hydrocarbons and are more tolerant of contaminants in the reactant streams. For this reason, the searches have concentrated in finding new materials for electrodes and electrolytes. There are several different types of fuel cells having their own strengths and weaknesses. Low operating temperature is desirable for the vehicle applications, despite the fact that higher temperatures result in higher reaction rates. Rapid operation and cogeneration capabilities are desirable for the stationary applications. Cogeneration refers to the capability of utilizing the waste heat of a fuel cell to generate electricity using conventional means.

### 6.1.1   FUEL CELL CHARACTERISTICS

Theoretically, fuel cells operate isothermally meaning that all free energy in a fuel cell chemical reaction should convert into electrical energy. The hydrogen 'fuel' in the fuel cell does not burn as in the internal combustion engines bypassing the thermal to mechanical conversion. Also, since the operation is isothermal, the efficiency of such direct electrochemical converters is not subject to the limitation of Carnot cycle efficiency imposed on heat engines. The fuel cell converts the Gibbs free energy of a chemical reaction into electrical energy in the form of electrons under isothermal conditions. The maximum electrical energy for a fuel cell operating at constant temperature and pressure is given by the change in Gibbs free energy

$$W_{el} = -\Delta G = nFE \tag{6.1}$$

where $n$=number of electrons produced by the anode reaction and $F$=Faraday's constant=96,485 C/mol and $E$ is the reversible potential. The Gibbs free energy change for the reaction $H_2(g) + (1/2)O_2(g) \rightarrow H_2O(l)$ at standard condition of 1 atmospheric pressure and 25°C is −236 kJ/mol or −118 MJ/kg. With $n$=2, the maximum reversible potential under the same conditions is $E_0 = 1.23\,V$, using (6.1). The maximum reversible potential under actual operating conditions for the hydrogen-oxygen fuel cell is given by the Nernst equation as follows [1]:

$$E = E_0 + \left(\frac{RT}{nF}\right)\ln\left[\frac{C_H \cdot C_O^{1/2}}{C_{H_2O}}\right] \tag{6.2}$$

where $T$ is the temperature in Kelvin, $R$ is the specific gas constant, and $C_H$, $C_O$ and $C_{H_2O}$ are the concentrations or pressures of the reactants and products.

The voltage-current output characteristic of a hydrogen/oxygen cell is illustrated in Figure 6.2. The higher potentials around 1 V per cell are theoretical predictions that are not achievable in a practical cell. The linear region where the reduction in cell potential is due to ohmic losses is where a practical fuel cell operates. The resistive components in the cell limit the practical achievable efficiency of a fuel cell. The working voltage of the cell falls with an increasing current drain, a knowledge that is very important in designing fuel cell-powered electric and hybrid vehicles. Since the cell potential is small, several cells are stacked in series to achieve the desired voltage. The major advantage of fuel cells is the lower sensitivity to scaling, which means that fuel cells have very similar overall system efficiencies from those in the kW range to those in the MW range.

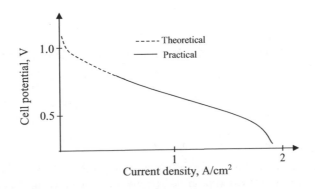

**FIGURE 6.2**   Voltage-current relationship of a hydrogen/oxygen cell.

### 6.1.2  FUEL CELL TYPES

The six major types of fuel cells are the alkaline, proton exchange membrane (PEM), direct methanol, phosphoric acid, molten carbonate and solid oxide fuel cells. A short description of the relevant characteristics of each type in the context of vehicular and stationary applications is given below [2,3].

#### 6.1.2.1  Alkaline Fuel Cell

In an alkaline fuel cell (AFC), an aqueous solution of potassium hydroxide (KOH) is used as the electrolyte. Compared to some other fuel cells where acidic electrolytes are used, the performance of the alkaline electrolyte is as good as the acid electrolytes, while being significantly less corrosive toward the electrodes. AFCs have been in actual use for a long-time delivering electrical efficiencies of up to 60%. They require pure hydrogen as fuel, and operate at low temperatures (at 80°C), and is therefore, suitable for vehicle applications. Residual heat can be used for heating, but the cell temperature is not sufficiently high to generate steam that can be used for cogeneration.

#### 6.1.2.2  Proton Exchange Membrane Fuel Cell

The PEM fuel cell uses solid electrolytes and operate at low temperatures (around 80°C). Nafion is an example of solid polymer electrolyte. These fuel cells are also known as solid polymer membrane fuel cells. The electrical efficiency of PEM fuels cells is lower than that of the alkaline cells (about 40%). However, the rugged and simple construction makes these types of fuel cells highly suitable for vehicle applications. The PEM fuel cell and the AFC are the two types that are currently being considered for vehicle applications. The advantage of PEM cells is that they can tolerate impurity in the fuel as compared to pure hydrogen needed in AFCs.

#### 6.1.2.3  Direct Methanol Fuel Cell

The direct methanol fuel cell (DMFC) is a result of the research on using methanol as the fuel that can be carried on-board a vehicle and reformed to supply hydrogen to the fuel cell. A DMFC works on the same principle as the PEM except that the temperature is increased to the range of 90°C–120°C such that internal reformation of methanol into hydrogen is possible. The electrical efficiency of DMFC is quite low at about 30%. This type of fuel cell is still in the design stages, since the search for a good electro-catalyst both to reform the methanol efficiently and to reduce oxygen in the presence of methanol is ongoing.

#### 6.1.2.4  Phosphoric Acid Fuel Cell

Phosphoric acid fuel cell (PAFC) is the oldest type whose origin extends back to the creation of the fuel cell concept. The electrolyte used is phosphoric acid and the cell operating temperature is about 200°C, which makes some cogeneration possible. The electrical efficiency of this cell is reasonable at about 40%. These types of fuel cells are considered too bulky for transportation applications, while higher efficiency designs exist for stationary applications.

#### 6.1.2.5  Molten Carbonate Fuel Cell

Molten carbonate fuel cell (MCFC), originally developed to operate directly from coal, operate at 600°C and require CO or $CO_2$ on the cathode side and hydrogen on the anode. The cells use carbonate as the electrolyte. The electrical efficiency of these fuel cells is high at about 50%, but the excess heat can be used for cogeneration for improved efficiency. The high temperatures required makes these fuel cells not particularly suitable for vehicular applications, but can be used for stationary power generation.

#### 6.1.2.6  Solid Oxide Fuel Cell

A solid oxide fuel cell (SOFC) uses a solid ionic conductor as the electrolyte rather than a solution or a polymer, which reduces corrosion problems. However, to achieve adequate ionic conductivity in such a ceramic, the system must operate at very high temperatures. The original designs, using yttria-stabilized zirconia as the electrolyte required temperatures as high as 1,000°C to operate, but the search for materials capable of serving as the electrolyte at lower temperatures resulted in the 'intermediate temperature solid oxide fuel cell'. This fuel cell also has high electrical efficiency of 50%–60%, and residual heat can also be used for cogeneration. Although not a good choice for vehicle applications, it is at present the best option for stationary power generation.

The several fuel cell features described above are summarized in Table 6.1. The usable energy and relative cost of various fuels used in fuel cells are listed in Table 6.2. The selection of fuel cells as the primary energy source in electric and hybrid vehicles depends on a number of issues ranging from fuel cell technology itself to infrastructure to support the system. Based on the discussion in this section, the choice of fuel cell for the vehicular application is an alkaline or proton exchange design, while for stationary applications it will be the solid oxide fuel cell. The size, cost, efficiency and start-up transient times of fuel cells are yet to be at an acceptable stage for electric and hybrid vehicles applications. The complexity of the controller required for fuel cell operation is another aspect that needs further attention. Although its viability has been well-proven in the space program, as well as in prototype vehicles, the immature status make it a longer-term enabling technology for electric and hybrid vehicles.

**TABLE 6.1**
**Fuel Cell Types**

| Fuel Cell Variety | Fuel | Electrolyte | Operating Temperature | Efficiency | Applications |
|---|---|---|---|---|---|
| Phosphoric acid | $H_2$, reformate (LNG, methanol) | Phosphoric acid | ~200°C | 40%–50% | Stationary (>250 kW) |
| Alkaline | $H_2$ | Potassium hydroxide solution | ~80°C | 40%–50% | Mobile |
| Proton exchange membrane | $H_2$, reformate (LNG, methanol) | Polymer ion exchange film | ~80°C | 40%–50% | EV/HEV, industrial up to ~80 kW |
| Direct methanol | Methanol, ethanol | Solid polymer | 90°C–100°C | ~30% | EV/HEVs, small portable devices (1 W–70 kW) |
| Molten carbonate | $H_2$, CO (coal gas, LNG, methanol) | Carbonate | 600°C–700°C | 50%–60% | Stationary (>250 kW) |
| Solid oxide | $H_2$, CO (coal gas, LNG, methanol) | Yttria-stabilized zirconia | ~1,000°C | 50%–65% | Stationary |

**TABLE 6.2**
**Usable Energy and Cost of Fuels**

| Fuel | Usable Energy, MJ/kg | Relative Cost/MJ |
|---|---|---|
| Hydrogen: | | |
| 95% pure at plant | 118.3 | 1.0 |
| 99% pure in cylinders | 120 | 7.4 |
| LPG (propane) | 47.4 | 0.5 |
| Gasoline | 46.1 | 0.8 |
| Methanol | 21.8 | 3.3 |
| Ammonia | 20.9 | 3.6 |

**FIGURE 6.3**   Fuel cell model based on the fundamental principles of electrochemistry.

## 6.1.3   Fuel Cell Model

A fuel cell is an electrochemical device similar to that of a battery where all the physical processes are essentially the same. The only difference between a fuel cell and battery is that the energy source in the former is external, whereas it is internally stored in a battery. A lumped parameter model for fuel cell has been developed by Lei Xia using the fundamentals of electrochemistry [4]. The structure of the fuel cell model is shown in Figure 6.3.

The parameters of the model are

Fuel concentration: $C_0 = 10$
Diffusion process parameters: $R_{TL} = 0.001\,\Omega$, $C_{TL} = 200\,\text{F}$
Open-circuit voltage (Nernst equation): $E = 1.4 + 0.052(2p_0)\ln C_d$ ($p_0$ is the normalized fuel flow rate)
Charge transfer polarization (Tafel equation): $E_{ct} = 0.1 + 0.26\ln(i_f)$
Ohmic resistance: $R_\Omega = 0.002\,\Omega$
Double-layer capacitor: $C_{dbl} = 3000\,\text{F}$
Concentration polarization: $E_c = 0.06\ln\left[1 - \dfrac{i}{100}\right]$

The given parameters are for a single cell. Several cells are stacked in series to make a fuel cell device for an application. The model is useful for predicting the output $i$-$v$ characteristics for a given flow rate.

The major difference between the lumped parameter models of the fuel cell and the battery is the representation of the diffusion process parameters. The diffusion process in a fuel cell is entirely different from that of a battery. In a battery, the electrolyte not only provides the medium for mass transport of ions, but also stores the energy. Therefore, the relative volume or physical size of the electrolyte needs to be relatively large in a battery. This difference in the amount of electrolyte used in a battery can be attributed to its much faster response characteristics compared to that of a fuel cell. In a fuel cell, the electrolyte functions only as the current conduction medium through the diffusion process. The electrolyte layer in a fuel is designed to be fairly thin, and just enough to provide the electrical insulation between the electrodes. The different nature of diffusion process in a fuel cell is represented in the model with an $RC$-network primarily to represent the transient response. The function for the concentration polarization is also represented differently in the fuel cell model; it is modeled as a function of the discharge current.

## 6.1.4   Hydrogen Storage Systems

The options for storage of hydrogen play a critical role in the future development of infrastructure for fuel cell-powered electric and hybrid vehicles. The hydrogen gas at atmospheric pressure has a fairly low energy density and is not a suitable fuel for storage. Hydrogen could be stored as compressed or liquefied gas, or in more advanced manner by using metal hydrides or carbon nanotubes. Gas storage in compressed form is an option that has been in use for a long time. In this method, a large amount of energy is required to compress the gas to a level that will make storage viable, usually at a pressure of several hundred atmospheres [5]. Generation of liquid $H_2$ requires further compression along with refrigeration to cryogenic temperatures, and is not likely to become a viable means of storage for vehicle applications.

Advanced methods for $H_2$ storage include the use of metal hydrides or carbon nanotubes. Here, the gas is compressed to a lower pressure level (a few to a few tens of atmospheres) and fed into a container filled with a material that can absorb and release $H_2$ as a function of the pressure, temperature and amount of stored hydrogen in the system. The use of metal hydrides reduces the volumetric and pressure requirements for storage, since when fully loaded these metal hydrides can actually contain twice as many hydrogen atoms than an equivalent volume of liquid hydrogen. The sole problem is that it is much heavier than the other solutions. However, current efforts are underway by several automakers to include this in the structure of the vehicle, which may result in an overall acceptable vehicle weight. The prospect of using carbon nanotube-based materials for hydrogen storage is highly exciting, since it could eliminate most of the weight penalty. However, it should be noted that the properties of carbon nanotubes regarding their usefulness as $H_2$ storage materials is still highly controversial.

One of the myths that must be overcome to popularize fuel cell EVs is the safety of carrying pressurized hydrogen on-board. The safety of hydrogen handling has been explored by both commercial entities as well as public institution, such as Air Products and Chemicals, Inc. [6] and Sandia National Laboratories [7]. The recommendations for its safe handling have been issued [6]. In addition, the Ford report suggests that with proper engineering, the safety of a hydrogen vehicle could be better than that of a propane or gasoline vehicle [5].

## 6.1.5 REFORMERS

Many automotive industries have been exploring the use of methanol, ethanol or gasoline as a fuel and reforming it on-board into hydrogen for the fuel cell. The reformer is the fuel processor that breaks down a hydrocarbon, such as methanol, into hydrogen and other byproducts. The advantage of the approach is the ease of handling of hydrocarbon fuel compared to that of hydrogen gas, substantiated by the difficulty in storage and generation of pure hydrogen.

The accepted methods of reforming technique for vehicular fuel cells are steam reforming, partial oxidation and auto-thermal processing. The two types of steam reformers available use methanol and natural gas as the fuel. Gasoline can also be used as the fuel, but reforming it is an expensive and complex process. Methanol is the most promising fuel for reformers, since it reforms fairly easily into hydrogen and is liquid at room temperature. A brief description of how a methanol steam reformer works is given in the following.

The first step in a methanol ($CH_3OH$) steam reformer is to combine the methanol with water. This methanol–water mixture is then heated to about 250°C–300°C and reacted with a catalyst at low pressure. Platinum is the most widely used catalyst in reformers, but other metals such as zinc and copper can also be used. The chemical reactions taking place in the methanol steam reformer are

$$CH_3OH \rightarrow CO + 2H_2$$

$$2H_2O \text{ (gas)} \rightarrow 2H_2 + O_2$$

$$H_2 + O_2 + CO \rightarrow CO_2 + H_2O$$

The catalyst first splits the methanol into its two constituents, carbon monoxide and hydrogen gas. The heat generated splits the water into hydrogen and oxygen. The leftover oxygen from the decomposition of water combines with the pollutant carbon monoxide to produce another greenhouse gas carbon dioxide. Therefore, the major pollutant released as exhaust from the methanol steam reformer is $CO_2$, although the concentration is minimal compared to the exhaust of internal combustion engines.

The argument used for using reformers is that the infrastructure for the production and distribution of such fuel is already in place, although widespread conversion to methanol systems is not straightforward for methanol fuels due to its high corrosivity [3]. While hydrogen gas would lead to true zero emission vehicles, it should be noted that reforming hydrocarbon fuels, including methanol and other possible biomass fuels, only shifts the source of emissions to the reformer plant. Other factors to consider are safety of methanol versus hydrogen handling, including the fact that methanol is violently toxic, whereas hydrogen is innocuous. The methanol vapors tend to accumulate in enclosed spaces like those of gasoline leading to the formation of potentially explosive mixtures, whereas hydrogen will easily escape even from poorly ventilated areas. The overall efficiency from the well to the wheel of methanol-based transportation will be comparable or even lower than that can be achieved today from gasoline-based internal combustion engine vehicles.

### 6.1.6   Fuel Cell Electric Vehicle

An FCEV consists of a fuel storage system that is likely to include a fuel processor to reform raw fuel to hydrogen, fuel cell stack and its control unit, power processing unit and its controller, and the propulsion unit consisting of the electric machine and drivetrain. The fuel cell has current source-type characteristics and the output voltage of a cell is low. Several fuel cells have to be stacked in series to obtain a higher voltage level, and then the output voltage needs to be boosted-up in order to interface with the DC/AC inverter driving an AC propulsion motor, assuming that an AC motor is used for higher power density. The block diagram of an FCEV system is shown in Figure 6.4. Fuel cell output voltage is relatively low; a DC/DC converter is used to boost and regulate the voltage before being fed to the electric motor drive. The power electronic interface circuit between the fuel cell and electric motor includes the DC/DC converter for voltage boost, DC/AC inverter to supply an AC motor, microprocessor/digital signal processor for controls and battery/capacitors for energy storage. The time constant of the fuel cell stack is much slower than that of the electrical load dynamics. A battery storage system is necessary to supply the power during transient and overload conditions and also to absorb the reverse flow of energy due to regenerative braking. A high-voltage battery-pack can interface directly with the high-voltage DC link as shown in Figure 6.4; this requires a large number of series cells for the battery-pack. Alternatively, a bi-directional DC/DC converter link can interface a lower voltage battery-pack and the high-voltage DC bus. The fuel cell electric output feeds into the lower voltage DC bus which is also maintained by the battery-pack. An FCEV architecture with a lower-voltage battery-pack is shown in Figure 6.5. The architecture is close to that used in Toyota Mirai FCEV and the component ratings are similar to Mirai as well [8]. The battery-pack in an FCEV. Powertrain can be replaced by ultracapacitors.

Fuel cell performance is sensitive to the load variations, because of the low voltage and high current output characteristics. The fuel cell controller using voltage and current feedback information regulates the flow of hydrogen into the fuel cell stack to achieve a reaction rate that delivers the required electrical power with minimum excess hydrogen vented. Attempts to draw more power out

**FIGURE 6.4**   Fuel cell-based electric vehicle architecture.

**FIGURE 6.5**  FCEV with architecture and component ratings similar to Toyota Mirai.

of the fuel cell without changing the flow rate depletes the concentration of hydrogen, which reduces the output voltage and may lead to damage to the fuel cell membrane [9]. The fuel cell characteristic curves as a function of flow rate are shown in Figure 6.6. When the hydrogen utilization rate approaches 100%, the cell goes into the current limit mode when it is dominated by high internal losses. The fuel cell controller must avoid operation in the current limit regime in order to maintain a decent efficiency of operation. The output power deliverability of the fuel cell stack reduces with reduced flow rate of hydrogen, but if lower power is required for traction then operating the fuel cell at reduced flow rate minimizes wasted fuel. The ideal controller delivers fuel to the cell at exactly the same rate at which it is consumed by the cell to generate the electricity for the desired propulsion power. However, due to the slow response characteristics of the fuel cell, a reserve of energy is required to provide uninterrupted operation.

The byproduct of the fuel cell reaction is water in the form of steam that exits the cell along with any excess hydrogen. The water vapor can be used for heating the inside of the vehicle, but the hydrogen that is vented out is a waste for the system.

### 6.1.6.1  Case Study: Toyota Mirai FCEV

The Toyota Mirai FCEV is a mid-size hydrogen fuel cell sedan manufactured by Toyota and first appeared at the November 2014 Los Angeles Auto Show. Mirai is a fuel-efficient hydrogen fuel cell vehicle with a total range of 312 miles on a full tank with a fuel economy rating of 66 mpgge in all three categories of city, highway and combined driving. Mirai has an acceleration rating of 0–60 mph in 9.0 s. The global sale of the vehicle exceeded 10,000 vehicles by the end of 2019 with sales in Japan, North America and Europe. The powertrain components in the Mirai and their specifications are given below based on the 2017 Toyota Mirai [8]:

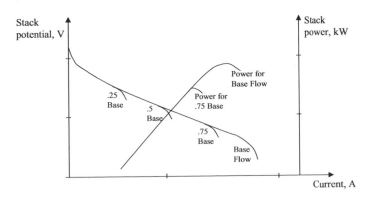

**FIGURE 6.6**  Fuel cell characteristics as a function of flow rate.

Curb mass: 1,930 kg

Fuel cell: Solid polymer electrolyte fuel cell; 370 cells in stack, 114 kW, 3.1 kW/L, 2.0 kW/kg

Hydrogen storage: 10,000 psi, 5 kg of $H_2$

Electric motor: Permanent magnet AC machine; peak power, 113 kW, peak torque 335 N m

Battery-pack: NiMH, 1.6 kWh, 245 V (nominal)

Powertrain DC/DC boost converter: 245–650 VDC

The air-cooled NiMH battery-pack is packaged in the trunk. The electric motor and the air compressor are packaged in-line between the front wheels. The fuel cell stack along with the Boost DC/DC converter is under the center of the vehicle. There are two hydrogen tanks located under the trunk and the rear passenger seats.

Mirai is a fuel cell dominant electric vehicle with a strong load following control strategy [8]. Fuel cell provides the majority of power during acceleration with assist from the battery-pack. With highly dynamic speed changes while cruising, fuel cell power follows the dynamic load changes. Fuel cell provides all the power when cruising at steady state with battery-pack being inactive. There is no fuel cell power output when the vehicle is stopped. Battery-pack provides all the power during coasting at low speed for short duration when hydrogen flow to fuel cell stack is stopped and the fuel cell open-circuit voltage drops. Fuel cell open-circuit voltage is 315 V and the voltage drops to around 225 V during heavy load. Fuel cell system peak efficiency is 63.7% at around 10% of full power and is around 58% at 25% of full power.

### Example 6.1

The current drawn by an electric motor of a fuel cell EV for a SAE schedule D J227A driving cycle is

$$I = \begin{cases} 9.36t + 1.482\text{E} - 3t^3 \text{ A} & \text{for } 0 < t < 28 \\ 61.42 \text{ A} & \text{for } 28 < t < 78 \\ 0 \text{ A} & \text{otherwise.} \end{cases}$$

The fuel flow rate for PEM fuel cell used in the vehicle is

$$N_f = \frac{405I}{nF} \text{ g/s}$$

a. Calculate the amount of fuel (hydrogen) needed for 1 cycle of schedule D.
b. Calculate the range of the vehicle using schedule D for the storage capacity of 5 kg of hydrogen.

### Solution

a. The fuel flow rate from the given equation is

$$N_f = \begin{cases} 0.01964t + 3.11\text{E} - 6t^3 & 0 < t < 28 \\ 0.1289 & 28 < t < 78 \\ 0 & \text{otherwise} \end{cases}$$

The amount of fuel (hydrogen) needed in one cycle can be obtained by integrating the $N_f(t)$ for $t = 0$ to $t = 78$ s.

Using numerical integration, we can show that

$$\int_0^{78} N_f(t)dt = 15.10 \text{ g}$$

b. For schedule D, 1 cycle is equivalent to 1 mile. Therefore, 5 kg of hydrogen will give a range of 5,000/15.1 = 331 miles.

## 6.2 ULTRACAPACITORS

Ultracapacitors and supercapacitors and are derivatives of the conventional capacitors where energy density has been increased at the expense of power density to make the devices function more like a battery. The terms ultracapacitors and supercapacitors are often interchangeably used. There are two types of ultracapacitors: Symmetrical and asymmetrical ultracapacitors. In the symmetrical ultracapacitors, there is no electrochemical reaction and the process is completely non-faradaic. These ultracapacitors use two identical polarizable carbon electrodes and is symmetrically designed. In this book, we will refer to these types as simply ultracapacitors. Asymmetrical ultracapacitors are designed for both faradaic and non-faradaic processes to take place simultaneously, which improves the energy density of the device. The asymmetrical ultracapacitors are more commonly referred to as supercapacitors.

### 6.2.1 SYMMETRICAL ULTRACAPACITORS

Capacitors are devices that store energy by the separation of equal positive and negative electrostatic charges. The basic structure of a capacitor consists of two conductors, known as plates separated by a dielectric, which is an insulator. The power density of the conventional capacitors are extremely high ($\sim 10^{12}$ W/m$^3$), but the energy density is very low ($\sim 50$ Wh/m$^3$) [10]. These conventional capacitors, commonly known as 'electrolytic capacitors' are widely used in electrical circuits as intermediate energy storage elements for time constants that are of a completely different domain and are of much smaller order compared to the energy storage devices that are to serve as the primary energy source for electric vehicles. The capacitors are described in terms of capacitance, which is directly proportional to the dielectric constant of the insulating material and inversely proportional to the space between the two conducting plates. The capacitance of a structure in terms of dimensional parameters is given by

$$C = \frac{\varepsilon A}{d}$$

where $\varepsilon$ is the permittivity of the dielectric material, $A$ is the area and $d$ is the separation distance of the charges. The capacitance of a conventional capacitor is established by wrapping metal foil plates separated by a dielectric film. The thickness of the dielectric film separates the charges built in the metal electrodes. The voltage rating of the capacitor is determined by the dielectric strength, given by $V/m$, and thickness of the film.

In terms of physical parameters, the capacitance is measured by the ratio of the charge magnitude between either plate and the potential difference between them, i.e.,

$$C = \frac{q}{V}$$

where $q$ is the charge between the parallel plates and $V$ is the voltage between them.

The structure of an ultracapacitor is completely different from that of a conventional capacitor although the physics of establishing the capacitance is the same. Ultracapacitors contain an electrolyte that enables the storage of electrostatic charge in the form of ions in addition to the conventional energy storage in electrostatic charges like in an electrolytic capacitor. The internal functions in an ultracapacitor do not involve any electrochemical reaction. The electrodes in ultra-capacitors are made of porous carbon with high internal surface area to help absorb the ions and provide a much higher charge density than is possible in a conventional capacitor. The ions move much more slowly than electrons enabling a much longer time constant for charging and discharging compared to electrolytic capacitors. There is no ion or electron transfer within an ultracapacitor; the process is simply charge separation or polarization. Therefore, the chemical process in the cell is entirely non-faradaic.

Instead of using a conventional dielectric, the ultracapacitors use activated carbon plates that are of two layers of the same substrate, facilitating charge separation distances of an ion diameter, which is about 1 nm. The structure of an ultracapacitor is shown in Figure 6.7a. The carbon plates are made of extremely small powder particles, which form a mushy structure facilitating large sur-face areas. The carbon mush or matrix is impregnated with conductive electrolytes. The effective charge separation across extremely small distances and large surface areas form the electric double layer (EDL) giving rise to extremely high capacitances. Positive and negative carbon matrixes in the ultracapacitor are separated by the electronic separator that is porous to ions. The EDL arises at the interfaces between the porous activated carbon and the electrolyte. The double layer includes a compact layer and a diffused layer [11]. The compact layer is formed at the interface of the solid electrode and the electrolyte contacts. The diffused layer penetrates into the electrolyte. Metal foils or electrodes for carrying currents to external circuits are placed against the positive and negative carbon matrixes. Each of the carbon matrixes forms a capacitor; hence, each ultracapacitor is essen-tially the series combination of two capacitors. The drawback of using the carbon matrix double layers instead of a solid dielectric is the low-voltage ratings that are in the range of 2–3 V.

The porosity of the EDL structure is shown in further detail in Figure 6.7b. The carbon matrix has three types of pores: macro-, meso- and micropores. The micropores are as small as 1.5–2 times an ion diameter, which means that no more than one complete ion would fit inside the pore. Pores smaller than an ion diameter termed as submicropores exist, but ions cannot enter into those. Ions accumu-late in layers in the macro- and mesopores resulting in the electric field within the electrolyte. As the capacitor gets charged, the electrolyte slowly becomes depleted of ions and the charging slows down.

The power density and energy density of ultracapacitors are of the order of $10^6$ W/m$^3$ and $10^4$ Wh/m$^3$, respectively. The energy density is much lower compared than those of batteries

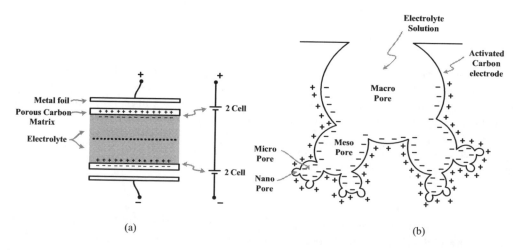

(a)                                                                                          (b)

**FIGURE 6.7** Ultracapacitor structure: (a) electric double-layer capacitance and (b) carbon matrix double layer.

(~5–25 × 10⁴ Wh/m³), but the discharge times are much faster (1–10 s compared to ~5 × 10³ s of batteries) and the cycle life is much more (~10⁵ compared to 100–1,000 of batteries) [10,12,13].

Current research and development aims to create ultracapacitors with capabilities in the vicinity of 4,000 W/kg and 15 Wh/kg. The possibility of using ultracapacitors as the primary energy source is quite far reaching, although it is likely that these can be improved to provide sufficient energy storage all by itself in hybrid vehicles. On the other hand, the ultracapacitors with high specific power are highly suitable as an intermediate energy transfer device in conjunction with batteries or fuel cells in electric and hybrid vehicles to provide the sudden transient power demand, such as during acceleration and hill climbing. The devices can also be used highly efficiently to capture the recovered energy during regenerative braking.

## 6.2.2 Asymmetrical Ultracapacitors

The symmetrical ultracapacitors with aqueous electrolyte first appeared in the late 1970s. Designs of asymmetrical ultracapacitors started in the 1980s. The asymmetrical devices use one polarizable carbon electrode and one non-polarizable electrode and a non-aqueous electrolyte. The chemical activities include both faradaic as well as non-faradaic processes which help increase the cell operating voltage. The asymmetrical ultracapacitors, which can also be termed a pseudo-battery, has higher energy density than a symmetrical ultracapacitor and is also capable of very high pulse power.

One design of asymmetrical ultracapacitor by ESMA in Russia uses a negative electrode of activated carbon like that in a symmetrical ultracapacitor and a positive non-polarizable, faradaic electrode [14]. The positive electrode is made of nickel oxyhydroxide. The electrolyte is an aqueous solution of KOH, which is used in alkaline batteries. The cell structure is shown in Figure 6.8. The capacitance of this positive electrode is significantly greater than the capacitance of a negative electrode having the same dimensions, which is different from the symmetrical ultracapacitors. The total capacitance of the asymmetrical ultracapacitor is approximately equal to the capacitance of the polarizable electrode.

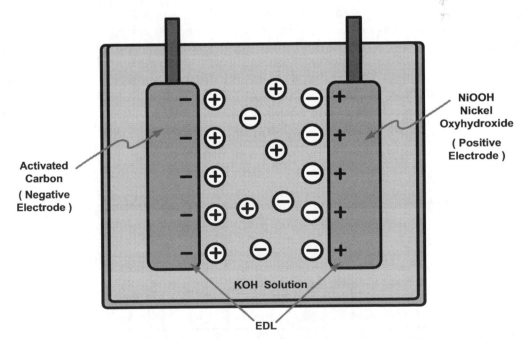

**FIGURE 6.8**   Asymmetrical ultracapacitor.

### 6.2.3 Ultracapacitor Modeling

Ultracapacitors rely on polarization of the electrolyte at carbon electrodes. The huge number of pores of the activated carbon increases the surface area allowing many electrons to accumulate. The number of electrons stored in the electrodes is proportional to the ultracapacitor capacitance. Since the size of pores in the activated carbon is not uniform, the capacitance depends on frequency. The ions in the electrolyte can charge the largest of the pores, the macropores, at highest frequency since these are closest to the current collectors and offers the least resistance path. The contribution to the total capacitance due to the macropores represents the high frequency behavior of the ultracapacitor with the fastest time constant. At medium frequencies, the ions are able to migrate to the mesopores as well. The capacitance for this part is lower, but the spreading resistance is higher compared to the macropores. At very low frequencies, ions are able to penetrate into the micropores establishing their contribution to the double-layer capacitance.

The behavioral models of ultracapacitor use a distributed $RC$-network with multiple-time constants. A three-branch non-linear model developed by Zubieta and Bonert is shown in Figure 6.9 [15]. The first $RC$ branch with the elements of $R_{fast}$, $C_{fast0}$ and $C_{fast1}$ models the charge accumulation behavior in the macropores. The components represent the highest frequency behavior in the time frame of seconds. The non-linear capacitance $C_{fast1}$ models the variation in the effective surface geometry as ions fill in the pores as a function of voltage. The second branch of $R_{med}$, and $C_{med}$ models the behavior around the mesopores in the time frame of seconds. The third branch with the parameters of $R_{slow}$, and $C_{slow}$ is the slowest branch representing the activity around the micropores and has the slowest time constant. The model also includes a parallel resistor to represent leakage and a series inductor for the terminals and electrodes. The model was developed to represent the behavior of ultracapacitor intervals of 30 min or less, which is sufficient for motor drive systems in electric and hybrid vehicles.

A three-time constant model developed at MIT and based on fast, medium and slow branches is shown in Figure 6.10 [16]. The model is a simplified version of the Toronto model where the non-linear dependence on voltage has been eliminated. The model describes the behavior of the ultracapacitor in the shorter term time frames.

Ultracapacitor models can also be developed based on frequency response data obtained using electrochemical image spectroscopy (EIS). EIS models the dynamic behavior of the system very well, but the derived model does not accurately predict the voltage-dependent behavior unless different DC biases are considered. The parameters are identified using the algorithm embedded in the EIS system. An EIS-based model, developed at Aachen is shown in Figure 6.11 [17]. The series resistance $R_s$ in the model represents the contact and electrolyte resistances, while the series inductance $L_s$ represents the terminal and electrode inductance. The parallel $RC$-network represents the complex pore behavior. The model does not include any leakage resistance to represent the longer-term behavior of ultracapacitors. The frequency domain impedance of the model is given by

$$Z(s) = R_s + sL_s + \frac{\tau}{\sqrt{s\tau}\,\tanh(\sqrt{s\tau})}$$

**FIGURE 6.9**  Toronto model.

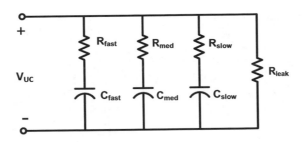

**FIGURE 6.10**   Short-term three-time constant model.

**FIGURE 6.11**   Aachen EIS model.

## 6.3   COMPRESSED AIR STORAGE

The compressed air storage is another alternative approach of energy storage where air is compressed and stored in a tank using electrical energy. The compressed air in the tank is expanded in a turbine converting stored energy into work done for the propulsion of a vehicle. The concept could be used solely for propulsion of an alternative vehicle or it could be combined with an IC engine or electric motor in a hybrid vehicle. The first compressed air vehicles were built in Paris in the mid-1800s, but the concept never transformed into commercialization even after repeated attempts to develop a viable prototype vehicle. In recent years, French developer MDI demonstrated advanced compressed air vehicles, but commercial production of such vehicles is yet to take place. At present, the low energy content of the compressed air in an acceptable tank size limits the range of the vehicle. However, the technology has merits as a viable alternative for clean and efficient local transportation, and further research and development is an attractive option. Some auto industries are pursuing the technology.

The components and the air flow for a compressed air vehicle is shown in Figure 6.12. The air compressor shown in Figure 6.12 is to be located in a filling station for the air vehicle where an electric motor compresses the air in a compressor, passes the gas through an air cooler before transferring it to the vehicle. Air compression produces substantial amount of heat, and hence, the working fluid is passed though heat exchanger for it to return to ambient temperatures. The vehicle itself has a tank that is filled with the compressed air at high pressures typically around 30 MPa or 300 bars. The compressed air drives two expansion turbines under suitable thermodynamic conditions for vehicle propulsion. The air coming out of the expansion turbine is extremely cold due to the thermodynamics involved in rapid expansion of the working fluid.

The efficiency of a compressed air vehicle is related to the thermodynamics of the compression and expansion processes. The thermodynamic analysis of compressed air energy storage showed that significant advantages are to be gained with much improved overall energy utilization when

**FIGURE 6.12**  Compressed air vehicle and its supply of energy.

both the compression and expansion processes are distributed over several stages with integrated inter-stage cooling [18]. In the compression process, the initial air volume is compressed to the vehicle tank volume followed by heat removal to bring the air temperature back to the original ambient temperature. The overall energy utilization can be improved if heat produced during air compression is otherwise used for domestic water and space heating. Similarly, the expansion process is also much more efficient when it is distributed over several stages with integrated inter-stage cooling. In a multi-stage turbine, the air is reheated using the ambient air at each stage before the working fluid enters the next turbine for further expansion. The multi-stage turbine is essentially extracting heat from the ambient which had been released during compression, although full recovery will never be possible. Both the compression and expansion processes must proceed as close as possible to the ideal isothermal limit; this can be done in practice with multi-stage polytropic processes with heat addition and removal during the intermediate stages. The efficiency improvements with multi-stage processes are significant compared to single-stage processes.

The exhaust for the compressed air vehicle is air which is clean, and hence, these vehicles will get certified as zero-emission vehicles. However, the source of energy for compressing the air at the filling station is electricity, and the well-to-wheel energy efficiency depends on how electrical energy is generated from a primary source. The ideal scenario is, of course, when electricity is produced from renewable sources. A wind-to-wheel energy analysis showed that the efficiency of compressed air vehicles is in between those of battery electric vehicles and FCEVs with the latter being the worse [19]. There is justification in pursuing the development of this compressed air alternative vehicle that uses an unconventional energy storage method. The engineering hurdles to overcome are associated with ice formation after expansion and inter-stage heat exchanger efficiency.

## 6.4  FLYWHEELS

The flywheel is the kind of energy supply unit that stores energy in a mechanical form. Flywheels store kinetic energy within a rotating wheel-like rotor or disk made of composite materials. Flywheels have a long history of usage in automobiles being routinely used in all of today's internal combustion engines to store energy and smoothen the power delivered by the abrupt pulses of the engine. However, the amount of energy storage required in flywheels of IC engines is small and is limited by the need of the vehicle to accelerate rapidly. The flywheel is currently being looked into for use in a number of different capacities. Flywheels can be used in HEVs with a standard IC engine as a power assist device. Alternatively, the flywheels can be used to replace chemical batteries in EVs to serve as the primary energy source or could be used in conjunction with batteries. However, technological breakthroughs in increasing the specific energy of flywheels are necessary before they can be considered as the energy source for EVs/HEVs. The flywheels of today are quite complex, large and heavy. Safety is also a concern with flywheels.

The flywheel design objective is to maximize the energy density. The energy U stored in the flywheel is given by

$$U = \frac{1}{2} J \omega^2$$

where $J$ is the polar moment of inertia and $\omega$ is the angular velocity. The energy storage is increased by spinning at higher velocities without increasing the inertia, which is directly proportional to mass. Increasing the angular velocity $\omega$ in turn increases the centrifugal stress, which must not exceed the failure stress with a given factor of safety. The stored energy per unit mass can be expressed as

$$\frac{U}{m} = k \frac{\sigma}{\rho}$$

where $k$ is a constant depending on the geometry, $\sigma$ is the tensile strength and $\rho$ is the density of the material. Therefore, the material to be used in flywheel must be lightweight with high tensile strength, conditions that are well satisfied by composite materials.

The flywheels have several advantages as the energy source, the most important one of which is the high specific power. Theoretically, specific power of flywheels has been shown to be of the order of 5–10 kW/kg, with 2 kW/kg easily achievable without exceeding safe working stresses. The other performance features that make the flywheels attractive can be attributed to its mechanical nature. The flywheels are not affected by temperature extremes. There are no concerns with toxic chemical processing and disposal of waste materials making flywheels environmentally friendlier than the chemical batteries. The flywheel energy storage is reliable that possess excellent controllability and repeatability characteristics. The state of charge in flywheels is precisely known at all times through measurement of the rotational speed. The energy conversion process to and from the flywheel approaches 98% compared to 75%–80% of batteries. The service life of a flywheel is many times than that of battery with very little maintenance requirement. The charging of flywheels is a fraction of that required by batteries, and can be less than 10 min for full recharge in a flywheel charging station. The ability to absorb or release high amount of power in a short period of time also aids the regenerative braking process.

Despite the several advantages, there are still a number of significant drawbacks with flywheels. The major difficulty in implementing a flywheel energy storage system is in the extra equipment needed to operate and contain the device. The extras are particularly difficult in electric and hybrid vehicle applications where the extra weight and expense make a big difference. In order to reduce windage losses, the flywheel needs to be enclosed in a vacuum chamber. The vacuum condition adds additional constraints on the bearings, since liquid-lubricated bearings do not survive in vacuum. The alternative is to use magnetic bearings, which themselves are in a development stage. The biggest extra weight in flywheels comes from the safety containment vessel, which is required to protect from the dangerous release of sudden energy and material in the case of a burst failure.

The flywheels, similar to a battery, go through a charge/discharge process to store and extract energy, which earned it the name 'electromechanical battery'. The rotor's shaft is coupled with a motor/generator, which during charging spin the rotor to store the kinetic energy and during discharging converts the stored energy into electric energy. Interface electronics is necessary to condition the power input and output and to monitor and control the flywheel. Modern flywheels are made of composite materials such as carbon fiber instead of steel to increase the energy density, which can be up to 200 Wh/kg. The composite material flywheel has the additional advantage that these disintegrate in the form of a fluid as compared to large metallic pieces for a steel made flywheel in the case of a catastrophic burst.

## PROBLEMS

### 6.1

The current drawn by an electric motor of a fuel cell EV for a SAE schedule D J227A driving cycle is

$$I = \begin{cases} 9.5t + 1.5 \text{ A} & \text{for } 0 < t < 28 \\ 55 \text{ A} & \text{for } 28 < t < 78 \\ 0 \text{ A} & \text{otherwise} \end{cases}$$

The fuel flow rate for PEM fuel cell used in the vehicle is

$$N_f = \frac{405I}{nF} \text{ g/s}$$

a. Calculate the amount of fuel (hydrogen) needed for 1 cycle of schedule D.
b. Calculate the amount of hydrogen needed for a range of 200 miles.

### 6.2

The efficiency of a fuel cell is related to the average voltage of each cell in the fuel cell stack $V_{fc}$. Referring to the lower heating value (LHV) of hydrogen, the efficiency of a fuel cell is given by

$$\eta_{fc} = \frac{V_{fc}}{E_0}$$

The practical average cell voltage has been used to determine the following equation for the rate of use of hydrogen in a PEM fuel cell

$$H_2 \text{ usage rate in kg/s} = 1.05 \times 10^{-8} \times \frac{P(t)}{V_{fc}}$$

The power required for a FCEV during a SAE J227a Schedule B driving cycle is

$$P_{TR}(t) = \begin{cases} 222t + 0.03t^3 & \text{for } 0 < t \le 19 \\ 830 & \text{for } 19 < t \le 38 \end{cases} \text{ W}$$

There is no regenerative braking in the driving cycle. Calculate the range of the FCEV with 8 kg of hydrogen. Consider the PEM fuel cell efficiency operating with pure hydrogen as 40% and reversible potential $E_0 = 1.23$ V.

# REFERENCES

1. A. J. Appleby and F. R. Foulkes, *Fuel Cell Handbook*, Van Nostrand Reinhold, New York, NY, 1989.
2. N. Andrews, "Poised for growth: DG and ride through power," *Power Quality*, 13(1), 10–16, January/ February 2002.
3. M.A. Laughton, "Fuel cells," *Power Engineering Journal*, 16(1), 37–47, February 2002.
4. L. Xia, *Behavioral Modeling and Analysis of Galvanic Devices*, PhD dissertation, University of Akron, Akron, OH, 2000.
5. Ford Motor Co, "Direct-Hydrogen-Fueled Proton-Exchange-Membrane Fuel Cell System for Transportation Applications: Hydrogen Vehicle Safety", Report no. DOE/CE/50389-502, Directed Technologies Inc, Arlington, VA, May 1997.
6. R.E. Linney and J.G. Hansel, *Hydrogen Energy Progress XI: Proceedings of 11th World Hydrogen Energy Conference*, T.N. Veziroglu (Editor), International Association for Hydrogen Energy, Stuttgart, Germany, 1996.
7. J.T. Ringland et al., "Safety Issues for Hydrogen Powered Vehicles," Report no. SAND-94–8226, UC407, Sandia National Laboratories, Albuquerque, NM, March 1994.
8. H. Lohse-Busch, M. Duoba, K. Stutenberg, S. Iliev and M. Kern. "Technology Assessment of a Fuel Cell Vehicle: 2017 Toyota Mirai," Argonne National Laboratory Report no. ANL/ESD-18/12, June 2018.
9. EC&G Services, Parson's Inc., *Fuel Cell Handbook*, 5th edition, U.S. Department of Energy, Office of Fossil Energy, Morgantown, WV, October 2000.
10. R.M. Dell and D.A.J. Rand, *Understanding Batteries*, Royal Society of Chemistry, London, 2001.
11. F. Belhachemi, S. Rael and B. Davat, "A physical based model of power electronic double-layer super-capacitors," *IEEE Industry Applications Society Conference Record*, 5, 3069–3076, October 2000.
12. S. Dhameja, *Electric Vehicle Battery Systems*, Newnes, Boston, MA, 2002.
13. D.A.J. Rand, R. Woods and R.M. Dell, *Batteries for Electric Vehicles*, John Wiley & Sons Inc., New York, NY, 1998.
14. I.N. Varakin, A.D. Klementov, S.V. Litvinenko, N.F. Starodubsev and A.B. Stepanov, "Application of ultracapacitors as traction energy sources," *7th International Seminar on Double Layer Capacitors and Similar Energy Storage Devices*, Deerfield Beach, FL, December 1997.
15. L. Zubieta and R. Bonert, "Characterization of double layer capacitors for power electronic applications," *IEEE Transactions on Industry Applications*, 36(1), 199–205, January/February 2000.
16. J.M. Miller, *Propulsion Systems for Hybrid Vehicles*, Institution of Electrical Engineers (IEE), London, 2004.
17. S. Buller, E. Karden, D. Kok and R. W. De Doncker, "Modeling the dynamic behavior of supercapacitors using impedance spectroscopy," *IEEE Transactions on Industry Applications*, 38(6), 1622–1626, November/December 2002.
18. U. Bossel, "Thermodynamic analysis of compressed air vehicle propulsion," *Proceedings of European Fuel Cell Forum*. Online www.efcf.com/reports, (E14).
19. P. Mazza and R. Hammerschlag, "Wind-to-wheel energy assessment," *Proceedings of European Fuel Cell Forum*, Institute for Lifecycle Environmental Assessment, Seattle, WA. Online www.efcf.com/reports, (E18).

# 7 Electric Machines

An electric machine is an electromechanical device used for energy conversion from electrical to mechanical and vice versa. In a vehicle system, the electric machine can be designed to process supplied energy and deliver power or torque to the transaxle for propulsion. The machine also processes the power flow in the reverse direction during regeneration when the vehicle is braking converting mechanical energy from the kinematics into electrical energy. The term 'motor' is used for the electric machine when energy is converted from electrical to mechanical and the term 'generator' is used when power flow is in the opposite direction with the machine converting mechanical energy into electrical energy. The braking mode in electric machines is referred to as regenerative braking. There are electrical, mechanical and magnetic losses during the energy conversion process in either direction in an electric machine, which affect the conversion efficiency. Some energy is always lost from the system for any energy conversion process. However, the conversion efficiency of electric machines is typically quite high compared to that of other types of energy conversion devices.

In electric vehicles, the electric motor is the sole propulsion unit, while in hybrid vehicles, the electric motor and the IC engine together in a series or parallel combination provide the propulsion power. In electric and hybrid vehicles, the electric traction motor converts electrical energy from the energy storage device to mechanical energy that drives the wheels of the vehicle. The major advantages of an electric motor over an IC engine is that the motor provides full torque at low speeds and the instantaneous power rating can be two or three times the rated power of the motor. These characteristics give the vehicle excellent acceleration with a nominally rated motor.

Electric motors can be DC type or AC type. The DC series motors were used in a number of prototype electric vehicles in the 1980s and prior to that due to its excellent match with the road load characteristics and ease of control. However, the size and maintenance requirements of DC motors are making their use obsolete not just in the automotive industry, but in all motor drive applications. The more recent electric and hybrid vehicles employ AC and brushless motors, which include induction motors, permanent magnet motors and switched reluctance motors. The AC induction motor technology is quite mature and significant research and development activities have taken place on induction motor drives over the past 50 years. The control of induction motors is much more complex than DC motors, but with the availability of fast digital processors, the computational complexity can be easily managed. Vector control techniques developed for sinusoidal machines make the control of AC motors similar to that of a DC motor through reference frame transformation techniques. The computational complexity arises from these reference frame transformations, but today's digital processors are capable of completing complex algorithms in a relative short time.

The competitor to induction motors is the permanent magnet motors. The permanent magnet (PM) AC motors have magnets on the rotor, while the stator construction is the same as that of the induction motor. The PM motors can be of surface mounted type or the magnets can be inset within the rotor in the interior permanent magnet (IPM) motors. The PM motor can also be classified as sinusoidal type or trapezoidal type depending on the flux distribution in the air gap. The trapezoidal motors have concentrated three-phase windings and are also known as brushless DC motors. The PM motors are driven by a six-switch inverter just like an induction motor, but the control is relatively simpler than that of the induction motor. The use of high density rare earth magnets in PM motors provides high power density, but at the same time the cost of magnets is on the negative side for these motors. For electric and hybrid vehicle applications, the motor size is relatively large compared to the other smaller power applications of PM motors, which amplifies the cost problem. However, the hybrid vehicle motors are much smaller than electric vehicle motors and the performance and efficiency achievable from PM motors may be enough to overcome the cost problem.

The IPM motors have excellent performance characteristics, much superior than the surface mount PM motors, but the manufacturing complexity is one of the drawbacks for these motors.

Another candidate for traction motors is the switched reluctance (SR) motors. These motors have excellent fault tolerance characteristics and their construction is fairly simple. The SR motors have no windings, magnets or cages on the rotor, which helps increase the torque/inertia ratio and allows higher rotor operating temperature. The constant power speed range is the widest possible in SR motors compared to other technologies, which makes it ideally suitable for traction applications. The two problems associated with switched reluctance motors are acoustic noise and torque ripple. There are well-developed techniques to address both; moreover, for several traction applications noise and torque ripple is not a big concern.

## 7.1 SIMPLE ELECTRIC MACHINES

The torque in electric machines is produced utilizing the basic principles of electromagnetic theory in one of two ways: (i) by the mutual interaction of two orthogonal magnetomotive forces (mmf) utilizing the Lorentz force principle, and (ii) by using a varying reluctance flux path where the rotor moves toward attaining the minimum reluctance position. The DC and AC machines including the PM machines work on the first principle, while the switched and synchronous reluctance machines work on the latter principle. The fundamental machine phenomena responsible for inducing voltage and producing torque is explained in this section followed by two simple machine configurations that operate based on the two different principles.

### 7.1.1 FUNDAMENTAL MACHINE PHENOMENA

An electric machine converts electrical energy to mechanical energy in the motoring mode and mechanical energy to electrical energy in the generating mode. The same electric machine can be used to serve either as a motor or a generator with appropriate changes in the control algorithm. Two basic phenomena responsible for this electromechanical energy conversion occur simultaneously in electrical machines. These are as follows:

1. Voltage is induced when a conductor moves in an electric field.
2. When a current carrying conductor is placed in an electric field, the conductor experiences a mechanical force.

#### 7.1.1.1 Motional Voltage $\vec{B}$

When a conductor is moving in a uniform magnetic field with a velocity $\vec{v}$, there will be voltage induced in the conductor given by

$$\vec{e} = (\vec{v} \times \vec{B}) \cdot l \tag{7.1}$$

The voltage induced is known as motional voltage or speed voltage. The above is a mathematical definition of Faraday's law of electromagnetic induction, which is written as

$$e = -\frac{d\lambda}{dt} = -N\frac{d\phi}{dt} \tag{7.2}$$

where $\lambda$ is the flux linkage, $\phi$ is the flux and $N$ is the number of turns.

For the conductor of length $l$ shown in Figure 7.1, which is moving with a velocity $\vec{v}$ in a magnetic field $\vec{B}$ that is perpendicularly directed into the plane of the paper, the induced voltage is

$$e = Blv \tag{7.3}$$

**FIGURE 7.1** Induced voltage in a conductor.

### 7.1.1.2 Electromagnetic Force

A current carrying conductor placed in a magnetic field experiences a force given by the Lorentz force equation. For a conductor carrying current $i$ in a uniform magnetic field $\vec{B}$, this electromagnetic force is given by

$$\vec{f} = i(\vec{l} \times \vec{B}) \tag{7.4}$$

Let us consider a magnetic field established by a pair of magnets and a conductor of length $l$ carrying current $i$, as shown in Figure 7.2. The force in this case is

$$f = Bil \tag{7.5}$$

### 7.1.2 Simple DC Machine

Let us consider a simple one turn loop placed in a magnetic field to understand the principles of voltage induced and torque developed. This magnetic field can be established by a magnet pole-pair directing flux from the North pole to the South pole as shown in Figure 7.3a. The one-turn loop is placed in the gap between the pole-pair where it can freely rotate around a pivot axis under the influence of the magnetic field. The magnet pole-pair and the one-turn loop forms the simple electric machine that we will use to discuss the principles of electromagnetic energy conversion. Another view of the one-turn loop under the influence of the magnetic field is shown in Figure 7.3b. The one-turn coil cuts the magnetic field as it rotates around its pivot axis.

### 7.1.2.1 Induced Voltage

The one-turn rotating part of the simple machine is the rotor, while the permanent magnets form the stator. The flux from the stator magnet pole pair establish the magnetic field for the machine, which is known as the field flux. Let us assume that the flux established in between the magnet pole pair is uniform flowing from the North pole to South pole in the negative $y$-direction as shown in Figure 7.3b. Now, if the single turn conductor rotates in this uniform magnetic field at a constant angular velocity $\omega$, a voltage will be induced in the sides of the coil according to Equation 7.1. The sides of the one-turn loop of length $l$, which passes under the pole faces, are called the *coil sides*.

(a)  (b)

**FIGURE 7.2** Force on a current carrying conductor in a magnetic field: (a) magnets and conductor, and (b) force, flux and current directions.

**FIGURE 7.3**    A one-turn coil in a magnetic field: (a) top view and (b) front view.

The side in the back of width $W$, which connects the coil sides, is known as the *end turn*. The one-turn coil rotating at an angular velocity of $\omega$ makes an angle $\theta$ with the magnetic field $\vec{B}$ as shown in Figure 7.3c. The cross product $(\vec{v} \times \vec{B})$ for the coil sides at any instant of time is $vB\cos\theta$, and this resultant is always parallel with the length $l$ of the coil sides. Therefore, the induced voltage in each of the coil sides is $vBl\cos\theta$ according to Equation 7.1. There will be no voltage induced on the end turn since $(\vec{v} \times \vec{B})$ is always perpendicular to the end turns that result in a zero dot product with the width $W$. Therefore, the total voltage induced in the one-turn loop accounting for the two coil sides and the end turn is

$$e_{ab} = 2vBl\cos\theta$$

Since the linear velocity $v$ can be expressed in terms of the angular velocity $\omega$ as $v = \omega(W/2) = \omega r$, the voltage induced in the one-turn loop can be expressed as

$$e_{ab} = 2Blr\omega\cos\theta \tag{7.6}$$

The induced voltage can also be derived from the alternative form of Faraday's law $\left(e = -N\dfrac{d\phi}{dt}\right)$ with the flux linkage for the one-turn coil expressed as

$$\phi(\theta) = -2Blr\sin\theta. \tag{7.7}$$

The peak flux linking the coil is

$$\phi_P = 2Blr \tag{7.8}$$

The simple electric machine of Figure 7.3 will produce sinusoidal voltages when rotated at a constant speed in the uniform magnetic field. The alternating voltage generated at the terminals *ab* need to be rectified into unidirectional voltages to obtain a DC output. This is achieved with pairs of commutators and brushes attached at the ends of the one-turn conductor for the simple machine to produce a DC voltage as seen in Figure 7.4. The commutators are connected to the ends of the turn and rotate with the coil. The brushes are stationary for connection with an external circuit. The two brushes are positioned in alignment with one of the stator magnetic poles such that they can collect the voltage created by that magnet pole and one of the coil sides through the commutator segment. The voltages seen by the brushes are thus unidirectional. The commutator and brush arrangement is a mechanical rectifier that converts the alternating voltage on the coil side $e_{ab}$ into a unidirectional

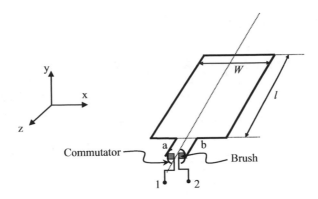

**FIGURE 7.4**  Commutators and brushes attached to the one-turn coil.

or DC voltage $E_{12}$. The field flux, the induced voltage and the DC voltage are shown in Figure 7.5. The average DC voltage at the terminal of the brushes is

$$E_{12} = \frac{2}{\pi} \int_{\frac{\pi}{2}}^{\frac{3\pi}{2}} \phi_P \omega \cos(\omega t) d(\omega t) = \frac{2}{\pi} \phi_P \omega \qquad (7.9)$$

### 7.1.2.2  Force and Torque

In the one-turn coil of Figure 7.4, the circuit is open at the terminals 1–2. If a resistor is connected between the terminals 1 and 2, current starts to flow within the coil as long as there is motion of the conductor in the presence of the magnetic field. This current is the armature current in a DC machine; for the one-turn coil, the current for a resistance $R$ is given by

$$I_a = \frac{e_{12}}{R} = \frac{2Blr}{R} \omega_m \cos\theta$$

The coil sides experience a force when current flows through the conductor according to Equation 7.5. The forces on the two coil sides, as shown in Figure 7.6, are given by

$$F_1 = F_2 = BI_a l$$

The electromagnetic torque of the machine can be derived from the two forces $F_1$ and $F_2$ forming a couple. The torque $T_e$ on the armature turn about the axis-of-rotation is

$$T_e = F_1 d = F_1 W \cos\theta$$

$$\Rightarrow T_e = \varphi_P I_a \cos\theta$$

The average torque produced is

$$T_e = \frac{2}{\pi} \int_{\frac{\pi}{2}}^{\frac{3\pi}{2}} \phi_P I_a \cos(\omega t) d(\omega t) = \frac{2}{\pi} \phi_P I_a \qquad (7.10)$$

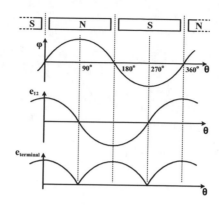

**FIGURE 7.5**   Field flux, the induced voltage and the DC voltage.

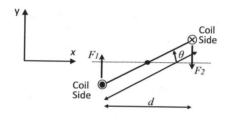

**FIGURE 7.6**   Forces on the coil sides due to current.

### 7.1.2.3   DC Machine Back-EMF and Torque

In a practical machine, the coil would be wound around an iron structure which is the rotor of the electric machine. The rotor in the magnetic circuit is free to turn about the vertical axis. The reluctance of the iron is much smaller than the reluctance of the air. The rotor iron material must have much higher relative permeability than air to facilitate the flux flow from one stator pole to another through the rotor. The rotor iron together with its curved shape provides a constant width air gap between the stator and the rotor. The uniform air gap maintained between the stator and rotor poles allows the flux to be radially directed between the stator and the rotor.

The simple machine of Figure 7.3 is shown to have two poles only, one N-pole and one S-pole. The number '2' in Equation 7.9 represents those two poles in the machine. In a practical machine, there can be more than two poles, but always in pairs, for better utilization of the space around the stator and rotor circumference, and also for different torque-speed characteristics of the machine. In general, the higher speed machines will have few number of pole pairs, and higher torque machines will have more number of pole pairs. In addition, the machine geometry is better utilized when there are multiple turns in a coil instead of the single turn shown in Figure 7.3 for the simple machine. The multiple turns will increase the induced voltage. The multi-turn arrangement, known as the *conductor*, is shown in Figure 7.7. The sides of the turn along the z-direction are known as the *coil side* similar to the one-turn coil. In the machine, many conductors are arranged radially along the rotor surface and connected in a series-parallel combination depending on the number of poles used. In DC machines, the conductor connectors are arranged in one of two winding patterns known as lap winding or wave winding. The induced voltage and torque equations for the simple machine can be generalized using the number of turns $N_t$ in each conductor, the number of poles $P$ and the type of winding arrangement used. The equations then become

$$E_a = K_m \phi_P \omega \tag{7.11}$$

$$T_e = K_m \phi_P I_a \tag{7.12}$$

**FIGURE 7.7**   A multi-turn conductor.

where $K_m$ is a machine constant given by $K_m = \dfrac{N_t P}{\pi a}$. $a$ is the number of parallel paths used in the conductor arrangement; $a = 2$ for wave winding, while $a = P$ for lap winding. $E_a$ is the induced voltage or motional voltage, more commonly known as back-emf of the machine. Equation 7.12 shows that for the DC machine, the back-emf $E_a$ is proportional to speed while the torque is proportional to current when the flux is held constant, since for a designed machine $K_m$ is constant.

The end turns in a conductor, as was shown earlier, does not contribute to voltage generation or torque production, but contributes only to losses due to the resistances in that segment of the coil length. Therefore, one of the objectives in machine design is to minimize the end turn lengths.

The flux in the simple machine shown is radially directed from the rotating component to the stationary component. The rotor rotates around the axis-of-rotation resulting in rotary motion. These machines are known as *radial flux machines*. Electric machines can also be constructed to deliver linear motion, which are known as *linear machines*. The movable component in a linear machine has linear or translator motion over the stationary structure.

### 7.1.3   SIMPLE RELUCTANCE MACHINE

The reluctance machines have a variable reluctance path for the magnetic flux as the rotor rotates about its axis-of-rotation. The saliencies in both the stator and the rotor poles provide a variable reluctance path for the magnetic flux as the rotor position changes. The windings are on the stationary member, while the rotor is a stack of laminations without any windings or magnets. A simple reluctance machine with only one phase is shown in Figure 7.8. The reluctance of the air gap varies as a function of the rotor angular displacement $\theta$. The reluctance of the air gap is minimum when the rotor and the stator are in perfect alignment at $\theta = 0°$. The minimum reluctance position corresponds to the maximum inductance seen by the current flowing through the coil. The reluctance becomes maximum when the rotor attains the position with the largest air gap, which occurs when $\theta = 90°$. The inductance in this position is the minimum. The stator coil inductance variation as a function $\theta$ can be expressed by

$$L(\theta) = L_1 + L_2 \cos(2\theta).$$

**FIGURE 7.8**   A simple reluctance machine.

The torque for the simple reluctance machine can be expressed as

$$T_e = \frac{1}{2} i^2 \frac{\partial L}{\partial \theta} \tag{7.13}$$

The single-phase simple reluctance machine operates as a synchronous machine when supplied with an AC voltage. The machine will produce torque as long as the stator excitation frequency is synchronized with the rotor speed. If the initial rotor position is $\delta$, the rotor angular displacement for a rotor speed $\omega$ is given by

$$\theta = \omega t + \delta.$$

The average torque produced for an excitation current of $i = I_m \cos \omega t$ at the synchronous speed is

$$T_e = -\frac{1}{4} L_2 I_m^2 \sin \delta.$$

The simple reluctance machine will produce the average torque only at synchronous speed. The torque will be maximum when the initial position is 45° and zero when it is 0°. The machine will not be able to start rotation if the rotor is in the aligned position initially.

The reluctance machines used for high power applications are of multiple phases irrespective of whether they are of synchronous or switched types. Power electronic inverters are used in both types of machines for controlling their torque and speed. However, the fundamental principle for torque production is essentially the same as that described in this section with the simple reluctance machine. The principles and characteristics of the switched reluctance machines will be discussed further later in the chapter.

## 7.2 MATERIALS FOR ELECTRIC MACHINES

An electric machine is made of both active materials that contribute to electromechanical energy conversion and passive materials for frame and support structure. The active materials in an electric machine are the current carrying conductors for electrical loading and the magnetic materials for magnetic loading. The passive materials include support structures, bearings for the rotating components, shafts for mechanical coupling with load or prime mover, and insulating materials. In a practical machine, there can be more than two poles, but always in pairs, for better utilization of the space around the stator and rotor circumference, and also for different torque-speed characteristics of the machine. In addition, the machine geometry is better utilized when there are multiple turns in a coil instead of the single turn to help increase the induced voltage. This multi-turn arrangement with two coil sides is known as the conductor. The two coil sides are the active elements and each are placed under the influence of opposite magnetic poles. In a machine, many conductors are arranged radially along the rotor surface and connected in a series-parallel combination depending on the number of poles used. The conductor segments active participating in torque production need to be connected through end turns which are necessary for completing the current loops, but do not contribute to voltage generation or torque production. One of the design objectives in machine design is always to minimize the end turn lengths to minimize the losses due to the resistances in that segment of the coil length.

### 7.2.1 CONDUCTORS

Electrical machines have windings made of electric conductors that conduct electric current or allow the flow of electrons. The materials for these windings need to have high conductivity to reduce their resistive losses to both improve efficiency and reduce the temperature rise of the winding, and nonmagnetic properties to eliminate magnetic losses. Copper is the material of choice for windings in electric machines due to their high electric conductivity. Copper also has great tensile strength, thermal conductivity and thermal expansion properties. Aluminum has a higher resistivity than copper, but is commonly used in the rotor bars of induction machines due to it low melting point. Although aluminum has about 60% of the conductivity of copper, it has only 30% of the weight of copper that makes it attractive for weight sensitive applications. Aluminum is also generally more inexpensive when compared to copper conductors. A new kind of conductor called copper clad aluminum (CCA) is emerging as one having the advantages of higher conductivity and reliable termination compared to aluminum. Litz wire is also an option to avoid excessive eddy current losses within the conductors, but these are quite expensive.

## 7.2.2 MAGNETIC MATERIALS

The parts of the electric machine that carries the magnetic fluxes are made of magnetic materials and permanent magnets, which are desired to be electrically non-conductive. This is because changing magnetic fields induce undesirable eddy-current currents in these materials which lead to extra losses. The flux carrying materials are ferromagnetic in nature that can be categorized into two kinds, soft materials and hard materials. Soft materials are easy to magnetize and demagnetize, and typically called the stator and rotor core lamination materials. Hard materials are the permanent magnets and require more energy to magnetize and demagnetize.

The electromagnetic properties of the machine core materials are defined by the $B$-$H$ relationship $B = \mu H$ where $B$ is the magnetic flux density in Tesla or weber/m$^2$, $H$ is the magnetic field intensity in Ampere-turn/m and $\mu$ is the permeability of the material. The permeability in turn is given by $\mu = \mu_0 \mu_r$ where $\mu_0 = 4\pi \times 10^{-7}$ H/m is the permeability of free space and $\mu_r$ is the relative permeability. The relative permeability of air is 1. The $B$-$H$ relationship of magnetic materials is non-linear and is difficult to describe by a mathematical function. The properties of core materials are often described graphically in terms of the $B$-$H$ characteristics as shown in Figure 7.9. The non-linearity in the characteristics is due to the saturation of flux for higher currents and the hysteresis effects. When an external magnetization force is applied through the currents in the windings, the magnetic dipole moments tend to align to orient in a certain direction. This dipole orientation establishes a large magnetic flux, which would not exist without the external magnetization force applied on the core. The magnetic dipole moments relax toward their random orientation up on removal of the applied magnetic force, but few dipole moments retain their orientation in the direction of the previously existing magnetization force. The retention of direction phenomenon of the dipole moments is known as magnetic hysteresis. The hysteresis causes magnetic flux density $B$ to be a multivalued function that depends on the direction of magnetization. The magnetic effect that remains in the core after the complete removal of the magnetization force is known as the residual magnetism (denoted by $B_r$ in Figure 7.9). The direction of the residual flux depends on the direction of field current change. The energy required to change the magnetic orientations is wasted in the core material and is referred to as hysteresis loss. The area of the hysteresis loop in the magnetization characteristics is proportional to the hysteresis loss. The saturation in the characteristics reflects the fact that more magnetic dipole moments remain to be oriented once sufficient magnetization force has been applied and the flux has reached the maximum or saturation level.

The energy required to cause change in the magnetic orientations is wasted in the core material and is referred to as hysteresis loss. The area of the hysteresis loop in the magnetization characteristics is proportional to the hysteresis loss.

The cross-sectional area available for Cu conductors decreases faster than the need for mmf as motor size decreases (resistive effects become more dominating). Therefore, in smaller electric machines, the per unit Cu losses increase and efficiency decreases; this is referred to as the excitation penalty associated with small machines. The almost loss free excitation of PM in smaller machines is advantageous, while in larger motors, the excitation penalty is small and magnet cost

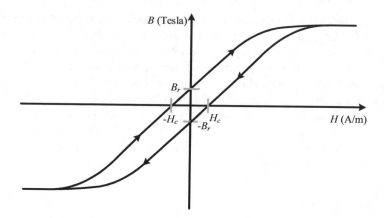

**FIGURE 7.9** *B-H* characteristics of magnetic materials.

becomes prohibitive. However, the permanent magnet machines are the popular choice in electric and hybrid vehicle applications due to the minimal excitation losses and high power density offered by these machines. PM machines are also being used in large wind turbine applications, although doubly fed induction machines remain the leading machine used in the wind industry.

The permanent magnets behave like a constant current source with $\mu_r$ just greater than air, i.e., $\mu_r \approx 1.05$–$1.07$. The magnet can be operated at any point of the linear $B$-$H$ characteristics and remain permanent. However, if the flux density is reduced beyond the knee of the characteristics ($B_d$), some magnetism will be lost permanently. In this case, on removal of the demagnetizing field greater than the limit, the new characteristics will be another straight line parallel to but lower than the original.

NdFeB, AlNiCo, SmCo and ferrites are among the magnet choices available for permanent magnet machines. Critical parameter values of few other soft magnetic materials are given in Table 7.1. For comparison, the parameter values for soft magnetic materials used in stator and rotor structures are given in Table 7.2. Neodymium-iron-boron (NdFeB) are of two types, sintered and bonded, with the

---

### TABLE 7.1
#### Parameters for Hard Magnetic Materials

| Material | $H_C$ (A/m) | $B_r$ (T) | $B_d$ (T) | $T_c$ (C) |
|---|---|---|---|---|
| Ferrite | 200,000 | 0.4 | 0.10 | 300 |
| AlNiCo | 119,366 | 0.68 | 0.02 | 860 |
| SmCo | 11,060 | 1.2 | 0.01 | 820 |
| NdFeB (sintered) | 636,620 | 1.5 | 0.10 | 310 |

---

### TABLE 7.2
#### Parameters for Soft Magnetic Materials

| Material | $H_C$ (A/m) | $B_{sat}$ (T) |
|---|---|---|
| M-47 | 22 | 2.08 |
| Soft magnetic composite (SMC) | 210 | 1.5 |
| Nanocrystalline | 4.6 | 1.8 |
| Vanadium permendur (cobalt steel) | 35 | 2.2 |

sintered option having higher flux densities that has driven the development and adoption of PM motors. Sintered NdFeB has a residual flux density $B_r$ in the range of 1.1–1.25 T at room temperature which is adequate to produce a flux-density between 0.8 and 0.9 T across a relatively large air gap, for example 1 mm, with a magnet thickness of 3–4 mm. Residual flux density $B_r$ decreases by about 0.1% for each degree rise in temperature. The knee-point of flux density ($B_d$) increases rapidly with temperature, which impose a limit on $T_{max}$ for NdFeB in the range of 100°C–140°C depending on the detailed composition. The cost of these sintered NdFeB materials is high mainly because of the manufacturing complexity of the sintering process. Fe (77%) and B (8%) cost relatively little, but Nd is one of the more prevalent rare earth elements. Bonded NdFeB magnets can be produced at a lower cost, but $B_r$ is lower, about 0.6–0.7 T.

Ferrites are the most abundant and lowest cost permanent magnets among all these magnets. The residual flux density $B_r$ at 0.3–0.4 T is much lower than the desired range of gap flux density. $B_d$ is higher for those ferrites for which $B_r$ is higher. Ferrites have high resistivity, low core losses, and can be operated up to 100°C. An increase in temperature increases $B_r$ and decreases $B_d$. The B-H characteristics of ferrite and other permanent magnets are shown in Figure 7.10. Samarium Cobalt (SmCo) permanent magnets have higher value of $B_r$, typically between 0.8 and 1.1 T. Flux density at the knee $B_d$ for SmCo is well into the third quadrant. Residual flux density $B_r$ decreases somewhat with temperature, while $B_d$ increases. These magnets have increased sensitivity to demagnetization as temperature increases. Resistivity is 50 times that of Cu, and the cost is relatively high reflecting the cost of rare earth element and an expensive metal.

One of the design requirements for PM machines is to ensure that magnets are protected against extreme points of operation as demagnetization may occur if flux density is reduced below the knee-point of flux density $B_d$. PM machines are designed to withstand considerable overload currents (2–5 times the rated) without damage to magnets. The major danger may arise from a short circuit of the stator following failure in the inverter. If $B_d$ is negative or zero, this short-circuit current can usually be tolerated without damage. However, steady-state short-circuit current is accompanied by an initial transient of equal magnitude. One way of providing protection is to design for additional stator leakage inductance. In a typical application, the demagnetization is most severe at the magnet corners and near the air gap, which can be solved by adding the air pockets on top of the inner barriers with magnets. The air pockets protect the magnets from the demagnetization at entire operating range with maximum operating current and temperature.

The resistance to demagnetization, and by extension, its high temperature performance is improved in NdFeB magnets by adding of dysprosium (Dy) or terbium (Tb) which are heavy rare earth (HRE) elements. The amount of Dy added is dictated, not only by demagnetizing stress, but also by the expected maximum temperature of the application. Dysprosium is never found in nature as a free element, though it is found in various minerals such as xenomite, the demand for Dy has

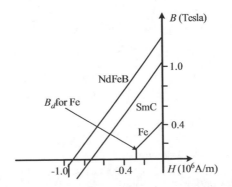

**FIGURE 7.10**   Characteristics of commonly used permanent magnets.

been surpassing its supply. NdFeB magnets can have up to 10% of the Nd substituted by Dy and at the current rate of use of dysprosium in clean energy applications like electric vehicles and wind turbine generators, and this would quickly exhaust its available supply.

The grain-boundary-diffused (GDB) NdFeB magnets are emerging one of the solutions for reducing HRE contents in permanent magnets. In the traditional approach, HRE materials are added to NdFeB in the initial melting process, which requires more HRE materials to be embedded in the entire magnet piece. In the grain-boundary-diffusion process, the HRE-rich compound is applied at the surface of the magnet which diffuses into the grain boundaries right below the magnet surface, but not so much in the grain boundaries in the interior of the magnet. The result of the diffusion process is that the corners and edges of the magnets are much more rich with HRE rather than in the interior [1]. This is highly compatible with what is needed in the IPM machine where the magnet corners and edges are more prone to permanent demagnetization that in the interior region. This can be observed from the demagnetization analysis of an IPM machine using finite element analysis.

## 7.3 DC MACHINES

DC machines have two sets of windings, one in the rotor and the other in the stator, which establish the two fluxes; hence, the mmfs that interact with each other produce the torque. The orthogonality of the two mmfs, which is essential for maximum torque production, is maintained by a set of mechanical components called commutators and brushes. The winding in the rotor is called the armature winding, while the winding in the stationary part of the machine is called the field windings. Both the armature and the field windings are supplied with DC currents. The armature windings carry the bulk of the current, while the field windings carry a small field excitation current. The armature and the field currents in the respective windings establish the armature and field mmfs. The magnitude of the mmfs is the product of the number of turns in the windings and the current. Depending on the number of supply sources and the type of connection between the armature and field windings, there can be several types of DC machines. When the armature and field windings are supplied from independently controlled DC sources, it is known as a separately excited DC machine. The separately excited DC machine offers the maximum flexibility of torque and speed control through independent control of the armature and field currents. The DC shunt machine has the similar parallel configuration of the armature and field windings as in the separately excited motor except that the same DC source supplies both the armature and field windings. In the shunt motors, the simplicity in power supply is compromised for the reduced flexibility in control. In another type of DC machine, known as the series DC machine, the armature and the series windings are connected in series and the machine is supplied from a single source. Since the armature and the field windings carry the same current, the field is wound with a few turns of heavy gauge wires to deliver the same mmf or ampere-turns as in the separately excited machine. The greatest advantage of the series machine is the very high starting torque that helps achieve rapid acceleration. However, the control flexibility is lost due to the series connection of armature and field windings.

The positive attributes of DC machines are as follows:

- Ease of control due to linearity
- Capability for independent torque and flux control
- Established manufacturing technology.

The disadvantages of DC machines are as follows:

- Brush wear that leads to high maintenance
- Low maximum speed
- EMI due to commutator action
- Low power to weight ratio.

The separately excited DC motor used in an electric or hybrid electric vehicle has two separate DC/DC converters supplying the armature and field windings from the same energy source as shown in Figure 7.11. The DC/DC converters process the fixed supply voltage of the energy source to deliver a variable DC to the armature and field circuits. The power rating of the converter supplying the armature windings is much larger than that of the converter supplying the field winding. The control inputs to the converter circuits are the desired torque and speed of the motor and the outputs of the converters are the voltages that are applied to the armature and field circuits of the DC motor.

The independent armature voltage and field current control, possible in separately excited DC machines or motors, offers the possibility of additional performance optimization in addition to meeting the torque-speed requirements of the machine. The indices used for measuring performance in motor drives include efficiency, torque per ampere, torque ripple, response time, etc. The weights on the individual performance indices depend on the application and the design requirements. The most critical performance index for electric and hybrid vehicle applications is the efficiency. The analysis to follow on DC motors, based on separately excited DC motors, is intended to set forth the premise for performance analysis of DC drives in the next chapter.

The armature equivalent cirucit of a DC motor is shown in Figure 7.12a. The circuit consists of the armature winding resistance $R_A$, the self-inductance of aramture winding $L_{AA}$ and the back-emf $e_A$. The variables shown in the figure are as follows:

$V_A$ = armature voltage,
$I_A$ = armature current,

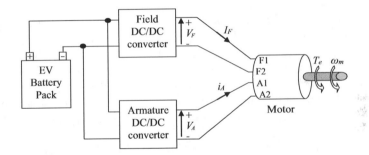

**FIGURE 7.11**  DC motor drive including the power electronics and battery source.

**FIGURE 7.12**  Equivalent circuit representation of a DC motor: (a) aramture circuit and (b) field circuit.

$T_e$ = developed motor torque,
$\omega_m$ = shaft speed,
$\phi$ = armature linking flux (primarily from field current).

Applying KVL around the armature circuit, the voltage balance equation is

$$V_A = R_A i_A + L_{AA} \frac{di_A}{dt} + e_A \tag{7.14}$$

where

$$e_A = K\phi\omega_m$$
$$T_e = K\phi i_A. \tag{7.15}$$

$e_A$ is known as the back-emf and $K$ is a machine constant that depends on the machine construction, number of winding and core material properties. The field equivalent circuit of the DC motor is shown in Figure 7.12b. The field circuit consists of the field winding resistance $R_F$ and the self-inductance of the field winding $L_{FF}$. $V_F$ is the voltage applied to the field.

The field circuit equation is

$$V_F = R_F i_F + L_{FF} \frac{di_F}{dt}.$$

The resistance of the field winding in separately excited and shunt DC motors is very high, since there are a lot of turns in the winding. The transient response in the field circuit is thus much faster than the armature circuit. The field voltage is also typically not adjusted frequently, and for all practical purpose, a simple resistor fed from a DC source characterizes the electrical unit of the field circuit. The field current establishes the mutual flux or field flux, which is responsible for torque production in the machine. The field flux is a non-linear function of field current and can be described by

$$\phi = f(i_F)$$

The torque-speed relationship of a DC motor can be derived from Equations 7.14 and 7.15 and is given by

$$\omega_m = \frac{V_A}{K\phi} - \frac{R_A}{(K\phi)^2} T_e \tag{7.16}$$

The positive torque axis represents the motoring characteristics, while the negative torque region represents the generating characteristics.

## 7.4 THREE-PHASE AC MACHINES

The primary difference between AC machines and DC machines is that the armature circuit of the former is located in the stationary piece of the structure while for the latter it is in the rotor. The advantage gained in having the armature circuit in the stator is the elimination of the commutator and brushes of the DC machines. The AC machines require alternating supply that can be derived from a DC source using a DC/AC inverter. The machines can be single phase or multiple phase types. Single phase AC machines are used for low-power appliance applications, while higher power machines are always of three-phase configuration. The second mmf required for torque production in AC machines (equivalent to the field mmf of DC machines) comes from the rotor circuit.

Depending on the way the second mmf is established, the AC machines can be induction type or synchronous type. For either of the two types of AC machines, the stator windings are similar in configuration.

### 7.4.1 SINUSOIDAL STATOR WINDINGS

The three-phase stator windings of AC machines are sinusoidally distributed spatially along the stator circumference as shown in Figure 7.13a to establish a sinusoidal mmf waveform. Although the windings are shown as concentrated in locations aa′, bb′ and cc′ for the three phases, the number of turns for each of the phase windings varies sinusoidally along the stator circumference. This space sinusoidal distribution of Phase-a winding is shown in Figure 7.13b, which has been represented by an equivalent concentrated winding a-a′ in Figure 7.13a. The equivalent distribution of the Phase-a windings in a horizontally laid stator axis as if the stator cross-section was split along the radius at $\theta = 0$ and developed longitudinally is shown in Figure 7.14a. The current passing through these Phase-a stator windings causes a sinusoidal Phase-a mmf $F_a(\theta)$, which is shown in Figure 7.14b. The mmf primarily exists in the air gap due the high permeability of the stator and rotor steel and tends to be radial in direction due to the short length of air gap relative to stator inside diameter. The sinusoidal distribution of the windings can be expressed as

$$n_{as}(\theta) = N_P \sin\theta, \quad 0 \le \theta \le \pi$$

$$= -N_P \sin\theta, \quad \pi \le \theta \le 2\pi$$

where $N_P$ is the maximum turns or conductor density expressed in turns per radian. Let the Phase-a winding has an $N_s$ equivalent number of turns (i.e., $2N_s$ conductors), which would give the same fundamental sinusoidal component as the actual winding distribution. Therefore, the integral of the conductor density in Figure 7.14b between 0 and $\pi$ has a total of $N_s$ conductors (accounting for half the turns in a winding-half), which is

$$N_s = \int_0^\pi N_P \sin\theta \, d\theta = 2N_P$$

$$\Rightarrow N_P = \frac{N_s}{2}$$

The sinusoidal conductor-density distribution in Phase-a winding is

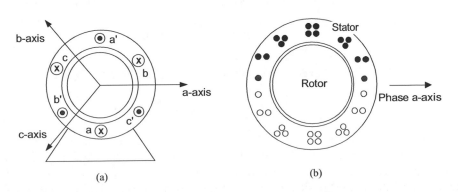

(a)                                                          (b)

**FIGURE 7.13**   (a) Three-phase winding and magnetic axes of an AC machine and (b) sinusoidal distribution of Phase-a winding along the stator circumference.

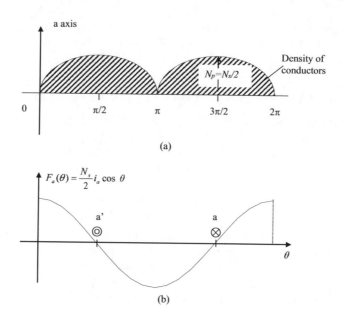

FIGURE 7.14   (a) Equivalent distribution of Phase-a winding and (b) mmf distribution of Phase-a.

$$n_s(\theta) = \frac{N_s}{2} \sin\theta, \ 0 \le \theta \le \pi \tag{7.17}$$

The equivalent conductor-density is used to calculate the air gap magnetic field parameters, which consist of field intensity, flux density and mmf. The basic relationship between magnetic field intensity $H$ and current $i$ is given by Ampere's law, which states that the line integral of $H$ around a closed path is equal to the net current enclosed $\left(\oint H \cdot dl = \sum Ni\right)$. $\sum Ni$ is the ampere-turn product defining the net current enclosed and is known as the total magnetomotive force (mmf) in magnetic circuit terms. The radial magnetic field intensity $H_a$ in the AC machine under discussion is established in the air gap when current $i_a$ flows through the Phase-a windings, which can be derived using Ampere's law as

$$H_a(\theta) = \frac{N_s}{2l_g} i_a \cos\theta$$

where $l_g$ is the length of the air gap. The flux density $B_a(\theta)$ and mmf $F_a(\theta)$ can be derived as

$$B_a(\theta) = \mu_0 H_a(\theta) = \frac{\mu_0 N_s}{2l_g} i_a \cos\theta$$

where $\mu_0$ is the permeability of free space or air and

$$F_a(\theta) = l_g H_a(\theta) = \frac{N_s}{2} i_a \cos\theta. \tag{7.18}$$

The mmf, flux intensity and field intensity are all 90° phase shifted in space with respect to the winding distribution. The angle $\theta$ is measured in the counter clockwise direction with respect to the Phase-a magnetic axis. The field distribution in Figure 7.14b is for positive current. Irrespective of the direction of current, the peak of the mmf (positive or negative) will always appear along the Phase-a magnetic axis, which is the characteristic of mmf produced by a single phase winding.

## 7.4.2 Number of Poles

The two equivalent Phase-a conductors in Figure 7.13a represent two poles of the machine. Electric machines are designed with multiple pairs of poles for efficient utilization of the stator and rotor magnetic core material. In multiple-pole pair machines, the electrical and magnetic variables (such as induced voltages, mmf and flux density) complete more cycles during one mechanical revolution of the motor. The electrical and mechanical angles of revolution and the corresponding speeds are related by

$$\theta_e = \frac{P}{2}\theta_m$$

$$\omega_e = \frac{P}{2}\omega_m$$

(7.19)

where $P$ is the number of poles. The 4-pole machine cross section is represented as shown in Figure 7.15a, while the Phase-a mmf $F_a$ as a function of $\theta_e$ or $\theta_m$ is illustrated in Figure 7.15b. The mmf is mathematically represented as

$$F_a(\theta_e) = \frac{N_s}{P} i_a \cos(\theta_e).$$

(7.20)

## 7.4.3 Three-Phase Sinusoidal Windings

Phases b and c of the three-phase machine have identical sets of windings as the Phase-a winding described in the previous section except that they are displaced 120° spatially with respect to each other as shown in Figure 7.13a. The resulting mmfs due to currents in Phases b and c can be expressed as

$$F_b(\theta) = \frac{N_s}{2} i_b \cos\left(\theta - \frac{2\pi}{3}\right)$$

$$F_c(\theta) = \frac{N_s}{2} i_c \cos\left(\theta + \frac{2\pi}{3}\right),$$

(7.21)

## 7.4.4 Space Vector Representation

The extensive amount of coupling existing among the circuits of three-phase AC machines makes the analysis a formidable task. Axes transformations or reference frame theory is necessary to decouple the voltage expressions of the phases as well as to implement control algorithms that achieve the

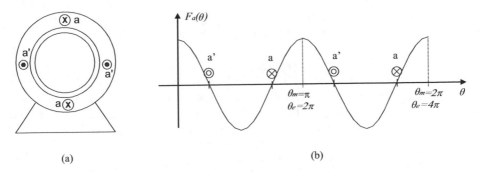

(a)                                                                 (b)

**FIGURE 7.15**   (a) Cross-section of a 4-pole machine showing Phase-a windings only and (b) Phase-a mmf distribution.

best performance. The *space vector representation* is a convenient method of expressing the equivalent resultant effect of the sinusoidally space distributed electrical and magnetic variables in AC
machines, in a way that is similar to the use of phasors in describing the sinusoidally time-varying
voltages and currents in electrical circuits. The space vectors provide a very useful and compact
form of representing the machine equations, which not only simplifies the representation of three-
phase variables, but also facilitates the transformation between three- and two-phase variables. The
two-phase system is an equivalent representation of the three-phase variables in a *dq* (two-axis) co-
ordinate system, which is necessary for control implementation. The *dq* coordinate system will be
elaborated in Section 7.4.6.

The concept of reference frame transformations originates from Parks transformations [2], which
provided a revolutionary new approach of analyzing three-phase electric machines by transforming
three-phase variables (voltages, currents and flux linkages) into two-phase variables with the help
of a set of two fictitious windings (known as *dq* windings) rotating with the rotor. The notations of
space vector evolved later as a compact set of representation of the three-phase machine variables
either in the three-phase *abc* reference frame or in the fictitious two-phase *dq* reference frame [3–5].
The space vectors are more complex than the phasors, since they represent time variation as well
as space variation. The space vectors, just like any other vectors, have a magnitude and an angle,
but the magnitude can be time varying. For example, the stator mmfs of the three phases in the AC
machine can be represented by space vectors as

$$\vec{F}_a(t) = \frac{N_S}{2} i_a(t) \angle 0°$$

$$\vec{F}_b(t) = \frac{N_S}{2} i_b(t) \angle 120° \qquad (7.22)$$

$$\vec{F}_c(t) = \frac{N_S}{2} i_c(t) \angle 240°$$

Note that space vectors are complex numbers and '→' is used to denote the vector characteristic.
The time dependence is also explicitly shown. The magnitude of the vector represents the positive
peak of the sinusoidal spatial distribution and the angle represents the location of the peak with
respect to the Phase-a magnetic axis (chosen by convention). The space vectors of the individual
phases can now be added conveniently by vector addition to give the resultant stator mmf as

$$\vec{F}_s(t) = \vec{F}_a(t) + \vec{F}_b(t) + \vec{F}_c(t) = \hat{F}_S \angle \theta_F \qquad (7.23)$$

where $\hat{F}_S$ is the stator mmf space vector amplitude and $\theta_F$ is the spatial orientation with respect to
the Phase-a reference axis.

In general, if $f$ represents a variable (mmf, flux, voltage or current) in a three-phase AC machine,
the corresponding resultant space vector can be calculated as

$$\vec{f}_{abc}(t) = f_a(t) + a f_b(t) + a^2 f_c(t).$$

where $f_a(t)$, $f_b(t)$ and $f_c(t)$ are the magnitudes of the phase space vectors of the variables and $a$
and $a^2$ are spatial operators that handles the 120° spatial distribution of the three windings one
with respect to the other along the stator circumference. The operators $a$ and $a^2$ are $a = e^{j2\pi/3}$ and
$a^2 = e^{j4\pi/3}$, and hence, the space vector can also be represented as

$$\vec{f}_{abc}(t) = f_a(t) + f_b(t) \angle 120 + f_c(t) \angle 240 \qquad (7.24)$$

The space vector can be used to represent any of the AC machine sinusoidal variables either in the stator circuit or in the rotor circuit. For example, the flux density, current and voltage space vectors of the stator can be expressed as

$$\vec{B}_S(t) = \frac{\mu_0 N_S}{2l_g} i_a(t) + \frac{\mu_0 N_S}{2l_g} i_b(t)\angle 120 + \frac{\mu_0 N_S}{2l_g} i_c(t)\angle 240 = \hat{B}_S \angle \theta_B$$

$$\vec{i}_S(t) = i_a(t) + i_b(t)\angle 120 + i_c(t)\angle 240 = \hat{I}_S \angle \theta_I \qquad (7.25)$$

$$\vec{v}_S(t) = v_a(t) + v_b(t)\angle 120 + v_c(t)\angle 240 = \hat{V}_S \angle \theta_V$$

The space vector $\vec{f}_{abc}$ for a balanced set of three phase variables $f_a$, $f_b$ and $f_c$ has a magnitude 3/2 times greater than the magnitude of the phase variables; its spatial orientation is at an angle $\omega t$ at time $t$ with respect to the reference Phase-a axis. Here, $\omega$ is the angular frequency of the phase variables. Therefore, the amplitude of the space vector is constant for balanced set of variables, but the phase angle (i.e., the spatial orientation) is a function of time. The space vector at any instant of time can be obtained by the vector sum of the three phase variables as shown in Figure 7.16 for stator currents. Note that there is a unique set of phase variables that would sum up to give the resultant space vector $\vec{f}_{abc}$, since $f_a + f_b + f_c = 0$ for a balanced set of variables. Examples with numerical values are given in the following to supplement the theory.

## Example 7.1

The stator currents of a three-phase machine at $\omega t = 40°$ are

$$i_a = 10\cos 40° = 7.66\,\text{A}$$
$$i_b = 10\cos(40° - 120°) = 1.74\,\text{A}$$
$$i_c = 10\cos(40° - 240°) = -9.4\,\text{A}$$

Calculate the resultant space vector.

## Solution

The space vector at $\omega t = 40°$ is

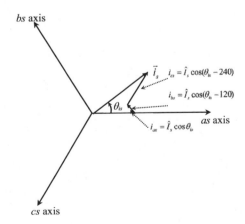

FIGURE 7.16  Space vector and its components in *abc* reference frame.

$$\vec{i}_S = i_a(t) + i_b(t)\angle 120 + i_c(t)\angle 240$$

$$= 7.66 + 1.74\angle 120 + (-9.4)\angle 240$$

$$= \frac{3}{2}(7.66 + j6.43)$$

$$= \frac{3}{2}\cdot 10\angle 40.$$

The projection of $\vec{i}_S$ on the Phase-a axis is $15\cos 40 = 11.49$, which is 3/2 times $i_a$.

## Example 7.2

a. The phase voltage magnitudes of a three-phase AC machine at time $\omega t = 0$ are $v_a = 240$ V, $v_b = -120$ V and $v_c = -120$ V. Calculate the resulting space vector voltage.
b. Recalculate the space vector at a different time when $v_a = 207.8$ V, $v_b = 0$ V and $v_c = -207.8$ V
c. Plot the space vector distribution in the air gap in the two cases.

### Solution

a. The resulting space vector using Equation 7.24 is

$$\vec{v}_S(t) = v_a(t) + v_b(t)\angle 120 + v_c(t)\angle 240$$

$$\Rightarrow \vec{v}_S(t_0) = 240 + (-120)(\cos 120° + j\sin 120°) + (-120)(\cos 240° + j\sin 240°)$$

$$= 360\angle 0° \text{ V}$$

b. The resulting space vector using Equation 7.24 is

$$\vec{v}_S(t) = v_a(t) + v_b(t)\angle 120 + v_c(t)\angle 240$$

$$\Rightarrow \vec{v}_S(t_0) = 207.8 + (0)(\cos 120° + j\sin 120°) + (-207.8)(\cos 240° + j\sin 240°)$$

$$= 360\angle 30° \text{ V}$$

c. The plot is in Figure 7.17.

**FIGURE 7.17** Plot of space vectors for Example 7.2a and b.

**FIGURE 7.18** (a) Resultant voltage space vector and (b) voltage space vector sinusoidal distribution in the air gap at $t_0$.

## Example 7.3

The phase voltage magnitudes of a three-phase AC machine at time $t_0$ are $v_a = 240$ V, $v_b = 50$ V and $v_c = -240$ V. Calculate the resulting space vector voltage and plot the space vector distribution in the air gap.

### Solution

The resulting space vector using Equation 7.24 is

$$\vec{v}_S(t) = v_a(t) + v_b(t)\angle 120 + v_c(t)\angle 240$$

$$\Rightarrow \vec{v}_S(t_0) = 240 + (50)(\cos 120° + j\sin 120°) + (-240)(\cos 240° + j\sin 240°)$$

$$= 418.69\angle 36.86° \text{ V}$$

The voltage space vector and its sinusoidal plot is shown in Figure 7.18.

The voltages given in Example 7.2 are a balanced set at two different times which corresponds to $\omega t = 0$ and $\omega t = 30°$ for parts (a) and (b), respectively. The peak magnitude of the of the resulting voltage space vector remain the same in the two cases and the location of these peaks along the machine axes are at $\theta = 0$ and $\theta = 30°$, which corresponds to the time dependence of the voltages. This is not coincidental, but will be so for balanced set of voltages. In Example 7.3, the voltages are unbalanced and the magnitude of the space vector depends on instantaneous values of the phase voltages.

### 7.4.4.1 Interpretation of Space Vectors

The space vectors, through one convenient and compact vector form, expresses the same resultant effect that the three individual phase variables would produce. For example, the stator mmf distribution in the air gap is result of three phase currents $i_a$, $i_b$ and $i_c$, while the equivalent space vector current $\vec{i}_S(t)$ is developed in such a way that this resultant current flowing through an equivalent winding of $N_s$ turns would produce the same resultant mmf distribution.

The relationships between electrical and magnetic quantities are conveniently expressed with the help of space vectors. Using Equations 7.22, 7.23 and 7.25, we can write

$$\vec{F}_S(t) = \frac{N_S}{2}\vec{i}_S(t). \tag{7.26}$$

The mmf and current vector magnitudes are related by the scalar constant $N_S/2$ and they have the same angular orientation.

The flux-density can be similarly shown to be

$$\vec{B}_S(t) = \frac{\mu_0 N_S}{2l_g}\vec{i}_S(t). \tag{7.27}$$

### 7.4.4.2 Inverse Relations

The phase quantities can be derived from the space vectors through the inverse relations established using the complex variable mathematics. We know that

$$|A|\angle\theta = |A|\cos\theta + j|A|\sin\theta.$$

Applying this to (7.24), we get

$$\vec{f}_{abc}(t) = f_a(t) - \frac{1}{2}(f_b(t) + f_c(t)) + j\frac{\sqrt{3}}{2}(f_b(t) - f_c(t)) = \frac{3}{2}f_a(t) + j\frac{\sqrt{3}}{2}(f_b(t) - f_c(t)),$$

since $f_a(t) + f_b(t) + f_c(t) = 0$ for balanced three-phase systems and for circuits without a neutral connection. Therefore, the inverse relation for the Phase-a variable is

$$f_a(t) = \frac{2}{3} \text{Re}\left[ \vec{f}_{abc}(t) \right] \tag{7.28}$$

Similarly, it can be shown that

$$f_b(t) = \frac{2}{3} \text{Re}\left[ \vec{f}_{abc}(t) \angle 240° \right] \tag{7.29}$$

and

$$f_c(t) = \frac{2}{3} \text{Re}\left[ \vec{f}_{abc}(t) \angle 120° \right]. \tag{7.30}$$

### 7.4.4.3 Resultant mmf in a Balanced System

In the typical operation of an AC machine, the stator windings are supplied with a balanced set of voltages, and since the windings are electrically symmetrical, a balanced set of currents flows through the windings. Let us assume that the rotor is open circuited and all the current that is flowing through the stator winding is the magnetizing current required to establish the stator mmf. The three phase currents have the same magnitude and frequency, but are 120° shifted in time with respect to each other. The currents in the time domain can be expressed as

$$i_a(t) = \hat{I}_M \cos \omega t$$
$$i_b(t) = \hat{I}_M \cos(\omega t - 120°) \tag{7.31}$$
$$i_c(t) = \hat{I}_M \cos(\omega t - 240°).$$

The space vector for the above balanced set of currents is (using Equation 7.24)

$$\vec{i}_M(t) = \frac{3}{2} \hat{I}_M \angle \omega t \tag{7.32}$$

The resultant stator mmf space vector is

$$\vec{F}_{ms}(t) = \frac{N_S}{2} \vec{i}_M(t) = \frac{3}{2} \frac{N_S}{2} \hat{I}_M \angle \omega t = \hat{F}_{ms} \angle \omega t \tag{7.33}$$

The result shows that the stator mmf has a constant peak amplitude $\hat{F}_{ms}$ (since $N_S$ and $\hat{I}_M$ are constants) that rotates around the stator circumference at a constant speed equal to the angular speed of the applied stator voltages. This speed is known as the synchronous speed. Unlike the single-phase stator mmf (shown in Figure 7.14b), the peak of the stator mmf resulting in the three-phase AC machine is rotating synchronously along the stator circumference with the peak always located at $\theta = \omega t$. The mmf peak position is time-varying for the three-phase winding, whereas the peak mmf position for the single-phase winding is not time-varying. The mmf wave is a sinusoidal function of the space angle $\theta$. The wave has constant amplitude and a space-angle $\omega t$, which is linear with respect to time. The angle $\omega t$ provides rotation of the entire wave around the air gap at a constant angular velocity $\omega$. Thus, at a fixed time $t_x$, the wave is a sinusoid in space with its positive peak displaced $\omega t_x$ from the reference $\theta = 0$. The resultant space vector at three different times is shown in Figure 7.19. The polyphase windings excited by balanced polyphase currents produce the same general effect as that of spinning a permanent magnet about an axis perpendicular to the magnet, or as in the rotation of the DC-excited field poles.

The three-phase stator mmf is known as the rotating mmf, which can be equivalently viewed as a magnet rotating around the stator circumference at a constant speed. Note that with the vector sum of $F_a(\theta_e)$, $F_b(\theta_e)$ and $F_c(\theta_e)$ as described in Equations 7.20 and 7.21 with $i_a(t)$, $i_b(t)$ and $i_c(t)$ replaced by the balanced set of Equation 7.31, we will arrive at the same result.

**FIGURE 7.19**   Resultant mmf space vector for $\omega t = -30°$, $0°$ and $90°$.

**Exercise 7.1**

Show that $F_a(\theta_e) + F_b(\theta_e) + F_c(\theta_e) = \dfrac{3}{2} \dfrac{N_S}{2} \hat{I}_M \angle \omega t$ with

$$i_a(t) = \hat{I}_M \cos \omega t$$
$$i_b(t) = \hat{I}_M \cos(\omega t - 120°)$$
$$i_c(t) = \hat{I}_M \cos(\omega t - 240°)$$

### 7.4.4.4   Mutual Inductance $L_m$ and Induced Stator Voltage

In an ideal situation, the equivalent electrical circuit for the stator windings with no rotor existing consists of the applied stator voltage source and a set of winding that is represented by an inductance known as magnetizing or mutual inductance. The practical circuit extends on this ideal circuit by adding the stator winding resistance and the stator leakage inductance in series with the magnetizing inductance. The magnetizing inductance for the three-phase AC machine including the effects of mutual coupling among the three phases can be shown to be [4,5]

$$L_m = \frac{3}{2}\left[ \frac{\pi \mu_0 r l}{l_g} \left( \frac{N_S}{2} \right)^2 \right] \tag{7.34}$$

where $r$ is the radius to the air gap, $l$ is the rotor axial length and $l_g$ is the air gap length. Note that the form of Equation 7.34 is the same as that of a simple inductor given by $L = \dfrac{N^2}{\mathfrak{R}}$, where $N$ is the number of turns and $\mathfrak{R} = \text{Reluctance} = \dfrac{\text{Flux-path length}}{\mu \times \text{Cross-sectional area}}$. The voltage induced in the stator windings due to the magnetizing current flowing through $L_m$ in space vector form is

$$\vec{e}_{ms}(t) = j\omega L_m \vec{i}_M(t) \tag{7.35}$$

The magnetizing flux-density $\vec{B}_{ms}(t)$ established by the magnetizing current $\vec{i}_M(t)$ is (from Equation 7.27)

$$\vec{B}_{ms}(t) = \frac{\mu_0 N_S}{2l_g} \vec{i}_M(t),$$

which gives

$$\vec{i}_M(t) = \frac{2l_g}{\mu_0 N_S} \vec{B}_{ms}(t). \tag{7.36}$$

Using the expression for $L_m$ from Equation 7.34 and the expression for $\vec{i}_M(t)$ in terms of $\vec{B}_{ms}(t)$, the induced voltage is

$$\vec{e}_{ms}(t) = j\omega \frac{3}{2}\pi r l \frac{N_S}{2} \vec{B}_{ms}(t).$$

The induced voltage can be interpreted as the back-emf induced by the flux-density $B_{ms}$, which is rotating at the synchronous speed. For a $P$-pole machine, the expression for the induced voltage is,

$$\vec{e}_{ms}(t) = j\omega\frac{3}{2}\pi rl\frac{N_S}{P}\vec{B}_{ms}(t) \tag{7.37}$$

### 7.4.5 Types of AC Machines

The second rotating mmf needed for torque production in AC machines is established by the rotor circuit. The interaction of the two rotating mmfs, essentially chasing each other at synchronous speed, is what produces torque. The method through which the rotor mmf is established differentiates the different types of AC machines. Broadly, the AC machines can be classified into two categories, synchronous machines and asynchronous machines. Figure 7.20 shows the cross-sections of the two types of AC machines. In synchronous machines, the rotor always rotates at synchronous speed. The rotor mmf is established either by using a permanent magnet or an electromagnet created by feeding DC currents into a rotor coil. The latter type synchronous machines are typically the large machines that are used in electric power generating systems. The permanent magnet machines are more suitable for the electric and hybrid vehicle applications, since these offer higher power density and superior performance compared to the rotor-fed synchronous machines. The several types of permanent magnet AC machines will be discussed later in the chapter. The rotor fed synchronous machines will not be discussed further in this book, since these are not of interest for the electric and hybrid vehicle applications. In the asynchronous type AC machine, the rotor rotates at a speed that is different but close to the synchronous speed. These machines are known as induction machines, which in the more common configurations are fed only from the stator. The voltages in the rotor circuit are induced from the stator, which in turn induces the rotor rotating mmf and hence the name induction machines. The induction machines that are generally labeled as AC machines are the subject of treatment in the following section.

### 7.4.6 *dq* Modeling

The *dq* modeling provides a methodology to analyze three-phase electric machines by transforming three-phase variables (voltages, currents and flux linkages) into two-phase variables with the help of a set of two fictitious windings, known as *dq* windings, that are in quadrature with each other. In the *dq* coordinate system, the *d*-axis is the direct axis aligned with a rotor related magnetic field, while the *q*-axis is in quadrature to the direct axis. The transformation allows three-phase variables in the *abc* coordinate system to be represented with *d*- and *q*-axes variable into an equivalent two-phase co-ordinate system that has an arbitrary speed in a given reference frame [2,4]. The reference frame relates to the rotational speed of the *dq*-axes. When the *dq* co-ordinates are stationary and the *d*-axis is aligned with

(a)              (b)              (c)

**FIGURE 7.20** Asynchronous and synchronous AC machines: (a) induction, (b) surface PM and (c) interior PM machines.

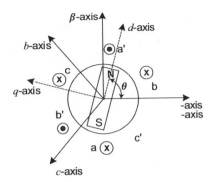

**FIGURE 7.21**    The *abc*, *dq* and $\alpha\beta$ coordinates of an elementary 2-pole AC machine.

the stationary *a*-axis, then the transformation is known as $\alpha\beta$-transformation. The coordinate variables with respect to the *abc* frame and the rotor mmf-axis is shown in Figure 7.21. The rotor magnet shown represents either a permanent magnet or a 2-pole rotor magnetic field induced in the rotor.

The objective of *dq* modeling is to transform the three phase *abc*-variables into *dq*-variables in a suitable reference frame so that the coupling between the stator and rotor variables of a three-phase AC machine disappears. The space vector approach is retained in the *dq* reference frame, since these vectors help express the complex three phase equations of AC machines in a compact form and also provides a simple relation for transformation between *abc* and *dq* reference frames.

Mathematically stated, for a general variable *f* (representing voltage, current or flux linkage), the *q* and *d*-axes variables in terms of the *a*, *b* and *c* variables are

$$f_q = \frac{2}{3}\left[f_a\cos\theta + f_b\cos(\theta - 120°) + f_c\cos(\theta + 120°)\right]$$

$$(7.38)$$

$$f_d = \frac{2}{3}\left[f_a\sin\theta + f_b\sin(\theta - 120°) + f_c\sin(\theta + 120°)\right].$$

The transformation relation holds good for stator as well as for rotor variables. A third variable is required to obtain a unique transformation, which comes from the neutral terminal. Representing the neutral terminal variable as a zero-sequence component, we have

$$f_0 = \frac{1}{3}\left[f_a + f_b + f_c\right].$$

$$(7.39)$$

For a balanced system or a Y-connected winding without a neutral connection, the zero-sequence component does not exist, resulting in

$$f_a + f_b + f_c = 0 \Rightarrow f_0 = 0.$$

Henceforth, we will consider the *d* and *q* variables ignoring the zero-sequence component.

The variables in the *dq* reference frame can be expressed in the space vector form as

$$\vec{f}_{qd}(t) = f_q(t) - jf_d(t) = \frac{2}{3}e^{-j\theta}\left[f_a(t) + e^{j\frac{2\pi}{3}}f_b(t) + e^{-j\frac{2\pi}{3}}f_b(t)\right]$$

$$= \frac{2}{3}e^{-j\theta}\vec{f}_{abc}(t)$$

$$(7.40)$$

The result shows that the *dq* space vector $\vec{f}_{qd}(t)$ is 2/3 of the space vector $\vec{f}_{abc}(t)$ along the *d* and *q*-axes. Equating the real and imaginary parts of the Equation 7.40, the transformation matrix between the *abc* and *dq* variables are

$$\begin{bmatrix} f_q(t) \\ f_d(t) \\ 0 \end{bmatrix} = T_{abc \to qd} \begin{bmatrix} f_a(t) \\ f_b(t) \\ f_c(t) \end{bmatrix}, \text{ where } T_{abc \to qd} = \frac{2}{3} \begin{bmatrix} \cos(\theta) & \cos(\theta - 2\pi/3) & \cos(\theta + 2\pi/3) \\ \sin(\theta) & \sin(\theta - 2\pi/3) & \sin(\theta + 2\pi/3) \\ 0.5 & 0.5 & 0.5 \end{bmatrix}$$

(7.41)

This transformation is known as Park's transformation. The *abc* variables are obtained from the *dq* variables through the inverse of the Park transform

$$T_{qd \to abc} = \begin{bmatrix} \cos(\theta) & \sin(\theta) & 1 \\ \cos(\theta - 2\pi/3) & \sin(\theta - 2\pi/3) & 1 \\ \cos(\theta + 2\pi/3) & \sin(\theta + 2\pi/3) & 1 \end{bmatrix}$$

(7.42)

The choice of the 2/3rd multiplying factor in Equation 7.38 is not unique. Several choices exist to define the relationship between the *abc*-axes variables and the *dq*-axes variables, since the transformation is from a three-phase set of variables to a two-phase set of variables. The choice of 2/3 makes the *dq*-variables to be 2/3 times the projection of $\vec{f}_{abc}$ on the *d* and *q* axes; $\frac{2}{3} \cdot \vec{f}_{abc}$ gives the same space vector magnitude as the peak value of the individual phase time-domain variables. Another possible choice is to take the *dq*-variables to be $\sqrt{2/3}$ times the projection of $\vec{f}_{abc}$ on the *d*- and *q*-axes. The $\sqrt{2/3}$ ratio between the *dq*-variables and the *abc*-variables conserves power without any multiplying factor in the *dq* and *abc* reference frames, and hence, is known as the power invariant transformation. In order for the equivalent *dq* windings to establish the same stator mmf $\vec{F}_S(t)$ as is done by the *abc* windings, the number of turns in the equivalent sinusoidally distributed orthogonal windings must be $2/3N_S$ or $\sqrt{2/3} N_S$, depending on the chosen transformation ratio. We shall arbitrarily choose the multiplying factor of 2/3 to define the transformation.

## 7.5  INDUCTION MACHINES

The two types of induction machines are the squirrel cage induction machines and the wound rotor induction machines. The squirrel cage induction machines are the workhorse of the industry, because of their rugged construction and low cost. The rotor windings consist of short-circuited copper bars that form the shape of a squirrel cage. The squirrel cage of an induction motor is shown in Figure 7.22. The rotor winding terminals of the wound rotor induction machines are brought outside with the help of slip rings for external connections, which are used for speed control. The squirrel cage induction motors are the one of greater interest for electric and hybrid vehicles and most other general purpose applications, and hence, are discussed further.

The stator windings of the induction machines are exactly the same as that discussed in the previous section. The rotor, usually made of stacked laminations, has copper or aluminum rotor bars molded around the periphery in axial direction. The bars are short-circuited at the ends through electrically conducting end rings. The electrical equivalent circuit of a three phase induction machine along with the direction of Phase-a stator and rotor magnetic axes are shown in Figure 7.23. The rotor windings have been short-circuited and the angle between the rotor and stator axes is $\theta_r$, which is the integral of the rotor speed $\omega_r$.

When a balanced set of voltages is applied to the stator windings, a magnetic field is established which rotates at synchronous speed as described in Section 7.3.4. By Faraday's law, as long as the

**FIGURE 7.22**   The squirrel cage of an induction motor.

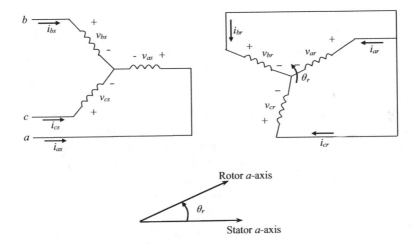

**FIGURE 7.23**   Stator and rotor electric circuit and magnetic axes of three-phase induction machine.

rotor rotates at a speed other than the synchronous speed (even at zero rotor speed), the rotor conductor are cutting the stator magnetic field and there is a rate of change of flux in the rotor circuit,
which will induce a voltage in the rotor bars. This is also analogous to transformer action where
a time varying AC flux established by the primary winding induces voltage in the secondary set
of windings. The induced voltage will cause rotor currents to flow in the rotor circuit, since the
rotor windings or bars are short-circuited in the induction machine. The induction machine can be
thought of as a transformer with a short-circuited secondary or rotor windings. The rotor induced
voltages and the current have a sinusoidal space distribution, since these are created by the sinusoidally varying (space sinusoids) stator magnetic field. The resultant effect of the rotor bar currents is
to produce a sinusoidally distributed rotor mmf acting on the air gap.

The difference between the rotor speed and the stator synchronous speed is the speed by which the rotor is slipping from the stator magnetic field, and is known as the slip speed:

$$\omega_{slip} = \omega_e - \omega_m \tag{7.43}$$

where $\omega_e$ is the synchronous speed and $\omega_m$ is the motor or rotor speed. The slip speed expressed as a fraction of the synchronous speed is known as the slip:

$$s = \frac{\omega_e - \omega_m}{\omega_e}. \tag{7.44}$$

The rotor bar voltages, current and magnetic field are of the slip speed or slip frequency with respect to the rotor. The slip frequency is given by

$$f_{slip} = \frac{\omega_e - \omega_m}{2\pi} = sf, \text{ where } f = \frac{\omega_e}{2\pi}. \tag{7.45}$$

From the stator perspective, the rotor voltages, currents and rotor mmf all have the synchronous frequency, since the rotor speed of $\omega_m$ is superimposed on the rotor variables' speed of $\omega_{slip}$.

### 7.5.1 Per-Phase Equivalent Circuit

The steady-state analysis of induction motors is often carried out using the per phase equivalent circuit. A single phase equivalent circuit is used for the three-phase induction machine assuming a balanced set as shown in Figure 7.24. The per-phase equivalent circuit consists of the stator loop and the rotor loop with the magnetic circuit parameters in the middle. The inductance representing the magnetization current path is in the middle of the circuit along with an equivalent core loss resistance. For the stator and rotor electrical parameters, the circuit includes the stator winding resistance and leakage reactance and the rotor winding resistance and leakage reactance. A slip-dependent equivalent resistance represents the mechanical power delivered at the shaft due to the energy conversion in the air gap-coupled electromagnetic circuit. The electrical input power supplied at the stator terminals converts to magnetic power and crosses the air gap. The air gap power $P_{ag}$ is converted to mechanical power delivered at the shaft after overcoming the losses in the rotor circuit.

Although the per phase equivalent circuit is not enough for designing controllers with good dynamic performance like that required in an electric or hybrid vehicle, the circuit helps develop the basic understanding of induction machines. The vast majority of applications of induction motors are for adjustable speed drives where controllers designed for good steady-state performance are adequate. The circuit does allow the analysis of a number of steady-state performance features.

The parameters of the circuit model are as follows:

$E_{ms}$ = Stator induced emf per-phase
$V_s$ = Stator terminal voltage per-phase
$I_s$ = Stator terminal current
$R_s$ = Stator resistance per-phase
$X_{ls}$ = Stator leakage reactance
$X_m$ = Magnetizing reactance
$X'_{lr}$ = Rotor leakage reactance referred to stator
$R'_r$ = Rotor resistance referred to stator
$I'_r$ = Rotor current per phase referred to stator

**FIGURE 7.24** Steady-state per-phase equivalent circuit of an induction motor.

Note that the voltages and currents described here in relation to the per-phase equivalent circuit are phasors and not space vectors. The power and torque relations are

$$P_{ag} = \text{Air gap power} = 3|I_r'|^2 \frac{R_r'}{s}$$

$$P_{dev} = \text{Developed mechanical power} = 3|I_r'|^2 \frac{(1-s)R_r'}{s}$$

$$= (1-s)P_{ag}$$

$$= T_e \omega_m$$

$$P_R = \text{Rotor copper loss} = 3|I_r'|^2 R_r'$$

The electromagnetic torque is given by

$$T_e = 3|I_r'|^2 \frac{(1-s)R_r'}{s\omega_m}$$

$$= \frac{3R_r'}{s\omega_s} \frac{V_s^2}{(R_s + R_r'/s)^2 + (X_s + X_r')^2} \tag{7.46}$$

The steady-state torque-speed characteristics of the machine are as shown in Figure 7.25. The torque produced by the motor depends on the slip and the stator currents among other variables. The induction motor starting torque, while depending on the design, is lower than the peak torque achievable from the motor. The motor is always operated in the linear region of the torque-speed curve to avoid the higher losses associated with the high slip operation. In other words, operating the machine at small slip values improves the efficiency.

The value of the rotor circuit resistance determines the speed at which the maximum torque will occur. In general, the starting torque is low and the maximum torque occurs close to the synchronous speed when the slip is small. The motor draws a large current during line starting from a fixed AC source, which gradually subsides as the motor reaches the steady-state speed. If the load requires a high starting torque, the motor will accelerate slowly. This will make a large current flow for a longer time, thereby creating a heating problem.

The non-linearity at speeds below the rated condition is due to the effects of the leakage reactances. At higher slip values, the frequencies of the rotor variables are large resulting in dominating impedance effects from the rotor leakage inductance. The air gap flux cannot be maintained at the rated value under this condition. Also, large values of rotor current (which flows at high slip values)

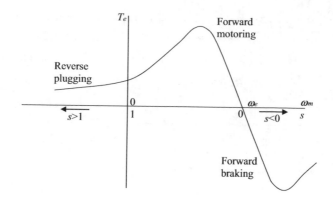

**FIGURE 7.25**   Steady-state torque speed characteristics of an induction motor.

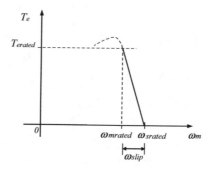

**FIGURE 7.26**   Torque-speed characteristics of induction motor for rated flux condition.

cause a significant voltage drop across the stator winding leakage impedance ($R_s + j\omega L_{ls}$), which reduces the induced voltage and in turn the stator mmf flux density $\hat{B}_{ms}$.

### 7.5.2  SIMPLIFIED TORQUE EXPRESSION

A simplified linear torque expression is sufficient to analyze the motor-load interaction, since the induction motor is invariably always operated in the linear region at maximum flux density $\hat{B}_{ms}$ with the help of a power electronic feed circuit. The segment of interest in the torque speed characteristic curve of the induction motor is shown by the solid line in Figure 7.26. The synchronous speed is set by the applied voltage frequency and the slope of the linear region is set by the design parameters and material properties. Hence, assuming that the stator flux density is kept constant at its rated value, the steady-state torque can be expressed linearly as a function of slip:

$$T_e = K_{IM}\omega_{slip}.$$

Here $K_{IM}$ is a constant; the constant originates from the dependence of torque production with the geometry and the number of turns of the induction machine. The electromagnetic torque is produced by the tendency of the stator and rotor mmfs trying to align with each other. The rotor mmf is due to the rotor current. The principle of torque production essentially lies in the Lorenz force law ($F = Bil$). Therefore, the electromagnetic torque produced in an induction machine at steady state can be expressed as

$$T_e = k_M \hat{B}_{ms} \hat{I}'_r \tag{7.47}$$

where $k_M$ is a machine constant. $\hat{B}_{ms}$ is the equivalent peak stator mmf flux density for the three-phase machine and $\hat{I}'_r$ peak equivalent rotor current. Note that these are different from the single phase equivalent circuit per phase quantities. Mohan [5] showed that this machine constant is $k_M = \pi r l \dfrac{N_S}{2}$ where $r$ is the radius to the air gap, $l$ is axial length of the machine and $N_S$ is the equivalent number of turns.

In order to find a relation between $\hat{B}_{ms}$ and rotor current $\hat{I}'_r$, let us denote the rotor mmf by the space vector $\vec{F}_r(t)$. The stator windings must carry currents in addition to the magnetizing current $\vec{i}_M(t)$ to support the currents induced in the rotor by transformer action to create $\vec{F}_r(t)$. These rotor currents referred to stator, or in other words, the additional stator current is represented by $\vec{i}'_r(t)$ (with magnitude $\hat{I}'_r$) and is related to $\vec{F}_r(t)$ by

$$\vec{i}'_r(t) = \frac{\vec{F}_r}{N_S/2}.$$

The total stator current is the sum of magnetizing current and referred rotor current

$$\vec{i}_S(t) = \vec{i}_M(t) + \vec{i}'_r(t). \tag{7.48}$$

These space vectors are shown in Figure 7.27. The rotor leakage inductance $L'_{lr}$ has been neglected in this diagram for simplification. Although this is an ideal situation, it is a very important assumption that helps one grasp the basic concepts of torque production in induction machines. Neglecting the rotor leakage reactance is equivalent to assuming that all of the flux created by the rotor bar currents crosses the air gap and links the stator windings, and that there are no leakage fluxes in the rotor. The rated speed on induction machines is close to the synchronous speed and the machine usually operates near the rated condition with a very small slip. At small slip values, the slip speed $\omega_{slip}$ is very small and it is justified to neglect the effect of rotor leakage inductance, which is small anyway. Mohan [5] showed that under this simplifying assumption, the rotor bar currents induced by Faraday's law are proportional to the stator flux density and slip speed, the peak of which can be given by

$$\hat{I}'_r = k_r \hat{B}_{ms} \omega_{slip} \tag{7.49}$$

where $k_r$ is a machine design constant.

Substituting $\hat{I}'_r$ from Equation 7.49 in the torque equation

$$T_e = k_m k_r \hat{B}_{ms}^2 \omega_{slip}.$$

The electromagnetic torque for fixed stator flux density is

$$T_e = K_{IM} \omega_{slip} \tag{7.50}$$

where $K_{IM} = k_m k_r \hat{B}_{ms}^2$.

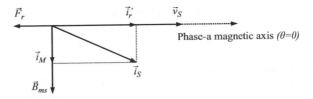

**FIGURE 7.27**  Space vector diagram of stator and rotor variables at $t = 0$.

The simple torque expression presents a convenient method of defining the toque-speed relationship of an induction machine linearly near the rated operating point very much similar to the DC machine relationship. The expression can be used to find the steady-state operating point of an induction machine driven electric and hybrid vehicles by finding the point of intersection of the machine torque-speed characteristics and the road load force-speed characteristics. When the motor rotates at synchronous speed, the slip speed is zero and the motor does not produce any torque. In practice, the machine never reaches the synchronous speed even in an unloaded condition, since a small electromagnetic torque is needed to overcome the no load losses that include the friction and windage losses. The slip speed is small up to the rated torque of the machine, and hence, it is reasonable to neglect the rotor leakage inductance, which gives the linear torque-speed relationship. The machine runs close to the synchronous speed under no load condition with a very small slip. As the machine is loaded from the no load condition, the slip starts to increase and the speed approaches the rated speed condition. Beyond the rated condition, the machine operates with a higher slip and the assumption of neglecting the leakage inductance starts to fall apart. This portion of the torque-speed characteristics is shown by a dotted curve in Figure 7.26.

The induction motors for electric and hybrid vehicles and other high performance applications are supplied from a variable voltage, variable frequency AC source. Varying the frequency changes the rated flux and synchronous speed of the machine, which essentially causes the linear torque-speed curve of Figure 7.26 to move horizontally along the speed axis toward the origin.

### Example 7.4

The vehicle road load characteristics on a level road are calculated as $T_{TR} = 24.7 + 0.0051\omega_{wh}^2$. The induction motor torque-speed relationship in the linear region is given by $T_e = K_{IM}(40 - \omega_m)$ including the gear ratio of the transmission system. The rated torque of 40 N m is available at a speed of 35 rad/s. Find the steady-state operating point of the vehicle.

### *Solution*

The induction motor torque constant is

$$K_{IM} = 40/(40 - 35) = 8 \text{ N m/rad/s.}$$

The steady-state operating point is obtained by solving the vehicle road load characteristic and the motor torque speed characteristic, which gives

$$\omega^* = 36.08 \text{ rad/s and } T^* = 31.34 \text{ N m.}$$

The torque and speed output of an induction machine is maintained through controlling the applied voltage and frequency by the motor drive unit according to the steady-state torque relation of Equation 7.46. Changing $f$ changes $\omega_e$ which is based on the frequency and synchronous speed relation $\omega_e = \dfrac{4\pi f}{p}$. What is needed to drive the induction motor is a power electronics converter that will convert the available constant voltage into a variable voltage, variable frequency output according to the command torque and speed.

Figure 7.28 shows the envelope of the torque speed characteristics of an induction motor. Using a power electronics-controlled drive, it is possible to achieve constant power characteristics from an induction motor at higher speeds, a feature that is so important for electric and hybrid vehicle motor drives. The first generation controllers of induction motor drives used in electric vehicles employed slip control (constant V/Hz control) using a table of slip versus torque. The performance of such a drive for vehicle applications is very poor, since the concept of V/Hz control is based on steady-state equivalent circuit of the machine. The dynamic performance of the machine improves significantly using vector control. The *dq*-axes transformation theory for induction motors pertaining to vector control theory will be covered in Chapter 8, which discusses high performance AC motor control methods.

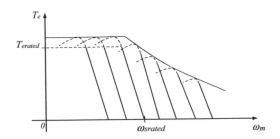

**FIGURE 7.28**    Torque-speed operating envelop for the induction motor.

### 7.5.3    REGENERATIVE BRAKING

One of the advantages of using electric motors for vehicle propulsion is to save energy during vehicle braking through regeneration. The regenerated energy can be used to recharge the batteries of an electric or hybrid vehicle. It is important to note that it will not be possible to capture all of the energy that is available during vehicle braking, especially when sudden stops are commanded. The energy that is available during braking is the kinetic energy that was acquired by the vehicle during acceleration. The energy is typically too high to be processed by the electric motor that is used for propulsion. Processing high energy at a relatively short time would require a large motor, or in other words a motor with very high power ratings, which is impractical. Hence, electric and hybrid vehicles must be equipped with the mechanical brake system even though the electric motor drive is designed with regeneration capability. However, regeneration can recapture a significant portion of kinetic energy extending the vehicle range. The vehicle supervisory controller decides the amount of braking that is needed from the mechanical system based on the driver braking command, the amount of regeneration possible and the vehicle velocity.

In the regenerative braking mode, the vehicle kinetic energy drives the shaft of the electric machine and the flow of energy is from the wheels to the energy storage system. The electric machine converts the mechanical power available from the vehicle kinetic energy and converts it to electrical energy. From the machine perspective, this is no different than operating the machine in the generator mode. Regenerative braking can increase the range of electric vehicle by a small percentage (about 10%–15%).

The induction machine works as a generator when it is operated with a negative slip, i.e. the synchronous speed is less than the motor speed ($\omega_m > \omega_e$). The negative slip makes the electromagnetic torque negative during regeneration or generating mode. In the negative slip mode of operation, the voltages and currents induced in the rotor bars are of opposite polarity compared to those in the positive slip mode. The electromagnetic torque acts on the rotor to oppose the rotor rotation, thereby decelerating the vehicle.

The motor drives for electric and hybrid vehicles are always four-quadrant drives meaning that the electric motor is controlled by the drive to deliver positive or negative torque at positive or negative speed. The transition from forward motoring to regeneration can be explained with the help of Figure 7.29 for four-quadrant induction motor drives. The linear segments of the induction motor toque-speed curves for several operating frequencies are shown in the figure. Consider the frequencies $f_1$ and $f_2$. The curves are extended in the negative torque region to show the characteristics during regeneration. Suppose initially, the vehicle is moving forward being driven by the positive torque delivered by the induction motor and the steady-state operating point in this condition is at point '1'. Now, the vehicle driver presses the brake pedal to slow down the vehicle. The vehicle system controller immediately changes the motor drive frequency to $f_2$ such that $\omega_{s2} < \omega_{m1}$. The operating point shifts to point '2' immediately, since the motor speed cannot change instantaneously due to the inertia of the system. At point '2', the slip and the electromagnetic torque are negative and the motor is regenerating. The vehicle will decelerate from

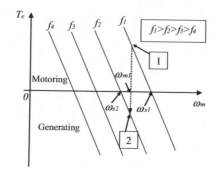

**FIGURE 7.29**  Transition from motoring to generating using a four-quadrant drive.

this condition onward. As the motor speed decreases and falls below the synchronous speed, the operating frequency needs to be changed to a lower value so that generating mode operation can be maintained. The power electronics drive is responsible for establishing the shifted linear torque-speed curves with different synchronous speeds for the induction machine at different frequencies as shown. The drive circuit does so by changing the frequency of the supply voltage. The regenerative braking mode continues as long as there is kinetic energy available and the driver wishes to slow down the vehicle. Similar to starting, the regeneration also has to be achieved in a controlled way so that the power rating of the machine is not exceeded. The amount of kinetic energy to be converted within the desired stopping time determines the power that is to be handled by the machine.

## 7.6   PERMANENT MAGNET MACHINES

The machines that use magnets to produce air-gap magnetic flux instead of field coils as in DC commutator machines or magnetizing component of stator current as in induction machines are the permanent magnet (PM) machines. This configuration eliminates the rotor copper loss as well as the need for maintenance of the field exciting circuit. The PM machines can be broadly classified into two categories:

- PM synchronous machines (PMSM): The machines have uniformly rotating stator field as in induction machines. The induced waveforms are sinusoidal and hence $dq$ transformation and vector control are possible.
- PM trapezoidal or brushless DC machines (PM BLDC): The induced voltages in these machines are trapezoidal in nature; the phase currents are rectangular or squarewave in nature. These PM machines are also known as squarewave or electronically commutated machines. The stator field is switched in discrete steps with square wave pulses.

There are several advantages of using permanent magnets for the field excitation in AC machines. The permanent magnets provide a loss free excitation in a compact way without complications of connections to the external stationary electric circuits. This is especially true for smaller machines, since there is always an excitation penalty associated with providing the rotor field through electrical circuits. The large synchronous machines use rotor conductors to provide the excitation, since the losses in the exciter circuit, referred to as excitation penalty, is small, especially when compared to the high costs of magnets. For smaller machines, the mmf required is small and the resistive effects often become comparable and dominating resulting in lower efficiency. The smaller cross-sectional area of the windings for small power machines further deteriorates the resistive loss effect. Moreover, the cross-sectional area available for winding decreases as the motor size gets smaller. The loss free excitation of PM in smaller machines with a compact arrangement is a definite plus with the only drawback being the high costs of the permanent magnets. Nevertheless, permanent magnet machines are a strong contender for electric and hybrid vehicle drives despite the larger size of these machines. All the production passenger hybrid vehicles use PM machines for the traction motor. The factors guiding the trend are the excellent performance and the high power density achievable from the PM machine drives.

### 7.6.1 PM Synchronous Motors

The permanent magnet synchronous motor (PMSM) is a synchronous motor with sinusoidal mmf, voltage and current waveforms where the field mmf is provided by permanent magnets. The use of rare earth magnet materials increases the flux density in the air gap and accordingly increases the motor power density and torque-to-inertia ratio. In high-performance motion control systems that require servo-type operation, the PMSM can provide fast response, high power density and high efficiency. In certain applications like robotics and aerospace actuators, it is preferable to have the weight as low as possible for a given output power. The PMSM, similar to the induction and DC machines, is fed from a power electronic inverter for its operation. The smooth torque output is maintained in these machines by shaping the motor currents, which requires a high-resolution position sensor and current sensors. The control algorithm is implemented in a digital processor using feedback from the sensors. A flux weakening mode that enables a higher speed operation in the constant power region is possible in PMSM by applying a stator flux in opposition to the rotor magnet flux. The motor high speed limit depends on the motor parameters, its current rating, the back-emf waveform, and the maximum output voltage of the inverter.

PMSM and induction motors have good performance in terms of torque response and have rugged motor structures, although broken magnet chips in PM machines is a concern. The slip speed calculation makes the induction motor control more complicated than that of the PMSM. Without a rotor cage, the PMSM has a lower inertia that helps the electrical response time, although the induction motor electrical response characteristics will be the fastest because of the smaller time constant. The electrical time constant of magnetic circuits is determined by the $L/R$ ratio. The load current transient in induction machines is limited only by the small leakage inductance, where the time constant inductance in PM machines is the much higher self-inductance. With a higher power density, the PMSM is smaller in size compared to an induction motor with the same power rating. The PMSM is more efficient and easier to cool due to the absence of rotor copper loss compared to the induction machines. The induction motor has lower cost and zero cogging torque, because of the absence of permanent magnets. Also, it is less sensitive to higher operating temperatures. The induction motor can sustain a higher peak stator current at several times the rated current without the danger of demagnetizing the magnets. Both the induction motors and the PMSM suffer from limited field weakening speed range.

The permanent magnets in PMSMs are not only expensive, but also sensitive to temperature and load conditions, which constitutes the major drawbacks of PM machines. Most of the PMSMs are found in small to medium power applications, although there are some high power applications for which PMSMs are being used.

PMSM has a stator with a set of three-phase sinusoidally distributed copper windings similar to the windings described in Section 7.2 on AC machines. A balanced set of applied three-phase voltages forces a balanced set of sinusoidal currents in the three-phase stator windings, which in turn establishes the constant amplitude rotating mmf in the air gap. The stator currents are regulated using rotor position feedback so that the applied current frequency is always in synchronism with the rotor. The permanent magnets in the rotor are appropriately shaped and their magnetization directions are controlled such that the rotor flux linkage created is sinusoidal. The electromagnetic torque is produced at the shaft by the interaction of these two stator and rotor magnetic fields.

The PMSMs are classified according to the position and shape of the permanent magnets in the rotors. The three common arrangements of the rotors are surface mounted, inset and interior or buried. The surface mounted and interior PM machine configurations are shown in Figure 7.34. The difference between surface mounted and inset magnets is that the magnets in the latter are inside the rotor surface, but still exposed to the air gap. The surface mounted and inset rotor PMSMs are often collectively called the surface mount PMSMs. In the surface-mounted PMSM, the magnets are epoxy-glued or wedge-fixed to the cylindrical rotor. Non-magnetic stainless steel or carbon fiber sleeves are also used to contain the magnets. The manufacturing of this kind of rotor is simple, although the mechanical strength of the rotor is only as good as that of the epoxy glue. In the inset PMSM, the magnets are put into the rotor surface slots, which make the magnet more secured.

The third type of PMSM is the interior PMSM (IPMSM), so named because the magnets are embedded inside the rotor. The manufacturing process is somewhat complex for the interior PMSM since the magnets has to be inserted after the lamination stacking of the rotor and then magnetized. However, the IPMSM has become the electric machine of choice for electric and hybrid vehicle applications due to the high power density and high efficiency offered by the design of these electric machines. The rotor structure is also robust since the magnets are buried inside and does not have the disadvantage of chipping off such as in SPMSMs. For electric and hybrid vehicle applications, the motor size is relatively large compared to the other smaller power applications of PM motors, which amplifies the cost problem due to the high cost of rare-earth magnet materials used in traction IPMSMs. The magnets in the rotor can have different arrangements such an I-type (shown in Figure 7.30c) or V-type or double-V type. A V-I type arrangement has also been used in production vehicles.

The stator circuit of a PMSM is similar to that of an induction motor or a wound rotor synchronous motor with the applied voltage being balanced by the stator winding resistance drop and the induced voltage in the winding. Assuming sinusoidally distributed stator mmf, the stator phase voltage equation in the stationary *abc* reference frame is

$$\vec{v}_{abcs} = \overline{R}_s \vec{i}_{abcs} + \frac{d}{dt} \vec{\lambda}_{abcs} \tag{7.51}$$

where the flux linkages are

$$\vec{\lambda}_{abcs} = \overline{L}_s \vec{i}_{abcs} + \vec{\lambda}_f.$$

$\overline{\lambda}_f$ is the flux in the stationary *abc* frame established by the PM flux. The eddy current and hysteresis losses are neglected in the model, since PM is a poor electrical conductor and eddy currents are negligible. Large armature currents can be tolerated in these machines without significant demagnetization. The flux and torque models for the Surface PMSM and Interior PMSM are discussed next.

### 7.6.1.1 Surface PMSM Flux and Torque

In surface PMSM, the permeability of the flux path between the stator and the rotor is equal around the stator circumference, and hence their *d* and *q*-axes inductances are approximately equal, which can be denoted by

$$L_m = L_{md} = L_{mq}.$$

The uniformity in the magnetic path despite the presence of magnets is because the permeability of magnets is approximately equal to that of the air. The space needed to mount the magnets increases the radial distance of the effective air gap, making the self-inductance relatively smaller in PMSMs. A simplified per-phase equivalent circuit will give significant insight in the torque production of

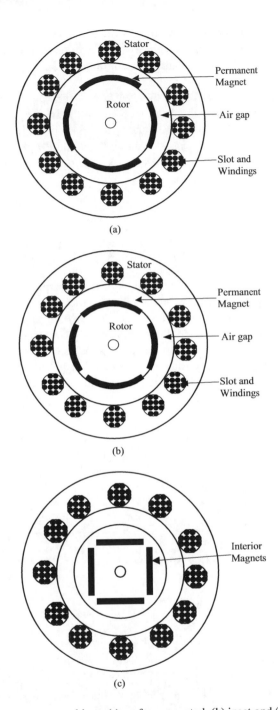

**FIGURE 7.30**   Permanent magnet machines: (a) surface-mounted, (b) inset and (c) interior.

surface PMSMs and also that for inset PMSMs when the $d$- and $q$-axes inductance differences are small. In the per-phase equivalent circuit, the fundamental frequency components of voltages and currents of the inverter driven machine is regarded as balanced three-phase sets for steady state and for slowly varying transient conditions. The PM machine can then be represented by the per-phase equivalent circuit shown in Figure 7.31a. The current source $I_F$ represents the rms value of the equivalent magnet current $i_{fd}$ that would create the PM flux $\lambda_f$. The PM flux in terms of the equivalent current is given by $\lambda_f = L_m i_{fd}$. Assuming sinusoidal distribution of stator windings, only the fundamental component of magnet flux density links with the stator windings. The magnetizing inductance $L_m$ for PM machines is much smaller than that of induction machines because of much larger effective air gap.

From the stator terminals, the effect of the PM flux is seen as a back-emf voltage given by $E = j\omega L_m I_m$. This back-emf or induced voltage is shown in the alternative representation of the per phase equivalent circuit in Figure 7.31b. The stator per phase rms current is denoted by $I_s$, which leads the reference axis (d-axis in this case) by an angle $\gamma$. The PM machine provides continuous torque only when rotor speed is synchronized with the stator frequency. For the per-phase model, the torque is given by

$$T_e = 3 \times \frac{P}{2} L_m I_F I_S \sin\gamma \qquad (7.52)$$

The torque is maximum when $\gamma = 90°$. The vector diagram for this maximum torque condition is shown in Figure 7.32a. The input power factor in this condition is lagging. Operation in this mode is practical up to the limit of the inverter supply voltage. At higher speeds, the appropriate operating condition is that for unity power factor, which maximizes the inverter volt-amp rating utilization. The vector diagram for this condition is given in Figure 7.32b. The motor can also be operated with a leading power factor by increasing the voltage angle $\delta$, as shown in Figure 7.32c. This condition is desired for some large synchronous drives that allows the use of a load-commutated inverter.

The torque equations signify that torque is maximized at $\gamma = 90°$ where the stator current is aligned in quadrature with the magnet field axis. Maintaining such orthogonality consistently and

**FIGURE 7.31**   PM synchronous motor equivalent circuits showing (a) equivalent magnet current and (b) induced voltage.

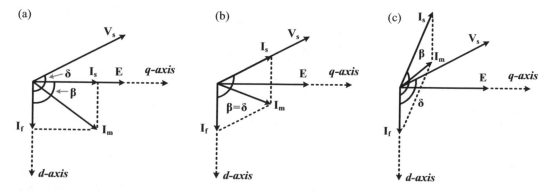

**FIGURE 7.32**   Vector diagrams with three power factors for the per-phase equivalent circuit: (a) lagging, (b) unity and (c) leading.

continuously through both magnitude and angle controls of the stator current form the basis of vector controls, which will be discussed in the next chapter. Motor operation for $\gamma > 90°$ is known as field weakening operation, which is necessary at higher speeds of operation. It can also be noted that for regeneration, the rotor angle $\gamma$ is made negative through current control.

### 7.6.1.2 Interior PMSM Flux and Torque

The direct and quadrature-axes inductances of a PMSM play an important role in the operation of the interior PMSM. Therefore, it is convenient to develop the machine models in the *dq* reference frame which is synchronized with the rotor speed for these machines. The magnets in the interior PMSMs are buried inside the rotor. This results in unequal *d*- and *q*-axes reluctances, since space is occupied by magnets in the direct axis and by iron in the quadrature axis. With the larger effective air gap along the *d*-axis flux path, the *d*-axis inductance $L_d$ is smaller than the *q*-axis inductance $L_q$, although the length of the air gap between the stator and rotor is the same. These inductances consist of the magnetizing inductances and the leakage inductances and are given as

$$L_q = L_{ls} + L_{mq} \tag{7.53}$$

$$\text{and } L_q = L_{ls} + L_{md}. \tag{7.54}$$

The larger difference in the *d* and *q*-axes inductances make the interior PM more suitable for flux weakening operation delivering a wider constant power region compared to the surface mount or inset PMSMs. The extended constant power range capability is extremely important for an electric and hybrid vehicle application to eliminate the use of multiple gear ratios. Because of the unequal reluctance paths in the direct and quadrature axes, a reluctance torque exists in buried and inset PMSMs.

When transformed to the *dq* reference frame, the interior PMSM voltage expressions in the *q*-axis and *d*-axis become

$$v_q = R_s i_q + \frac{d}{dt}\lambda_q + \omega_r \lambda_d$$
$$v_d = R_s i_d + \frac{d}{dt}\lambda_d - \omega_r \lambda_q \tag{7.55}$$

where the *q*- and *d*-axis flux linkages are

$$\lambda_q = L_q i_q$$
$$\lambda_d = L_d i_d + \lambda_f$$

Here $i_d$, $i_q$ are the *dq* axis stator currents, $R_s$ is the stator phase resistance, $\omega_r$ is the rotor speed in electrical rad/s and $\lambda_f$ is the amplitude of the flux linkage established by the permanent magnet. Ideally, there is no PM flux component in *q*-axis. The different stator slot/pole combinations and rotor magnet arrangements are reflected in the model parameter values.

The electromagnetic torque is given by

$$T_e = \frac{3}{2}\frac{P}{2}\left[\lambda_f i_q + (L_d - L_q)i_d i_q\right] \tag{7.56}$$

where $P$ is the number of poles. Since $L_d < L_q$, the reluctance torque contribution can be increased with increased negative $i_d$ current. The distribution between the mutual toque component and the reluctance torque component depends both on design and controls.

## 7.6.2 PM BRUSHLESS DC MOTORS

The permanent magnet AC machines with trapezoidal back-emf waveforms are the PM brushless DC (PM BLDC) machines [6]. The trapezoidal shaped back-emf waveforms in these machines are due to the concentrated windings of the machine used instead of the sinusoidally distributed windings used in the PMSMs. The PM BLDC motors are used in a wide variety of applications ranging from computer drives to sophisticated medical equipment. The reason behind the popularity of these machines is the simplicity of control. Only six discrete rotor positions per electrical revolution are needed in a three-phase machine to synchronize the phase currents with the phase back-emfs for effective torque production. A set of three Hall sensors mounted on the stator facing a magnet wheel fixed to the rotor and placed 120° apart can easily give this position information. This eliminates the need for a high resolution encoder or position sensor required in PMSMs, but the penalty paid for position sensor simplification is in the performance. Vector control is not possible in PM BLDC machines, because of the trapezoidal shape of the back-emfs.

The three-phase back-emf waveforms and the ideal phase currents of a PM BLDC motor are shown in Figure 7.33. The back-emf waveforms are fixed with respect to the rotor position. Square wave phase currents are supplied such that they are synchronized with the peak back-emf segment of the respective phase. The controller achieves this objective using rotor position feedback information. The motor basically operates like a DC motor with its electronic controller; hence, the motor is called as the brushless DC motor.

### 7.6.2.1 PM BLDC Machine Modeling

The PM in the rotor can be regarded as a constant current source, giving rise to the back-emfs in the stator windings. The three stator windings for the three phases are assumed to be identical with 120° (electrical) phase displacement among them. Therefore, the stator winding resistances and the self-inductance of each of the three phases can be assumed to be identical. Let

$R_s$ = stator phase winding resistance,
$L_{aa} = L_{bb} = L_{cc} = L$ = stator phase self-inductance and
$L_{ab} = L_{ac} = L_{bc} = M$ = stator mutual inductance.

The voltage balance equations for the three-phases are

**FIGURE 7.33**  Back-emf and ideal phase currents in the three phases of a PM brushless DC motor.

$$\begin{bmatrix} v_a \\ v_b \\ v_c \end{bmatrix} = R \cdot \begin{bmatrix} i_a \\ i_b \\ i_c \end{bmatrix} + \begin{bmatrix} L & M & M \\ M & L & M \\ M & M & L \end{bmatrix} \cdot p \cdot \begin{bmatrix} i_a \\ i_b \\ i_c \end{bmatrix} + \begin{bmatrix} e_a \\ e_b \\ e_c \end{bmatrix} \quad (7.57)$$

where $p$ is the operator $d/dt$, and $e_a$, $e_b$ and $e_c$ are the back-emfs in the three phases. The back-emf is related to the phase flux-linkage as

$$e = \frac{d\lambda}{dt} = \frac{d\lambda}{d\theta} \cdot \frac{d\theta}{dt}$$

However, $\dfrac{d\theta}{dt} = \omega_r$ which is the rotor speed. Then

$$e = \omega_r \cdot \frac{d\lambda}{d\theta} \quad (7.58)$$

Similar to the back-emfs, the currents are also shifted by 120°, and they satisfy the condition $i_a + i_b + i_c = 0$. Therefore, we have $M \cdot i_b + M \cdot i_c = -M \cdot i_a$; similar expressions exist for the two other phases. Equation 7.57 can then be simplified as

$$\begin{bmatrix} v_a \\ v_b \\ v_c \end{bmatrix} = R \cdot \begin{bmatrix} i_a \\ i_b \\ i_c \end{bmatrix} + \begin{bmatrix} L-M & 0 & 0 \\ 0 & L-M & 0 \\ 0 & 0 & L-M \end{bmatrix} \cdot p \cdot \begin{bmatrix} i_a \\ i_b \\ i_c \end{bmatrix} + \begin{bmatrix} e_a \\ e_b \\ e_c \end{bmatrix}$$

The rate of change of currents with the applied voltages can be expressed as

$$p \cdot \begin{bmatrix} i_a \\ i_b \\ i_c \end{bmatrix} = \frac{1}{L-M} \cdot \left[ \begin{bmatrix} v_a \\ v_b \\ v_c \end{bmatrix} - R \cdot \begin{bmatrix} i_a \\ i_b \\ i_c \end{bmatrix} - \begin{bmatrix} e_a \\ e_b \\ e_c \end{bmatrix} \right] \quad (7.59)$$

The electrical power transferred to the rotor is equal to the mechanical power $T_e\omega_r$ available at the shaft. Using this equality, the electromagnetic torque for the PM BLDC motor is

$$T_e = \frac{e_a \cdot i_a + e_b \cdot i_b + e_c \cdot i_c}{\omega_r} \quad (7.60)$$

For the control strategy described previously where only two phase-currents are active at a time, the torque expression for equal currents in two phases simplifies to

$$T_e = \frac{2 \cdot e_{max} \cdot I}{\omega_r} \quad (7.61)$$

Since the currents are controlled to synchronize with the maximum back-emf only, $e_{max}$ has been used in Equation 7.61 instead of $e$ as a function of time or rotor position. Assuming magnetic linearity, Equation 7.58 can be written as

$$e = K \cdot \omega_r \cdot \frac{dL}{d\theta}.$$

Hence, the maximum back-emf is

$$e_{max} = K \cdot \left[ \frac{dL}{d\theta} \right]_{max} \cdot \omega_r \text{ or } e_{max} = K' \cdot \omega_r. \quad (7.62)$$

Equations 7.61 and 7.62 are very similar to the $T = K \cdot \phi \cdot I$ and $E = K \cdot \phi \cdot \omega$ equations associated with regular DC machines. Therefore, with a rotor position feedback information and an inverter to commutate from one phase to another, the PM BLDC machine can be considered to behave like that of a DC machine.

## 7.7 RELUCTANCE MACHINES

The electric machine types based on the torque production using the magnetic reluctance principle have windings on the stator, and the rotor is fairly simple and low-cost without any windings or magnets. The types of reluctance machines are:

- Synchronous reluctance machine
- PM-assisted synchronous reluctance machine
- Switched reluctance machine
- Mutual coupled reluctance machines.

Cross-sections of three of these types of reluctance machines are shown in Figure 7.34. The synchronous reluctance (SyncRel) machines have stator winding arrangement similar to that of induction and PM synchronous machines designed to produce sinusoidal rotating mmf in the air gap. The rotor saliency causes a reluctance variation along the air gap which is utilized to produce torque using the reluctance principle. While it may be difficult to achieve the power density and wide speed range requirements of a traction electric machine with synchronous reluctance machines, it may be possible to achieve targets for some applications with the PM-assisted synchronous reluctance (PM-SyncRel) machines. The fundamental operating principles of PM-SyncRel machines are very much the same as IPMSMs, but the reluctance torque segment is of higher proportion in the former. Another candidate for traction motors is the switched reluctance (SR) motors. The switched reluctance machines have concentrated windings around the stator teeth with each phase independently producing torque during their segment of torque production. The mutual coupled switched reluctance machine (MCSRM) is a variant of the SR machine designed with full-pitched winding where mutual inductance variation instead of self-inductance variation is used for torque productions. The MCSRMs enable the use of three-phase voltage source converters in place of the asymmetric half-bridge converters used for conventional SRMs.

### 7.7.1 Synchronous Reluctance Machines

Torque is produced in a SyncRel machine through the interaction between rotor reluctance and stator magnetomotive force ($mmf_s$). In a three-phase SyncRel machine, the sinusoidally distributed stator windings produce the $mmf_s$ which is constant in amplitude but rotating at synchronous speed $\omega_s$ around the air gap between the stator and rotor as shown in Figure 7.35 with a conceptual 2-pole

(a) (b) (c)

**FIGURE 7.34** Reluctance machines: (a) synchronous, (b) mutual coupled and (c) switched reluctance.

stator-rotor configuration of a SyncRel machine. The reluctance to the stator mmf$_S$ is minimum along the $d$-axis of the rotor reluctance while it maximum along the $q$-axis of the rotor. With the stator energized, the rotor tries to align itself to its minimum reluctance position with the stator mmf ($\theta = 0$). Therefore, if there is an angle difference between $d$-axis and the direction of mmf$_S$, an electromagnetic torque will be produced in the counter-clockwise direction as shown in Figure 7.35. When a constant load angle $\theta$ is maintained through controls with the rotor rotating at synchronous speed, electromagnetic energy will continuously be converted into mechanical energy.

Stator current in a SyncRel machine is responsible for producing both magnetization (stator mmf$_S$) and torque production. Park's equations, which describe the conventional wound-field synchronous machine, can be used to model the SyncRel as

$$v_{ds} = r_s i_{ds} + p\lambda_{ds} - \omega\lambda_{qs} \tag{7.63}$$

$$v_{qs} = r_s i_{qs} + p\lambda_{qs} + \omega\lambda_{ds} \tag{7.64}$$

Here, $v$ and $i$ represent stator voltage and currents, respectively, $r_s$ is stator resistance per phase, $\omega$ is the electrical angular speed of the reference frame, and $\lambda$ represents flux linkages which can be written as

$$\lambda_{ds} = (L_{ls} + L_{md})i_{ds} = L_d i_{ds} \tag{7.65}$$

$$\lambda_{qs} = (L_{ls} + L_{mq})i_{qs} = L_q i_{qs} \tag{7.66}$$

Here, $L_{ls}$ is stator leakage inductance and $L_{md}$ and $L_{mq}$ are the direct and quadrature axis magnetizing inductance, respectively. The general expression of electromagnetic torque of SynRM is given by

$$T_e = \frac{3}{2}\frac{P}{2}[\lambda_{ds}i_{qs} - \lambda_{qs}i_{ds}] \tag{7.67}$$

where $P$ is the number of poles. In terms of $dq$-axes inductances and constant current operation the torque expression can be re-written as

$$T_e = \frac{3}{2}\frac{P}{2}(L_{ds} - L_{qs})i_{ds}i_{qs} \tag{7.68}$$

In synchronous reluctance machines, the difference of $dq$-axes inductances ($L_{ds} - L_{qs}$) and the ratio of the two inductances ($L_{ds}/L_{qs}$) are two critical parameters. To achieve higher performances, it is the best if these two parameters are made as large as possible. A large saliency ratio is required in order to achieve a wide constant power and a high power factor in SynRM drives. The large saliency

**FIGURE 7.35**    Stator rotating mmf$_S$ and equivalent 2-pole conceptual rotor in a SyncRel machine.

ratio can be achieved in both axially and transversally laminated rotor structures with multiple flux barriers. The placement, shape and number of flux barriers are critical parameters that are subject to optimization for a specific design target for an application. The multi-barrier synchronous reluctance rotor designs are the practical types which target high torque density and power factor improvement and/or torque ripple minimization.

### 7.7.2 PM Assisted Synchronous Reluctance Machines

Adding permanent magnets within the ribs of the rotor flux barriers is an approach to increase the performance and power density of synchronous reluctance machines which are called PM-SyncRel machines. A PM can be inserted in each of the rotor flux barrier. The rotor magnets are placed radially with magnetization direction suppressing the $q$- axis flux which in turn contributes to saliency ratio. Effectively, the magnet flux contributes to the SynRM $d$- axis flux. The $d$- and $q$- axes flux linkages as a function of currents can be expressed as

$$\lambda_{ds} = (L_{ls} + L_{md})i_{ds} = L_{ds}i_{ds} \tag{7.69}$$

$$\lambda_{qs} = (L_{ls} + L_{mq})i_{qs} - \lambda_f = L_{qs}i_{qs} - \lambda_f \tag{7.70}$$

Neglecting saturation and torque oscillations, the average torque can be expressed as

$$T_e = \frac{3}{2}\frac{P}{2}(L_{ds} - L_{qs})i_{ds}i_{qs} + \lambda_f\ i_{ds} \tag{7.71}$$

### 7.7.3 Switched Reluctance Machines

The switched reluctance machine (SRM) is a doubly-salient, singly-excited reluctance machine with independent phase windings on the stator. The stator and the rotor are made of magnetic steel laminations, with the latter having no windings or magnets. The SRMs can be of various stator-rotor pole combinations related to different phase configurations. The cross-sectional diagrams of a four-phase, 8–6 SRM and a three-phase, 12–8 SRM are shown in Figure 7.36. The three-phase, 12–8 machine is a two-repetition version of the basic 6–4 structure within the single stator geometry. The two-repetition machine can alternately be labeled as a four poles/phase machine, compared to the 6–4 structure that can be called a two poles/phase machine. The stator windings on diametrically opposite poles are connected either in series or in parallel to form one phase of the motor.

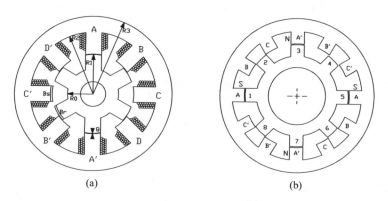

(a)                                    (b)

**FIGURE 7.36** Cross-sections of three-phase SR machines: (a) four-phase 8/6 structure and (b) 12/8, two-repetition (two-channel) structure.

When a stator phase is energized, the most adjacent rotor pole-pair is attracted toward the energized stator in order to minimize the reluctance of the magnetic path. Therefore, it is possible to develop constant torque in either direction of rotation by energizing consecutive phases in succession.

The aligned position of a phase is defined to be the orientation when the stator and rotor poles of the phase are perfectly aligned with each other attaining the minimum reluctance position. The unsaturated phase inductance is maximum ($L_a$) in this position. The phase inductance decreases gradually as the rotor poles move away from the aligned position in either direction. When the rotor poles are symmetrically misaligned with the stator poles of a phase, the position is said to be the unaligned position. The phase has the minimum inductance ($L_u$) in this position. Although, the concept of inductance is not valid for a highly saturating machine like SRM, the unsaturated aligned and unaligned inductances are two key reference positions for the controller.

Several other combinations of the number of stator and rotor poles exist, such as 10–4, 12–8, etc. A 4–2 or a 2–2 configuration is also possible, but they have the disadvantage that if the stator and rotor poles are aligned exactly then it would be impossible to develop a starting torque. The configurations with higher number of stator/rotor pole combinations have less torque ripple and do not have the problem of starting torque.

The switched reluctance machines or motors possess few unique features that make them strong competitors to existing AC and DC motors in various adjustable speed drive and servo applications. The machine construction is simpler due to the absence of rotor winding and permanent magnets. The bulk of the losses in the machine occur in the stator, which is relatively easier to cool. The starting torque of the SRM can be very high without the problem of excessive inrush current due to its higher self-inductance. Another great advantage for SRMs is that the maximum permissible rotor temperature is higher. The SRMs can be designed with a wide constant power region, which is a feature particularly attractive for traction applications. The SRM also has some unique fault tolerance features that do not exist with the other AC machines. Since each phase winding is connected in series with converter switching elements, there is no possibility of shoot-through faults between the DC buses in the SRM drive converter. The independent stator phases enable drive operation in spite of loss of one or more phases, and the drive can be brought to a safe shutdown instead of a sudden stop.

The SRM also comes with a few disadvantages among which the torque ripple and the acoustic noise are the most critical. The double saliency construction and the discrete nature of torque production by the independent phases lead to higher torque ripple compared to other machines. The higher torque ripple also causes the ripple current in the DC supply to be quite large necessitating a large filter capacitor. The acoustic noise of the SRM could be comparatively higher due to the resonance between the excitation forces and the lower order circumferential mode-shapes of the stator.

The absence of permanent magnets imposes the excitation burden on the stator windings and converter, which increases the converter kVA requirement. Compared to PM brushless machines, the per-unit stator copper losses will be higher reducing the efficiency and torque per ampere. However, the maximum speed at constant power is not limited by the fixed magnet flux as in the PM machine, and hence, an extended constant power region of operation is possible in SRMs. The control can be simpler than the field oriented control of induction machines, although for torque ripple minimization significant computations may be required for an SRM drive.

### 7.7.3.1 SRM Principles of Operation

The regular choice of the number of rotor poles in an SRM is

$$N_r = N_s \pm k_m \qquad (7.72)$$

where $k_m$ is an integer such that $k_m \bmod q \neq 0$ and $N_s$ is the number of stator poles. The most common choice of (7.72) for the selection of stator and rotor pole numbers is $k_m = 2$ with the negative sign. The fundamental cycle frequency is given by

$$f = \frac{n}{60} N_r \ \text{Hz} \tag{7.73}$$

where $n$ is the motor speed in rev/m and $N_r$ is the number of rotor poles. The 'step angle' or 'stroke' of an SRM is given by

$$\text{Step angle } \varepsilon = \frac{2\pi}{N_{ph} \cdot N_{rep} \cdot N_r} \tag{7.74}$$

The stoke angle is an important design parameter related to the frequency of control per rotor revolution. $N_{rep}$ represents the multiplicity of the basic SRM configuration, which can also be stated as the number of pole pairs per phase. $N_{ph}$ is the number of phases. $N_{ph}$ and $N_{rep}$ together set the number of stator poles.

The SRM is always driven into saturation to maximize the utilization of the magnetic circuit, and hence, the flux-linkage $\lambda_{ph}$ is a non-linear function of stator current and rotor position given by

$$\lambda_{ph} = \lambda_{ph}(i_{ph}, \theta)$$

The electromagnetic profile of an SRM is defined by the $\lambda$–$i$–$\theta$ characteristics shown in Figure 7.37. The highest possible saliency ratio (the ratio between the maximum and minimum unsaturated inductance levels) is desired to achieve the highest possible torque per ampere, but as the rotor and stator pole arcs are decreased the torque ripple tends to increase. The torque dip observed in the $T$-$i$-$\theta$ characteristics of an SRM (see Figure 7.38) is an indirect measure of the torque ripple expected in the drive system. The torque dip is the difference between the peak torque of a phase and the torque at an angle where two overlapping phases produce equal torque at equal levels of current. The smaller the torque dip, the less will be the torque ripple. The $T$-$i$-$\theta$ characteristics of the SRM depend on the stator-rotor pole overlap angle, pole geometry, material properties, number of poles and number of phases.

**FIGURE 7.37**   Flux-angle-current characteristics of a four-phase SRM.

The design objectives for an SRM are to minimize the core losses, to have good starting capability, to minimize the unwanted effects due to varying flux distributions and saturation and to eliminate mutual coupling. The fundamental design rules governing the choice of phase numbers, pole numbers and pole arcs are discussed in detail by Lawrenson et al. [7] and also by Miller [8]. A comprehensive design methodology of SRM appears in [9].

The general equation governing the flow of stator current in one phase of an SRM can be written as

$$V_{ph} = i_{ph}R_s + \frac{d\lambda_{ph}}{dt} \tag{7.75}$$

where $V_{ph}$ is the DC bus voltage, $i_{ph}$ is the instantaneous phase current, $R_s$ is the winding resistance and $\lambda_{ph}$ is the flux linking the coil. Assuming magnetic linearity (where $\lambda_{ph} = L_{ph}(\theta)i_{ph}$), the voltage expression can be simplified as

$$V_{ph} = i_{ph}R_s + L_{ph}(\theta)\frac{di_{ph}}{dt} + i_{ph}\frac{dL_{ph}(\theta)}{dt}\omega. \tag{7.76}$$

where $k_v$ is the current dependent back-emf co-efficient and $\omega = \dfrac{d\theta}{dt}$ is the rotor angular speed.

The last term in Equation 7.76 is the 'back-emf' or 'motional-emf' and has the same effect on SRM as does the back-emf has on DC motors or PM BLDC motors.

### 7.7.3.2 Energy Conversion

The energy conversion process in an SRM can be evaluated using the power balance relationship. Multiplying Equation 7.76 by $i_{ph}$ on both sides, the instantaneous input power can be expressed as

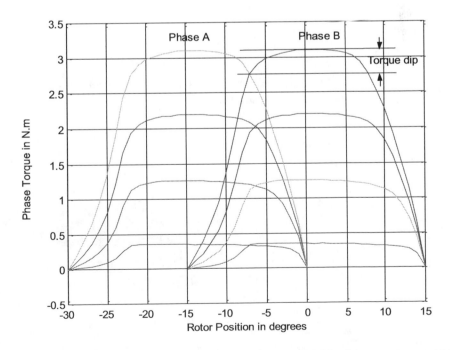

**FIGURE 7.38**  Torque-angle-current characteristics of a four-phase SRM for four constant current levels.

$$P_{in} = V_{ph}i_{ph} = i_{ph}^2 R_s + \left( L_{ph}i_{ph}\frac{di_{ph}}{dt} + \frac{1}{2}i_{ph}^2\frac{dL_{ph}}{d\theta}\omega \right) + \frac{1}{2}i_{ph}^2\frac{dL_{ph}}{d\theta}\omega$$

$$= i_{ph}^2 R + \frac{d}{dt}\left( \frac{1}{2}L_{ph}i_{ph}^2 \right) + \frac{1}{2}i_{ph}^2\frac{dL_{ph}}{d\theta}\omega. \tag{7.77}$$

The first term represents the stator winding loss, and the second term denotes the rate of change of magnetic stored energy, while the third term is the mechanical output power. The rate of change of magnetic stored energy always exceeds the electromechanical energy conversion term. The most effective use of the energy supplied is when the current is maintained constant during the positive $\frac{dL_{ph}}{d\theta}$ slope. The magnetic stored energy is not necessarily lost, but can be retrieved by the electrical source if an appropriate converter topology is used. In the case of a linear SRM, the energy conversion effectiveness can be at most 50% as shown in the energy division diagram of Figure 7.39a. The drawback of lower effectiveness is the increase in converter volt-amp rating for a given power conversion of the SRM. The division of input energy increases in favor of energy conversion if the motor operates under magnetic saturation. The energy division under saturation is shown in Figure 7.39b.

### 7.7.3.3 Torque Production

The torque is produced in the SRM by the tendency of the rotor to attain the minimum reluctance position when a stator phase is excited. The general expression for instantaneous torque for such a device that operates under the reluctance principle is

$$T_{ph}(\theta,i_{ph}) = \left.\frac{\partial W'(\theta,i_{ph})}{\partial \theta}\right|_{i=\text{constant}} \tag{7.78}$$

where $W'$ is the co-energy defined as

$$W' = \int_0^i \lambda_{ph}(\theta,i_{ph})\,di.$$

Obviously, the instantaneous torque is not constant. The total instantaneous torque of the machine is given by the sum of the individual phase torques

 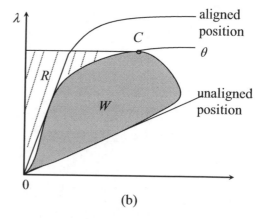

(a)                                          (b)

**FIGURE 7.39** Energy partitioning during one complete working stroke: (a) linear assumption and (b) practical case. $W$ = energy converted into mechanical work. $R$ = energy returned to the DC supply.

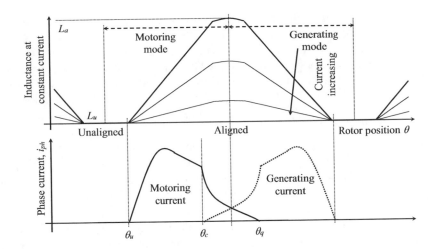

**FIGURE 7.40**  Phase currents for motoring and generating modes with respect to rotor position and idealized inductance profiles.

$$T_{inst}(\theta, i) = \sum_{phases} T_{ph}(\theta, i_{ph}). \tag{7.79}$$

The SRM electromechanical properties are defined by the static $T-i-\theta$ characteristics of a phase shown in Figure 7.38. When magnetic saturation can be neglected, the instantaneous torque expression becomes

$$T_{ph}(\theta, i) = \frac{1}{2} i_{ph}^{2} \frac{dL_{ph}(\theta)}{d\theta}. \tag{7.80}$$

The linear torque expression also follows from the energy conversion term (last term) in Equation 7.77. The phase current needs to be synchronized with the rotor position for effective torque production. For positive or motoring torque, the phase current is switched such that rotor is moving from the unaligned position toward the aligned position. On the other hand, the phase current must coincide with the decreasing inductance region for braking or generating torque. The phase currents for motoring and generating modes of operation are shown in Figure 7.40 with respect to the phase inductance profiles. The direction of current is immaterial in torque production. The optimum performance of the drive system depends on the appropriate positioning of phase currents relative to the rotor angular position. Therefore, a rotor position transducer is essential to provide the position feedback signal to the controller.

## 7.8  TRACTION IPM MACHINE DESIGN

The auto industry focused on performance of the electric drivetrain while working toward customer acceptance of electric and hybrid electric vehicles and considering system aspects of higher range or reduced battery mass with a goal of overall system cost reduction. In the process, the IPM synchronous machines utilizing NdFeB magnets became the design choice of traction electric machines primarily due to the unparallel power/torque density and efficiency that can be achieved with these machines to meet the demanding requirements of an electric traction drivetrain.

In the process, traction electric machine sustainability and cost was initially overlooked when almost all of the vehicle manufacturers employed IPM synchronous machine which uses rare-earth and heavy rare-earth materials for the production vehicles. In some applications, induction machines have been used although these machines cannot machines cannot match the power density of IPMSMs. There is ongoing research effort to develop alternative machines with good performance that do not use rare-earth magnet materials or minimize the use of rare-earth and heavy rare-earth magnet materials. Nevertheless, the IPMSM still remains the most widely used traction electric machine, and hence, the design of such a machine will be discussed in this section.

### 7.8.1 INITIAL MACHINE SIZING: ELECTROMAGNETIC DESIGN

The electric machine design starts with the electromagnetic design based on the specifications which will include certain performance parameters and constraints while several parameters have to be assumed during the design process. An initial analytical sizing equation which relates the rotor volume with the electric and magnetic loading of the machine is the starting point for the electromagnetic design [10]. The electric loading (A) is associated with the electrical conductors and how hard these are stressed in relation with the rms current density. The magnetic loading is related to how hard the magnetic materials are stressed, and is measured in terms of the peak radial magnetic flux density in the air gap ($B_{g,max}$). Core material saturation and core losses set the limit in driving $B_{g,max}$ to the maximum achievable point.

The design constraint of machine's electrical ($A_{pe}$) and mechanical ($A_{pm}$) area products, given by $A_{pm} \geq A_{pe}$, determines the slot RMS current density $J_{RMS}$ for the machine. The RMS current density for traction electric machines which are forced cooled is around 20 A/mm$^2$. The torque developed in the electric machine can be represented by [10]

$$T = 3 \times N_{ph} \times r_g \times L \times B_g \times A_c \times J_{rms} \tag{7.81}$$

where $N_{ph}$ is the number of turns per stator phase, $A_c$ slot conductor area, and $r_g$ the rotor air-gap radius. Typical torque per unit volumes for the traction motors are in the range of 50–100 kN m/m$^3$ [11]. The air gap between the rotor and stator is typically between 0.6 and 1 mm for traction machines.

### 7.8.2 THERMAL ANALYSIS

In the process of electromechanical energy conversion from electrical to mechanical or vice versa in an electric machine, losses are inevitable which ultimately limits the rating of the machine. The various losses within the machine translate to heat which needs to be rejected at a rate that balances with the rate of heat generation. The thermal design is as critical as the electromagnetic design requiring in-depth analysis. A power loss analysis is required to identify and model all the heat sources prior to building the thermal model in order to analyze and design the thermal system.

The losses in an electric machine can be categorized into electrical loss, magnetic loss, and mechanical loss in all electric machines. The electrical loss comprises of DC or copper loss and AC loss made up of skin and proximity losses. The magnetic loss or core loss consists of hysteresis loss and eddy loss in the lamination materials and the eddy loss in the PMs. The mechanical losses are the friction and windage losses. Any loss in an electric machine not accounted for in these categories are lumped into stray losses. All these losses need to be modeled accurately as these losses are the input for thermal analysis. The heat sources and the heat transfer coefficients which depend on the material properties allow the designer to build the thermal model of the machine using which one can estimate the temperature distribution inside the motor.

### 7.8.3 MECHANICAL/STRUCTURAL ANALYSIS

Mechanical stress analysis for structural integrity is another step in the machine design process in parallel with the electromagnetic and thermal analysis. For an electric machine, two types of forces need to be considered in stress analysis: (i) electromagnetic radial force occurring from its excitation and torque production and (ii) centrifugal force that is acting on its rotor due to rotational speed. In the elastic region, stress is proportional to applied strain following Hooke's law. The deformed material comes back to its original form after the removal of stress in this region. The maximum strain boundary of elastic region is defined by the material yield strength ($\sigma_y$). Beyond its elastic limit is the plastic region where Hooke's law no longer applies and non-recoverable deformation occurs. Elastic region is typically smaller than the plastic region. The analysis of interest is to evaluate electric machine stresses under the rated operating condition to verify if it remains within the elastic region of its material and is not permanently deformed.

The electric machine design leads to the torque and power envelopes as a function of the operating speed as shown in Figure 7.41. The thermal analysis helps to find the maximum continuous output torque or power without exceeding the maximum allowable steady-state temperature limit.

### 7.8.4 STATOR AND WINDING DESIGNS

The stator design includes the selection of the conductors and the slot/pole combination. The two types of conductors used in traction electric machines are the stranded ones and the bar types. The bar wound stator holds the advantages of higher slot fill factor, shorter end winding, better thermal performance, improved high voltage protection, and fully automated manufacturing process. However, the well-known issue with the bar wound design is the AC winding effect can lower motor efficiency at higher speeds. The stranded conductors are more suitable for high speed machine designs since there is much more flexibility in the selection of the number of turns.

The selection of the machine pole number $P$ depends on the operating speed range, maximum switching frequency of the drive, available DC link voltage and core loss constraints. Moreover, the selection of the winding configuration and stator structure also determines the rotor pole numbers with suitable winding factors. However, the leakage flux increases with pole numbers and very high pole machines (such as $P > 16$) suffer from lower power factor and reduced torque density. The slot/pole combination for a design is chosen based on a number performance factors including noise, winding design, back-emf harmonics and torque ripple, fundamental frequency. The winding distribution can be integer or fractional depending on the slot/pole/phase quantity which is denoted as $q$. Table 7.3 shows example slot/pole combinations of several electric machines. Although several choices are available, $q = 2$ is a compromise among average torque, losses, and moderate harmonics content which is the most commonly found with the commercially available vehicles. A higher $q$ design is going to

**FIGURE 7.41** Traction motor torque-speed envelop.

**TABLE 7.3**

**Slot/Pole Combinations of Electrical Machines in Electric Vehicles**

| Slot/Pole/Phase, $q$ | Pole, $P$ | Slot ($3 \times q \times P$) | Mode, $m$ | Example Vehicle |
|---|---|---|---|---|
| 2 | 8 | 48 | 8 | 2017 Toyota Prius |
| 2 | 8 | 48 | 8 | Nissan Leaf |
| 2 | 12 | 72 | 12 | 2016 BMWi3 |
| 3 | 12 | 108 | 12 | Example not in production |

provide inherently more sinusoidal back-emf, lower PM loss, higher average torque, but will also have higher conductor loss and thinner teeth which will increase the core loss compared to $q = 2$. It has to be noted that only fractional slot design where $q = 1.5$ can offer possible parallel path winding design where the vibration mode order will still be reasonable for traction motor applications.

For the winding design, series or parallel connections among the conductors can be made depending on primarily the available DC link voltage and rated speed. For series connection, the phase current has to go through each conductor which will increase the size of the conductor for a constant current density. As the number of parallel paths increases, the current and the size of the conductor reduce for the constant current density. It is also found that the parallel winding connection reduces the unbalanced magnetic pull (UMP) compared to the series connected configuration [12–14]. Additionally, it has to be ensured that there are no circulating current among the parallel paths. The maximum current density for liquid cooling in stranded conductor is in the range of 19–20 A/mm², and in bar conductors, it is 24–26 A/mm². The current density and maximum allowable current dictate the size of the conductor.

### 7.8.5 ROTOR DESIGN

The rotor design for the IPM machine involves the selection and sizing of magnets and the rotor configuration. Among the permanent magnets, sintered NdFeB-type magnets are common in electric vehicle applications because of their high-energy product. The design candidates for rotor magnet configurations are single-V, double-V, and delta with the double-V shape being the most commonly used configuration in the production electric and hybrid-electric vehicles. The double-V shape provides lower ripple, higher average torque, and higher saliency compared to the single V-shape rotor configurations. The delta-shaped configuration is a compromise for performance and manufacturing complexity, and hence, is used in a few production vehicle types. An example double-V shape design is shown in Figure 7.42.

The length and width of the magnets affect the flux distribution, maximum average torque, torque ripple as well as the total magnet weight. The angle between the two magnets, the flux barriers, and the length of the center bridge affect the maximum average torque and torque ripple. Therefore, the dimensions and angle of the magnets need to be optimized to achieve the average torque, maximum speed and power requirement. There are two main bridges that exist in the rotor, namely top bridge (close to air gap) and center bridge. As the bridge thickness increases, it reduces the mechanical stress and increases the leakage flux. The thicknesses of both the bridges are recommended to be greater than 1.4 mm from the manufacturing point of view. Rounding the edges at the corner also helps to reduce the mechanical stress and torque ripple.

### Example 7.5

Design an electric motor for an electric vehicle system using the software design tool MotorCAD for the given specifications and constraints. The electric machine is to be used in the propulsion system of an electric vehicle that requires 150 kW power to reach a vehicle speed of 45 miles/hour

**FIGURE 7.42**  Double-V rotor layout with bar windings in stator.

(mph) from 0 mph. The radius of the wheel is 0.35 m. The maximum vehicle speed is 150 mph. Consider a torque reduction ratio of 10:1 from vehicle level to motor level. Design an electric motor that can meet the requirement mentioned above using Motor-CAD.

**Constraints:**

DC bus voltage: 650 V
Power factor: $\geq 0.65$
Slot current density: $\leq 28$ A(rms)/mm$^2$
Efficiency @ 45 mph: $\geq 0.95$
Power density: 30 kW/L
Design outputs required are: (a) torque-speed profile of the motor; (b) power-speed profile of the motor; (c) efficiency map, conductor loss, and core loss; (d) flux plot during peak power condition; and (e) parameters of the designs ($L_d$, $L_q$, $R$, BEMF constant).

*Answer*

Initial sizing is carried out for a given torque target and TRV, which will give rotor volume, using the following relationships

$$ROD \leftarrow \frac{TRV}{Rotor\ Volume} \text{ and } SOD = \frac{ROD}{SR}$$

where $ROD$ = rotor outer diameter, $TRV$ = torque per unit rotor volume, $SOD$ = stator outer diameter and $SR$ = split ratio (i.e., $ROD/SOD$ which is typically between 0.5 and 0.8).

The line-line rms voltage and line current are given by

$$V_{LLrms} = \sqrt{6}/\pi \times V_{dc} \times 0.9 \text{ and}$$

$$I_L = P_{max}/(\sqrt{3} \times V_{LLrms} \times pf \times \eta)$$

The motor was designed with eight poles and $q = 2$ resulting in 48 slots for a three-phase machine. The number of conductors per phase is calculated for an electrical frequency of $f_{elec} = 320$ Hz as

$$Conductor/phase = \frac{V_{ph}\ (rms)}{4.44 f_{elec} k_{w1} \lambda_{m1}}$$

where $k_{w1}$ is the winding factor and $\lambda_{m1}$ is the fundamental component of the PM flux linkage. The winding factor is takes as $k_{w1} = 0.945$. The fundamental PM flux linkage is related to the geometry as

$$\lambda_{m1} = B_{m1} \times ROD \times \frac{1_{stk}}{Pole/2}$$

where $B_{m1}$ is the fundamental airgap flux density in the range of 0.9–1 Tesla.

The designed machine geometry and parameters are given in Table 7.4.

The cross-sectional structure of the machine designed is shown in Figure 7.43. The electrical specifications of the motor are provided in Table 7.5. The simulation output of the torque and power envelop of the designed machine is given in Figure 7.44; the simulated characteristic plots of the designed machine are given in Figure 7.45.

### TABLE 7.4
### 150 kW Designed IPM Geometry and Parameters

| Parameter | Specification | Unit |
| --- | --- | --- |
| Phase current | 404 | A |
| Rotor outer diameter | 150.5 | mm |
| Stator outer diameter | 214 | mm |
| Length | 138 | mm |
| Base speed | 5500 | rpm |
| Max speed | 18,200 | rpm |
| Aspect ratio | 0.7 | - |
| Split ratio | 0.7 | - |
| Slots | 48 | - |
| Poles | 8 | - |
| Winding factor | 0.945 | - |
| Slot fill | 0.4 | - |

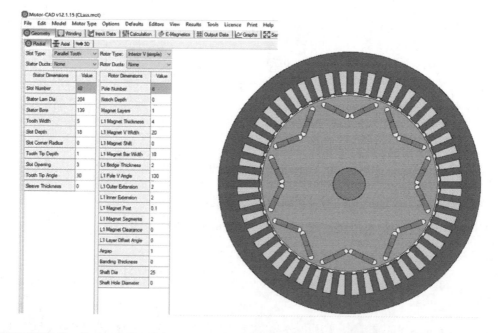

**FIGURE 7.43**   Cross-sectional structure of machine designed using MotorCad.

**TABLE 7.5**
**150 kW IPM Electrical Parameters**

| Parameter | Specification | Unit |
|---|---|---|
| $L_d$ | 0.2387 | mH |
| $L_q$ | 0.4482 | mH |
| $R$ | 0.02465 | Ω |
| BEMF constant ($K_e$) | 0.8222 | V s/rad |

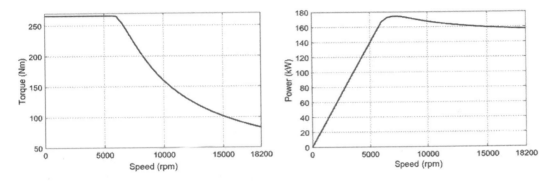

**FIGURE 7.44** Torque and power envelop over the operating speed range.

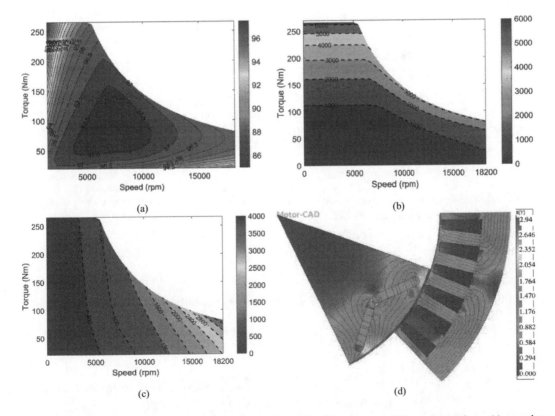

**FIGURE 7.45** Characteristics of the designed machine: (a) efficiency map, (b) conductor loss, (c) core loss and (d) flux at peak power.

## PROBLEMS

### 7.1

A 460 V, 60 Hz, six pole, 1,176 rpm, Y-connected induction motor has the following parameters referred to the stator at rated condition:

$$R_s = 0.19\,\Omega,\ R_r = 0.07\,\Omega,\ X_s = 0.75\,\Omega,\ X_r = 0.67\,\Omega \text{ and } X_m = \infty.$$

Find the speed of the motor for a braking torque of 350 N-m and the inverter frequency of 40 Hz. when the motor is supplied at rated voltage.

### 7.2

A three-phase induction machine is operated from a variable voltage, fixed frequency source.

a. Derive an expression for machine efficiency in terms of slip (not in terms of torque and speed). Include only stator and rotor copper losses and core loss in $P_{loss}$. Model core loss is modeled as a constant resistance in the equivalent circuit. To simplify the analysis, assume that core loss resistance and magnetizing reactance are large compared to the other parameters. Under this assumption, you can use an approximate equivalent circuit where the core loss resistance and magnetizing reactance are directly across the stator terminals.
b. Does motor efficiency depend on terminal voltage? Calculate the slip that maximizes motor efficiency.

### 7.3

Find the condition of operation that minimizes the losses in a separately excited DC machine. (Start by writing an equation for $P_{loss}$ in terms of the field currents and armature currents. Assuming linearity for all the non-linear functions, establish the relation between armature current and field current and then find the condition for minimum $P_{loss}$.)

### 7.4

Present an argument why it is impossible to achieve maximum efficiency at every operating point $(T^*, \omega^*)$ for a permanent magnet DC machine. (Start by writing an equation for $P_{loss}$ in terms if $T$, $\omega$ and machine flux $\phi$).

### 7.5

Proceeding as in Problem 7.2, explain why it is impossible to minimize losses at any operating point $(T^*, \omega^*)$ for a series DC motor.

### 7.6

a. A PM brushless DC has a torque constant of 0.12 N-m/A referred to the DC supply. Estimate its no-load speed in rpm when connected to a 48 VDC supply.
b. If the armature resistance is 0.15 $\Omega$/phase and the total voltage drop in the controller transistors is 2 V, determine the stall current and the stall torque.

## 7.7

Consider a three-phase 6/8 SRM. The stator phases are excited sequentially with a total time of 25 ms required to excite all the three phases. Find the angular velocity of the rotor. Express your answer both in rad/s and rpm.

## 7.8

The following flux equation describes the non-linear characteristics of a three-phase, 6/4 SRM:

$$\lambda_j(i,\theta) = \lambda_s(1 - \exp(-i_j f_j(\theta))), \ i_j \geq 0$$

where $\lambda_S$ = saturation flux = 0.2 V-s and $f(\theta) = a + b * \cos(N_r\theta - (j-1)2\pi/m)$.
Here, $j = 1, 2, 3$ denotes the phase number and $m = 3$. Also, given $a = 0.024$ and $b = 0.019$.

a. Derive the expression for the phase torque $T_j(i, \theta)$.
b. Plot the $\lambda$-$i$-$\theta$ characteristics for six angles between and including the unaligned and aligned positions. Take the maximum current as 100 A.
c. Plot the $T$-$i$-$\theta$ characteristics between the unaligned and aligned rotor positions. Take the maximum current as 100 and 10 A current steps for the torque characteristics.

## REFERENCES

1. M.P. Thompson, E. Chang, A. Foto, J.G. Citron-Rivera, D. Haddad, R. Waldo and F.E. Pinkerton, "Grain-boundary-diffused magnets," *IEEE Electrification Magazine*, 5(1), 19–27, March 2017.
2. R.H. Park, "Two-reaction theory of synchronous machines – Generalized method of analysis – Part I," *AIEE Transactions*, 48, 716–727, July 1929.
3. P. Vas, *Electric Machines and Drives: A Space-vector Theory Approach*, Oxford University Press, Oxford, 1992.
4. D.W. Novotny and T.A. Lipo, *Vector Control and Dynamics of AC Drives*, Oxford University Press, Inc., New York, NY, 1997.
5. N. Mohan, *Electric Drives – An Integrated Approach*, MNPERE, Minneapolis, MN, 2001.
6. T.J.E. Miller, *Brushless Permanent Magnet and Switched Reluctance Motor Drives*, Oxford University Press, Oxford, 1989.
7. P.J. Lawrenson, J.M. Stephenson, P.T. Blenkinsop, J. Corda and N.N. Fulton, "Variable-speed switched reluctance motors," *IEE Proceedings, Part B*, 127(4), 253–265, July 1980.
8. T.J.E. Miller, *Switched Reluctance Motors and their Control*, Magna Physics Publishing, Hillsboro, OH and Oxford Science Publications, Oxford, 1993.
9. M.N. Anwar, I. Husain and A.V. Radun, "A comprehensive design methodology for switched reluctance machines," *IEEE Transactions on Industry Applications*, 37(6), 1684–1692, November–December 2001.
10. D.A. Torrey, *AC Electric Machines and their Control*, E-Man Press LLC, Amsterdam, NY, 2010.
11. J.R. Hendershot, *Design of Brushless Permanent-Magnet Machines*, Motor Design Books, Venice, FL, 2010.
12. Y. Yang, S.M. Castano, R. Yang, M. Kasprzak, B. Bilkin, A. Sathyan, H. Dadkhah and A. Emadi, "Design and comparison of interior permanent magnet motor topologies for traction applications," *IEEE Transactions on Transportation Electrification*, 3(1), 86–97, March 2017.
13. M. Sarif Islam, A. Ahmed, I. Husain and A. Sathyan, "Asymmetric bar winding for high speed traction electric machine," *IEEE Transactions on Transportation Electrification*, 6(1), 3–15, March 2020. doi:10.1109/TTE.2019.2962329.
14. M.A. Kabir, *High Performance Reluctance Motor Drives with Three-phase Standard Inverter*, Doctoral Dissertation, Electrical Engineering, NC State University, December 2017.

# 8 Control of AC Machines

The robustness of the AC electric machines compared to DC machines makes them attractive in various motor drive applications including those for electric and hybrid vehicles. The robustness advantage is of benefit only when AC motor controllers can deliver performance comparable or better than of those of DC machines. The control simplicity in DC machines is due to the mechanical arrangements of commutators and brushes that maintain the orthogonality between the stator and rotor fluxes without any controller involvement. Fast response is a critical requirement for traction applications; motor drives must respond instantaneously with torque changes following a command change. In DC machines, the torque is directly proportional to the armature current without any dynamics involved, which makes the response instantaneous. The AC motor drives can be designed with fast response characteristics, but at the expense of controller complexity.

The scalar control methods of AC machines discussed earlier in Chapter 7 do not have the fast response characteristics desired in traction applications. The desired control method for AC induction machines is the *vector controls* where both the magnitude and the phase angle of the excitation current are controlled [1,2]. Vector control of the stator current is used in AC machines to overcome the effects of stator resistance, inductance and induced voltage in the same manner as in DC machines. The stator current is transformed into a reference frame where the two parameters can be controlled independently, one for the rotor flux and the other for the electromagnetic torque. A 90° spatial orientation of the rotor flux is maintained with respect to the stator torque producing current component using sensor feedback signals and model-based computations. The first section of the chapter addresses the required *dq* modeling essential for vector controls, and then the control algorithms are presented.

The vector control methods based on *dq* modeling are also used for permanent magnet (PM) synchronous machines. Any machine with sinusoidal excitations can employ the vector control method. Vector controls are difficult to be applied to machines where the machine electrical variables cannot be transformed into a suitable two-axe reference frame. The PM brushless DC (BLDC) and switched reluctance (SR) machines use square wave-type excitations for torque production, and the controller algorithms are mostly developed for independent phases with smoothing controls during phase commutations.

## 8.1  VECTOR CONTROL OF AC MOTORS

The electric and hybrid electric vehicle propulsion drive requires accurate torque control with fast response characteristics. The induction motor drive is capable of delivering high performance similar to that of DC motors using the vector control approach. Although vector control complicates the controller implementation, the lower cost and rugged construction of the induction machines are advantages over the DC machines.

The key variable for control in speed- and position-controlled applications is the torque. Although torque is never measured directly, torque estimators from machine models are frequently used to generate the current commands. A current controller in the innermost control loop regulates the motor current by comparing the command currents with feedback current measurements coming from the sensors. Speed control, if necessary, is achieved in the outer loop by comparing command speed signal with the feedback speed signal. With the two loops arranged in a cascade, the speed controller output of the outer loop is the current command for the inner loop. In certain high-performance position-controlled applications, such as in the actuator drives for accessories in electric and conventional vehicles, the position is controlled in the outermost loop putting the speed controller in an intermediate loop. The ability to produce a step change in torque with a step change in command generated from the outer loop represents the degree of control over the motor drive system for high-performance applications. The vector control in induction motors enables the machine to produce step changes in torque with instantaneous transition from one steady state to another steady state, which dramatically improves the dynamic performance of the drive system [3].

The objective of vector control or field orientation is to make the induction motor emulate the separately excited DC motor or the PM BLDC motor (i.e., PM trapezoidal motors). To understand vector control, let us revisit the torque production mechanism in DC machines. A simplified diagram of a DC motor with the field produced by separate excitation is shown in Figure 8.1. The field flux linkage space vector $\vec{\lambda}_f$ is stationary and is along the $d$-axis of the motor. The armature current space vector $\vec{i}_a$ is always along the $q$-axis due to action of the commutators and brushes, even though the rotor is revolving. The orthogonality between the field and armature current ensures the optimal condition for torque production providing the highest torque per ampere ratio. The electromagnetic torque of the DC machine is given by

$$T_e = k_T \lambda_f i_a \tag{8.1}$$

where $k_T$ is a machine constant depending on geometry and design parameters of the machine. The vector notations are dropped, since these variables are constants in DC machines. The armature and field circuits in a separately excited DC machine are completely independent or decoupled allowing independent control over torque and magnetic field. The independent flux control is especially desirable for electric vehicle-type applications where flux weakening is used at higher speeds above rated torque conditions in the constant power region of torque-speed characteristics. The constant power range helps minimize the transmission gear requirements for propulsion drives.

In the case of PM BLDC motors, the rotor position sensor and power electronic converter replace the mechanical commutators and brushes of DC motors; these components work in synchronism to maintain the orthogonality between the stator current space vector $\vec{i}_s(t)$ and the rotor flux vector $\vec{\lambda}_r(t)$ on an average basis. The back-emfs in these machines are trapezoidal, and not sinusoidal; hence, vector control is not possible. Torque ripple is a problem in PM BLDC motors, since square wave currents are used for torque production in synchronism with the trapezoidal back-emfs. In contrast, the orthogonality between armature and field mmfs is continuously maintained in DC commutator machines that help deliver a smoother torque. However, in the case of PM synchronous machines, the back-emfs are sinusoidal, and using vector control, smooth torque control can be achieved like that in an induction machine.

In light of the discussion presented above, the primary requirements of instantaneous torque control are controllability of the armature current, a controlled or constant field flux, and an orthogonal spatial angle between stator mmf axis and rotor mmf axis. In the case of DC and PM BLDC motors,

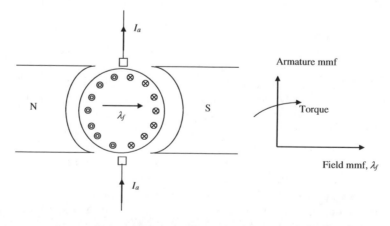

**FIGURE 8.1**  Torque in a separately excited DC machine.

the last two requirements are automatically met with the help commutators and brushes, and position sensors and inverter switching, respectively. However, note that the orthogonality is maintained on an average basis only for PM BLDC motors, the effect of which shows up in performance. In the case of induction machines and PM synchronous machines, these requirements are met with the help of *dq* models and reference frame transformations. Instantaneous torque control is achieved when the three requirements are met at every instant of time. Note that the armature of a machine is the component that carries the bulk of the current delivered by the source. In DC machines, the armature is in the rotor, whereas for AC machines, the armature is in the stator. The control of armature currents is achieved with the help of current regulators, such as the hysteresis current regulator or a PI current regulator. Armature current control is necessary to overcome the effects of armature winding resistance, leakage inductance and induced voltage in the stator windings. For field-weakening operation, the rotor flux needs to be reduced, which is achieved through field current control. The task is simple in separately excited DC machines. In induction and PM sinusoidal machines, *dq* modeling that decouples the torque and flux producing components of currents and subsequent control of these components helps achieve the objective.

## 8.2   AC MACHINE MODELING FOR CONTROLS

The AC machine controls starts with the *dq* modeling which provides all the necessary transformation equations required to implement the torque controller. The electromagnetic torque $T_e$ expression in terms of machine variables (current, flux linkage, etc.) in the *dq* model is often used to estimate the torque for closed loop control. These machine variables are measurable using sensors, which is much simpler than torque measurement. The steady-state torque expression of Equation 7.46 and the simplified torque expression of Equation 7.50 are inadequate for a dynamic controller implementation, which is due to the significant coupling between the stator and rotor variables of a three-phase AC machine.

We have seen earlier in Chapter 7 that a balanced set of three-phase currents $i_a(t)$, $i_b(t)$ and $i_c(t)$ flowing through 120° space displaced balanced set of *a*, *b* and *c* stator windings, respectively, establishes a rotating mmf $\vec{F}_S(t)$; this resultant rotating mmf has a constant peak amplitude which rotates around the stator circumference at synchronous speed. The *dq* transformation is based on the concept that *d*- and *q*-axes equivalent stator currents, designated as $i_{ds}(t)$ and $i_{qs}(t)$, flowing through a fictitious set of orthogonal windings along the *d*- and *q*-axes establishes the same stator rotating mmf $\vec{F}_S(t)$. The transformation to a *dq* reference frame from the *abc* reference frame in terms of a general variable *f* (representing voltage, current or flux linkage) is given by (repeated here from Chapter 7 for convenience)

$$f_q = \frac{2}{3}[f_a \cos\theta + f_b \cos(\theta - 120°) + f_c \cos(\theta + 120°)]$$

$$f_d = \frac{2}{3}[f_a \sin\theta + f_b \sin(\theta - 120°) + f_c \sin(\theta + 120°)].$$

(8.2)

$$f_0 = \frac{1}{3}[f_a + f_b + f_c].$$

The transformation in space vector form is

$$\vec{f}_{qd}(t) = \frac{2}{3}e^{-j\theta}\vec{f}_{abc}(t)$$

(8.3)

The transformation relation holds good for stator as well as for rotor variables. All the three-phase systems considered here are assumed to be balanced.

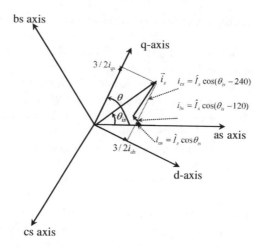

**FIGURE 8.2** Transformation from three-phase variables to $dq$ axes variables.

The projections from both the $abc$ frame and the $dq$ frame to form the same space vector for a three-phase AC machine current variable are shown in Figure 8.2. The orientation of the $dq$ axes with respect to the $abc$-axes is at an arbitrary angle $\theta$. The direct- and quadrature-axis stator currents $i_{ds}$ and $i_{qs}$ are a set of fictitious two-phase current components, and the same is true for other $dq$ variables. The $dq$ reference frame can be stationary with respect to the stator or rotating at an arbitrary speed, such as at rotor speed or at synchronous speed. Again, when a stationary $dq$ reference frame is used, the $dq$ axes may be at any arbitrary angle with respect to our chosen reference Phase-$a$ axis.

### 8.2.1 ROTATING REFERENCE FRAME

Although the speed of the $dq$ winding can be arbitrary, three of those are the most suitable for machine analysis. These three speeds of $dq$ windings are 0, $\omega_m$ and $\omega_e$. The zero speed is known as the stationary reference frame, where more commonly the stationary $d$-axis is aligned with the Phase-$a$ axis of the stator. The angle of transformation $\theta$ in Equations 8.2 and 8.3 is 0 in this case. The $d$- and $q$-axis variables oscillate at the synchronous frequency in the balanced sinusoidal steady state. When $\omega_e$ is chosen as the speed of the reference $dq$ frame, all the associated variables in the stator and in the rotor $dq$ windings appear as DC variables in the balanced sinusoidal steady state. For an arbitrary speed of the reference $dq$ windings, the angle of transformation is

$$\theta = \int_0^t \omega(\xi)\, d\xi + \theta_0. \tag{8.4}$$

**Example 8.1**

The three-phase currents in an AC machine are

$$i_a(t) = 10\cos 377t$$

$$i_b(t) = 10\cos\left(377t - \frac{2\pi}{3}\right)$$

$$i_c(t) = 10\cos\left(377t + \frac{2\pi}{3}\right)$$

Calculate the currents in the $dq$ reference frame in the (a) stationary reference frame and (b) in the synchronous reference frame.

### Solution

a. Using Equation 8.2 and $\theta = 0$, the $dq$ current variables in the stationary reference frame are

$$i_d{}^s(t) = -10\sin(377t)$$

$$i_q{}^s(t) = 10\cos(377t)$$

b. Using Equation 8.2 and $\theta = \omega t = 377t$ with $\theta_0 = 0$, the $dq$ current variables in the synchronously rotating reference frame are

$$i_d{}^e(t) = 0$$

$$i_q{}^e(t) = 10$$

## 8.2.2 Induction Machine $dq$ Model

Let us assume that the stator and rotor voltages and currents in the three-phase model vary arbitrarily in time. The voltage balance equations in the stator and rotor circuits of the three-phase induction machine in space vector form are

$$\vec{v}_{abcs} = R_s \vec{i}_{abcs} + p\vec{\lambda}_{abcs}$$

$$\vec{v}_{abcr} = R_r \vec{i}_{abcr} + p\vec{\lambda}_{abcr}$$

The rotor winding voltage $\vec{v}_{abcr}$ is zero for squirrel cage induction machine with short-circuited rotor windings, but will be represented as such for generality. The rotor variables are represented here without the rotor-to-stator referral symbol for the sake of simplicity, but are implicitly incorporated in the equations. The stator and rotor flux linkages include coupling effects between the windings of stator and rotor circuits as well as between stator and rotor windings. Accounting for all the magnetic coupling and assuming magnetic linearity ($\lambda = Li$), the phase-variable form of the voltage equations in the $abc$ frame can be derived as

$$\vec{v}_{abcs} = R_s \vec{i}_{abcs} + L_s(p\vec{i}_{abcs}) + L_m(p\vec{i}_{abcr})e^{j\theta_r} + j\omega_r L_m \vec{i}_{abcr} e^{j\theta_r} \tag{8.5}$$

$$\vec{v}_{abcr} = R_r \vec{i}_{abcr} + L_r(p\vec{i}_{abcr}) + L_m(p\vec{i}_{abcs})e^{-j\theta_r} - j\omega_r L_m \vec{i}_{abcs} e^{-j\theta_r}, \tag{8.6}$$

where $\omega_r = p\theta_r = \dfrac{d\theta_r}{dt}$ is the rotor speed and $L_s = L_{ls} + L_m$ and $L_r = L_{lr} + L_m$. $L_{ls}$ and $L_{lr}$ are the stator and rotor leakage inductances, respectively. The derivation can be carried out using either the space vector approach [1] or reference frame transformation [4].

Multiplying by $e^{j\theta}$ and applying $dq$ transformation, Equations 8.5 and 8.6 can be transformed into a general reference frame rotating at a speed $\omega$ as

$$\vec{v}_{qds} = R_s i_{qds} + L_s(p\vec{i}_{qds}) + L_m(p\vec{i}_{qdr}) + j\omega(L_s \vec{i}_{qds} + L_m \vec{i}_{qdr}) \tag{8.7}$$

$$\vec{v}_{qdr} = R_r i_{qdr} + L_r(p\vec{i}_{qdr}) + L_m(p\vec{i}_{qds}) + j(\omega - \omega_r)(L_r \vec{i}_{qdr} + L_m \vec{i}_{qds}). \tag{8.8}$$

The matrix form of the induction motor model in the arbitrary $dq$ reference frame is

$$
\begin{bmatrix} v_{ds} \\ v_{qs} \\ v_{dr} \\ v_{qr} \end{bmatrix} = \begin{bmatrix} R_s & -\omega L_s & 0 & -\omega L_m \\ \omega L_s & R_s & \omega L_m & 0 \\ 0 & -(\omega-\omega_r)L_m & R_r & -(\omega-\omega_r)L_r \\ (\omega-\omega_r)L_m & 0 & (\omega-\omega_r)L_r & R_r \end{bmatrix} \begin{bmatrix} i_{ds} \\ i_{qs} \\ i_{dr} \\ i_{qr} \end{bmatrix}
$$
(8.9)
$$
+ \begin{bmatrix} L_s & 0 & L_m & 0 \\ 0 & L_s & 0 & L_m \\ L_m & 0 & L_r & 0 \\ 0 & L_m & 0 & L_r \end{bmatrix} \begin{bmatrix} pi_{ds} \\ pi_{qs} \\ pi_{dr} \\ pi_{qr} \end{bmatrix}.
$$

The $dq$ equivalent circuit model for the induction machine in circuit schematic form is shown in Figure 8.3.

### 8.2.3 Power and Electromagnetic Torque

Power into the three-phase machine needs to be analyzed in terms of $dq$ variables to arrive at the electromagnetic torque expression, which is used in the motor control loop. The power into the induction machine is the product of the phase voltage and phase currents given as

$$
P_{in} = (v_{as}i_{as} + v_{bs}i_{bs} + v_{cs}i_{cs}) + (v_{ar}i_{ar} + v_{br}i_{br} + v_{cr}i_{cr})
$$
(8.10)

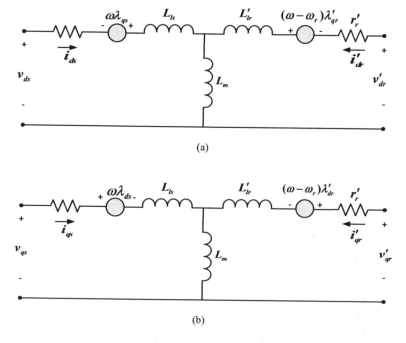

FIGURE 8.3 $d$- and $q$-axes equivalent circuits of the induction machine: (a) $d$-axis circuit and (b) $q$-axis circuit.

The input power is embedded in the real part of the product of the voltage space vector and the current space vector conjugate of the stator and rotor variables. The real part can be calculated as follows:

$$\text{Re}\left(\vec{v}_{abc}\vec{i}_{abc}^*\right) = \text{Re}[(v_a + v_b\angle120 + v_c\angle240)\cdot(i_a + i_b\angle-120 + i_c\angle-240)]$$

$$= \frac{3}{2}(v_a i_a + v_b i_b + v_c i_c).$$

Using the above relation in the power input equation for the induction machine, we get

$$P_{in} = \frac{2}{3}\left[\text{Re}\left(\vec{v}_{abcs}\vec{i}_{abcs}^*\right) + \text{Re}\left(\vec{v}_{abcr}\vec{i}_{abcr}^*\right)\right]$$

Now, using Equation 8.3,

$$P_{in} = \frac{2}{3}\left[\text{Re}\left[\left(\frac{3}{2}e^{j\theta}\vec{v}_{qds}\right)\left(\frac{3}{2}e^{-j\theta}\vec{i}_{qds}^*\right)\right] + \text{Re}\left[\left(\frac{3}{2}e^{j\theta}\vec{v}_{qdr}\right)\left(\frac{3}{2}e^{-j\theta}\vec{i}_{qdr}^*\right)\right]\right]$$

$$= \frac{3}{2}\left[\text{Re}\left(\vec{v}_{qds}\vec{i}_{qds}^*\right) + \text{Re}\left(\vec{v}_{qdr}\vec{i}_{qdr}^*\right)\right]. \tag{8.11}$$

The input power expression in scalar form is

$$P_{in} = \frac{3}{2}(v_{ds}i_{ds} + v_{qs}i_{qs} + v_{dr}i_{dr} + v_{qr}i_{qr}) \tag{8.12}$$

The multiplying factor 3/2 is due to the choice of the factor 2/3 for the ratio of $dq$ and $abc$ variables. The input power expression of Equation 8.12 would not have this 3/2 factor, had we chosen $\sqrt{2/3}$ as the proportionality constant between the $dq$ and $abc$ variables.

Upon expanding the right-hand side of Equation 8.12 and extracting the output electromechanical power $P_e$ [1], we get

$$P_e = \frac{3}{2}\text{Im}\left[\omega_r L_m \vec{i}_{qds}\vec{i}_{qdr}^*\right] \tag{8.13}$$

where $\omega_r$ is the rotor angular velocity of a two-pole machine. The electromagnetic torque for a $P$-pole machine is, therefore,

$$T_e = \frac{3}{2}\frac{P}{2}L_m\,\text{Im}\left[\vec{i}_{qds}\vec{i}_{qdr}^*\right] = \frac{3}{2}\frac{P}{2}L_m(i_{qs}i_{dr} - i_{ds}i_{qr}). \tag{8.14}$$

Several alternative forms of the electromagnetic torque can be derived using the stator and rotor flux linkage expressions. A couple of these torque expressions are

$$T_e = \frac{3}{2}\frac{P}{2}\text{Im}\left[\vec{i}_{qds}\vec{\lambda}_{qdr}^*\right] = \frac{3}{2}\frac{P}{2}(\lambda_{ds}i_{qs} - \lambda_{qs}i_{ds}) \tag{8.15}$$

$$T_e = \frac{3}{2}\frac{P}{2}\frac{L_m}{L_r}\text{Im}\left[\vec{i}_{qds}\vec{\lambda}_{qdr}^*\right] = \frac{3}{2}\frac{P}{2}\frac{L_m}{L_r}(\lambda_{dr}i_{qs} - \lambda_{qr}i_{ds}). \tag{8.16}$$

The torque expressions in terms of $dq$ variables are used in the vector control of induction motor drives. The vector control implementations are accomplished in one of the several available choices of reference frames, such as rotor-flux-oriented reference frame, stator-flux-oriented reference frame or air gap-flux-oriented reference frame. The $abc$ variables at the input of the controller are converted to $dq$ variables in the chosen reference frame. The control computations take place in terms of $dq$ variables and the generated command outputs are again converted back to $abc$ variables. The inverter controller executes the commands to establish the desired currents or voltages in the drive system.

The torque expression derived in this section is useful for motor controller implementation, while the simplified torque expression of Equation 7.50 is useful for system-level analysis.

## 8.3 INDUCTION MACHINE VECTOR CONTROL

Vector control refers to the control of both magnitude and phase angles of the stator and rotor critical variables in a chosen reference frame. More specifically, the control methods used in high-performance induction motor drives is known as field-oriented controls. The term *field orientation* is used as a special case of vector control where a 90° spatial orientation between the stator and rotor mmfs is continuously maintained by the motor controller. The term vector control is general and is also used for controls where the angle between the rotor and stator critical variables is different from 90°.

Transformation of the variables into a rotating reference frame facilitates the instantaneous torque control of an induction machine similar to that of a DC machine. Consider the electromagnetic torque expression in Equation 8.16 in the $dq$ reference frame:

$$T_e = \frac{3}{2}\frac{P}{2}\frac{L_m}{L_r}(\lambda_{dr}i_{qs} - \lambda_{qr}i_{ds}).$$

If we choose a reference frame that rotates at synchronous speed with the rotor flux linkage vector $\vec{\lambda}_{qdr}(t)$ continuously locked along the $d$-axis of the $dq$ reference frame, then $\lambda_{qr} = 0$. The resulting torque equation is then

$$T_e = \frac{3}{2}\frac{P}{2}\frac{L_m}{L_r}\lambda_{dr}i_{qs}. \tag{8.17}$$

Now, note the similarity between the above torque expression and the DC motor torque expression in Equation 8.1. An instantaneous change in $i_{qs}$ current with constant $\lambda_{dr}$ will result in an instantaneous change in torque similar to the situation in DC motors. We can conclude that an AC machine can be made to appear like a DC machine with appropriate reference frame transformations, and hence, controlled similarly. There are several ways of implementing the vector control on induction motors. The implementation can be carried out through transformation into any one of the several synchronously rotating reference frames, such as the rotor flux reference frame, air gap flux reference frame and stator flux reference frame [1,5]. The task is the simplest in the rotor-flux-oriented reference frame, which will be described in the next section. In addition, according to the method of rotor flux angle measurement, the vector control is labeled as either direct vector control or indirect vector control.

### 8.3.1 ROTOR-FLUX-ORIENTED VECTOR CONTROL

The rotor flux linkage vector direction is chosen as the $d$-axis of the reference frame in the rotor-flux-oriented vector control methods. The reference frame is also assumed rotating at the speed of the rotor flux vector. In the rotor-flux-oriented reference frame, $q$-axis rotor flux $\lambda_{qr}{}^{rf} = 0$ and the torque is

$$T_e = \frac{3}{2}\frac{P}{2}\frac{L_m}{L_r}\lambda_{dr}{}^{rf}i_{qs}{}^{rf}. \tag{8.18}$$

The instantaneous control of the $q$-axis stator current in the rotor flux reference frame results in an instantaneous response of the motor torque provided that the rotor flux is held constant. The current controller can be assumed to have a high bandwidth so that it establishes the stator command currents instantaneously. Therefore, the dynamics of the controller are primarily associated with the rotor circuit. The rotor flux and current and the stator current in the rotor-flux-oriented reference frame are shown in Figure 8.4. The rotor voltage and current equations in the rotor flux reference frame, derived from Equation 8.9, are

$$v_{qr}{}^{rf} = R_r i_{qr}{}^{rf} + p\lambda_{qr}{}^{rf} + (\omega_{rf} - \omega_r)\lambda_{dr}{}^{rf}$$

$$v_{dr}{}^{rf} = R_r i_{dr}{}^{rf} + p\lambda_{dr}{}^{rf} - (\omega_{rf} - \omega_r)\lambda_{qr}{}^{rf}.$$

The flux linkages from Figure 8.3 are

$$\lambda_{qr}{}^{rf} = L_{lr} i_{qr}{}^{rf} + L_m\left(i_{qs}{}^{rf} + i_{qr}{}^{rf}\right) = L_m i_{qs}{}^{rf} + L_r i_{qr}{}^{rf}$$

$$\lambda_{dr}{}^{rf} = L_{lr} i_{dr}{}^{rf} + L_m(i_{ds}{}^{rf} + i_{dr}{}^{rf}) = L_m i_{ds}{}^{rf} + L_r i_{dr}{}^{rf}.$$

The rotor voltages are identically zero in squirrel cage induction machines. Moreover, the $q$-axis flux linkage is zero in the rotor-flux-oriented reference frame ($\lambda_{qr}{}^{rf} = 0$). Therefore, the rotor $dq$-circuit voltage balance equations becomes

$$0 = R_r i_{qr}{}^{rf} + (\omega_{rf} - \omega_r)\lambda_{dr}{}^{rf} \tag{8.19}$$

$$0 = R_r i_{dr}{}^{rf} + p\lambda_{dr}{}^{rf}. \tag{8.20}$$

An important relation required to implement one form of vector control (indirect method) is the slip relation, which follows from Equation 8.19 as

$$\omega_{rf} - \omega_r = s\omega_{rf} = -\frac{R_r i_{qr}{}^{rf}}{\lambda_{dr}{}^{rf}} = \frac{R_r}{L_r}\frac{L_m i_{qs}{}^{rf}}{\lambda_{dr}{}^{rf}}. \tag{8.21}$$

From the $q$-circuit flux linkage expression, we get

$$\lambda_{qr}{}^{rf} = L_m i_{qs}{}^{rf} + L_r i_{qr}{}^{rf} = 0 \Rightarrow i_{qr}{}^{rf} = -\frac{L_m}{L_r} i_{qs}{}^{rf} \tag{8.22}$$

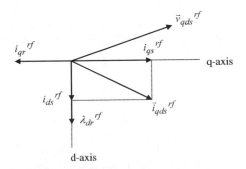

**FIGURE 8.4** $d$- and $q$-axes currents in the rotor-flux-oriented reference frame.

Equation 8.22 describes that there will be an instantaneous response without any delay in the rotor current following a change in the torque command stator current $i_{qs}{}^{rf}$. The major dynamics in the rotor-flux-oriented vector control method is in the behavior of $d$-axis rotor flux $\lambda_{dr}{}^{rf}$. $\lambda_{dr}{}^{rf}$ is related to the $d$-axis rotor and stator currents according to

$$\lambda_{dr}{}^{rf} = L_r i_{dr}{}^{rf} + L_m i_{ds}{}^{rf} \tag{8.23}$$

Now, using Equations 8.20 and 8.23, the following dynamic relations can be easily established

$$i_{dr}{}^{rf} = -\frac{L_m p}{R_r + L_r p} i_{ds}{}^{rf} \tag{8.24}$$

$$\lambda_{dr}{}^{rf} = \frac{R_r L_m}{R_r + L_r p} i_{ds}{}^{rf} \tag{8.25}$$

Equation 8.24 shows that $i_{dr}{}^{rf}$ exists only when $i_{ds}{}^{rf}$ changes, and is zero in the steady state. Equation 8.25 gives the dynamics associated in bringing a change in the rotor flux $\lambda_{dr}{}^{rf}$. In steady state, the rotor flux is

$$\lambda_{dr}{}^{rf} = L_m i_{ds}{}^{rf}.$$

Therefore, in order to change the rotor flux command, $i_{ds}{}^{rf}$ must be changed which will cause a transient occurrence of $d$-axis rotor current $i_{dr}{}^{rf}$. The time constant associated with these dynamics is $\tau_r = \dfrac{L_r}{R_r}$, which is commonly known as the rotor time constant.

## 8.3.2 Direct and Indirect Vector Controls

The key to the implementation of the vector control is to find the instantaneous position of the rotor flux with respect to a stationary reference axis. Let this angle be defined as $\theta_{rf}$ with respect to the Phase-$a$ reference axis as shown in Figure 8.5. The vector control methods can be implemented in one of two ways defined as direct and indirect methods according to the nature of measuring or calculating the rotor flux angle.

### 8.3.2.1 Direct Vector Control

In direct vector control methods, the rotor flux angle is calculated from direct measurements of machine electrical quantities. Using the $dq$ model of the machine, the measurements are used to calculate the rotor flux vector, which directly gives the rotor flux angle $\theta_{rf}$. The measurements of electrical variables can be carried out in one of several different ways. For example, flux sensing coils or Hall sensors placed in the air gap can be used to measure the air gap flux $\vec{\lambda}_{qdm}$. The subscript '$m$' stands for mutual flux in the air gap between the stator and the rotor. The $dq$ model of the induction machine gives the following mathematical relations:

$$\vec{\lambda}_{qdm}{}^s = L_m \left( \vec{i}_{qds}{}^s + \vec{i}_{qdr}{}^s \right) \tag{8.26}$$

$$\vec{\lambda}_{qdr}{}^s = L_m \vec{i}_{qds}{}^s + L_r \vec{i}_{qdr}{}^s \tag{8.27}$$

The superscript '$s$' is used for the reference frame, since the air gap flux measurements are with respect to the stator in the stationary reference frame. Now, the objective is to write $\vec{\lambda}_{qdr}$ in terms of measurable quantities. From Equation 8.26, the rotor current can be written as

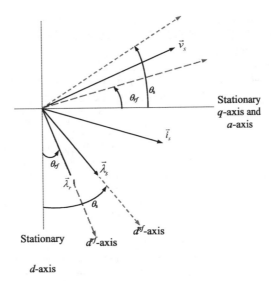

**FIGURE 8.5** Relationship among stationary, rotor flux (*rf*) oriented and stator flux (*sf*) oriented reference frames.

$$\vec{i}_{qdr}{}^{s} = \frac{\vec{\lambda}_{qdm}{}^{s}}{L_m} - \vec{i}_{qds}{}^{s}.$$

Substituting the rotor current in Equation 8.27

$$\vec{\lambda}_{qdr}{}^{s} = \frac{L_r}{L_m}\vec{\lambda}_{qdm}{}^{s} - (L_r - L_m)\vec{i}_{qds}{}^{s}$$

$$\Rightarrow \lambda_r = \left|\vec{\lambda}_{qdr}{}^{s}\right|, \ \theta_{rf} = \angle \vec{\lambda}_{qdr}{}^{s}$$

The approach is very straightforward requiring the knowledge of only two motor parameters, rotor leakage inductance, $L_r - L_m = L_{lr}$ and the ratio $L_r/L_m$. The rotor leakage inductance is a fairly constant value, while the $L_r/L_m$ ratio varies only a little by magnetic flux path saturation. However, the big disadvantage is the need for flux sensors in the air gap.

The flux sensors can be avoided by using voltage and current sensors to measure the stator applied voltages and currents. The measurements are used to calculate the stator flux by direct integration of the phase voltage

$$\vec{\lambda}_{qds}{}^{s} = \int \left(\vec{v}_{qds}{}^{s} - R_s\vec{i}_{qds}{}^{s}\right)dt$$

The rotor flux vector can be obtained from the stator flux vector using the following mathematical relationship:

$$\vec{\lambda}_{qdr}{}^{s} = \frac{L_r}{L_m}\left(\vec{\lambda}_{qds}{}^{s} - L_s'\vec{i}_{qds}\right)$$

where $L_s' = L_s - \dfrac{L_m^2}{L_r}$. The method requires the knowledge of three motor parameters $R_s$, $L_s'$ and $\dfrac{L_r}{L_m}$. The major difficulty of the method is the significant variation of the stator resistance $R_s$ due to temperature dependence and the integration of the phase voltage to obtain stator flux at low speeds. The integration is especially inaccurate at low speeds due to the dominating resistive voltage-drop term.

### 8.3.2.2 Indirect Vector Control

In the indirect vector control scheme, which is more commonly used, a rotor position sensor is used to derive the speed and rotor position information, and the slip relation of Equation 8.24 is used to derive the rotor flux angle. The implementation of rotor flux angle calculation in the indirect vector control method is shown in Figure 8.6.

### 8.3.2.3 Vector Control Implementation

The vector-controlled drive has three major components like any other motor drive system: Electric machine, power converter and controller. An implementation block diagram of a speed regulated vector-controlled drive is shown in Figure 8.7. The controller processes the input command signals and the feedback signals from the converter and the motor, and generates the gating signals for the PWM inverter or converter.

In the closed loop speed-controlled system, the input is a speed reference, which is compared with the measured speed feedback signal to generate the control signals for maintaining the desired speed. The vector controller requires reference frame transformations and several computations that are typically implemented in a digital signal processor. The sensors provide current feedback

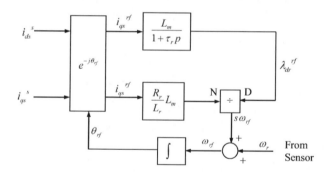

**FIGURE 8.6**  Rotor flux angle calculation in indirect vector control method.

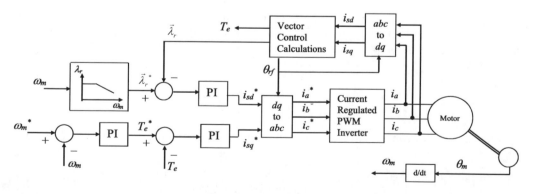

**FIGURE 8.7**  Implementation of vector control.

information to the controller for vector calculations. The first step in the vector controller is the transformation calculations of the feedback current signals to a suitable *dq* reference frame. The following steps are the torque and reference frame angle calculations. The vector controller outputs the three-phase reference currents $i_a^*$, $i_b^*$ and $i_c^*$ for the current-regulated PWM inverter. The current controller in the subsequent stage generates the PWM gating signals for the power electronics converter switches to establish the desired currents in the electric machine. The torque and angle calculations can be in the rotor flux reference frame where torque Equation 8.18 and the block diagram of Figure 8.7 are used. For speeds up to the rated speed of the machine, rated rotor flux $\vec{\lambda}_r$ is used. For higher speeds, the flux command is reduced to operate the machine in the constant power mode. This mode of operation is known as the flux-weakening mode. In the indirect control method, position and speed sensors are used to provide the rotor position and motor speed feedback information (the implementation is shown in Figure 8.7).

## 8.4 PM SYNCHRONOUS MACHINE VECTOR CONTROL

The PM machines used in electric and hybrid vehicles are designed with sinusoidal mmfs where vector control is applied to obtain the fastest response characteristics with smooth torque control.

### 8.4.1 VOLTAGE AND TORQUE IN REFERENCE FRAMES

For vector control of PM synchronous machines, the *abc* variables are transformed into the rotor reference frame which is also the synchronous reference frame for synchronous machines in steady state. The *dq* equations of the PMSM were presented earlier in Chapter 7 and are repeated here for convenience:

$$v_q = R_s i_q + \frac{d}{dt}\lambda_q + \omega_r \lambda_d$$

$$v_d = R_s i_d + \frac{d}{dt}\lambda_d - \omega_r \lambda_q$$

(8.28)

where the *dq* axes flux linkages are

$$\lambda_q = L_q i_q$$

$$\lambda_d = L_d i_d + \lambda_f$$

The *d* and *q*-axis inductances are

$$L_d = L_{ls} + L_{md} \text{ and } L_q = L_{ls} + L_{mq}.$$

$L_{ls}$ is the leakage inductance.

The equivalent circuit representations in the *q*- and *d*-axes are shown in Figure 8.8.

The electromagnetic torque is given by

$$T_e = \frac{3}{2}\frac{P}{2}\left[\lambda_f i_q + (L_d - L_q)i_d i_q\right]$$

(8.29)

where *P* is the number of poles.

The rotor position information gives the position of *d*- and *q*-axes which is given by

$$\theta_r = \int_0^t \omega_r(\xi)d\xi + \theta_r(0).$$

FIGURE 8.8 IPM synchronous machine model in $dq$ reference frame: (a) $q$-axis circuit and (b) $d$-axis circuit.

The control objective is to regulate the voltages $v_d$ and $v_q$ or the currents $i_d$ and $i_q$ by controlling the firing angles of the inverter switches.

## 8.4.2 PMSM Simulation Model

The state-space representation of the PMSM $dq$ model is useful for the computer simulation of the motor. The representation in the commonly used $dq$ synchronous reference frame is

$$\frac{di_d}{dt} = -\frac{R_s}{L_d}i_d + \frac{L_q}{L_d}\omega_r i_q + \frac{v_d}{L_d}$$

$$\frac{di_q}{dt} = -\frac{R_s}{L_q}i_q - \frac{L_d}{L_q}\omega_r i_d - \frac{1}{L_q}\omega_r \lambda_f + \frac{v_q}{L_q}$$

$$\frac{d\omega_m}{dt} = \frac{1}{J}\left(T_e - T_l - B\omega_m - F\frac{\omega_m}{|\omega_m|}\right)$$

$$\frac{d\theta_r}{dt} = \frac{P}{2}\omega_m$$

(8.30)

where $J$ is the rotor and load inertia, $F$ is the coulomb friction, $B$ is the viscous load, $T_l$ is the load torque, $P$ is the number of poles, $\omega_r$ is the electrical rotor speed and $\theta_r$ is the electrical rotor position, while $\omega_m$ is the mechanical rotor speed and $\theta_m$ is the mechanical rotor position. The electrical rotor position is related to the mechanical rotor position $\theta_r$ as

$$\theta_r = \frac{P}{2}\theta_m.$$

The electrical rotor speed is related to the mechanical rotor speed as

$$\omega_r = \frac{P}{2}\omega_m.$$

### 8.4.3 PM SYNCHRONOUS MACHINE DRIVES

The advantage of a PM synchronous machine is that it can be driven in the vector-controlled mode delivering high performance, unlike the PM trapezoidal machine which has to be driven with square-wave currents. Of course, a high-precision position information is needed to implement the vector control in PM synchronous machines. A typical PM synchronous motor drive consists of a PM synchronous motor, a three-phase bridge inverter, gate drivers, position sensor, current or voltage sensors, a microprocessor or digital signal processor, and interfacing circuits, as shown in Figure 8.9.

The vector control of a PM synchronous motor is simpler than that of an induction motor, since the motor always rotates at synchronous speed. In vector calculations, only the synchronously rotating reference frame is necessary. The system controller sets the reference or command signal, which can be position, speed, current or torque. The variables needed for the controller are the feedback signals from the sensing circuits (position, speed, current or voltage) or estimated values obtained within the signal processor. The error signals between the reference and actual variable signals are transformed to gate control signals for the inverter switches. The switches follow the gate commands to decrease the error signals by injecting desired stator currents into the three-phase stator windings.

Vector control is used for the PM synchronous motor drives in the electric and hybrid vehicle applications to deliver the required high performance. The torque expression in Equation 8.29 for the PM synchronous motor shows that if the $d$-axis current is maintained constant, the generated torque is proportional to the $q$ axis current. For the special case when $i_d$ is forced to be zero $\lambda_d = \lambda_f$ and

$$T_e = \frac{3}{2} \cdot \frac{P}{2} \cdot \lambda_f \cdot i_q$$

$$= k_e i_q$$

(8.31)

where $k_e = \dfrac{3}{2} \cdot \dfrac{P}{2} \cdot \lambda_f =$ Motor constant. Since the magnetic flux linkage is a constant, the torque is directly proportional to the $q$-axis current. The torque equation is similar to that of a separately excited DC machine. Therefore, using reference frame transformations, the PM synchronous motor

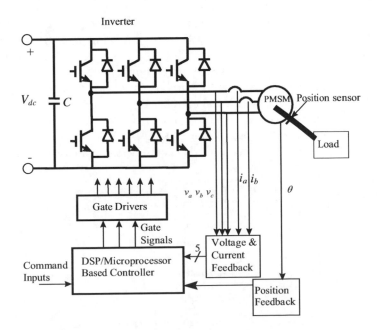

**FIGURE 8.9** A typical PM synchronous motor drive structure.

can be controlled like a DC machine. For a given torque command, the command $i_q$ below base speed is obtained from the machine electromagnetic torque equation as

$$i_q^* = \frac{2}{3} \times \frac{2}{P} \times \frac{T_e^*}{\lambda_f}$$  (8.32)

### 8.4.3.1 Flux Weakening

The PM synchronous motor can be operated in the field-weakening mode similar to the DC motor to extend the constant power range and achieve higher speeds. An injection of negative $i_d$ will weaken the air gap flux. The implementation technique for the field weakening mode is shown in Figure 8.10.

Above the machine base speed, the flux-weakening algorithm is used to find the demagnetizing component of the stator current satisfying the maximum current and voltage limits. Based on the speed of the machine, the flux-weakening algorithm calculates a constant as

$$f(\omega_r) = \frac{\omega_b}{\omega_r}; \quad \omega_b < \omega_r < \omega_{max}$$

$$= 1; \quad 0 < \omega_r < \omega_b$$  (8.33)

where $\omega_b$ is the base speed, $\omega_r$ is the rotor speed and $\omega_{max}$ is the maximum machine speed. For rotor speeds below base speed, $f(\omega_r) = 1$ and the $i_d$ command is zero. For speeds above base speed, the flux-weakening component of the stator current is given by

$$i_d^* = \frac{\lambda_m^* - \lambda_{af}}{L_d} \times k_f \times \frac{\omega_b}{\omega_r}.$$  (8.34)

### 8.4.3.2 Current and Voltage Controllers

The current regulators in a PM synchronous motor drive can be designed in the $dq$ reference frame where $d$- and $q$-axis current commands are generated by the outer loop controller. These $dq$ current commands are then converted to $abc$-current commands using the rotor position feedback information. Current controllers in the $abc$-reference frame then generate the gate signals for the inverter. The simplified block diagram of a current controller is shown in Figure 8.11. The current controller then converts the commanded currents into a PWM signals using feedback current signals which are applied to the voltage source inverter (VSI) through a driver circuit.

An alternative approach of implementing the current controller is to convert the $dq$ current commands into $dq$ voltage commands using a PI controller to convert the $dq$ current commands into $dq$ voltage commands. The voltage command signals can then be used for a voltage PWM scheme, such as the sinusoidal PWM or the space vector PWM. The block diagram of such a method is shown in Figure 8.12. Further details on the current controllers are discussed in Section 8.6.

**FIGURE 8.10**  Vector controller structure for PMSM with field weakening.

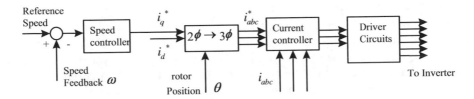

**FIGURE 8.11**   PM synchronous drive controls using a current controller.

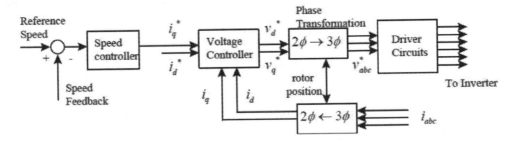

**FIGURE 8.12**   PM synchronous drive controls using a PWM voltage controller.

### 8.4.4   IPM Synchronous Machine Controls

The interior permanent magnet (IPM) synchronous motor can provide high power and/or torque density and high efficiency from the electric machine perspective while being compatible with extended speed-range operation from the controls side which made the technology widely adopted for electric and hybrid vehicle applications despite the high magnet costs. The extended speed range feature stems from the difference in $d$- and $q$-axis inductances that enables flux-weakening controls through stator current control to counter the constant magnetic airgap flux generated by the permanent magnets. The motor controller functionality is to generate the commands for the power drive circuit which is the PWM-controlled VSI for electric and hybrid vehicle systems. The controller operates within the constraints of inverter and motor current limits and the supply voltage constraints. The desirable control features are torque per ampere maximization or winding loss minimization at lower speeds, maximum torque per voltage maximization during extended speeds, and smooth transitions into and out of the flux-weakening modes and fast response to driver demands.

#### 8.4.4.1   Current Constraint

The current limit of the electric drive depends on the rated current of the inverter and the thermal rating of the electric machine. The inverter limit is set by the switching and conduction losses of the power devices. For the electric machine, the limit is set by the electrical, magnetic and mechanical losses of the AC machine with the electrical or copper loss and magnetic or iron loss dominating the losses. The thermal time constant of the machine (which can be from several seconds for less than a kW sized machines to several minutes for large machines) is much larger than that of the inverter (which can be several tens of milliseconds) due to the thermal mass of the former for which the inverter needs to be rated at 150%–300% of the electric machine rating to meet the for higher acceleration torque.

Let us assume that the maximum current of an AC electric machine is defined as $I_{s,max}$ which would limit the $d$- and $q$-axis current commands within a circle given by

$$i_d^{s*2} + i_q^{s*2} = i_d^{e*2} + i_q^{e*2} \le I_{s,max}^2 \tag{8.35}$$

### 8.4.4.2  Voltage Constraint

The motor controller must also operate under the voltage constraint limit as the power converter is limited by the maximum DC-link voltage and the modulation method. The voltage constraint becomes more prominent as the speed increases since the supply is constrained in forcing current into the machine against the machine back-emf which is proportional to the speed. If the maximum phase voltage under the DC-link and modulation method is $V_{s,max}$, then the voltage constraint can be represented as

$$V_d^{s*2} + V_q^{s*2} = V_d^{e*2} + V_q^{e*2} \leq V_{s,max}^2 \tag{8.36}$$

In steady state, neglecting $R_s$,

$$V_d = -X_q I_q$$

$$V_q = X_d I_d + \omega_r \lambda_f$$

Also, $V_s^2 = V_d^2 + V_q^2$

$$\Rightarrow V_s^2 = \left(X_q I_q\right)^2 + \left(X_d I_d + \omega_r \lambda_f\right)^2$$

$$\Rightarrow \left(\frac{V_s}{X_q}\right)^2 = I_q^2 + \left(\frac{X_d}{X_q}\right)^2 \left(I_d + \frac{\omega_r \lambda_f}{X_d}\right)^2 \tag{8.37}$$

Alternatively this can be written in terms of flux linkages as

$$\lambda_s^2 = \left(\lambda_f + L_d I_d\right)^2 + \left(L_q I_q\right)^2 \tag{8.38}$$

Since $V_s = \omega_r \lambda_s$ in steady state, for a given $V_s$ and $\omega_r$ (which fixes $\lambda_s$), the $I_q - I_d$ trajectory is an ellipse. The voltage and current constraints for an IPMSM using Equations 8.35 and 8.38 are shown graphically in Figure 8.13. The commanded current and voltage vector pair must simultaneously satisfy the steady-state motor equations and the regulator imposed limits. Since the voltage constraint is speed dependent, the objective of torque maximization is achieved under current and voltage constraints as a function of speed.

### 8.4.4.3  Maximum Torque per Ampere (MTPA)

The stator current magnitude is given by $I_s = \sqrt{I_d^2 + I_q^2}$ which can be inserted in the torque equation as

$$T_e = \frac{3}{2}\frac{P}{2}\left[\lambda_f + (L_d - L_q)I_d\right]\sqrt{I_s^2 - I_d^2}$$

The only variable in the equation is $I_d$. Hence, we can obtain the condition for MTPA by taking the derivative of torque with respect to $I_d$ and setting the expression equal to zero, i.e., $\frac{\partial T_e}{\partial I_d} = 0$. The resulting MTPA condition is

$$I_d^2 + I_d \frac{\lambda_f}{L_d - L_q} - I_q^2 = 0 \tag{8.39}$$

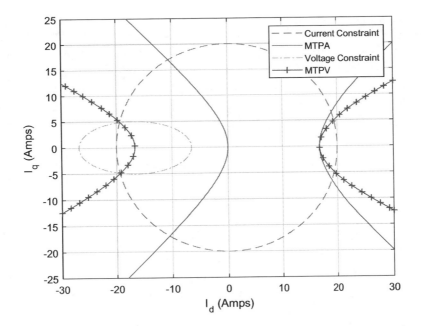

**FIGURE 8.13**  IPMSM voltage and current constraints along with MPTA and MTPV trajectories.

### 8.4.4.4  Maximum Torque per Voltage (MPTV)

The torque equation and the voltage constraint of an IPMSM is given by

$$T_e = \frac{3}{2}\frac{P}{2}[\lambda_f + (L_d - L_q)I_d]I_q;$$

Replacing $I_q$ with the voltage constraint, the torque equation is

$$T_e = \frac{3}{2}\frac{P}{2}[\lambda_f + (L_d - L_q)I_d]\frac{\sqrt{\left(\dfrac{V_s}{\omega_r}\right)^2 - (\lambda_f + L_dI_d)^2}}{L_q}$$

The only variable in the equation is $I_d$, and hence, we can take the derivative of the torque with respect to $I_d$ to derive the condition for maximum by equating the equation to zero, i.e., $\dfrac{\partial T_e}{\partial I_d} = 0$. The resulting MTPV condition is

$$(L_d - L_q)\cdot(L_d \cdot L_q)^2 - [\lambda_f + (L_d - L_q)I_d]\cdot(\lambda_f \cdot L_d + L_d^2 \cdot I_d) = 0 \tag{8.40}$$

For each value of reference torque $T_e^*$, unique values of $I_q^*$ and $I_d^*$ are obtained according to one of the optimization criteria at a given speed provided the current limit and flux limit are not exceeded. The MTPA and MTPV curves using Equations 8.39 and 8.40 are shown in Figure 8.13.

### 8.4.4.5  Characteristic Current, Finite Drive System and Infinite Drive System

In a finite drive system, the voltage constraint limits the maximum operating speed even if there is no mechanical limit on the speed. In this case, the center of the ellipse is outside the circle, i.e., $[\lambda_f > L_d, I_{s,max}]$ [6]. In an infinite drive system, the maximum speed is limited by mechanical constraints such as centrifugal forces or the stress on the bearing. The maximum speed is not limited by current or voltage constraints and the center of the ellipse is inside the circle, i.e., $[\lambda_f < L_d, I_{s,max}]$.

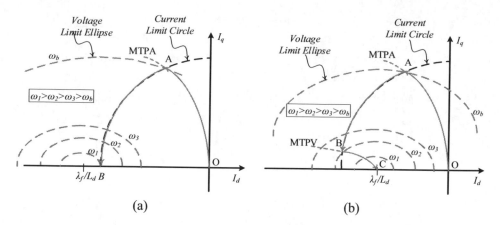

**FIGURE 8.14** (a) Finite drive system and (b) infinite drive system.

The $I_q^*$ and $I_d^*$ command trajectory to be followed for given torque commands as a function of increasing operating speed is shown in Figure 8.14a and b for a finite drive system and an infinite drive system, respectively.

The magnetic loading, machine inductance and characteristic current have an effect on the power factor and the torque-speed operating speed region. The IPMSM design defines whether a machine is a finite drive system or an infinite drive system based on the relationship between the operating speeds and the characteristic current given by

$$I_c = \frac{\lambda_f}{L_d}$$

When the characteristic current is smaller which could result from a weak magnetic loading or larger $d$-axis inductance, a small advance angle would result in $I_d$ current reaching the current constraint limit. Further extension of the constant power speed range would require the $q$-axis current magnitude to reduce, which means that the CPSR is essentially very limited. The situation is adversely affected by higher inductance values which also results in poor power factor. In low power factor machines, armature inductive voltage composes the majority of the terminal phase voltage. The infinite drive system field weakening operation is illustrated in Figure 8.14b, where point A represents the intersection of current limit with the base speed $\omega_b$, point B represents the maximum weakening of PM's field at rated current, and B to C represents the extended speed operating region with reduced current magnitude.

### Example 8.2

The vehicle parameters for the Tesla Model 3 are: vehicle mass = 1611 kg, wheel radius = 0.447 m, frontal area = 2.16 m² and wheelbase = 2.7 m. The electric motor parameters are: $L_d = 0.42$ mH, $L_q = 0.52$ mH, $R_{ph} = 0.028\,\Omega$, Motor torque constant $K_e = 0.24$ (phase, peak) and $\lambda_f = 0.06\,\frac{Vs}{rad}$ (phase, peak). The battery is rated at 75 kWh with a nominal DC bus voltage of 375 V.

Develop the simulation model with the controller operating under MTPA conditions using the highway drive cycle and plot motor $i_d$ and $i_q$ currents and motor torque.

### Solution

Let us first derive the $i_d$ and $i_q$ currents as a function of torque from the stator current and PMSM torque equations under MTPA conditions. The stator current rms magnitude $i_s$ is related to the motor $i_d$ and $i_q$ components as

$$\sqrt{2}i_s = \sqrt{i_d^2 + i_q^2}$$

The PM motor torque is given by

$$T_e = \frac{3}{2}\frac{P}{2}[\lambda_f + (L_d - L_q)i_d]i_q$$

Following a similar procedure as in Section 8.4.4.3, the MPTA condition relating $i_q$ and torque $T_e$ can be obtained. By substituting $i_d$ in terms of $i_q$ and the commanded torque in the stator current equation, and setting $\frac{\partial T_e}{\partial i_q} = 0$, we get a 4th-order transcendental equation which represents the MTPA condition given by

$$i_q^4 + \frac{4T_e\lambda_f i_q}{3P(L_d - L_q)^2} - \left(\frac{4T_e}{3P(L_d - L_q)}\right)^2 = 0$$

For a given torque, four solutions are obtained solving for $i_q$ where only one is valid. In the simulation, the smallest of the solutions were considered. Once $i_q$ is obtained, $i_d$ can be calculated from

$$i_d = \frac{4T_e}{3P(L_d - L_q)i_q} - \frac{\lambda_f}{L_d - L_q}$$

For obtaining the $i_d$ and $i_q$ currents as a function of time for the highway drive cycle, the vehicle simulation model, shown in Figure 3.25, is run with the Tesla Model 3 motor parameters where the machine is loaded with the vehicle road load model. The vehicle controller generates the torque command which is used to calculate the reference $i_d$ and $i_q$ currents under the MTPA condition without considering bus voltage limitation. The results are plotted in Figure 8.15.

## 8.5 CURRENT CONTROL METHODS

The current control loops constitute the inner control loop to generate PWM signals for the inverter gates using current feedback information from sensors. The measured three-phase currents are compared with the three reference current commands generated by the outer-loop controller. The error between the measurements and the reference signals are utilized in a PWM scheme to generate the gate switching signals. A number of current-controlled PWM methods have been developed ranging from fairly simple to rather complex ones. Some of these methods are hysteresis current controller, PI-current controller, predictive current controller, etc. Two of the simpler methods, the hysteresis current controller and the PI-current controller are described in the following.

### 8.5.1 Hysteresis Current Controller

In the hysteresis current controller, the error between the measured current and the reference current is compared with a hysteresis band as shown in Figure 8.16. If the current error is within the band, then PWM output remains unchanged. If the current error exceeds the band, then the PWM output is reversed forcing a sign change of the *di/dt* slope. Mathematically stated, the PWM output is obtained from

$$PWM = \begin{cases} 0 & \text{if } \Delta i < -h/2 \\ 1 & \text{if } \Delta i > h/2 \end{cases}.$$

(a)

(b)

**FIGURE 8.15** IPM motor current and torque for operating under MTPA conditions for the highway drive cycle: (a) $i_d$ and $i_q$ currents and (b) torque $T_e$.

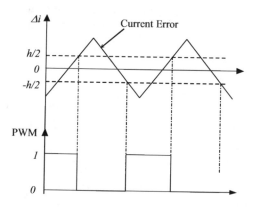

**FIGURE 8.16** Hysteresis current control and PWM output.

A '0' PWM output signal cuts off the supply voltage in the controlled phase forcing current to decay, while an '1' PWM output applies voltage to the phase resulting in an increase of current. The voltage will then force the current to vary in such a way that it remains within the hysteresis band.

The advantage of such a controller is that the error remains within a certain band, which is known by the user. In the hysteresis controller, the switching frequency is unknown, which makes it difficult to design the filters. The switching frequency should be carefully monitored so that the inverter limits are not exceeded. In practical implementations, a frequency limit is used so as not to exceed the inverter maximum switching frequency. The hysteresis band is designed according to the limits of the device switching frequency. If the hysteresis band $h$ is chosen to be very narrow, then the switching frequency will be very high, and not be compatible with the maximum switching frequency of the power devices. On the other hand, if the band is too wide, then the current error will be too large.

The hysteresis current controller can be used in a three-phase PWM inverter with each phase having its own PWM controller. If the actual current is higher than the reference current by the amount of half of the hysteresis band, the lower leg switch of the bridge inverter is turned on to reduce the phase current. The difficulty in three-phase hysteresis control is that there may be conflicting requirements of switch conditions for the phases based on the output of the hysteresis controller. The difficulty arises from the interaction of the phases of the three-phase system and the independent hysteresis controllers for each phase. The consequence of this difficulty is that the current does not remain within the hysteresis band. For example, a current-increase command in Phase-a needs a return path through Phase-b or Phase-c lower legs. If Phase-b and Phase-c happen to have upper leg switches on during this instant, the current in Phase-a will not increase to follow the command, but will freewheel. In this case, it is possible that the current error of Phase-a will exceed the hysteresis current band. Using the $dq$ transformation theory, it is possible to first transform the three-phase currents into two-phase $dq$ currents and then impose the hysteresis control in the $dq$ reference frame.

### 8.5.2 PI CURRENT REGULATOR

The most commonly used current regulator for electric motor vector controls implementation is the PI controllers that can be designed to generate $v_{ds}$ and $v_{qs}$ and add the feedforward compensating terms to derive $v_d$ and $v_q$ commands. The current controller is implemented in the $dq$ reference frame such that it is easier to tune the PI parameters using the DC variables instead of tuning it for the sinusoidally varying current variables in the $abc$ reference frame. The inverter is controlled using a space vector pulse width modulation (SVPWM) in both generating and motoring modes. This arrangement requires that the $dq$ current command be converted into a $dq$ voltage command. The machine $abc$ phase currents are fed back into the controller, where the variables are transformed into the $dq$ reference frame using Park's transformation. The phase current feedback is transformed to the $dq$ variables and then $dq$ voltage commands are generated which are implemented using a voltage source PWM inverter. The compensation terms are the speed-dependent back-emf terms which can be assumed to be constant for the design of the PI compensator.

The PI current regulator design is based on a linearized plant transfer function. To derive the relationship between the current command and the voltage command $v_q^*$, the $q$-axis machine model is linearized to give

$$v_q' = v_q^* - \omega_r \left( L_d i_d + \lambda_f \right) \approx R_s i_q + L_q \frac{di_q}{dt} \tag{8.41}$$

Therefore, the $q$-axis transfer function for the linearized machine model is

$$\frac{i_q}{v_q'} = \frac{1}{R_s + sL_q} = \frac{(1/L_q)}{s + (R_s/L_q)}$$

The transfer function for the $d$-axis phase circuit is similar to the $q$-axis equation. The $d$-axis linearized model can be derived as

$$v_d' = v_d^* + \omega_r \left( L_q i_q \right) - \frac{d\lambda_f}{dt} \approx R_s i_d + L_d \frac{di_d}{dt} \tag{8.42}$$

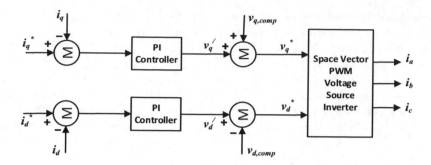

**FIGURE 8.17** Control block diagram for generating the motor phase currents.

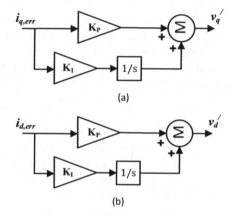

**FIGURE 8.18** PI compensators: (a) $q$-axis and (b) $d$-axis.

The PM flux is constant, and hence, the derivative of $\lambda_f$ is zero in Equation 8.42. Therefore, the $d$-axis transfer function for the linearized machine model is

$$\frac{i_d}{v_d'} = \frac{1}{r + sL_d} = \frac{(1/L_d)}{s + (r/L_d)}$$

With the linearized transfer function, the PI compensator parameters $k_p$ and $k_i$ can be tuned using the standard compensator design techniques using bode plots and specified gain and phase margins. The controller eliminates the error in the current signal and generates the $dq$ voltage commands. The control block diagram for generating the $v_q^*$ and $v_d^*$ space vector commands is shown in Figure 8.17. The $v_{q,\,comp}$ and $v_{d,\,comp}$ feedforward compensating terms are obtained from Equation 8.41 and Equation 8.42, respectively. The VSI converter applies the PWM voltages to the motor windings which establishes the $i_a$, $i_b$ and $i_c$ motor phase currents. The PI compensator blocks for the $d$- and $q$-axes are shown in Figure 8.18.

## 8.6  SRM CONTROLS

Appropriate positioning of the phase excitation pulses relative to the rotor position is the key in obtaining effective performance out of an SR motor drive system [7]. The turn-on time, the total conduction period and the magnitude of the phase current determine torque, efficiency and other performance parameters. The type of control to be employed depends on the operating speed of the SRM.

## 8.6.1   Control Parameters

The control parameters for an SRM drive are the turn-on angle $(\theta_{on})$, the turn-off angle $(\theta_{off})$ and the phase current. The conduction angle is defined as $\theta_{dwell} = \theta_{off} - \theta_{on}$. The complexity of determination of the control parameters depends on the chosen control method for a particular application. The current command can be generated for one or more phases depending on the controller. In voltage-controlled drives, the current is indirectly regulated by controlling the phase voltage.

At low speeds, the current rises almost instantaneously after turn-on due to the negligible back-emf, and the current must be limited by either controlling the average voltage or regulating the current level. The type of control used has a marked effect on the performance of the drive. As the speed increases, the back-emf increases and opposes the applied bus voltage. Phase advancing is necessary to establish the phase current at the onset of rotor and stator pole overlap region. The voltage PWM or chopping control is used to force maximum current into the motor in order to maintain the desired torque level. Also, the phase excitation is turned off early enough so that the phase current decays completely to zero before the negative torque-producing region is reached.

At higher speeds, the SRM enters the single-pulse mode of operation, where the motor is controlled by advancing the turn-on angle and adjusting the conduction angle. At very high speeds, the back-emf will exceed the applied bus voltage once the current magnitude is high and the rotor position is appropriate, which causes the current to decrease after reaching a peak even though a positive bus voltage is applied during the positive $dL\!/\!d\theta$ region. The control algorithm outputs $\theta_{dwell}$ and $\theta_{on}$ according to speed. At the end of $\theta_{dwell}$, the phase switches are turned off so that negative voltage is applied across the phase to commutate the phase as quickly as possible. The back-emf reverses polarity beyond the aligned position and may cause the current to increase in this region if the current does not decay to insignificant levels. Therefore, the phase commutation must precede the aligned position by several degrees so that the current decays before the negative $dL\!/\!d\theta$ region is reached.

In the high speed range of operation, when the back-emf exceeds the DC bus voltage, the conduction window becomes too limited for current or voltage control and all the chopping or PWM has to be disabled. In this range, $\theta_{dwell}$ and $\theta_{adv}$ are the only control parameters and control is accomplished based on the assumption that approximately $\theta_{dwell}$ regulates torque and $\theta_{adv}$ determines efficiency.

### 8.6.1.1   Advance Angle Calculation

Ideally, the turn-on angle is advanced such that the reference current level $i^*$ is reached just at the onset of pole overlap. In the unaligned position, phase inductance is almost constant, and hence, during turn-on back-emf can be neglected [8]. Also, assuming that the resistive drop is small, the SRM phase voltage equation can be written as

$$V_{ph} = L(\theta)\frac{\Delta i}{\Delta \theta}\omega \qquad\qquad (8.43)$$

Now, $\Delta i = i^*$ and $\Delta \theta = \theta_{overlap} - \theta_{on} = \theta_{adv}$, where $\theta_{overlap}$ is the position where pole overlap begins, $\theta_{on}$ is the turn-on angle and $\theta_{adv}$ is the required phase turn-on advance angle. Therefore, we have

$$\theta_{adv} = L_u\omega\frac{i^*}{V_{dc}}. \qquad\qquad (8.44)$$

The above simple advance angle $\theta_{adv}$ calculation approach is sufficient for most applications, although it does not account for the errors due to neglecting the back-emf and the resistive drop in the calculation.

**FIGURE 8.19** Current-controlled drive.

### 8.6.1.2 Current-Controlled Drive

In torque-controlled drives, such as in high-performance servo applications, the torque command is executed by regulating the current in the inner loop as shown in Figure 8.19. The reference current $i^*$ for a given operating point is determined from the load characteristics, the motor speed and the control strategy. A wide-bandwidth current transducer provides the current feedback information to the controller from each of the motor phases. This mode of control allows rapid resetting of the current level and is used where fast motor response is desired. For loads whose torque increases monotonically with speed such as in fans or blowers, speed feedback can be introduced in the outer loop for accurate speed control.

The simpler control strategy is to generate one current command to be used by all the phases in succession. The electronic commutator (see Figure 8.19) selects the appropriate phase for current regulation based on $\theta_{on}$, $\theta_{off}$ and the instantaneous rotor position. The current controller generates the gating signal for the phases based on the information coming from the electronic commutator. The current in the commutated phase is quickly brought down to zero applying negative $V_{dc}$, while the incoming phase assumes the responsibility of torque production based on the commanded current. The phase transition in these drives is not very smooth, which tends to increase the torque ripple of the drive.

## PROBLEMS

### 8.1

An induction motor has the following parameters:

5 hp, 200 V, three-phase, 60 Hz, star connected.

| | | |
|---|---|---|
| $R_s = 0.28\ \Omega$, | $L_s = 0.055$ H | Turns ratio = 3 |
| $R_r = 0.18\ \Omega$, | $L_r = 0.056$ H | $L_m = 0.054$ H |

The motor is supplied with its rated voltages. Find the $d$- and $q$-axis steady-state voltages and currents in (a) synchronous reference frame and (b) rotor reference frame when the rotor is locked (i.e., $\omega_r = 0$).

### 8.2

The parameters of a 440 V, 10 hp, 4-pole, 60 Hz induction machine with an indirect field-oriented control are given as

| | | | | |
|---|---|---|---|---|
| $R_s = 0.768\ \Omega$ | $X_{ls} = 2.56\ \Omega$ | $X_m = 51.2\ \Omega$ | $R_r = 0.768\ \Omega$ | $X_{lr} = 2.56\ \Omega$ |

Sketch the reference frame phasor diagrams for this machine for the following conditions:

a. $\omega_r = \omega_{rated}$
   I.  $T_e = 40$ N-m
  II.  $T_e = 0$
b. $\omega_r = 0$
   I.  $T_e = 40$ N-m
  II.  $T_e = 0$

The phasor diagrams should include the complex vector variables $\vec{\lambda}_r, \vec{I}_r, \vec{\lambda}_s, \vec{I}_s$ and $\vec{V}_s$
(e.g., $\vec{\lambda}_r = \lambda_{qr} - j\lambda_{dr}$).

## 8.3

The parameters of a 10 hp, 60 Hz, three-phase, wye-connected, 6-pole, squirrel-cage induction motor are given as follows:

Rated voltage = 220 V
Rated speed = 1,164 rpm

| | | | |
|---|---|---|---|
| $R_s = 0.294\ \Omega$/ph | $X_{ls} = 0.524\ \Omega$/ph | $R_r' = 0.156\ \Omega$/ph | $X_{lr}' = 0.279\ \Omega$/ph |
| $X_m = 15.457\ \Omega$/ph | $J = 0.4$ kg-m² | | |

a. The motor operates in steady state under rated operating conditions. Calculate the stator and rotor currents in the stator reference frame and then calculate the developed torque.
b. The motor operates under the same condition as in part (a). Utilizing results obtained in (a) calculate the airgap flux and rotor flux vectors.

## 8.4

An induction motor is used as the traction motor in a small electric vehicle sedan similar to the size of Nissan Leaf. The parameters of a 30 kW, 295 Hz, three-phase, wye-connected, 4-pole, squirrel-cage induction motor are given as: Rated phase voltage = 280 V; rated speed = 8,846 rpm; $R_s = 87.6$ m$\Omega$/ph; $L_{ls} = 0.1506$ mH/ph; $R_r' = 36.14$ m$\Omega$/ph; $L_{lr}' = 0.1149$ mH/ph; $L_m = 2.367$ mH/ph; and $J = 0.3$ kg-m².

The motor is connected to the wheel axle through a 15:1 ratio gear. The vehicle weighs 1,500 kg, and has a wheel radius of 0.3 m. The vehicle driver follows a speed profile as given below:

- 0–1 s, standstill
- 1–5 s, linear acceleration from 0 to 36 mph
- 5–6 s, constant speed at 36 mph
- 6–9 s, linear deceleration from 36 to 10 mph
- 9–10 s, constant speed at 10 mph

The loads for the vehicle include

- Aerodynamic drag force Newton is $F_{AD} = \dfrac{1}{2}\rho C_D A_F v^2$, in which $\rho = 1.225\,\text{kg/m}^3$ is the density of air, $C_D = 0.35$ is drag coefficient, and $A_F = 2.3\,\text{m}^2$ is vehicle frontal area, $v$ is vehicle speed in m/s.
- Rolling resistance force in Newton is $F_R = C_{rr} mg$, in which $C_{rr} = 0.03$ is rolling resistance coefficient, $m$ is the mass of vehicle, and $g$ is 9.8 N/kg.
- Gravitational force on a road with a grade is $F_g = mg\sin(\arctan(\alpha))$, in which $\alpha = 10\%$ is grade of the road.

Develop a simulation model to

a. Develop the vehicle road load model based on the vehicle speed
b. Construct a subsystem that simulates vehicle mechanical dynamics
c. Design an outer speed control loop to follow the given speed command
d. Simulate the vehicle and motor using the indirect rotor flux orientation system. Give the plots of command speed, vehicle actual speed, induction motor torque and stator currents $i_{ds}$ and $i_{qs}$ (in the rotor flux reference frame), all with respect to time.

## REFERENCES

1. D.W. Novotny and T.A. Lipo, *Vector Control and Dynamics of AC Drives*, Oxford University Press, Oxford, 1996.
2. B.K. Bose, *Modern Power Electronics and AC Drives*, Prentice Hall, Upper Saddle River, NJ, 2001.
3. W.V. Lyon, *Transient Analysis of Alternating Current Machinery*, John Wiley & Sons, Inc., Hoboken, NJ, 1954.
4. P.C. Krause and O. Wasynchuk, *Analysis of Electric Machinery*, McGraw Hill, New York, NY, 1986.
5. N. Mohan, *Electric Drives – An Integrated Approach*, MNPERE, Minneapolis, MN, 2001.
6. S.-K. Sul, *Control of Electric Machine Drive Systems*, John Wiley and IEEE Press, Hoboken, NJ, 2011.
7. T.J.E. Miller, *Switched Reluctance Motors and their Control*, Magna Physics Publishing, Hillsboro, OH and Oxford University Press, Oxford, 1993.
8. T.L. Skvarenina (Editor), *Power Electronics Handbook: Chapter 13 Switched Reluctance Machines*, CRC Press, Boca Raton, FL, 2001.

# 9 Power Electronic Converters

Power electronic circuits convert electrical energy from one voltage level and frequency to another for an electrical load. The basis of the power electronics circuits are the power semiconductor devices. Power devices act as an electronic switch in a power circuit to change circuit configuration. Power devices are available commercially since the 1970s and have seen tremendous advancements over the past 40 years. These devices are now available with ratings up to thousands of volts and thousands of amps in a single package. Two or six switch configurations, suitable for certain power converter topologies, are available in a single package.

The power devices are connected to form a circuit or topology that can assume two or more configurations depending on the device switching states. Commands generated in a controller circuit bring about the changes in the switching states. These power electronic circuit topologies are known as power converter circuits. Additional energy storage circuit elements of inductors and capacitors are often used in the power converter circuits. Resistors are not used in power converters to avoid losses, but parasitic resistances of power devices, storage elements, wires and connectors invariably exist. The converters process power based on signals from a control unit. Four basic power converter circuits are as follows:

- *DC/DC converter*: Converts DC voltages from one level to another.
- *DC/AC inverter*: Converts DC voltage to AC voltages. The AC voltages can be square wave or sinusoidal voltages comprised of pulse-width modulated (PWM) signals.
- *AC/DC converter or rectifier*: Rectifies AC voltages to DC voltages.
- *AC/AC converter*: Converts AC voltages at one level and frequency directly into another voltage level and frequency. These are known as cycloconverters.

In this book, the power converter circuits used in the electric and hybrid vehicle powertrain and high-voltage segments will be discussed. The DC/DC converters are used both in the electric power transmission path as well as for power supply to the 12 V electronics. There are many different topologies available for DC/DC power conversion. The DC/AC inverters are used for the electric drive for AC electric machines. The converter topologies and their implementation for electric and hybrid vehicles will be discussed in detail in this chapter.

## 9.1 POWER ELECTRONIC SWITCHES

The power electronic devices or switches are either of two terminals or three terminals; the third terminal, when it exists, is for the small signal control input. Device operation switches from 'on' to 'off' state or vice versa based on either signal changes to its control terminal or changes in circuit conditions. Two terminal devices change state when circuit conditions dictate, whereas three terminal devices change state with changes in its control input.

Let us consider an ideal controlled switch shown in Figure 9.1a prior to discussing the practical power devices. The switch has three terminals for power connections and a control input. Switch operation is defined in terms of quadrants established by the voltage and current axes. The quadrants are labeled in Figure 9.1b in the counter-clockwise direction of the *i-v* plane of switch conduction. The ideal switch shown is a four-quadrant switch, which means that it can handle bi-directional current as well as bi-directional voltage. In the ideal switch, there is no voltage drop across the device when it conducts. Ideally, the operating point will be along the axes with the ideal switches either

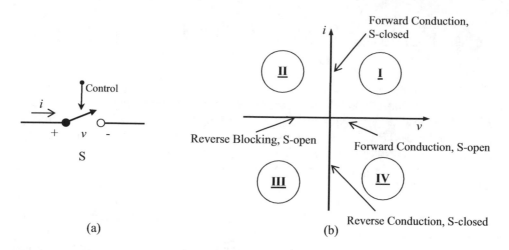

**FIGURE 9.1**  Ideal switch and its conduction characteristics. (a) Switch symbol; (b) switch characteristics in four quadrants.

carrying current with zero voltage drop across it or blocking a voltage with zero current flowing through it. The ideal switch also turns on and off instantaneously without any delay; consequently, ideal switch has no power loss. The practical semiconductor switch differs considerably from the ideal switch. Practical switches have conduction voltage drops and require finite time to turn-on and turn-off; furthermore, practical devices do not have four-quadrant capability unless it is combined with one other device.

The practical devices used in power converters have their own specific characteristics [1]. The particular application and its power requirements determine the type of device to be used in a converter topology. The bipolar junction transistors (BJTs) have higher power ratings and excellent conduction characteristics, but the base drive circuit is very complicated, since these are current-driven devices. On the other hand, the metal oxide semiconductor field effect transistors (MOSFETs) are voltage-driven devices, and hence, the gate drive characteristics are much simpler. The switching frequency of a MOSFET is much higher compared to BJT, but the maximum available device power ratings would be much smaller for the former. The insulated gate bipolar transistor (IGBT) device, invented in the early 1980s, combines the attractive features of both the MOSFET and the BJT. The IGBT is the device of choice today in most medium to high-power applications due to their availability in high power ratings, although SiC and GaN FETs are making their entries with higher frequency, lower loss, and higher temperature operation features. In early years of EV development, when DC motors were the primary machine choice, the high-power converters were typically made of silicon controller rectifiers (SCRs), which are available in very high power ratings. However, unlike the other devices SCRs cannot be turned off through a gate signal and a commutation circuit is required to turn them off. The gate turn-off thyristor (GTO) device is similar to SCR except that it can be turned off through a gate signal, although the current required in the gate signal to turn them off is typically four to five times the current required to turn them on. Attempts to combine the gating characteristics of a MOSFET and the conduction characteristics of an SCR resulted in the device called MOS-controlled thyristor (MCT) in the late 1980s. However, the failure of the MCTs under certain conditions did not make these devices popular. In addition to the switches mentioned above, there is an additional two-terminal device called diode, which is universally used in all converters. The diodes are used in conjuction with other controlled devices in the power converter to provide current paths for inductive circuits or for blocking reverse voltages. The operating characteristics of the devices that have a significance in electric and hybrid vehicle applications are discussed in the following.

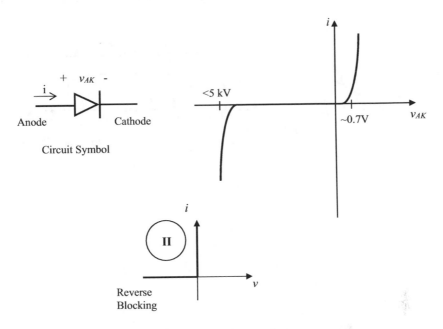

**FIGURE 9.2** Diode symbol, characteristics and operating quadrant.

### 9.1.1 DIODE

The diode is a two-terminal, uncontrollable switch, which is turned on and off by the circuit. A positive voltage across the anode and the cathode of the diode turns the device on allowing current conduction up to its rated value. There will be a small forward voltage drop during diode conduction as shown in Figure 9.2. The diode conducts current in one direction only and blocks voltage in the negative direction, which makes it a quadrant II switch. The diode can block a reverse voltage up to its breakdown level.

### 9.1.2 BJT

The BJT is a three-terminal controlled switch. BJTs are the type of transistors that use both negative charge carriers, i.e., electrons, and positive charge carriers, i.e., holes, and hence, they are bipolar devices as the name implies. The circuit symbol and the $i$-$v$ characteristics of a BJT are shown in Figure 9.3. When sufficient positive base current $i_B$ flows through the base of an npn-BJT, the transistor action allows large positive collector current $i_C$ to flow through the junctions of the device with a small positive collector to emitter voltage $v_{CE}$ (known as saturation voltage) drop. The amplitude of the base current determines the amplification in the collector current. The power BJT is a controllable switch that can be turned on or off with the help of the base current. The power BJTs are always operated as a switch either at saturation with high enough base current or at cut-off with zero base current. The device allows forward current or blocking voltage, and hence, is a quadrant I switch. Steady-state operation in quadrants II and IV is not possible.

### 9.1.3 MOSFET

The MOSFET is a controlled switch similar to the BJT. However, the MOSFETs are unipolar devices where the semiconductor channel conduction is due to either the negative charge carriers, i.e., electrons, or positive charge carriers, i.e., holes. The three terminals of the MOSFET are gate, drain and

(a)

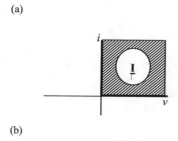

(b)

**FIGURE 9.3** An npn power BJT: (a) device symbol and $i$-$v$ characteristics and (b) operating quadrant.

source, which are analogous to the base, collector and emitter, respectively, of the BJT. Similar to the BJT, the MOSFET is a quadrant one switch allowing forward flow of current and blocking forward voltage between drain and source. Unlike the BJT, MOSFET is a voltage-driven device in that they do not need any biasing current like a bipolar transistor and is controlled through applying a voltage between gate and source. The voltage control also enables much faster switching capabilities for the MOSFET. The current-voltage characteristics of a MOSFET are illustrated in Figure 9.4a. This allows power MOSFET operation at much higher frequencies compared to the BJT, although the available maximum device voltage and current ratings are much smaller than the BJT.

### 9.1.4   JFET

A junction gate field-effect transistor (JFET) is a three-terminal device similar to a MOSFET that can be used as an electronically controlled switch. It is also a unipolar device like a MOSFET and is voltage controlled. Unlike a MOSFET, a JFET is usually a normally ON device where electric charge flows through a semiconducting channel between source and drain terminals when there is no voltage between its gate and source terminals. A reverse bias voltage needs to be applied between the gate and source terminals to 'pinch' the conducting channel and impede the electric current and switch off the device.

### 9.1.5   IGBT

The excellent conduction characteristics of the power BJT have been combined with the excellent gate characteristics of the power MOSFET in the IGBT. The IGBT has high input impedance like that of a MOSFET, and low conduction losses like that of a BJT. There is no second breakdown problem in the IGBT. By chip design and structure, the equivalent drain-to-source resistance $R_{DS}$ is controlled to behave like that of a BJT. The conduction characteristics of an IGBT are shown in Figure 9.4b.

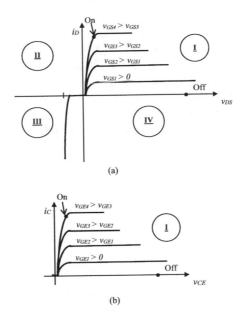

**FIGURE 9.4**   Current-voltage characteristics of (a) MOSFET and (b) IGBT.

## 9.1.6   BI-DIRECTIONAL SWITCH

Electric and hybrid vehicles can recapture energy during vehicle braking or when it slows down through regenerative mode of operation of the electric machine, which can be used to recharge the batteries. For the regenerative mode of operation, power converters need to allow bi-directional power flow, which requires the power devices or switches of the DC/DC or DC/AC converter topologies to be bi-directional. Figure 9.5 gives an example of how bi-directional switches can be made by combining a BJT and a diode.

## 9.1.7   ELECTRICAL PROPERTIES

The electrical properties of a power semiconductor device influence the switching and conduction characteristics which are vital for evaluating the losses and other performance attributes such as thermal limits, electromagnetic interference, and short-circuit capabilities. The maximum values of current, voltage, temperature, and power dissipation are related to the electrical properties and are

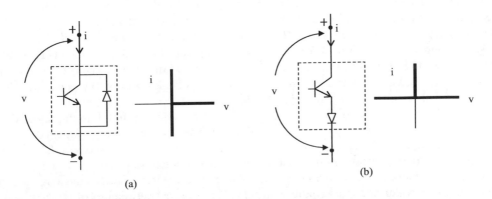

**FIGURE 9.5**   (a) Bi-directional current switch and (b) bi-directional voltage switch.

recommended by the manufacturers for their product types. Few electrical properties and ratings critical to the choice of a device for an application are described in the following.

*Collector Current ($I_C$):* The collector current $I_C$ indicates the current carrying capacity of a bipolar device such as the IGBT. The collector current is also categorized into continuous and peak ratings. The continuous current is referred to as the continuous current carrying capacity of the device, while the peak collector current $I_{CP}$ indicates the maximum pulse current that the device can handle which is higher than the rated continuous current. The manufacturer's datasheet typically would give the ratings at 25°C, which has to be derated for higher temperature operation based on the junction temperature.

*Drain Current ($I_D$):* The drain current $I_D$ indicates the current carrying capacity of a MOSFET type device. The drain current is categorized into continuous and peak ratings. The continuous current is referred to as the continuous current carrying capacity of the device, while the peak drain current or pulsed drain current $I_{D,pulse}$ indicates the maximum pulse current that the device can handle which is higher than the rated continuous current. The manufacturer's datasheet typically would give the ratings at 25°C, which has to be derated for higher temperature operation based on the junction temperature.

*Collector-to-Emitter Voltage ($V_{CE}$):* The collector to emmitter votlage $V_{CE}$ is the maximum voltage the collector-to-emitter junction can support in BJTs and IGBTs at 25°C with gate and emitter terminals shorted together.

*Forward Biased Safe Operating Area (FBSOA):* This shows the collector current $I_C$ as a function of collector-emitter voltage $V_{CE}$ at different operating pulses.

*Gate-to-Emiter Voltage ($V_{GE}$):* Gate-to-emitter voltage $V_{GE}$ stands for the allowable range between the gate and emitter terminals. Exceeding $V_{GE}$ may result in permanent device degradation due to oxide breakdown and dielectric rupture.

*Maximum Power Dissipation:* The maximum power dissipation of a device is related to a given case temperature ($T_C$), the maximum junction temperature ($T_J$) and the thermal resistance $\left( R_{th(J-C)} \right)$. The maximum power dissipation of the device is given by

$$P_{total} = \frac{T_{Jmax} - T_C}{R_{th(J-C)}}$$

The allowable power dissipation of the device increases with increasing junction temperature.

The thermal resistance $R_{th}$ relates to the heat conduction properties of the device given by temperature per unit of power (°C/W).

*Collector-to-Emitter Saturaiton Voltage ($V_{CE(sat)}$):* $V_{CE(sat)}$ is the on-state collector-to-emitter voltage drop and relates to the BJT or IGBT power dissipation during the conduction time. The voltage is a function of collector current ($I_C$), gate-emitter voltage ($V_{GE}$) and junction temperature, and it is specified at the rated $I_C$. The range of $V_{CE}$ is within the saturation region where $V_{CE(sat)}$ increases with increasing $I_C$, but reduces with increasing $V_{GE}$ which rises the channel conductivity.

*Short-Circuit Withstand Time ($t_{sc}$):* When load current overload occurs, collector current rises rapidly allowing the power device to limit the current amplitude to a safe level for a period of time that allows the control circuit to detect the fault condition and turn the device off. This is a particularly useful feature in motor drive applications for safe shutdown using the power device and manage a load or equipmet short-circuit condition.

*Turn-On Time:* The turn-on time ($t_{on}$) of a device is the total time required for the device collector or drain current to reach the 100% level. The time is the sum of the turn-on delay time ($t_{d,on}$) and the current rise time ($t_{rise}$). During the current rise time, the voltage across the device falls from the blocking voltage to the collector-emitter saturation voltage or the drain-source conduction voltage. $t_{d,on}$ is measured between the 10% value of the base-emitter or gate-source voltage and the 90% value of drain-source or collector-emitter voltage. $t_{rise}$ is measured between the 90% value and the 10% value of the collector-emitter or drain-source voltage.

*Turn-off time*: The turn-off time ($t_{off}$) of a device is the total time required for the device collector or drain current to reach zero and the device completely turns off. The time is the sum of the turn-off delay time ($t_{d,off}$), and the current fall time ($t_{fall}$). $t_{d,off}$ is measured between the 90% value of the base-emitter or gate-source voltage and the 10% value of collector-emitter or drain-source voltage. $t_{fall}$ is measured between the 10% value and the 90% value of collector-emitter or drain-source voltage.

*Junction Temperature*: This is the temperature at the pn-junction of a power device. Since the temperature cannot be measured directly, but can only be determined by indirect means, the term 'virtual' is often used with junction temperature. The junction temperature during switching operation of semiconductors is the most relevant parameter for the thermal system design and is also the one to be used for estimating lifetime. The point where the product of the voltage and current, i.e., the power dissipation loss is the maximum, will be the hottest point which will be at the pn junction.

*Turn-on Energy ($E_{on}$)*: The energy generated inside a device during the turn-on and turn-off of a power device is the contributor to the switching loss and subsequently to efficiency and thermal management of the system. The turn-on energy is measured during the turn-on of a single collector or drain current pulse and is given by

$$E_{on} = \int_0^{t_{Eon}} v_{CE}(t) \cdot i_C(t) dt \text{ (for BJT and IGBT) or}$$

$$E_{on} = \int_0^{t_{Eon}} v_{DS}(t) \cdot i_D(t) dt \text{ (for MOSFET)}$$

where $t_{Eon}$ is the time span that starts at the moment when the collector or drain current has risen to 10% of its nominal value and ends when the collector-emitter or drain-source voltage has dropped to 2% of its nominal value.

*Turn-off Energy ($E_{off}$)*: The turn-on energy is measured during the turn-off of a single collector or drain current pulse and is given by

$$E_{off} = \int_0^{t_{Eoff}} v_{CE}(t) \cdot i_C(t) dt \text{ (for BJT and IGBT) or}$$

$$E_{off} = \int_0^{t_{Eoff}} v_{DS}(t) \cdot i_D(t) dt \text{ (for MOSFET)}$$

where $t_{Eoff}$ is the time span that starts at the moment when the collector-emitter or drain-source voltage has risen to 10% of its nominal value and ends when the collector or drain current has fallen to 2% of its nominal value.

*Reverse Recovery Time ($t_{rr}$) and Energy ($E_{rec}$)*: The charge stored in a diode during its on-state needs to be completely removed immediately following the diode conduction period before the diodes blocking capability is resumed. This charge is known as the reverse recovery charge. The energy generated inside the diode during the turn-off is the reverse recovery energy. The higher the switching rate of the current ($di/dt$), the higher the reverse recovery charge. The time needed for the removal of the reverse recovery charge is the reverse recovery time ($t_{rr}$). The reverse recovery energy is given by

$$E_{rec} = \int_0^{t_{rr}} v_R(t) \cdot i_F(t) dt$$

where $t_{rr}$ is the time span that starts at the moment when the diode voltage $v_R$ has risen to 10% of its nominal value and ends when the reverse diode current $i_{RM}$ has fallen to 2% of its nominal value.

*Gate-Source Voltage $V_{GS}$*: Gate-source voltage of a MOSFET affects the on-state resistance and is deterministic of the device's output characteristics. Device manufacturers will specify the allowable range of the gate-source voltage in the datasheet.

*Drain-Source on-State Resistance $R_{DS,on}$*: The drain-source on-state resistance $R_{DS,on}$ is a key parameter of a MOSFET. The $R_{DS,on}$ changes significantly with the applied gate-source voltage. A lower value of $V_{GS}$ can be applied for applications where the conduction loss due to higher $R_{DS,on}$ is less critical such as in synchronous rectification. The $R_{DS,on}$ affects the conduction loss of a MOSFET and is given by

$$R_{DS,on}(I_D) = \frac{V_{DS}}{I_D}$$

Typical and maximum values of $R_{DS,on}$ are provided in the datasheet by the manufacturer at room temperature. In addition, $R_{DS,on}$ characteristic curves as a function of junction temperature are also provided, since the on-state resistance increases as the junction temperature rises. Because of this positive temperature coefficient, it is possible to parallel several MOSFET devices.

*MOSFET Capacitances*: MOSFETs have capacitances between gate-source ($C_{GS}$), gate-drain ($C_{GD}$) and drain-source ($C_{DS}$), which are critical parameters affecting the gate drive design and the device switching characteristics. These capacitances cannot be measured directly, but can be calculated from measurable input, output and reverse transfer characteristics. The relationships among the capacitances are given by

$$C_{iss} = C_{GS} + C_{GD}$$

$$C_{oss} = C_{DS} + C_{GD}$$

$$C_{rss} = C_{GD}$$

*Avalance Characteristics*: The avalanche characteristics of a MOSFET define the avalanche time duration $t_{AV}$ during which pulsed avalanche current $I_{AV}$ can be sustained. Operation under the pulse avalanche current limits is allowed with consideration of the maximum junction temperature. The longer the avalanche pulse, the lower the maximum allowed avalanche current.

### 9.1.8  Si, SiC and GaN Power Devices

Semiconductors are the type of materials that have bound electrons occupying distinct energy levels around an atomic nucleus which are the valence band and the conduction band. In semiconductor devices, electrons moving up to the conduction band from the valence bond under a biasing condition constitute current flow. The Si-based semiconductor power devices constitute a mature technology and are widely used in the power industry. Si devices are almost exclusively used in the automotive industry for both auxiliary power converters and motor drives as well as for traction inverters due to their maturity and reliability. For low-voltage motor drives, Si MOSFET is the device of choice, while for electric and hybrid electric vehicle traction systems, the device of choice is Si-IGBT.

The next generation of power electronic devices based on wide bandgap semiconductors, particularly silicon carbide (SiC) and gallium nitride (GaN) devices, have made significant strides in recent years to come to the forefront and find their place in many applications. The energy required by the electrons to move up the band in WBG devices is much greater than that of Si. For example, SiC requires 3.2 electron-volts (eV) and GaN requires 3.4 eV compared to that of 1.1 eV for Si. The increased energy required translates to higher electric field breakdown performance for WBG devices compared to Si of the same scale. This also leads to the WBG device capability of withstanding higher temperatures before failure. In addition, the thermal conductivity of SiC is 3.5 times that of Si. These attributes have led to the development of WBG devices with high-frequency, high-temperature operation at higher voltage and power levels. Faster switching, and lower power losses in SiC and GaN power devices compared to Si devices enables systems design with smaller and compact footprint while simultaneously delivering superior performance. SiC devices are now commercially available at voltage levels of 900, 1,200, 1,700, and 3,300 V, while 6,600 and 10,000 V devices are emerging. GaN devices are available up to 600 V levels, while higher voltage level devices are being developed. The SiC MOSFETs are highly attractive for traction inverters as well as for the chargers. The various available devices in the power and frequency spectrum are shown in Figure 9.6. As the electric vehicles are moving toward 800 V nominal battery voltages, SiC MOSFETs is an increasingly attractive proposition as inverters exceeding 99% efficiency levels become feasible. A table of three commercially available power devices with similar ratings is given in Table 9.1.

It is to be noted that Si-IGBTs are bipolar devices, while SiC MOSFETS are unipolar devices where the conduction charaterics and current waveforms are fundamentally different when comparing these devices for any application. While utilizing higher switching frequecies in SiC MOSFETs can lead to reduced filter requirements and better motor current regulation, the EMI effects would be enhanced and need to be mitigated through other means. Alternatively, the SiC MOSFETs can be used with switching speed the same as that of a Si-IGBT to maintain the *dv/dt* and *di/dt* rates such that the EMI effects remain the same, but the efficiency advantages can help the fuel economy at the system level and/or reduce the battery capacity requirement.

## 9.2 DC/DC CONVERTERS

The DC/DC converters change the system voltages from one level to another. The input to the converter is a filtered DC voltage, although it may be unregulated. The output is a regulated DC voltage; multiple outputs are also designed for many applications. The converters have inductive

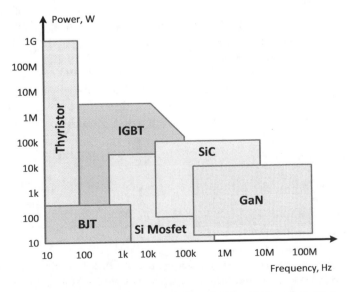

**FIGURE 9.6** Semiconductor power devices with respect to power and frequency levels.

**TABLE 9.1**

**Comparison of Three Commercial Power Devices in Terms of Their Ratings and Key Parameters**

|  | Si Superjunction IPP65R045C7 | SiC MOSFET C3M0065090J | E-mode GaN GS66508B |
|---|---|---|---|
| Voltage | 700 V | 900 V | 650 V |
| Current | 46 A at 25°C; 29 A at 100°C; | 35 A at 25°C; 22 A at 100°C; | 30 A |
| $R_{DS,on}$ mΩ | 45 | 65 | 50 |
| $R_{DSA}$ mΩ-cm² | 10 | 3.5 | 6.6 |
| $R_{ds} * E_{OSS}$ mΩ-μJ | 462 | 1,040 | 350 |
| $V_{th}$ (V) | 3.5 | 2.1 | 1.3 |
| Avalanche | Yes | Yes | No |
| Gate voltage rating | ±20 | +19/−8 | +/−10 |
| Diode behavior | Poor | Excellent | Excellent |

and capacitive storage elements in addition to the switching devices. The switching frequency of the power devices are very high often reaching as high as a few hundreds of kHz. The high switching frequency helps minimize the size of the storage elements. The efficiencies of these switching converters are also very high in the upper 90 percentages.

Depending on whether or not transformer isolation is used, the switching converters can be broadly classified into isolated and non-isolated DC/DC converters. The basic non-isolated DC/DC converter has a single switch and a single diode; these types of converters may also have one inductor and one capacitor as the energy storage elements. There are also other types of non-isolated DC/DC converters that use two switches and two diodes in the circuit topology and additional energy storage elements. A lot of applications, including certain ones in electric and hybrid vehicles, require electrical isolation between the input and the output. The isolated DC/DC converters are derived from the basic topologies, but have high frequency transformer isolation.

The high-power DC/DC converters are primarily used in three places of electric and hybrid electric vehicles: Voltage boost for electric powertrain, high- to low-voltage interface for 12 V electronics, and converters for energy storage cell balancing. A non-isolated DC/DC converter is often used in the powertrain of electric and hybrid vehicles to boost the battery voltage to higher levels for the propulsion electric motor drive. The 12 V electronics in the electric and hybrid vehicles are supplied with a high-voltage to low-voltage DC/DC converter, which needs to be of isolated type. These non-isolated and isolated converter topologies are discussed below in this section. The DC/DC converters used in energy storage cell balancing are discussed in Section 9.4.

### 9.2.1 Non-isolated DC/DC Converters

DC/DC converters can be designed to either step-up or step-down the input DC voltage. Depending on the location of the two switches and the inductor and capacitor, the three basic second-order DC/DC converter topologies are buck, boost and buck-boost converters. A buck converter is a step-down converter, and a boost converter is a step-up converter, while a buck-boost converter can be operated in either mode. Improved topologies are available with two switching devices and two diodes, and additional storage elements. Consequently, the order of the converter also increases with the additional components. Examples of higher-order converters are Cuk and Sepic converters. All of these DC/DC converters are used to convert an unregulated DC voltage into a regulated DC output voltage; hence, the converters are known as switching regulators.

The DC/DC converters can be operated either in the *continuous conduction mode* (CCM) or in the *discontinuous conduction mode* (DCM). The conduction relates to the inductor current in the DC/DC converters. If the inductor current remains continuous and is above zero at all times, then the converter is in CCM. If the lowest value of the inductor current is zero, then the converter is in DCM. The converter operations are explained below with the help of CCM waveforms.

### 9.2.1.1 Buck Converter

The circuit topology of a buck converter with a MOSFET implementation is shown in Figure 9.7a. A BJT could also be used for the switch $S$. The voltage and current waveforms in the circuit are shown in Figure 9.7b. The average output voltage $\langle v_o \rangle$ is smaller than the input DC voltage $V_{in}$; hence, the circuit is known as a buck converter. The operation of the converter primarily involves the switching of the power device according to the controller command. The transistor switch is turned on for a duty cycle $D$ defined as

$$D = \frac{\text{Switch-on time}}{\text{Time period }(T)} \tag{9.1}$$

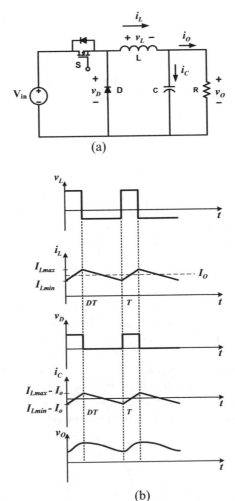

(a)

(b)

**FIGURE 9.7** (a) Buck converter with MOSFET-diode implementation and (b) voltage and current waveforms.

The time period $T$ is fixed and sets the switching frequency of the converter. The circuit operation has two modes, one when the switch S is on and the second mode is when the switch is off. The switch is on for a period of $DT$ s and off for a period of $(1-D)T$ s. The inductor current increases when the switch is on thereby charging the inductor. When the switch is off, the diode is forced to turn-on to maintain the continuity of the inductor current; the inductor gets discharged and its current decreases. Through the charging and discharging of the inductor, energy gets transferred from the input to the output. The filter capacitor $C$ along with the output resistor $R$ provides a very large time-constant compared to the switching frequency. Hence, the output voltage ripple will be very low; typically, the ripple is less than 1%.

The input and output average voltages and currents are related to the duty cycle as

$$\frac{\langle v_o \rangle}{V_{in}} = \frac{\langle i_{in} \rangle}{I_o} = D \tag{9.2}$$

where $\langle v_o \rangle$ and $\langle i_{in} \rangle$ are the average output voltage and the average input current, respectively. $I_o = \langle i_o \rangle$ is the average output current.

### 9.2.1.2  Boost Converter

A boost converter steps up a DC voltage from one level to another. The circuit topology of a boost converter with a MOSFET implementation is shown in Figure 9.8a. A BJT could also be used for the switch S. The current and voltage waveforms are shown in Figure 9.8b. The circuit has two modes of operation in a switching cycle, depending on whether the switch is on or off. When the switch is on for a period of $DT$ s, the input current $i_{in}$ increases, thereby storing energy in the inductor. Input current is the same as the inductor current $i_L$. When the switch is turned off, the diode becomes forward biased and starts conducting. Energy from the inductor flows to the load. The inductor current decreases until the end of the period when the switch is turned on again. A large filter capacitor $C$ is required compared to the buck converter since high rms current flows through it.

The input and output average voltages and currents are related to the duty cycle as

$$\frac{\langle v_o \rangle}{V_{in}} = \frac{\langle i_{in} \rangle}{I_o} = \frac{1}{1-D} \tag{9.3}$$

where $\langle v_o \rangle$ and $\langle i_{in} \rangle$ are the average output voltage and the average input current, respectively. $I_o = \langle i_o \rangle$ is the average output current.

### 9.2.1.3  Buck-Boost Converter

The buck-boost converter topology can either step up or step down the input voltage; hence, the name of the converter. The circuit topology of a buck-boost converter with a MOSFET implementation is shown in Figure 9.9a. The current and voltage waveforms are shown in Figure 9.9b. Similar to the buck and boost converters, the buck-boost converter also has two modes of operation in one switching cycle. When the switch S is on for a period of $DT$ s, the input current flows through the inductor storing energy in it. The diode is reverse biased in this mode, and the filter capacitor $C$ maintains the load current. When the switch is off for the period $(1-D)T$ s, the diode becomes forward biased and the stored inductor energy is transferred to the load. The inductor current decreases until the switch is turned on again in the CCM. The output voltage polarity of a buck-boost converter is inverted.

The input and output average voltages and currents are related to the duty cycle as

$$\frac{\langle v_o \rangle}{V_{in}} = \frac{\langle i_{in} \rangle}{I_o} = \frac{D}{1-D} \tag{9.4}$$

where $\langle v_o \rangle$ and $\langle i_{in} \rangle$ are the average output voltage and the average input current, respectively. $I_o = \langle i_o \rangle$ is the average output current.

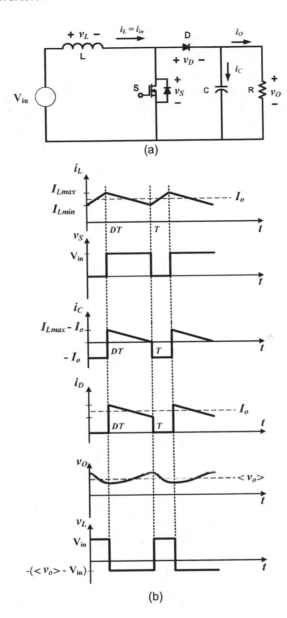

**FIGURE 9.8** (a) Boost converter with MOSFET-diode implementation and (b) voltage and current waveforms.

The CCM of the basic converters have been discussed so far. The boundary between the CCM and DCM depends on the size of the inductor relative to the other parameters of the circuit. The converters enter the DCM when the inductor size is reduced below the critical size $L_{crit}$ provided other parameters remain the same. The smaller the $L_{crit}$ value, the wider is the choice for inductor design. For the same switching frequency and load resistance, the buck converter has the highest $L_{crit}$, while the boost converter has the smallest $L_{crit}$.

In the DCM, the minimum inductor current in each of the three basic topologies is zero. For a short interval, the inductor current remains zero. The DC/DC converters frequently enter DCM, since they often operate under no load conditions. In the DCM, the voltage gain is not only a function of $D$, but also of switching frequency, load and circuit parameters; this makes the analysis in DCM much more complicated. The readers are referred to the references [2,3] for analysis of the DCM operation.

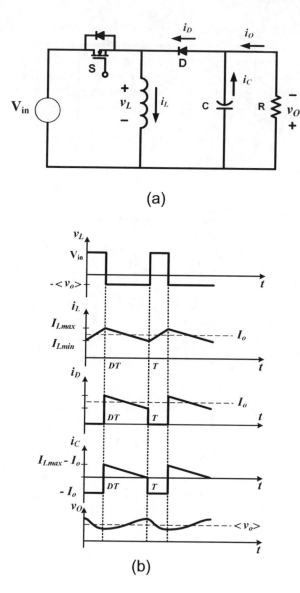

FIGURE 9.9 (a) Buck-boost converter with MOSFET-diode implementation and (b) voltage and current waveforms.

### 9.2.1.4 Fourth-Order DC/DC converters

The DC/DC converters presented so far have only one switch and a diode, and are of second order. The minimal switch number ensures high efficiency of the converters, although the stress on the switches will also be high. However, the basic converters are not suitable under certain input-output conditions, especially when the input voltage has a wide range. Cascade and cascode combinations of the basic converters result in other attractive DC/DC converter topologies such as the Sepic and Cuk converters [3]. These converters have two inductors and two capacitors; hence, the order of the converter is fourth.

### 9.2.1.5 Cascading of Converters

In DC/DC converters, power is transferred from the input to the output load either through a direct process or through an indirect process. In the indirect process, the switching devices use intermediate energy storage in the passive components for the power transfer; in the direct process, the power is transferred directly without the requirement of any intermediate energy storage. For the single-switch DC/DC converters discussed so far, the buck and the boost converters transfer power using both direct and indirect mechanisms. The ratio of direct and indirect power depends on the voltage conversion ratios; the power is processed entirely by the direct method when the conversion ratio is unity. For the converters that process all of the input power through the switching of the devices, the switch component stresses and the energy storage requirements are higher. For the single switch buck-boost, Cuk and Sepic converters, the power is processed using the indirect mechanism in its entirety. However, with a minimized number of switches, these converters are suitable for applications up to only about 300 W, but not for higher-power applications. Additionally, the converters are also not suitable when the input voltage has a wide range.

In electric and hybrid vehicle applications, converter configurations that offer high efficiency and reliability are desired. The ability to provide direct power transfer paths reduces the component stresses and energy storage requirements, which leads to higher efficiencies; these types of converter topologies can be derived by cascading two DC/DC converters in series as shown in Figure 9.10. The efficiency performance of these converters is comparable to those of simple buck or boost converters. The overall gain of two converters with gains *Conv*1 and *Conv*2 connected in series (cascade) (Figure 9.10) is

$$G_{cascade} = \frac{V_{out}}{V_{in}} = G_{Conv1} \cdot G_{Conv2}$$

### 9.2.1.6 Synchronous Rectification

The ability of the MOSFET channel to conduct current in the reverse direction by reversing the source and the drain connections makes it possible to use a MOSFET switch where a diode would otherwise be used. The device is operated in the third quadrant of its *i-v* characteristics where the current flows from the source to the drain. This third quadrant operation of the MOSFET is known as synchronous rectification. The device is blocking negative voltage and conducting positive current. An example of a converter with synchronous rectifier is shown in Figure 9.11 where the diode of a buck converter has been replaced by a MOSFET. The use of a MOSFET in the synchronous rectification mode helps minimize the power loss during reverse current conduction since otherwise the use of a conventional diode rectifier would contribute significantly to the power loss due to its relatively large forward voltage drop. For a diode, the conduction loss is proportional to the product

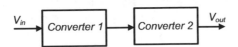

**FIGURE 9.10** Cascade connection of two converters.

**FIGURE 9.11** Boost converter with synchronous rectifier.

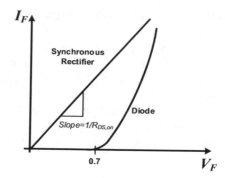

**FIGURE 9.12** Synchronous rectifier and diode characteristics.

of its forward-voltage drop $V_F$, and the forward conduction current $I_F$. On the other hand, the rectifier with MOSFET switches presents resistive $i$-$v$ characteristics as shown in Figure 9.12. The MOSFET conduction loss is equal to $I_{rms}^2 R_{DS,on}$ where $I_{rms}$ is the switching rms current and $R_{DS,on}$ is the MOSFET on-state resistance. A MOSFET with a lower $R_{DS,on}$ can be used to increase converter efficiency, but usually at some increased cost.

In the synchronous rectification mode, the device is controlled in such a way that it operates in the 'on' state when a diode would normally conduct and in the 'off' state when the diode would be reverse biased. The dead times inserted in gate switching controls lead to the conduction of the body diode in the MOSFET, and the energy that must be dissipated with the reverse voltage depends on the diode conduction time. Once the MOSFET is turned on for synchronous rectification, the switch undergoes soft-switching with current commutation from diode to the MOSFET channel.

## 9.2.2 Isolated DC/DC Converters

Transformers are also useful in applications that require large step-up or step down of the input voltage. The concept is equally useful in power electronic converters where large voltage ratios are required between the input and output side of power electronic converters. The voltage and current stresses on the transistors and switches can be minimized to improve efficiency by the proper choice of the transformer turns ratio. The output voltage polarity can also be easily set with the transformer winding polarity. Multiple DC outputs are possible with transformers by using multiple secondary windings and converter secondary side circuits. In addition, a number of applications, including some segments of the EV/HEV system, require electrical isolation between the input and the output. The voltage stepping and isolation is provided by incorporating a high frequency transformer made of ferrite, amorphous or nanocrystalline materials. The operation at higher switching frequencies in the range of tens or hundreds of kilohertz helps minimize the size and weight of these transformers drastically compared to the power transformers operating at 50 or 60 Hz. Additional controls may also be needed in the converter to avoid transformer core saturation. However, adding a transformer in a DC-DC converter will increase the size and weight compared to a non-isolated converter and will also impact the efficiency. There can be switching frequency limitations due to the parasitic elements introduced by the transformer.

There are several approaches for the primary and secondary winding connections with the power devices giving rise to different converter topologies. The primary winding arrangements can be single-ended, push-pull, half-bridge or full-bridge as shown in Figure 9.13 [3]. The secondary arrangements can be half-wave, center-tapped full-wave, or full-bridge full-wave. Two of these secondary arrangements are shown in Figure 9.14. With multiple windings, the critical design consideration is to ensure volt-sec balance for each winding. Failure to maintain the volt-sec balance will lead to core saturation that will destroy the converter.

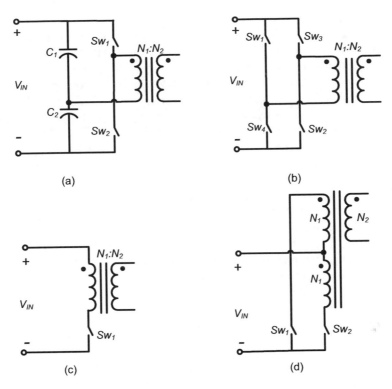

**FIGURE 9.13** Primary winding arrangements: (a) single-ended, (b) push-pull, (c) half-bridge and (d) full-bridge.

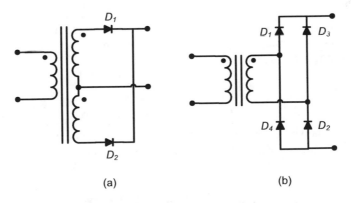

**FIGURE 9.14** Secondary winding arrangements: (a) center-tapped half wave and (b) full-bridge full-wave.

The isolated DC/DC converters can be derived from either the buck topology or the boost topology. In addition, depending on the number of switches used, the DC/DC converters can be single-switch type or multiple-switch type. The single-switch converters are similar to the buck or boost converter, but with a transformer isolation. The two single-switch isolated DC/DC converters are the forward and flyback converters. The forward converter is derived from the buck topology, whereas the flyback converter is derived from the boost topology. These are the simplest isolated DC/DC converters with the lowest component count. However, the magnetic components are used in a unipolar, single-quadrant mode. The switching stress on the power device is $2V_{in}$. These topologies are used in low power applications, about 100 W or less.

The multi-switch DC/DC converters fully utilize the transformer magnetics, and are used in higher-power applications. Depending on the number of switches and the type of transformer used, there are three types of isolated multi-switch DC/DC converters: Push-pull, half-bridge, and full-bridge. The input side of push-pull converters uses a center-tapped transformer, while half-bridge and full-bridge converters use non center-tapped transformers. The secondary side of the transformers can use a half-bridge diode configuration with a center tap or a full-bridge diode configuration without a center tap. The multi-switch converters can be either buck-derived or boost-derived. The full-converter topology is the most suitable for applications exceeding 500 W. The common high-power DC/DC converter in electric and hybrid vehicle applications for the high- to low-voltage interface is of the full-bridge converter type.

The circuit topology of a buck-derived push-pull converter is shown in Figure 9.15. The circuit uses two switches on the input side and an inductor for energy storage on the output side. The center-tapped transformer is used for voltage scaling and electrical isolation. Switches S1 and S2 are turned on and off alternately with equal duty ratios within one switching period. The duty ratio for each switch can be varied between 0 and 0.5. A minimum dead time when both switches are off is guaranteed by the controller between the switching transition of the two devices to avoid the possibility of shoot-through across the supply voltage. The voltage gain of the push-pull converter is

$$\frac{V_o}{V_{in}} = 2\frac{N_2}{N_1}D, \quad 0 < D < 0.5$$

The converter topology is simpler than the half- and full-bridge topologies, but the main disadvantage is that the diode and power device switching stresses are in excess of $2V_{in}$. In addition, the transformer core is prone to saturation due to any slight non-ideality in the switching pattern. The push-pull isolated converter is used in medium power applications up to about 500 W.

The half-bridge converter use active switches to generate symmetrical AC waveforms at the primary side of the transformer. The transformer core flux is excited with bi-directional waveforms, which gives better core utilization and makes it less prone to flux saturation. The circuit topology of a half-bridge converter with a center-tapped secondary is shown in Figure 9.16. The switches operate the same way as in the push-pull converter, and the maximum duty cycle for each switch is 0.5. The voltage gain of the half-bridge converter is

$$\frac{V_o}{V_{in}} = \frac{N_2}{N_1}D, \quad 0 < D < 0.5$$

The maximum blocking voltage for each switch in the half-bridge converter is $V_{in}$ rather than $2V_{in}$ like that in the push-pull converter. The half-bridge converter is the most commonly used isolated

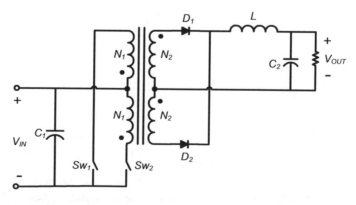

**FIGURE 9.15** Push-pull isolated DC/DC converter.

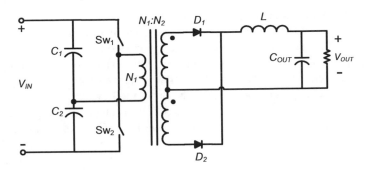

**FIGURE 9.16**   Half-bridge isolated DC/DC converter.

DC/DC converter in the medium power range. The switching device stress is $V_{in}$, and the switch count is less than the full-bridge converter.

The full-bridge converter topology also generates symmetrical AC waveforms at the primary side of the transformer, but with four active switches. The circuit topology of a full-bridge converter with a full diode bridge at the secondary side is shown in Figure 9.17a. The switches are operated in pairs; switches $Sw_1$-$Sw_4$ and $Sw_2$-$Sw_3$ are switched alternately with the maximum duty ratio for each switch being 0.5. A dead time is also inserted between the transitions from one pair to another to avoid shoot-through across the supply voltage. The voltage gain of the full-bridge converter is

$$\frac{V_o}{V_{in}} = 2\frac{N_2}{N_1}D, \quad 0 < D < 0.5$$

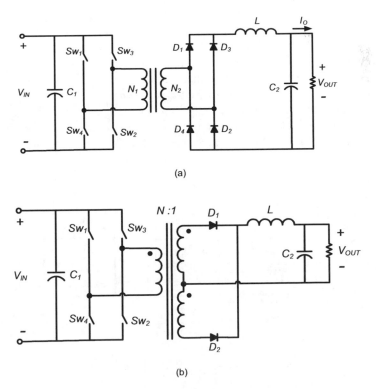

(a)

(b)

**FIGURE 9.17**   Full-bridge isolated DC/DC converters: (a) diode bridge secondary and (b) center tap secondary.

An alternative to the diode bridge used on the low-voltage side of the full bridge converter is to use a center-tap transformer with two diodes. The topology is shown in Figure 9.17b. The alternative is often used for cost minimization, since the diodes carry large currents and are expensive. The topology shown in Figure 9.17b is unidirectional, but can easily be converted into a bi-directional topology by replacing the two diodes with two controlled switches. The appropriate control of the secondary switches allows the topology to be operated in the boost mode with power flowing from the low-voltage side to the high-voltage side. The use of switches is also more efficient than using diodes.

The typical power rating of the high- to low-voltage DC/DC converter in mid-size electric or hybrid vehicles is around 2 kW. The low-voltage output supplies the 12 V electronics in the vehicle. The 12 V ground is always connected to the vehicle chassis; hence, the requirement for this converter topology to be of isolated type. The converter topology commonly used for this application is one of the full-bridge types. The switching frequency of this converter used in vehicles is around 100 kHz. In most electric and hybrid vehicles, this converter is unidirectional, although there are advantages of using a bi-directional converter. The boost mode operation, possible with the topologies shown in Figure 9.17 but with switches in the secondary, helps eliminate the 12 V starter for IC engines in hybrid electric vehicles. The hybrid vehicles have a high-power electric machine that can start the engine more efficiently and much faster than the conventional 12 V starter. The boost mode operation also helps in extreme weather starting conditions. In extremely cold cranking situations, the high-voltage battery may not be able to provide all of the required engine cranking power; the 12 V battery can supply additional starting power to the high-power electric machine to help start the IC engine.

## 9.3  EV POWERTRAIN CONVERTERS

The primary power electronic converters in an EV powertrain are the inverter for providing power to the traction electric machine, the DC/DC converter for connecting the high-voltage system with the low-voltage system, and the on-board charger (OBC) for plug-in electric vehicles. The power converters used in an EV or a PHEV with respect to their locations are shown in Figure 9.18. The inverter in the powertrain can be a boosted type or a non-boosted type depending on whether a higher DC-link voltage than the battery-pack voltage is used for powering the electric machine or not. A higher DC-link voltage is preferred so that the electric machine can be designed with higher maximum operating speed. The reliability of the boosted/non-boosted inverter is critical and has to be designed with constraints of short-circuit capability and long lifetime. The charger is not in the critical operation path of the electric powertrain and also its operational duty cycle is less. It needs to be mentioned that the gate drivers for the primary DC/DC converters, and the traction inverter

**FIGURE 9.18**  Power electronic converters in an EV/PHEV electric powertrain.

and various auxiliary power supplies have DC/DC converters that are buck or flyback or push-pull type with smaller power ratings. The choice and sizing of the different powertrain converters are discussed below.

## 9.3.1  POWERTRAIN BOOST CONVERTER

A boost-type non-isolated DC/DC converter is used in the electric power transmission path in many electric and hybrid vehicles. The DC/DC converter boosts the battery-pack output voltage to a higher level for efficient operation of the traction electric drive in a battery equipped electric or hybrid electric vehicle. The converter needs to be bi-directional to recover and recharge the battery-pack during vehicle regenerative braking; however, it does not have to be isolated. The higher DC-link voltage enables the electric machine to operate at higher speeds by overcoming the higher back-emf voltage which is proportional to the speed. Therefore, to operate the electric machine at higher speeds for the same power output, the DC-link voltage needs to be increased. The higher machine operating speeds for the same power output helps minimize its size and increase its power density. Also, boosting the voltage to higher levels facilitates the generator mode of operation for the electric machine, since the DC-link voltage has to be higher than the back-emf voltage at the maximum operating speed for a controlled generation. Also, with a higher voltage DC bus, the motor will draw less current for the same power from the DC link. As a result, the DC bus current/voltage ripple will be less. This will help to reduce the filter size at the inverter input. The electric machine electrical losses will be reduced with lower current, which will also reduce the requirements on the cooling system. From the battery sizing point of view, the use of a boost stage can help minimize the number of battery cells in series. Reduced number of cells in a series results in component and cost savings for the battery management system in addition to reducing the equivalent battery series resistance. The pack capacity is not affected by reducing the number of cells, since it is determined by the capacity of each cell connected in a series string. The other advantages of adding the boost converter are reduction in filter choke and DC-link capacitor sizes of the motor drive, and reduction in wiring harness size due to lower current requirements. DC-link bus voltage can be modulated as a function of the motor operating speed and power requirement to minimize the switching losses of the inverter. The drawbacks of adding the boost segment in the electric powertrain are increase in cost, requirement of an input side filter and increase in the number of failure points. One needs to evaluate the entire powertrain including the battery at the system level to compare a boosted system against a non-boosted system.

The boost DC/DC converter is essential in the powertrain of a fuel cell electric vehicle, since the output voltage of a fuel cell is typically low and unregulated. The DC/DC converter increases the voltage level and regulates the output voltage. This converter topology needs to be of unidirectional only, since regenerative fuel cells are yet to be developed. The DC/DC converters can also be used to interface between two energy storage devices in an electric or hybrid vehicle. For example, when a battery-ultracapacitor combination is used for the energy storage system, one of the components is connected directly to the DC bus, while the other is buffered through a DC/DC converter. The ultra-capacitor can be used to capture as much of regenerative braking energy as possible, since its power density is high; the battery-pack can be designed to provide the zero emission range of the vehicle.

The half-bridge bi-directional non-isolated DC/DC converter, derived from the basic topologies, is one of the most commonly used converter topology used for boost operation of the main DC bus. The topology is shown in Figure 9.19a. Power flows from the low-voltage side (which would be the battery-pack side) to the high-voltage DC-link side in the boost mode with lower switch $S_2$ and the diode $D_1$ in operation. In buck mode, upper switch $S_1$ and the diode $D_2$ come into operation; controlling $S_1$ allows power to flow from the high-voltage DC-link side to the battery-pack. An interleaved structure can be designed for the boost converter which enables significant reduction in the ripple current supplied from the battery. Also, on the DC-bus side, lower ripple current in the DC bus capacitors can be observed with an interleaved converters which results in lower requirements on

**FIGURE 9.19** DC-DC half-bridge boost converter: (a) single-phase non-interleaved and (b) three-phase interleaved.

the DC-link bus capacitors [4,5]. A three-phase interleaved boost converter is shown in Figure 9.19b. Interleaved boost structure inherently requires multiple boost inductors and an increased number of switches. However, an optimized converter can be designed with proper selection and sizing of the passive components to obtain system-level benefits.

The two other converter topologies suitable for the mains DC-boost is shown in Figure 9.20a and b [6]. Figure 9.20a shows the Cuk converter which boosts voltage when power flows from $V_{in}$ to DC bus $V_{DC}$. In this boost mode, $S_1$ and $D_2$ are active, and $S_2$ and $D_1$ are inactive. In the buck mode, voltage is stepped down from $V_{DC}$ to $V_{in}$ when $S_2$ and $D_1$ are active, and $S_1$ and $D_2$ are inactive. $C_t$ and $C_2$ are transfer capacitor and DC-link capacitor, respectively. Figure 9.20b shows the combined SEPIC/Luo converter, which operates as a SEPIC converter when voltage boost operation is required and as a Luo converter when buck operation is required. In the SEPIC operation mode, power flows from low-voltage battery-pack side to high-voltage DC-link side boosting the input battery voltage $V_{in}$. In this mode, $S_1$ and $D_2$ are active, and $S_2$ and $D_1$ are inactive. In the Luo operation mode, power flows from the high-voltage DC-link side to the low-voltage battery-pack side stepping down the input DC-link voltage. In this mode, $S_2$ and $D_1$ are active, and $S_1$ and $D_2$ are inactive. Table 9.2 shows the stress on active and passive components for the three converter topologies [6]. For comparison, the advantages of half-bridge converter over Cuk and SEPIC/Luo converters are: a smaller size of inductor, reduced voltage and current ratings of active components, less number of components, less point of failure and higher efficiency. The main drawback of half-bridge is that output current might become discontinuous due to small inductor size, which impacts the size of the DC-link capacitor.

In some EV/HEV applications where a DC/DC converter is used to buffer the energy storage system with the high-voltage inverter DC-link, the two DC voltages may overlap depending on the electric powertrain design, the energy storage system components and design, and the operating condition. Traction batteries have a rated or nominal voltage, but always operate with a range that depends on the state of charge of the battery. For example, a Li-ion battery pack made of 50 cells

**FIGURE 9.20** DC boost converters: (a) Cuk and (B) SEPIC/Luo.

with a nominal rating of 144 V operates within a range of 126–172 V; the output of the DC/DC boost converter stage may overlap with the input battery pack operating range. In a fuel cell electric vehicle, the output voltage of the fuel cell varies over a wide operating range, and may require both buck and boost operation of the DC/DC converter to deliver power to the electric drive system. In these types of situations, the cascaded DC/DC converter with bi-directional buck and boost operation, such as the one shown in Figure 9.21, is a suitable converter topology. The cascaded topologies have higher switch counts, but during operation only one bridge is switching while the other is passive. The cascaded boost-buck or buck-boost bi-directional converters have significantly lower component stress that helps achieve improved efficiency. Furthermore, phase interleaving of these half bridge-based converters provides additional benefits of ripple cancellation.

**TABLE 9.2**

**Stresses on Active and Passive Components in Non-isolated DC/DC Converters**

| | Half-Bridge | Cuk | SEPIC/Luo |
|---|---|---|---|
| Transfer capacitor voltage rating | — | $V_{in} + V_o$ | $V_{in}$ |
| Switch voltage rating | $V_o$ | $V_{in} + V_o$ | $V_{in} + V_o$ |
| Diode voltage rating | $V_o$ | $V_{in} + V_o$ | $V_{in} + V_o$ |
| Inductor average current[a] | $\dfrac{I_o}{1-d_1}$, boost $\dfrac{I_o}{d_2}$, buck | $I_{L1} = I_o\dfrac{d_1}{1-d_1}$ $I_{L2} = I_o$ | $I_{L1} = I_o\dfrac{d_1}{1-d_1}$ $I_{L2} = I_o$, boost $I_{L1} = I_o\dfrac{(1-d_2)}{d_2}$ $I_{L2} = I_o$, buck |

[a] $d_1$ and $d_2$ are duty cycle for boost and buck operation, respectively.

**FIGURE 9.21**    Boost-buck cascaded DC-DC converter.

## 9.3.2  TRACTION INVERTER

The six-switch voltage source inverter (VSI) is used in electric and hybrid vehicle applications where the source typically delivers a stiff voltage at the DC-link. The function of the inverter is to convert the available on-board DC power to a high-fidelity AC current and voltages required to meet the driver demands for vehicle propulsion. The three-phase current controlled six-switch VSI is current choice of power converter universally adopted by the automotive industry. The inverter is labeled as a non-boosted type when the DC source or battery-pack output voltage directly feeds into the DC-link of the inverter, whereas it will be a boosted type when a front end DC-DC stage is used to step up the battery-pack voltage to a higher DC-link voltage level. The non-boosted traction inverter topology is shown in Figure 9.22. The six-switch VSI topology is used for induction machines, interior permanent magnet or any other three-phase synchronous machine. The VSI which is a two-level inverter is typically hard switched. Three-level inverters such as the T-type are also good candidates for the inverter depending on the unique application requirements. Whether 2 or 3L is the choice, the overarching design goal for traction inverters is enhanced high efficiency and reliability while maintaining low cost, size and mass.

A boosted inverter topology which allows the increase of the DC-link bus voltage for higher motor maximum speeds is shown in Figure 9.23. The inverter topologies are shown with SiC MOSFET devices, but can similarly be implemented with IGBT devices. The DC-DC boost converter is three-phase interleaved which can significantly reduce the ripple. The DC-DC boost stage can be operated with zero-voltage switching which will improve system efficiency and reduce the battery-pack bus filtering requirements.

The power device of choice adopted by the automotive industry since the introduction of the first modern day electric vehicle EV1 in 1996 is the Si-IGBT which is still favored due to cost, decent efficiency, developed EMI management approaches around its 5–10 kHz switching frequencies and good

**FIGURE 9.22**    Powertrain non-boosted traction inverter.

**FIGURE 9.23**   Powertrain-boosted inverter with interleaved DC/DC stage.

short-circuit capability of about 10 µs. SiC and GaN power devices have made tremendous progress over the past 10 years and are now challenging Si-IGBTs for traction applications. Several EVs have already adopted the SiC technology. SiC MOSFETs are more mature and near term compared to GaN HEMTs, although GaN has the potential to be the eventual choice in the future. For high-voltage systems such as 800 V, SiC MOSFETs offer unique advantages of lower device losses and higher-frequency operation to enable better current regulation and reduced dead time to contribute towards less voltage and current distortion. Another big advantage of SiC MOSFETs over Si-IGBT is the elimination of the anti-parallel diodes, which is essential in the case of the latter. In a MOSFET, both positive and negative currents can flow since the channel can conduct in both directions.

The traction inverter is integrated with the motor controller which generates the gate switch signals for the inverter power devices using a PWM method and control commands to process the power flow and deliver the output voltage at the desired voltage and frequency. The traction inverter consists of the power devices, the gate driver, power stage or busbar, DC bus and EMI filter, heat sinks, controller and sensors. Each of the components is designed to meet the inverter system requirements and packaging constraints. The overall objectives of the traction inverter design are efficiency and power density, which are critical for electric/hybrid vehicle fuel economy and space constraints. On the operational aspect, the inverter is designed to operate both in the six-step mode and in the PWM mode. The motor control and inverter PWM controls will be discussed further in Chapter 10; here we focus on the inverter design aspects.

### 9.3.2.1   Power Device Selection

The power device is selected based on the current rating, voltage rating, device losses and short-circuit capability. The current rating is based on the maximum current that the deivce can carry for the peak power level of the traction motor for the minimum specified battery-pack voltage or DC-link voltage. The device losses comprised of both switching loss and conduction loss are intimately related to the maximum continuous current rating since the device current ratings are always derated at higher ambient temperatures. At peak power level, the device losses are at a maximum which elevates the device junction temperatures and the current capability has to be derated for the device to remain within the safe operating area. The device voltage ratings are specified based on the voltage levels that the devices have to withstand including the overshoots during switch turn-off transient and the maximum rms current that the devices have to carry including some safety margin. In relation to the DC-link voltage, the voltage rating can be obtained from

$$V_{DC,\,rating} = V_{nom,DC} \times \left(1 + \frac{s_1}{100}\right)$$

(9.4)

where $s_1$ is the safety margin.

The power device switching losses also depend on the gate drive which can be adjusted for a trade-off among EMI (related to *dv/dt*), voltage overshoot, switching losses and short-circuit capability. Further discussion on this appears in the gate drive section.

There are several choices available for packaging and thermal management of the power devices. In terms of packaging, either TO-247 type discrete devices can be used with several of them placed in parallel to increase the current carrying capability or modules of either half-bridge or six-pack can be used. The TO-247 packages have been optimized over time and offer the flexibility of overall inverter packaging with its cooling components. The modules can be of either flat baseplate type or integrated pin fin type. Flat baseplate modules are less expensive but they require the use of a thermal interface module (TIM) such as one made of aluminum nitride. The heat from the devices is extracted through coolant fluid (typically, 50/50 water-glycol mix) forced through the channels or tubes placed within the heat sink underneath the TIM. With the pin fin modules, direct water flow over the pin fin area is possible, which is a more efficient heat removal process due to reduced thermal impedance. Another technique that is emerging is the double sided cooling possible with modules designed for heat removal from both top and bottom surfaces of the device. Although the heat removal process is significantly improved with very low thermal impedance, double-sided cooling does complicate the overall mechanical packaging.

### 9.3.2.2 Busbar and Packaging

Conventional power electronic converter packages use copper bar-based laminated bus structures and power device modules. The overall goal is to build an integrated power electronic module (IPEM) with full digital control. With increased demand for high power density converters, busbar form-factor and interconnection with power modules play a significant role in the overall system-level design. The alternative to laminated design is the printed circuit board (PCB)-based design. The PCB bus bars are an attractive alternative owing to ease of design, manufacturability and simplified system assembly [5,7]. While the majority passenger electrical vehicle manufactures now adopts 400 V system for the traction inverter, which has a DC-link voltage of 150 V–450 V, an 800 V system which has DC-link of up to 870 V has come into market which provides system-level benefits to the EV powertrain. Compared with 800 V system, the 400 V system needs to operate with much higher phase current that increases temperature and loss of the busbar and power cable. Moreover, high current operation also reduces reliability of the DC-link capacitors since paralleling of capacitor cells are needed sacrificing power density and cost.

Busbar design is an important design element for traction applications where the goal is to minimize the DC-loop inductance due to the inherent presence of parasitic components for enhanced system performance, reliability, and efficiency, as well as for reduced electromagnetic emissions. The commutation loop is formed by the DC-link capacitors, the conduction path inside the power module and the stray inductance on the busbar between them. A minimized loop inductance ensures constrained voltage overshoot on power semiconductor switches during power device turn-off which must be below the device voltage rating. The design is even more critical with WBG systems where higher operating frequencies are desired with attendant increase in signal edge rates. Low ESL DC-link capacitor, optimized busbar layout and high-performance module all help to reduce the loop inductance. The busbar form-factor and interconnection with power modules play significant roles in the overall system-level design.

There are a number of parasitic components in the inverter power stage that are unavoidable due to the busbars, circuit conductor traces, and connectors. An equivalent circuit model of parasitic inductances is shown in Figure 9.24 where $L_{DS}$ represents the lumped parasitic inductance of the power module and $L_{P1}$ and $L_{P2}$ are associated with the busbar. $L_{P3}$ and $L_{P4}$ denote the stray inductance between the input DC terminals to the capacitor/module terminals. The parasitic inductance in the loop consisting of a power module and DC-link storage capacitor is large because of their dimensions and a compensation may be required for EMI mitigation. Adding low ESL decoupling capacitor in close vicinity to the power module terminals is another effective method to reduce the loop inductance [7]. These decoupling capacitors are shown as a lumped parameter $C_{decoup}$ in the equivalent circuit of Figure 9.24. This arrangement creates two loops; with the decoupling capacitors placed close to the module terminal, the inductance of Loop 1 is significantly smaller than that of Loop 2. This effectively helps reduce the DC-loop inductance for the inverter. Busbar design adopting a central electrolytic DC-link capacitor can result in unsymmetrical commutation loops for different phases and cause the switch voltage overshoot as well as switching loss for one particular phase. Therefore, the commutation loops for the inverter should be designed as symmetrical as possible especially for high-power applications.

### 9.3.2.3   DC Bus Filtering

The DC bus voltage filtering components include the bulk capacitors for energy storage and the common mode and differential mode filters for EMI reductions. The inverter along with the filters, gate drive, sensors and controller are shown in Figure 9.25. As the battery-pack terminal is at a distance from the inverter, there will be a few microhenries of line inductance which necessitates a local energy storage in the inverter which is served by the bulk DC-link capacitors (denoted as $C_{bulk}$ in Figure 9.25). The DC-link bulk capacitor has to sink and source the ripple currents, which are caused by the PWM switching of the inverters to protect the battery and other components. The bulk capacitors used in automotive traction inverters are large polypropylene film capacitors chosen for the working voltage (1.2–1.5 times the DC-link nominal voltage), rms current, operating temperature, lifetime and parasitic inductance and resistance. The current requirements are obtained from different use cases such as high currents during acceleration or moderate currents over an extended time such as highway cruising on a steep grade over an extended duration. The vehicle-level simulation with a mission profile helps generate these requirements from the system-level consideration.

**FIGURE 9.24**   Commutations loops involving the DC-link capacitor and decoupling capacitor in a half-bridge configuration.

**FIGURE 9.25**   Traction inverter with associated filter components and controller.

The inverter power devices, the shielded AC cables and the motor all have significant parasitic capacitances to the ground which in the case of a vehicle is the chassis. The high $dv/dt$, i.e., the rate of change of voltage for each PWM switching event at the AC inverter terminals induces common mode (CM) pulses to the ground which cause severe EMI. To mitigate the EMI, CM filters are included within the inverter or busbar cabling in the form of a CM choke and Y-Caps (shown as $L_{CM}$ and $C_y$ in Figure 9.25); $L_{CM}$ and $C_y$ together work as a second-order noise filter to mitigate EMI. The amount of CM choke and Y-Caps allowed on the DC bus is, however, limited by the SAE 1772 DC charging [8].

The parasitic capacitance of the traction electric motor between its winding and chassis ground (denoted by $C_{p2}$ in Figure 9.25) can be significant typically in the range of 5–25 nF. In systems where the inverter and the motor are separated by a distance and connected through shielded AC cables, there will be additional parasitic capacitance. These capacitances and the switching $dv/dt$ from the PWM voltage waveforms of the inverter will result in significant common mode currents such as motor inter-turn currents and bearing currents which essentially has to be supplied by the inverter. This would lead to not only inverter losses and derating, but also insulation damage of the motor windings. An output filter with a CM choke can be placed before the motor terminals to mitigate the issue. However, the best solution is a tightly coupled packaging such as mounting the inverter directly to the motor housing as has been done in the Chevy Volt [9].

### 9.3.2.4 Gate Drive Design

The gate driver receives the PWM gating signals from the motor drive controller and buffers them to deliver to the gate of the power devices of the VSI with complete electrical isolation. As a critical part of the power converter system, the gate driver design requires isolation, driving capability, minimum delay and reliable operation. The motor controller is referenced to the vehicle chassis which is isolated from the high-voltage DC system. The gate driver provides this isolation and ensures that all the power device gate connections are floating with respect to the controller ground. A typical isolated gate driver block diagram is shown in Figure 9.26 which consists of control signal transfer, isolated bias power supply and driver stage that may include current booster circuit. This bias supply actually shares the same floating ground with the switching device, which poses stringent voltage isolation requirement especially for high-voltage applications. Appropriate voltage level needs to be maintained all the time and a negative bias is used to prevent $dv/dt$-induced turn-on. Meanwhile, the capacitive coupling across the isolation barrier also becomes critical, especially if SiC devices are used with their high switching $dv/dt$. As the power device is switching with high voltages, the isolated controller signals must be immune from those high-voltage transients. This immunity is characterized by the gate drive parameter called common mode noise immunity (CMTI) which is measured by kV/µs.

**FIGURE 9.26**   Block diagram of a typical isolated gate driver.

Another important functionality of the gate driver is to provide hardware-based fast fault protection. The protection features that are included in a gate drive circuit include desaturation, anti-shoot-through, overcurrent, undervoltage and over temperature. Desaturation protection prevents the power device from operating in the linear region which would cause tremendous power dissipation leading to its quick failure. The collector voltage (for IGBT) or drain voltage (for MOSFET) must remain below certain threshold value when the device is gated on. Desaturation protection provides one of the fastest ways to prevent device failure and is implemented by monitoring the collector or drain voltage using a comparator circuit. This is particularly useful for SiC MOSFETs which has very short duration short-circuit rating capability of around 2 μs. The short-circuit current duration capability for IGBT is around 10 μs. The anti-shoot-through protection is essential to prevent simultaneous turn-on of both the upper and lower device of a half-bridge phase leg; this protection is implemented using hardware circuits for fast response. Overcurrent protection is implemented in hardware with comparator circuits for the fastest response preventing the flow of more than the maximum current limit for the inverter. Undervoltage detection is used in the gate driver to ensure that there is always sufficient gate voltage so that the device is always in full saturation.

### 9.3.2.5 Controller and Sensors

The controller card, i.e., the electronic control module (ECM), for the motor drive houses the gate driver, the DSP that hosts the motor and inverter controller, the voltage and current sensors, and the interfaces to the vehicle control module. The control algorithm is entirely dependent on the current sensors and the rotor positions sensors.

Accurate and reliable current sensing is essential to maintain the integrity of the traction motor drive system. The current-sensed signal must be isolated from the current carrying conductor. The AC output terminals high-voltage switching voltages which require the current sensing circuit to have high noise immunity. An EV inverter maximum AC rms current can be as high as 1,000 A depending on the power rating and the DC-link voltage. The current sensors are placed in the bus bars which will have losses and increased temperature due to the high current flowing through them. Hence, high temperature capability, up to 125°C, is needed for the current sensors. Sensor bandwidth is also a critical parameter which is important for good closed loop control of the motor drive system. A bandwidth of 40 kHz or higher depending on the PWM switching frequency and with minimal phase shift up to the maximum fundamental frequency is required. The maximum fundamental frequency is typically in the range of 500–1,200 Hz depending on the electric machine pole number and the maximum operating speed. The key requirements for the current sensor are measurement range, accuracy, bandwidth, voltage isolation, noise immunity, temperature range, form factor, weight and cost. The current sensor circuit design must address offset, gain imbalance, delay and quantization. The types of current sensors that can be used are (i) Hall sensor, (ii) current transformer, (iii) resistive shunt and (iv) giant magneto resistive (GMR) sensor. The Hall sensors can be either with core or coreless and provides the highest accuracy measurement of all types of current sensors. The core-type Hall sensors are widely used as automotive traction inverter current sensors. The measured output signal is isolated from the current-carrying power conductors and the delay introduced is relatively small. Physical size and mass and limited measurement range due to finite core saturation are the drawback of these core-type Hall sensors. Coreless Hall sensors are emerging to overcome the drawbacks of core-type Hall sensors. Current transformers use the transformer principle as the name implies, and hence, can only be used for AC current measurement. The measurement is isolated but the accuracy is somewhat limited. The resistive shunts provide the easiest approach for all to be integrated into the power stage of the converter with small footprint. However, although the resistance value is small, there will be losses and a heatsink is needed for thermal management. The signal sensed has to be processed through an isolation barrier before being fed to the controller, which is always challenging due to the noise prone environment. A trade-off is needed between the losses and noise immunity while selecting the shunt. GMR

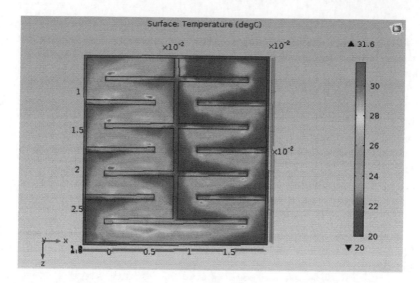

**FIGURE 9.27** Surface temperature simulation of turbulator cell beneath power module baseplate [5].

sensors are becoming attractive due to its small and compact form, high bandwidth and isolated measurement. GMR uses materials whose resistance varies depending on the magnitude of current flowing. The accuracy is lower than that of Hall sensors.

### 9.3.2.6 Thermal Design

Thermal design is critical for power electronic converters especially with high-power modules in integrated packaging. Power semiconductor devices and the passive components, specifically the inductors, in an electric drivetrain require cooling in order to operate below their fusing currents and maximum junction temperature. Ultimately, the more effectively heat can be extracted from the power modules and the inductors, the more current can be pushed through the electric drivetrain, resulting in higher power density design. Effective cooling also ensures long-term reliability as most failure mechanisms in electronics are due to the inability to remove heat from the active and passive components. Based on the planar, stacked structure design methodology, a cold plate can be mounted directly to the baseplate of the power modules to provide cooling. The heat distribution of a cooling approach based on ShowerPower cooling technique developed by Danfoss obtained from a thermal finite element simulation analysis is shown in Figure 9.27.

### Example 9.1

A SiC inverter is used to drive a traction motor using SVPWM from a battery-pack with 800 V nominal voltage. The inverter is made of Wolfspeed SiC CAB450M12XM3 MOSFET whose parameters are: $V_{DS} = 1,200$ V, $I_{DS} = 450$ A, $R_{ds,on} = 4.625$ m$\Omega$, $E_{on} = 11.7$ $\mu$J, and $E_{off} = 11.3$ $\mu$J. It is required to evaluate the power devices and the inverter performance for a given steady-state operating point of the traction AC motor. The operating point data are: Motor input power = 250 kW; $V_{DC} = 800$ V; modulation index $M = 0.907$ and power factor $\varphi = 0.7$. The junction temperature can be assumed to be 100°C for the simulation.

Using an equivalent electrical circuit representation for the AC electric motor in a simulation model, estimate the inverter power device thermal losses (conduction and switching).

### Solution

An equivalent circuit model representing the AC motor load for the given operating point can be derived in the form of a simplified $R$-$L$ model. This is obtained from the phase voltage and phase angle. The rms phase voltage can be calculated from the given data as

$$V_{phase} = M \frac{V_{DC}}{\sqrt{2}\sqrt{3}}$$

The motor equivalent resistance $R_{eq}$ is obtained from

$$R_{eq} = \frac{1}{3} \frac{V_{phase}^2}{P}$$

where $P$ = real power of the system (mechanical power); $V_{phase}$ = rms phase voltage;

The equivalent inductance $L_{eq}$ models the motor power factor which can be determined from

$$\text{Phase angle } \varphi = \tan^{-1} \left( \frac{\omega L_{eq}}{R_{eq}} \right)$$

The motor load is driven by a switching inverter model built in PSIM or PLECS to obtain the rms current and voltage across the power devices. The simulation model is shown in Figure 9.28. The resulting voltage and current waveforms are shown in Figure 9.29, which were obtained using SVPWM in a PSIM platform. The rms current and voltage across the power devices are then used to evaluate the dominant conduction and switching losses using device datasheet values of $R_{ds,on}$, $E_{on}$, $E_{off}$ under a certain junction temperature $(T_j)$.

The resulting data from simulation are: $P_{out} = 250.82$ kW, $P_{loss} = 2.19$ kW and inverter efficiency = 99.13%. Here, the device junction temperature $(T_j)$ has been assumed to be 100°C.

For evaluating the thermal stress on the device (i.e., the junction temperature rise), the device and heatsink thermal model can be implemented using given $R_{\theta(junction\text{-}case)}$ and $R_{\theta(heatsink)}$ values. For a coolant/ambient temperature $(T_{coolant})$, the junction temperature can be updated for the calculated losses in a dynamic simulation as shown in Figure 9.28. From the thermal stress imposed on the devices for the specific loading condition, the safe operation capability and efficiency can be determined to compare performance of the inverter using different power devices.

**FIGURE 9.28** Simulation model to evaluate power devices performance using equivalent motor model at a given operating point.

**FIGURE 9.29** PWM voltage and current waveforms obtained using SVPWM in PSIM.

### 9.3.3 High- to Low-Voltage DC/DC Converter

High- to low-voltage DC/DC converters are used in an EV/HEV to supply the 12 V electronics. The typical power rating of the high- to low-voltage DC/DC converter in mid-size electric or hybrid vehicles is around 2–3 kW. The low-voltage output supplies the 12 V electronics in the vehicle. The 12 V ground is always connected to the vehicle chassis; hence, the requirement for this converter topology is to be of isolated type. The converter topology used for this application is typically the full-bridge type with either the diode with a center tap as shown in Figure 9.30 or synchronous rectifiers. The switching frequency of this converter used in EV/HEV is around 100 kHz.

The HV to 12 V converter is unidirectional in most EV/HEV, although there are certain advantages of using a bi-directional converter. The converter in Figure 9.30 can easily be converted into a bi-directional topology by replacing the two diodes with two controlled switches.

The alternative is often used for cost minimization, since the diodes carry large currents and are expensive. The appropriate control of the secondary switches allows the topology to be operated in the boost mode with power flowing from the low-voltage side to the high-voltage side. The use of switches is also more efficient than using diodes. The boost mode operation of this 12 V-HV DC/DC converter facilitates the elimination of the 12 V starter in hybrid electric vehicles. The hybrid vehicles have a high-power electric machine that can start the engine more efficiently and much faster than the conventional 12 V starter. When boost mode operation is available, additional starting power is available to the high-power electric machine from the 12 V battery under extreme starting conditions such as during cold cranking. In extreme cold situations, the HV battery may not be able to provide all of the engine cranking power; in that situation the 12 V battery can supplement the additional power required through the 12 V-HV converter operated in the boost mode. Also, the boost operation may enable some functions on the HV side, if the HV battery fails.

### 9.3.4 On-Board Battery Charger

A vehicle's OBC connects to a residential or commercial single-phase AC supply either at 110 or 240 VAC or to a commercial 400 VDC fast charger. The OBCs can be designed as a universal component that can be plugged to either a single-phase AC source or a three-phase AC-source with

**FIGURE 9.30** High voltage to 12 V DC/DC converter with sensors and controller.

capability of handling a wide input voltage range and supplying a regulated output voltage to the vehicle battery pack based on the battery state-of-charge.

Currently used OBCs are based on cascaded design of two converters with the front-end converting the grid AC voltage into an intermediate DC voltage (typically up to 400 V level), while the second stage is an isolated DC/DC converter with a large DC-link storage capacitor in between to filter the AC grid frequency. Two topologies are popular for the front-end converter, one is the interleaved power factor correction (PFC) boost converter with a diode bridge and the second is a bridgeless PFC boost converter. The two topologies are shown in Figure 9.31. The efficiency of the two converters are about the same with both being around 98% with Si IGBTs, but the current and voltage sensing requirements are more complex in the bridgeless PFC topology. The filter components for EMI also tend to be larger for the bridgeless PFC topology.

Multiple topologies are suitable for the DC/DC stage of the OBC such as the phase shifted full-bridge (PSFB) and the LLC resonant converters, with the former being the most popular among the automotive industries. The PSFB uses a fixed frequency PWM with a control technique to allow zero voltage switching (ZVS) of the power devices. ZVS helps reduce the switching losses and also helps with the EMI reduction. The LLC resonant converter topology enables both ZVS and zero current switching (ZCS) virtually eliminating all switching losses for the entire operating range. This loss reduction helps achieve about 3% efficiency gain over the PSFB. The control is somewhat more complex for the resonant LLC compared to the PSFB, but the EMI filtering requirements are less. Chevy Volt Gen 1 used the PSFB topology, but in Gen 2, the topology was switched to the LLC resonant converter [10].

The design objectives for an OBC include power density, high efficiency, performance, reliability and cost. High power density is desirable for the OBC similar to any other power component for electric vehicles. Small form factor and high power density allow the vehicle maker to have more usable space for the customer and decrease the overall vehicle mass. High efficiency also contributes to power density in addition to reducing the energy loss from the power drawn from the AC grid.

The circuit schematic of a typical battery charger used in electric and plug-in hybrid vehicles including the sensor and controller IC blocks is shown in Figure 9.32. The circuit consists of a bridge rectifier at the input followed by a PFC circuit, and then a full-bridge DC/DC converter. The interleaved boost DC/DC converter is shown as the PFC circuit in the battery charger. The boost converter is used in the boundary conduction mode (BCM) to minimize the losses and the cost for the diodes. In BCM, the MOSFET on time is kept fixed, but the off-time is varied and the new switching interval starts as soon as the inductor current reaches zero. With the MOSFET turned on for a fixed time, the peak inductor current is proportional to the input voltage. The average current in each switching interval is proportional to the input voltage, since the current waveform is triangular in shape. If the input voltage is sinusoidal, the input current follows the sinusoidal waveform

**FIGURE 9.31**    Front-end topologies for OBC: (a) interleaved PFC topology and (b) bridgeless PFC topology.

**FIGURE 9.32**  OBC circuit topology.

with highly accurate consumption of sinusoidal current from the source. The two interleaved boost DC/DC converters in the PFC circuit are synchronized with the other with a 180° phase shift. With this interleaved topology, the high-frequency ripple currents cancel and the EMI filter requirements are reduced.

## 9.4  CELL-BALANCING CONVERTERS

The individual battery cell voltages as well as the charge will vary in a series-connected string as the entire battery-pack goes through charge-discharge cycles. The charge imbalance in a series connected string of cells reduces the overall capacity as well as the average life of the pack. Battery cell charge equalization is used to avoid long-term imbalance. Individualized cell-balancing methods monitor and balance the charge or the voltage during charging and discharging of an electrochemical pack using passive or active components. The cell-balancing electronics can also monitor *SoC* and/or voltage during discharge so that the capacity of the pack is not limited by the weakest cell in the string. The overall cell management methods were discussed earlier in Chapter 4. In this section, the power electronics included in the balancing electronics are presented. Some of the cell-balancing circuits is dissipative in nature, while others use DC/DC converter circuits to transfer charges from one cell to another or between a cell and the supply. Based on the operational feature, the balancing methods can be classified broadly into two types: Passive or dissipative balancing methods and active or non-dissipative balancing methods. The two types of cell-balancing circuits are discussed below.

### 9.4.1  PASSIVE BALANCING METHODS

In passive balancing methods, the individual cell voltages are equalized by either dissipating the excess energy or providing a shunt path to bypass the charging current. In the most common approaches, a dissipative component such as a resistor or a zener diode is connected across a cell to prevent overcharging of the cell. The dissipative resistors connected directly across each cell will always draw currents from the cells as shown in Figure 9.33a, but a large resistor value is used so that the current bleeding is minimal. The value of the resistor is chosen to ensure that charges are equalized during both cell charging and discharging. The magnitude of the current drawn by the resistor is larger for the higher voltage cells; the cells with higher voltages discharges faster and the current gradually decreases as the voltage drops. All the cells in the series string achieve balance through this power dissipation in the resistors.

An improvement over the continuous dissipation in the resistors can be achieved by adding a switch in series with the resistor as shown in Figure 9.33b [11]. The switch can be realized using a

**FIGURE 9.33**  Passive cell voltage equalization: (a) resistive shunt, (b) resistor with switch and (c) analog shunt equalization.

MOSFET or a BJT. Each cell voltage is measured and monitored to control the turn-on and turn-off of the switches. Cell voltage monitoring and control of switches can be done centrally by a micro-processor. During cell charging, all the switches will remain open initially. Once a cell voltage reaches its limit, the switch for that cell is turned on and the charging current is bypassed through the resistor. The switched resistor method minimizes the loss in the resistors, but adds cost and com-plexity of the switches, voltage sensors and the central processor. The use of a central processor can be avoided by using a local analog shunt electronic circuit as shown in Figure 9.33c [12]. An elec-tronic circuit monitors and compares each cell voltage against a reference value, which is set to the limit of the cell voltage. When the cell reaches the reference voltage, the op-amp comparator turns the Darlington switch connecting the resistor $R$ in parallel to the cell. The current is proportionally shunted through the resistor, and the cell is charged at a constant voltage thereafter. The battery-pack charging continues until all the cells are completely charged. The analog shunt equalization circuit can balance the voltage of even highly unmatched cells, and is completely local to each cell.

The cell-balancing circuits using zener diodes are shown in Figure 9.34. In one method, a sharp-knee zener clamping diode is connected across each cell or a group of cells to provide a current shunt path for cell voltage equalization. The balancing circuit is shown in Figure 9.34a. The minimum available zener voltage is higher than the voltage of most electrochemical cells; hence, a zener has

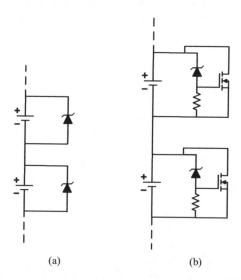

**FIGURE 9.34**  Passive cell voltage equalization: (a) zener diode clamping and (b) zener with switch.

to be connected across at least a pair of cells. The zeners break down when the cell voltages reach the zener breakdown voltage, clamping the voltage across two or more cells to the zener breakdown voltage. The drawback of the method is the large power dissipation when the zener diode clamps the cell voltage, especially when the cell is being recharged with high charging currents.

An analog equalization method can be designed with a shunt transistor switch and zener diode is shown in Figure 9.34b. The zener clamping diode breaks down when the cell voltage reaches its upper limit. The zener diode and resistor circuit then provides the turn-on signal for the transistor switch, which then bypasses the charging current. The entire equalization circuitry is local and there is no need for a central processor.

The main drawback of the passive methods is the wastage of energy in the dissipative components. Additionally, relatively high currents may need to be bypassed through the equalizing circuit for cell balancing. The components in the analog balancing circuitry also have strong dependence on temperature, which may not be tolerable. These methods are otherwise less expensive and easier to implement.

## 9.4.2 ACTIVE BALANCING METHODS

In active cell-balancing methods, non-dissipative elements (capacitors and inductors) are used in conjunction with switches to selectively transfer energy from the overcharging cells to the undercharged cells. The electronic switches and associated circuitry actively controls the turn-on and turn-off of the switches to transfer energy among cells. A central microprocessor monitors the pack and cell conditions to control the switches for cell voltage equalization. The current charge/discharge rates in energy storage systems of electric and hybrid vehicles are fairly high with short durations. Consequently, the charge equalization currents could be of the same order of magnitude. The charge transfer among the cells using non-dissipative elements for cell equalization minimizes the energy losses in electric and hybrid vehicles. The active balancing circuits are more complex and difficult to implement, but ensures the highest possible charge/discharge efficiency. In some active balancing methods, charges are locally redistributed among neighboring cells for cell voltage equalization, while in more complex methods charges are globally redistributed relative to a constant reference voltage.

The concept of cell balancing using transfer of energy from the strongest cell to the weakest cell can be explained using a switched capacitor network. The circuit schematic of a switched capacitor network for N-number of cells with a pair of generic switches and a flying capacitor across each battery cell is shown in Figure 9.35 [13]. Each neighboring cells has a similar circuit. The equalizer needs single-pole, double-throw (SPDT) switches. The switches can be implemented using two transistor switches, zener diodes and transformer; alternative transformerless SPDT implementations are also possible, which are given in [13]. The transformer-coupled switches are desirable

**FIGURE 9.35**  Switched capacitor circuit.

for equalizers that have high isolation requirements. The charge from one cell can be transferred to the neighboring cell of lower voltage using the flying capacitors. For example, when cell 1 in the figure reaches its limit, flying capacitor $C_1$ across $Sw_1$ and $Sw_2$ are connected to the top rails until $C_1$ is charged to the level of cell 1 voltage. The voltage of cell 1 drops by a small amount in the process. The switch network then connects $C_1$ to cell 2 to bring up its voltage to the same level. Using this charge pump technique, charges can be transferred across neighboring cells, and subsequently to distant cells to balance the entire pack. The disadvantage of the method is that the voltages are equalized with neighboring cells rather than with respect to a reference voltage. This charge transfer technique is inherently slow for a long series string of cells.

Charge can be transferred among the battery cells using DC/DC converters instead of routing them through flying capacitors. The degree of cell voltage equalization and efficiency of charge transfer depend on the type of DC/DC converter circuit used [14,15]. Also, charges can be transferred to distant or neighboring cells depending on the circuit topology used. Three categories of DC/DC converter-based cell-balancing circuits are discussed; these are: (i) individual DC/DC converter, (ii) centralized DC/DC converter and (iii) current diverter DC/DC converter.

### 9.4.2.1 Individual DC/DC Converter

The charge equalization method using isolated DC-DC converters is shown in Figure 9.36a. The DC-DC converters can be unidirectional transferring energy only in one direction from the overcharged cell to the battery DC-bus during charging or can be bi-directional transferring energy back and forth from the unbalanced cells to the battery-pack DC-bus or to other cells. The method is highly efficient and precisely regulates the voltage across each cell. However, the high component count with individual DC/DC converters for each cell increases the cost of cell-balancing circuitry. The DC/DC converter modules can be connected across a group of cells instead of individual cells for large battery systems, such as that in electric and hybrid vehicles.

A unidirectional flyback DC-DC converter module for a group of cells is shown in Figure 9.36b. When an overvoltage is detected in the group of cells, the excess energy is transferred to the DC-bus by PWM control of the transistor switch allowing precise regulation of the cell voltage. The control of the switch can be either from a central microprocessor or a simple comparator with a preset voltage. The isolation transformer turns-ratio must satisfy the condition $a \leq N$, where $N$ is the number of cell groups. A bi-directional flyback DC–DC converter circuit for cell voltage equalization is shown in Figure 9.36c. The bi-directional cell equalization circuit transfers energy during both charging and discharging, thereby increasing pack utilization and enhancing cell life. Energy can be transferred in either direction by controlling the two switches of each module. Cell equalization

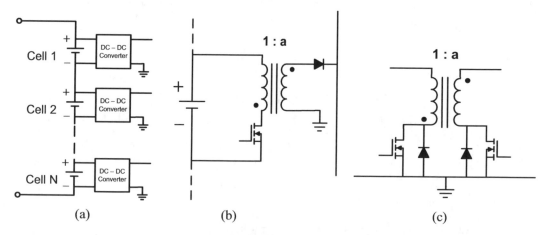

**FIGURE 9.36** Active cell voltage equalization with: (a) isolated DC-DC converters, (b) unidirectional flyback converter and (c) bi-directional flyback converter.

during charging takes place the same way as with the flyback DC-DC converter with the anti-parallel diode of the switch conducting during energy transfer from the magnetization inductance to the DC-bus. The transistor switch on the DC-bus side is turned off during this mode. During pack discharging, energy can be transferred from the DC-bus to the weaker cells by PWM control of the converter switch on the DC-bus side thus maintaining cell voltage equalization.

### 9.4.2.2 Centralized DC/DC Converter

The control and hardware complexity with individual DC-DC converters can be simplified by using a centralized flyback or forward DC-DC converter built with a multi-winding transformer [14,15]. A flyback converter configuration with centralized DC/DC converter is shown in Figure 9.37a. The primary of the transformer is connected to the DC-bus, while the secondaries are distributed among $N$ group of cells. The isolation transformer turns-ratio must satisfy the condition $a \leq N$,

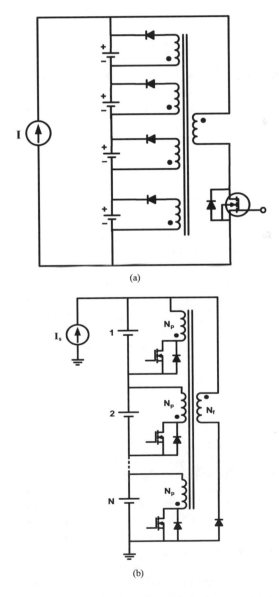

(a)

(b)

**FIGURE 9.37** Charge equalization with: (a) centralized flyback converter and (b) centralized forward converter.

where $N$ is the number of cell groups. The cell equalizing circuit is designed to transfer energy from the battery-pack to the weaker cells that have the undervoltages. The centralized DC/DC converter uses only one switch that is kept off until a weak cell is detected. When undervoltage is detected in one of the cells or cell groups during charging, the switch is turned on to transfer pack energy to the magnetizing inductance of the transformer. Once the magnetizing inductance is charged, the switch is turned off and the charging currents are automatically steered to the cell equalizer circuit segment that has the lowest voltage at the cathode of its diode. In the ideal case, the largest portion of the stored energy will be transferred to the cells with the lowest voltage without any additional control. Thus, the flyback converter preferentially transfers the energy to the cell with the lowest voltage. The charge transfer continues until all the cell voltages are equalized. In practice, transformer parasitics, especially the transformer's leakage inductance dictates the distribution of the magnetizing inductance stored energy among the cells. The transformer leakage inductance $L_{ls}$ is the main component for controlling the charging current. The charging current is given by

$$I_{ch}(t) = \frac{V_{bat} - aV_{bx}}{L_{ls}} t \qquad (9.5)$$

where $V_{bat}$ is the total battery voltage and $V_{bx}$ is the cell-group module voltage.

The practical difficulty is the matching of all the leakage inductances among the secondary windings. The co-axial winding transformers can be used for these converters to tightly control the parasitics [15].

Forward converters and a multi-winding transformer, as shown in Figure 9.37b, can also be used to transfer energy from the overcharged cells to the weak cell-group modules. When a cell group becomes overcharged, the corresponding DC-DC converter module switch is turned on to transfer the energy from that cell to the others via the magnetizing inductance of the transformer. Energy is transferred from the overcharged module to the weaker modules with the most energy diverted to the lowest voltage module. The charge transfer current is directly proportional to the difference between the terminal voltages of the overcharged module and the weaker module, and inversely proportional to the leakage inductance in the secondary windings similar to Equation 9.5. Consequently, the lowest-voltage cell group accepts the most charge. The leakage inductance plays a critical role in determining the charge transfer currents. The winding $N_f$ and the diode $D_f$ provides a guaranteed reset path when all the active switches are turned-off and there is still stored energy left in the magnetizing inductance. The diodes of the modules also turn-off when all the switches are off. The residual energy in that case is returned to the pack DC-bus through diode $D_f$. The turns ratio between the reset winding and the module windings is given by

$$a = \frac{N_f}{N_m} \leq N$$

where $N$ is the number of batter cell-group modules.

### 9.4.2.3 Current Diverter DC/DC Converter

The current diverter cell equalization circuits transfer energy to the neighboring cells using DC/DC converters [14]. A current diverter circuit that can only transfer energy downward through a stack of series connected cells is shown in Figure 9.38a. Each diverter module consists of a MOSFET switch, a diode and an energy storage element. A flyback converter module is necessary for the last cell group to transfer excess energy back to the battery pack when required.

A bi-directional current diverter circuit topology is shown in Figure 9.38b with two MOSFET switches and an inductor per module. Charge can be transferred to the cell either above or below an overcharged cell. There is also no need for a separate flyback module for the last cell. The diverter modules along with two corresponding pack cell groups form a half-bridge converter feeding an inductive load. During normal operation, the diverter modules are disabled. When a cell group is

(a)                                                                    (b)

**FIGURE 9.38**   Current diverter circuits: (a) unidirectional and (b) bi-directional.

overcharged, the corresponding MOSFET switch is turned on to transfer energy from the cell group to the inductor. When the switch is turned off, the stored energy in the inductor transfers to the cell group up or down the stack depending on the location of the inductor.

## REFERENCES

1. B.J. Baliga, *Power Semiconductor Devices*, PWS Publishing Company, Boston, MA, 1995.
2. J.G. Kassakian, M.F. Schlecht and G.C. Verghese, *Principles of Power Electronics*, Addison Wesley Publishing Company, Reading, MA, 1991.
3. I. Batarseh, *Power Electronic Circuits*, John Wiley & Sons Inc., Hoboken, NJ, 2004.
4. D. Rahman, A. Morgan, R. Gao, W. Yu, D.C. Hopkins and I. Husain, "Design methodology for a planarized high power density EV/HEV traction drive using SiC power modules," *IEEE Energy Conversion Congress & Expo (ECCE2016)*, Milwaukee, WI, September 2016.
5. M.A. Awal, D. Rahman, Y. Luo, W. Yu and I. Husain, "Dynamic interleaving of multi-phase synchronous DC-DC converters with ZVS," *Applied Power Electronics Conference (APEC2019)*, Anaheim, CA, March 2019.
6. R.M. Schupbach and J.C. Balda, "Comparing DC-DC converters for power management in hybrid electric vehicles," *IEEE International Electric Machines and Drives Conference*, 3, 1369–1374, June 2003.
7. R. Sree Krishna, B. Aberg, M. Olimmah, L. Yang, D. Rahman, A.N. Lemmon, W. Yu and I. Husain, "Estimation, minimization, and validation of commutation loop inductance for a 135 kW SiC EV traction inverter," *IEEE Journal of Emerging and Selected Topics in Power Electronics*, 8(1), 286–297, 2020.
8. S.E. Shultz, "Exploring the high-power inverter," *IEEE Electrification Magazine*, 5(1), 28–35, March 2017.
9. M. Anwar, M. Hayes, A. Tata, M. Teimorzadeh and T. Achatz, "Power dense and robust traction inverter for the second-generation Chevrolet volt extended-range EV," *SAE International Journal on Alternative Power*, 4(1), 145–152, 2015.
10. D. Cesiel and C. Zhu, "A closer look at the on-board charger," *IEEE Electrification Magazine*, 5(1), 36–42, March 2017.
11. M.J. Isaacson, R.P. Hollandsworth, P.J. Giampaoli, F.A. Linkowsky, A. Salim and V.L. Teofilo, "Advanced lithium ion battery charger," *The Fifteenth Annual IEEE Battery Conference on Applications and Advances*, pp. 193–198, Long Beach, CA, January 2000.

12. Y. Eguchi, H. Okada, K. Murano and A. Sanpei (inventors), Sony Corporation (assignee), Battery Protection Circuit, US patent 5,530,336, 1993.
13. C. Pascual and P.T. Krein, "Switched capacitor system for automatic series battery equalization," *IEEE Applied Power Electronics Conference*, Twelfth Annual, 2, 848–854, February 1999.
14. N.H. Kutkut and M. Deepak Divan, "Dynamic equalization techniques for series battery stacks," *IEEE Telecommunications Energy Conference*, pp. 514–521, Boston, MA, October 1996.
15. N.H. Kutkut, H.L.N. Wiegman, D.M. Divan and D.W. Novotny, "Charge equalization for an electric vehicle battery system," *IEEE Transactions on Aerospace and Electronic Systems*, 34(1), 235–246, January 1998.

# 10 Electric Motor Drives

The electric motor drive is the integrated power electronic converter and motor controller that processes and controls the electrical energy flowing from the source to the electric machine or vice versa in response to a user demand. In a BEV, the drive converts the stiff DC battery voltage to either a DC voltage for DC motors or an AC voltage for AC motors. The controller generates the gating signals for the power electronic circuit devices based on the driver input command, the sensor feedback signals and the control algorithm for the type of electric machine used. The driver input is translated into a torque command for the motor drive. The torque command in conjunction with the feedback signals set up the operating point parameters for the electric motor and accordingly controls the turn-on and turn-off of the power switches inside the drive system. The drive controller includes the inverter control modulation scheme in the case of AC drives to convert the motor control current commands into gate signals for the power converter. During vehicle propulsion, the motor drive delivers power at the desired voltage and frequency to the motor, which in turn provides the desired torque at the wheels. During regeneration, the motor drive processes power flow from the wheels to the energy storage system.

## 10.1 ELECTRIC DRIVE COMPONENTS

A motor drive consists of a power electronic converter and the associated controller. The power electronic converter handles the flow of bulk power from the source to the motor input terminals. The function of the controller is to process information and generate the switching signals for the power converter semiconductor switches. The interaction between the components of the motor drive with the source and the electric motor is shown schematically in Figure 10.1. The power converter can be either a DC drive supplying a DC motor or an AC drive supplying an AC motor. The converter functions of the two types of drives are shown in Figure 10.2. A power converter is made of high-power fast-acting semiconductor devices, such as those discussed in Chapter 9. The tremendous advances in the power semiconductor technology over the past two decades enabled the development of compact, efficient and reliable DC and AC electric motor drives. The commonly used power device for the electric motor drive in electric and hybrid vehicles is the IGBT.

The drive controller manages and processes the system information to control the flow of power in the electric drivetrain. The controller acts on the command input from the user while following a motor control algorithm such as those discussed in Chapter 8. The motor drive for the electric powertrain requires fast response characteristics with high efficiency; hence, these fall under the category of high-performance drives. These motor drive control algorithms are computationally intensive requiring faster processors and interfacing with a relatively higher number of feedback signals. The modern controllers are digital instead of analog, which helps minimize drift and error and improves performance through their capability of processing complex algorithms in a short time. The controllers are essentially an embedded system where microprocessors and digital signal processors are used for signal processing along with peripherals and interface electronic modules. The interface circuits consisting of A/D and D/A converters are required for communication between the processor and the other components of the system. The digital I/O circuitry brings in the digital input signals and carries out the gate driver signals for the power semiconductor devices. Further details of the controller hardware will be discussed in Chapter 11.

The chapter discusses the DC and AC drives used for controlling the power flow and energy conversion in electric machines with emphasis to those used in electric and hybrid vehicle propulsion. Although DC machines are complex in construction, the DC drives are much simpler than their AC

**FIGURE 10.1**  Block diagram of a motor drive.

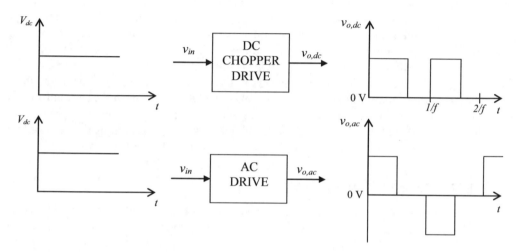

**FIGURE 10.2**  DC-DC and DC-AC converter functions.

counterparts. The simpler DC drive models serve as a useful tool in understanding the interaction between the propulsion system and the vehicle road load. On the other hand, the complexity of AC motor drives is in the drive system, although the AC electric machines are less complicated than the DC machines. The AC drives use a standard six switch inverter topology and a PWM strategy to generate the three-phase sinusoidal waveforms in the machines. The switched reluctance motor (SRM) drives require an asymmetric half-bridge power converter topology which is discussed toward the end of the chapter.

## 10.2  DC DRIVES

The DC drives for electric and hybrid vehicle applications are the DC/DC converters, such as DC choppers, resonant converters or isolated full-bridge converters. DC choppers are more commonly used for the propulsion DC electric motor drives. A two-quadrant chopper will be analyzed in this chapter as a representative DC drive. The simplicity of the two-quadrant chopper and the torque-speed characteristics of the separately excited DC motor will be used to present the interaction of a power electronic motor drive and the vehicle road load. The details on various other types of DC drives can be found in several textbooks on electric motor drives [1–4].

### 10.2.1  Two-Quadrant Chopper

The two-quadrant DC chopper allows bi-directional current and power flow with unidirectional voltage supply. The schematic of a two-quadrant chopper is shown in Figure 10.3. The motor current $i_0$ is inductive current, and therefore cannot change instantaneously. The transistor $Q_1$ and diode

**FIGURE 10.3** DC electric motor drive.

$D_1$ combined make the bi-directional current switch $S_1$. Similarly, switch $S_2$ is made of transistor $Q_2$ and diode $D_2$. The on and off conditions of the two switches make four switching states (SWS), two of which are allowed and two are restricted as shown in Table 10.1. In the allowed switching states SWS1 and SWS2, the switches $S_1$ and $S_2$ have to withstand positive voltage when they are off and both positive and negative currents when they are on. Therefore, bi-directional current switches have been used.

In quadrant 1 operation, turning on $Q_1$ allows current and power to flow from the battery to the motor. Both the motor terminal voltage $v_o$ and current $i_o$ are greater than or equal to zero. $Q_2$ is required to remain continuously off in quadrant 1 operation, and hence, $i_{b2} = 0$. When $Q_1$ turns off $D_2$ turns on, since $i_0$ is continuous. Quadrant 1 operation takes place during the acceleration and constant velocity cruising of a vehicle. The chopper operating modes toggle between switching states 1 and 2 in this quadrant as shown in Figure 10.4.

**TABLE 10.1**
**Switching States of Two-Quadrant Chopper**

| Switching State | $S_1$ | $S_2$ | Comments |
|---|---|---|---|
| SWS0 | 0 (OFF) | 0 (OFF) | Not applicable in CCM, since $i_0$ is inductive |
| SWS1 | 0 | 1 (ON) | $v_0 = 0$; $v_{S1} = v_{IN}$ (allowed) $i_{IN} = 0$; $i_{S2} = -i_0$ |
| SWS2 | 1 | 0 | $v_0 = v_{IN}$; $v_{S2} = v_{IN}$ (allowed) $i_{IN} = i_0$; $i_{S1} = i_0$ |
| SWS3 | 1 | 1 | Not allowed since $v_{IN}$ will get shorted |

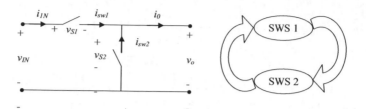

**FIGURE 10.4**   Quadrant I operation.

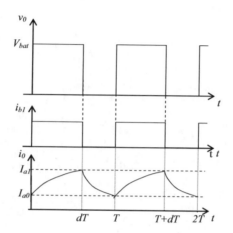

**FIGURE 10.5**   Output voltage, gate drive for $Q_1$ and motor current.

The transistor $Q_1$ switches at fixed chopper frequency to maintain the desired current and torque output of the DC motor. The motor current $i_0$ is shown in Figure 10.5 with exaggerated ripple, where in practice the ripple magnitude is much smaller compared to the average value of $i_0$. The filtering requirements set the time period of switching such that a smooth current and torque output is available. The output of the outer-loop vehicle controller desiring a specific torque output of the motor is the duty ratio $d$, which sets the on-time of the transistor $Q_1$. $d$ is a number between 0 and 1, which when multiplied by the time period $T$ gives the on-time of the transistor. The gate drive signal for $Q_1$ is a function of $d$, and consequently, assuming ideal switching conditions, the input voltage to the motor is also dependent on $d$. The circuit configurations in the allowed switching states are shown in Figure 10.6 to aid the steady-state analysis of the drive system. The steady-state analysis is carried out assuming the ideal conditions that there are no switching losses and no delay in the turn-on and turn-off of the devices.

## 10.2.2   Open Loop Drive

From a systems perspective, the two-quadrant chopper drives the DC motor that delivers power to the transmission and wheels for vehicle propulsion as shown in Figure 10.7. The input to the system comes from the driver of the vehicle through the acceleration pedal and the brake pedal. The acceleration and constant speed cruising is controlled by $Q_1$ in quadrant 1 operation, while braking is controlled by $Q_2$ in quadrant 2 operation. In a simplified vehicle control strategy, the slope of the acceleration pedal dictates the desired vehicle response and the angle of the pedal is used to set the duty ratio $d_1$ for $Q_1$. The drive signals for the two switches are shown in Figure 10.8. Similarly, the slope of the brake pedal relates to the amount of braking desired and the angle of the brake pedal is used to set the duty ratio $d_2$ for $Q_2$. The two pedals must not be depressed simultaneously.

**FIGURE 10.6**    Circuit condition for (a) switch $Q_1$ on and (b) for switch $Q_1$ off.

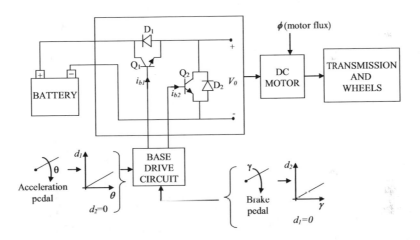

**FIGURE 10.7**    Open loop drive for bi-directional power flow.

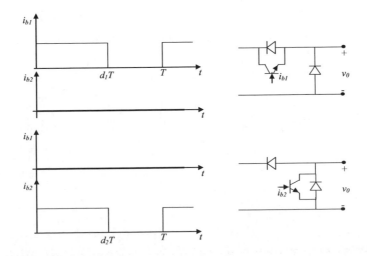

**FIGURE 10.8**    Base drive signals for the two transistors during acceleration and regeneration.

As mentioned in Chapter 7, one of the advantages of using electric motors for vehicle propulsion is to save energy during vehicle braking through regeneration. The energy from the wheels is processed by the power converter and delivered to the battery or any other type of energy storage device during regenerative braking. For the two-quadrant chopper, the amount of regeneration per cycle is a function of the duty ratio as will be shown later. Therefore, the real duty ratio commands of an electric or hybrid vehicle will be non-linearly related to the pedal angle than is assumed in the simplified analysis to follow. However, the simplistic assumption will give a good insight into the system control.

### 10.2.2.1  Steady-State Analysis of Quadrant 1

During acceleration of the vehicle with the two-quadrant chopper, the power and the current flow into the motor from source. The current can be continuous or discontinuous depending on the required torque, although the average value of the current is a non-zero positive value. These two scenarios give the two modes of operation of the two-quadrant chopper, namely, the continuous conduction mode (CCM) and the discontinuous conduction mode (DCM). Let us first analyze the CCM by assuming that the required torque and the chopping frequency to propel the vehicle forward are high enough to maintain a positive current into the motor continuously as shown in Figure 10.5. The current $i_o$ is the armature current. Therefore, $i_o = i_a$. Neglecting ripple in the back-emf $E$ due to ripple in $\omega$, we can assume that $E$ is a constant.

During $0 \leq t \leq dT$, the equivalent circuit of the motor is shown in Figure 10.9. Applying Kirchhoff's voltage law (KVL) around the circuit loop,

$$V_{bat} = R_a i_a + L_a \frac{di_a}{dt} + E$$

The initial condition is $i_a(0) = I_{a0} > 0$. This is a first-order linear differential equation solving which one gets

$$i_a(t) = \frac{V_{bat} - E}{R_a}\left(1 - e^{-t/\tau}\right) + I_{a0}e^{-t/\tau}.$$

The final condition of SWS2 is

$$i_a(dT) = \frac{V_{bat} - E}{R_a}\left(1 - e^{-dT/\tau}\right) + I_{a0}e^{-dT/\tau} = I_{a1}. \tag{10.1}$$

During $dT < t \leq T$, the equivalent circuit of the motor is as shown in Figure 10.10.
   Let $t' = t - dT$. Applying KVL,

$$0 = R_a I_a + L_a \frac{di_a}{dt} + E.$$

Solving the linear differential equation,

**FIGURE 10.9**   Equivalent circuit with $Q_1$ on.

**FIGURE 10.10** Equivalent circuit when $Q_2$ is off.

$$i_a(t') = -\frac{E}{R_a} + \left(I_{a1} + \frac{E}{R_a}\right)e^{-t'/\tau} = \frac{E}{R_a}\left(-1 + e^{-t'/\tau}\right) + I_{a1}e^{-t'/\tau}.$$

In steady state, $i_a(t' = T - dT) = I_{a0}$. Therefore,

$$I_{a0} = \frac{E}{R_a}\left(-1 + e^{-T(1-d)/\tau}\right) + I_{a1}e^{-T(1-d)/\tau}. \tag{10.2}$$

Using Equations 10.1 and 10.2 to solve for $I_{a0}$ and $I_{a1}$, we get

$$I_{a0} = \frac{V_{bat}}{R_a}\left(\frac{e^{dT/\tau} - 1}{e^{T/\tau} - 1}\right) - \frac{E}{R_a},$$

$$I_{a1} = \frac{V_{bat}}{R_a}\left(\frac{1 - e^{-dT/\tau}}{1 - e^{-T/\tau}}\right) - \frac{E}{R_a}.$$

The armature current ripple is

$$\Delta i_a = I_{a1} - I_{a0}$$

$$= \frac{V_{bat}}{R_a}\left[\frac{1 + e^{T/\tau} - e^{dT/\tau} - e^{(1-d)T/\tau}}{e^{T/\tau} - 1}\right]. \tag{10.3}$$

If the armature current $i_a$ has ripple, motor torque $T_e$ will have ripple, since the motor torque is proportional to the armature current ($T_e = K\varphi i_a$). The speed is also proportional to the electromagnetic torque (see Equation 7.16 in Chapter 7). Therefore, for electric and hybrid vehicle applications, significant ripple in $T_e$ is undesirable, since ripple in torque causes ripple in speed $\omega$, resulting in a bumpy ride. For a smooth ride, ripple in $T_e$ needs to be reduced.

### 10.2.2.2 Ripple Reduction in $i_a$

The armature current ripple can be reduced in one of two ways: (i) adding a series armature resistance and (ii) increasing the chopper switching frequency.

Adding a series inductance in the armature increases the electric time constant $\tau$. The new time constant is

$$\tau = \frac{L_f + L_a}{R_a}$$

where $L_f$ is the added series inductance (Figure 10.11). As $\tau$ increases, $\Delta i_a$ decreases for fixed switching period $T$. The trade-off is the increase in $i^2R$ losses due to $L_f$, since practical inductances has series resistance. Also, the electrical response time will increase due to the increase in the time constant.

**FIGURE 10.11** Series inductance $L_f$ added in series with the chopper.

Increasing the switching frequency of the chopper, i.e., decreasing $T$ will also reduce the arma-ture current ripple. The upper limit on switching frequency depends on type of switch used. The switching frequency must also be smaller than the controller computational cycle time, which depends on the speed of the processor used and the complexity of the control algorithm. The trade-off of using a higher switching frequency is the higher switching losses in the power devices.

### 10.2.2.3  Acceleration (Continuous Conduction Mode, CCM)

In the acceleration mode, the current and the power are flowing into the motor from the battery or energy source. The condition for CCM mode is

$$I_{a0} > 0 \Rightarrow I_{a0} = \frac{V_{bat}}{R_a}\left(\frac{e^{d_1 T/\tau}-1}{e^{T/\tau}-1}\right) - \frac{E}{R_a} > 0$$

$$\Rightarrow V_{bat}\left(\frac{e^{d_1 T/\tau}-1}{e^{T/\tau}-1}\right) > E.$$

Note that $0 \le \dfrac{e^{d_1 T/\tau}-1}{e^{T/\tau}-1} \le 1$, since $0 \le d_1 \le 1$. It follows that $V_{bat} > V_{bat}\left(\dfrac{e^{d_1 T/\tau}-1}{e^{T/\tau}-1}\right)$. Therefore, the condition for CCM is

$$V_{bat} \ge V_{bat}\left(\frac{e^{d_1 T/\tau}-1}{e^{T/\tau}-1}\right) > E. \tag{10.4}$$

The electrical time constant of the power converter is much faster than the mechanical time constant of the motor and the vehicle. The analysis of the interaction between the motor torque-speed char-acteristics and the vehicle force-velocity characteristics is best conducted on an average basis over one time period. The KVL applied around the motor aramature circuit loop gives

$$v_a(t) = R_a i_a(t) + L_a \frac{di_a}{dt} + K\phi\omega(t).$$

Averaging both sides yields

$$\langle v_a \rangle = R_a \langle i_a \rangle + k\phi\langle\omega\rangle. \tag{10.5}$$

The average aramture circuit can be represented by circuit in Figure 10.12. The average armature voltage in the CCM is

$$\langle v_a \rangle = \frac{1}{T}\int_0^T v_a(\tau)\,d\tau = \frac{V_{bat}d_1 T}{T} = d_1 V_{bat}. \tag{10.6}$$

**FIGURE 10.12** Average armature circuit.

The average torque equation is

$$T_e(t) = K\phi i_a(t)$$

$$\Rightarrow \langle i_a \rangle = \frac{\langle T_e \rangle}{K\phi}.$$

Substituting the average current in Equation 10.6

$$d_1 V_{bat} = R_a \frac{\langle T_e \rangle}{K\phi} + K\phi\langle\omega\rangle$$

$$\Rightarrow \langle\omega\rangle = \frac{d_1 V_{bat}}{K\phi} - \frac{R_a}{(K\phi)^2}\langle T_e \rangle. \tag{10.7}$$

The average speed-torque characteristic of a separately excited DC motor driven by a two-quadrant chopper in the CCM given by Equation 10.7 is shown qualitatively in Figure 10.13. The effect of increasing the duty ratio $d_1$ in the acceleration mode is to shift the no-load speed and rest of the characteristics vertically upward in the first quadrant.

#### 10.2.2.4 Acceleration (Discontinuous Conduction Mode, DCM)

When the torque required from the motor in the acceleration mode is not high enough, the chopper may enter the DCM where the armature current becomes discontinuous as shown in Figure 10.14. In the DCM, $I_{a0} \leq 0$ and $V_{bat} > E$ (since power is still flowing from the energy source into the motor). The operation is still in quadrant 1. The condition for DCM of operation is

$$V_{bat}\left(\frac{e^{d_1 T/\tau} - 1}{e^{T/\tau} - 1}\right) \leq E < V_{bat}. \tag{10.8}$$

The motor armature current cannot go negative without the use of switch $Q_2$ in the DCM. $Q_1$ is used to control the flow of power from the source to the motor only. In the interval between $d_1 T + \Delta T$ and $T$, for $i_a$ to become negative, $D_1$ must turn on. However, during this interval $v_0 = V_{bat} > E$; hence, $i_a$

**FIGURE 10.13** Torque-speed characteristics of the chopper-fed DC drive.

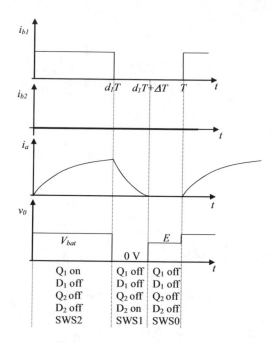

**FIGURE 10.14** Voltage and current waveforms during acceleration in the DCM.

cannot go negative. Also, $i_a$ cannot become positive since that would require $v_0 = V_{bat}$, which would require $Q_1$ to be on, but $i_{b1} = 0$. Hence, $i_a = 0$ over this interval.

### 10.2.2.5 Acceleration (Uncontrollable Mode, UNCM)

When a vehicle is rolling down a steep slope, it is possible for the propulsion motor to attain a large value of back-emf. In such a case, if $E > V_{bat}$, current cannot be forced into the motor and the use of $Q_1$ becomes meaningless. The supply voltage saturation limit prevents the driver from supplying more power into the motor to move faster than the velocity attained due to gravity. Therefore, the driver cannot control the vehicle using the acceleration pedal; he can only slow down the vehicle by using the brake pedal. If the brake pedal is not used in this situation, then the vehicle enters the uncontrollable mode. When $E > V_{bat}$, $i_a$ starts to decrease and once it reaches zero, diode D1 becomes forward biased and turns on. $i_a$ continues to increase in the negative direction until it reaches its steady-state value of

$$i_a = \text{Constant} = \frac{-E + V_{bat}}{R_a}. \tag{10.9}$$

The mode of operation in this stage is in quadrant II. The current and switch conditions are shown in Figure 10.15. Depressing the acceleration pedal to increase $d_1$ doesn't control the vehicle in any way, and the vehicle is in fact rolling downward while regenerating into the source in an uncontrolled way. The controller fault protection algorithm must kick in at this stage to prevent any overcharging of the batteries. Of course, the driver can regain control by switching to the brake pedal from the acceleration pedal and forcing controlled regeneration through the use of $Q_2$. This will help slow down the vehicle on a downhill slope.

### 10.2.2.6 Braking Operation (CCM in Steady State)

The most efficient way of recovering energy during vehicle braking is through regeneration in the motor drive system. Let us assume that $E < V_{bat}$ and the brake pedal is depressed. $Q_1$ is kept off during this period, while braking is controlled through the gate signal $i_{b2}$. For regeneration, the

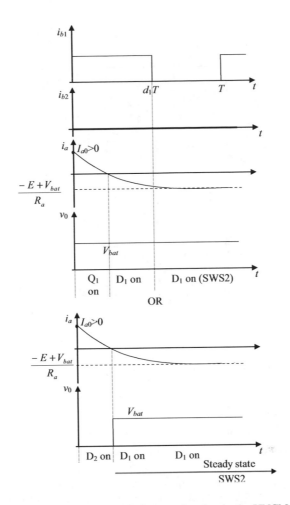

**FIGURE 10.15**   Voltage and current waveforms during acceleration in the UNCM.

power flow must be from the motor to the energy source storage requiring armature current $i_a$ to be negative. Turning $Q_2$ on helps $i_a$ become negative (from a previously positive value) and an average negative current can be established in a relatively short time for vehicle braking and regeneration. The voltage and current waveforms during braking operation in CCM are shown in Figure 10.16.

An analysis similar to the CCM during acceleration will yield the $I_{a1}$ and $I_{a2}$ values in the steady-state CCM during braking as

$$I_{a1} = \frac{1}{R_a}\left\{V_{bat}\left(\frac{1-e^{-d_2'T/\tau}}{1-e^{-T/\tau}}\right) - E\right\}, \, d_2' = 1 - d_2,$$

(10.10)

$$I_{a2} = \frac{1}{R_a}\left\{V_{bat}\left(\frac{e^{d_2'T/\tau}-1}{e^{T/\tau}-1}\right) - E\right\} \, < 0.$$

The current ripple during braking is

$$\Delta i_a = \frac{V_{bat}}{R_a}\left[\frac{-e^{-d_2'T/\tau}+1+e^{T/\tau}-e^{d_2T/\tau}}{e^{T/\tau}-1}\right].$$

(10.11)

**FIGURE 10.16**   Voltage and current waveforms during braking operation in the CCM.

During braking CCM, $I_{a1} < 0$ and $E < V_{bat}$. Also, note that $0 < \left( \dfrac{1 - e^{-d_2'T/\tau}}{1 - e^{-T/\tau}} \right) = \dfrac{e^{T/\tau} - e^{d_2T/\tau}}{e^{T/\tau} - 1} < 1$.
Therefore, the condition for continuous conduction during braking is

$$0 < V_{bat} \left( \frac{1 - e^{-d_2'T/\tau}}{1 - e^{-T/\tau}} \right) < E < V_{bat}. \tag{10.12}$$

The average voltage equation in the braking CCM is

$$\langle v_a \rangle + R_a \langle i_a \rangle + 0 = E = K\phi \langle \omega \rangle. \tag{10.13}$$

The average motor torque is

$$\langle T_e \rangle = -K\phi \langle i_a \rangle. \tag{10.14}$$

The average motor terminal voltage is

$$\langle v_a \rangle = \frac{1}{T} \int_0^T v_a(\tau) d\tau = \frac{1}{T} V_{bat}(T - d_2 T) = (1 - d_2) V_{bat}. \tag{10.15}$$

Substituting $\langle v_a \rangle$ from Equation 10.15 and $\langle i_a \rangle$ from Equation 10.14 into Equation 10.13 gives

$$(1 - d_2) V_{bat} - \frac{R_a}{K\phi} \langle T_e \rangle = K\phi \langle \omega \rangle.$$

The average speed-torque characteristics is (Figure 10.17)

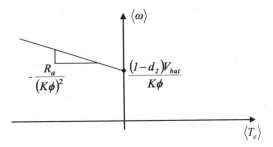

**FIGURE 10.17**   DC motor drive speed-torque characteristics during braking.

$$\langle \omega \rangle = \frac{(1-d_2)V_{bat}}{K\phi} - \frac{R_a}{(K\phi)^2}\langle T_e \rangle, \quad \text{for } \langle T_e \rangle < 0, \langle \omega \rangle > 0 \tag{10.16}$$

### 10.2.2.7  Regenerative Power

The power is regenerated into the energy source only during part of the cycle when current flows into the battery from the motor as shown in Figure 10.18. When transistor $Q_2$ is on, power is only being dissipated in the switch and contact resistances. When $Q_2$ is off and diode $D_1$ is conducting, the current termed $i_{bat}(t)$ is flowing into the battery. Therefore, the instantaneous regenerative power is $P_{reg}(t) = V_{bat} \times i_{bat}(t)$. The average regenerative power is

$$\langle P_{reg} \rangle = \frac{1}{T} \int_{d_2T}^{T} P_{reg}(\gamma)d\gamma. \tag{10.17}$$

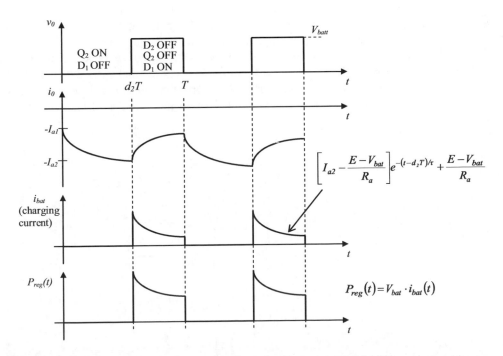

**FIGURE 10.18**   Voltage, current and power waveforms during regenerative braking.

Using an analysis similar to that done for the CCM during acceleration and the results of Equation 10.10, the battery current can be derived as

$$
i_{bat}(t) = \begin{cases} \left[ I_{a2} - \dfrac{E - V_{bat}}{R_a} \right] e^{-(t - d_2 T)/\tau} + \dfrac{E - V_{bat}}{R_a} & \text{for} \quad d_2 T < t \le T \\ 0 & \text{otherwise.} \end{cases}
\tag{10.18}
$$

The average regenerative power obtained by inserting Equation 10.18 into Equation 10.17 and integrating is

$$
\langle P_{reg} \rangle = \frac{V_{bat}^{\,2}}{R_a} \left[ \left( \frac{E}{V_{bat}} - 1 \right)(1 - d_2) + \frac{\tau}{T} \left\{ \frac{e^{(1 - d_2)T/\tau} + e^{d_2 T/\tau} - e^{T/\tau} - 1}{1 - e^{T/\tau}} \right\} \right].
\tag{10.19}
$$

The regenerative energy per cycle is

$$
\int_0^T P_{reg}(\gamma)d\gamma = \int_{d_2 T}^T P_{reg}(\gamma)d\gamma = \langle P_{reg} \rangle T.
$$

## 10.3  OPERATING POINT ANALYSIS

The following discussion presents the steady-state operating point analysis of the vehicle system at the intersection of the motor torque-speed characteristics with the road-load characteristics. Four operating points are chosen for analysis in three different quadrants of the motor speed-torque plane representing four chopper operating modes discussed in the previous section. These modes are acceleration CCM in quadrant 1 (scenario 1), acceleration CCM in quadrant IV (scenario 2), acceleration UNCM in quadrant 2 (scenario 3) and braking CCM in quadrant 2 (scenario 4). The four scenarios are shown in Figure 10.19.

Now, recall that the tractive force vs. vehicle speed characteristics of Chapter 2, which essentially defines the speed-torque characteristics of the electric or hybrid vehicle load. The tractive force versus velocity characteristics of Figure 2.11 can be converted into an equivalent vehicle load speed-torque characteristics knowing the transmission gear ratio and the vehicle wheel radius. The steady-state operating point of the vehicle for certain conditions of the motor drive system and road-load characteristics can be obtained by overlaying the two speed-torque characteristics on the same plot. The steady-state operating points at the intersection of the motor and road-load characteristics are shown in Figure 10.20.

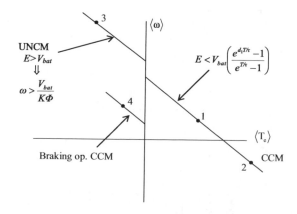

**FIGURE 10.19**  Motor speed torque characteristics for four chopper modes.

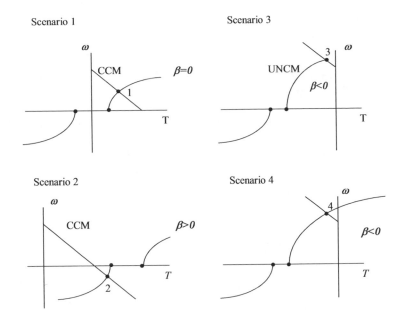

**FIGURE 10.20** Operating point analysis for the scenarios.

*Scenario 1*
In this scenario, the vehicle is moving forward on a level roadway with a constant velocity. The chopper is in the acceleration CCM of operation.

*Scenario 2*
The chopper is operating in the acceleration CCM, yet the vehicle is moving backward on a steep uphill road. If the duty ratio has not yet reached 100%, $d_1$ can be increased all the way up to 1 by depressing the acceleration pedal further and increasing the torque output of the motor. Increasing $d_1$ will raise the motor speed-torque characteristics vertically upward enabling a possible steady-state operating point in the first quadrant. If the motor rating has reached its limit, then the torque cannot be increased further to overcome the road-load resistance. The slope is too steep for the capacity of the motor and the vehicle rolls backward. The wheel back drives the motor in this case.

*Scenario 3*
The vehicle is going downhill with the chopper operating in the acceleration mode. The angle of the acceleration pedal will have no bearing on the steady-state operating point. There will be uncontrolled regeneration into the energy source.

*Scenario 4*
The vehicle is going downhill in a controlled fashion using the brake pedal. The speed of the vehicle going down the slope is in control of the driver.

## Example 10.1

An electric vehicle drivetrain with a 72 V battery pack is powered by a two-quadrant chopper as shown in the Figure 10.7. $d_1$ is the duty ratio for the acceleration operation, while $d_2$ is the duty ratio for braking operation.
The various parameters are given below:
The EV parameters are

$m = 1,000$ kg, $C_D = 0.2$, $A_F = 2$ m$^2$, $C_0 = 0.009$, $C_1 = 0$,
$\rho = 1.1614$ kg/m$^3$ and $g = 10.81$ m/s$^2$.
$r_{wh}$ = radius of wheel = 11 in. = 0.28 m.

Motor and controller parameters are

Rated armature voltage $V_{a,rated} = 72\,V$,
Rated armature current $I_{a,rated} = 400\,A$,
$R_a = 0.5\,\Omega$, $L_a = 8\,mH$, $k\phi = 0.7$ V-s,
$f_s$ = chopper switching frequency = $400\,Hz$

a. Find the series filter inductance $L_f$ so that worst-case motor armature current ripple is 1% of $I_{a,rated}$.
b. The vehicle road-load characteristics on a level road is $T_{TR} = 24.7 + 0.0051\omega_{wh}{}^2$. What is the EV steady-state speed on a level road if $d_1 = 0.7$? Assume an overall gear ratio of 1 for the transmission system. Find the chopper mode of conduction *[Scenario 1]*.
c. What is the percent ripple in the armature current for the operating point in (b)?
d. The vehicle road-load characteristics on a grade of 5.24% ($\beta = 3°$) is $T_{TR} = 119.1 + 0.0051\omega_{wh}{}^2$. What is the EV steady-state speed for $d_1 = 0.7$? *[Scenario 2]*.
e. What is the EV speed on grade of −5.24% using brake pedal with $d_2 = 0.5$? *[Scenario 4]*.

## Solution

a. From (10.3) with $x = e^{T_p/\tau}$, $x > 1$

$$\Delta i_a = I_{a1} - I_{a0}$$

$$= \frac{V_{bat}}{R_a}\left[\frac{1 + x - x^{d_1} - x^{(1-d_1)}}{x-1}\right]$$

The worst-case condition is when $d_1 = 0.5$. Therefore,

$$0.01 \times 400 = \frac{72}{0.5}\left[\frac{1 + x - x^{1/2} - x^{1/2}}{x-1}\right] \Rightarrow 1.0278 + 0.972x - 2\sqrt{x} = 0.$$

Solving for $x$ we get, $x = 1$, 1.1110. Since $x > 1$, take $x = 1.1110$. Therefore,

$$1.118 = e^{T_p/\tau} \Rightarrow \tau = 8.96T_p = 22.4 \text{ ms}.$$

Now,

$$\tau = \frac{L_a + L_f}{R_a} = 22.4 \times 10^{-3}$$

$$\Rightarrow L_f = 3.2 \text{ mH}.$$

b. The motor steady-state torque speed characteristic using Equation 10.7 is

$$\langle\omega_m\rangle = \frac{0.7 \times 72}{0.7} - \frac{0.5}{0.7^2}\langle T_e\rangle \Rightarrow \langle\omega_m\rangle = 72 - 1.02\langle T_e\rangle.$$

The steady-state operating point is the point of intersection of the motor torque-speed characteristic and the vehicle road-load characteristic $T_{TR} = 24.7 + 0.0051\omega_{wh}{}^2$. Solving the two equations, the operating point is

$$T^* = 32.4 \text{ Nm and } \omega^* = 38.9 \text{ rad/s}.$$

Now,

$$V_{bat}\left(\frac{e^{d_1 T_P/\tau} - 1}{e^{T_P/\tau} - 1}\right) = 72 \cdot \frac{e^{0.7*2.5/22.4} - 1}{e^{2.5/22.4} - 1} = 49.6.$$

And $E = k\varphi\langle\omega\rangle = 0.7*(38.9) = 27.2$.

Therefore, $V_{bat}\left(\dfrac{e^{d_1 T/\tau} - 1}{e^{T/\tau} - 1}\right) > E$, and hence, the chopper is operating in CCM. It can

also be shown that $I_{a0} > 0$, verifying that the operation is indeed in CCM.

c. The ripple in the armature current for the operating point in part (b) is

$$\Delta i_a = \frac{72}{0.5}\left[\frac{1 + 1.118 - 1.118^{0.7} - 1.118^{(1-0.7)}}{1.118 - 1}\right] = 3.37 \text{ A}.$$

The ripple current magnitude is still less than 1% of rated current.

$$\langle i_a \rangle = \frac{\langle T^* \rangle}{k\varphi} = \frac{32.4}{0.7} = 46.3 \text{ A}$$

Therefore, the percentage ripple is

$$\% \text{ ripple} = \frac{\Delta i_a}{\langle i_a \rangle} \times 100\% = \frac{3.37}{46.7} \times 100\% = 7.28\%.$$

d. The steady-state operating point for a grade of 5.24% is at the intersection of the motor torque-speed characteristic $\langle \omega_m \rangle = 72 - 1.02\langle T_e \rangle$ and the vehicle road-load characteristic $T_{TR} = 119.1 + 0.0051\omega_{wh}^2$. The two solutions are $\omega^* = -40.8, 233$. The correct solution is $\omega^* = -40.8$, since the other speed is too high. The vehicle in this case is actually rolling backward due to insufficient power from the propulsion unit. It can be verified that the maximum gradability of the vehicle is 2.57%.

e. The vehicle road-load characteristic for a slope of −5.24% is $T_{TR} = -119.1 + 0.0051\omega_{wh}^2$. The motor torque speed characteristic in the braking CCM from Equation 10.14 is $\langle \omega_m \rangle = \dfrac{(1-d_2)V_{bat}}{K\phi} - \dfrac{R_a}{(K\phi)^2}\langle T_e \rangle \Rightarrow \langle \omega_m \rangle = 51.4 - 1.02\langle T_e \rangle$. Solving for the operating point from the two torque–speed characteristics,

$T^* = -57.4, 347$. The negative value is the solution since the chopper is in braking mode. This gives the steady-state speed as $\omega^* = 51.4 - 1.02(-57.4) = 109.9$ rad/s. The vehicle speed is $V^* = 0.28*109.9 = 30.77$ m/s = 68.8 mph.

Now, $E = 0.7*109.9 = 76.9 \geq 72\dfrac{1 - e^{-0.5*0.1116}}{1 - e^{-0.1116}} = 37$, which satisfies the condition of CCM for braking given by Equation 10.12.

## 10.4  AC DRIVES

The synchronous speed of AC machines is proportional to the supply frequency $(\omega_s = \dfrac{120f}{P})$, which means that the speed can be controlled by varying the frequency of the AC input voltage. The power electronic converter, more commonly referred to as the inverter, supplies the variable voltage, variable frequency output to an AC machine (induction or synchronous) from the available energy source which is typically in the form of a fixed DC voltage. The inverter consists of six switches, and through appropriate control, shapes the available DC voltage into balanced three-phase AC voltage of the desired magnitude and frequency. The voltage source inverter, shown in Figure 10.21, is common for electric and hybrid vehicle applications where the source has a stiff voltage.

**FIGURE 10.21**    Six-switch voltage source inverter.

The inverter can be operated in either the six-step mode or in the pulse width modulation (PWM) mode, but are typically designed to minimize the voltage spikes, devices stresses and electromagnetic interference for operation at the designated PWM frequency. The PWM frequency depends on the inverter power device capability and the maximum operating speed of the traction motor. For a traction machine with $P$ poles, the fundamental frequency for a maximum operating speed of $N_{max}$ rpm is given by

$$f_1 = \frac{N_{max} \times P}{120}$$

The PWM frequency is typically chosen an order of magnitude higher than the fundamental frequency to provide adequate bandwidth for good current regulation. For example, if the maximum speed of an eight-pole traction machine is 12,000 rpm, then the fundamental frequency is 800 Hz and an 8 kHz PWM frequency is adequate. With IGBT-based inverters, the PWM switching frequency is typically limited between 5 and 10 kHz to minimize the device switching losses and maintain a decent inverter efficiency. Controllers are designed to reduce the switching frequency for lower motor speeds and even go into a six-step switching mode where the switching frequency equals the fundamental frequency in order to reduce inverter losses. With SiC- and GaN-based inverters, it is possible to use high PWM switching frequency while maintaining high efficiency and the higher bandwidth available can be utilized for better current regulation improving the torque output performance of the traction motor.

The inverter output invariably has a number of harmonic components in addition to the desired fundamental voltage component. The PWM is used to minimize the harmonic contents of the output voltage signal. There are several methods of generating the PWM signals, such as sinusoidal PWM, state vector PWM, uniform sampling PWM and selective harmonic elimination. The electronic controller generates the gate switch signals for the inverter power devices using a PWM method and control commands to process the power flow and deliver the output voltage at desired voltage and frequency.

## 10.4.1   SIX-STEP OPERATION

The six-step operation is the simplest approach of generating AC voltage using the six-switch inverter. For the sake of analysis, let us replace the transistor and diodes with ideal switches, which results in a simplified equivalent inverter circuit shown in Figure 10.22. The DC voltage is represented here as $V_{dc}$. The characteristics of the ideal inverter are: (i) switches can carry current in both directions, and (ii) the total number of possible switching states is $2^6 = 64$. Some of the switching states are not allowed. For example, $S_1$ and $S_4$ cannot be on at the same time. The operation of the inverter can be divided into six intervals between 0 and $2\pi$ radians with each interval being of $\pi/3$

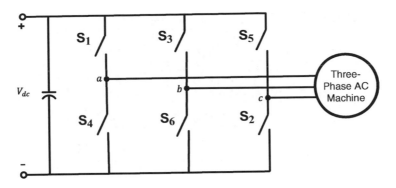

**FIGURE 10.22** Ideal six-switch voltage source inverter.

radians duration. In each interval, three of the switches are on and three are off. This operation is known as six-step operation. The six interval periods identified with the operating switches during that period are as follows:

$$1 \rightarrow 0 < wt < \pi/3: \qquad S_1 S_5 S_6$$
$$2 \rightarrow \pi/3 < wt < 2\pi/3: \qquad S_1 S_2 S_6$$
$$3 \rightarrow 2\pi/3 < wt < \pi: \qquad S_1 S_2 S_3$$
$$4 \rightarrow \pi < wt < 4\pi/3: \qquad S_4 S_2 S_3$$
$$5 \rightarrow 4\pi/3 < wt < 5\pi/3: \qquad S_4 S_5 S_3$$
$$6 \rightarrow 5\pi/3 < wt < 2\pi: \qquad S_4 S_5 S_6$$

The gating signals for the electronic switches and the resulting output AC voltage for six-step operation are shown in Figure 10.23. The line-to-line voltage and the line-to-neutral voltage, i.e., voltage of one phase, are shown in the figure.

In three-phase machines, three-wire systems are used where the line terminals $a$, $b$, and $c$ are connected to the motor with neutral terminal $n$ kept hidden. The relationships between line-to-line voltages (i.e., line voltages) and line-to-neutral voltages (i.e., phase voltages) are

$$v_{ab} = v_{an} - v_{bn}$$

$$v_{bc} = v_{bn} - v_{cn} \qquad (10.20)$$

$$v_{ca} = v_{cn} - v_{an}.$$

There are three unknowns and two linearly independent equations ($v_{an}, v_{bn}, v_{cn}$). Therefore, we need another equation to find the inverse solution. For a balanced three-phase electrical system, we know that $v_{an} + v_{bn} + v_{cn} = 0$. Therefore, the line and phase voltage relationships can be written in matrix format as

$$\begin{bmatrix} 1 & -1 & 0 \\ 0 & 1 & -1 \\ -1 & 0 & 1 \\ 1 & 1 & 1 \end{bmatrix} \begin{bmatrix} v_{an} \\ v_{bn} \\ v_{cn} \end{bmatrix} = \begin{bmatrix} v_{ab} \\ v_{bc} \\ v_{ca} \\ 0 \end{bmatrix}.$$

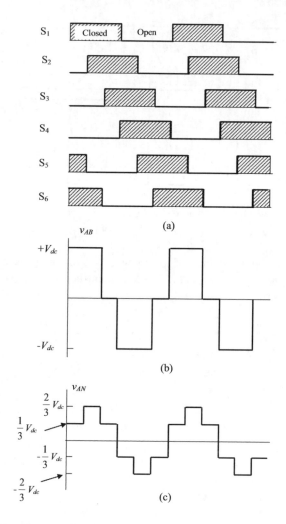

**FIGURE 10.23**  Six-step inverter gate signals and output voltages.

The solutions for the phase voltages are

$$v_{an} = -\frac{1}{3}[v_{bc} + 2v_{ca}]$$

$$v_{bn} = \frac{1}{3}[v_{bc} - v_{ac}] \qquad (10.21)$$

$$v_{cn} = -\frac{1}{3}[v_{bc} + v_{ac}].$$

The phase voltages are useful for per phase analysis of the three-phase systems. The phase voltage $v_{an}$ of the six-step inverter output can be derived using Equation 10.21 as shown in Figure 10.24. Now, the question is what type of switches is required for the inverter. Let us first consider switch $S_1$. When $S_1$ is off, $v_{S1} = V_{dc}$. When $S_1$ is on, $S_4$ is off. The phase voltage of the six-step inverter is shown in Figure 10.24. The output voltage can be filtered to make the supply more sinusoidal. The supply is naturally filtered when supplying an inductive load, such as the electric motor. It is only the fundamental component of the supply that contributes to electromagnetic torque production, while

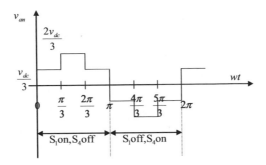

**FIGURE 10.24**  Phase voltage during switch $S_1$ operation.

the higher harmonic components are responsible for part of the losses in the system. The interaction of the induction motor with the higher harmonic components is analyzed in Section 10.4.1.1. The fundamental component of the phase voltage and the current through the switch into phase a winding is shown in Figure 10.25. Since the motor is inductive, line current lags the phase voltage. Therefore, we must use bi-directional current switches since $i_a$ is both positive and negative.

### 10.4.1.1  Harmonic Analysis

Let us consider the switching interval number three where $2\pi/3 < \omega t < \pi$. The switches that are on during this period are $S_1$, $S_2$ and $S_3$. The inverter configuration in this interval is shown in Figure 10.26. The line-to-line square wave voltage can be written in terms of the fundamental and harmonic components using the Fourier series analysis as

$$v_{ab} = \frac{2\sqrt{3}}{\pi} V_{dc} \left\{ \sin\left(\omega t + \frac{\pi}{6}\right) + \frac{1}{5}\sin\left(5\omega t - \frac{\pi}{6}\right) + \frac{1}{7}\sin\left(7\omega t + \frac{\pi}{6}\right) + \cdots \right\} \qquad (10.22)$$

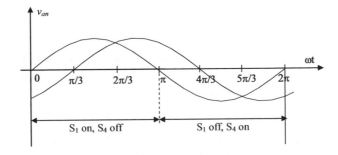

**FIGURE 10.25**  Phase voltage and current during $S_1$ operation.

**FIGURE 10.26**  Inverter switch connection in switching interval number 3.

**FIGURE 10.27**  Dominant harmonic components in inverter output voltages.

Note that the harmonics present are the $6n \pm 1$ ($n$ is an integer) components and that the triplen harmonics are absent. The harmonic phase voltages that are 30° phase shifted from the line voltages are

$$v_{an} = \frac{2}{\pi} V_{dc} \left\{ \sin(\omega t) + \frac{1}{5}\sin(5\omega t) + \frac{1}{7}\sin(7\omega t) + \cdots \right\}. \tag{10.23}$$

The dominant harmonic components are shown in Figure 10.27.

The harmonics do not contribute to the output power, but they certainly increase the power losses that reduce the efficiency and increase the thermal loading of the machine. The harmonic losses do not vary significantly with the load. The interactions of fundamental air gap mmf with harmonic air gap mmfs produce torque pulsations, which may be significant at low speeds.

## 10.4.2  Pulse Width Modulation

The pulse width modulation techniques are used to mitigate the adverse effects of harmonics in the inverter [3,5]. The harmonics in the output PWM voltage are not eliminated, but shifted to a much higher frequency, which makes the filtering a lot easier. The controllability of the amplitude of the fundamental output voltage is another advantage of PWM. The PWM techniques developed over the years are sinusoidal PWM, uniform sampling PWM, selective harmonic elimination PWM, space vector PWM and random PWM. The two commonly used PWM techniques, the sinusoidal PWM and the space vector PWM, are discussed in the following.

### 10.4.2.1  Sinusoidal PWM

In the sinusoidal PWM method, a sinusoidal control signal $V_a$ is compared with a high-frequency triangular waveform $V_T$ to generate the inverter switch gating signals. The frequency of $V_T$ estab-lishes the inverter switching frequency $f_c$. The magnitude and frequency of the sinusoidal signal are controllable, but the triangular signal magnitude and frequency are kept constant. The sinusoidal control signal $V_a$ modulates the switch duty ratio, and its frequency $f$ is the desired fundamental fre-quency of the inverter. For the three-phase voltage generation, the same $V_T$ is compared with three sinusoidal control voltages $v_A$, $v_B$ and $v_C$, which are 120° out of phase with respect to each other to produce a balanced output. The switches are controlled in pairs $(S_1,S_4)$, $(S_2,S_5)$ and $(S_3,S_6)$. When one switch in a pair is closed, the other switch is open. In practice, there has to be a blanking pulse between the change of control signals for the switches in a pair to ensure that there is no short circuit in the inverter. This is necessary since practical switches take finite time to turn on and turn off. The three-phase sinusoidal pulse width modulation signals are shown in Figure 10.28. The switch control signals follow the logic given below:

$S_1$ is on when $v_A > V_T$
$S_2$ is on when $v_C > V_T$
$S_3$ is on when $v_B > V_T$
$S_4$ is on when $v_A < V_T$
$S_5$ is on when $v_C < V_T$
$S_6$ is on when $v_B < V_T$

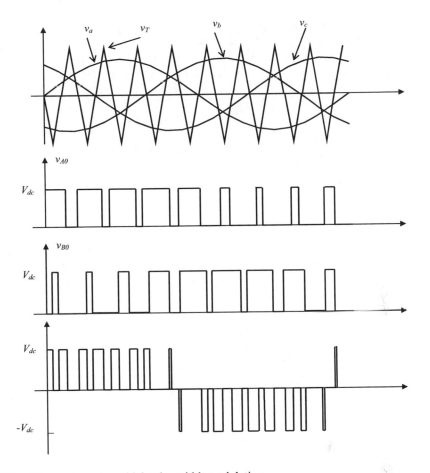

**FIGURE 10.28** Three-phase sinusoidal pulse width modulation.

The amplitude modulation index is

$$m = \frac{V_{a,peak}}{V_{T,peak}} = \frac{A}{A_m} \qquad (10.24)$$

where $A$ = amplitude of the reference sine wave and $A_m$ = amplitude of the triangular carrier wave. Let us define the ratio of carrier frequency and fundamental frequency as

$$p = \frac{f_C}{f}$$

The rms value of the fundamental inverter output phase voltage $V_{ph}$ is

$$V_{ph,1} = m\frac{V_{dc}}{2\sqrt{2}}, \quad m \leq 1 \qquad (10.25)$$

where $V_{dc}$ is the DC input voltage to the inverter. Note that $V_{ph,1}$ increases with $m$ until $m = 1$. For $m > 1$, modulation ceases to be sinusoidal PWM wherein it is referred to as over-modulation. The rms value of the fundamental in the line to line voltage is

$$V_{LL,1} = m\frac{\sqrt{3}\,V_{dc}}{2\sqrt{2}}, \quad m \leq 1. \qquad (10.26)$$

There are two types of modulation depending on the value of $p$, called synchronous modulation and asynchronous modulation. In synchronous modulation $p = 3n$, $n = 1, 2, \ldots$, making the carrier wave symmetrical with respect to the three-phase reference voltages $v_a$, $v_b$ and $v_c$. Otherwise, the modulation is called asynchronous modulation. The characteristics of asynchronous modulation are as follows:

1. Pulse pattern does not repeat itself identically from cycle to cycle.
2. Sub-harmonics of $f$ and a DC component are introduced.
3. Sub-harmonics cause low-frequency torque and speed pulsations known as frequency beats.
4. For large $p$, frequency beats are negligible. For small $p$, frequency beats may be significant.
5. For small $p$, synchronous modulation is used. Preferably, $p$ is an odd multiple of three.

The boundary of sinusoidal modulation is reached when $m = 1$. The relationship between the fundamental component of phase voltage and $m$ ceases to be linear for values greater than 1. For sufficiently large values of $m$, the output phase voltage becomes a square wave with maximum amplitude of the fundamental equal to $2V_{dc}/\pi$ (relate to Equation 10.23). This is essentially the six-step operation of the inverter. Note that the amplitude of the fundamental on the boundary of linear sinusoidal PWM is only 78.5% of the maximum value. The modulation with $m > 1$ is known as overmodulation; lower-order harmonics are introduced in this range of modulation.

### 10.4.2.2 Harmonics in Sinusoidal PWM

The inverter output phase voltage contains harmonics that are of odd multiples of the carrier frequency $f_C$ (i.e., $f_C$, $3f_C$, $5f_C$, ...). The waveform also contains sidebands centered around multiples of $f_C$ and given by

$$f_h = k_1 f_C \pm k_2 f = (k_1 p \pm k_2) f$$

where $k_1 + k_2$ is an odd integer. The harmonic frequency centers are at $k_1 f$ for odd integers of $k_1$, while the side bands are symmetrically located without a center for even integers of $k_1$. Note that the magnitudes of band frequency harmonics decrease rapidly with increasing distance from band center. The harmonic frequency components for $k_1 = 1$ and $k_1 = 2$ along with the bandwidth are shown in Figure 10.29. The bandwidth of harmonics is the range of frequency over which the harmonics are considered dominant. The frequency bandwidth increases with $m$. The dominant harmonics among the sidebands are at frequencies $(p \pm 2)f$ and $(2p \pm 1)f$.

### 10.4.2.3 Space Vector (SV) PWM

The voltage space vectors embedded in the $dq$ models and vector controllers of AC machines present a highly compatible method for the control of three-phase PWM inverters. The $dq$ voltage commands for the direct and quadrature axes voltages generated by the controller to drive a motor are converted into an equivalent PWM signal to be applied to the gates of the six inverter switches. For variable frequency drive applications, space vector PWM is very popular because of its superior performance compared to other voltage PWM techniques.

The three-phase voltage source inverter can assume one of eight ($2^3 = 8$) states only, since each switch in a phase leg can assume either an *on* or *off* position. Each of these eight states is associated with a specific set of values of the three-phase voltages. Based on the state, the machine phase winding terminals are connected to the upper or lower side of the DC link. For the terminal voltages, eight voltage vectors are defined using 3-bit digital states as 000, 100, 110, 010, 011, 001, 101 and 111. For example, the state 011 stands for Phase-a connected to the lower side of the DC bus, while Phases b and c connected to the upper side. Alternatively, a 0 indicates the lower switch is turned on and a 1 indicates that the upper switch is on. This means that the inverter can generate eight

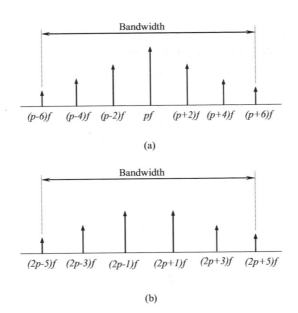

(a)

(b)

**FIGURE 10.29**  Harmonic frequency components for $k_1 = 1$ (a) and $k_1 = 2$ (b).

stationary voltage vectors $\vec{V}_0$ through $\vec{V}_7$ with the subscript indicating the corresponding state of the inverter. These voltage vectors are

$$\vec{V}_0 = \begin{bmatrix} 0 \\ 0 \\ 0 \end{bmatrix}, \quad \vec{V}_1 = \begin{bmatrix} 1 \\ 0 \\ 0 \end{bmatrix}, \quad \vec{V}_2 = \begin{bmatrix} 1 \\ 1 \\ 0 \end{bmatrix}, \quad \vec{V}_3 = \begin{bmatrix} 0 \\ 1 \\ 0 \end{bmatrix}$$

$$\vec{V}_4 = \begin{bmatrix} 0 \\ 1 \\ 1 \end{bmatrix}, \quad \vec{V}_5 = \begin{bmatrix} 0 \\ 0 \\ 1 \end{bmatrix}, \quad \vec{V}_6 = \begin{bmatrix} 1 \\ 0 \\ 1 \end{bmatrix}, \quad \vec{V}_7 = \begin{bmatrix} 1 \\ 1 \\ 1 \end{bmatrix}$$

The switching states, voltage vectors and the associated switch conditions are given in Table 10.2.

The eight voltage vectors represent two null vectors ($\vec{V}_0$ and $\vec{V}_7$) and six active-state vectors forming a hexagon (Figure 10.30). A simple circuit analysis will reveal that the phase voltage magnitudes vary between $\pm\frac{2}{3}V_{dc}$ in steps of $\frac{1}{3}V_{dc}$ in the six active states. This is analogous to the six-step operation where the voltage magnitude variations are similar for the six steps. For example, in vector state $\vec{V}_1$ switches $S_1$, $S_2$ and $S_6$ are on with Phase-a connected to the upper side of the DC bus, and Phase-b and Phase-c connected to the lower side. In this state, the inverter phase voltages are $v_{an} = \frac{2}{3}V_{dc}$, $v_{bn} = -\frac{1}{3}V_{dc}$ and $v_{cn} = -\frac{1}{3}V_{dc}$. This is the step in the interval $\pi/3 < \omega t < 2\pi/3$ in Figures 10.23 and 10.24 for six-step operation. Transforming the three-phase *abc* variables into *dq* variables, the *d* and *q* voltages are $v_d = \frac{2}{3}V_{dc}$ and $v_q = 0$. Therefore, voltage vector $\vec{V}_1$ has a magnitude of $\frac{2}{3}V_{dc}$ and is along the *d*-axis in the *dq*-plane. It can be shown similarly that each of the six active-state vectors has a magnitude of $\frac{2}{3}V_{dc}$ and is displaced by 60° with respect to each other in the *dq*-plane. The six active-state vectors form a hexagon as shown in Figure 10.30 with the null vectors remaining in the origin. The six active-state vectors can be represented in space vector form as

**TABLE 10.2**

**Space Vector Switching States**

| Switching State | On Devices | Voltage Vector |
| --- | --- | --- |
| 0 | S4S6S2 | $\vec{V}_0$ |
| 1 | S1S6S2 | $\vec{V}_1$ |
| 2 | S1S3S2 | $\vec{V}_2$ |
| 3 | S4S3S2 | $\vec{V}_3$ |
| 4 | S4S3S5 | $\vec{V}_4$ |
| 5 | S4S6S5 | $\vec{V}_5$ |
| 6 | S1S6S5 | $\vec{V}_6$ |
| 7 | S1S3S5 | $\vec{V}_7$ |

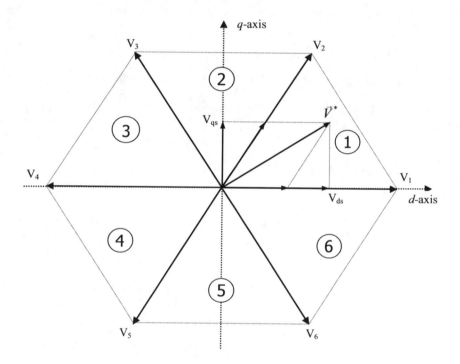

**FIGURE 10.30**  Inverter switching states and space vectors.

$$\vec{V}_k = \frac{2}{3}V_{dc}e^{j(k-1)\pi/3},$$
(10.27)

where $k = 1, \dots, 6$. Note that the same notation $\vec{V}_k$ is used to denote the voltage vector in the *abc* frame in relation to the switch location and the space vector in mathematical terms. The space vector can be easily related to the *d* and *q* variables in the two co-ordinate *dq* reference frame.

The SV PWM operates in a modulated fashion including the null vectors within a fixed time period in contrast to the six-step operation of the inverter. The six-step operation uses only the six active states moving in the sequence $\vec{V}_1 \rightarrow \vec{V}_2 \rightarrow \vec{V}_3 \rightarrow \vec{V}_4 \rightarrow \vec{V}_5 \rightarrow \vec{V}_6 \rightarrow \vec{V}_1$ with a duration of 60° in each one of the states. The objective in SV PWM is to generate the gating signals such that harmonically optimized PWM voltage is obtained at the output of the inverter.

### 10.4.2.4 Generation of SV PWM Switching Signals

The continuous space vector modulation technique is based on the fact that every reference voltage vector $\vec{V}^*$ inside the hexagon can be expressed as a combination of the two adjacent active-state vectors and the null-state vectors. Therefore, the desired reference vector imposed in each cycle is achieved by switching among four inverter states. The sector where the space vector $\vec{V}^*$ lies determines the two active-state vectors that will be used in generating the gate switching signals of a PWM period [6]. The phase angle is evaluated from $\theta = \arctan\left(\dfrac{V_{qs}}{V_{ds}}\right)$ and $\theta \in [0, 2\pi]$. The phase angle is related to the relative magnitudes of $V_{qs}$ and $V_{ds}$. For example, in sector 1, $0 \leq \arctan\left(\dfrac{V_{qs}}{V_{ds}}\right) < \dfrac{\pi}{3}$; hence, $0 < V_{qs} < \sqrt{3}V_{ds}$. The following conditions are used to determine the sector where the space vector is located.

Sector 1: $0 < V_{qs} < \sqrt{3}V_{ds}$;
Sector 2: $V_{qs} > \left|\sqrt{3}V_{ds}\right|$;
Sector 3: $0 < V_{qs} < -\sqrt{3}V_{ds}$;
Sector 4: $0 > V_{qs} > \sqrt{3}V_{ds}$;
Sector 5: $V_{qs} < -\left|\sqrt{3}V_{ds}\right|$;
Sector 6: $0 > V_{qs} > -\sqrt{3}V_{ds}$.

Let us assume that $\vec{V}_k$ and $\vec{V}_{k+1}$ are the components of the reference vector $\vec{V}^*$ in sector $k$ and in the adjacent active sectors $(k+1)$, respectively. In order to obtain optimum harmonic performance and minimum switching frequency for each of the power devices, the state sequence is arranged such that the transition from one state to the next is performed by switching only one inverter leg. This condition is met if the sequence begins with one zero-state and the inverter poles are toggled until the other null-state is reached. To complete the cycle, the sequence is reversed, ending with the first zero-state. If, for instance, the reference vector sits in sector 1, the state sequence has to be...0127210... whereas in sector 4 it is...0547450... The central part of the space vector modulation strategy is the computation of both the active and zero-state times for each modulation cycle. These are calculated by equating the applied average voltage to the desired value. Figure 10.31 demonstrates the on-times of vectors.

In the following, $T_k$ denotes the required on-time of active-state vector $\vec{V}_k$, $T_{k+1}$ denotes the required on-time of active-state vector $\vec{V}_{k+1}$ and $(T_0 + T_7)$ is the time for the null-state vector to cover the complete time period $T_s$ [6]. The on-time is evaluated by the following equation:

$$\int_0^{T_s/2} \vec{V}dt = \int_0^{T_0/2} \vec{V}_0 dt + \int_{T_0/2}^{T_0/2+T_k} \vec{V}_k dt + \int_{T_0/2+T_k}^{T_0/2+T_k+T_{k+1}} \vec{V}_{k+1} dt + \int_{T_0/2+T_k+T_{k+1}}^{T_s/2} \vec{V}_7 dt, \quad (10.28)$$

where $T_0 + T_k + T_{k+1} + T_7 = T_s$.

By taking $\vec{V}_0$ and $\vec{V}_7$ to be zero vectors, and $\vec{V}^*$, $\vec{V}_k$ and $\vec{V}_{k+1}$ to be constant vectors in a PWM period, Equation 10.28 can be simplified as

$$\frac{T_s}{2}\vec{V} = \frac{T_0}{2}\vec{V}_0 + \frac{T_k}{2}\vec{V}_k + \frac{T_{k+1}}{2}\vec{V}_{k+1} + \frac{T_7}{2}\vec{V}_7$$

$$\Rightarrow T_s\vec{V} = T_k\vec{V}_k + T_{k+1}\vec{V}_{k+1}.$$

(10.29)

**FIGURE 10.31**  Diagram of on-times of vectors.

Using the space vector relation for $\vec{V}$ and Equations 10.27 and 10.29, it can be shown that

$$
\begin{bmatrix} T_k \\ T_{k+1} \end{bmatrix} = \frac{\sqrt{3}T_s}{V_{dc}} \begin{bmatrix} \sin\dfrac{k\pi}{3} & -\cos\dfrac{k\pi}{3} \\ -\sin\dfrac{(k-1)\pi}{3} & \cos\dfrac{(k-1)\pi}{3} \end{bmatrix} \begin{bmatrix} V_{ds} \\ V_{qs} \end{bmatrix}.
\tag{10.30}
$$

The duty ratios are related to the on-time as

$$
\begin{bmatrix} T_k \\ T_{k+1} \end{bmatrix} = T_s \begin{bmatrix} D_k \\ D_{k+1} \end{bmatrix}
\tag{10.31}
$$

Comparing Equation 10.30 with Equation 10.31, one can obtain the duty ratios as

$$
\begin{bmatrix} D_k \\ D_{k+1} \end{bmatrix} = \sqrt{3} \begin{bmatrix} \sin\dfrac{k\pi}{3} & -\cos\dfrac{k\pi}{3} \\ -\sin\dfrac{(k-1)\pi}{3} & \cos\dfrac{(k-1)\pi}{3} \end{bmatrix} \begin{bmatrix} \dfrac{V_{ds}}{V_{dc}} \\ \dfrac{V_{qs}}{V_{dc}} \end{bmatrix}.
\tag{10.32}
$$

The on-time for the null vectors are obtained as follows:

$$
\begin{bmatrix} T_0 \\ T_7 \end{bmatrix} = 1/2 \begin{bmatrix} T_S - T_k - T_{k+1} \\ T_S - T_k - T_{k+1} \end{bmatrix}
\tag{10.33}
$$

Therefore, Equations 10.31 and 10.33 give the on-times $T_k$, $T_{k+1}$, $T_0$ and $T_7$ with the duty ratio given by Equation 10.32 within a PWM period. The on-times of the three-phase PWM generator for the controller are determined as follows:

$$\begin{bmatrix} T_A \\ T_B \\ T_C \end{bmatrix} = \begin{bmatrix} \vec{V}_k & \vec{V}_{k+1} & \vec{V}_7 \end{bmatrix} \begin{bmatrix} T_k \\ T_{k+1} \\ T_7 \end{bmatrix} \quad (k = 1,\ldots,6) \tag{10.34}$$

where $T_A$, $T_B$ and $T_C$ are the on-times of each phase, and $\vec{V}_k$ is one of the six active operating states defined previously. For the instance shown in Figure 10.29, $\vec{V}^*$ is in sector 1. The on-times are obtained as

$$\begin{bmatrix} T_A \\ T_B \\ T_C \end{bmatrix} = \begin{bmatrix} \vec{V}_1 & \vec{V}_2 & \vec{V}_7 \end{bmatrix} \begin{bmatrix} T_k \\ T_{k+1} \\ T_7 \end{bmatrix} = \begin{bmatrix} 1 & 1 & 1 \\ 0 & 1 & 1 \\ 0 & 0 & 1 \end{bmatrix} \begin{bmatrix} T_k \\ T_{k+1} \\ T_7 \end{bmatrix}$$

The on-times of the switching gates are set up by the SV PWM controller by decomposing the rotating reference vector $\vec{V}^*$ into two components made of its neighboring space vectors. The duty cycles calculated from the two space vectors help establish the balanced three-phase voltages for the AC electric machine.

It was shown that only 78.5% of the inverter's capacity is used with sinusoidal PWM method. In SV PWM method, inverter's capability is improved by using a separate modulator for each of the inverter legs, generating three reference signals forming a balanced three-phase system. In this way, the maximum obtainable output voltage is increased with ordinary SV PWM up to 90.6% of the inverter capability. The SV PWM algorithm is fairly complex and computation intensive, but still well within the capabilities of the digital signal processors available today.

## Example 10.2

A SiC six-switch voltage source inverter is used as the inverter to drive the electric motor of a Nissan Leaf whose parameters are: vehicle mass = 1,521 kg, wheel radius = 0.4 m, frontal area = 2.16 m$^2$ and wheelbase = 2.7 m. The electric motor parameters are: $L_d$ = 1.52 mH, $L_q$ = 1.54 mH, $R_{ph}$ = 0.046 $\Omega$, motor torque constant $K_e$ = 0.46 (phase, peak) and $\lambda_m = 0.115 \dfrac{\text{Vs}}{\text{rad}}$ (phase, peak). The battery is rated at 40 kWh with a nominal DC bus voltage of 360 V.

The device parameters for the AEC-Q101 Automotive Grade N-channel Rohm SCT3022ALHR SiC MOSFET (discrete TO-247 package) selected for the inverter are: $V_{DS}$ = 650 V, $I_{DS}$ = 65 A, $R_{ds,on}$ = 22 m$\Omega$, $E_{on}$ = 252 µJ and $E_{off}$ = 201 µJ.

Using a computer simulation model and analysis, compute and plot the inverter rms current, inverter losses and motor power and energy demand as a function of time for the highway drive cycle.

## Solution

The simulation and analysis is carried out in two steps first generating data from a vehicle simulation model and then using equation-based models. The vehicle simulation model shown in Figure 3.25 and developed using MATLAB-Simulink is used for the highway drive cycle to derive the motor and inverter operating points. The drive cycle is given in terms of speed versus time which is regulated using the driver model. The vehicle simulation model then generates the motor input voltages $v_d$ and $v_q$, motor and inverter currents $i_d$ and $i_q$, and motor output torque $T$ and speed $\omega$. In this vehicle simulation model, the inverter details are not modeled since this would be computationally intensive requiring a long time to process for one drive cycle.

Using the simulation data of $v_d(t)$, $v_q(t)$, $i_d(t)$ and $i_q(t)$ components, motor peak voltage $v_{a,peak}(t)$ and motor peak current $I(t)$ are obtained. Using these data, modulation index $M(t)$ and power factor $\varphi(t)$ can be calculated from

$$M(t) = \frac{\sqrt{3}V_{a,peak}(t)}{V_{DC}}$$

$$\phi(t) = \tan^{-1}\frac{Q}{P}$$

where real power $P(t) = v_d \cdot i_d + v_q \cdot i_q$ and reactive power $Q(t) = v_q \cdot i_q - v_d \cdot i_q$.

From the above-calculated values, and using the device parameter values, the loss incurred by the inverter power devices can be calculated. The device rms current can be calculated as follows [7,8]:

$$I_{q,rms}(t) = I(t)\sqrt{\frac{1}{8} + \frac{1}{3\pi}M(t)\cos\phi(t)}$$

where $I(t)$ = peak output current, $M(t)$ = modulation index and $\varphi(t)$ = power factor.

The conduction loss of each device is

$$P_{cond,Q}(t) = R_{ds(on)}\left(I(t)\sqrt{\frac{1}{8} + \frac{1}{3\pi}M(t)\cos\phi(t)}\right)^2$$

The switching loss for each device is

$$P_{sw,Q}(t) = \frac{1}{\pi}f_{sw}(E_{on} + E_{off})\frac{I_{rms}V_{dc}}{I_{rms(nom)}I_{dc(nom)}}$$

The inverter rms current and power loss plots are given in Figure 10.32. Sinusoidal currents have been assumed for these loss calculations. Due to synchronous rectification of the MOSFET devices, SiC diodes conduct for a very small amount of time, and thus the loss associated with diodes can be neglected in drive cycle energy analysis.

The motor power output and energy are calculated from the simulation torque and speed data; the results are plotted in Figure 10.33.

(a)

(b)

**FIGURE 10.32** SiC Inverter operation in highway drive cycle: (a) inverter rms current and (b) inverter total power loss.

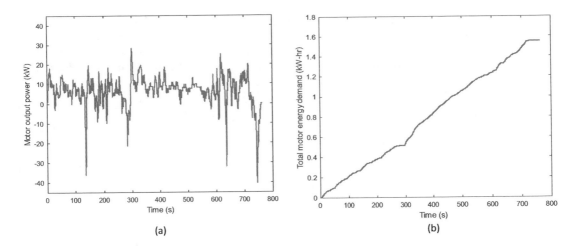

(a)

(b)

**FIGURE 10.33**  Electric motor operation in highway drive cycle: (a) motor output power and (b) energy demand.

## 10.5  SRM DRIVES

The power electronic drive circuits for SRM drives are quite different from those of AC motor drives. The torque developed in an SRM is independent of the direction of current flow. Therefore, unipolar converters are sufficient to serve as the power converter circuit for the SRM unlike induction motors or synchronous motors, which require bi-directional currents. This unique feature of the SRM together with the fact that the stator phases are electrically isolated from one another generated a wide variety of power circuit configurations. The type of converter required for a particular SRM drive is intimately related to motor construction and the number of phases. The choice also depends on the specific application.

The most flexible and the most versatile four-quadrant SRM converter is the bridge converter shown in Figure 10.34, which requires two switches and two diodes per phase [9,10]. The switches and the diodes must be rated to withstand the supply voltage plus any transient overload. During the magnetization period, both the switches are turned on and the energy is transferred from the source to the motor. Chopping or PWM, if necessary, can be accomplished by switching either or both the switches during the conduction period according to the control strategy. At commutation, both switches are turned off and the motor phase is quickly defluxed through the freewheeling diodes. The main advantage of this converter is the independent control of each phase, which is particularly important when phase overlap is desired. The only disadvantage is the requirement of two switches and two diodes per phase. This converter is especially suitable for high-voltage, high-power drives.

**FIGURE 10.34**  Converter topology for SRM: classic bridge power converter.

A number of other types of converters were developed for SRM with the primary objective of reducing the number of power devices by taking advantage of the phase independence character-istics of SRMs [11,12]. These converters include the split-capacitor converter, the Miller converter and the energy-efficient C-Dump converter. Converters with a reduced number of switches are less fault tolerant, and hence, not suitable for traction applications.

## PROBLEMS

### Parameters for Problems 10.1 and 10.2

$$V_{bat} = 144 \text{ V}, \ k\phi = 0.6 \text{ V-s}, \ L_a = 8\text{E-4 H}, \ R_a = 0.1 \ \Omega, \ f_s = 500 \text{ Hz}.$$

### 10.1

The time $\gamma$ (see Figure P10.1) in the DCM during acceleration of a two-quadrant chopper can be derived as

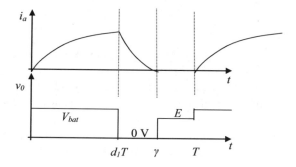

**FIGURE P10.1**

$$\gamma = -\tau \ln\left[\frac{E}{E + V_{bat}(e^{d_1 T/\tau} - 1)}\right] \text{ where } \tau = \frac{L_a}{R_a}$$

Derive the $\langle \omega \rangle$-$\langle T \rangle$ characteristics for acceleration operation of the two-quadrant chopper operat-ing in the DCM. (Do not substitute numerical values for parameters yet.) Do not try to solve $\langle \omega \rangle$ in terms of $\langle T \rangle$. Instead solve for $\langle T \rangle$ in terms of $\langle \omega \rangle$. Plot $\langle T \rangle$ versus $\langle \omega \rangle$ for the given parameters and $d_1 = 0.9, 0.5$ and $0.1$.

### 10.2

Calculate the worst-case armature current ripple in CCM for the given parameters. If the worst-case ripple is required to be less than 10 A what is the value of the filter inductance, or what value should the switching frequency be changed to?

### 10.3

Find the regions in the $T$-$\omega$ plane for DCM, CCM and UNCM acceleration operation of a two-quadrant chopper-fed DC motor. That is, find the restrictions on T and $\omega$ for each mode.

Hint: Start with the condition on $E$. Solve the inequality for $d_1$. Then, use the $\omega$-$T$ characteristics to eliminate $d_1$. Also, remember $0 \le d_1 \le 1$.

Plot these regions for the given parameters and also plot the safe operating area given:

$-100\,\text{N m} \le T \le 100\,\text{N m}$
$-300\,\text{rad/s} \le \omega \le 300\,\text{rad/s}$
$-30\,\text{hp} \le P \le 30\,\text{hp}$

## 10.4

Describe the UNCM of braking operation. Draw waveforms of armature current and terminal voltage. Calculate the speed torque characteristics for this mode. What quadrant in the $\omega$-$T$ plane is this mode?

## 10.5

Consider the electric vehicle drivetrain driven by a two-quadrant chopper shown in Figure P10.5. $d_1$ is the duty ratio for the acceleration operation, while $d_2$ is the duty ratio for braking operation. The various parameters are given below:

**FIGURE P10.5**

The EV parameters are

$m = 1{,}050\,\text{kg}, M_B = 150\,\text{kg}, C_D = 0.25, A_F = 2\,\text{m}^2, C_0 = 0.01, C_1 = 0,$
$\rho = 1.1614\,\text{kg/m}^3$ and $g = 10.81\,\text{m/s}^2,$
$r_{wh} = \text{radius of wheel} = 0.28\,\text{m}.$

Motor and controller parameters are

$R_a = 0.1\,\Omega, L_a = 2\,\text{mH}, k\phi = 0.6\,\text{V-s}, I_{a,rated} = 200\,\text{A},$
$f_s = \text{chopper switching frequency} = 500\,\text{Hz},$
$L_f = \text{series filter inductance} = 1.6\,\text{mH}.$

In each of the following cases, determine whether steady-state operation is in CCM, DCM or UNCM.

    a. $d_1 = 0.4, d_2 = 0, V = 25\,\text{m/s},$
    b. $d_1 = 0.8, d_2 = 0, V = 45\,\text{m/s},$
    c. $d_2 = 0, V = 25\,\text{m/s}, T = 40\,\text{N m}.$

Note: $V$ is the vehicle steady-state velocity, and $T$ is the motor torque. Also neglect friction and windage losses, and assume zero power loss between the motor shaft and the vehicle wheels.

## 10.6

An AC inverter is operated in a sinusoidal pulse mode. The transistor base current waveforms are shown in Figure P10.6. Sketch line-to-line voltages $v_{AB}$, $v_{BC}$ and $v_{CA}$, and line-to-neutral voltage $v_{AN}$ in Figure P10.6. Briefly comment on the voltages. Are they balanced? ($i_{cj}$ is for $j = 1$ to 6 are the base currents for transistors 1 to 6, respectively).

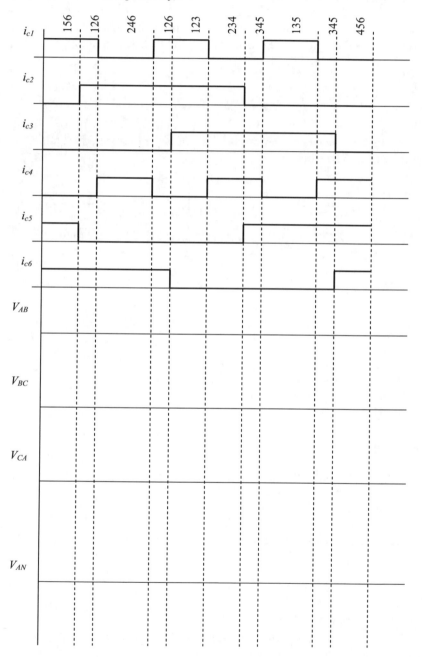

**FIGURE P10.6**

## 10.7

A 460 V, 60 Hz, 6 pole, 1,176 rpm, Y-connected induction motor has the following parameters referred to the stator at rated condition:

$$R_s = 0.19\ \Omega,\ R_r = 0.07\ \Omega,\ X_s = 0.75\ \Omega,\ X_r = 0.67\ \Omega \text{ and } X_m = \infty.$$

The motor is fed by a six-step inverter. The inverter is fed from a battery pack through a DC/DC converter.

The battery pack voltage is 72 V. Neglecting all the losses:

  i. Determine the output of the DC/DC converter.
  ii. Mention the type of the converter and its conversion ratio.

## 10.8

The motor in Problem 10.7 is employed to drive an electric vehicle which requires 300 N-m to propel the vehicle on a level road at constant velocity. The configuration is shown in Figure P10.8. Determine its operating speed and slip, while the frequency and voltage are kept constant at rated value.

**FIGURE P10.8**

## 10.9

The vehicle in Problem 10.7 is moving downward so that it requires 250 N m.

  i. What will be the input voltage for the motor from the inverter? Hence, determine the conversion ratio of the converter. Frequency is kept constant at rated value and the motor is running at the rated speed.
  ii. What should be the operating frequency of the inverter if the input voltage to the motor is kept constant at rated value and the motor is running at rated speed?

## 10.10

The DC-link voltage of a PWM inverter feeding a vector controlled induction motor drive is 300 VDC. Space vector PWM is used to supply the command voltages to the motor through the inverter. The voltage command in the stationary reference frame is $\vec{V}^s = 210e^{j0.44}$. What is the sector for this voltage command? Which two inverter voltage vectors are to be used? Calculate the $x$, $y$ and $z$ percentages to apply the command voltage.

## 10.11

The following flux equation describes the non-linear characteristics of a three-phase, 6/4 SRM:

$$\lambda_j(i,\theta) = \lambda_s(1 - \exp(-i_j f_j(\theta))),\ i_j \geq 0$$

where $\lambda_s$ = saturation flux = 0.2 V-s and $f(\theta) = a + b * \cos(N_r\theta - (j-1)2\pi/m)$.

Here, $j = 1, 2, 3$ denotes the phase number and $m = 3$. Given that $a = 0.024$ and $b = 0.0110$. Also given, phase resistance $R_{ph} = 0.3$.

Write a computer program and plot the phase-a currents when the motor is energized in the single pulse mode between the mechanical angles of 45° and 75° for speeds of 100, 1,000 and 10,000 rpm. The applied voltage is 24 V.

## REFERENCES

1. J.G. Kassakian, M.F. Schlecht and G.C. Verghese, *Principles of Power Electronics*, Addison Wesley Publishing Company, Reading, MA, 1991.
2. M.H. Rashid, *Power Electronics: Circuits, Devices and Applications*, Prentice Hall, Upper Saddle River, NJ, 2003.
3. N. Mohan, T.M. Undeland and W.P. Robins, *Power Electronics: Converters, Applications and Design*, John Wiley & Sons. Inc., Hoboken, NJ, 1995.
4. G.K. Dubey, *Power Semiconductor Controlled Drives*, Prentice Hall, Englewood Cliffs, NJ, 1989.
5. A.M. Trzynadlowski, *Introduction to Modern Power Electronics*, John Wiley & Sons Inc., Hoboken, NJ, 2016.
6. C. Hou, *DSP Implementation of Sensorless Vector Control for Induction Motors*, MS Thesis, University of Akron, Akron, OH, 2001.
7. K. Berringer, J. Marvin and P. Perruchoud, "Semiconductor power losses in AC inverters," *Conference Record of the 30th IEEE Industry Applications Society Conference and Annual Meeting*, 1, 882–888, Orlando, FL, 1995.
8. B. Ozpineci, L.M. Tolbert, S.K. Islam and M. Hasanuzzaman, "Effects of silicon carbide (SiC) power devices on HEV PWM inverter losses," IECON'01, *27th Annual Conference of the IEEE Industrial Electronics Society* (Cat. No. 37243), 2, 1061–1066, Denver, CO, 2001.
9. R.M. Davis, W.F. Ray and R.J. Blake, "Inverter drive for switched reluctance motor: circuits and component ratings," *IEE Proceedings*, 128(pt. B, 2), 126–136, March 1981.
10. T.J.E. Miller, *Switched Reluctance Motors and Their Control*, Magna Physics Publishing, Hillsboro, OH and Oxford University Press, Oxford, 1993.
11. C. Pollock, "Power converter circuits for switched reluctance motors with the minimum number of switches," *IEE Proceedings*, 137(pt. B, 6), 373–384, November 1990.
12. S. Mir, I. Husain and M. Elbuluk, "Energy-efficient C-dump converters for switched reluctance motors," *IEEE Transactions on Power Electronics*, 12(5), 912–921, September 1997.

# 11 Vehicle Controllers and Communication

In electric and hybrid vehicles, controllers are required for various powertrain components such as electric motor drives, power electronic converters, battery management, IC engine, transmission and fuel cell. Hybrid electric vehicles also require a supervisory controller to generate the commands for the various powertrain subsystems. Ancillary systems such as electric power steering (EPS), anti-lock braking system (ABS), multimedia entertainment unit and climate control system also require a controller for their operation. The controller is responsible for generating output command signals for the actuator based on command inputs and feedback signals following a control law and algorithm. The controllers also host the communications module through which the components and subsystems communicate with each other. The command signals, the sensor feedback signals and the system output variables interconnect the vehicle driver, the supervisory controller and the subsystems, and components are transferred from one unit to another through an automotive communication network. Controller area network (CAN) is the most commonly used protocol used for such communication. CAN uses a serial multi-master communication protocol with each controller hosting the physical layer of the network.

The first two sections of this chapter cover the vehicle controllers, microcontrollers and the controller software, while the two other sections discuss vehicle communications and CAN.

## 11.1 VEHICLE CONTROLLERS

Controller devices or processors are available today with high computational power and speed due to the tremendous advances in the very large-scale integrated circuit (VLSI) technology over the past few decades. Powertrain and ancillary components are controlled based on an algorithm and sensor feedback signals which are implemented in a microprocessor control unit (MCU) which is essentially a microcontroller. These are also known as the embedded controller units which include the control algorithm software and the MCU hardware [1,2]. The tasks of the controller include the following:

- Control law implementation to generate command signals for the actuators.
- Protection and fault management based on system variables, constraints and sensor feedback signals.
- Data processing and logging for display to the user for testing during development and maintenance during operation.

The MCU or a microcontroller is a highly integrated device which includes the parts needed to perform an application control function. Depending on the processing power and features needed, a 4-, 8-, 16- or 32-bit microcontroller can be chosen for an application. The embedded control unit of a system, particularly that of a powertrain component, is known as an electronic control unit (ECU). The ECU module is the brain of each system of an automobile. At the heart of this ECU lies the microcontroller that coordinates and controls the functions of the system; system performance is driven by the features and capabilities of the microcontroller. In a modern vehicle, there are about 50–100 microcontrollers as compared to about 15 in the mid-1990s. In addition to the powertrain component ECUs, microcontrollers are used in an automobile in a variety of applications such as

Electric and Hybrid Vehicles

fuel injection, trip computer, window lift, keyless entry, seat belt fastener, airbag system and dashboard display.

The control task can be managed by one controller device or more depending on the system and requirements. The designer can choose from a wide selection of processors to implement the control algorithm of the system available from various suppliers.

### 11.1.1 Microcontroller Types

The microcontroller is a miniaturized integrated circuit with all of the components needed for a controller built in a single chip. The complete microcontroller integrates the central processor unit (CPU) with the memory and various peripheral components, such as timer/counter units, analog-to-digital (A/D) converters, serial interface unit, communication units, input/output (I/O) ports and pulse-width modulation (PWM) modules on the single IC. The CPU of a microcontroller is the microprocessor which is the more elemental device used for computations. Microcontrollers have all the memory and peripheral components required for an event-driven control application integrated in one piece of silicon. Different memory types include read-only memory (ROM), random access memory (RAM) and erasable programmable ROM (EPROM). The organization of the microcontroller components with respect to its bus structure is shown in Figure 11.1.

Digital signal processors (DSPs) are also used in automotive embedded control applications especially for the powertrain components that have intensive computational requirements. DSPs are designed with dedicated hardware circuitry for fast processing of signals. Examples of automotive applications where DSPs are used include electric motor drives, power electronics control, voice synthesis and recognition, communication systems, radar signal analysis and image processing.

Microcontrollers and DSPs can be divided into floating point processors or fixed-point processors in terms of number representation, although high-end microcontrollers are available that support both type of number handling. A floating point processor allows allotting point arithmetic units to solve this issue with an added cost. Algorithm development time for a floating point system can be dramatically shorter due to the programming flexibility. In fixed-point processors, special representations of non-integer values are required to execute mathematical operations which are known as fixed-point arithmetic. A fixed-point processor makes it more difficult to calculate mathematical expressions that involve non-integer variables. However, there is an advantage of fixed-point processors in applications where control execution times need to be managed critically. Multiplications and divisions are managed by register shift left or right, respectively, by the corresponding number of bits to minimize code execution time since the CPU operates in base two. The shift by one bit is equivalent to multiplying or dividing by a power of two depending on shifting left or shifting right. With shift operations, control loop times can be accurately controlled and cycle execution time overruns can be eliminated.

The automotive microcontroller manufacturers have resorted to multicore architectures to meet the stringent and demanding performance requirements in powertrain-type ECUs as well as in multimedia applications. In multicore architectures, two or more CPU cores are implemented within the same die. In comparison with the single-core microcontroller, a dual-core microcontroller offers

**FIGURE 11.1**　Microcontroller organization block diagram.

close to double the performance at the same frequency depending on the SW architecture. An additional benefit for improved performance is that the power generation and the heat dissipation are lower in a multicore processor compared to a single-core processor for the execution of the same tasks [3].

The ARM processors have gained significant popularity in recent years for various automotive MCU applications. ARM, which evolved from advanced RISC machine, is a family of reduced instruction set computing (RISC) architectures for computer processors configured for various environments. ARM processors are built with one of its core architectures both as a system-on-chip (SoC) and system-on-module (SoM) which include memory and various interfaces. Processors that have a RISC architecture typically require fewer transistors than those with a complex instruction set computing (CISC) architecture which helps reduce cost, power consumption and heat dissipation.

There is also a trend of including logic resources, such as field programmable gate array (FPGA) into the SoC and SoM digital control platform to enable new opportunities for the digital control system. First, the embedded logic resource of SoC significantly enhances the configuration flexibility of the peripherals. The pin-out and number of specific peripherals are no longer constrained by the IC manufacturer. Second, the FPGA can be programmed as a computation core dedicated to particular tasks to reduce the program execution time. Finally, the FPGA can be used to implement more precise, efficient and advanced PWM.

With more stringent safety standards and heated competition among automotive OEMs, there are more advanced technology features in new cars, like ADAS (advanced driver assistance systems), infotainment systems with OTA (over-the-air) upgrade functionality and active chassis/body control. With the adaptation of these new features, the number of MCUs would also increase. There is a trend to integrate the functionality of multiple MCUs into one massive MCU to simplify the vehicle's electrical system architecture, like combining motor drive MCU with the vehicle control MCU. The FPGA-embedded SoC digital platform, as mentioned above, with high degree of flexibility and performance, would be an ideal candidate. With the introduction of ASIC dedicated to autonomous driving from Tesla, it is not hard to imagine that there will be specialized ASIC for vehicle control and powertrain control with even higher performance in the future.

Microcontrollers offered by manufacturers typically belong to a family. The family has similar type of microcontrollers but with different capabilities in terms of memory size, maximum frequency, package compatibility, embedded number of peripherals and even enhanced peripherals. An application developed on a microcontroller can be easily ported to another microcontroller within the same family. Hence, during the selection of a microcontroller, a family should be chosen such that it provides a growth path for future upgrades.

### 11.1.2 MICROCONTROLLER COMPONENTS

The primary components of a microcontroller are: central processing unit (CPU), memory, data bus and address bus, data I/O circuitry and peripherals. Brief descriptions of these components are provided below.

#### 11.1.2.1 Central Processing Unit

CPU of a microcontroller is the elemental microprocessor where instructions are executed and decisions are made. One or more independent actual processors (also known as cores) form the single computing unit that read and execute program instructions (i.e., software codes). The program instructions and data are stored in internal or external memory that can be sequentially accessed by the CPU via the address bus. The CPU reads the instructions from memory via the data bus and executes the instructions. The main processing part of the CPU is the arithmetic logic unit (ALU) that performs the mathematical and logic operations. The data specified by an instruction is loaded into the ALU for processing. After execution, the result is stored in the defined register or memory area. Microcontrollers are digital systems using the binary numbering system which are the bits representing either '1' or '0' in the boolean logic. A common approach of referring to a microcontroller, microprocessor or DSP is by the data width of the CPU. The CPU can process either a 4-, 8-, 16-, 32- or 64-bit data at a time depending on the hardware design.

### 11.1.2.2   Memory and Registers

There are five basic types of memory: RAM, ROM, EPROM, electrically erasable programmable ROM (EEPROM) and flash memory. A RAM has the capability to both read and write so that the stored information can be retrieved (read) and new information can be stored (write). This type of memory is typically of static type, which means that the memory contents are lost once the microcontroller is powered down. The ROM allows data to be read from, but do not allow writing into the memory. ROM is a non-volatile memory that retains its contents even after power is removed. ROM is used for storing the user code that does not change during execution of the software instructions. The EPROM devices allow the user to apply ultraviolet ray to erase the contents of the memory and reprogram it. EPROMs are generally used during the development stage when the user's code often changes. The EEPROM is a type of ROM whose contents can be erased electrically and reprogrammed. Flash memory is the latest type of non-volatile memory similar to an EEPROM. Once programmed, the contents of the flash memory remain intact until an erase cycle is initiated through software, and the device has not been powered down. The contents of flash memory can be erased electrically.

Microcontroller on-chip memory typically consists of ROM, flash memory and partially of RAM. Initialization programs are stored in ROM so that the controller is basically initialized after reset during the start-up phase automatically. The flash memory contains the application code including the control algorithms, which is executed after the start-up phase. If the RAM is used for code, then an external or internal memory device plus communication is needed to load the program into the embedded controller RAM at start-up or during run-time phase.

The registers are used for temporary data storage location, while a user's software code is being executed. The register file consists of the memory locations used for data storage. The register files are typically made of RAM memory locations. Microcontrollers also contain special function registers (SFRs) which allow the user to configure and define the functionalities of the peripherals. A microcontroller pin can be configured either as a general purpose I/O or as a special function pin through appropriate configurations set in the corresponding SFR. The pins are interrupt driven when configured as a special function pin, and are used for special operation with precise timing synchronized with microcontroller clock signals.

### 11.1.2.3   Timers and Counters

A microcontroller is equipped with several timers that provide the time base for triggering events or executing a certain piece of user code. The timer/counter is a digital counter that increments or decrements at a fixed frequency. For a 16-bit timer/counter, the counting could go on until $2^{16}$ or 65,536 before it overflows. The counter can be reset according to the instructions set by the user in a SFR. The timers can be clocked from either the microcontroller crystal clock source or from an external clock. The frequency of counting is also configurable. An event counter SFR can also be loaded with set value; once the set value is reached by counting up or down in synchronism with the clock frequency, an action is triggered such as setting an interrupt or generating a pulse.

Modern microcontroller supports special timer and counter for dedicated applications. For example, PWM generation and position sensor interfaces are included for electronic motor control, while signal debouncing, angle speed frequency generation and PWM signaling are built-in for combustion engine control.

The internal timer is ideal to set a constant frequency such as that required for PWM generation. On the other hand, capturing the encoder pulses for position and speed calculations of a rotating device based on the rising or falling edge on the I/O port pin is an example of using an external timer.

For safety reasons, most of the microcontrollers are also fitted with a *watchdog timer*. This could be a hardware or software timing device that triggers a system reset when there is some fault in the processor, such as a hang-up of the processor. The processor is supposed to service the watchdog timer routinely, and a failure to do so means something is wrong. The intent of the watchdog timer is to generate a reset of the microcontroller.

### 11.1.2.4  Peripherals

The on-chip peripherals are what make microcontrollers the most suitable for ECU implementations in automobiles. The type and capabilities of the peripherals play the most important roles in selecting a microcontroller for an application. They can help to off load the main CPU by, e.g., handling serial interface protocols (CAN, SPI, UART, Flexray), calculating special filter types (FIR) and generating control signals (such as PWM outputs). Communication ports, I/O ports, PWM generator and A/D converter are among the important peripherals in a microcontroller which are discussed in the following.

Communication modules in a microcontroller help a control unit communicate with external devices, such as back-up processors, shift registers, data loggers, data converters, diagnostics modules, monitoring devices, sensors or other controllers on the vehicle. Serial interface is often used in many automotive applications using communication modules such as CAN, SPI (serial peripheral interface) and LIN (local interconnect network). Serial communication modules transfer a group of data bits, one at a time, sequentially over a single data line. Microcontrollers may also be equipped with a parallel port that functions the same way as the serial port except that the data are in parallel format. Parallel communication is much faster than the serial communication, but requires address decoding. In automotive applications, parallel ports are used for external memory bus such as in DRAM or Flash.

The I/O pins in a microcontroller allow to read signals from an external source and to output signals for other electronic components. The external source could be a sensor or another microcontroller. The output signals are required for power electronic gate drivers, actuators or other digital devices. The I/O pins can be configured as a general purpose pin for manual read or write option by the user or as a special purpose pin for dedicated peripherals.

PWM peripherals allow the user to generate digital signals at a specified frequency and duty ratio with minimal hardware and software overhead. Microcontrollers or DSPs feature a number of digital PWM outputs, with associated timers that can generate PWM signals with minimal CPU supervision. Once the PWM dedicated registers are initialized, the only operation needed from the CPU is to update the duty cycle. This peripheral is especially useful for electric motor drives or power converters that require generating the gate signals for the power semiconductor devices.

A/D converters are used to convert external analog signals to digital format for the microcontroller. For example, the measured feedback currents for an electric motor drive are analog which needs to be converted to digital format for the controller to use it. On-chip A/D converters can convert that command input into digital format. Conversely, D/A converters will transform a digital information within the microcontroller into an analog signal that the outside world will understand. While A/D converters are a common peripheral device, a D/A converter may also exist on-chip in a microcontroller. The time required for the complete analog to digital conversion in the A/D converter is critical in ensuring proper execution of a control algorithm. The time depends on the two steps of sampling and conversion that are needed for the complete conversion. The digital value can be stored in 8-, 10- or 12-bit depending on the A/D converter used.

### 11.1.3  FUNCTIONAL SAFETY STANDARD ISO 26262

The functional safety requirements of electrical and electronic systems in production road vehicles is guided by the standard ISO 26262 as defined by the International Organization for Standardization (ISO) in 2011. ISO 26262 focuses on the specific safety needs of those vehicle systems throughout their entire lifecycles. The requirements and guidelines for software development and design are also included in this standard.

The electronic control system has seen increasing utilization in the automotive industry with the system becoming more complex. Software failure could be catastrophic, compromising the safety of the vehicle. Software developers need to ensure that under no circumstance, failure could occur. However, exhaustive testing is not practical. Therefore, systems should be designed to prevent failure in the first place or ensure failure happens in a controlled manner.

The systems on vehicles that need to comply with ISO 26262 include driver assistance system, passive and active safety systems and propulsion system. ISO 26262 provides guidelines for developers to mitigate the risks of failure.

## 11.2 CONTROLLER SOFTWARE DEVELOPMENT

The tasks and operations in the microcontroller hardware are governed by the software developed through a process of coding, debugging, optimization, testing and validation. The software development starts with coding using a programming language, which can be either a *high-level language* (such as C or C++) or a *modeling language* (such as MATLAB/Simulink) [4]. Assembly languages were used decades ago, but with the availability of efficient compilers, the use of high-level languages started due to the ease of programming. The process of code generation is more rapidly moving toward auto-code generators using modeling languages, such as MATLAB/Simulink or Universal Modeling Language (UML). The use of auto-code generation, software encapsulation and hardware-independent application software (such as AUTOSAR) allows greater reusability of the software across several hardware platforms [5].

### 11.2.1 AUTOSAR

The AUTOSAR (AUTomotive Open System ARchitecture) is a software architecture platform designed to manage the functions of the ECU implementation and to address the software standardization across a common platform. The AUTOSAR consortium was founded in 2003 by BMW, DaimlerChrysler, Bosch, Continental, Volkswagen and Siemens VDO to address the microcontroller software development needs in the automotive industry. Ford, General Motors, Toyota and PSA (Peugeot Citroen) joined the consortium later as core members (http://www.autosar.org/). The consortium describes the AUTOSAR architecture as an open and standardized automotive software architecture, jointly developed by automobile manufacturers, suppliers and tool developers. Software standardization helps the automotive industry to execute the same software operation by several different microcontrollers and to utilize prior software assets in different and expanded applications. The AUTOSAR standard will serve as a platform for future vehicle developments with cost reduction. The primary motivation for AUTOSAR is to manage software complexity and to provide flexibility with product modification, upgrade and update.

The fundamental design concept of AUTOSAR is separation between infrastructure and application. AUTOSAR masks the software codes that are microcontroller dependent through the real-time environment (RTE) and basic software (BSW). The automotive ECU manufacturers can then develop ECUs without having to consider the type of microcontroller. This software exists on top of the RTE and is hardware independent. The AUTOSAR software configuration is shown in Figure 11.2.

The RTE is the middleware layer that interfaces the AUTOSAR software and/or sensor and actuator components with the BSW. The RTE allows the AUTOSAR software components to be independent from the mapping to specific ECUs.

The BSW is mostly hardware-independent middleware connecting the RTE with the microcontroller; however, it contains the operating system. The BSW is composed of the service layer, ECU abstraction layer, microcontroller abstraction layer (MCAL) and other software components.

**FIGURE 11.2** AUTOSAR software configuration.

The service layer of the BSW provides the application software with the following operating system services: network communications and management services, memory services, diagnostics and ECU control status.

The ECU abstraction layer responds to the functions of the application software and connects to the MCAL. This layer provides interfaces to the drivers in the MCAL, and drivers for external devices. This is achieved through an application programming interface (API) for access to peripherals and devices regardless of their physical location, and their connectivity.

The MCAL is a device driver positioned in the bottommost layer of the BSW. It can directly access the memory that is mapped with the peripheral and external devices inside the microcontroller. The MCAL segment of the BSW is hardware dependent.

## 11.2.2 Software Development Tools

The software code development requires an integrated development environment (IDE) which is typically provided by the microcontroller manufacturer. The IDE tool includes the compiler, debugger, linker and simulator/emulator. The debugger has the capabilities of debugging at the source level. The simulation environment provided models the microcontroller, memory configuration and interrupt mechanism. The block diagram of the development process using a tool is shown in Figure 11.3. An application developer starts with an evaluation board based on a specific microcontroller during the development stages of an application. The evaluation boards are typically used to evaluate the application software at a very early state when the target ECU is still under development. Control cards with the microcontroller installed are then developed for an application. The IDE tool is then used to download the software into the target device.

Hardware-in-the-loop (HIL) simulation environment is another useful method to validate microcontroller-based control card for development cost reduction or when the complete system is not available. The system is simulated is an HIL simulator with the real control hardware connected to it. For example, during the development of a motor drive system (plant), a real motor controller (hardware) can be connected to a virtual motor and load model which will be running in real time in a HIL simulator. In HIL simulation, the dynamic behavior of the plant will be very close to real plant with an accurate plant model.

**FIGURE 11.3**   Microcontroller software development environment.

### 11.2.3  APPLICATION CONTROLLER IMPLEMENTATION

A microcontroller-based hardware development project for a system starts with the determination of the system requirements. The requirements analysis consists of defining what the system should do, how it will interface with other systems or the user, how it should respond to different input conditions, etc. The next step is the microcontroller selection which is chosen based on the bus size (8-, 16- or 32-bits), the number and type of inputs and outputs, the processing power and speed, amount and types of memory, support tools and the peripherals required. The peripherals include GPIO, PWM I/O, communication ports, A/D converters and memory. The memory size within the microcontroller in terms of Flash for the main program, RAM and EEPROM are important considerations. The speed of the microcontroller is critical which is related to the frequency of the clock source, as well as the internal bus, the CPU core and/or internal PLL. The temperature range is considered for both operating and storage. An example of a motor controller implementation is given below.

#### 11.2.3.1  Motor Controller

A high-performance motor controller algorithm is needed for either the traction electric motor drive or a servo-type drive such as the electric power steering. The controller development stages are similar although the algorithm, sensors, resolution and faults management would be customized for each application. The processing and flow of signals in the controller of a generic motor drive system are shown in Figure 11.4. The motor controller algorithm resides in the memory of the microcontroller and is processed by its CPU. The controller receives the command signals from the user, which could be a higher-level controller of the vehicle. The control command could be either the desired torque or speed of the motor. Communication between the user and the CPU is shown through the CAN module. Microcontroller analog and digital ports can input signals only up to a certain voltage level. Also, PWM output signals are needed at much higher levels (18 V or more) at the input of the inverter gate driver; the microcontroller PWM output signals are typically around 3.3 V. An interface electronic signal circuit board conditions the microcontroller input and output for interfacing with the external devices, such as various sensors and gate drivers. The figure shows position sensor and three Hall effect current sensors for position, speed and phase current feedback signals.

*Signal Conditioning Circuits*: The feedback circuits measure and scale the sensor signals into voltages within the range of the microcontroller inputs. The Hall effect sensors or resistive shunt sensors are used to measure currents. The signal outputs of the sensors are bi-directional for AC motor phases currents that they are sensing. This current has to be converted into a voltage that would be within the ADC input range. The DC bus voltage feedback is also needed for the motor controller which is easier to handle since it is a strictly positive voltage. The only necessary operation is to scale down the high voltage such that ADC ratings are never exceeded. Analog circuit examples for current and voltage sensing are shown in Figure 11.5.

**FIGURE 11.4** Microcontroller implementation of an electric motor drive controller.

**FIGURE 11.5** Analog circuits for (a) current sensing and (b) voltage sensing.

*Interrupt Services*: Embedded control systems can be classified into event-triggered or time-triggered based on the method of control execution. In an event-triggered system, a processing algorithm or activity is initiated as a consequence of the occurrence of an event. In a time-triggered system, the activities are initiated periodically at predetermined instants in real time. Many of the automotive applications are event-driven control systems, which means that the normal code execution must be halted to allow a higher-priority task to be executed. When an interrupt occurs, the CPU branches to an interrupt service routine (ISR) and executes the instructions stored in that routine. Upon completion of the ISR, the CPU returns to the instruction from where it branched off to the ISR. A higher-priority interrupt may occur while servicing an interrupt; the CPU would branch off to the ISR of the higher-priority interrupt, and would return to the lower priority interrupt after servicing the higher-priority interrupt.

*PWM Generation*: PWM is generated by having a timer configured to count either upward, or upward and downward (symmetric or asymmetric PWM) up to a value chosen by the user at a rate also set by the user. As a result, both PWM precision and frequency can be accurately selected. The timer value is then compared at each step with a variable contained in another register, called the compare register. It is also possible to associate two PWM outputs with one timer and compare value in order to control the two switches that form an inverter leg. Various interrupts can be generated to synchronize the programs with PWM. An interrupt function is a program that is executed when a preprogrammed event occurs such as PWM period or underflow. This can be useful, for example, to synchronize the various program measurements, such as analog to digital conversions, with the PWM. The PWM module includes deadbeat timer to introduce a user specified dead-time delay to prevent shoot-through faults in an inverter. This feature is essential for AC drives.

*Analog to Digital Conversion*: For AC motor control applications, microcontrollers or DSPs with two or three sample and hold units are useful to measure the AC phase currents for controller feedback signals. In automotive applications, all three phase currents are measured using the A/D channels. However, two-phase currents can be sampled to reduce cost as is used in many applications. The total A/D conversion time is the sum of the sampling time and conversion time. Higher sampling time ensures the capacitor to charge up to the analog input voltage. Higher conversion time ensures higher accuracy of representative digital values. The sampling and conversion times are set during initialization in the A/D configuration registers. This synchronization is important for optimal precision of the two measured phase currents. The ADC can be automatically synchronized with the PWM circuits so that conversions can be started when specific events occur, without any CPU supervision for optimal precision.

*Quadrature Encoder*: Motor control microcontrollers and DSPs are equipped with a special quadrature encoder unit for processing position feedback signal information. The encoder outputs, which are two square-waves in quadrature, are decoded so that they either increment or decrement the counter value in a timer. The microcontroller detects the rotor movement direction from the leading of the two signals and the timer's value is updated accordingly. In addition to this, the encoder has an index output, which is a digital output that gives a small pulse once per revolution. An initial alignment phase through an off-line test is necessary to synchronize the index pulse with a particular location of the rotor with respect to the stator. This allows the program to get absolute rotor position once the index pulse is received. The three signals are processed in this peripheral module to calculate the position and direction of rotation without any CPU overhead.

*CAN Communications*: Microcontrollers for automotive ECUs require a CAN module to support distributed real-time control with a very high level of security at a given communication rate. The CAN module can transmit and receive prioritized messages of up to eight bytes in data length using a multi-master serial bus with an arbitration protocol and an error-detection mechanism for a high level of data integrity. CAN modules are desired with time-stamping feature to provide a versatile and robust serial communication interface. Further details on CAN communications are presented in Section 11.4.

*Program Execution Times*: In a motor control algorithm, different code segments have to be executed within certain rates to ensure proper execution of the codes, and hence, the proper operation of the system. For example, current feedback updates must be available to the processor at the PWM rate so that the updated PWM duty ratio is based on the latest current sampled data and not the one stored in the previous PWM cycle. However, speed calculations need not be updated at the PWM rate since a machine mechanical dynamics is much slower than the electrical dynamics. Figure 11.6 shows an example of program segmentation in a PWM clock cycle to execute various functionalities synchronized with the PWM counter. A symmetric PWM carrier is shown here with the PWM timer counting up and down from zero to a chosen period value that sets the PWM frequency. The time '$t_{ADC}$' in Figure 11.6 corresponds to the time at which ADC conversions are triggered. This time is chosen so that the data used in the 'A' programs would use measurements that would be as recent as possible. The different segments are described below.

Segment A: This segment of the program includes high-priority time-critical applications. They are executed on a timer underflow (zero-value) interrupt, at the beginning of the PWM period. These

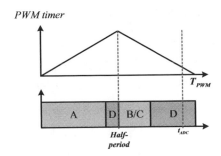

**FIGURE 11.6** Program executions as a function of time.

programs include: Park transformation of currents in AC drives, ADC result treatment, position update, current control and PWM algorithm.

Segment B/C: This segment represents control codes that need not be run in every PWM cycle, but at a fixed slow rate. An example is parameter adaptation algorithms that do not need to be executed in every PWM cycle, but is related to the slower thermal time constant of the machine. These segments are chosen to be synchronized with the timer period interrupt and consequently have a high priority.

Segment D: Most of the programs included in this block have a low priority and stop their execution whenever an interrupt occurs. Exceptions can be allowed with interrupts provided the interrupt service execution time is very small. For example, the interrupt associated with the encoder index, which resets the rotor position and has a very small execution time, can be executed in this segment. The other programs in this category are not time critical, such as data conversion and serial transmission to external device. The speed control program could also be included in these blocks. The segment could also include diagnostics and a supervising program.

## 11.3  VEHICLE COMMUNICATIONS

The components and systems in a vehicle are linked together through a system of networked communication. The command signals, the sensor feedback signals and the system output variables interconnect the vehicle driver, the supervisory controller and the subsystems, and components are transferred from one unit to another through the automotive communication network. The type of networked communication used in automobiles is known as CAN. CAN is a special type of local area network (LAN) that uses a serial multi-master communication protocol. CAN supports distributed real-time control with a very high level of security, and a communication rate of up to 1 Mbps. The CAN bus is ideally suitable for applications operating in noisy and harsh environments, such as in the automotive and other industrial fields that require reliable communication or multiplexed wiring.

Communications via Ethernet are used for in-vehicle communication, measurement and calibration, diagnostics and communication between electric vehicles and charging stations. Ethernet is also being used for automated and autonomous driving as well as infotainment. For vehicle-to-vehicle (V2V) and vehicle-to-infrastructure (V2I) external communications, 5G mobile networks will play a key role in the future as discussed earlier in Section 4.2.2. In this chapter, we will focus on the CAN protocol after an introduction on the OSI (Open Systems Interconnection) seven-layer model.

### 11.3.1  OSI Seven-Layer Model

The fundamental of networked communications is the OSI seven-layer network model, which describes the protocol for communication among computer nodes over a common network. The model was developed by the ISO in 1983 to provide an open communication protocol for the

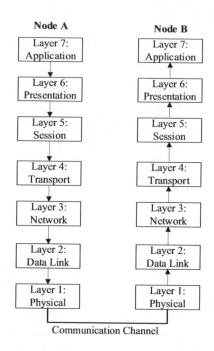

**FIGURE 11.7**   Communication of two nodes via seven-layer OSI network model.

industry to use and build systems with defined interfaces at the physical link. The seven-layer OSI model is structured in a top-to-bottom arrangement starting with the application layer at the top [6]. Figure 11.7 shows the communication of two computer nodes, one a transmit node and the other a receive node, via the seven layers of the network for each system. The application layer serves as the human-machine interface (HMI) for the computer node of a system. The bottom layer of OSI provides the physical link to the communication channel through which data is transferred to other systems built with a similar communication model. The seven layers of OSI are described below.

*Layer 7: Application* – The end-user interacts with the machine through an executable application in this layer. The layer supports a collection of miscellaneous protocols for high-level applications. Examples are electronic mail, command execution, file transfer and connecting remote terminal.

*Layer 6: Presentation* – The presentation layer is concerned with the semantics of the bits. This layer isolates the application layer of sending Node A from the particulars of the environment and can tell the receiving Node B of the format. For example, this layer describes how floating point numbers can be exchanged between nodes with different math formats. The layer is responsible for protocol conversion and data cryptography, if implemented.

*Layer 5: Session* – This layer ensures that the context of all packets sent by the other layer is preserved. This is an enhanced version of the transport layer and very few applications use it.

*Layer 4: Transport* – The transport layer acknowledges message transmission across the network and validates that the transmission has occurred without any loss of data. The layer divides the message into smaller packets, assigns sequence number and transmits them. The receiving computer re-assembles the packets. If a data packet is lost and arrives out of order, the layer resends the data packet placing it back in the correct sequence.

*Layer 3: Network* – The network layer is responsible for the transmission of packets routing them either through the shortest distance route or through the fastest route whichever is the best path. The layer is responsible for managing network problems such as packet switching, data congestion and routines. As an example, the internet protocol (IP) resides in this layer.

*Layer 2: Data Link* – The data link layer is responsible for controlling the error between adjacent nodes and transfer the frames to other computer via the physical layer. Data link layer is used by hubs and switches for their operation. The layer groups the bits into bit stream and ensures their correct delivery. It adds few bits at the beginning and end of each frame and also adds the checksum. The receiving node verifies the checksum; if the checksum is incorrect, it sends a control message requesting retransmission.

*Layer 1: Physical* – The physical layer is responsible for transmitting the bit stream over the physical cable. The physical layer defines the hardware items such as modems, cables, cards and voltages. The bit rate and the voltage levels for '0' and '1' are defined in this layer. The transmission may be one-way or bi-directional.

## 11.3.2  IN-VEHICLE COMMUNICATIONS

In-vehicle communication protocols have been categorized into classes A through D according to the data-handling speed with class A being the slowest. Within a class, there are several different types of communication protocols. The network classes, the data-handling speed ranges for the four classes and the types of communication protocols in a class are listed in Table 11.1. The data-handling speed requirements of the various systems in a vehicle determine the class of protocol that would be used for that system; not all devices need to communicate at the same speed. For example, the powertrain components need to be networked through a high-speed protocol since these are drive critical components of the vehicle. On the other hand, passenger seat operation is not drive critical, and hence, can be managed through a slower communication protocol.

Class A is the slow-speed protocol used for vehicle body electrical functions, such as power seat, power windows and power mirrors. Protocols under class A are LIN and time-triggered protocol/A (TTP/A).

Class B network is used for instrumentation and data display to the user; for example, dash-board display and cabin climate control. The most common class B protocol is the SAE J 1850.

Class C network is used for real-time control applications, such as those in vehicle dynamics control, powertrain controls, engine controls and hybrid component controls.

Class D networks include the fastest communication protocol in the automobiles. This class targets future protocols for in-vehicle communications as well. Media-oriented systems transport (MOST) and Flexray are example protocols for Class D, which are making their way into modern automobiles. MOST is the vehicle communication bus standard intended for interconnecting multimedia components. A reliable, high-speed communication network is also essential for safety critical components for today's automobiles, particularly as drive-by-wire systems get introduced in a vehicle. Drive-by-wire technologies include steer-by-wire, brake-by-wire, throttle-by-wire, etc.; these technologies will replace all the existing hydraulic and mechanical systems currently in place. In addition, the control command for all of the electric powertrain in hybrid and electric vehicles are by-wire technologies. The safety-critical and propulsion components require reliable and deterministic time triggered protocols instead of event triggered protocol such as that in the CAN.

**TABLE 11.1**
**Vehicle Communication Networks**

| Network Class | Speed | Communication Protocols | Application |
|---|---|---|---|
| Class A | <10 kbps | CAN (basic), LIN, SAE J2602, TTP/A | Vehicle body electrical accessories |
| Class B | 10–125 kbps | CAN (low-speed) SAE J1850, ISO 9141-2 | Diagnostics and data sharing |
| Class C | 125 kbps–1 Mbps | CAN (high-speed), SAE J 1039 | Real-time controls |
| Class D | >1 Mbps | Flexray, MOST | Safety-critical, multimedia |

The Flexray protocol, which is being developed by the Flexray consortium, provides high-speed, deterministic, fault-tolerant message transmission essential in drive-by-wire and electric powertrain components.

## 11.4 CONTROLLER AREA NETWORK

The CAN was originally developed by Bosch in 1985 for in-vehicle communications among the devices, sensors and actuators. Prior to CAN, the automotive industry used point to point wiring which required digital and analog inputs and outputs to every electronic device in the vehicle. This required a heavy wiring harness that increased weight, cost and complexity of the in-vehicle wiring. The problem compounded as the number of electronic devices used in vehicles gradually increased. CAN provides an inexpensive, reliable network that enables all the electric control units or the electronic interface of vehicle components communicate with each other. The automotive industry quickly adopted CAN since its original development because of its flexibility and advantages. Realizing the advantages of CAN, other industries have also adopted CAN for networked communications. CAN is widely used in aerospace applications, such as aircraft ECUs of components, flight-state sensors and navigation systems. Rail transportation systems extensively use CAN for communications at various levels ranging from ECUs of components to keeping track of the number of passengers. CAN communications is widely used in HMI units of industrial equipment. CAN protocols have applications in medical equipment and in hospital operating rooms.

The focus on CAN in this book is on in-vehicle communications where systems or devices require distributed real-time control including fault management and diagnostics. Operating points of powertrain and ancillary components are transmitted from the vehicle supervisory controller to the CAN nodes of the respective components. Similarly feedback information from the components are transmitted into the CAN bus. An example CAN layout with three classes of networks in a hybrid electric vehicle is shown in Figure 11.8. The three classes serve three types of vehicle systems or devices categorized based on their data-handling speed requirement. The faster class C-type CAN, which is also known as full CAN, is used for powertrain devices. The class A-type basic CAN, which is of lower speed, used for vehicle body communications is shown in Figure 11.8. The class B-type CAN is used for devices requiring medium speed communications such as the cabin climate control unit.

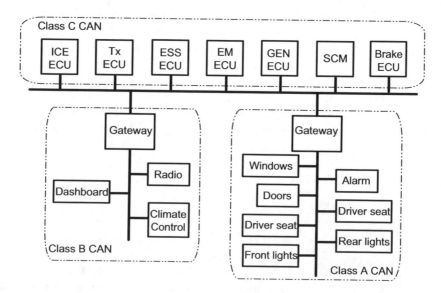

**FIGURE 11.8** Typical CAN layout in a hybrid electric vehicle.

Each of the vehicle components that need to receive and transfer a command or a message has a CAN controller to connect to the CAN bus. The controller is often referred to as a *CAN node* for the system or the device. The requirements of a CAN controller are simple interface to the device, message filtering and buffering, protocol handling and a physical layer interface. The ECUs of the powertrain devices have dedicated hardware for CAN communications to reduce its primary control processor's overhead. The devices on the slow network may not have a microprocessor-based control unit, but do require a CAN controller to interface the device with the CAN bus. A device could be something as simple as sensor providing information for the ECUs of one of the powertrain components or a much more complex unit such as the vehicle supervisory controller.

In the CAN communication protocol, commands, feedback signals or any information is converted into a message format for transmission into the CAN. On the other hand, the messages can be picked up by any of the devices connected to the network and decoded. Each component sees all the messages and can decide on the appropriate message to pick up. The messages have a priority structure; if two CAN nodes attempt to transmit two messages at the same time then the one with higher priority gets transmitted while the other one has to wait. On the other hand, multiple nodes may receive data and act upon the message simultaneously. The CAN is highly flexible; adding a node or removing a defective node does not require any hardware or software change of the remaining CAN.

The details of these CAN communication protocols are described below in terms of the physical layer, transfer layer and programming.

## 11.4.1  CAN Transfer Protocol

The CAN protocol defines only the two lower layers of the OSI seven-layer communication model: Data link layer and physical layer. The data link layer has the transfer layer dealing with message frame coding, message arbitration, overload notification, bus access control, identifying message reception, error detection and error signaling. The data link layer also includes an interface with the application layer of the device including deciding which messages are to be transmitted and received. The physical layer performs the actual transfer of bits between the CAN node of a device and the CAN bus. The layer has the transreceivers, wires and connectors.

A CAN node can be either a transmitter or a receiver. A node that originates a message transmission is called the *transmitter*. The CAN communication is based on carrier sense multiple access (CSMA) protocol. Any node can start transmitting a message when the network bus is idle, which is the multi-master feature of the CAN protocol. Each node must monitor the bus for a period of no activity before transmitting a message. If multiple nodes start transmitting at the same time then the node with the highest priority will be successful in transmitting a message. A node remains a transmitter until it finishes the transmission and the bus becomes idle or when it loses a message transmission arbitration with another node. A node becomes a *receiver* when it is not sending a message, but another node is transmitting keeping the bus busy.

The information is transmitted to the CAN bus from a node using a defined format called *messages*. The messages are framed containing the data and other relevant information pertaining to the data. For example, each message has a unique identifier that describes the meaning of the transmitted data. The identifier also defines the priority of the message during bus access. Each node can decide whether or not to act on the data upon receiving it. The application layer of the device utilizes the data that is useful. It is also the application layer that decides on the information to be transmitted.

Messages are transmitted at a fixed baud rate. This is also known as *bit rate*. The transmission speed may be different for different networks, but the *bit rate* is fixed and uniform for a given network.

The magnitude of the CAN bit signal is known as *bus value*. The CAN bus values are defined as *dominant* and *recessive* using the reverse logic.

## 11.4.2   CAN Transfer Layer

The CAN transfer layer protocol is described in this section in terms of bit timing, message frames, message arbitration, error detection and error signaling.

### 11.4.2.1   Bit Timing

The CAN transfer layer handles the bit timing, transfer protocol and message frames. The bit timing depends on the CAN class used. Several CAN buses exist within a vehicle for communication at different rates. For each class of CAN protocol, the message is transmitted within the time period known as the *nominal bit time*. The *nominal bit rate* is the reciprocal of the nominal bit time given by

$$\text{Nominal bit rate} = \frac{1}{\text{Nominal bit time}}.$$

The nominal bit rate for the CAN bus can be anything less than 1 Mbps.

Nominal bit time in a CAN protocol is partitioned into four time segments as shown in Figure 11.9. Message transmission starts with synchronization segment *Sync_seg* which is used to synchronize the various nodes in the bus. The rising edge of a signal is expected to lie within this segment. This is the smallest time segment. The segment *Prop_seg* accounts for the physical propagation delays in the network. The remaining two segments *Phase_seg1* and *Phase_seg2* are used to compensate for the edge phase errors. *Phase_seg1* is used for positive phase edge errors and can be lengthened by resynchronization. *Phase_seg2* is used for negative phase edge errors and can be shortened by resynchronization. The data sample point is in between *Phase_seg1* and *Phase_seg2*. *Phase_seg2* length should be large enough for information processing. The lengths of the phase segments can be adjusted for edge phase errors. The lengths of the various segments are defined in terms of a fixed time quantum $T_Q$, which is related to the oscillation period as

$$T_Q = n \times T_{osc}$$

Here $n$ is a prescaler integer number ranging between 1 and 32. The lengths of the segments are

$$Sync\_seg = 1 \times T_Q$$

$$Prop\_seg = n_p \times T_Q, \ \ n_p = 1,2,\ldots,8$$

$$Phase\_seg1 = n_1 \times T_Q, \ \ n_1 = 1,2,\ldots,8$$

$$Phase\_seg2 = n_2 \times T_Q, \ \ n_2 \geq n_1$$

For the purpose of synchronization, a *synchronization jump width* (*SJW*) is used, which is defined as the largest allowable adjustment of *Phase_seg1* and *Phase_seg2*. SJW is given as

$$SJW = n_{SJW} \times T_Q$$

**FIGURE 11.9**   Four segments within the nominal bit time of a CAN message.

All the CAN controllers in a common CAN bus must have the same bit rate and bit length. If the clock frequencies of the individual controllers are different, then the bit rate and bit length has to be adjusted using the $T_Q$.

### 11.4.2.2 CAN Message Frames

There are four types of message frame in a CAN protocol: data frame, remote frame, error frame and overload frame. The *data frame* transmits data from a transmitting node to the receiving nodes. The *remote frame* is used by a node to request the transmission of a data frame by another node with the same message identifier. An *error frame* is transmitted by a node after detecting a bus error. An *overload frame* is used to provide additional delay between two data and remote frames. The error frame and overload frame are not necessarily used in all CAN implementations.

The CAN *data frame* consists of seven fields each with a varying bit number to serve a specific purpose. The data frame structure is shown in Figure 11.10. The fields are described below.

*SOF (Start-of-frame)*: The SOF marks the beginning of a data frame. It has only a single dominant bit. All nodes have to synchronize with the leading edge of the SOF bit.

*Arbitration field*: The field has the 11-bit message identifier and a remote transmission request (RTR) bit in a standard frame format. The RTR bit is dominant for a data frame and recessive for a remote frame. In an extended message format, message identifier is of 29-bits. There is also the RTR-bit, SRR (substitute remote request)-bit and IDE (identifier extension)-bit.

*Control field*: The control field has six bits. The first two bits are reserved for future expansion and must be transmitted as dominant. The remaining four bits indicate the length of the data.

*Data field*: The data field contains the data to be transmitted. The number of bits can be 0–8 bits with the most significant bit being sent first.

*CRC field*: The CRC field has 15-bit sequence followed by a CRC delimiter. The CRC delimiter is a single recessive bit.

*Acknowledge field*: The acknowledge field consists of two bits, one for the acknowledge slot and the other for the acknowledge delimiter. The transmitting node sends a recessive bit for the acknowledge slot, while all the receiving nodes send a dominant bit through this slot after receiving a valid message. The acknowledge delimiter is always a recessive bit.

*EOF (End-of-frame)*: The end of a frame is designated by seven recessive bits.

The *remote frame* is transmitted by a CAN node to request certain data that it needs from a remote node. The remote frame has six fields: SOF, Arbitration, Control, CRC, ACK and EOF. There is no data field, regardless of the value in the data length code (DLC). The remote frame structure is shown in Figure 11.11.

The *error frame* is transmitted by a CAN node when it detects an error in the bus. The error frame structure is shown in Figure 11.12. The frame consists of two fields: error flag field and error delimiter. The error flag field contains the superposition of the error flags generated by the different nodes. The error flags can be an active flag or a passive flag. The active error flag consist of six consecutive dominant bits. The passive error flag consists of six consecutive recessive bits unless

**FIGURE 11.10** Data frame.

**FIGURE 11.11**   Remote frame.

**FIGURE 11.12**   Error frame.

it is overwritten by dominant bits from other nodes. The error delimiter consists of eight recessive bits. A node sends a recessive bit after the transmission of an error flag and monitors the bus until it detects a recessive bit. After detecting the recessive bit, the node starts sending seven more recessive bits.

The *overload frame*, similar to the error frame, consists of two fields: overload flag field and overload delimiter. The overload frame structure is shown in Figure 11.13. A node transmits an overload frame when it detects one of two conditions: (i) when receiving node requires a delay for the next data frame or the next remote frame due to internal conditions, and (ii) when a node detects a dominant bit during bus intermission. The overload flag field consists of six dominant bits, and the overload delimiter consists of eight recessive bits.

The *interframe* space, shown in Figure 11.14, separates the data frames and remote frames with the help of three recessive bits. No other node is allowed to start transmission of a data or remote frame during the inter-frame space. The only action permitted during this intermission is signaling of an overload condition. The bus may remain idle for any arbitrary length of time after the interframe space or accept a new frame. Any node having to transmit a message can start a transmission when the bus is idle with a dominant bit which indicates the SOF. A node with a pending message due to the bus being busy starts transmitting with the first bit following the intermission.

**FIGURE 11.13**   Overload frame.

**FIGURE 11.14**   Interframe space

### 11.4.2.3 Message Arbitration

If two nodes start to transmit at the same time, a collision occurs in the bus. The resolution of bus collision through bitwise evaluation is known as *message arbitration*. The process includes collision detection as well as arbitration so that all the messages can be transmitted eventually without having to lose any message. The transmitting node monitors the bus to see if the logic state that it is trying to send already exists in the bus or not. If the level of the bit transmitted is the same as the level monitored on the bus, then the node will continue message frame transmission. However, if a recessive level is sent by a node and a dominant level is monitored on the bus, then that node has lost arbitration and must stop transmitting any further bits. The message with the dominant bit gets through, while the other node waits for the bus to become idle without destroying its message. A dominant bit state (logic '0') will always win arbitration over a recessive bit state (logic '1'), which means that the message with a lower identifier value has the higher priority. The collision is essentially resolved with the message having the lower identifier going through first.

### Example 11.1

Let two nodes start transmitting messages at the same time with the following message identifiers:

Node-1 – 0010010...
Node-2 – 0010110...

Determine the message that will get through in the bus.

### *Solution*

For the 5th identifier bit, Node-2 will notice that the bus has dominant bit when it is trying to transmit a recessive bit. Node-2 loses arbitration at this step, and immediately stops transmitting. The node also turns itself into a message receiver from a message transmitter. Node-1 will continue to finish transmission of its message, while Node-2 will wait for next bus idle period and try to transmit its message again.

### 11.4.2.4 Error Detection and Error Signaling

A high level of data integrity is maintained in a CAN through measures of self-evaluation, error detection, and error signaling at each node. Each transmitting node compares the level of bit transmitted with the level monitored on the bus. Any node that detects an invalid message transmits the error frame. These corrupted messages are aborted and retransmitted automatically.

Error detection in the CAN protocol takes place at both the message level and the bit level. At the message level, the three error detection methods are: cyclic redundancy check (CRC), frame check and acknowledgement error check. At the bit level, there are two methods of error management: bit error and bit stuffing.

The CRC sequence included in the data frame of a transmitted message consists of the CRC calculation results. The CRC sequence is calculated by the transmitter using a predefined algorithm. A receiving node calculates the CRC using the same algorithm as the transmitter. A CRC error is detected if the calculated result does not match the transmitted CRC sequence.

The receiving node does a *format check* on a message by evaluating the bits in CRC delimiter, ACK delimiter, EOF bit-field and interframe space. If an invalid bit is detected in one of the above positions by the receiver, a format or frame error is flagged.

All nodes on the bus acknowledge each valid message. The receiving nodes acknowledge a consistent message, but would flag any inconsistency in the message. A consistent message is acknowledged by sending a dominant bit into the ACK slot of the frame by each of the receiving nodes. If a transmitter determines that a message has not been acknowledged, then an ACK error is flagged. The ACK error may occur because of transmission error or if there is no active receiver.

A transmitting node monitors the bus simultaneously as it transmits a bit on the bus. When the bit transmitted is different from the bit monitored then the node interprets the situation as a *bit error*. The exceptions are when sending a recessive bit during message arbitration or seeing a dominant bit in the bus in the ACK slot due to the acknowledgment from the receiving nodes. A node detecting an error bit starts transmission of an error flag immediately at the next bit transmission time.

Error is confined in CAN in terms of transmit and receive error counts. The transmit error count increases when a node transmits error flags and the receive error count increases when a receiving node detects an error. The transmit error count is decremented when the node successfully transmits a message. Similarly, when a receiving node successfully receives a message, it reduces it's receive error count. A node is an Error-Active node when the error count is between 1 and 127, and it is Error-Passive when the error count is between 128 and 255. The node will be in a bus-off status if the error count is greater than 255. An Error-Active node transmits an active error flag, while an Error-Passive node transmits a passive error flag. A bus-off node is not allowed to have any influence on the CAN bus.

The CAN controllers are designed for the receiver to synchronize on recessive to dominant transitions. The method of *bit stuffing* is used to guarantee that there are enough transitions in the NRZ (non-return-to-zero) bit stream to maintain synchronization. If five identical and consecutive bit levels are transmitted within a message from SOF to CRC, the transmitting node automatically inserts or stuffs one bit of the opposite polarity into the bit stream. Receiving nodes will automatically delete the stuffed bits from the message. A stuff error is flagged if any node detects six consecutive bits of the same level. For example, a message with ID 0x340 will be transmitted as

$$....111 \quad 0 \quad 011 \quad 0100 \quad 000(1)0$$

SOF            3     4     1   Stuffed bit

### 11.4.3 CAN Physical Layer

Several different physical layers can be established for the CAN. The physical layer defines the bus topology, signal methods, bus termination, maximum baud rates and several other features. The most common physical layer is the high-speed CAN. The bus topology consists of a two-wire differential bus and allows communication transfer rates up to 1 Mbps. Class B-type low-speed CAN is also implemented with two wires, which allows transmission rates up to 125 kbps. In these two-wire CAN buses, one wire carries the CANH (CAN High) signal and the other wire carries the CANL (CAN Low) signal without any clock signal. Class A-type basic CAN uses a single-wire plus ground CAN interface with data transfer rates up to 33.3 kbps. Basic CAN is used for devices not depending on critical communications. The CAN signals are NRZ serial data, which is inherently not self-synchronizing.

There can be long periods of inactivity in a device connected to the CAN bus. During that period the CAN node can be put to sleep to conserve resources. The activities of that node can be restored through a wake-up signal by any bus or by changes in internal conditions of the device. CAN nodes can distinguish between short disturbances and permanent failures. Temporary disturbances may be caused by voltage spikes or other electrical noise. Permanent failures may be caused by CAN controller failures, faulty cables, bad connections, transreceiver failures or extended external disturbances. When a CAN node becomes defective, it is switched off and will have no further effect on the CAN bus.

The two-wire CAN bus network with a straight line topology where nodes can be connected anywhere in that line is shown in Figure 11.15. The nodes from the vehicle devices are all connected in parallel. The two ends of the bus are the terminating nodes, which in its simplest form can be a resistive termination. A terminating impedance with a bypass capacitor and two 60 Ω resistances can also be used to reduce the common-mode noise. Resistive and capacitive terminations of the

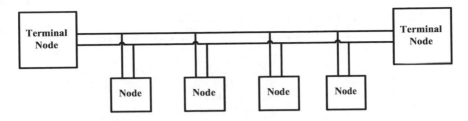

**FIGURE 11.15** CAN bus network in a straight line topology.

CAN bus terminations with pure resistance and with resistance-capacitance combination are shown in Figure 11.16a and b, respectively.

The *dominant* and *recessive* CAN bus values in the network have magnitudes as follows:

Logic '0' = 'dominant'; CANH = 5 V and CANL = 0 V.
Logic '1' = 'recessive'; CANH = CANL = 'floating' (a weak pull to 2.5 V).

Note that the CAN bus values use the reverse logic.

A typical CAN node hardware associated with the ECU of a powertrain component or any other vehicle device consists of a CAN transreceiver, such as MCP 2551 and a CAN controller. CAN controllers are available either in a microprocessor or as a CAN I/O expander. A CAN node hardware is shown in Figure 11.17. The CAN controller hardware is available in microcontrollers and DSPs designed for automotive and other industrial applications.

The CAN bus is in a '0' state when it is busy. Although only one node is allowed to transmit at a given time, two nodes can start transmitting at the same time when both sees the bus to be idle. During simultaneous transmission of dominant and recessive bits, the resulting bus value will be dominant. The arbitration process resolves the issue of which node gets to transmit its message first as was described earlier.

### 11.4.4 CAN PROGRAMMING

The basic concepts of the CAN layers and protocols are essential in developing a CAN interface for the electronic units of a vehicle component. The specifics of a CAN controller in a certain microprocessor must also be evaluated for developing the CAN software program. The general structure of a CAN program is essentially the same for the various CAN controllers that are available in

**FIGURE 11.16** CAN bus termination: (a) resistive termination and (b) resistance-capacitance termination.

**FIGURE 11.17**   CAN node hardware.

various microcontrollers and DSPs; they include register configuration, timer configuration and ISR programming.

The task of register configuration includes defining the bit timing message frame constants for the type of CAN protocol to be used. The transfer and receive buffer registers for managing manages also need to be configured. The transfer layer configuration includes the following:

- Define $T_Q$
- Define $SJW$
- Define $Prop\_seg$, $Ph\_seg1$, and $Ph\_seg2$ (together with $Sync\_seg = 1 \times T_Q$; this sets the bit period)
- Define other processor specific parameters.

The transmit and receive buffer register configurations include the following:

- Transmit identifiers, DLCs
- Receive identifiers (filters and masks)
- Receive configuration bits.

Messages are transmitted based on the times calculated in the timers. The timer registers and timer interrupts are set accordingly to transmit messages periodically. Messages are also received on an interrupt basis. Interrupts are defined and enabled on the registers associated with receiving a message.

The ISR manages to transmit and receive messages. The ISR programming includes the following:

- Load transmit buffers with data to be sent and request transmission
- Read receive buffers, copy data to local variables and clear the receive buffer flag
- Reset interrupt flags and re-enable interrupts.

The number of nodes is only theoretically limited by the number of identifiers available. The drive capabilities of the devices impose the practical limitation. The bit rate depends on the total length of the bus and the delays associated with the trans-receivers.

The very first step in developing a CAN is to define the messages for the various systems that need to be communicated. This is accomplished through developing a message list. An example message list segment is shown in Figure 11.18. The list includes a subset of messages from the generator control module (GCM), system health monitor (SHM) and supervisory control module

| Tx | Rx | Signal Frame | CAN ID | Timing | Signal |
|---|---|---|---|---|---|
| GCM | SCM, SHM | Generator status | 0 × 440 | 10 ms | Mode of operation |
| | | | | | Generator current actual |
| | | | | | Generator speed actual |
| | | | | | HV bus voltage |
| GCM | SHM | GCM fault mode status | 0 × 468 | 100 ms | Inverter temperature |
| | | | | | System critical fault |
| | | | | | Local critical fault |
| | | | | | Local non-critical fault |
| | | | | | Local diagnostic fault |
| | | | | | Rolling count |
| | | | | | Critical communications with UALAN lost |
| | | | | | Critical inverter overheat |
| | | | | | Critical error on inverter phase A |
| | | | | | Critical error on inverter phase B |
| | | | | | Critical error on inverter phase C |
| | | | | | Critical error in computed speed |
| | | | | | Critical instantaneous overcurrent |
| | | | | | Critical continuous overcurrent |
| | | | | | Critical undervoltage |
| | | | | | Critical overvoltage |
| | | | | | Critical persistent invalid position sequence |
| | | | | | Non-critical speed high |
| | | | | | Non-critical inverter overheat |
| | | | | | Invalid position sequence |
| | | | | | Invalid position sensed |
| SCM | GCM | Generator command | 0 × 340 | 10 ms | Connect generator |
| | | | | | Clear faults |
| | | | | | Rolling count |
| | | | | | Generator current commanded |

| CAN ID | Bytes | Bits before stuffing | Worst case bits after stuffing | Worst case transmit time | Periodic interval | Worst case % bus utilization | Best case transmit time | Best case % bus utilization per signal |
|---|---|---|---|---|---|---|---|---|
| 0 × 440 | 6 | 92 | 112 | 0.000225 | 0.01 | 0.02245 | 0.00018 | 0.0184 |
| 0 × 468 | 3 | 68 | 82 | 0.000165 | 0.1 | 0.001645 | 0.00014 | 0.00136 |
| 0 × 340 | 3 | 68 | 82 | 0.000165 | 0.01 | 0.01645 | 0.00014 | 0.0136 |

**FIGURE 11.18** An example CAN message list.

(SCM) of a hybrid electric vehicle. The node that will transmit the message and the nodes that will receive and use the message are identified in the message list. Each message is given a unique identifier according to the priority of the message. The signal information contained within the message is detailed in the message list. Once the hardware is configured according to the message list and the CAN nodes are physically connected to the network, the messages can be evaluated through a CAN analyzer. The CAN analysis and development tools are extremely useful during the development process of a device as well as for system integration, testing and debugging.

## REFERENCES

1. N. Navet and F. Simonot-Lion, *Automotive Embedded Systems Handbook*, CRC Press, Boca Raton, FL, 2009.
2. R. Jurgen (Editor-in-Chief), *Automotive Electronics Handbook*, Second Edition, McGraw-Hill Professional, New York, NY, 2019.
3. P. Leteinturier, S. Brewerton and K. Scheibert, "Multicore benefits & challenges for automotive applications," SAE Publication 2008-01-989, SAE International, Warrendale, PA, 2008.
4. Y. Dajsuren and M. van den Brand, (Editors), *Automotive Systems and Software Engineering: State of the Art and Future Trends*, Springer, Cham, Switzerland, 2019.
5. M. Staron, *Automotive Software Architecture: An Introduction*, Springer, Cham, Switzerland, 2017.
6. J.M. Miller, *Propulsions Systems for Hybrid Vehicles*, Institute of Electrical Engineers, London, 2004.

# 12 Electric Vehicles and the Power Grid

Plug-in electric vehicles (PEVs) interact with the power systems through the charging and discharging functions of the vehicle's energy storage unit. Charging the batteries to replenish the energy capacity, i.e., restoring the battery SOC as the batteries get exhausted due to the operation of the vehicle is the most common and frequent interaction mode between the PEV and the power grid. There are emerging technologies and evolving concepts that enable energy transfer from the PEV to the grid to support grid functionalities such as meeting consumer electricity load demands, and grid voltage and frequency support. There are three modes of interaction between an electric vehicle and the power grid based on the charging/discharging capability of the PEVs which are grid-to-vehicle (G2V), vehicle-to-grid (V2G) and vehicle-to-home (V2H). The three modes of interaction bond the transportation system with the power system where the grid is the fuel delivery system for the electric transportation, while the vehicle is either a load or a distributed energy resource (DER). The electric vehicle storage system functioning as a DER can provide ancillary services to the power grid through discharging of the PEV energy storage. The technologies involved in this framework are the power electronics-based chargers and charging stations, information and communication platforms and protocols, battery technology and optimization strategies.

## 12.1 VEHICLE GRID INTERFACE

Electric vehicles and the power grid have a symbiotic relationship where one can help the other in a sustainable business relationship while providing desirable services to the customer. PEVs or battery electric vehicles (BEVs) require available electricity supply dispensed through the charging stations, while the power grid needs to maintain adequate infrastructure for maintaining the supply under varying power demand conditions. This mode of energy transfer from the power grid to the vehicle using either an on-board charger or a charging station is designated as the more conventional G2V mode. The electric transportation sector can play a key role in contributing toward a clean environment only if the electricity to charge the batteries in PEVs is produced from clean and renewable energy sources such as wind or solar.

The power system infrastructure has capacity constraints, and the primary objective of the utility is to reliably deliver power to the customer under varying load conditions. The power load demand peaks during certain times of the day and also during extreme weather conditions. The challenge of meeting supply with demand is exacerbated when generation has uncertainties such as with renewable energy (with solar and wind) generations. Intermittent nature of solar and wind adversely affects the grid voltage and frequency stability and overall grid management. The power provider, i.e., utility, needs compensation or some type of infrastructure to address the variability of renewable generation for grid management. Compensation becomes complicated in distribution systems encompassing residential areas where small-scale DERs are being integrated. Real and reactive power management through controls based on dispatch signals from a system operator even at the residential level is the most attractive proposition. Addition of energy storage at both utility scale and residential levels is a solution to address both the variability of renewable power generation and reliable management of the grid. The cost of storage is an issue, but the growth of electric vehicles is driving down the cost of battery storage.

PEVs can play a role in helping the power grid during peak demands through discharging the battery utilizing the V2G mode in the emerging concept of smart grid. PEVs carry a sizeable energy storage unit which is capable of delivering energy back to the grid via the bi-directional charger or charging station. This energy delivery back to the grid can be in support of meeting high load demands by providing real power during extreme scenarios such as in a hot summer day when the demand can be high to provide adequate air-conditioning. The power electronics of the charger or charging station is also capable of providing reactive power to the grid in support of voltage regulation. The V2G mode can become very effective when PEV penetration increases such that there is sufficient energy stored in the fleet of PEVs to make a significant contribution in mitigating the peak power demand. The benefit to the utility industry is that they do not have to bear the burden of maintaining the peaker plants which is not only expensive to own but also to operate.

## 12.1.1   G2V, V2G, V2V AND V2H FRAMEWORKS

The G2V, V2G, V2V and V2H frameworks provide the infrastructure for the interactions between vehicle, grid and home. The available infrastructure thus far is only that of G2V technology which is essential for vehicle charging of charge-depleting-type electric vehicles. A PEV charger with bi-directional power flow capability is the enabler for V2H and V2G. Vehicle-to-vehicle (V2V) technologies are intended for either information exchange or energy exchange, although the latter requires an intermediary.

The PEVs, or EVs in short, use electricity to charge the on-board batteries instead of fossil fuel unless the vehicle is a charge sustaining plug-in hybrid vehicle with very limited zero emission range. The EV storage with bi-directional power flow capability can serve either as a load to the grid or as a source to a household or the grid. V2G and V2H provide the opportunity to turn a PEV into a DER where the vehicle energy storage unit along with its bi-directional power converter can supply power to the bulk grid or the residential grid when needed, provided the vehicle has excess capacity. The scenario becomes more likely with increasing deployment of EVs. For V2G operation, an aggregate of PEVs and an infrastructure is needed, whereas for V2H a single-household PEV can respond to the power demand of that residence. The addition of a DER with the help of PEVs would certainly enhance the reliability and resiliency of the electric grid as well as enable increasing the efficiency of supply and utilization of resources through energy management optimization algorithms.

V2H allows the PEV to be connected to a home for charging and/or discharging by the on-board or an off-board bi-directional charger. The V2H framework is established within a small microgrid established in a single house involving one or two PEVs owned by the household (smart home). The functionalities of a V2H microgrid are as follows:

- Smoothing of daily household load profile with active power exchange.
- Providing reactive power to the home or even to a community microgrid. It is to be noted that reactive power can be provided independent of the battery usage since the charger itself can deliver this functionality.
- Power reserve can be maintained within the community reducing power and trading loss between community and power grid.
- V2H avoids the infrastructure and tariff needs associated with V2G operation. Load and generation are co-located in V2H operation, which minimizes transmission and distribution losses compared to electricity supply from a centralized station.

The V2V concept for information exchange is useful for driving safety and autonomous driving. This is an emerging technology area focused on communications with 5G or other future networks. On the energy aspect, V2V allows PEVs to transfer storage energy using bi-directional chargers to a local grid and then distribute the energy to other PEVs through a controller managed by a business aggregator. The aggregator's business model allows collection of PEVs and enables interaction among the PEVs and with the local grid for energy request over a V2V platform. Examples of aggregators are the EV charging station operator or a community microgrid operator. New business models are expected to evolve in the future where aggregators will work with fleet operators. The features of V2V technology for energy transfer are as follows:

- Involves multiple PEVs.
- Uses smart homes and charging stations, parking lots or community microgrids for energy exchange.
- Requires simpler infrastructures compared to V2G operation and incurs small transmission losses, but requires an aggregator business model.
- V2V can be cooperated with DERs for community microgrid operation.

The energy storage unit within the EVs has the potential to transfer power to the grid to alleviate peak power demand and provide ancillary services in a way similar to the use of other energy storage devices. These EV services are referred to as V2G services. V2G allows PEVs to be connected to the grid and feed energy back to the grid using a bi-directional charger. An aggregate of PEVs will have sufficient energy storage capacity to deliver enough power and have an impact on grid management. For the V2G concept to be effective, an aggregator turns to a group of PEVs for providing grid support services. The factors affecting the efficiency of V2G operation are the number of available vehicles, SOC of the energy storage units within the vehicles and the availability of the vehicles whose owners chose to participate on a particular type of V2G operation. The vehicle owner must commit to have the vehicle available for a certain amount of time with a set limit of discharge capacity available after ensuring that sufficient charge remains to complete the journey after the V2G operation. The aggregators also need to have a statistical guarantee that a certain number of vehicles would be available to participate in a V2G operation with the utility.

The features of V2G technology are as follows:

- V2G has the cumulative effect for a larger number of PEVs.
- V2G can be enabled through smart homes, parking lots and fast charging stations for power exchange.
- Optimization strategies can be incorporated for efficient energy usage and cost reduction.
- V2G can be used for peak shaving, frequency and voltage regulation and spinning reserve.

## 12.2 ELECTRIC VEHICLE CHARGING

The charging of an electric vehicle is facilitated by a number of components including on-board charger, home charger, fast chargers and connectors with communication protocols and charging stations. The EVs and PEVs are equipped with an on-board battery charger to recharge the battery pack which can be connected to either a 120 V/240 V AC supply or a 400 V DC supply depending on what is provided. Alternatively, the vehicle can also recharge from a higher power AC or DC charger installed off-board in a charging station. The simplest solution is the vehicle's on-board charger which connects to a residential or commercial single-phase AC supply. The so-called Level 1 and Level 2 AC chargers serve as an interface between the 120 V (Level 1 chargers) and 240 V (Level 2 chargers) supply line and the on-board charger, and can deliver up to 1.92 kW and 19.2 kW to the vehicle for Level 1 and Level 2, respectively. The IEC classification (IEC 61851) allows up to 26.6 kW for Level 2 home AC chargers. The on-board chargers are limited in their power capacity and would require over 8 h to add 200 miles of range using the standard 208 V or 240 V plug available within the US homes. The different AC and DC charging levels with their power capacities as defined in SAE J1772 and SAE J1773 standards are given in Table 12.1 [1].

**TABLE 12.1**
**AC and DC Charging Levels with Current and Power Limits**

| Charger Coupling | Nominal Voltage | Maximum Current (A) | Continuous Power (kW) |
|---|---|---|---|
| AC Level 1, single-phase | 120 VAC | 20 | 1.92 |
| AC Level 2, single-phase | 240 VAC | 80 | 19.2 |
| AC Level 3, three-phase | 208 VAC, 480 VAC and 600 VAC | 400 | <100 |
| DC Level 1 | 200–450 VDC | 80 | <36 |
| DC Level 2 | 200–450 VDC | 200 | <90 |
| DC Level 3 | 200–600 VDC | 400 | <240 |

## 12.2.1 DC Fast Chargers

An indirect solution to the range anxiety of electric vehicle users is a fast charging option to provide similar refueling experience that is experienced by the drivers of the ICEVs. DC fast chargers rated 120 kW or more with a 400 VDC–800 VDC charging option which is a Level 3-type charger are designed to provide a quick charging option to address the slow charging rates of Level 1 and Level 2 AC chargers. While PEV owners would still utilize the convenience of home charging with a Level 1 or Level 2 charger, the fast chargers are installed in a public charging station with multiple units available to simultaneously serve multiple vehicles. The PEVs also need to be equipped with a DC port, while the power grid needs the capacity to deliver the power at a high charging rate. The fast chargers started appearing in stations with 50 kW rating, but to meet the growing need of EV users, both the power rating of the chargers and the number of installations are growing rapidly. More recently, 120 kW chargers have been installed in the United States, and power levels up to 350 kW are evolving. A fast charger rated at 50 kW requires over 1 h to deliver enough charge for a 200-miles trip, while a 350 kW extreme fast charger (XFC) would only take about 10 min to deliver the same amount of energy.

### 12.2.1.1 480 V Fast Charger

DC fast chargers are supplied from a three-phase AC outlet at either 480 VAC or 400 VAC line-to-line voltage and typically have two power conversion stages: a three-phase AC/DC rectification stage and a DC/DC stage that provides galvanic isolation. The front end includes a power factor correction (PFC) component to ensure acceptable power quality on the grid side. The functional block diagram of a DC fast charger power stage is shown in Figure 12.1a. The rectifier stage in state-of-the-art fast chargers is made with diode bridges, and hence, the power flow is unidirectional, but in the future, this is expected to be replaced by an active front end (AFE), as shown in Figure 12.1b, to facilitate bi-directional power flow for V2G applications.

The front end converts the three-phase AC voltage to a DC voltage, while the subsequent DC/DC stage converts the DC voltage to a regulated DC voltage required by the electric vehicles and also provides galvanic isolation. The AFE stage is typically operated in a current-controlled mode using pulse-width modulation (PWM) with PFC functions, while the DC/DC stage is used for power flow control. The AFE is based on power semiconductor modules which are typically based on reverse conducting IGBTs, and operate at switching frequencies not higher than 10 kHz. In future topologies, SiC power modules will replace these IGBT modules with switching frequencies in excess of 30 kHz. In the bi-directional mode of the AFE, when power is flowing from the grid to the vehicle, PWM rectifier control algorithms are used, while for V2G operation, PWM inverter control algorithm needs to be employed.

The DC/DC stage in the fast charger is essentially a multi-stage converter where the DC is first converted into a high-frequency AC with a switching power bridge and then converted back to DC by an output bridge. The input and output bridges are coupled through a medium-frequency (MF)

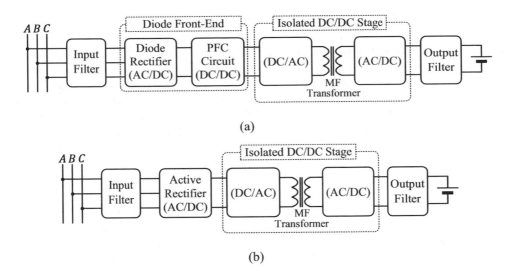

**FIGURE 12.1** Power stages in three-phase DC fast chargers: (a) using a diode front end and (b) using an active front end (AFE).

transformer which transfers energy electromagnetically across an electrical isolation. This unit is what is known as a solid-state transformer (SST) which transfers electrical energy through an electromagnetic coupling field with input and output voltages and currents processed through power electronic converter bridges [2,3]. The DC/DC converter stage, particularly the low-voltage stage, can be made with SiC MOSFETs which are the emerging technologies. The galvanic isolation isolates the vehicle from the grid and also allows for the charger output stages to be easily connected in parallel. By maintaining system isolation, the charging system respects the protection scheme designed for the vehicle battery. The medium-frequency transformer requires careful design to avoid magnetic saturation and high-voltage insulation breakdown.

### 12.2.1.2 MV Fast Charger

A more efficient fast charger system can be built when the three-phase AC power is supplied from a distribution system at medium voltage (MV) level provided by the utility [4]. The distribution voltage level is 12.47 kVAC (line-to-line) or 13.2 kVAC (line-to-line) for many utility systems before it is stepped down to 480 VAC (line-to-line) by a 60 Hz (i.e., low-frequency) distribution transformer in the conventional approach. In contrast, deploying an SST-based fast charger connected directly to the MV level will provide efficiency and power density benefits in addition to the many smart control features that can be incorporated within the fast charger. The SST is a power electronics-based controllable transformer wherein communications and intelligence can be integrated for demand-side management, control of voltage and power factor on the grid side, elimination of customer-side harmonics, and for providing isolation and protection features. The SST eliminates the bulky low-frequency step-down transformer and also adds a number of smart grid features. A key feature that distinguishes the SST from a traditional transformer is its ability to decouple and buffer medium-voltage distribution grids from the low-voltage feeder sections. The SST provides the potential for revolutionizing the power distribution side with the replacement of the traditional iron-core distribution transformer with at least 10 times size and weight reduction, and with a significant intelligence incorporated; the SST is also an enabler for the future smart agent for markets and energy transactions. The bi-directional power flow capability of the SST provides possibilities to feed locally generated power back to the grid in a controlled way, which makes it an ideal choice for electric vehicle fast charging.

The power electronics stages of an SST-based fast charger consists of a front-end rectifier stage, which converts high-voltage AC to high-voltage DC and a dual-active bridge (DAB) stage which converts high DC voltage to a low DC voltage as shown in Figure 12.1b. The galvanic isolation is provided by the medium-frequency transformer within the DAB DC/DC power conversion stage. For the MV fast charger, the power converter stage is much more complex requiring the use of multi-level or cascaded converter topologies due to the high-voltage connection and the limited availability of high-voltage power devices. An example of a three-phase power converter for a MV fast charger system utilizing cascaded three-phase bridges as active front ends and dual active bridge (DAB) type isolated DC/DC converter stages is shown in Figure 12.2 [4]. The converter is composed of stackable three-phase AC to DC converter blocks series cascaded in the medium-voltage three-phase AC supply side while parallel coupled on the low-voltage DC (LVDC) side where the vehicle load is to be connected to deliver higher levels of charging currents at the nominal DC voltage of the vehicle battery system. The series connected configuration is possible by DAB DC-DC converters that provide isolation between the load and isolated DC buses for the active front-end bridges. For stable DC bus voltage minimal energy storage is required in any of the medium- or low-voltage buses. The LVDC bus can be designed to deliver power to a single voltage level EVs or to multiple types of EVs with different battery-pack voltages through the use of another DC/DC power conversion stage. The configuration is fully bi-directional enabling both G2V power supply for current use and V2G power flow for future power and transportation systems' coupled applications.

The use of higher voltage SiC MOSFETs enables a more compact and efficient power stage design compared to Si-IGBT-based solutions. The ability of SiC devices to operate at higher switching frequencies (a few tens of kHz, as opposed to less than 10 kHz for Si devices) enables significant reduction in size of the inductors and the transformers used for the filter components and galvanic isolation, thereby reducing the overall system size and weight.

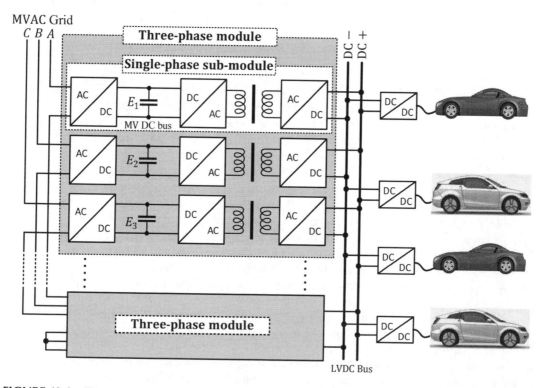

**FIGURE 12.2**   The medium-voltage fast charger.

## Example 12.1

An extreme fast charging station is to be built with a front-end MV SST connected to 13.2 kV (LL RMS) medium-voltage AC (MVAC) grid with an allowable voltage variation of ±5%. The fast charging station is built with a modular topology as shown in Figure 12.2. The front-end power converter is built with a multi-level topology of cascaded H-bridges consisting of six three-phase modules with each module having three single-phase sub-modules. Each sub-module consists of an AC/DC front stage and an isolated DC/DC stage to establish the LVDC distribution bus. The charging station is designed to deliver a rated power of 1 MW to the LVDC bus and is capable of sourcing/sinking 445 kVAR on the MVAC side.

Calculate the following:

a. Total apparent power capacity at the MVAC side (assuming overall efficiency of 99%)
b. Nominal and maximum input AC voltage level for each front-end AC/DC stage (sub-module)
c. Nominal and maximum current rating for each front-end AC/DC stage (sub-module)
d. Thermal load (i.e., total loss incurred) in each sub-module and the station
e. Nominal voltage value ($E_k$, $k = 1,2,...$) for MVDC buses (assume 15% boost from input AC voltage)
f. Sketch the power flow through each AC/DC stage (sub-module) for 1 MW consumption at LVDC bus assuming a power factor of 1 and nominal AC input voltage at the MVAC side and a grid frequency of 60 Hz
g. Sketch the voltage variation on the MVDC bus at same condition as (f); assume constant power flow through DC/DC stages and 500 uF capacitance on each MVDC bus.

### *Solution*

a. For efficiency $\eta = 99\%$ and rated output power of 1 MW, the rated input power is

$$P_{mvac,nom} = \frac{1 \text{ MW}}{0.99} = 1,012.1 \text{ kW}$$

For rated reactive power capacity of $Q_{mvac,nom} = 445$ kVAR, the apparent power capacity is obtained as

$$S_{mvac} = \left( P_{mvac,nom}^2 + Q_{mvac,nom}^2 \right)^{0.5} = 1.104 \text{ MVA}$$

b. Nominal input AC voltage: For line-to-line (RMS) voltage $V_{LL0} = 13.2$ kV, the line-to-neutral voltage is

$$V_{LN,nom} = \frac{13.2}{\sqrt{3}} = 7.621 \text{ kV RMS}$$

Nominal input AC voltage for the AC/DC front-end stage in each sub-module is

$$V_{sm,nom} = \frac{7.621 \text{ kV}}{6} = 1.27 \text{ kV RMS}$$

Maximum input AC voltage: For +5% maximum allowable overvoltage, the maximum LL voltage is

$$V_{LL,max} = 13.2 \times 1.05 = 13.86 \text{ kV RMS}$$

Following similar steps, the maximum input AC voltage is obtained as

$$V_{sm,max} = 1.33 \text{ kV RMS}$$

c. The rated power at the MVAC side is $P_{mvac,nom} = 1,012.1$ kW (from (a)). The total number of sub-modules is $N = 3 \times 6 = 18$. Rated power capacity for the AC/DC stage in each sub-module is

$$P_{mvac,sm,nom} = \frac{P_{mvac,max}}{N} = 56.12 \text{ kW}$$

The nominal current is given as

$$I_{mvac,nom} = \frac{P_{mvac,sm,nom}}{V_{sm,nom}} = 44.18 \text{ A RMS}$$

The AC/DC front-end stage draws maximum current while transferring $P_{mvac,\,sm,nom}$ at the lowest allowable AC input voltage. The lowest allowable voltage is

$$V_{sm,min} = V_{sm,nom} \times 0.95 = 1.21 \text{ kV RMS}$$

Therefore, the maximum current rating is obtained as

$$I_{mvac,max} = \frac{P_{mvac,\,sm,nom}}{V_{sm,min}} = 46.51 \text{ A RMS}$$

d. Assuming 99% efficiency, the total loss incurred in each sub-module is obtained as

$$P_{loss,sm} = P_{mvac,sm,nom} \times 0.01 = 0.56 \text{ kW}$$

0.56 kW of heat needs to be extracted from each sub-module at rated operation. The total loss of the charging station (18 sub-modules) is

$$P_{loss} = P_{loss,sm} \times 18 = 12.1 \text{ kW}$$

e. The maximum AC input voltage for each sub-module is $V_{sm,max} = 1.33$ kV RMS which gives a peak voltage of

$$V_{sm,peak,max} = V_{sm,max} \times \sqrt{2} = 1,886.1 \text{ V}$$

For 15% boost, the nominal MVDC bus voltage value should be set as

$$E_k = V_{sm,peak,max} \times 1.15 = 2,169 \text{ V}$$

f. Let the AC input voltage and AC current for the AC/DC stage in a sub-module is

$$v_{sm}(t) = \sqrt{2} V_{sm,nom} \cos(2\pi f_1 t); \; i_{sm}(t) = \sqrt{2} I_{mvac,nom} \cos(2\pi f_1 t)$$

where $f_1 = 60$ Hz. The power flow is given as

$$P_{sm}(t) = v_{sm}(t) \times i_{sm}(t) = V_{sm,nom} I_{mvac,nom}[1 + \cos(4\pi f_1 t)] = P_{av}[1 + \cos(4\pi f_1 t)]$$

The AC input voltage, current and power for the medium-voltage sub-module are shown in Figure 12.3.

g. The rate of change of stored energy in the MVDC bus capacitor is given by

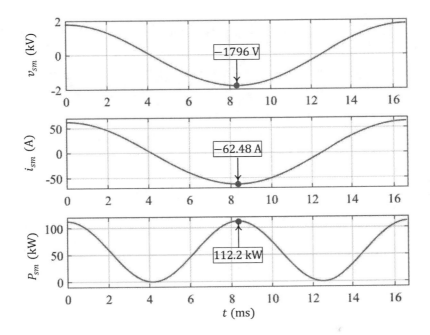

**FIGURE 12.3**    Active front-end sub-module voltage, current and power.

$$\frac{d}{dt}\left(\frac{1}{2}C_{mvdc}v_{mvdc}^2\right) = P_{sm}(t) - P_{DC/DC}$$

Here, $P_{sm}(t)$ denotes the power through the AC/DC stage from the MVAC side to the MVDC bus and $P_{DC/DC}$ denotes the power flow through the isolated DC/DC stage and hence

$$P_{DC/DC} = P_{mvac,sm,nom} = 56.12 \text{ kW}$$

Now, the AC component of the capacitor voltage/MVDC bus voltage $v_{mvdc}$ can be derived as

$$\hat{v}_{mvdc} = \frac{1}{C_{mvdc}v_{mvdc}} \int [P_{sm}(t) - P_{DC/DC}]dt$$

For simplicity, the reference value for $v_{mvdc} = E_k$ can be used on the right side

$$\hat{v}_{mvdc} = \frac{1}{C_{mvdc}E_k} \int [P_{sm}(t) - P_{DC/DC}]dt = \frac{1}{C_{mvdc}E_k} \int P_{av}\cos(4\pi f_1 t)dt = \frac{P_{av}\sin(4\pi f_1 t)}{4\pi f_1 C_{mvdc}E_k}$$

Note that $P_{sm} = P_{av}[1 + \cos(4\pi f_1 t)]$ and $P_{DC/DC} = P_{av}$. Therefore, the overall voltage is given as

$$v_{mvdc} = E_k + \hat{v}_{mvdc} = E_k + \frac{P_{av}\sin(4\pi f_1 t)}{4\pi f_1 C_{mvdc}E_k}$$

The voltage variation is shown in Figure 12.4.

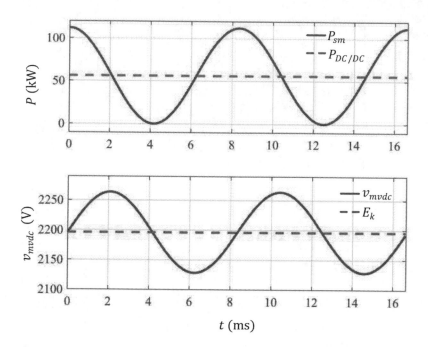

**FIGURE 12.4**  Medium-voltage DC voltage and power waveforms.

## 12.2.2 Electric Vehicle Charging Station

Electric vehicle charges are installed either as isolated units in a business entity or as a cluster of chargers configured for a charging station similar to a gas station with multiple types of charging nodes to supply multiple vehicles from the same power grid. Charging stations with fast chargers are gradually evolving and more are expected in the future as the charger technology further improves and matures.

There are two different aspects to consider for the grid coupling of these fast chargers: first, whether the coupling of the charger with the power grid is at low voltage or medium voltage of the power distribution system, and second, whether fast charger stations are AC coupled or DC coupled. The currently commercialized fast chargers are AC coupled where the charging system connects to a three-phase power supply node with line-to-line voltage of up to 480 VAC. Since this supply is not readily available in public installations, a dedicated service transformer is used to step down medium voltage at 12–35 kVAC levels of the power distribution system and provide three-phase supply at 480 VAC or lower levels to a single DC fast charger or to multiple fast charging units in a charging station. The medium- and low-voltage power levels depend on the particular power distribution system of a country or locality. Each fast charger unit has an AC/DC rectifier and a DC/DC converter to deliver DC power to the vehicle battery as shown in Figure 12.5. A fast charging station may include local storage to help mitigate demand charges that are incurred during peak power consumption requirements at the station. Power dispensing at lower voltage levels requires large conductors and bulky low-voltage distribution and switchgear equipment, and the service transformer operating at 60 Hz adds cost.

Alternatively, a DC distribution system can be envisioned which is established centrally by converting the MVAC to a lower user-level DC voltage. This central conversion can be accomplished either with a step-down 60 Hz low-frequency transformer coupled with a single AC/DC power electronic converter or through the use of an SST. The DC distribution line delivers power to individual DC fast charger units that has an internal DC/DC converter. The two types of DC-coupled EV fast charging stations are shown in Figure 12.6a and b. The DC distribution system eliminates multiple

**FIGURE 12.5** Charging station concept with AC coupling.

**FIGURE 12.6** EV charging station based on DC coupling: (a) with a low-frequency transformer (LF XFR) and AC/DC central rectifier, and (b) with an SST technology.

AC/DC and DC/DC conversion stages, and facilitates energy storage and other renewable generation integration which output DC power such as solar PV systems. In contrast, an AC-connected
system is more complicated to control than DC-connected systems since they need to deal with
inverter synchronization, and voltage and frequency regulation during islanded operation of the
system. In AC- and DC-coupled charging stations, the system benefits from load diversification by
sharing a large common power supply to serve varying PEV battery capacities with different SOC
conditions. The system power demand can be substantially lowered from the rated value by adjusting the charging profile based on the battery requirement.

   The concept of using an SST connected directly to the medium voltage to establish the DC distribution system is an emerging one facilitated by the developments of power electronics topologies,
controls and SiC devices. The SST-based DC-coupled EV charging station is shown in Figure 12.6b.
The advent of the high-voltage SiC power devices with high-frequency and high-temperature operation capability is enabling the development of MV EV fast chargers [5].

## 12.2.3 Grid Impacts of Fast Chargers

The power demand from the grid for charging a large capacity battery-pack like that in a PEV is
significant. The power demand is also varying depending on the battery size and battery state-of-
charge. On top of these, there will be a large variation in the power demand when multiple EVs
charge simultaneously. This puts a lot of strain on the utility both in terms on grid power flow
management as well as for meeting bursts of peak power demands. A suitable solution to address
the power supply challenges is to include a local storage capability within the charging station for
system-level benefits as shown in Figure 12.6a and b. The local storage allows the station owner to
profile the power demand from the station, while still delivering the desired power to individual customers. The storage also enables the station owner to be responsive to the needs of the local utility
while avoiding high peak-demand charges, which could be a significant percentage of the electricity
costs depending on the utility rate structure. The downside of adding the storage is the additional
investment cost for the charging station owner.

   The number and rating of fast chargers, and especially XFCs powered from the grid are expected
to grow rapidly as the number of EVs grows in the roadways. An individual XFC unit can be rated at
360 kW or higher to give the fast and convenient charging service to the customer. An EV charging
station with multiple XFCs would require an order of magnitude more power compared to systems
deployed today with the total power rating of the system in the multi-MVA range. A multi-MVA
charging stations may severely influence the power quality on the feeder that supplies it. Recent studies show that the additional load at a single point can lead to feeder overload and voltage variations
along the feeder that are beyond the allowable limits [6]. One way to mitigate the negative effects of
XFCs on the distribution grid is to allow the utility to control the station's demand during hours of
peak consumption. Additionally, the charging station can be designed to provide ancillary services
to the grid to help mitigate power quality issues on its feeder. The fast chargers connected to today's
grid are designed to absorb power from the grid at a unity power factor. In the case of XFCs, if the
front end of the charging station is designed for bi-directional power flow along with power factor control, then these can also be utilized for providing the ancillary grid services such as voltage
and frequency regulation and optimal dispatch. The capability to inject reactive power from power
electronics-interfaced DERs is extremely important to simplify the utility's voltage control problem.

### Example 12.2

An EV charging station has ten fast chargers each rated at 240 kW. Average power demand is 60%
of the peak power rating. Roundtrip efficiency of storage power converter is 94%. Average utilization of the station at full power per day is 20%. If the grid tie is sized for average power, calculate
the storage capacity in kWh needed.

*Solution*

Energy consumption of the charging station per day is

$$240 \times 0.2 \times 24 = 1,152 \text{ kWh}$$

If average power rating is 60% of the peak power rating, then the energy storage needs to be sized to supply the demand for power needed above the average power demand. The storage capacity requirement is

$$1,152 \times 0.4 = 460.8 \text{ kWh}$$

Accounting for the roundtrip efficiency of the storage and its power converter, the energy storage size is

$$460.8/0.94 = 490 \text{ kWh}$$

## 12.3  ELECTRIC VEHICLES IN MICROGRIDS

The V2H, V2V and V2G operations and functionalities fall within the scope of a microgrid system which can be as small as in single-household microgrid or a large network microgrid with multiple sources, multiple storages and distributed loads. In this section, we will discuss the role of an electric vehicle within a microgrid and the associated controls for their symbiotic existence.

### 12.3.1  MICROGRIDS AND CONTROLS

A microgrid is a group of interconnected DERs that acts as a single controllable entity with respect to the power grid to which it is connected. The DERs are the distributed generators (including solar PV, wind power, wave energy converter, diesel generator and fuel cells), storage devices and controllable loads. Microgrids can be operated in a controlled, coordinated way either while connected to the main power network or while islanded. Microgrids can also operate in standalone, islanded modes when power grid is not available or out-of-service due to a failure. The microgrid would be connected to the larger power grid at a single node known as the point of common coupling (PCC). These are orders of magnitude smaller than the bulk power system, but these can coordinate assets and present them to the power grid at scale in a manner that is consistent with grid operations. Microgrids reduces the operational complexity introduced by DERs by adopting a system-level approach for managing a group of these DERs and loads rather than an ad-hoc approach for operating them individually. The overall system efficiency can be enhanced through minimization of overall energy consumption with reduced environmental impact. At the same time, reliability can be enhanced utilizing the DERs through providing congestion relief, voltage and frequency control, and supply security. Evolving transportation systems with PEVs can be an integral component of the microgrid being connected as a DER to provide services to both the homeowner and collectively with a cohort of PEVs to the grid.

#### 12.3.1.1  Primary- and Secondary-Level Controls

Microgrid operations are managed through a hierarchical control structure that distributes the control objective among the three control layers of primary, secondary and tertiary to achieve the desired performance by leveraging time-scale separation among the consecutive layers. The hierarchical control architecture is shown graphically in Figure 12.7. The control layers are shown for the droop-based controls and oscillator-based controls, which are the two approaches used for microgrid controls. The primary control layer is responsible for stabilizing the voltage and frequency, enable plug-n-play capability of DERs, avoid circulating currents and islanding detection

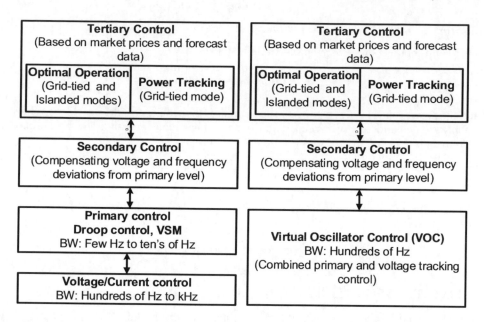

**FIGURE 12.7**   Hierarchical controls in microgrid for droop- and oscillator-based controls.

with the ability to work both connected to the network and in a islanded condition. The objectives of the secondary control are to restore the microgrid voltage and frequency in case of deviations from nominal set-points, enhancement of power quality and synchronization between microgrid and main power network. The combined control objective is one and unique which is to maintain power balance among load, generation and storage despite the multiple implementation levels. The interfaces between the DERs and the tie-lines are power electronic converters which have their own voltage and current tracking controllers underneath the hierarchical control structure. These converter controllers are labeled as the local controller which is at the lowest layer but have the fastest response time and are designed to track references provided by the primary control layer. These tracking control loops are typically updated at the same or twice the converter switching frequency with bandwidths ranging from hundreds of Hz to a few kHz; the control bandwidth is limited by the passive filter components, converter switching frequency, and the controller implementation delay [7]. One of the key differences between droop-based controls and oscillator-based controls is that the latter merges the local controls with the primary control layer. The next two sections describe the two types of controls in further details.

## 12.3.1.2   Droop-Based Controls

The primary control layer exists on top of the voltage and/or current tracking controllers to ensure the power balance by instantaneously matching the generation with the load [8,9]. The most widely used primary control methods are the droop-based methods which enables decentralized power balance by allowing deviation from the nominal voltage and frequency, where the deviation provides the necessary signal to locally adjust the set-points of the generation source. The method does not require explicit communication among the interconnected units within the microgrid. The control methodology is based on controlling voltage and frequency at the interconnection node and allowing these variables to deviate from the nominal values for power balance. The low-voltage distribution networks are predominantly resistive where real power flow is strongly correlated to voltage magnitude while reactive power is strongly linked to the phase angle. In the microgrid, the dispatchable DERs, such as energy storage or distributed generation units are operated to emulate the appropriate droop response, such as real power versus voltage and reactive power versus frequency. The droop control method is used in the bulk power systems as well, but those networks

**FIGURE 12.8**  Simplified power network formed by two power electronic inverters.

being predominantly inductive where the droop relations used are real power versus frequency and reactive power versus voltage.

The primary layer control problem for droop-type implementations can be formulated based on the network formed by two power electronic converter-based DERs, a load and tie-line impedances as shown in Figure 12.8.

The power flow equations for the network shown in Figure 12.6 for real and reactive power are

$$P_k = \left( \frac{E_k V}{Z_k} \cos\delta_k - \frac{V^2}{Z_k} \right) \cos\theta_k + \frac{VE_k}{Z_k} \sin\delta_k \sin\theta_k$$

$$Q_k = \left( \frac{E_k V}{Z_k} \cos\delta_k - \frac{V^2}{Z_k} \right) \sin\theta_k - \frac{VE_k}{Z_k} \sin\delta_k \cos\theta_k$$

for $k = 1, 2$. Here, $P$ is the real power, $Q$ is the reactive power, $E$'s are the voltages at the inverter output terminals and $\delta$'s are the power angles. For a purely or predominantly resistive line impedance, the power flow equations simplify to

$$P_k = \frac{VE_k}{R_k} \cos\delta_k - \frac{V^2}{R_k} \text{ and } Q_k = -\frac{VE_k}{R_k} \sin\delta_k$$

The power angle $\delta_k$ is typically very small, and hence, as $\delta_k \to 0$, $P_k \approx \dfrac{V(E_k - V)}{R_k}$ and $Q_k \approx -\dfrac{VE_k}{R_k}\delta_k$.

By adjusting the amplitude of the inverter voltage and the power angle (which affects frequency), the real and reactive power flow in the network can be dynamically controlled. The droop curves for predominantly resistive output impedance are

$$E_k = E_0 - n_{P,k}(P_k - P_{0,k}) \text{ and } \omega_k = \omega_0 + n_{Q,k}(Q_k - Q_{0,k})$$

The droop curves are graphically shown in Figure 12.9. Typical selections of droop coefficients are

$$n_{P,k} = \frac{\Delta E}{2P_{max}} \text{ and } n_{Q,k} = \frac{\Delta\omega}{2Q_{max}}$$

For predominantly or purely inductive line impedance, the power flow equations can be simplified as

$$P_k = \frac{VE_k}{X_k} \sin\delta_k \text{ and } Q_k = \frac{VE_k}{X_k} \cos\delta_k - \frac{V^2}{X_k}$$

The power angle $\delta_k$ being typically very small, as $\delta_k \to 0$, $P_k \approx \dfrac{VE_k}{X_k}\delta_k$ and $Q_k \approx \dfrac{V(E_k - V)}{X_k}$

**FIGURE 12.9** Real power versus voltage and reactive power versus frequency droop control curves in a predominantly resistive network.

The associated droop control curves are used for the bulk power systems.

A subset of the droop method is the virtual synchronous machine (VSM)-based method that incorporates a virtual inertial response with droop control to emulate synchronous machine behavior by an inverter. A simple first-order low-pass filter in the power computation step modifies the droop controller to have a virtual inertial response in the VSM. The VSM controller exhibits a different transient response, but the same steady-state response as the droop controller.

### 12.3.1.3 Oscillator-Based Controls

Another emerging microgrid control method is the oscillator-based controls that achieve much faster global asymptotic synchronization and power sharing despite output impedance mismatch among different converter units [10–12]. Virtual oscillator control (VOC), dispatchable VOC and unified VOC (uVOC) are the types of oscillator-based controls that have emerged in recent times both for faster response characteristics with superior synchronization property and for providing theoretical foundation for analysis, design and implementation. In general, an oscillator-based control is a time domain controller that combines the voltage tracking control layer with primary control. Unlike droop and VSM controls, oscillator-based controls do not require explicit calculation of real and reactive power control. The oscillator model is implemented in the controller, i.e., within the microcontroller or digital signal processor. The power electronic converter is used only as a voltage amplifier that couples the oscillators in different controller units through a physical electrical network. In the oscillator-based system, no voltage tracking or current tracking loops are required. Oscillator-based controllers are time-domain controllers in contrast to the phasor domain droop-based controllers. Any modification in the oscillator parameters directly affects the dynamic response of output voltage. The converter units automatically achieve real and reactive power sharing without any explicit power calculation by the controllers. However, real and reactive power dispatch signals can be provided from higher-level slower time-scale controllers.

Secondary controllers are needed in a droop, VSM or oscillator control-based microgrid for eliminating any steady-state error caused by both real and reactive power perturbations from nominal conditions. These controllers use closed-loop compensators to update the nominal power setpoints of all the dispatchable generators relying on some type of communication among the DERs. The overall objective of the secondary controller is to retain steady-state operation at nominal frequency and to restore desired voltage at various nodes of the network while maintaining the real and reactive power sharing among all generators [13,14].

### 12.3.1.4 Tertiary Control

Tertiary control is the highest level of control for microgrid operation producing longer-term setpoints depending on the requirements of the host power system based on the information received about the status of the DER units, market signals, and other system requirements. Tertiary control manages more of the global responsibilities to ensure the stable and economic operation of a microgrid, while keeping the balance between the power production and power consumption and making the most use of renewable generation systems. A centralized optimal power flow controller can be employed to minimize the operational costs and maximize the overall energy efficiency of the microgrid. Furthermore, tertiary control exchanges information with the distribution system operator (DSO) to optimize the microgrid operation within the utility grid. The control challenges at the tertiary level arise from the different characteristics of multiple generators and loads, bi-directional power flow and the versatile infrastructures of a microgrid.

### 12.3.2  V2H AND H2V POWER CONVERTER

EVs require electricity from the grid for battery charging, but any excess charge stored within the vehicle battery can be used to meet household electricity demand in price or supply constrained scenarios using the EV battery charger. This is particularly useful in areas where the cost of electricity is high and time-of-use (TOU) rates are available. The power converter, capable of V2H operation in addition to the essential G2V and/or H2V which is required for charging, needs to have bi-directional capability. The V2H mode is intended for providing electricity to the home in case of emergency or for load sharing in conjunction with renewable energy resources in a smart home configuration. The V2H mode can level the household electricity demand profile by responding to sharp power increases associated with running high power appliances for short periods of time. The smoother demand is beneficial to the electric suppliers allowing more manageable, efficient and cost-effective electricity generation. V2H operation also enables better utilization of renewable energy sources where excess generation can be stored and used for smoothing household load profile.

An example power converter capable of V2H and H2V operations is shown in Figure 12.10. The power converter connects to the vehicle battery pack to convert the DC high voltage to AC voltage of either 110 Vrms or 240 Vrms depending on the region of operation. The power converter enables the charging of the vehicle battery with power flowing from the AC supply side to the battery DC voltage in the G2V or H2V operation mode. The power converter digital controller regulates the charging of the battery. In the reverse direction in V2H mode, power flows from the vehicle battery to the home AC loads. Electric vehicle battery packs have high capacity and reliability; hence, by charging up the vehicle battery pack at night when the electricity demand from the grid is low and the utility provider may provide price breaks, the stored energy can be used during the daytime to alleviate power consumption in peak periods when the demand is high. A smart algorithm with user set preferences will ensure that there is enough charge in the battery left to meet the driving needs. In addition, the stored energy can be leveraged as back-up power supply during emergencies. The power converter connects to the household's power distribution board.

**FIGURE 12.10**  Power electronics converter capable of V2H and H2V modes of operation.

### 12.3.3 SOLAR GENERATION INTEGRATION WITH ELECTRIC VEHICLES

Along with the increase in EV usage, solar PV installations for residential applications also have a modest growth rate in recent times. Customers are also seeing added benefits of adding a storage unit to the solar panels. A typical solar PV power generation and household load profile is shown in Figure 12.11 which shows the mismatch between generation and load demand. When a storage is added with PV, the excess generation during the day can be stored and used later when the demand is higher which also results in higher electricity cost. Although significant cost and value barriers are obstacles to the deployment of combined solar PV and energy storage systems, a homeowner may consider a PV-storage hybrid installation for the reliability and utilization benefits. It is also likely that the PV with storage homeowners may also own an EV where the storage units in combination and coordination may provide significant value to the homeowner. An ideal scenario can be envisioned when the EV storage is recharged utilizing electricity generated from renewable energy sources such as solar PV. Homeowners with both an EV and a PV with storage can manage and control their equipment's operation in a coordinated way to reduce electricity and transportation costs; however, an automated and optimized algorithm is necessary to maximize the benefits.

The storage unit within the EV can provide the customer with the various functionalities at the household level such as electricity purchase cost minimization, voltage regulation and load regulation. The V2H controller can control the charge/discharge actions of the EV considering different objectives. Homeowners would be interested in reducing monthly electricity purchase cost utilizing the EV asset which is a significant investment in itself. If homeowners can be assured that they will have the required amount of charge in the EV when leaving home to make the necessary trip, then the electricity purchase cost per day can be reduced with an effective control strategy. For V2G operations, effective communication is required which comes with the risk of jeopardizing the privacy issues of the customer. The EV utilization for V2H capabilities are simpler and easier to integrate within a household without challenging communication requirements.

The power electronics required for integrated operation of solar PV and EV is a multiport converter that has a port to connect to the vehicle battery, home loads, home generation and power grid with intelligent controls managing the power and energy flow among the sources, loads and storage. A multiport power converter (MPC) configuration that can integrate home PV unit with storage and PEV along with the household load is shown in Figure 12.12 [15]. This MPC is configured to form a DC-coupled architecture where a DC bus connects the renewable generation source, energy storage and the grid through separate power electronic converters. Two separate DC/DC converters connect the renewable generation source and the energy source, while a DC/AC converter connects to the

**FIGURE 12.11**  Solar generation and household load demand profiles for a summer day.

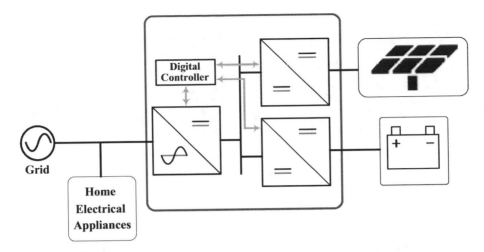

**FIGURE 12.12**   Multiport converter capable of V2H, H2V, V2G and G2V operations.

grid. The household load is connected to the AC line at the PCC where the MPC connects to the power grid. With the MPC architecture shown, the intermediate DC-link voltage level can be configured to be compatible with the EV storage battery level so that power can flow in either direction from the EV storage to the home storage or household load with minimum power conversion stages.

### 12.3.3.1   Coordinated Control of Solar PV Generation, Storage and PEV

A scenario and problem formulation for a household system that owns both PEV and PV with storage is provided as an example of coordinated control and usage at the residential level in this section [16]. The coordinated control of the two storage devices in the PV system and in the PEV can be used to provide benefits to both the customer and the utility. Homeowners will be able to control the available storage devices in their household according to their requirements. The system overview with coordinated control is shown in Figure 12.13. The coordinated control problem can be defined through a mathematical optimization model with the representation of the management problem through decision variables, parameters, objective function and constraints. The data related to electricity demand, solar PV generation and storage device characteristics are to be included in the optimization process. If the objective is to control the charge/discharge profiles of the storage devices for a particular day then the day-ahead forecast data of these parameters is needed. The goal of the coordinated controller is to make optimal control decisions for the storage devices in a particular day.

Considering electricity demand and solar PV generation as deterministic parameters-based historical data, the household electricity usage optimization can be handled by using off the shelf methods for solving linear programming, mixed-integer linear programming, quadratic programming and dynamic programming. When TOU rate-based cost structures are available for the electricity purchase from the utility, reduction of electricity purchase costs is possible by controlling the storage device charge/discharge scheduling using dynamic programming (DP). DP approaches ensure reaching the global optimal path by considering all of the possible paths which is exhaustive [17]. A specific algorithm for DP is the deterministic dual dynamic programming (DDDP) which considers a deterministic forward path. However, in the real-world problem, both the solar PV generation and the electricity demand are uncertain parameters. Therefore, to ensure an accurate coordination of the system resources, these uncertainties need to be considered with a stochastic model when developing a robust and realistic coordinated control scheme. Stochastic models can be optimized through model predictive control, stochastic gradient descent method, stochastic dual dynamic programming (SDDP), approximate dynamic programming (ADP), and machine

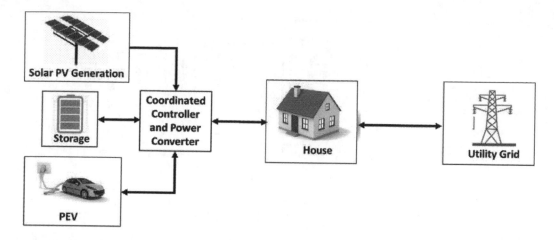

**FIGURE 12.13** System overview with coordinated control at the residential level and benefits at different levels.

learning algorithms. The dynamic programming-based control strategies will always outperform the commonly used state flow-based heuristic approaches.

The greatest benefit of combined usage of PV-storage hybrid system and PEV storage at the residential level is energy security during distribution or transmission-level power outages. The homeowners with a PV-storage unit and a PEV can control energy usage and storage in a coordinated way considering the priority, availability and outage duration when the gird is unavailable either due to bad weather or rolling blackouts due to higher load demand. The controller and converter allow the homeowner to have greater independence on energy usage and can also participate in transactive energy exchange with grid or other consumers. The impact of load regulation with the coordinated control strategy is shown in Figure 12.14 for the household with the same capacities of PV storage and PEV. If both of the storage devices are controlled in coordination, then the electricity demand variance is reduced by controlling them individually which is a benefit to both the homeowner and the utility. The utility benefits from the coordinated control through load regulation, reduction of back feeding of power, deferral of asset replacement and network upgrade. Overall, a partnership with the homeowner through an optimized and coordinated control allows utility to supply power more reliably and with improved power quality. The coordinated usage of solar PV generation, storage and PEV demonstrates the close linkage between the power and transportation systems.

**FIGURE 12.14** Regulated household profile with coordinated energy management control.

# REFERENCES

1. Society of Automotive Engineers (SAE), *Electric Vehicle and Plug in Hybrid Electric Vehicle Conductive Charge Coupler*, Standard SAE J1772, Warrendale, PA, October 2017.
2. R. Gao, X. She, I. Husain and A. Huang, "Solid-state transformer interfaced permanent magnet wind turbine distributed generation system with power management functions," *IEEE Transactions on Industry Applications*, 53(4), 3849–3861, 2017.
3. A.A. Milani, M.T.A. Khan, A. Chakrabortty and I. Husain, "Equilibrium point analysis and power sharing methods for distribution systems driven by solid-state transformers," *IEEE Transactions on Power Systems*, 33(2), 1473–1483, March 2018.
4. M.A. Awal, I. Husain, M.R.H. Bipu, O.A. Montes, F. Teng, H. Feng, M. Khan, and S. Lukic, "Modular medium voltage ac to low voltage dc converter for extreme fast charging applications," 2020, doi: arXiv:2007.04369. [Online] Available at: https://arxiv.org/abs/2007.04369
5. H. Tu, H. Feng, S. Srdic and S. Lukic, "Extreme fast charging of electric vehicles: A technology overview," *IEEE Transactions on Transportation Electrification*, 5(4), 861–878, 2019.
6. T. Ortmeyer, L. Wu and D. Dean, "Parameter identification for optimal electric vehicle rate structures," NYSERDA Report 16-32, New York, NY, 2016.
7. M.A. Awal, I. Husain, and W. Yu, "Passivity based predictive-resonant current control for resonance damping in LCL-equipped VSCs," *IEEE Transactions on Industry Applications*, 56(2), 1702–1713, 2020.
8. J. Vasquez, J. Guerrero, A. Luna, P. Rodriguez and R. Teodorescu, "Adaptive droop control applied to voltage-source inverters operating in grid-connected and islanded modes," *IEEE Transactions on Industrial Electronics*, 56(10), 4088–4096, October 2009.
9. Y. Sun, X. Hou, J. Yang, H. Han, M. Su and J.M. Guerrero, "New perspectives on droop control in AC microgrid," *IEEE Transactions on Industrial Electronics*, 64(7), 5741–5745, July 2017.
10. M.A. Awal and I. Husain, "Unified virtual oscillator control for grid-forming and grid-following converters," *IEEE Journal of Emerging and Selected Topics in Power Electronics*, doi: 10.1109/JESTPE.2020.3025748.
11. B.B. Johnson, M. Sinha, N.G. Ainsworth, F. Dorfler and S.V. Dhople, "Synthesizing virtual oscillators to control islanded inverters," *IEEE Transactions on Power Electronics*, 31(8), 6002–6015, August 2016.
12. M.A. Awal, H. Yu, H. Tu, S. Lukic and I. Husain, "Hierarchical control for virtual oscillator based grid-connected and islanded microgrids," *IEEE Transactions on Power Electronics*, 35(1), 988–1001, 2020.
13. A. Bidram, A. Davoudi, F.L. Lewis and J.M. Guerrero, "Distributed cooperative secondary control of microgrids using feedback linearization," *IEEE Transactions on Power Systems*, 28(3), 3462–3470, August 2013.
14. J.W. Simpson-Porco, Q. Shafiee, F. Dorfler, J.C. Vasquez, J.M. Guerrero and F. Bullo, "Secondary frequency and voltage control of islanded microgrids via distributed averaging," *IEEE Transactions on Industrial Electronics*, 62(11), 7025–7038, November 2015.
15. A.K. Bhattacharjee, N. Kutkut and I. Batarseh, "Review of multiport converters for solar and energy storage integration," *IEEE Transactions on Power Electronics*, 34(2), 1431–1445, February 2019.
16. F. Hafiz, A.R. de Queiroz and I. Husain, "Coordinated control of PEV and PV-based storages in residential system under generation and load uncertainties," *IEEE Transactions on Industry Applications*, 55(6), 5524 – 5532, December 2019.
17. F. Hafiz, D. Lubkeman, I. Husain and P. Fajri, "Energy storage management strategy based on dynamic programming and optimal sizing of PV panel-storage capacity for a residential system," *IEEE Transmission and Distribution Conference and Exposition*, Denver, CO, 2018.

# 13 Internal Combustion Engines

Internal combustion (IC) engines are energy conversion devices that extract stored energy in a fuel through the combustion process and deliver mechanical power. The devices are also known as heat engines in the broader sense. Reciprocating-type IC engine is the primary choice of power plant in today's production hybrid vehicles. The IC engine is assisted by an electric motor of similar or lower power capability in these vehicles. IC engines for conventional vehicles are designed to operate over a wide range, and compromise is often necessary to deliver acceptable efficiency and performance throughout its operation regime. On the other hand, IC engines in hybrid vehicles require operation within a narrow band of torque-speed characteristics, especially in those with series-type hybrid architectures. However, IC engines are yet to be designed specifically for hybrid vehicles; significant opportunity exists to explore improved IC engine designs for hybrid vehicles.

The prime objectives of hybridization of road vehicles are to enhance fuel economy and reduce emissions. Fuel economy depends on the operating points of the IC engine, while emission control units target eliminating harmful pollutants from the exhaust stream. After developing an understanding of the working principles of IC engines, this chapter addresses fuel economy calculations and exhaust emission control methods. Discussions on IC engines include operation principles, air standard cycles and combustion characteristics. For understanding engine operation efficiency, practical parameters such as brake mean effective pressure (BMEP) and brake-specific fuel consumption have been used.

## 13.1    HEAT ENGINES

The devices that convert heat transfer to work are known as heat engines. Heat engines operate in cycles undergoing constant pressure, constant volume, constant entropy, etc., strokes within one cycle to convert thermal energy into useful work. The ideal cycle used for thermodynamic analysis is the Carnot cycle, although practical heat engines work with different cycles that have theoretical efficiencies lower than that of the Carnot cycle. The practical cycles have evolved due to the practical limitations of the Carnot cycles, and also because of the difference in characteristics of the choices available for the energy source, working fluid and hardware materials.

The heat engines of interest for the hybrid vehicle applications, primarily the IC engine and the gas turbine, will be discussed in this section. An IC engine is a heat engine that utilizes gas as a working fluid. The IC engines use heat cycles that gain their energy from combustion of fuel within the engine. The IC engines can be reciprocating type, where the reciprocating motion of a piston is converted to linear motion through a crank mechanism. The IC engines used in automobiles, trucks and buses are of the reciprocating type where the processes occur within reciprocating piston-cylinder arrangement. The gas turbines used in power plants are also IC engines where the processes occur in an interconnected series of different components. The Brayton cycle gas-turbine engine has been adapted to automotive propulsion engine and has the advantage of burning fuel that requires little refining and the fuel burns completely. The gas turbines have fewer moving parts since there is no need to convert the rotary motion of the turbine. The disadvantages of gas turbines for automotive applications are complex construction, high noise levels and relatively lower efficiency for smaller-sized engines. Nevertheless, gas turbines have been considered for hybrid electric vehicles and prototype vehicles have been developed.

The performance of a heat engine is measured by the efficiency of the heat engine cycle defined as the ratio of the net work output per cycle $W_{net}$ to the heat transfer into the engine per cycle. Another way of defining the performance of heat engines is to use the mean effective pressure MEP.

The MEP is the theoretical constant pressure that, if exerted on the piston during the expansion stroke between the largest specific volume and the smallest volume, would produce the same net work as actually produced by the heat engine. Mathematically stated,

$$\text{MEP} = \frac{|W_{net}|}{\text{Displacement Volume}} \qquad (13.1)$$

The heat engine cycle performance analysis is carried out from the information available at certain convenient state points in the cycle. The parameters needed at the state points are pressure, temperature, volume and entropy. If two parameters are known at two state points, then the unknown parameters are usually obtained from the process that the working fluid undergoes between the two state points (such as isobar and isentropic) and the laws of thermodynamics. The discussion of the laws of thermodynamics and efficiency analysis of heat engine cycles are beyond the scope of this book. Only a general introduction to the heat engine cycles of interest will be given. The concepts of entropy discussed earlier in Chapter 5 will be used here while discussing the thermodynamic cycles of the heat engines.

### 13.1.1 RECIPROCATING ENGINES

The two types of reciprocating IC engines are the spark-ignition engine (SI) and the compression-ignition (CI) engine. The two engines are commonly known as gasoline/petrol engine and diesel engine based on the type of fuel used for combustion. The difference in the two engines is in the method of initiating the combustion and in the processes of the cycle. In a spark-ignition engine, a mixture of air and fuel is drawn in and a spark plug ignites the charge. The intake of the engine is called the charge. Electronically controlled direct fuel injection is used in modern gasoline engine vehicles, which helps to measure out the right amount of fuel in response to driver demand. In a compression-ignition engine, air alone is drawn in and compressed to such a high pressure and temperature that combustion starts spontaneously when fuel is injected. The spark-ignition engines are relatively light and lower in cost and used for lower power engines as in the conventional automobiles. The compression-ignition engines are more suitable for power conversion in the higher power range, such as in trucks, buses, locomotives, ships and in auxiliary power units. The fuel economy of compression-ignition engines is better than the spark-ignition engines justifying their use in higher power applications [1].

Although gasoline engines have thus far been used in passenger hybrid vehicles, diesel engines have a lot of potential for replacing those in the future. Diesel engines are increasingly being used in several models of passenger IC engine vehicles, which give high gas mileages because of their high fuel efficiency. The problem of $NO_x$ emissions in diesel engines can be addressed through catalytic conversion and emission after-treatment components. More on emissions and their controls appear in Section 13.4.

The sketch of a representative reciprocating IC engine including the terms standard for such engines is given in Figure 13.1. The engine consists of piston that undergoes a reciprocating motion within the engine cylinder. The position of the piston at the bottom of the cylinder when the volume inside is maximum is known as the *bottom dead center* (BDC). The position of the piston at the top of the cylinder when the volume inside is minimum is called the *top dead center* (TDC). This cylinder minimum volume when the piston is at the TDC is known as the *clearance volume*. A crank mechanism converts the linear motion of the piston into rotary motion and delivers the power to the crankshaft. The volume swept by the piston as it moved from the TDC to the BDC is known as the *displacement volume*, which is a parameter commonly used to specify the size of an engine. The *compression ratio* is defined as the ratio of the volume at BDC to the volume at TDC.

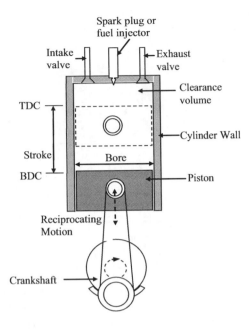

**FIGURE 13.1**   A reciprocating IC engine.

The diameter of the cylinder is called the *bore*. The bore in automotive spark-ignition engines are typically between 70 and 100 mm. Too small a bore leave no room for valves while exceedingly large bores mean more mass and longer flame travel time. The smaller bores enable higher rpm of the engines. The vertical distance traversed by the piston from the BDC to the TDC is called the *stroke*. The stroke is typically between 70 and 100 mm. Too short a stroke means there will not be enough torque. The length of the stroke is limited by the piston velocities. The minimum displacement of a cylinder can be 250 cc, while the maximum can be up to 1,000 cc. The acceptable bore and stroke lengths lead to multiple cylinder engines. The multiple cylinders can be arranged inline, flat or in a V-shaped configuration depending on the number of cylinders. The typical arrangements are given in Table 13.1.

For a good primary balance, the power strokes of the multiple cylinders are equally spaced. The engine arrangements that have good primary balance are: Inline 4 and 6 cylinders, 90° V 8 cylinders and flat 4 and 6 cylinders. The arrangements that have poor primary balance are 90° V 6 cylinders and Inline 3 cylinders. In the arrangements with poor primary balance, counter-rotating balance shafts are used to cancel vibration.

The valve arrangement in the cylinder is known as the valve train. The valve train can be overhead valve (OHV), single overhead cam valve (SOHC) or dual overhead cam valve (DOHC). The OHV

**TABLE 13.1**
**Arrangement of Automotive Engine Cylinders**

| No. of Cylinders | Cylinder Arrangement |
| --- | --- |
| 3 | Inline |
| 4 | Inline, flat |
| 5 | Inline |
| 6 | Inline, flat, V (narrow, 60°, 90°) |
| 8 | V (90°) |
| 10 | V (90°) |
| 12 | V, flat (for exotics) |

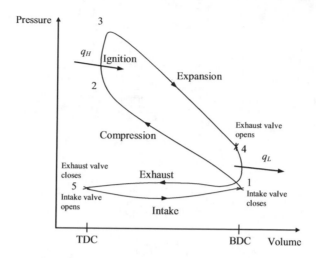

**FIGURE 13.2**   Pressure-volume diagram of a reciprocating-type IC engine.

has camshaft, push rod, rocker and valve, while the SOHC and DOHC have camshaft(s), rocker and valve. The SOHC has one camshaft placed in the cylinder head, while DOHC has two camshafts in the cylinder head, one for the inlet valves and the other for the exhaust valves. There can be 2, 3, 4 or 5 valves in a cylinder. The number of valve selection depends on the tradeoff between flow and complexity.

### 13.1.2  PRACTICAL AND AIR-STANDARD CYCLES

The automobile IC engines are typically four-stroke engines where the piston executes four strokes of the cylinder for every two revolutions of the crankshaft. The four strokes are: *intake, compression, expansion* and *exhaust*. The operations within the four strokes are illustrated in the pressure volume diagram of Figure 13.2. The numbers 1–5 in the diagram represent the distinct state points between processes of the cycle. The *intake* is the process of drawing the charge into the cylinder with the intake valve open. The working fluid is compressed in the *compression* stage with the piston traveling from the BDC to the TDC. Work is done by the piston in the compression stage. In the next stage, heat is added during ignition of the compressed fluid by ignition for spark ignition or spontaneous combustion for compression-ignition engines. The next stage is the *expansion* process, which is also known as the power stroke. In this stroke, work is done by the cylinder on the piston. The *exhaust* process starts at the BDC with the opening of the exhaust valve. Unutilized heat is rejected from the engine during the exhaust process.

The practical cycle entails significant complexity due to the irreversibilities associated with friction, pressure and temperature gradients, heat transfer between the gases and the cylinder walls, and the work required to compress the charge and to discharge the products of combustion. The complexity of the process typically calls for computer simulation for performance analysis. However, significant insight can be gained into the processes by making simplifying assumptions about the behavior of the processes that make up the cycle. Idealized processes can substitute the combustion and expansion processes within the cylinder. These idealized cycles are known as air-standard cycles. The air-standard analysis assumes that the working fluid is an ideal gas, the processes are all reversible and the combustion process is replaced by a heat transfer process from an external source. A brief description of the two air-standard cycles, the Otto cycle and the Diesel cycle are given in the following.

#### 13.1.2.1  Air-Standard Otto Cycle

The Otto cycle is the idealized air-standard version of the practical cycle used in spark-ignition engines. The air-standard Otto cycle assumes that the heat addition occurs instantaneously under constant volume when the piston is at the TDC. The cycle is illustrated on a *p-v* (pressure-volume)

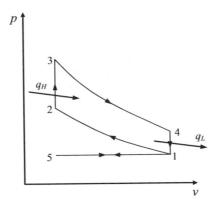

**FIGURE 13.3**   *p-v* diagram of an air-standard Otto cycle.

diagram in Figure 13.3. The *intake stroke* starts with the intake valve opening at the TDC to draw a fresh charge into the cylinder. The intake valve is open between 5 and 1 to take the fresh charge, which is a mixture of fuel and air. The volume of the cylinder increases as the piston moves down to allow more charge into the cylinder. The stroke ends with the piston reaching the BDC when the intake valve closes at that position. This state point at the BDC is labeled as 1. In the next cycle between 1 and 2, work is done on the charge by the piston to compress it thereby increasing its temperature and pressure. This is the *compression stroke* when the piston moves up with both the valves closed. Process 1–2 is an isentropic (i.e. reversible as well as adiabatic) compression as the piston moves from the BDC to the TDC. The combustion starts near the end of the compression stroke in spark-ignition engines when the high-pressure, high-temperature fluid is ignited by the spark plug. The pressure thus rises at constant volume (i.e. almost instantaneously) to state point 3. Process 2–3 is the rapid combustion process when heat is transferred near the TDC to the air from the external source. The next stroke is the *expansion or power stroke*, when the gas mixture expands and work is done on the piston forcing it to return to the BDC. Process 3–4 represents the isentropic expansion when work is done on the piston. The final stroke is the *exhaust stroke*, which starts with the opening of the exhaust valve near 4. The piston begins to move upwards purging the combustion products from the cylinder along the way. During process 4–1, the most of the heat is rejected while the piston is near BDC. Process 1–5 represents the exhaust of the burnt fuel at essentially constant pressure. At 5, the exhaust valve closes and the intake valve opens; the cylinder is now ready to draw in fresh charge for a repeat of the cycle.

The spark-ignition engines can be a four-stroke engine or a two-stroke engine. The two-stroke engines run on two-stroke Otto cycle where the intake, compression, expansion and exhaust operations are all accomplished in one revolution of the crankshaft. The two-stroke cycles are used in smaller engines, such as those used in motorbikes.

Most spark-ignition engines, or gasoline engines as it is more commonly known, run on a modified Otto cycle. The air-fuel ratio used in these engines is between 10/1 and 13/1. The compression ratios are in the range of 9–12 for most production vehicles. The compression ratio of the engine is limited by the octane rating of the engine. A high compression ratio may lead to auto-ignition of the air-fuel mixture during compression, which is absolutely undesirable in a spark-ignition engine. The spark-ignition engines have been originally developed by limiting the amount of air allowed into the engine using a *carburetor* placed in the path of air intake. The function of the carburetor is to draw the fuel by creating a vacuum following 'Bernoulli's principle'. However, fuel injection, which is used for diesel engines, is now common for gasoline engines with spark ignition instead of the carburetor. The control objective for fuel injection systems is to compute the mass flow rate of air into the engine at any instant of time and to mix the correct amount of gasoline with it, such that the air and fuel mixture is right for the engine running condition. In recent years, the requirements to meet the strict exhaust gas emission regulations have increased the demand for fuel injection systems.

The torque-speed characteristics of a spark-ignition or gasoline engine are shown in Figure 13.4. The engine has a very narrow high torque range, which also requires high-enough rpm of the engine. The narrow high-torque region burdens the transmission gear requirements of spark-ignition engines.

The spark-ignition engines are widely used in automobiles, and continuous development has resulted in engines that easily meet current emission and fuel economy standards. Currently, spark-ignition engines are of the lowest cost engine, but the question remains whether it will be possible to meet future emission and fuel economy standards at a reasonable cost. The spark-ignition engine also has a few other drawbacks, which include the throttling plate used to restrict the air intake. The partial throttle operation is poor in spark-ignition engines due to throttle irreversibility, a problem that is non-existent in diesel engines. In general, the throttling process leads to reduction in efficiency of the spark-ignition engine. The losses through bearing friction and sliding friction further reduce the efficiency of the engine.

### 13.1.2.2   Air-Standard Diesel Cycle

The practical cycles in diesel engines are based on the Diesel cycle. The Diesel cycle attempts to approach the Carnot efficiency as closely as possible. The air-standard Diesel cycle assumes that the heat addition takes place at constant pressure, while heat rejection occurs under constant volume. The cycle is shown on a $p$-$v$ (pressure-volume) diagram in Figure 13.5.

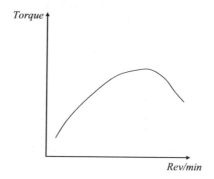

**FIGURE 13.4**   Torque-speed characteristics of a gasoline engine.

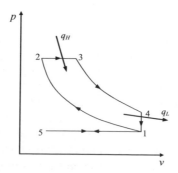

**FIGURE 13.5**   $p$-$v$ Diagram of an air-standard Diesel cycle.

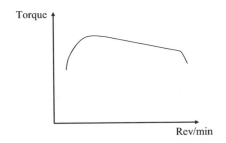

**FIGURE 13.6** Torque-speed characteristics of a diesel engine.

The cycle begins with the *intake* of fresh air into the cylinder between 5 and 1. The intake valve is open between 5 and 1. The next process 1–2 is the same as in the Otto cycle when isentropic (constant entropy) *compression* takes place as the piston moves from the BDC to the TDC. With a sufficiently high compression ratio, the temperature and pressure of air reach such a level that the combustion starts spontaneously due to injection of fuel near the end of the compression stroke. The heat is transferred to the working fluid under constant pressure during combustion in process 2–3, which also makes up the first part of the *expansion* or power stroke. The isentropic expansion in process 3–4 makes up for the rest of the power stroke. The *exhaust* valve opens at state point 4 allowing the pressure to drop under constant volume during the process 4–1. Heat is rejected during this process, while the piston is at BDC. The exhaust of the burnt fuel takes place during 1–5 at essentially constant pressure. The exhaust valve then closes and the intake valve opens, and the cylinder is ready to draw in fresh air for a repeat of the cycle.

The nominal range of compression ratios in compression-ignition engines is 13/1 to 17/1 and the air-fuel ratios used lie between 20/1 and 25/1. The higher compression ratio aided by the work produced during combustion results in higher efficiency in diesel engines compared to gasoline engines. The diesel engine has a lower specific power than the gasoline engine. The diesel engines also have a broad torque range as shown in Figure 13.6.

The major drawbacks of diesel engines include the requirement of stronger and heavier components that increase the mass of the engine and the speed limitation of the injection and flame propagation time. The improvements in diesel engine are directed toward reducing the nitrogen oxides in the exhaust, and the noise, vibration and malodorous fumes from the engine. The recent automotive diesel engines developed addressing the aforementioned issues make them excellent candidates for hybrid electric vehicle applications.

### 13.1.3 Gas Turbine Engines

Gas turbines are used for stationary power generation as well as for transportation applications such as in aircraft propulsion and marine power plants. The gas turbines can be either an open type or a closed type. In the open type, the working fluid gains their energy from combustion of fuel within the engine, whereas in a closed type the energy input by heat transfer is from an external source. The open type is used in vehicle propulsion systems and will be considered here. The use of gas turbines in transportation applications can be attributed to the favorable power output to weight ratio of gas turbines, which again makes it a viable candidate for hybrid electric vehicles.

The gas turbine engine runs on a Brayton cycle, which uses constant pressure heat transfer processes with isentropic compression and expansion processes in between. The major components of a gas turbine are shown in Figure 13.7a along with the directions of energy flow. The corresponding *p-v* diagram for an air-standard cycle is illustrated in Figure 13.7b, which ignores the irreversibilities in air circulation through the components of the gas turbine. The constant entropy processes are shown as $s = c$.

The working fluid of air is considered to be an ideal gas in the air-standard analysis. At the beginning of the cycle at state 1, atmospheric air is continuously drawn in and compressed in the

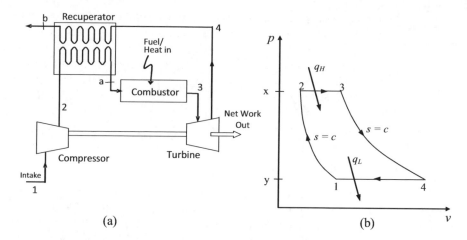

**FIGURE 13.7**   (a) Air-standard gas turbine cycle and (b) $p$-$v$ diagram of ideal Brayton cycle.

compressor to raise its pressure and temperature. The compressor is usually of the radial flow type for automotive applications. The air then moves into the combustion chamber or combustor, where combustion takes place with fuel injected to raise the temperature of the air. The high temperature, high pressure mixture is then expanded and cooled in the turbine, which produces power and delivers work. The hot gas turbine exhaust gas is utilized in a recuperator to preheat the air exiting the compressor before entering the combustor. This reduces the fuel needed in the combustor and increases the overall efficiency of the system. In the open-type gas turbine, fresh air is drawn in and exhaust gases are purged after going through the recuperator in each cycle. The turbine is designed to deliver work output that is greater than the required compressor work input. The excess work available at the shaft is used to propel a vehicle in automotive gas turbines or to generate electricity in stationary applications. The enclosed area in the figure represents the network output. In particular, the area 12xy1 in the $p$-$v$ diagram represents the compressor work input per unit mass and the area 34yx3 represents the turbine work output per unit mass.

The power output of a turbine is controlled through the amount of fuel injected into the combustor. Many turbines have adjustable vanes and/or gearing to decrease fuel consumption during partial load conditions and to improve acceleration. The major advantage of a gas turbine is that the only moving part is the rotor of the turbine. The turbine has no reciprocating motion, and consequently runs smoother than a reciprocating engine. Another big advantage of gas turbines is its multi-fuel capability. The turbine has the flexibility of burning any combustible fuel injected into the air-stream, because the continuous combustion is not heavily reliant on the combustion characteristics of the fuel. The fuel in a gas turbine burns completely and cleanly, which keeps the emissions at a low level.

The gas turbine engine has a few drawbacks, which have prevented its widespread use in automotive applications. The complicated design of gas turbines increases the manufacturing costs. The response time of the gas turbine to changes in throttle request is slow relative to a reciprocating engine. The efficiency of the gas turbine decreases at partial throttle conditions making it less suitable for low-power applications. The turbine requires intercoolers, regenerators and/or reheaters to reach efficiencies comparable to the spark-ignition or compression-ignition engines, which adds significant cost and complexity to a gas turbine engine [2].

## 13.2   BMEP AND BSFC

Although torque is a measure of a particular engine's ability to do work, mean effective pressure (MEP) is a more useful parameter for standardized comparison of several different engines as was indicated earlier. For reciprocating engines, BMEP is the more practical parameter, which measures the engine's work done per cycle per cylinder displaced volume. To understand BMEP, we first need to define indicated mean effective pressure (IMEP) and friction mean effective pressure (FMEP). The word 'indicated' refers to the net work performed by the working mixture in the cylinder of the engine over the compression and expansion strokes. Part of this work goes into overcoming engine mechanical friction and losses to induct air-fuel mixture and expel excess charge. The remaining work or torque is what is available at the engine crankshaft. 'Brake' refers to the work or torque available at the engine crankshaft as measured at the flywheel by a dynamometer. The dynamometer measurements help avoid mechanical losses associated with the powertrain of a vehicle. In terms of mean effective pressures, we can write

$$IMEP = BMEP + FMEP$$

The result of calculated BMEP gives the value for a theoretical constant pressure exerted in the combustion chamber as a result of combustion. While it does not describe the actual combustion pressure, it is a good standard for comparison.

Work done per cycle using the engine's output power is

$$\text{Work per cycle} = \frac{P_b n_R}{N} \tag{13.2}$$

where $P_b$ is engine brake output power, $n_R$ is the number of crankshaft revolutions per power stroke and $N$ is the engine speed in rev/s. $n_R$ is the number of power strokes, which is 2 for a four-stroke engine. It must be noted that the engine power is the power output for the entire engine rather than just one cylinder. Therefore, the BMEP is obtained by dividing by the engine's entire displacement volume $V_d$ as

$$BMEP = \frac{P_b n_R}{V_d N} \tag{13.3}$$

To simplify the computation, power can be expressed as the product of brake torque $T_b$ and engine speed $N$. Note that to be unit consistent with Equation 13.3, engine speed has to be expressed in terms of revolutions per unit time; thus, multiplication by $2\pi$ is necessary. Using these values in Equation 13.3, the proper unit for BMEP with torque expressed in N·m is

$$\frac{\left(\dfrac{\text{rev}}{\text{cycle}}\right)\left(2\pi\dfrac{\text{rad}}{\text{rev}}\right)(N\,m)}{(m^3/\text{cycle})} \Rightarrow \frac{N}{m^2} \text{ or Pa (Pascal)} \ (1\text{ bar}=100\text{ kPa})$$

BMEP in terms of torque is given by

$$BMEP = \frac{4\pi \times T_b}{V_d}\left(N/m^2\right) \tag{13.4}$$

The volume of one cylinder can be calculated from

$$V_d = \frac{\pi}{4} \times \text{Bore}^2 \times \text{Stroke (m}^3)$$

**FIGURE 13.8** Example efficiency map of a diesel IC engine.

Fuel consumption in IC engines is measured in terms of fuel mass flow per unit time $\dot{m}_f$. The fuel flow rate per unit output power, called the *specific fuel consumption* (SFC), is a measurement of how effectively the engine is converting the stored chemical energy in the fuel into mechanical energy. For practical purposes, the more commonly used parameter is the ratio of the fuel's mass flow rate $\dot{m}_{fuel}$ and the measured output power $P_b$. Similar to BMEP, this parameter is called the *brake specific fuel consumption* (BSFC) for reciprocating engines, indicating that power $P_b$ or torque $T_b$ is measured at the engine crankshaft using a dynamometer. The engine's output power at the flywheel can be expressed as the product of the measured engine brake torque and speed. The resulting equation for calculating BSFC is

$$\text{BSFC} = \frac{\dot{m}_f}{P_b} = \frac{\dot{m}_f}{T_b\,2\pi N} \tag{13.5}$$

Contour maps of BSFC under the engine's peak torque curve are obtained empirically through laboratory testing of the engine at a variety of speed/load combination set-point. Performance curves of engine power, torque and BSFC versus speed are a useful tool for analyzing IC engines. An example efficiency map for a diesel engine is shown in Figure 13.8 with BSFC contours plotted in g/kWh [3]. Representative scales for BMEP in kPa and corresponding engine torque in N m have been used in the figure. Engine power available at the crankshaft for an operating point can be obtained from the product of the brake torque and the engine speed.

## 13.3   VEHICLE FUEL ECONOMY

The fuel economy is a key performance measure of a vehicle related to the efficiency of the powertrain components. The fuel economy is calculated based on fuel consumption over a standard drive cycle. Fuel economy of a production or already built vehicle can be calculated by actually driving the vehicle on the road or in a chassis dynamometer following a standard drive cycle such as a highway drive cycle or an urban drive cycle. Real-world fuel economy is consumer specific; however, if representative highway or urban standard drive cycles are used by a consumer, then the fuel economy should be close to the numbers obtained in a laboratory with a dynamometer.

   The design of a vehicle can be evaluated by predicting the fuel economy through simulation. Subsystem models or characteristics obtained from test or simulation data are used to characterize the vehicle. Dynamic models of subsystems are avoided to simplify the vehicle-level simulation. Standard drive cycles along with the vehicle model and road-load characteristics can predict the fuel economy reasonably well in simulation with fairly accurate characterization of the subsystems.

In order to predict the fuel economy, the engine output power at the crankshaft and the fuel consumed to produce that power are necessary.

The resultant BSFC and the specific gravity of the fuel at prevailing conditions are necessary to predict the fuel economy. The BSFC of an engine is the mass of fuel consumed at the engine to produce a certain amount of energy. The specific gravity of the fuel is assumed constant for the drive cycle. This is an approximation since the specific gravity depends on temperature and other factors.

The fuel economy of a vehicle is given by

$$\text{FE(m/L)} = \frac{\text{Vehicle velocity, } v \text{ (m/s)}}{\text{Fuel flow rate, } Q_f \text{ (L/h )} \times \text{(h/3600 s)}} \quad (13.6)$$

The fuel flow rate is obtained from the mass flow rate of fuel as

$$Q_f \text{ (L/h)} = \frac{\text{Mass flow rate, } \dot{m}_f \text{ (g/h)}}{\text{Specfic gravity, } \rho_{fuel} \text{ (g/L)}} \quad (13.7)$$

The mass flow rate is obtained from the engine power at the crankshaft and the BSFC as

$$\dot{m}_f = P_b \text{ (kW)} \cdot \text{BSFC (g/kW h)} \quad (13.8)$$

The fuel flow rate is then

$$Q_f \text{ (L/h)} = \frac{P_b \text{ (kW)} \times \text{BSFC (g/kW h)}}{\rho_{fuel} \text{ (g/L)}}$$

Finally, the fuel economy is given by

$$\text{FE(m/L)} = \frac{3600 \times v \text{ (m/s)} \times \rho_{fuel} \text{ (g/L)}}{P_b \text{ (kW)} \times \text{BSFC (g/kW h)}} \quad (13.9)$$

The fuel economy in mi/gal is given by

$$\text{FE(mi/gal)} = \frac{3600 \times v \text{ (m/s)} \times \rho_{fuel} \text{ (g/L)} \times (3.79 \text{ L/gal}) \times \text{mi/1609 m)}}{P_b \text{ (kW)} \times \text{BSFC (g/kW h)}}$$

$$= 8.4797 \frac{v \times \rho_{fuel}}{P_b \times \text{BSFC}} \quad (13.10)$$

The engine power can be obtained from the traction power if the drivetrain efficiency is available. For a given traction power and drivetrain efficiency, the engine power is

$$P_b = \frac{P_{TR}}{\eta_{DT}} \quad (13.11)$$

While BSFC can be useful in standardized examination of fuel usage relative to power output, evaluation of fuel efficiency tells what percentage of fuel being put into the engine is being used for mechanical work output. Efficiency for a combustion engine can be tabulated by dividing the measured brake power by the potential power of the injected fuel. Power potential of a particular fuel depends on both its energy content and the rate that it is injected. Standard fuel economy validation requires standard fuel formulation with well-established heat values. Energy content can be expressed in terms of a fuel's higher heating value (HHV) which is the amount of heat released per unit quantity when combusted and allowed to cool to its initial temperature (and the water in the exhaust is condensed). The product of HHV and the fuel mass flow rate gives the power potential of the fuel. The following expression is used to calculate efficiency for an internal combustion engine:

$$\text{Fuel efficiency} = \frac{\text{Measured power}}{\text{Fuel power potential}} = \frac{P_b}{\dot{m}_f \text{HHV}} = \frac{T_b N}{\dot{m}_f \text{HHV}} \tag{13.12}$$

It must be emphasized that for efficiency calculations involving different chemical energy carriers the HHV of fuels must be considered, and not the lower heating value (LHV) [4]. The definition of HHV is derived from the heat of formation which includes all the energy changes of a chemical reaction between the initial state at 25°C and the final state, also at 25°C. The primary difference between HHV and LHV is that the latent heat of water vapor present in the combustion products is included in the former, i.e., water is assumed to be condensed at 1 atm and 25°C. The HHV is based on the true energy content representing the heat released by oxidation of a fuel with air. As an example, the HHV of common diesel is 19,733 BTU/lb.

### 13.3.1 Fuel Economy in Hybrids

In charge-sustaining hybrids, all of the power is delivered by the engine. Even if the vehicle is driven with electric propulsion for a certain period of time, the energy coming from the energy storage system (battery or ultracapacitor or both) was originally supplied by the on-board fuel through the engine at some point in time. This is why state of charge (SoC) correction algorithms have to be used to make sure that all of the energy supplied by the fuel has been utilized to drive the vehicle. Otherwise, the fuel used to charge the energy storage system will be left unaccounted for resulting in a worse fuel economy than what it actually is. On the other hand, if fuel used for charging the energy storage system is not accounted for in calculating the fuel economy, a better than actual result will be obtained. With the SoC corrections, the energy storage system is maintained at the same SoC at the beginning and end of the drive cycle for which fuel economy is being measured.

The fuel economy of plug-in hybrids must be calculated accounting for both the on-board fuel used and the off-board fuel supplied. The fuel economy in plug-in hybrids are measured according to the standard SAE J1711, which states that the total fuel supplied during the drive cycle is the sum of the on-board fuel consumed and the fuel equivalency of the off-board supplied electric charge. For the correct fuel economy calculation, the on-board energy storage system is recharged from the wall outlet until the SoC matches the initial value. The equivalent fuel for recharging the on-board energy storage system is obtained from

$$F_{elec} = \frac{E_{ob}}{\zeta_{fuel}} \tag{13.13}$$

where $\zeta_{fuel} = 38.322$ kWh/gal is the fuel equivalency of the electric energy supplied and $E_{ob}$ is the off-board electrical energy supplied by the utility.

### Example 13.1

A hybrid electric vehicle has a downsized engine, an electric motor/generator and an ultracapacitor-bank for electric propulsion assistance. The vehicle is driven for 30 min at a constant velocity of 25 m/s with engine operating at BSFC = 270 g/kWh and electric motors. The traction power required for this constant velocity cruise is 15.2 kW. However, the ultracapacitor-bank has additional 960 kJ of energy captured during a regenerative braking. Calculate the fuel economy when all of the ultracapacitor energy is utilized for propulsion within the 30 min constant velocity cruising period.

### Solution

Velocity $v = 25$ m/s; energy captured by ultracapacitor $= 960$ kJ

Power supplied by ultracapacitor in 30 min $= \dfrac{960 \times 1000 \text{ J}}{30 \text{ min} \times 60 \text{ s/min}} = 533.33 \ W$

Given, $P_{TR} = 15.2$ kW

Drivetrain efficiency $\eta_{DT} = 90\%$

Power to the wheels is delivered both by ultracapacitor-bank and engine over 30 min. Therefore,

$$P_{UC} + P_{Eng} = P_{TR}/\eta_{DT}$$

Engine power $P_{Eng} = 15.2/0.9 - 0.533 = 16.36$ kW

Fuel flow rate $Q_f = \dfrac{P_{TR}/\eta_{DT} \times \text{BSFC}}{\rho_{fuel}} = \dfrac{(16.36) \times 270}{720} = 6.135$ L/h

Fuel economy

$$\text{FE} = \frac{v}{Q_f} = \frac{25 \text{ m/s} \times 3600 \text{ s/h}}{6.135 \text{ L/h}} = 14670 \text{ m/L}$$

$$= \frac{14670 \text{ m/L} \times 3.79 \text{ L/gal}}{1609 \text{ m/mi}} = 34.55 \text{ mi/gal}$$

## 13.4  EMISSION CONTROL SYSTEM

The exhaust stream of both spark and compression-ignition engines are significant sources of environmental pollution [5]. Gasoline fueled spark-ignition engine exhaust gases contain oxides of nitrogen ($NO_x$), carbon monoxide (CO) and hydrocarbons (HC). Diesel exhaust emissions contain lower levels of CO and HC, but similar levels of $NO_x$ compared to gasoline engines. CO is a highly toxic substance and must be converted to $CO_2$ before being released to the atmosphere. $CO_2$ is not toxic, but does contribute to the greenhouse gases.

### 13.4.1  GENERATION OF POLLUTANTS

The origin of the pollutants in the exhaust stream of IC engines is in the combustion process itself. Complete combustion of hydrocarbons with excess oxygen would result in the formation of only water and carbon dioxide as follows:

$$[C_x H_y] + [O_2] \rightarrow [H_2O] + [CO_2]$$

However, due to practical limitations and constraints placed on IC engine operation, complete combustion of hydrocarbons is not possible. Intermediate reaction products are formed since chemical reactions depend on pressure, temperature, concentration of species and time. Exhaust streams contain much different types of hydrocarbons. While most of these hydrocarbons are intermediate reaction products, some unburned high-molecular-weight hydrocarbon fuel may also be present. Carbon monoxide is produced when there is insufficient oxygen. Retarded ignition in gasoline engines also aid in carbon monoxide production.

Atmospheric nitrogen present in the intake stream reacts with excess oxygen at high combustion temperatures to produce the undesirable and highly toxic $NO_x$ compounds. At high combustion temperatures, molecular nitrogen ($N_2$) and oxygen ($O_2$) in the combustion air disassociate and bond with each other; a process commonly referred to as thermal $NO_x$ generation. Most of the $NO_x$ generated in combustion is of the form nitric oxide (NO) and is governed by the following reactions:

$$O + N_2 \rightarrow NO + N$$

$$N + O_2 \rightarrow NO + O$$

$$N + OH \rightarrow NO + H$$

Although in much less quantities, a significant pollution source is the generation of nitrogen dioxide ($NO_2$), which is produced through the combination of NO and oxygen as follows:

$$2NO + O_2 \rightarrow 2NO_2$$

NO released to the atmosphere will combine with oxygen to form $NO_2$, which is a toxic pollutant.

Both gasoline and diesel fuels contain some amount of sulfur with diesel fuel having a much greater content at 0.1%–0.3% weight as compared to less than 0.06% weight for gasoline. Combustion of sulfur in the engine compartment leads to the emission of sulfur oxides ($SO_x$).

Combustion of diesel fuel results in particulate material (PM) emissions in addition to the exhaust components discussed above. About 0.1%–0.5% of the fuel is emitted as small particulates, which consist primarily of soot with some additional adsorbed hydrocarbon material. Particulates smaller than 0.1 μm that is present in both spark and compression engine exhaust streams has the greatest deposition efficiency in lungs [6]. Soot emission is composed of small pieces of solid carbon matter emitted from the combustion of fuel in highly rich conditions, when there is insufficient amount of oxygen present to fully combust the fuel. Particulate matter is more of a problem with diesel engines compared to gasoline, even though the former always operate with excess air. This is because the fuel and air for a spark ignited engine are premixed before entering the combustion chamber, and the fuel content is almost fully vaporized and only small portions of the mixture contains liquid fuel. Although this portion does contribute to particulate matter production in gasoline engines, the amount produced is considered to be negligible. Since the fuel in a diesel engine is injected into the combustion chamber after the air has been compressed, a brief period of time elapses where a high concentration of atomized (but not vaporized) fuel is present in the injection region creating significant amounts of soot emission. Actual formation of soot concentration is largely dependent on the design of the injection system and combustion chamber as well as engine operating speed and load [7].

The 1970 Clean Air act and subsequent legislations set the limit to the amount of pollutants that can be released into the atmosphere from the tail pipe of a vehicle. United States Environmental Protection Agency (USEPA) has categorized emission levels into tier levels based on vehicle mass. For example, light-duty vehicles with a maximum curb mass of 2,721 kg (6,000 lb) and a maximum gross vehicle weight rating of 3,855 kg (8,500 lb) must meet USEPA tier 2 emissions requirements. Tier 2 emissions requirement has been broken up into 10 bins having different limitations of exhaust emissions for different compounds classified as harmful. The legislation specifies maximum limits on pollutants irrespective of the fuel type. Two of the bins were part of a phase-in policy and have since been deleted at the end of the 2006 model year. Remaining eight bins are permanent. Table 13.2 shows the allowable emission limits for tier 2 vehicles per bin for the eight permanent bins. USEPA specifies that vehicle manufacturers are required to meet a light-duty vehicle fleet average to the tier 2, bin 5 specifications. While production vehicles are allowed to be sold at the bin 8 specifications, their sales must be offset by an equal sales volume of bins lower than 5.

Sulfur in diesel fuel is not of particular concern because its content can be controlled during the manufacture of the fuel, and hence not included among the pollutants in the bins. USEPA has

**TABLE 13.2**
**USEPA Legislation for Tier 2 Classified Vehicles**

| Bin # | USEPA Allowable Emission Limits Per Bin – g/mile | | | | |
|---|---|---|---|---|---|
| | NMHC | CO | $NO_x$ | PM | HCHO |
| 8 | 0.125 | 4.2 | 0.20 | 0.02 | 0.018 |
| 7 | 0.090 | 4.2 | 0.15 | 0.02 | 0.018 |
| 6 | 0.090 | 4.2 | 0.10 | 0.01 | 0.018 |
| 5 | 0.090 | 4.2 | 0.07 | 0.01 | 0.018 |
| 4 | 0.070 | 2.1 | 0.04 | 0.01 | 0.011 |
| 3 | 0.055 | 2.1 | 0.03 | 0.01 | 0.011 |
| 2 | 0.010 | 2.1 | 0.02 | 0.01 | 0.004 |
| 1 | 0.000 | 0.0 | 0.00 | 0.00 | 0.000 |

Abbreviations: NMHC – non-methane hydrocarbons; CO – carbon monoxide; $NO_x$ – Nitrogen oxides; PM – Particulate matter; HCHO – formaldehyde.

mandated that all diesel fuel produced for highway use shall contain less than 15 ppm (0.015% weight) of sulfur after June 30, 2006 [8].

Legislation as well as installation of emission control components led to the dramatic reduction of pollutant emissions into the atmosphere. For example, CO emission levels dropped from 87 to 1.7 g/mile from pre-control days of 1966 to emission controlled days of 2004 [6]. Similarly, HC and $NO_x$ emission levels dropped from 8.8 and 3.6 g/mile to 0.09 and 0.07 g/mile, respectively, during the same period. The 2004 numbers are corporate averages for all emissions.

### 13.4.2   Effect of Air-fuel Ratio on Emissions

Improvements in exhaust emissions have been achieved through both the advancements in IC engine technology and the developments of emission control components. Advances in IC engine technology through the use of fuel injection systems, precision ignition timing, accurate fuel flow metering and computerized engine management system have led to more complete combustion of fuels and increased efficiencies that helped reduce emissions. Despite all the advances in engine technology, the amount of pollutants in the exhaust stream of automobiles is still significant without additional treatment. Emission control components placed in the path of the exhaust stream help bring the level of pollutants within acceptable levels.

For a given IC engine, the parameters that can be controlled by the hybrid control strategy to affect the fuel efficiency and emissions are the engine speed and load. In order to maximize fuel economy, the best region to operate the engine is where BSFC is the lowest. For hybrid vehicles operating in the series mode, the IC engine operating point should be in this lowest BSFC region when driving the electric generator for reduced fuel usage. The high fuel efficiency in an IC engine is a result of high thermal efficiency; consequently, the engine chamber temperature is also the highest in this region. However, this may not be the desired operating region as far as emissions are concerned. Emissions are strongly related to the air/fuel ratio of the mixture for combustion in the IC engine. Gasoline engines are typically operated at the stoichiometric ratio to maximize the fuel efficiency. Stoichiometric means that the air and fuel ratio of the mixture is just right for complete combustion. An equivalence ratio $\lambda$ which is the ratio of stoichiometric mixture and the actual air-fuel mixture is often used in describing the relative air/fuel ratio in practical engines. In mathematical terms, the equivalence ratio is

$$\lambda = \frac{\text{Stochiometric ratio}}{\text{Actual air/fuel ratio}}$$

**FIGURE 13.9** Effect of air-fuel ratio on emission pollutants in a gasoline engine under full load conditions.

The relative effects of the equivalence ratio in a gasoline engine on the three major pollutants CO, HC and $NO_x$ are shown qualitatively in Figure 13.9. The graph shows that the highest levels of $NO_x$ are produced for $\lambda \approx 1.1$, which is also the ratio for best fuel economy [9]. $NO_x$ generation is expected to be high in these areas of high fuel economy, since the temperatures are also higher. On the other hand, gasoline engines develop the best power around $\lambda \approx 0.9$ where the $NO_x$ emissions are lower, but the CO and HC emissions are higher. Thus, a compromise between fuel efficiency and emissions is necessary to set the engine operating point so that acceptable results may be obtained for both parameters. The control objective is often to run the engine at the stoichiometric ratio, i.e., at $\lambda \approx 1$ so that there is no oxygen in the exhaust stream. An oxygen sensor placed in the exhaust stream provides feedback to the engine control unit so that appropriate air/fuel ratio can be maintained for the engine to minimize all three emissions. In a hybrid electric vehicle, the hybrid control strategy must function in conjunction with the engine management system to achieve the desired goals.

### 13.4.3 $NO_x$ FLOW RATE

The total mass flow rate of exhausted $NO_x$ is the sum of the mass flow rates of exhausted NO and $NO_2$.

$$\dot{m}_{NO_x,exh} = \dot{m}_{NO,exh} + \dot{m}_{NO_2,exh} \tag{13.14}$$

In terms of engine mapping, nitrogen oxide mass flow rate can be presented as simply the $NO_x$ mass flow rate values obtained from Equation 13.14 over the relevant domain. This will facilitate computational modeling of a vehicle's $NO_x$ output per mile over a particular drive cycle. However, expression of $NO_x$ mass flow rate relative to power output allows performance mapping of an engine that can be used in standardized comparison among several engines. As with fuel use analysis, brake specific values are again calculated. *Brake-specific $NO_x$ emission* (BSNO$_x$) is simply the $NO_x$ mass flow rate divided by the engine's measured brake power [10].

$$BSNO_x = \frac{\dot{m}_{NO_x,exh}}{P_b} = \frac{\dot{m}_{NO_x,exh}}{T_b 2\pi N} \tag{13.15}$$

where $P_b$ is the output power, $T_b$ is the brake torque and $N$ is the engine speed (in rev/s).

Baseline mapping of a warmed engine under steady-state conditions in an engine dynamometer test stand is useful to gain an understanding of the engine's $NO_x$ emission characteristics and examine the tradeoff of reduced emission and fuel economy. The test stand with emissions sampling, fuel flow measurement and engine diagnostics recorder can be configured as shown in Figure 13.10. Results from tests conducted in the laboratory with a dynamometer on a 1.9 L diesel engine over its expected range of operation is shown in Figures 13.11 and 13.12 [10,11]. In the tests designed for collecting data to develop a hybrid control strategy, diesel engine torque load and speed were modulated and read by the dynamometer controller. Fuel use was measured by the flow-meters, and read off the dynamometer controller. The mass air flow rate was read from a sensor via the engine's diagnostics port. A sample of exhaust gas was taken downstream of the turbocharger. The collected data for the engine's intake air and fuel mass flow as well as volumetric exhaust content data was used to determine levels of engine-out mass flow of $NO_x$ over the engine's operating domain. The BSFC and $BSNO_x$ raw data, calculated using Equations 13.5 and 13.15, was regressed to develop the baseline engine maps given in Figures 13.11 and 13.12. The BSFC is required for IC fuel usage comparison as discussed earlier in Section 13.2.

In a hybrid electric vehicle, a starter/generator can be coupled to the IC engine through a transmission for starting the engine as well as for supplying propulsion energy to the electric powertrain. The transmission is a single-stage speed reducer designed to match operating speed ranges of the electric machine and the IC engine. Combined efficiency of engine and starter/generator is useful to develop the hybrid control strategy for such hybrid systems, which is given by

**FIGURE 13.10**   Dynamometer test stand for collecting emissions data.

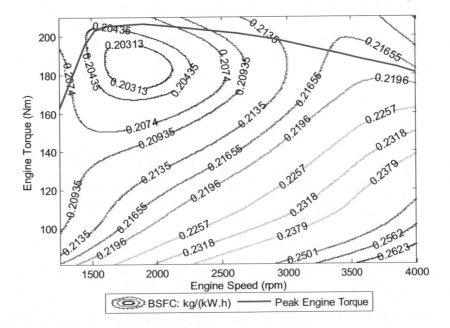

**FIGURE 13.11**   BSFCs for 1.9 L diesel engine [11].

**FIGURE 13.12** Brake-specific $NO_x$ emissions for 1.9 L diesel engine [11].

$$\text{Combined efficiency} = \frac{\text{Generator output power}}{\text{Fuel power potential}}$$

(13.16)

$$= \frac{P_{gen,out}}{\dot{m}_{fuel}\text{HHV}} = \frac{V_{DC}I_{DC}}{\dot{m}_{fuel}\text{HHV}}$$

In the series mode of hybrid vehicle operation, the IC engine and the starter/generator are cycled on and off to maintain the energy storage system within the desired SoC band. The 'on' operating point may be chosen based on fuel economy, emissions and the characteristics of the starter/generator electric machine. If only high fuel economy is targeted, the engine should operate in a region of low BSFC. The engine maps of Figures 13.11 and 13.12 show that the regions of operation with low fuel consumption also yield high $NO_x$ generation. Therefore, the optimal IC engine operating point has to be selected with a compromise between high fuel efficiency and reduced emissions. The selection of the 'on' operating point for the hybrid control strategy is discussed in Chapter 13.

### Example 13.2

The mass flow rate during series mode operation of a diesel hybrid electric vehicle is 2.3 kg/h. A permanent magnet starter/generator is belt coupled to the engine with a gear ratio of 2.8:1. The starter/generator input torque and speed are 28.93 N m and 3,500 rpm. Assume the coupling losses between the engine and starter/generator shafts to be negligible. Generated output voltage and current are 300 VDC and 31.8 A, respectively. Calculate engine BSFC, engine efficiency and combined engine-starter/generator efficiency.

### Solutions

IC engine brake torque is $T_b = 28.93 \times 2.8 = 81$ N m
IC engine speed is $N = 3{,}500/2.8 = 1{,}250$ rpm
Therefore, IC brake power output, neglecting belt coupling losses is

$$P_b = 81 \times 1{,}250 \times \frac{\pi}{30} = 10.6 \text{ kW}$$

IC engine BSFC is

$$\mathrm{BSFC} = \frac{\dot{m}_f}{P_b} = \frac{2.3}{10.602} = 0.217 \text{ kg/kW h}$$

This is equal to 0.357 lb/hp-h.
Diesel HHV is 19,733 BTU/lb, which is equivalent to

$$\mathrm{HHV} = 19733 \times 1055 \times 2.205 \text{ J/kg} = 45904.38 \times 10^3 \text{ J/kg} = 12.75 \text{ kW h/kg}$$

IC engine input power calculated from the fuel potential is

$$P_{in} = \dot{m}_f \times \mathrm{HHV} = 2.3 \times 12.75 = 29.32 \text{ kW}$$

Therefore, IC engine efficiency is $\eta_{ICE} = \dfrac{10.602}{29.32} = 36.2\%$

The combined efficiency is $\eta_{combined} = \dfrac{300 \times 31.8}{29.32} = 32.5\%$

### 13.4.4 EMISSION CONTROL COMPONENTS

The emission control components in a vehicle depend on the type of IC engine used, although some of the components are similar in both gasoline and diesel engines. Emission is controlled is gasoline engines through providing a chamber in the exhaust stream path for further oxidation and reduction of pollutants, and reintroducing part of the exhaust stream back into the engine compartment. The component used for oxidation and reduction of pollutants is known as the catalytic converter, while the second method is known as exhaust gas recirculation (EGR). A catalytic converter and EGR is highly effective in the wwwreduction of all pollutants in gasoline engine vehicle. The diesel engines require additional after-treatment components for bringing the pollutant levels within acceptable levels. We will discuss the EGR and catalytic converter in general in this section, and then address the specific needs for emission controls in diesel engine vehicles.

#### 13.4.4.1 Exhaust Gas Recirculation

EGR is used for reducing the $NO_x$ levels at the tail pipe of the vehicle. The method uses the EGR valve to reintroduce part of the exhaust stream into the air/fuel intake system to reduce the engine chamber temperature. The exhaust gas added dilutes the air/fuel ratio and reduces $\lambda$ which helps reduce the combustion chamber temperature. The lower the engine operating temperature the lower will be the amount of $NO_x$ produced. EGR action dilutes the rich air/fuel mixture (rich with fuel) to a lean mixture (lean with fuel) which has the negative effect of reducing engine performance. Therefore, EGR action is disabled when full engine power is required or when the engine is cold.

#### 13.4.4.2 Catalytic Converter

Catalytic converters convert harmful pollutants in the exhaust stream into more acceptable compounds through oxidation and reduction. Catalytic converter designed only for two oxidation processes is known as a two-way catalytic converter, while that using two oxidation and one reduction processes is known as a three-way catalytic converter. The two oxidation processes reduce the carbon monoxide and hydrocarbons in the exhaust stream. The two-way catalytic converters first came into use for gasoline engines, but their inability to reduce $NO_x$ in the emissions led to the development of three-way catalysts, which is now universally used. Currently, two-way catalytic converters are used in diesel engines along with additional after-treatment components to reduce $NO_x$ and particulate matter.

Three-way catalytic converters use catalysts for the following three actions:

1. Reduction of $NO_x$ into nitrogen and oxygen; $2NO \rightarrow O_2 + N_2$ and $2NO_2 \rightarrow 2O_2 + N_2$
2. Oxidation of carbon monoxide (CO) to carbon dioxide ($CO_2$); $2CO + O_2 \rightarrow 2CO_2$
3. Oxidation of hydrocarbons to carbon dioxide ($CO_2$) and water ($H_2O$); $[C_xH_y] + [O_2] \rightarrow [H_2O] + [CO_2]$

The chemical reactions are aided by catalysts that speed up the process. Platinum and rhodium are used as reduction catalysts, while platinum and palladium are used as oxidation catalysts.

Three-way catalytic converters are highly effective in reducing CO, $NO_x$ and HC emissions when IC engines operate within a narrow band around the stoichiometric ratio. Engine management and fuel injection systems work in conjunction with the catalytic converter to effectively reduce the amount of pollutants. The oxygen sensor in the exhaust stream provides feedback to the engine management system, which controls the ratio of the air/fuel mixture through the fuel injection system within the narrow band around the stoichiometric ratio. However, at part-load conditions of the engine or during heavy demand conditions, it may not be possible to maintain the ratio around the stoichiometric ratio. Outside the band around stoichiometric ratio when the air/fuel mixture is lean, oxidation is favored since the exhaust stream has more CO and HC. Again, when the air/fuel mixture is rich reduction is favored since the exhaust will contain more $NO_x$ due to the high engine chamber temperatures. Metal oxide (cerium oxide) used within the catalytic converter has the ability to store oxygen when there is excess available and release when required. This type of oxides is known as stabilizers. Metal oxide stores oxygen during lean operating condition where there is excess oxygen in the exhaust stream, and release it during rich operating condition when sufficient oxygen is not available to aid the oxidation process.

In addition to the catalytic converter, secondary air injection (SAI) method is applied to the exhaust stream in spark-ignition engines under certain conditions to burn off excess hydrocarbons. The method is predominantly used during engine start-up to control emissions when the catalytic converter did not have sufficient time to warm up.

### 13.4.5 Treatment of Diesel Exhaust Emissions

Diesel engines are attractive for hybrid vehicles since these can deliver a higher level of fuel economy compared to gasoline engines. Some of the latest technology diesel engines utilizing high-speed direct injection for fuel atomization can achieve up to 35% lower volumetric fuel consumption than equivalent performance gasoline engines [12]. Smaller efficient diesel engines for passenger vehicles are already available particularly from the European auto industry. The use of a diesel engine as the primary power source for a hybrid vehicle can lead to a significant improvement in fuel economy when compared to common gasoline-fueled vehicles. However, if diesel engines are to be used in hybrid vehicles, an after-treatment system must be employed to meet EPA requirements.

While it is possible to reduce emissions output in diesel engine exhaust by varying engine operating parameters, achievements are typically at the cost of fuel efficiency. This section focuses on the after-treatment components of diesel exhaust; after-treatment refers to methods of emission reduction in the exhaust stream, which is post combustion.

#### 13.4.5.1 Diesel Oxidation Catalysts

Significant reduction of unburned hydrocarbons and carbon monoxide can be achieved by use of oxidation catalysts in the exhaust stream. Similar to the gasoline exhaust catalytic converters, diesel exhaust catalytic converters oxidize hydrocarbons and carbon monoxide in the exhaust stream through the promotion of the chemical reaction using precious metal catalysts. However, the design of the oxidation catalytic converter for diesel engines differs significantly from those of gasoline engines, since performance has to be optimized for operation at much lower exhaust temperatures seen in the diesel exhaust [13]. The lower temperatures are due to the fact that diesel engines always operate with excess air.

### 13.4.5.2 Diesel Particulate Filters

Particulate mass can be reduced by treating with a diesel oxidation catalyst, since it contains hydrocarbons. Currently, oxidation catalysts are the only type of particulate control used in production light-duty diesel vehicles. However, to effectively control particulate materials, which mostly contain soot, a diesel particulate filter (DPF) is necessary. Several designs for DPFs exist, but the most common and effective designs are the wall-flow type. The filter provides channels for exhaust flow that force the gases through blocked ends requiring it to flow through a clay derived material that traps the particles. Filters of this design are reported to have trapping efficiency of almost 100% [14]. The problem in DPF use lies in rapid clogging and blockage that require periodic cleaning of the filter.

The method for clearing particle mass from DPFs is known as regeneration, which simply involves combusting the soot particles. Regeneration can occur either passively or actively. Passive regeneration is accomplished by maintaining a high-enough exhaust temperature so that particle oxidation can take place during normal vehicle operation. Unfortunately, the required temperature is in the range of 550–600°C which is often unreasonable for the diesel exhaust stream. Heavy-duty diesel vehicles used in the commercial industry have engines sized for fuel economy; high-load operation is common as most driving is done on the highway making DPF usage ideal for such vehicles. Light-duty passenger vehicles operate more frequently in urban driving conditions where high-load operation creating high exhaust temperatures is not frequently encountered. Lower exhaust temperatures are not enough for regeneration, hence the lack of DPF usage in typical production diesel passenger vehicles. In active regeneration, catalyst additives are added to the fuel to reduce particulate combustion temperature. Catalyst addition can be combined with a complex engine management strategy in which fuel injection rates are altered to provide higher exhaust temperature.

An advantage of using light-duty diesel engines in hybrid vehicles is that hybrid control strategy can ensure high load on the engine even in urban driving conditions by operating in the series mode. The electric generator can load the engine sufficiently for all of city driving with excess energy being used for battery charging when possible. With high-enough engine temperature at high load, passive regeneration of DPF is possible. In development of a vehicle of this type, engine selection or development should consider the criteria for passive regeneration.

### 13.4.5.3 Methods of NO$_x$ Reduction

NO$_x$ reduction through the catalytic converter is not so effective in diesel engines as compared to gasoline engines, since the diesel exhaust temperature is lower and the exhaust stream is oxygen rich. Chemical reactions always occur in the simplest way possible, and excess oxygen in the diesel exhaust stream will bond before promoting dissociation of NO$_x$ in the catalyst. Reduction of NO$_x$ compounds in the diesel exhaust by catalytic promotion is further complicated when the operating scenario of a hybrid vehicle is considered. Hybrid control strategies may require high efficiency from an engine, such as in the series mode of operation. High fuel efficiency is accomplished by running the engine at high load for a given speed, a situation in which high NO$_x$ is also generated. This operating scenario for hybrids would be typical in urban driving. Highway driving would always require engines to be operated at high loads for hybrid vehicles. This would result in the IC engine for a hybrid vehicle to be always operated with high-load conditions which would dramatically increase NO$_x$ levels over a drive cycle compared to a conventional IC engine vehicle.

Two modern technologies applied for diesel NO$_x$ control are lean traps that are capable of storing NO$_x$ at low operating temperatures until higher loads are seen and a process called selective catalyst reduction (SCR) in which ammonia is used to treat engine exhaust for NO$_x$ reduction [10].

Lean NO$_x$ trap is a technology for NO$_x$ adsorption under lean (oxygen-rich) operating conditions and then later decomposing into non-harmful water and nitrogen in a fuel rich environment.

The system operates by use of a catalyst that promotes adsorption and storage of $NO_x$ in a lean environment by forming a new compound [15]. The inherent problem is that in order to create the fuel rich environment, excess fuel must be injected into the exhaust stream frequently for regeneration which would reduce fuel economy. Lean $NO_x$ traps are being introduced into diesel passenger vehicles only recently. Mercedes Benz was the first auto maker to introduce a model equipped with a lean $NO_x$ trap in the 2007 model year production vehicle.

SCR involves injection of a reducing agent into the exhaust, which is capable of bonding with $NO_x$ compounds to form non-harmful ones. The most effective reducing agent that can be used in the process is ammonia ($NH_3$). The term 'selective' is demonstrated in ammonia's unique ability to selectively react with $NO_x$ compounds rather than be oxidized to form $N_2$, $N_2O$, and NO [16].

$$4NH_3 + 4NO + O_2 \rightarrow 4N_2 + 6H_2O \tag{13.17}$$

$$2NH_3 + NO + NO_2 \rightarrow 2N_2 + 3H_2O \tag{13.18}$$

$$8NH_3 + 6NO_2 \rightarrow 7N_2 + 12H_2O \tag{13.19}$$

Greater than 90% of $NO_x$ from diesel emissions is composed of NO and thus reaction (13.17) accounts for most of the reduction as it occurs with NO and $NH_3$ at a 1:1 ratio in excess oxygen. Reaction (13.18) is most desirable because it occurs at a lower temperature than the others, but requires a 1:1 ratio of NO and $NO_2$. Reaction (13.19) takes care of the remaining $NO_2$ that cannot be reduced by (13.18) due to insufficient NO.

Efficient bonding of ammonia and $NO_x$ compounds is only possible with the aid of a specially designed catalytic converter. Three types of catalysts have been developed for commercial use: noble metals, metal oxides and zeolites. Noble (precious) metal catalysts have proven highly active in $NO_x$ reduction, but also effectively oxidize $NH_3$ rendering it almost useless as a reducing agent. For this reason, slightly less effective metal oxide (compounds composed of metals and oxygen) catalysts are the most common for conventional SCR applications. Zeolite catalysts that are composed of minerals having micro-porous structures can also be used in SCR systems; however, their use are more suited to gas-fired cogeneration plants rather than diesel engines.

While ammonia can be an effective $NO_x$ reduction agent, storage and transportation becomes an issue as ammonia itself is a toxic chemical regulated by the EPA. The solution is to inject an aqueous urea solution into the hot exhaust stream, which will quickly decompose into ammonia and carbon dioxide [17]. The dissociation of excess urea yielding ammonia leads to a discharge of raw ammonia out the tail pipe termed as ammonia slippage. Additionally, it is desired that only the correct amount of urea be added to the exhaust stream so that the supply be conserved, thus maximizing the time before refill of urea is necessary.

An injector unit comparable to common fuel injectors found on gasoline engines can be used for urea injection. The injection rate can be controlled by sending the correct injection frequency through a pulse-width modulated (PWM) signal to the injector. The required injection pressure is usually maintained by a pressure regulator fitted to an air reservoir. Commercial systems intended for retro-fit an application typically have a compressor and motor that re-pressurizes the air tank as needed. For the control of urea injection, monitoring of exhaust temperature provides adequate feedback information to determine the injection rate. More sophisticated control systems include interfacing with the engine electronic control unit (ECU) which provides engine speed and fuel injection rate feedbacks for controlling the urea injection rate. A sensor for determining the ammonia content downstream of the catalyst is ideally suitable for developing the feedback controller for urea injection; however such sensors are currently in the prototype phase.

## PROBLEMS

### 13.1

A hybrid electric vehicle has the following parameter values: $\rho = 1.16\,\text{kg/m}^3$, $m = 692\,\text{kg}$, $C_D = 0.2$, $A_F = 2\,\text{m}^2$, $g = 9.81\,\text{m/s}^2$, $C_0 = 0.009$ and $C_1 = 1.75*10^{-6}\text{s}^2/\text{m}^2$. The type of internal combustion engine that will be used for the vehicle has the force (at wheel) versus velocity characteristics of $F = 2.0\sin(0.0285x)$ N for $5 < x < 100$, where $x$ is the vehicle speed in mph. Determine the displacement of the ICE for a rated cruising velocity of 60 mph on a 2% slope.

## REFERENCES

1. M.J. Moran and H.N. Shapiro, *Fundamentals of Engineering Thermodynamics*, sixth edition, John Wiley & Sons, Inc., New York, NY, 2008.
2. J.P. O'Brien, *Gas Turbines for Automotive Use*, Noyes Data Corporation, Park Ridge, NJ, 1980.
3. J.B. Heywood, *Internal Combustion Engine Fundamentals*, McGraw-Hill, Inc., New York, NY, 1988.
4. U. Bossel, "Well-to-wheel studies, heating values, and the energy conservation principle," in *Proceedings of European Fuel Cell Forum*, 2003. Online www.efcf.com/reports, (E10).
5. G.C. Koltsakis and A.M. Stamatelos, "Catalytic automotive exhaust aftertreatment," *Progress in Energy and Combustion Science*, 23, 1–39, 1997.
6. R. Stone and J.K. Ball, *Automotive Engineering Fundamentals*, SAE International, Warrendale, PA, 2004.
7. J.P.A. Neeft, M. Makkee and J.A. Moulijn, "Diesel particulate emission control," *Fuel Processing Technology*, 47, 1–69, 1996.
8. Environmental Protection Agency "Technical amendments to the highway and nonroad diesel regulation; final rule and proposed rule," 40 CFR Part 80, Federal Register, vol. 71, no. 83, May 2006.
9. H.H. Braess and U. Seiffert, *Handbook of Automotive Engineering*, SAE International, Warrendale, PA, 2005.
10. R.N. Paciotti, An Evaluation of Nitrogen Oxide Emission from a Light-Duty Hybrid Electric Vehicle to Meer U.S.E.P.A. Requirements Using a Diesel Engine, MS Thesis, Mechanical Engineering, The University of Akron, August 2007.
11. S.M.N. Hasan, I. Husain, R.J. Veillette and J.E. Carletta, "A PM brushless DC starter/generator system for a series/parallel $2 \times 2$ hybrid electric vehicle," *IEEE Transactions on Industry Applications*, 16(2), 12–21, March–April 2013.
12. R.B. Krieger, R.M. Siewert, J.A. Pinson, N.E. Gallopoulos, D.L. Hilden, D.R. Monroe, R.B. Rask, A.S.P. Solomon and P. Zima, "Diesel engines: One option to power future personal transportation vehicles," SAE International 972683, 1997.
13. J.C. Clerc, "Catalytic diesel exhaust aftertreatment," *Applied Catalysis B: Environmental*, 10, 99–115, 1996.
14. P. Walker, "Controlling particulate emissions from diesel vehicles," *Topics in Catalysis*, 28, 1–4, 165–170, April 2004.
15. A. Hinz, L. Andersson, J. Edvardsson, P. Salomonsson, C.J. Karlsson, F. Antolini, P.G. Blakeman, M. Lauenius, B. Magnusson, A.P. Walker and H.Y. Chen, "The application of a $NO_x$ absorber catalyst system on a heavy-duty diesel engine," SAE International 2005-01-1084, 2005.
16. P. Forzatti, "Present status and perspectives in de-$NO_x$ SCR catalysis," *Applied Catalysis A: General*, 222, 221–236, 2001.
17. M. Chen and S. Williams, "Modeling and optimization of SCR-exhaust aftertreatment systems," SAE International 2005-01-0969, 2005.

# 14 Power Transmission, Brakes and Cooling Systems

Internal combustion engines transfer power to the wheels through a power transmission path known as powertrain. The key mechanical power transmission components of clutch, gear, transmission and differential in the powertrain are presented in this chapter along with a few ancillary components. The IC engine and the powertrain together form the mechanical power transmission path. Some of these powertrain components are also essential for the electric vehicles and for blending power from IC engine and electric motor. The electric vehicle power transmission includes the electrical path from the energy storage system to the electric motor as well as the mechanical path from the motor shaft to the wheels. The powertrain of a hybrid electric vehicle is more complex than that of the electric vehicle, because of the coupling necessary to blend the torque outputs of the electric motor and the IC engine. This chapter also discusses the hybrid powertrain after the primary powertrain components are presented.

Near the end of the vehicle power transmission path lays a critical element, which is the vehicle brake. The braking system dynamics are similar to the propulsion dynamics except that braking forces have to be evaluated in order to stop the vehicle from motion. Modern vehicles are seeing increasing usage of electrical components replacing hydraulic-based systems. In many cases, this electrification relates to replacing hydraulic actuators with electrical motor-driven actuators. Electric power steering and electronic valve control are examples of such components. This trend in IC engine vehicles resulted in improved performance and better fuel economy. While some of these electrical components are already in usage, others are in queue for implementation in future vehicles. Electromechanical brake (EMB) system is an example of such a system. These components are the enabling technologies for the by-wire systems envisioned to integrate modern vehicle system functionalities through electronic control and communications. Vehicle control enhancements stem from the relatively easier controllability of electrical systems that are predicated on highly dynamic behavior from the motor drives in these systems. A brief overview of the EMB system is presented in this chapter following the description of conventional brakes.

There are several systems within a vehicle that are required as supporting systems, some for the powertrain components and some for the vehicle occupants. Some of the ancillary systems in a vehicle are designed for the safety and comfort of passengers. The mission of some of these systems could be as critical as the powertrain itself. The cooling systems in a vehicle serve both the comfort and safety requirements of the occupants and the powertrain components. In this chapter, we also discuss the cooling systems of a vehicle. While a vehicle has many ancillary systems, the objective here is not to present a comprehensive coverage, but to highlight the importance of these ancillary systems.

## 14.1 POWER TRANSMISSION COMPONENTS

The *powertrain* of a vehicle starts with the IC engine or the electric motor that processes the stored energy and ends with the delivery of the power at the wheels. The powertrain is also often referred to as the *drivetrain* of the vehicle. The engine, transmission, electric motor, gear set, clutch, transmission, driveshafts and the final drive are the major components of the powertrain. The energy in the vehicle is initially stored in the diesel or gasoline fuel for the IC engines or in the chemicals of a battery for electric motors. The IC engine or the electric motor converts the stored energy into mechanical form. The mechanical power or energy still needs to be delivered to the end point which is at the wheel of the vehicles. The next component in the powertrain is the transmission with an IC engine, while it could be a simple gearbox for speed reduction with an electric motor. The transmission and the differential consist of different types of gears and gear sets. The components of the powertrain excluding the propulsion unit (IC engine and transmission or electric motor and gear set or the combination of the two sets) are collectively known as the *driveline.*

The final part of the power train is the *final drive* that reduces the output speed of the transmission/gearbox or drive shaft. It consists of a gear set made of two or more gears working together. The final drive includes the *differential* that accommodates unequal speeds of the inside and outside wheels when the the vehicle turns around a corner. The differential is necessary for the driven wheels on an axle since they are linked together so that the propulsion unit can transmit power to both the wheels. This is not a concern for the non-driven wheels which are not linked and can spin freely. The power from the differential is transferred to the final drive at the driven wheels by the *half-shafts.* The half-shafts transmit half of the power coming down the powertrain to the differential. The transmission or the gearbox out of the propulsion unit is not usually in the same plane as the differential; power needs to be transferred across the driveline at an angle. The universal joints (U-joints) and constant-velocity joints (CV-joints) are used to accomplish the task.

The powertrain components used also depend on whether the vehicle is a front-wheel drive or a rear-wheel drive. The powertrain assembly after the IC engine or the electric motor in a *front-wheel drive* are compact and usually integrated into one device. Front-wheel drives which are popular in passenger vehicles have their transmissions located behind the engine with a change in output direction. In a *rear-wheel drive*, the power is transferred across the length of the vehicle using the *driveshaft* when the propulsion unit is located in the front of the vehicle. The driveshaft delivers power to the differential using joints in the rear-wheel drive vehicle. Rear-wheel drives are used in some passenger vehicles and more commonly in light trucks. Vehicles where power is transferred to both the front wheels and the rear wheels are known as *all-wheel drive* vehicles. All wheel drives have a front differential and a rear differential.

In some passenger vehicle, the transmission, driveshaft, differential and the final drive are combined into one lightweight device known as *transaxle.* It is typically used with transverse mounted engines such that its rotating axis is parallel to that of the drive axles and engine crankshaft. The arrangement does not require a change in direction enabling more efficient power transmission.

In the following, we will review the powertrain of electric vehicles to present an overview of the integration of components with simpler configurations. The discussions on the components along with relevant analysis appear in the subsequent sections.

## 14.1.1 ELECTRIC VEHICLE POWERTRAIN

The components for an electric vehicle powertrain consist of the electric motor, gear box, driveshaft, differential, half-shafts and wheels. The ability of electric motors to start from zero speed and operate efficiently over a wide speed range makes it possible to eliminate the clutch that is used in IC engine vehicles. A single gear ratio is sufficient to match the wheel speed with the motor speed. Electric vehicles can be designed without a gear, but the use of a speed reducer allows the electric motor to operate at much higher speeds for given vehicle speeds, which minimizes the motor size because of lower torque requirment at higher speeds.

In the case of a front wheel drive, the electric motor drives the gear box which is mounted on the front axle as shown in Figure 14.1. This configuration is for a electric vehicle using a single propulsion motor. The single motor drives the transaxle on a common axis, delivering power to the two wheels differentially through a hollow motor shaft [1]. The powertrain is more complex in the case of a rear wheel drive, which requires a differential to manage the cornering of the vehicle. A typical rear wheel drive electric vehicle powertrain configuration is shown in Figure 14.2.

The use of two motors driving two front wheels simplifies the powertrain and eliminates the differential. Several configurations are possible with two propulsion motors driving two wheels. In one

**FIGURE 14.1**   Typical front-wheel drive.

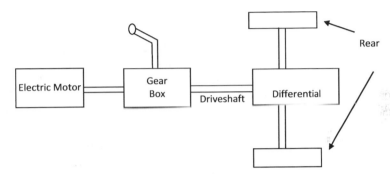

**FIGURE 14.2**   Typical rear-wheel drive.

arranagment, the motors, mounted to the chassis, can be connected to the wheels through two short half-shafts. The suspension system of the vehicle isolates the wheels and its associated parts from rest of the components of the vehcile for easier handling of the vehicle depending on roadway condition. The wheels are able to move freely without the weight of the motors when they are mounted on the chassis. In an alternate arrangement, the motors are mounted on the half-shafts with the motor drive shaft being part of the half-shaft. The half-shafts connect the wheels on one side and the chassis through a pivot on the other side. In-wheel mounting of motors is another arrangement possible in electric vehicles. The difficulty in this case is that the unsprung weight of the vehicle increases due to motors inside the wheels, making traction control more complex. To minimize the unsprung weight of the vehicle and because of the limited space available, the in-wheel motors must be of high-power density. As mentioned at the beginning, the use of a speed reducer is desirable which adds to the constraint of limited space. The cost of a high-power, high-torque motor is the primary impediment in using in-wheel motors for electric vehicles. Another problem with in-wheel motor is the heating due to braking comopounded by the limited cooling capability in the restricted space. Nevertheless, the powertrain simplicity has led to many projects for the development of in-wheel motors for electric vehicles.

## 14.2   GEARS

The gear is a simple machine used for mechanical power transmission with a mechanical advantage through increase in torque or reduction in speed. This mechanical device uses the law of conservation of energy maintaining the steady flow of power or energy, since torque times speed is power that remains constant in the transmission process. In an ideal gearbox, the motion is frictionless, and the power and energy supplied at the input point of the gear are equal to the power and energy available at the delivery point. The gearbox is not used to increase the shaft speed of an electric motor, since this means that a high-torque motor is unnecessarily designed where the size of a motor

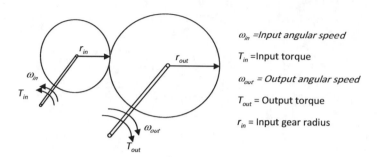

**FIGURE 14.3** Gear mechanism.

is proportional to the torque output. Therefore, the gear can be used as a torque multiplier or speed reducer. A typical gear mechnism is shown in Figure 14.3.

A gear structurally is a round disk with teeth cut at equal intervals around the rim designed to engage with similar teeth of another disk. The round disks, placed in combination, transmit power from one gear to another. The teeth at both the disks lock the driving and the driven shafts together to transfer the energy through contact with little, if any, loss.

The four principle types of gears are: spur, helical, bevel and worm gears. Almost all types of gears can be found in an automobile. Spur gears are the simplest of all types whose teeth connect in parallel to the axis of rotation. Power is transmitted to parallel shafts connected by the spur gear. Helical gears have teeth inclined to the axis of rotation, but transmit power between parallel shafts just like the spur gear. Bevel gears transmit power between shafts that intersect, but are not in parallel. The differential of an automobile uses bevel gears. Hypoid gears are a type of bevel gear whose teeth form circular arc and the shafts are nonintersecting. These gears connect shafts that are neither parallel, nor do they intersect such as in the final drive of the power train. The gear schematic in Figure 14.3 represents either a spur gear or a helical gear. This representation is used below to develop the gear input-output relationships.

The power transmission equations through gears will be established using an ideal gear box assumption, which are as follows:

1. $P_{losses} = 0$, Efficiency = 100%.
2. Gears are perfectly rigid.
3. No gear backlash (i.e., no space between teeth).

The variables used in deriving the steady-state model are given in Figure 14.4. Additional variables are shown in Figure 14.4 with respect to a single disk.

## 14.2.1 GEAR RATIO

For a disk with radius $r$, the tangential and the angular velocity are realted by

$$\omega r = v$$

The tangential velocity at the gear teeth contact point is the same for the two gear disks shown in Figure 14.3 with different radius

$$r_{in}\omega_{in} = v = r_{out}\omega_{out}$$

The gear ratio is defined in terms of the ratio of speed transformation between the input shaft and the output shaft.

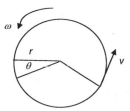

**FIGURE 14.4**   Variables in a gear.

$$GR = \frac{\omega_{in}}{\omega_{out}} = \frac{r_{out}}{r_{in}} \qquad (14.1)$$

Assuming 100% efficiency of the gear train

$$P_{out} = P_{in}$$

$$\Rightarrow T_{out}\omega_{out} = T_{in}\omega_{in}$$

The gear ratio in terms of the torque at the two shafts are

$$GR = \frac{T_{out}}{T_{in}} = \frac{\omega_{in}}{\omega_{out}} \qquad (14.2)$$

The gear ratio can be alternately derived with the help of Figure 14.5. At the point of gear mesh, the supplied and delivered forces are the same. This is an example of Newton's third law of motion, which states that every action has an equal and opposite reaction. The torque at the shaft is the force at the mesh divided by the radius of the disk. In the two-gear combination, the change is torque between the two gears which is proportional to the ratio of gear disks radius.

The torque of the inner disk in terms of its radius and force at the gear mesh is

$$T_{in} = Fr_{in}$$

$$\Rightarrow F = \frac{T_{in}}{r_{in}}$$

Similarly, for the outer disk with radius $r_{out}$, the force at the gear mesh is

$$F = \frac{T_{out}}{r_{out}}$$

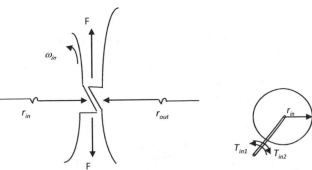

**FIGURE 14.5**   Force and torque working in a gear.

The two forces and the troques are working in opposite directions. The gear ratio can be obtained from equating the two equal but opposite forces as

$$GR = \frac{T_{out}}{T_{in}} = \frac{r_{out}}{r_{in}} \tag{14.3}$$

For any gear, the diameter is proportional to the number of teeth, which gives

$$\frac{d_{out}}{d_{in}} = \frac{r_{out}}{r_{in}} = \frac{N_{out}}{N_{in}} \tag{14.4}$$

$N_{out}$ and $N_{in}$ are the numbers of teeth, and $d_{out}$ and $d_{in}$ are the diameters of the output and input gears. Using Equations 14.2–14.4, the gear law can be written as

$$\frac{T_{out}}{T_{in}} = -\frac{r_{out}}{r_{in}} = -\frac{N_{out}}{N_{in}} = -\frac{\omega_{in}}{\omega_{out}} \tag{14.5}$$

The negative sign signifies that the direction of torque in the two gear meshes is opposite.

The gear law can be extended to multiple gear meshes such as the four-gear device shown in Figure 14.6. The arrangement of multiple gear meshes to transfer power is known as gear train. In the gear train shown, gear 2 is the driver, while gear 4 is the driven member. If $N_2$, $N_3$ and $N_4$ are the numbers of teeth in the four gears, the input-output torque ratio is given by

$$\frac{T_4}{T_3} \cdot \frac{T_3}{T_2} = \left(-\frac{N_4}{N_3}\right)\left(-\frac{N_3}{N_2}\right) = \left(-\frac{\omega_3}{\omega_4}\right)\left(-\frac{\omega_2}{\omega_3}\right)$$
$$\Rightarrow \frac{T_4}{T_2} = \frac{N_4}{N_2} = \frac{\omega_2}{\omega_4} \tag{14.6}$$

Notice that the middle gear has no effect on the final torque ratio, but it made the output shaft rotate in the same direction as the input shaft. These techniques can be used to get the desired direction of rotation out of a gear train.

A compound gear train made up of five gears is shown in Figure 14.7 [2]. Gear 3 serves the same function as in the middle gear of Figure 14.6, which is to affect the direction of rotation for the final gear 6 without affecting the input-output torque ratio. Gears 4 and 5 form a compound gear stage with both gears mounted on the same shaft. The input-output torque and speed relation for the gear train is

$$\frac{T_2}{T_6} = -\frac{\omega_6}{\omega_2} = -\frac{N_2}{N_3} \cdot \frac{N_3}{N_4} \cdot \frac{N_5}{N_6} \tag{14.7}$$

Gears 2, 3 and 5 are drivers, while gears 3, 4 and 6 are driven members in this gear train. The angular speed and torque directions between the input and output gears are opposite since the number

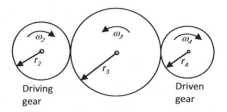

**FIGURE 14.6**  Two-mesh gear train.

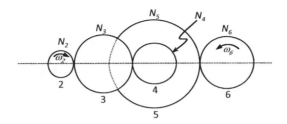

**FIGURE 14.7** Compound gear train.

of gear meshes is 3. This type of gear train is commonly used in the transmission of a vehicle. In general, the sign of the direction is given by $(-1)^n$ where $n$ is the total number of gear meshes; the gear ratio or the train value is given by

$$GR = \frac{\text{Product of driving tooth numbers}}{\text{Product of driven tooth numbers}} \tag{14.8}$$

## 14.2.2 Torque-Speed Characteristics

The advantage of using a gear will be shown in this section considering a DC motor-driven electric vehicle system. Part of the electric vehicle drivetrain including the electric motor coupled with a gear box is shown in Figure 14.8. The drivetrain will be analyzed in terms of the system torque-speed characteristics.

Electric motors are typically designed to operate at higher speeds to minimize the size of the motor. The gear box functions as a torque multiplier to deliver high torque at a reduced speed at the vehicle wheels. Let the overall gear ratio between the electric motor and the vehicle wheel be $GR$ with $\omega_m$ and $T_m$ representing the motor speed and torque, respectively. The torque and speed at the wheels are $\omega_{out}$ and $T_{out}$, respectively. For a separately excited DC motor, the speed-torque relationship at steady state is

$$\omega_m = \frac{V_t}{k\phi} - \frac{R_a}{(k\phi)^2} T_m \tag{14.9}$$

However,

$$\frac{\omega_m}{\omega_{out}} = GR = \frac{T_{out}}{T_m}$$

Substituting in (14.9),

$$\omega_{out} = \frac{V_t}{GR(k\phi)} - \frac{R_a}{(GRk\phi)^2} T_{out} \tag{14.10}$$

**FIGURE 14.8** Connection of a gear with the motor.

## Example 14.1

The powertrain of an electric vehicle is shown in Figure 14.9.
    Given, $V_t = 50\,V$, $R_a = 0.7\,\Omega$, $k\phi = 1.3$, $mg = 7,848\,N$.
    Gear box gears: First $GR_1 = 2$, second $GR_2 = 1$, $r_{wh}$ = wheel radius = 7 in. = 0.178 m.
    Find the vehicle maximum % gradability for each gear.

### *Solution*

$$\text{Max.\% grade} = \frac{100 F_{TR}}{\sqrt{(mg)^2 - F_{TR}^2}}$$

The torque-speed relationship is

$$\omega_{out} = \frac{V_t}{GR(k\phi)} - \frac{R_a}{(GRk\phi)^2} T_{out}$$

To find $F_{TR}$, set $\omega_{out} = 0$.

$$0 = \frac{V_t}{GR(k\phi)} - \frac{R_a}{(GRk\phi)^2} T_{out}$$

$$\Rightarrow T_{out} = \frac{V_t}{GR(k\phi)} \times \frac{(GRk\phi)^2}{R_a} = \frac{GR(k\phi)V_t}{R_a}$$

The relationship between $F_{TR}$ and $T_{out}$ is
    $F_{TR} = 2$ ($F_{TR}$ per rear wheel)
    $F_{TR}$ per rear wheel = torque per wheel/$r_{wh}$ = $(1/2 T_{out})/r_{wh}$
    Therefore,

$$F_{TR} = 2 \frac{\frac{1}{2} T_{out}}{r_{wh}} = \frac{T_{out}}{r_{wh}}$$

Substituting,

$$F_{TR} = \frac{(GRk\phi)V_t}{r_{wh}R_a} = \frac{GR(1.3)50}{(0.178)(0.7)} = 521.7 GR$$

In first gear,

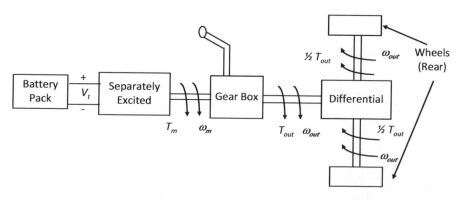

**FIGURE 14.9**   EV power train for Example 14.1.

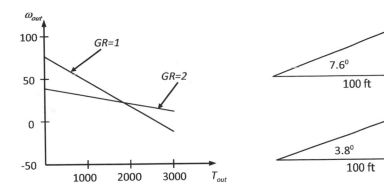

**FIGURE 14.10** Plots for Example 14.1.

$F_{TR} = 1,043\,\text{N}$

$$\text{Max. grade} = \frac{100(1,043)}{\sqrt{(7,878)^2 - (1,043)^2}} = 13.4\%$$

In second gear,
$F_{TR} = 521.7\,\text{N}$, max. grade = 6.7%

The steady-state torque-speed characteristics for the separately excited DC motor connected to the gear box for the first two gears are shown in Figure 14.10. The maximum percentage grades for the two gears are also shown in the figure.

## 14.2.3 PLANETARY GEAR SET

The planetary gear set is a gear system consisting of three components: the outer ring gear, the planet carrier and the central sun gear as shown in Figure 14.11. The planet gears are mounted on a movable arm or carrier which itself may rotate with respect to the ring or sun gear. In a planetary gear set, one of the basic components is typically held stationary, while power is transferred through

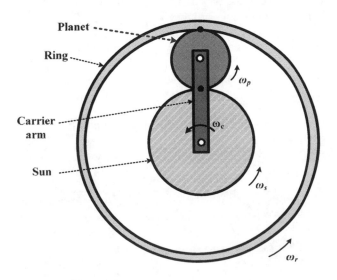

**FIGURE 14.11** Planetary gear set.

the other two components; however, all three components can actively participate in the power transfer such as in the power-split hybrid vehicles.

The planetary gear has the advantages of high power density and large gear reduction in a small volume. In hybrid vehicles, these gears enable multiple kinematic combinations and coaxial shafting of three powertrain components. The disadvantages of planetary gears are high bearing loads and design complexity.

There are several ways in which the input rotation applied through one of the components can be converted to output rotation of the one or two of the other gears. The speed relationships of the three gears are given by

$$(r_r + r_s)\omega_p = r_r\omega_r + r_s\omega_s \tag{14.11}$$

where $r_r$ is the radius of the ring gear, $r_p$ is the radius of the planet carrier and $r_s$ is the radius of the sun gear. The torque is transferred from the input device to the output devices through the force acting at the gear teeth. If a force $F$ is working on the planet, then equal but half of the forces act as reaction forces on the contact area of the ring and sun gears. This is shown in Figure 14.12.

The planet applies torque to the ring and sun gear in proportion to their radii. The torque relationships among the three gears are

$$T_p r_r = T_r(r_r + r_s) \text{ and } T_p r_s = T_s(r_r + r_s)$$

where $T_p$ is the planet carrier torque, $T_r$ is the ring gear torque and $T_s$ is the sun gear torque. From the balance of torques in the three gears, we have

$$T_p = T_r + T_s$$

$$= \frac{r_r}{r_r + r_s}T_p + \frac{r_s}{r_r + r_s}T_p \tag{14.12}$$

The ratios of the radii for the three gears are set by design, which results in a fixed ratio of torque distribution between the ring gear and the sun gear. If the power is supplied through the planet carrier, and delivered to the ring and sun gears, then we must have

$$P_p = P_r + P_s$$

$$\Rightarrow T_p\omega_p = \frac{r_r\omega_r}{r_r + r_s}T_p + \frac{r_s\omega_s}{r_r + r_s}T_p \tag{14.13}$$

where $P_p$ is the planet carrier power, $P_r$ is the ring gear power and $P_s$ is the sun gear power.

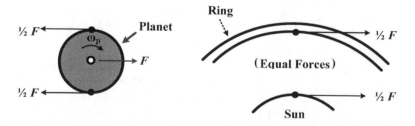

**FIGURE 14.12**  Reaction forces on sun and ring gears due to an applied force in planet carrier.

In the power-split hybrid vehicles, the planet carrier is connected to the engine, the sun gear is connected to the starter/generator and the ring gear is connected to the electric motor which is also connected to the differential and hence the wheels. The torque applied to the planet carrier is transferred to the wheels and the starter/generator through the ring and sun gear. The control strategy for the power-split hybrid using the planetary gear set is discussed in Section 15.2.1.

## 14.3 CLUTCHES

The clutch is a mechanical device used to smoothly engage or disengage the power transmission between a prime mover and the load. The most common use of a clutch is in the transmission system of an automobile, where it links the IC engine with transmission system of the vehicle. The clutch allows the power source to continue running, while the load is freely running due to inertia or is idle. The clutch engages and disengages the IC engine from the road load as the gear ratio of the transmission is changed to match vehicle speed with the desired IC engine speed. Clutches can be eliminated in electric vehicles, since the motor can start from zero speed and operate all the way to its maximum speed using a single gear ratio.

The type of clutch used to link the transmission with the engine in a vehicle is known as friction clutch. The clutching action brings the rotational speed of one disk to that of the other disk. The clutching action can be brought about by electrical, pneumatic or hydraulic action in addition to mechanical means discussed here.

The friction clutch used in a manual transmission of an automobile is engaged and disengaged by the driver. The components of the clutch used in the manual transmission are: cover, pressure plate and a friction disk. The cover is bolted to the flywheel of the engine; hence, it always rotates with the engine. The pressure plate is inside the cover, which also rotates with the engine. The disk with friction facings is positioned in between the cover and the pressure plate. The disk is connected to the transmission through a splined shaft [3]. The transmission is engaged for the power to be transmitted from the engine with the help of a series of springs attached to the pressure plate. When engaged, the pressure plate squeezes the friction disk against the flywheel to complete the mechanical linkage. The driver must depress the clutch pedal to disengage the transmission when the pressure plate moves away from the friction disk.

The mechanical brakes of both the disk and drum types are examples of friction clutch. The brakes will be discussed in detail in Section 14.6.

## 14.4 AUTOMOBILE DIFFERENTIAL

The automobile differential provides a mechanism for differential movement of the wheels on the rear axle. When a vehicle is turning a corner, the rear wheel to the outside of the curve must rotate faster than the inside wheel, because the former has a longer distance to travel. The type of gear used in automobile differential is made of planetary and bevel gears, where a set of gear train operates in a coordinated manner. A simplified schematic of an automobile differential is given in Figure 14.13. The figure omits the teeth of the gears for simplicity. The drive shaft connected to the engine drives the pinion that is connected to the bevel (perpendicular) gear. The bevel gear is connected to the differential cage, which drives the wheel axles. The cage is connected to only one of the wheel axles, connecting the other axle only by means of the differential pinion. The differential pinion connecting the differential gears does not rotate as long as the speeds of the two wheels on the axle are the same. If one of the wheels slows down due to cornering, the differential pinion starts rotating to produce a higher speed on the other wheel. The system described above is a simple differential that is not suitable for full torque transfer in low-traction condition, such as on ice [4].

**FIGURE 14.13**   Simplified schematic of an automobile differential.

## 14.5   TRANSMISSION

The mechanical assembly that delivers the power from the IC engine to the driveshaft most effectively under various driving conditions of speed, acceleration, roadway grades and vehicle turns is called the *transmission*. A transmission assembly includes various rotating parts, such as gears, clutches, levels, bearings and shafts. The transmission allows the vehicle to operate over the entire speed range of the vehicle starting from standstill to the maximum vehicle speed. The transmission is designed and controlled to operate to match the engine speed and vehicle speed. The transmission engages different gear ratios to satisfy the torque and speed requirements of the driver while satisfying the conflicting requirements of acceleration, speed and fuel economy. The tractive force delivered by the transmission for four gear ratios of a four-speed transmission is shown in Figure 14.14 plotted against vehicle speed.

The three primary types of transmission are: *manual, automatic* and *continuously variable* transmissions (CVTs). With the manual transmission, the driver shifts the gears manually in relation to the vehicle speed using the clutch pedal for engagement and disengagement. The driver skill plays a big role with manual transmissions for maximizing the performance of the vehicle. In automatic transmissions, the gear shifting is accomplished through the vehicle controllers without any intervention of the driver. These transmissions also allow the engine to idle when the vehicle is stopped.

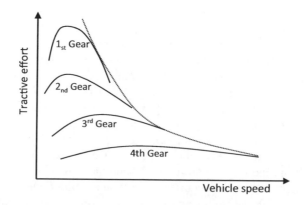

**FIGURE 14.14**   Tractive force versus vehicle speed for a four-speed transmission.

The CVT also does not require any driver intervention, but provides an infinite number of gear ratios rather than a fixed set. A general overview of the three transmissions is given in the following.

### 14.5.1 MANUAL TRANSMISSION

The manual transmission is a gear train with several shafts, countershafts, spur gears, synchronizers and safety devices to facilitate multiple gear ratios for power transmission from engine to the drive shaft. Different gear meshes lock and unlock through the use of clutch, gear lever, synchronizer and the lock/unlock mechanisms in the transmission [3]. The simplified schematic of a four-speed manual transmission is shown in Figure 14.15. The transmission has the input shaft, output shaft, one counter-shaft, eight gears, an idler and two synchronizers. The functions of the synchronizer are to ensure that the driving gear and the shaft are rotating at the same speed prior to engagement, and then to lock the gear to the shaft after engagement. The synchronizer eliminates the need for double clutches.

The forward and reverse gear ratios for the gear train and synchronizer arrangement shown in Figure 14.15 can be calculated based on the number of teeth in the gears. For example calculations, the numbers of teeth on gears 1 through 8 are assumed to be 35, 15, 28, 21, 24, 26, 20 and 31, respectively. In the first gear, the input shaft transmits power to the countershaft through the 20/31 gear mesh. The countershaft transmits power to the output shaft through the 15/35 gear mesh. Both the synchronizers remain disengaged in a neutral position. Therefore, the first gear ratio is

$$GR_1 = \frac{T_{out}}{T_{in}} = \frac{31}{20} \cdot \frac{35}{15} = 3.617$$

In the second gear, synchronizer 2 engages the second gear (28 teeth) to the output shaft. The input shaft transmits power to the output shaft through the right half of the countershaft and the second gear counter gear (21 teeth). The second gear ratio is

$$GR_2 = \frac{T_{out}}{T_{in}} = \frac{31}{20} \cdot \frac{28}{21} = 2.067$$

In the third gear, synchronizer 1 locks the third gear (24 teeth) to the output shaft. The input shaft transmits power to the countershaft and then to the output shaft through the 26/24 third gear mesh. The third gear ratio is

$$GR_3 = \frac{T_{out}}{T_{in}} = \frac{31}{20} \cdot \frac{24}{26} = 1.431$$

**FIGURE 14.15**  A manual four-speed transmission.

In the fourth gear, synchronizer 1 locks the input shaft to the output shaft. Power flows directly from the input to the output, and the fourth gear ratio is 1.

In the reverse gear, the idler is used to change the direction of rotation between the input and output shafts. The power is transmitted from the input shaft to the countershaft through the 20/31 gear mesh. The idler is engaged in between the 15/35 gear mesh to change the direction of rotation. Both the synchronizers remain disengaged in this condition. The reverse gear ratio is

$$GR_{Rev} = \frac{T_{out}}{T_{in}} = -\frac{31}{20} \cdot \frac{35}{15} = -3.617$$

### 14.5.2  Automatic Transmission

The automatic transmission uses a fluid coupling and a planetary gear set to transmit power from the engine to the driveshaft. The fluid coupling device is known as the *torque converter*, while is central to the operation of the automatic transmission. Torque converters allow the IC engine to idle without additional driver intervention when the vehicle is stopped. This eliminates the need for the clutch pedal that exists in manual transmission vehicles.

The other significant component of the automatic transmission is the gear set. The planetary gear set used produces different gear ratios using the unique torque and speed relationships among the sun, ring and planet carriers. One of the elements in the planetary gear set must be held fixed for torque transfer. In automatic transmission, this is achieved using clutches and bands. A set of clutches, actuated by hydraulics, engage and disengage the different gears of the planetary set. The bands are also actuated by hydraulics to wrap around a gear train and connect to the housing. The planetary gear set along with the clutches and bands establishes the various gear ratios for the transmission.

The construction and operation of the torque converter is discussed in further detail below since this is a key component in the automatic transmission.

#### 14.5.2.1  Torque Converter

Torque converter is a type of fluid coupling device that allows power transfer from the engine to the transmission at different vehicle speeds. When the vehicle is stopped and the engine is idling, only a small amount of torque is transferred to the transmission. As the engine speed increases with increased power demand from the driver, the torque transfer amount also increases.

Torque converter consists of a turbine, an impeller or pump, the housing and transmission fluid. The parts of a torque converter are shown in Figure 14.16. The pump is the driving member of the converter, while the turbine is the driven member. The pump is of centrifugal type and is connected to the engine crankshaft. The turbine is splined to the input shaft of the transmission. The converter is completely filled with transmission fluid, which serves as the only connection between the pump and the turbine. It is the dynamics of the fluid that transmits power for the engine to the transmission. Engine rotation causes fluid to enter the pump through the middle and exit through the periphery. In the turbine, fluid enters through the peripheral blades and exits through the middle. As the fluid enters the turbine and pushes against the turbine blades, the turbine starts to rotate in the same direction as that of the pump. As the engine speed increases, more fluid is pumped into the turbine and the torque transmitted increases. When the pump speed is much higher than that of the turbine, the fluid enters the turbine with great force.

Torque converter has a *stator* that prevents the returning fluid from the turbine from hitting the pump with a high velocity in the opposite direction. The stator is mounted on a stationary shaft attached to the transmission and is positioned in between the pump and the turbine. The stator remains stationary and locked to the shaft in one direction when the pump velocity is high relative to the turbine. In this position, the stator redirects the fluid toward the pump in the same direction of rotation. This prevents the drag on the pump and loss of engine power. When the pump is rotating

**FIGURE 14.16** Torque converter.

at almost the same velocity as the turbine at higher vehicle speeds, the fluid leaves the turbine with little residual velocity. The fluid strikes the back of the stator, which is then able to rotate freely in the opposite direction.

As mentioned previously, the engine, and hence, the pump speed is almost the same as turbine velocity at higher vehicle speeds which is highway speeds. The transmission output shaft speed is the same as the turbine speed. Ideally, the transmission speed should match the engine speed exactly since the difference corresponds to power loss. However, in practice there is always slippage resulting in power loss in the torque converter. The power dissipation appears in the form of heat in the fluid. The heat is removed in passenger vehicles by air-cooling the torque converter housing, or in trucks and utility vehicles by a adding a transmission cooling loop with a secondary radiator. The power loss in the torque converter is the primary reason why automatic transmissions are less efficient than a manual transmission.

Modern torque converters can multiply the engine torque by two to three times when the engine speed is higher compared to the output shaft speed. This allows the torque converter to deliver high torque when a vehicle accelerates from a stop. At higher vehicle speeds, the engine speed matches the output shaft speed, and there is no torque multiplication.

#### 14.5.2.2 Automatic Transmission in Hybrids

Automatic transmissions including the torque converter were used in hybrid vehicles prior to the development of the power-split hybrid architectures. For crankshaft mounted and belt-driven starter/generator hybrid vehicles, the automatic transmission is still a preferred choice. Three main types of step-ratio automatic transmissions considered for hybrid vehicle applications are Simpson, Wilson and Lepelletier types [5]. The three types differ mainly in the number and type of planetary gear sets, and number and type of clutches and bands required. In crank shaft mounted starter/generator systems, the electric machine is packaged around the torque converter with the rotor mounted to the torque converter at the flex plate of the impeller.

### 14.5.3 Continuously Variable Transmission

CVT does not have a gearbox with a fixed set of gear ratios, but instead uses a sliding mechanism that allows an infinite number of gear ratios between the highest and lowest gear ratios possible with the system. The two common types of CVTs used are the belt-pulley system and the toroidal system. In either type, there are three major components: a driving shaft part connected to the engine, a driven

shaft part connected to the transmission and a coupling mechanism providing the variability. In the belt-pulley system, the input and output shafts are connected to two pulleys and a belt is used for the coupling. In the toroidal systems, two disks are connected to the shafts, and wheels or rollers slide over the disks for coupling the input to the output. In addition, the CVTs have an electronic control unit (ECU) and various sensors to provide feedback to the controller. The controller adjusts the operating point of the CVT to maximize fuel economy and vehicle acceleration. The belt-pulley system, which is also known as the Van Doorne system is more suitable for low-power systems, especially in front-wheel drive vehicles. The toroidal CVTs have been built in larger systems [3].

The schematic of a belt-pulley CVT is shown in Figure 14.17a. The three primary components shown are: a high-power metal or rubber belt, an input driving pulley and an output-driven pulley. Both the pulleys have cone-shaped structures and the belt rides on top of the cones. Each pulley has two cones which can get closer or move away from each other; this movement varies the diameter of the pulleys. When the cones get closer, the diameter of the pulley increases. When the cones move further apart, the belt sits low in the groove with a smaller diameter. By adjusting the cone positions of the two pulleys, a continuous variation of the gear ratio is possible from a maximum gear ratio (low gear; when the drive pulley diameter is the smallest and the driven pulley diameter is the largest) to a minimum gear ratio (high gear; when the drive pulley diameter is the largest and the driven pulley diameter is the smallest). The drive pulley is connected to the engine crankshaft, while the driven pulley is connected to the transmission.

The toroidal CVT, shown in Figure 14.17b, has a cone-shaped disk connected to the engine (drive disk) and another one connected to the transmission (driven disk). The rollers or wheels slide on the two disks transferring power from the drive disk to the driven disk. The rollers function as the coupling device for power transmission similar to the belt in the belt-pulley CVT. The gear ratio is 1 when the rollers are in the middle with the two disks rotating at the same velocity as shown in the figure. The gear ratio is the higher when the rollers in the driving disk are in contact near the center, while those in the driven disk are near the edge. The gear ratio is lower when the contact scenario is the opposite.

FIGURE 14.17 CVTs: (a) belt-pulley type and (b) toroidal type.

## 14.5.4 eCVT/HEV Transmission

In the power-split hybrid vehicles, the planetary gear set along with electronic controls is used for power transmission between the engine and electric motor to the wheels. The planet carrier of the planetary gear set is connected to the engine, the sun gear is connected to the starter/generator and the ring gear is connected to the electric motor which is also connected to the differential and hence the wheels. The torque applied to the planet carrier is transferred to the wheels and the starter/generator through the ring and sun gear. From Equation 14.12,

$$T_p = T_r + T_s$$

$$\Rightarrow T_{engine} = T_{wheels} + T_{gen}$$

The use of the planetary gear set in the power-split results in a fixed ratio of torque distribution between the wheels and the starter/generator gear. A split ratio of 72%–28% between the motor/wheels and the starter/generator is used in some production hybrid vehicles.

The power relationship in the power-split hybrid vehicle is

$$T_p \omega_p = \frac{r_r \omega_r}{r_r + r_s} T_p + \frac{r_s \omega_s}{r_r + r_s} T_p$$

$$\Rightarrow P_{engine} = P_{engine\ to\ ring} + P_{engine\ to\ sun}$$

In the power-split hybrid vehicles, all of the power comes from the stored fuel through the IC engine. The control strategy algorithm varies the generator or loading to split the power from the engine between the wheels and the starter/generator. The electric motor can add power to the wheels in addition to what comes directly from the IC engine through electronic control. Since the power split is controlled electronically, these types of transmissions are known as electronic CVT (eCVT). The details of the control strategy for the power-split hybrid vehicle are given in Section 15.2.1 of Chapter 15.

## 14.6 VEHICLE BRAKES

Vehicle braking system converts the kinetic energy of the vehicle into thermal (heat) energy to provide the driver with a mechanism to stop the vehicle or reduce its speed. The brakes in automobiles are mechanical clutches that uses friction to slow down a rotational disk. The driver controls the brake action through a foot-operated linkage. The friction clutch is composed of two disks, each connected to its own shaft. As long as the disks are not engaged, one disk can spin freely without affecting the other. When the rotating and the stationary disks are engaged through the operation action, friction between the two disks reduces the speed of the rotating disk. The kinetic energy of the vehicle transfers directly between the disks and is wasted due to friction.

### 14.6.1 Conventional Brake System

Conventional braking systems use the hydraulic technology to actuate the friction clutches for the braking action. The entire hydraulic system is filled with a special brake fluid, which is pressurized and forced through the system by the movement of the master cylinder pistons. Simplified views of the two main types of conventional brakes, which are the disk-type brakes and the drum-type brakes, are also shown in Figure 14.18 [6].

The disk brakes are the preferred choice for both front and rear wheels of passenger vehicles. The pads of the disk-type brakes are forced against the machined surfaces of a rotating disk

**FIGURE 14.18** Conventional brake systems.

called the rotor which is attached to the wheel. The disk brakes have friction pads controlled by a caliper arrangement, which when engaged clamps to the rotor and the wheel. The brake pads are designed to assist cooling and resist fading. Fading causes the braking friction coefficient to decrease with temperature rise. The high force required for caliper actuation is typically supplied from a power assist device following the brake command input from the driver.

Drum brakes, which has been gradually replaced by the disk brakes, use an internally expanding brake shoes that are forced against the inside machined surface of a rotating drum. The drum-type brake units have cylindrical surfaces and shoes instead of pads that hold the friction material. Drum brakes are highly suitable for hand brakes; they are still used in rear wheels of some vehicles. The shoes press against the drum cylinder up on a brake command input from the driver. The shoes can be arranged to press against the outer or inner surface of the rotating drum to retard the wheel rotation. If the shoes are applied to the inner surface, then the centrifugal force of the drum due to rotation will resist disk engagement. If the shoes are pressed against the outer drum surface, the centrifugal force will assist engagement, but at the same time may cause overheating.

When the driver applies the brakes, a command is executed to exert a brake force acting in opposition to the motion of the car. The dynamics of the braking forces are similar to the vehicle dynamics studied in Chapter 2 except that braking forces are now applied at the wheels instead of tractive forces from the propulsion unit. The braking conditions are governed by the tire-road interface friction coefficients. Let us consider $F_{bf}$ and $F_{br}$ as the braking forces applied at the front and rear wheels to understand the braking dynamics. From Newton's second law,

$$\sum F_{xT} = m_v a_{xT} = F_{bf} + F_{br} + m_v g \sin(\theta) + F_{Roll} + F_{AD} \tag{14.14}$$

where $a_{xT}$ is the linear acceleration or deceleration in the $x_T$ direction. The rolling resistance force $F_{Roll}$ and aerodynamic drag force $F_{AD}$ assist in braking action, and the function of the gravitational force depends on the roadway slope.

The time and the distance traveled during a velocity change with uniform deceleration can also be derived from Newton's second law as

$$t = \frac{m_v}{\sum F_{xT}}(V_0 - V_f)$$

$$x = \frac{m_v}{\sum F_{xT}}\left(V_0^2 - V_f^2\right)$$

where $V_0$ and $V_f$ are the initial and final velocities, respectively, of the vehicle during braking. The uniform deceleration approximation indicates that the time to stop is proportional to the vehicle velocity and the stopping distance is proportional to the square of the vehicle velocity.

Let us consider the maximum sustained deceleration requirement of 0.65 g which corresponds to a panic stop from 60 mph [3]. Braking forces will be much larger compared to the rolling resistance and aerodynamic drag forces for harder braking actions. Also if we assume a level roadway, then for the panic stop situation, Equation 14.14 simplifies to

$$F_{bf} + F_{br} = m_v a_{xT} \tag{14.15}$$

The average power dissipated with a uniform deceleration is

$$P_{b,avg} = (F_{bf} + F_{br}) \times \frac{V_f + V_0}{2} \tag{14.16}$$

The initial power with uniform deceleration is going to be twice the value of $P_{b,avg}$. The rate of heat dissipation must be evaluated for braking system design, since the friction brakes convert the kinetic energy of the vehicle into heat energy.

The free body diagram of the vehicle under braking action is shown in Figure 14.19. The static weight distribution of the vehicle between the front and rear axles is

$$W_f = \frac{m_v g b}{(a+b)}$$

$$W_r = \frac{m_v g a}{(a+b)}$$

There will be a dynamic shift in vehicle weights under braking action. Let the dynamic weights of the vehicle be $W_f'$ and $W_r'$. Applying Newton's second law in the $y_T$-direction

$$\sum F_{yT} = 0 = W_f' + W_r' - m_v g \tag{14.17}$$

$$\Rightarrow W_f' + W_r' = m_v g$$

The dynamic weights can be calculated using the moment of the forces around the vehicle center of gravity. The moment forces are

$$\sum M_{cg} = 0 = F_{bf} \cdot h - W_f' \cdot a + F_{br} \cdot h + W_r' \cdot b \tag{14.18}$$

$$\Rightarrow m_v a_{xT} h = W_f' \cdot a - W_r' \cdot b$$

**FIGURE 14.19**   Free-body diagram of a vehicle under braking action.

Equation 14.15 has been used in deriving the above relationship. Multiplying both sides of Equation 14.17 with $b$ and adding with Equation 14.18, we can obtain

$$W_f' = \frac{m_v g b}{(a+b)} + \frac{m_v a_{xT} h}{(a+b)} \tag{4.19}$$

and

$$W_r' = \frac{m_v g a}{(a+b)} - \frac{m_v a_{xT} h}{(a+b)} \tag{14.20}$$

The first terms on Equations 14.19 and 14.20 are the same as the static weights; the second terms are the dynamic weights added or subtracted from the front and rear axles due to braking action. The equations show that during braking the front axle bears heavier weight than the rear axles. This means that the front axles sustain higher braking forces than the rear axles.

The ratio of dynamic weights between the front and rear axles is

$$\frac{W_f'}{W_r'} = \frac{b + h a_{xT}/g}{c - h a_{xT}/g} \tag{14.21}$$

The front braking action to rear braking action can be distributed as

$$\frac{F_{bf}}{F_{br}} = \frac{W_f'}{W_r'} \tag{14.22}$$

The braking force acting on the vehicle is also function of the tire to road interface, as mentioned earlier in Chapter 2. The maximum braking force possible for a wheel is equal to the coefficient of friction times the normal force

$$F_{b,max} = \mu W_{wh}' \tag{14.23}$$

where $\mu$ is the tire-to-road friction coefficient and $W_{wh}'$ is the dynamic weight on the wheel. Friction coefficients for three different road conditions are shown in Figure 14.20. The friction co-efficient limits the maximum braking force that can be applied in different road conditions beyond which wheels lock-up. In addition, the friction force limit is a non-linear function of the vehicle slip speed. Therefore, the force applied to the brake pads in each wheel of the vehicle has to be carefully optimized in order to ensure maximum effectiveness.

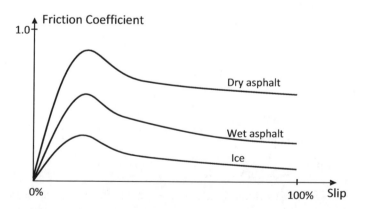

FIGURE 14.20   Friction coefficient variations as a function of tire to road slip.

Brake systems are designed to apportion the applied brake force between the front and rear brakes according to the dynamic weight ratios. The front and back wheels of the vehicle will consequently have different braking behaviors and requirements due to the dynamic load transfer during braking in two-axle vehicles. Front brakes are designed to carry out higher percentage of braking due to the increase in dynamic weight during braking in the front axles. The brakes must also be prevented from locking up for good braking performance. The vehicle losses steering control when the front brake lock up and the vehicle tends to sway when the rear wheels lock-up. Anti-lock braking systems (ABS) use control algorithms to prevent wheels from locking up.

Additional brake system analysis reveals that to obtain maximum braking power it is necessary to consider front and back braking forces together. The front and rear brake are highly interdependent in contrast to the simplified analysis presented here. Advanced designs also have to consider overall vehicle stability, and optimization of the force applied to the rotor, along with critical safety considerations.

In addition to the previous considerations, controller design of the brake system must consider the non-linear characteristic of the rotor and pad interaction. The braking pad displacement has a nonlinear relationship with rotor clamping force and is also temperature dependent. The desired braking force is achieved by applying the corresponding pad displacement according to the actuator characteristic. The use of a highly dynamic and controllable electromechanical actuator will allow vehicle manufacturers to achieve better performance and higher reliability. An EMB system is discussed next.

## Example 14.2

A 2,000 kg vehicle traveling at 85 mph has to be stopped with a maximum sustained deceleration of 0.65 g. The vehicle has a wheelbase of 2.5 m and a front/rear static weight distribution of 49%/51%. The center of gravity is at a height of 0.5 m from the ground.

    a. Find the total force and average power required to bring the vehicle to a stop.
    b. Find the average power absorbed by the brakes.
    c. Find the front and rear weight distribution during braking.

### Solution

    a. The force required to stop the vehicle is

$$F_b = F_{bf} + F_{br} = m_v a_{xT} = 2{,}000 \times 0.65 \times 9.81 = 12.753 \text{ kN}$$

    b. The average power dissipated in the brakes is

$$P_{b,avg} = \frac{1}{2} F_b V_f = \frac{12.753 \times 37.97}{2} = 242.12 \text{ kW}$$

    c. The front and rear weight distribution is

$$\frac{W_f'}{W_r'} = \frac{1.275 + 0.5 \times 0.65 \text{ g/g}}{1.225 - 0.5 \times 0.65 \text{ g/g}} = 64\%/36\%$$

## 14.6.2 ELECTROMECHANICAL BRAKE SYSTEM

EMB system is an alternative to conventional brake system where electromechanical components replace the hydraulic actuators and controls [7,8]. EMB avoids the use of hydraulic fluid in the brake system and facilitates improved performance with modern braking control systems such as ABS or

VSC (vehicle stability control). EMB technology allows for the introduction of pure brake-by-wire systems, which removes brake fluids and hydraulic lines entirely. The braking force is generated directly at each wheel by high-performance electric motors that are controlled by an ECU and actuated by signals from an electronic pedal module. This specific mechanism in conjunction with the underlying control structure translates into the most direct and individual wheel control, and therefore, increases braking performance.

The layout and communication between the control unit of an EMB system and its actuators are shown in Figure 14.21. EMB system allows complete separate corner assembly of the components near the wheels while commands are to be executed through electronic signals only. The feel of the brake pedal can be easily tuned and adjusted to individual needs since brake pedal displacement is now completely independent from changes in brake actuator travel. An EMB system does not exhibit the often undesirable noise and vibration pedal feedback experienced in conventional hydraulic brake systems during ABS and other control modes. In addition, EMB systems are environmentally friendlier than conventional systems since no hydraulic fluid is required, while at the same time they allow for an easy and straightforward 'plug & bolt' assembly process.

Electric machines and their controllers enable electromechanical actuation to meet the specifications required in braking systems. Each wheel of the vehicle is equipped with its own brake actuator, which can be controlled independently from the other wheels. Individual control of each wheel's braking behavior can then be used to achieve optimal braking ability and improved vehicle stability. This makes it possible for the vehicle to remain stable during a braking phase even when wheels are subject to different surface conditions. Electric motor-driven actuators allow implementation of advanced control algorithms to improve the braking behavior of the entire vehicle, which is otherwise not possible with hydraulic actuation. In addition to that, software upgrades can provide for an easy tuning of the entire system, while minimizing mechanical changes.

EMB systems have very specific requirements in terms of dynamic response and steady-state operation. When a braking operation is required, the motor must have a fast response and a sufficiently high no-load speed to bring the disengaged brake into contact with the brake rotor. On the other hand, in order to apply the necessary braking force, the motor has to generate high torques at low speeds down to a complete stall, once the pad is applied. The electric machine must have fast response in both directions of rotation, since both engagement and disengagement functions have to be randomly available. Therefore, it is necessary to have a controller and machine suitable for four

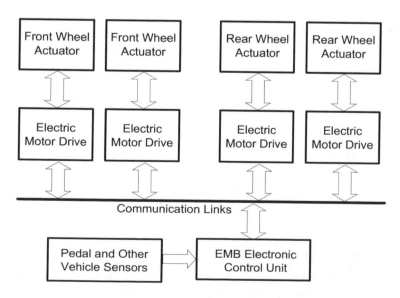

FIGURE 14.21   EMB system in a vehicle.

quadrant operation, which can be appreciated from the typical operation cycle for an EMB motor as shown in Figure 14.22. The electric machine is operated in the torque controlled mode with maximum speed limits.

EMB system shown in Figure 14.23 consists of a rotary motor coupled to a planetary-gear and ball-screw assembly that converts the motor torque and rotation into linear force and travel suitable for operation in a caliper brake. Components of one actuator to be located in a corner wheel assembly are shown in Figure 14.23. There will be four such actuators in the four corner wheel assemblies in a four-wheel vehicle equipped with EMB system. A high-speed/low-torque electric machine along with the gears helps minimize the package size. The gears reduce the high motor speed and increase the output torque for brake actuation. The system controller can be operated in a force-controlled mode in the outer loop with force feedback from the calipers. The force commands are issued through the brake pedal. The force controller located in the ECU issues signals to the individual wheel actuators to achieve desired performance. The force controller generates the torque command for each of the electric motor controllers. The motor controller processes the command signal and the feedback signals to generate the gating signals for the power converter. Pulse-width modulation or hysteresis current controllers are commonly used for this purpose. The power converter drives the motor, which produces the desired torque and creates the desired force on the brake calipers.

The type of electric machines suitable for EMB systems is either the PM machine or the switched reluctance machine. PM machine does offer a higher power density, but temperature sensitivity has to be carefully evaluated since the friction heat generated due to braking could damage the magnets. On the other hand, switched reluctance machine offer simple and low rotor inertia and is also amenable to discrete position sensorless operation.

EMB is not yet widely accepted mainly because of the safety critical nature of brake systems. A first alternative to the conventional braking systems could be to combine the advantage of electronic control with hydraulic actuators. This makes it possible to implement control algorithms that will improve the performance of the braking system and user comfort. With electrohydraulic braking (EHB), the hydraulic link between the brake pedal and the wheel brake is replaced with a by-wire-transmission which offers considerable advantages. The hydraulic structure of the system is simplified and control of the actuator is made easier. EHB control unit receives inputs from sensors connected to the brake pedal. In normal operation, a backup valve is kept closed and the controller activates the brakes of the wheel through an electric motor driven hydraulic pump. When the controller goes into a fail-safe mode, the backup valve is opened, which allows the brakes to be controlled through a conventional hydraulic circuit. This redundancy makes the system very reliable in case of an electrical failure.

**FIGURE 14.22** Four-quadrant operation of electric motor to engage and disengage EMB.

**FIGURE 14.23**  EMB system with an electric actuator.

## 14.7  COOLING SYSTEMS

Ancillary systems unique to electric and hybrid electric vehicles are either adapted from existing ones or developed from basics. An electric motor drive powered by the traction battery is required to drive the compressor of the air-conditioning system in electric vehicles. The electric machines and inverters for propulsion require a powertrain electronic cooling system to be developed. The traction batteries require adequate cooling for their operation and safety. Two cooling systems are discussed in this section, one related to the safety and comfort of the passengers which is the climate control system, while the other is the powertrain component cooling system which is critical to the reliable and safe operation of the powertrain components. The climate control system presented is also required in an IC engine vehicle.

### 14.7.1  CLIMATE CONTROL SYSTEM

Cabin climate in a vehicle is controlled using one of the refrigeration cycles. A working fluid circulates in a closed loop through two heat exchangers to cool the vehicle cabin. A typical air-conditioning unit in a passenger vehicle requires about 2 kW of power under steady-state conditions, but could require up to three times that during peak conditions. The work input to the system is through the component called *compressor* that compress the working fluid.

In conventional IC engine vehicles, the compressor is belt driven by the IC engine, but in hybrid vehicles an electric motor drive is required for electric only operation modes when the engine is off. Hybrid electric vehicles that do not employ an electric motor drive for the compressor must turn the engine on when air-conditioning is demanded by the user. In electric vehicles, an electric motor drive has to be used to the drive compressor. The remaining components in the climate control system are the same in electric and hybrid electric vehicles as those in the IC engine vehicles.

In this section, the thermodynamics of the refrigeration cycle used in cabin climate control is discussed followed by descriptions of vehicle air-conditioning system components.

### 14.7.1.1    Vapor Compression Refrigeration Cycle

The most common refrigeration systems of today use the vapor-compression refrigeration cycle, which has been derived from the ideal Carnot vapor refrigeration cycle. Reversing the Carnot vapor power cycle gives the ideal refrigeration cycle. This cycle is completely reversible, but not a practical one. Let us first evaluate the ideal vapor cycle before discussing the practical vapor cycle. In the ideal cycle, refrigerant circulates through a series network of components while operating between a cold region and a warm region. The schematic of the ideal cycle and the associated temperature-entropy ($T$-$s$) diagram is shown in Figure 14.24 [9]. The components in the system are evaporator, compressor, condenser and turbine. Evaporators and condensers are heat exchangers where heat is exchanged between the refrigerant and the two regions at different temperatures. The refrigerant enters the evaporator as a two-phase liquid vapor mixture at state 4. In the evaporator, the refrigerant receives heat from the cold region while some of it changes state from liquid to vapor. The temperature and pressure remain constant during this process from state 4 to state 1. The refrigerant is then compressed adiabatically (constant entropy) from state 1 to state 2 by the compressor. Compressor requires work input to increase the pressure and temperature of the refrigerant. In state 2, the refrigerant is in a saturated vapor condition. The refrigerant then enters the condenser where heat is transferred to the warm region under constant temperature and pressure conditions. The refrigerant changes state from saturated vapor to saturated liquid as a result of the heat transfer in the condenser. The liquid refrigerant at state 3 enters the turbine where it expands adiabatically. Both temperature and pressure drops in the turbine as the refrigerant returns to its initial state 4. In this ideal Carnot cycle, all processes are internally reversible; heat transfer between refrigerants and the two regions takes place without any change in temperature.

In the practical vapor compression refrigeration cycle, the most significant departure from the ideal condition is related to the heat transfers that cannot be accomplished reversibly in the heat exchangers. In particular, the temperature of the refrigerant at the evaporator needs to be maintained several degrees below the cold region temperature $T_C$ with a practical size evaporator to maintain a sufficient heat transfer rate. Also, the temperature in the condenser needs to maintained several degrees higher than the warm region temperature $T_H$. Another important point of departure from the ideal cycle is in the phase of the refrigerant during compression. As mentioned earlier, the refrigerant during compression is in a liquid-vapor mixed phase; this is known as wet compression. In practice, wet compression is avoided since liquid droplets damage the compressor. In the practical vapor cycle, refrigerant has to be completely vaporized; such process is

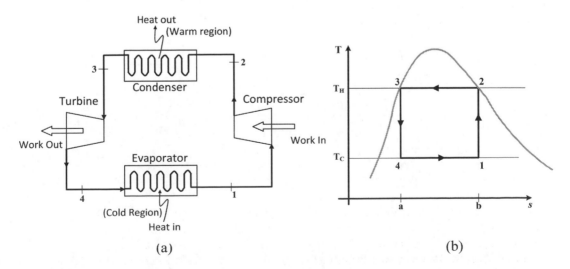

(a)                                                                                                (b)

**FIGURE 14.24**    Carnot vapor refrigeration cycle: (a) components and (b) temperature-entropy diagram.

known as dry compression. Another impractical aspect of the ideal cycle is the expansion process in the turbine from state 3 to state 4 where saturated liquid is converted to liquid-vapor mixture. This process produces very little work output by the turbine compared to the work input at the compressor. This is because turbines working under these conditions have very low efficiencies. In the practical vapor refrigeration cycle, the turbine is replaced with a simple expansion valve. This is a very cost effective solution although work output of the turbine has to be sacrificed.

The vapor-compression refrigeration system and the operating $(T\text{-}s)$ diagram are shown in Figure 14.25 [9]. Let us analyze the heat transfers and work done in the system components starting with the evaporator. The work and energy transfers are positive in the directions indicated. Kinetic and potential energy changes in the processes will be neglected. We will also assume that there are no extraneous heat transfer and the pressure changes take place only in the expansion valve and the compressor.

In the evaporator, heat is transferred from the refrigerated space to the refrigerant which results in vaporization of the refrigerant. The heat transfer rate per unit mass of refrigerant is given by the enthalpy change between the two states as

$$\frac{\dot{Q}_C}{\dot{m}} = H_1 - H_4 \tag{14.24}$$

where $\dot{Q}_C$ is the heat transfer rate and $\dot{m}$ is the mass flow rate of the refrigerant. $\dot{Q}_C$ is also known as refrigeration capacity with units of kW in SI units or Btu/h in English units. Another commonly used unit for refrigeration capacity is *ton of refrigeration* which is equal to 12,000 Btu/h.

The compressor pump compresses vapor refrigerant out of the evaporator into high-pressure vapor while simultaneously increasing the temperature. Assuming there is no heat transfer to or from the compressor, the rate of energy input per mass of refrigerant is given by the enthalpy change between the two states as

$$\frac{\dot{W}_c}{\dot{m}} = H_2 - H_1 \tag{14.25}$$

In the condenser, heat transfer takes place from the refrigerant to the warm region under constant pressure (isobar). The heat transfer rate per unit mass of refrigerant is

$$\frac{\dot{Q}_H}{\dot{m}} = H_2 - H_3 \tag{14.26}$$

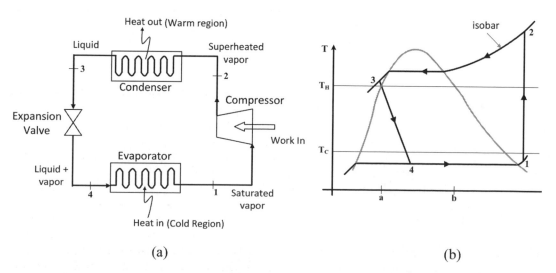

(a)                                                          (b)

**FIGURE 14.25**  Vapor compression refrigeration cycle: (a) components and (b) temperature-entropy diagram.

The refrigerant then expands to the evaporator pressure from state 3 to state 4 in the expansion valve. This process is irreversible when the pressure decreases along with an increase in entropy. Again, assuming there is no heat transfer to or from the compressor, energy transfer rate per unit mass of refrigerant is

$$\frac{\dot{W}_{out}}{\dot{m}} = H_3 - H_4 \tag{14.27}$$

Since there is no work output in the expansion valve, $\dot{W}_{out} = 0$, and hence,

$$H_4 = H_3$$

The objective of the air-conditioning system or refrigerator is the removal of heat, called the cooling load from a low-temperature environment. The performance of a refrigeration cycle is measured in terms of coefficient of performance which is the ratio of the refrigeration effect to the net work input required to achieve that effect [10]. For the vapor compression cycle, the coefficient of performance is

$$COP_R = \frac{\text{Cooling effect}}{\text{Net work input}} = \frac{\dot{Q}_C}{\dot{W}_C} = \frac{H_1 - H_4}{H_2 - H_1} \tag{14.28}$$

The above equations apply to both practical vapor compression cycles with irreversibilities and idealized compression cycles where such effects are absent since the above equations have been derived from mass and energy rate balances. Although practical cycles deviate from the ideal cycles due to the irreversibilities in evaporator, compressor and condenser, it is insightful to evaluate systems with the idealized cycles; the idealized evaluations do establish the upper limit on the performance of a practical refrigeration system.

### 14.7.1.2  Vehicle Air-Conditioning System

The automotive air-conditioning system runs on the vapor compression refrigeration cycle with similar components shown in Figure 14.25a. The only addition is a receiver/dryer which is placed in between the condenser and the expansion valve. The types of components and their functionalities in an automotive air-conditioning system are described below.

Compressor is responsible for compressing the low-pressure refrigerant gas to high pressure and high temperature. The compressor is essentially a pump with a suction side and a discharge side. The suction side draws the low-pressure refrigerant from the outlet of the evaporator. In some cases, the suction is drawn through an accumulator. The high-pressure compressed fluid at the discharge side is delivered to the condenser.

Compressors play a determining role in the cabin climate control of a vehicle. Either a belt coupled to the IC engine output shaft or an electric motor drives the compressor. The common compressor types used for climate control in the automotive industry are scroll compressor, rotary vane compressor and swashplate compressor. Of these, scroll compressors deliver high efficiency at medium speeds and also have the ability to withstand high rotational speeds. Hence, these are suitable for use with electric motors which can operate at higher speeds. Electric motor-driven compressors also have the advantage of adjustable speeds through motor control that would improve performance of the air-conditioning system.

A unidirectional, speed-controlled electric motor drive is required for compressors that are operated without an IC engine. Either PM machines or SR machines are suitable for the application. The drive structure is similar to that presented earlier in Chapters 7 and 10 except that regeneration is not required. PM synchronous machines are in use currently for the compressor drives used in the Toyota and Lexus hybrid electric vehicles. Pressure sensors from the high-pressure and low-pressure sides provide feedback to the motor controller to regulate the motor speed and torque for maintaining the desired cabin temperature. Position sensorless vector control with space vector PWM is the common choice of motor control used for these PM electric motor drives. Indirect position sensing is essential since there is not enough space available for mounting mechanical position sensors with the compressor integrated with the electric motor. The cold side of the compressor is conveniently used for cooling the IGBTs of the electric drive inverter.

The condenser provides the area for heat release of the refrigerant into the atmosphere. As the refrigerant fluid goes through the condenser, it cools off and condenses into high-pressure liquid which exits from the bottom. The condenser must be located in a position where there is sufficient air-flow. Engine-cooling fan can be utilized to radiate the heat from the condenser; alternatively, one or more electric cooling fans can be added for effective heat radiation.

The receiver-drier is located in the high-pressure side of the system right after the condenser. Its function is to store liquid refrigerant and remove moisture and dirt as the refrigerant circulates through the system. Removal of dirt is critical so as not to clog the expansion valve orifice which is next in line of the air-conditioning system.

The expansion valve receives the high-pressure liquid from the receiver-drier and allows the refrigerant pressure to drop so that it can change phase and become liquid. The valve controls the amount of refrigerant passing through its orifice so that liquid refrigerant can be delivered to the evaporator for evaporation.

The evaporator serves as the heat absorption unit and is located inside the vehicle. The liquid refrigerant evaporates by extracting heat from the warm air blown over the evaporator fins thereby cooling the cabin air. Refrigerants have very low boiling point and hence can absorb large amount of heat from the passing air and boil to low-pressure gas as it exits the evaporator. The heat carried off by the refrigerant is eventually released to the atmosphere at the condenser. Evaporator also serves as a dehumidifier adding to the passenger comfort level inside the cabin. As warmer air travels through the cooler fins of the evaporator, the moisture in the air condenses on its surface. Evaporator also acts as an air filter attracting dust and small particles from the air to stick to its wet surfaces which drains off to the outside of the vehicle.

Accumulators are connected at the outlet end of the evaporator to collect liquid refrigerant and also to remove moisture and dirt from the system similar to the receiver-drier. Function of the accumulator is critical to the compressor which can only compress gas and not liquid.

Climate control unit maintains the cabin temperature in a vehicle by controlling refrigerant pressure and flow into the evaporator. Pressure sensors, one in the high-pressure line and one in the low-pressure line, provide feedback to the control unit to maintain the pressure in the evaporator low to prevent it from freezing.

Refrigerant used in the automobiles is R-134a, which replaced the previously used Refrigerant R-12 due to the environmental concerns. R-134a operates at higher pressure levels than the R-12 which requires a more powerful compressor.

## 14.7.2 POWERTRAIN COMPONENT COOLING SYSTEM

Thermal system design and thermal management is a critical component in the performance and reliability of power electronics and electric machines. Electric and hybrid vehicles require adequate thermal management for the electric machines and drives as well as for additional power electronics component used such as the DC/DC converter for the high-voltage to low-voltage interface.

Heat energy is removed from the electric motor, motor drive and power electronic components by the methods of radiation and convection. *Thermal radiation* is the process by which energy is transported by electromagnetic waves with or without any intervening medium. This means that thermal radiation can take place even in vacuum. Electronic configuration changes in the atoms or molecules within a material result in thermal radiation. The rate of energy transfer from a system through thermal radiation is complicated involving the properties of the radiating surfaces and the energy absorbing medium. A modified form of the Stefan-Boltzmann law macroscopically quantifies the rate of energy transfer as [9]

$$\dot{Q}_{rad} = \varepsilon \sigma A T_b^{\,4} \qquad (14.29)$$

where $A$ is the surface area, $\varepsilon(\,0 \leq \varepsilon \leq 1)$ is the emissivity of the surface, $\sigma$ is the Stefan-Boltzmann constant and $T_b$ is the absolute temperature of the surface.

*Convection* refers to energy transfer between a solid surface at one temperature and an adjacent moving gas or liquid (to be referred to as fluid) at another temperature. Heat energy is conducted from the solid surface to the moving fluid through the combined effects of conduction within the fluid and the bulk motion of the fluid. The rate of energy transfer through convection can be evaluated through the following empirical formula [9]:

$$\dot{Q}_{conv} = hA(T_b - T_f) \qquad (14.30)$$

where $A$ is the surface area, $T_b$ is the temperature on the surface and $T_f$ is the fluid temperature. The heat transfer coefficient $h$ is an empirical parameter relating the properties and flow rate of the fluid, and the geometry of the system; this is not a thermodynamic property. Convection can be of two types; *forced* and *natural*. Fans or pumps used for forced convection would result in a higher heat transfer coefficient than in natural convection.

Development of the cooling system for electrical components starts with identifying the requirements which depend on the vehicle architecture and the rating of components within that architecture. The liquid cooled components and the air cooled components in the vehicle need to be identified first. The type of cooling to be employed depends on the cooling requirement as well as on the location of the component within the vehicle. Most of the power electronics and electric powertrain traction components use liquid cooling for compact packaging. In some cases, a liquid cooling system may already be available for other components in the vehicle, and it then becomes only an extension to add the electric drive components in the loop. The IC engine and automatic transmission are also liquid cooled. Traction batteries, especially those of NiMH types, and small electronics may be air cooled. However, advanced Li-ion batteries need to be liquid cooled. In determining the cooling requirements, the worst case operating scenarios of the components have to be evaluated. These include steep grades, hill holding, extreme temperatures and altitudes. Duty cycle of operation in the worst case scenarios have to be evaluated to distinguish between transient and continuous cooling loads. The continuous and maximum temperature ratings of the powertrain and electronic components vary widely depending on design and mission of the vehicle, and the type of component. In order to design for reliability and durability, the component cooling systems are often sized for peak operating conditions at maximum allowable temperatures. Power electronic components are highly sensitive to excessive temperatures compared to mechanical devices such as IC engines and transmission due to their much lower thermal mass.

Representative temperatures of powertrain and electronic components in a light-duty vehicle are given in Table 14.1 as a general reference. The allowable operating temperatures and liquid/air-flow rates are typically specified by the component manufacturer. The performance characteristics provided by the manufacturer showing efficiencies at various loads is very useful in targeting the operating points through the vehicle supervisory controller. Efficiencies along with the power ratings give a good starting point to calculate the heat load to be removed by the cooling system.

Liquid-cooled system includes a heat exchanger to reject heat into the environment and a coolant pump for forced circulation of the liquid coolant. Thermal analysis of the system yields the heat rejection, coolant mass flow rate and pump size required. In the case of air-cooled systems, fans and blowers are sized based on the amount of heat removal required.

**TABLE 14.1**

**Example Temperatures in Vehicle Components**

| Component | Continuous | Maximum |
|---|---|---|
| IC engine and transmission | 95°C | 120°C |
| Traction electric motor | 65°C | 75°C |
| Traction inverter, DC/DC converter | 65°C | 75°C |
| Electronic controllers | 65°C | 75°C |
| Traction batteries | 30°C | 55°C |

In a hybrid electric vehicle, multiple loops may be desired due to significantly different allowable operating temperatures. The number of coolant loops depends on the maximum component operating temperatures, coolant flow requirements, packaging of the component and proximity to other components within the same loop. The coolant loop design objective is to minimize plumbing complexity, length and restriction. The fill points and coolant reservoirs have to be incorporated within the coolant loops ensuring appropriate venting and degassing.

An example of hybrid electric vehicle powertrain component cooling system is shown in Figure 14.26. The powertrain architecture has two electric machines and an IC engine that needs to be liquid cooled. The inverters for the electric machines and the DC/DC converter also need to be liquid cooled. The battery is air-cooled using cabin air. Liquid cooling system is arranged in three loops: first loop is for cooling the IC engine and transmission, the second loop is for the traction motor and its inverter, and the third loop for the generator, its inverter and the DC/DC converter. Temperatures are monitored using sensors in the coolant loop for controlling the speed of the coolant pump. Devices will have internal temperature monitoring for thermal management, but it is advisable to monitor coolant temperatures at least in inlet locations especially during the development stages.

Three heat exchangers are shown in Figure 14.26 stacked in series which would be located in the front of the vehicle. IC Engine has a separate heat exchanger (i.e., radiator), while two electrical component cooling loops use one heat exchanger. The third heat exchanger is for the air-conditioning system of the vehicle which is not shown in the figure. Series arrangement of the heat

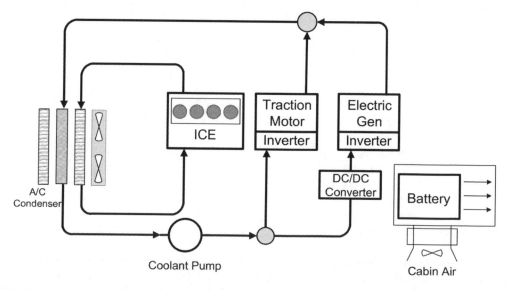

**FIGURE 14.26** Cooling loops in a hybrid electric vehicle.

exchangers provides efficient packaging, but requires higher total fan power requirements due to increased airside pressure loss, and shared fan control. In the series stacking, the lowest temperature heat exchanger must be placed first in the direction of airflow. Parallel stacking of heat exchangers maximizes the frontal area. Airflow into each heat exchanger can be optimally controlled by individual fan control. Forward-facing heat exchangers can benefit greatly from dynamic air pressure created by vehicle motion, but adequate airflow is necessary at lower speeds. Lower vehicle speeds provide the more challenging cooling system design requirements due to higher loads for the devices and inadequate airflow.

## PROBLEMS

### 14.1

An EV drive train employs a separately excited DC motor which drives the EV rear axle through a gear box as shown below in Figure P14.1.

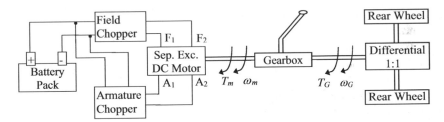

**FIGURE P14.1**

The vehicle is traveling in the fourth gear on a level road at constant velocity of 60 mph. All necessary parameters are as follows:

$mg = 6{,}867\,\text{N}$, $C_0 = 0.009$, $C_1 = 1.75\text{E-6}\,\text{s}^2/\text{m}^2$, $A_F = 2\,\text{m}^2$, $C_d = 0.2$, $\rho = 1.16\,\text{kg/m}^3$, $r_{wh} =$ wheel radius $= 7.5\,\text{in.}$, gear ratio GR $= 0.4$.
Motor parameters: $R_a = 0.2\,\Omega$, $R_F = 150\,\Omega$, $K = 0.8\,\text{V-s/Wb}$, $\phi = 3.75 I_F$, $B_g = 1.2 I_F$.

In the following calculations, assume no power loss from motor output to wheels and use motor power loss model given in class. Assume chopper outputs are pure DC.

    a. Calculate the operating speed and torque of the motor.
    b. For $0.5 \leq I_F \leq 4$ A, plot $I_A$ versus $I_F$.

## REFERENCES

1. R.L. Willis and J. Brandes, "Ford next generation electric vehicle powertrain," *12th Electric Vehicle Symposium*, Anaheim, CA, pp. 449–458, December 1994.
2. R.G. Budynas and J.K. Nisbett, *Mechanical Engineering Design*, McGraw Hill, New York, NY, 2008.
3. R. Stone and J.K. Ball, *Automotive Engineering Fundamentals*, SAE International, Warrendale, PS, 2004.
4. T.E. Scott, *Power Transmission Mechanical, Hydraulic, Pneumatic, and Electrical*, Prentice Hall, Upper Saddle River, NJ, 2000.
5. J.M. Miller, *Propulsions Systems for Hybrid Vehicles*, Institute of Electrical Engineers, London, 2004.
6. S. Underwood, A. Khalil, I. Husain, H. Klode, B. Lequesne, S. Gopalakrishnan and A. Omekanda, "Switched reluctance motor based electromechanical brake-by-wire system," *International Journal of Vehicle Autonomous Systems*, 2(3–4), 278–296, 2004.

7. A. Omekanda, B. Lequesne, H. Klode, S. Gopalakrishnan and I. Husain, "Switched reluctance and permanent magnet brushless motors in highly dynamic situations: A comparison in the context of electric brakes," *IEEE Industry Applications Magazine*, 15(4), 35–43, July/Aug. 2009.

8. H. Klode, A. Omekanda, B. Lequesne, S. Gopalakrishnan, A. Khalil, S. Underwood and I. Husain, "The potential of switched reluctance motor technology for electro-mechanical brake applications," Simulation and Modeling Mechatronics, SP2030, SAE Publication, Warrendale, PA, 2006.

9. M.J. Moran and H.N. Shapiro, *Fundamentals of Engineering Thermodynamics*, sixth edition, John Wiley & Sons, Inc., New York, NY, 2008.

10. R. Stone and J.K. Ball, *Automotive Engineering Fundamentals*, SAE International, Warrendale, PA, 2004.

# 15 Hybrid Vehicle Control Strategy

A hybrid electric vehicle powertrain comprises both electrical mechanical power transmission paths. The powertrain consists of multiple power sources and energy converters; the operation of each of these components needs to be coordinated. The powertrain components are arranged in various configurations depending on the vehicle architecture, although the most general ones are the series, parallel and power-split architectures. The control problem is to manage the power flow through the electrical and mechanical transmission paths through the coordinated use of the multiple components with a certain objective, such as maximizing fuel efficiency. The control strategy developed for the purpose is implemented in the vehicle supervisory controller. The supervisory controller shields the driver from a complicated control problem and ensures that the driver demand is continuously and consistently satisfied.

The control strategy is essentially an algorithm that determines the operating points of the vehicle powertrain components. The primary objective of the control strategy is to ensure that the driver demand is met, while the powertrain system efficiency is optimized. The primary inputs to the supervisory controller are the vehicle speed and the pedal inputs. Secondary inputs of roadway, traffic and GPS information may also be used in more advanced supervisory controllers. The outputs of the controller are the command signals for the powertrain components, such as electric motor or IC engine torque requests, and on/off commands for certain components.

The battery-pack or energy storage system (ESS) state of charge (SoC) levels must also be maintained within levels that extend the life of the system. The control strategy determines when and how much of deep discharge of the ESS will be allowed to meet a driver demand. Moreover, vehicle kinetic energy can be recuperated and stored in the ESS using regenerative braking when vehicle brake commands are in effect from the driver.

Additional goals targeted by the control strategy algorithm include all or some of the following: enhancing powertrain efficiency and/or fuel economy, reducing emissions and maintaining good drivability. Increasing fuel efficiency and reducing emissions are contending requirements; an optimization algorithm can be used to determine the best operating points of the IC engine. Drivability is also a key parameter for customer acceptance of hybrid vehicles; the controller must ensure that driver feel is almost the same as that of a conventional IC engine vehicle. The command changes for the various propulsion units must be carefully coordinated to maintain high drivability quality of the vehicle. Drivability can be measured in terms of gear shifting and driveline vibrations.

## 15.1 VEHICLE SUPERVISORY CONTROLLER

Vehicle supervisory controller sits in the middle of a multi-level hierarchical structure for the control of the hybrid vehicle powertrain. At the top control level is the driver, who uses speed and position feedback to set the accelerator and brake pedal inputs. The supervisory controller accepts the driver commands and accordingly controls the various powertrain subsystems. The subsystems, such as the electric motor drive, energy storage device, IC engine and starter/generator drive have their own controllers, but the operating set-points depend on the commands issued by the supervisory controller. The interactions between the driver, vehicle and supervisory controller in a simplistic representation are shown in Figure 15.1. The control strategy in the supervisory controller is implemented using feedback signals from all of the subsystem control modules. The supervisory controller communicates with the subsystems through a controller area network (CAN) and may

**FIGURE 15.1**   Driver interface with SCM and vehicle.

also receive direct inputs from sensors through A/D channels. The sensor data are not only used for control purposes, but can also be logged for performance analysis or for failure analysis if one or more subsystem components malfunction in the vehicle.

The driver communicates with the supervisory controller through the ignition switch, transmission shifter, accelerator pedal and brake pedal. The driver is at the top level of the controller who uses vehicle speed and driving condition feedback to set the accelerator and brake pedal inputs. Once the vehicle is ready to be driven, the pedal inputs are converted from position to driver demand. The supervisory controller-driver interface makes the control system transparent by interpreting the accelerator and brake pedal depressions as propulsion/braking power and torque requests.

The objective of the supervisory control strategy is to ensure that the driver demand is met, while the powertrain system efficiency is optimized. The inputs to the supervisory controller are the drive requests, and vehicle operating conditions such as speed and acceleration. Secondary inputs of roadway, traffic and GPS information may also be used in more advanced supervisory controllers. The outputs of the controller are the command signals for the powertrain components, such as electric motor or ICE torque requests, battery charging set points and on/off commands for certain components. Battery-pack or ESS demands are set within certain limits to extend the life of the system. The control strategy determines when and how much of deep discharge will be allowed to meet a driver demand. Supervisor controller also regulates the amount of kinetic energy should be recovered to recharge the batteries during vehicle braking.

The complexity of the control strategy depends on whether the hybrid architecture is compound, such as series-parallel or simple, such as series or parallel. The control strategy in a compound hybrid architecture can be implemented in a two-level structure: mode selection strategy and modal control strategy. The mode selection strategy determines the powertrain mode of operation, such as series or parallel. The modal control strategy addresses the controls within a specific hybrid operating mode. In simple hybrid architectures, such as in series or parallel hybrids, a one-level algorithm is sufficient; the supervisory controller implements the modal control strategy for hybrid operation. The two levels of control strategy are discussed in separate sections of this chapter. The mode selection strategy applies to only compound hybrid architectures, while the modal selection strategy applies to both compound and simple hybrid architectures.

## 15.2   MODE SELECTION STRATEGY

The mode selection strategy discussed in the context of a compound hybrid architecture assumes that there is one IC engine and at least two electric machines in the powertrain of the vehicle. Up to four fundamental operating modes are possible in the hybrid vehicle, which are electric only, series, parallel and power split. The mode selection strategies will be discussed in general since the constraints on the series mode of operation will be similar for a series hybrid electric vehicle to that of a vehicle that allows additional modes. Furthermore, the control strategies discussed are examples of a possible method of implementation. There can be various other mode selection strategies depending on the powertrain components available in the compound hybrid architecture, the relative sizes of the components and the goal of the control strategy.

The first decision to be made by the supervisory controller is the mode of operation of the powertrain. The decision is made primarily based on the driver demand and the vehicle speed. The torque request issued by the driver through the acceleration pedal input is converted into a driver power demand through the multiplication of the torque request with the vehicle speed. A propulsion mode is selected based on the driver power demand and the vehicle speed.

In the electric only mode, the stored energy in the battery or other ESS is used to drive one or more of the electric drive motors for propulsion. In the series mode, the energy stored in the fossil fuel is converted by the IC engine to mechanical form that runs an electric generator to produce electrical energy. The generated electricity is used by the electric drive motor to deliver traction power to the wheels. In the power-split mode, the IC engine provides traction power to the wheels through both the series electrical path and the direct mechanical path. The power from the IC engine is split through the mechanical and electrical transmission paths. For either series or split operation, the ESS can supply or absorb power depending on the power demand, the storage system SoC and IC engine efficiency considerations. In the parallel mode, the IC engine is operated up to its maximum capacity and the electric machines are operated in the motoring mode to provide propulsion power using stored energy from both the ESS and fossil fuel. The power-split mode differs from the parallel mode in that one of the electric machines is operated as a generator.

The mode selection for hybrid operation is governed by rule-based control laws that depend on current and past states of the vehicle operating point, driver power demand, the vehicle speed, and the ESS SoC. The rules are generated based on the operating limits of the subsystems, models or performance maps of subsystems, designer experience and heuristics. The concept of 'load-leveling' for energy management is often used in rule-based strategies. In this type of controls, one of the energy converters, such as the IC engine, is primarily used to supply propulsion power, while a subsidiary subsystem component, such as an electric motor, is called in to assist the IC engine to shift the operating point of the latter to a different location of increased fuel economy and reduced emissions. The rule-based strategies can be further divided into two categories as follows [1]:

*Deterministic Rule-Based Methods*: Deterministic rules are developed to determine the mode of hybrid operation and the conditions for switching from one mode to another [2,3]. The most popular deterministic rule-based strategy that is used in production hybrids is the power follower approach. The driver input is interpreted as a power request to decide the operating mode. Figure 15.2 shows

**FIGURE 15.2**  Hybrid vehicle modes of operation.

an example qualitative dependence of the operating mode on the driver power demand (accelerator input) and the vehicle speed. In a parallel or series-parallel hybrid vehicle, at low power demand levels only the electric motor is used below a minimum vehicle speed. If the power demand exceeds the minimum level, the engine turns-on. In a parallel hybrid, the electric motor would assist the engine only if the power demand is greater than the maximum engine power. In a series-parallel or power-split architecture, the powertrain would be in a power-split mode after the electric only mode. A series mode may be used between the electric only and split-mode for low power demands. Only at very high power demand levels, the parallel mode will be used. The battery SoC is also maintained within a preset band by using the drive electric motor in the generator mode in a pure parallel hybrid or using the generator of a series-parallel hybrid vehicle. The main disadvantage of the method is that the overall powertrain efficiency is not optimized.

The supervisory controller may also use a state machine to implement the mode selection strategy. The state machine executes the transitions between the various hybrid modes based on driver demand, vehicle speed, and subsystem operating limits and faults, if any. The implementation of supervisory controller through state machines facilitates fault management. Although powertrain efficiency optimization is typically not addressed at the state transition levels, such optimization can be addressed at the modal control algorithms.

*Fuzzy-Rule-Based Methods*: The hybrid powertrain is a nonlinear, multi-dimensional, time-varying plant, where fuzzy-logic-based mode selection strategy can be particularly useful [4–6]. The fuzzy-logic-based control systems uses the driver demand, vehicle speed, SoC, component torque outputs and estimated road load as inputs and a fuzzy-rule base to determine the operating mode of the vehicle. The main advantage of the fuzzy-rule base compared to a deterministic rule base is its robustness toward imprecise measurements and parameter variations. A well-designed fuzzy-rule base can give suboptimal performance of the powertrain in real time. The fuzzy rule-base includes weighted parameters that can be adapted in real time depending on the driving condition. A fuzzy-rule-based control algorithm can also be effectively utilized to develop a modal control strategy within a hybrid operating mode.

Deterministic rule-based method of control strategy is further elaborated with the help of series-parallel hybrid electric vehicle architectures. Series-parallel hybrid architectures with two electric machines and one IC engine can be implemented either using the mechanical device of planetary gear set or using electronic controls. The mode selection strategies for the two types of series-parallel hybrid vehicles appear below.

## 15.2.1  Mechanical Power-Split Hybrid Modes

The mechanically enabled power-split architecture uses a planetary or epicyclic gear set without any driveline clutches. The concept of power split using planetary gear set was first introduced by TRW [7,8]. The non-shifting transmission in a planetary gear set offers continuously variable transmission (CVT) like performance while enabling mounting of three powertrain components in a single driveline. The mechanical power-split architecture has rapidly become the design choice for hybrid sedans, light trucks and SUVs. The mechanical power-split design offers compactness and ease of assembly with the motor, generator and IC engine mounted in a single driveline.

A series-parallel power-split powertrain architecture using a planetary gear set similar to that used in the Toyota Prius is shown in Figure 15.3. As was presented earlier in Section 14.2.1, the planetary gear set has three gears, the ring, the sun and the planet carrier. The output shaft of the IC engine is connected to the planet carrier of the planetary gear set. The mechanical power is transferred to the final drive and the wheels from the IC engine indirectly through the ring gear. There is no direct coupling between the IC engine and the final drive. The generator is connected to the sun gear; the motor along with the wheels is connected to the ring gear. The IC engine power can be split and part of it be transferred to the final drive and the wheels through the sun gear and the electrical power transmission path. The IC engine drives the generator which either charges the

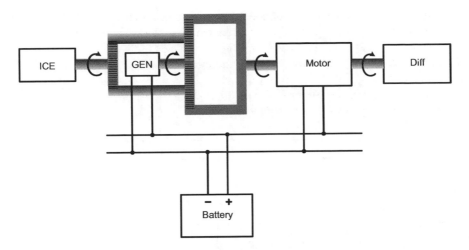

**FIGURE 15.3** Series-parallel HEV powertrain component arrangements with a planetary gear set.

battery or supplies electrical power to the motor or does both. The generator operation develops the reaction torque against the planet gear to which the shaft of the IC engine is coupled. The motor can add torque to the ring gear to provide additional power to the wheels. The generator can also be operated in the motoring mode during peak acceleration demand to add torque to the planet gear which then gets transmitted to the wheels through the ring gear. Both the electric machines can act either in the motoring mode or in the generating mode. During vehicle braking, the motor acts as a generator to capture regenerative braking energy, which is converted to electrical energy and stored in the battery. The several modes of operation possible through the planetary gear coupling and dual modes of the electric machines are described in further detail.

The speed-torque relationships among the ring, sun and planet carrier gears discussed earlier in Section 14.2.1 apply to the hybrid powertrain architecture presented here, and will be used in this section. The power relationship in the power-split hybrid vehicle from Equation 14.13 is

$$P_{engine} = P_{engine\,to\,ring} + P_{engine\,to\,sun}$$

$$\Rightarrow T_p \omega_p = \frac{r_r \omega_r}{r_r + r_s} T_p + \frac{r_s \omega_s}{r_r + r_s} T_p \tag{15.1}$$

The rotational directions shown in Figure 15.3 for the three gears connected to the three powertrain components will be assumed to be the positive direction of rotation.

### 15.2.1.1 Electric Only (Low Speeds, Reverse, Battery Charging)

In this mode, the IC engine is off and the planet carrier is stationary, i.e., $\omega_p = 0$. The starter/generator rotates freely under no-load condition in the reverse direction. The speed relation between the starter/generator and the electric motor is given by (from Equation 14.11)

$$r_r \omega_r = -r_s \omega_s.$$

The electric motor supplies the traction power to the wheels being driven by the battery energy as shown in Figure 15.4. No power is transmitted through the planetary gear set. The accelerator position (power demand) and vehicle speed determine the motor current set point.

$$I_{motor} \propto T_{motor} = \frac{P_{motor}}{\omega_r} \tag{15.2}$$

**FIGURE 15.4**  Electric-only mode of operation.

The batteries can be recharged using the regeneration control strategy with the electric machine operated in the generator mode when the vehicle is coasting or braking and the engine turned off.

### 15.2.1.2  Engine Starting (Low Speeds)

The starter/generator operates in the motoring mode to crank the engine. The motoring mode is enabled with a positive torque command while it is rotating in the reverse direction causes the power to flow from the battery to the starter/generator to the IC engine. The vehicle may be moving during engine starting with the traction power provided by the electric motor. The source of energy during engine starting is the battery.

### 15.2.1.3  Parallel Mode (Heavy Acceleration)

The powertrain operates in the parallel mode for heavy acceleration which can be demanded during vehicle launch. The starter/generator and motor both assist the IC engine using battery power. The power flow in the parallel mode is shown in Figure 15.5.

**FIGURE 15.5**  Parallel operation of electrical and mechanical powertrain components.

The starter/generator power using Equation 15.1 is given by

$$P_{sun\,to\,ring} = \frac{r_s \omega_s}{r_r + r_s} T_p, \quad \omega_s < 0 \tag{15.3}$$

The sun gear rotates in the reverse direction, i.e., counter-clockwise looking into the generator shaft from the gear, which makes $P_{sun\,to\,ring} < 0$. The reverse rotation of the sun gear increases IC engine torque enabling the starter/generator to deliver motoring torque to the final drive. The starter/generator input is electrical power from the battery.

### 15.2.1.4 Power-Split Mode (Cruise, Light Acceleration)

In this mode, the IC engine power is split between the starter/generator and the motor shaft as shown in Figure 15.6. The motor assists the engine by adding more torque to the differential input shaft of the final drive. At the same time, some engine power may be diverted to the sun gear to run the starter/generator in the generating mode to charge the battery. The starter/generator is rotating in the forward direction. The IC engine power flow to the starter/generator, and hence to the battery, is regulated by controlling the IC engine speed, since the percentage of engine torque transferred to the starter/generator is mechanically fixed. The battery power required determines the starter/generator current, which is turn, sets the starter/generator torque. The IC engine speed control will be discussed further later.

$$I_{gen} \rightarrow T_s = \frac{r_s}{r_r + r_s} T_p \tag{15.4}$$

This sun gear torque in turn fixes the engine torque $T_p$; therefore, the IC engine must be speed controlled.

### 15.2.1.5 Engine Brake Mode (Driver Selectable Mode)

In this mode, the IC engine is idling and absorbs some power. The motor is rotating freely ($I_{motor} = 0$). The starter/generator is rotating in the reverse direction and generating. The power flow in this mode is shown in Figure 15.7.

**FIGURE 15.6** Power-split mode of operation.

**FIGURE 15.7**   Engine brake mode of operation.

### 15.2.1.6   Regeneration Mode (Vehicle Braking)

In this mode, the generator is rotating freely ($I_g = 0$). The motor is being driven by the kinetic energy of the vehicle and is regenerating delivering energy to the battery. The power flow in this mode is shown in Figure 15.8.

### 15.2.2   SERIES-PARALLEL 2 × 2 HYBRID MODES

The series-parallel $2 \times 2$ architecture is an electronically controlled power-split architecture (see Figure 15.9). The IC engine is coupled to the front wheels through a clutch and transmission while the starter/generator is coupled to an output shaft of the IC engine. The electric motor powers the rear wheels providing a four-wheel drive capability. The architecture allows for great flexibility in the modes of operation of the hybrid electric vehicle

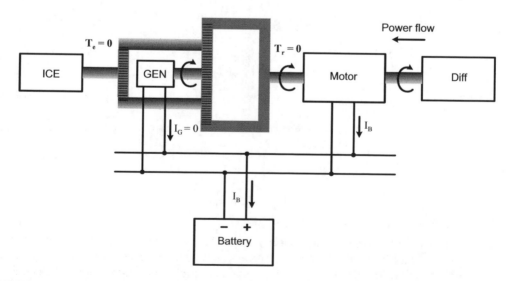

**FIGURE 15.8**   Vehicle regeneration mode.

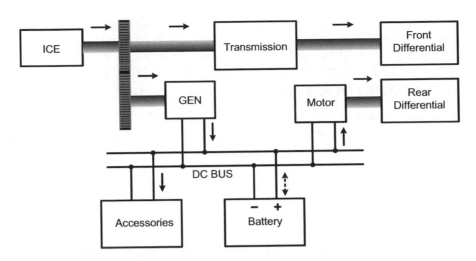

**FIGURE 15.9**   Series-parallel $2 \times 2$ architecture.

### 15.2.2.1   Electric Only (Low Speeds, Reverse, Battery Charging)
Keeping the IC engine off and leaving the clutch disengaged, the vehicle can be operated as an electric vehicle by using the rear traction motor. The stored energy in the battery or any other type of storage device is used to power the electric motor which supplies traction power to the rear wheels through the rear differential. The batteries can be recharged using the regeneration control strategy with the electric motor operated in the generator mode when the vehicle is coasting or braking and the engine turned off.

### 15.2.2.2   Series Mode (Lower Speeds)
The vehicle can also be operated as a series hybrid within the limitations of the electric generator especially in urban driving conditions when the driver power demand is relatively low. The total IC engine torque is delivered to the generator which supplies the electric motor with the storage system acting as the buffer. The electric motor delivers traction power to the rear wheels. The transmission is held in neutral in the series mode.

### 15.2.2.3   Power-Split Mode (Cruise, Light Acceleration)
When the speed reaches a threshold or the power requested is more than that can be provided in the series mode, the clutch is engaged and the IC engine provides propulsion power through the transmission. In this mode of operation, the IC engine speed is set by the power-split control mode algorithm which will be discussed later. Power from the IC engine is delivered to the front wheels and the rear wheels through the mechanical transmission path and the electrical transmission path, respectively. Using both the electric machines this power-split operation is similar to the mechanical power-split that has a planetary gear set. The power-split ratio between the mechanical and electrical transmissions can be arbitrarily chosen by the generator loading in contrast to the mechanical power-split hybrid. The power-split proportions may be chosen to optimize ESS usage and to maintain a desirable front-to-rear traction force ratio, subject to transient smoothing considerations.

### 15.2.2.4   Parallel Mode (Heavy Acceleration)
In the parallel mode which is used during high driver demands, the IC engine and the two electric machines all work in parallel to deliver traction power to the wheels. The electric generator is operated in the motoring mode, and the IC engine and electric generator torque blended at the IC engine-generator coupling is delivered to the front wheels. The electric motor simultaneously

delivers traction power to the rear wheels. The energy for both the electric machines comes from the ESS; this is a charge depleting operation, and hence, is not sustainable for long duration. This can be used as a boost mode of the vehicle utilized during heavy acceleration demands.

## 15.3   MODAL CONTROL STRATEGIES

The modal control algorithms uses the driver demand and system feedback inputs to satisfy the demand while optimizing the driveline system efficiency and minimizing the emissions. The energy storage SOC is also maintained within a preset band to meet the performance requirements without damaging the system. Control laws within the modal control strategy determine the best reference torques for the energy converters and the best gear ratio for the transmission. The control laws can be generated based on an optimization algorithm where a cost function representing fuel economy, emissions, motor efficiency, or battery life is minimized. A global optimization to achieve the best fuel efficiency depends on a priori knowledge of power demand and driving conditions, which is only possible in simulation. A global optimization based on fixed driving cycles can be used to determine the rules for real-time power flow management. In real driving scenarios, a real-time optimization-based control strategy can be developed [9–10]. An instantaneous cost function defined in terms of real-time variables is used for such an optimization strategy.

The powertrain subsystems place constraints on the maximum continuous and peak power that the can be provided in the series, parallel and power-split modes. However, the modal control algorithms share common calculations to determine the maximum power that the IC engine, motor and generator can provide. The calculations are based on the device ratings, temperature, DC-link bus voltage, vehicle speed and other parameters that determine the limits on the operating points for each subsystem. For example, the motor power limit can be reduced as a function of bus voltage. The bus voltage depends on the energy storage SoC. The objective of motor power reduction for reduced voltages is to ensure acceptable drivability by eliminating sudden reduction in acceleration if the electric motor enters a shutdown mode when the battery runs out of energy. The power limit for the electric motor also depends on the temperature. The motor ratings are derated for elevated temperatures of operation.

Series, parallel and power-split modes require different control algorithms. The optimization techniques, if used, for the different modal control strategies are also different. The following discusses modal control strategies along with examples of optimization techniques. It must be mentioned that the modal control strategies discussed in this section are only examples; there can be various other ways of implementing a modal control strategy depending on the size of the powertrain components available, and the desired optimization strategy.

### 15.3.1   SERIES CONTROL

In a series hybrid or in the series mode of a multi-mode hybrid, the electric motor provides all of the traction power demand measured off of the accelerator pedal. The IC engine, the generator and the ESS must ensure that sufficient electrical power is available for the electric motor at all times to meet the driver demand. In urban driving, the power demand varies greatly due to variations in vehicle speed and frequent start/stop operation; the hybrid electric vehicle undergoes a highly variable battery discharge/charge profile. The average power required by the motor is relatively low, compared to the peak transient power requirements during the peak acceleration demands.

The IC engine is buffered from the vehicle load variations by a passive control algorithm of the ESS charge which is independent of the active vehicle powertrain control. The ESS control is based on an on/off control method, which is also known as thermostat control of the IC engine. The criterion for on-off control can be set by the SoC limits of the battery. The maximum and minimum SoC limits are set such that the driver demand can be met by the electric motor at all times. The thermostat control of the engine to maintain the SoC within specified limits is shown in Figure 15.10.

The objective in the series mode is to maintain the IC engine speed and torque at the most efficient operating point. An example selection of the IC engine 'on' operating point in series mode is explained with the help of the torque-speed characteristics of the engine and the generator. The 'on' operating point of the IC engine may be chosen based on fuel economy, emissions and the characteristics of the electric generator. If only high fuel economy is targeted, the engine should operate in a region of low brake-specific fuel consumption (BSFC). The baseline engine maps including the BSFC and BSNOx data of a 1.9 L diesel engine are shown in Figures 15.11 and 15.12 [11]. The continuous and peak torque curves of a permanent magnet electric generator reflected through engine-generator coupling gear are superimposed on both plots. The engine maps show that the regions of operation with low fuel consumption also yield high $NO_x$ generation. Considering the generator characteristics, the target operation should be at the point where the generator goes from torque to power limited along the continuous generation threshold where its efficiency is also relatively high. The generator is torque limited below the corner speed and not capable of its maximum possible continuous power generation; operation in this region will increase the time that the IC engine must run to recharge the ESS in series mode before it is shut down.

Selecting the 'on' operating point near corner point of the PM generator will cause a slight increase in the BSFC from the minimum of 0.20313 kg/(kWh), but works out quite favorably in terms of emissions. The $NO_x$ emissions around the corner point are significantly below the maximum of 0.0097 kg/(kWh). The optimum 'on' operating point is in the corner region where it produces relatively low emissions, and exhibits reasonable efficiency while allowing the generator to run close to its maximum continuous power rating (37.5 N m, 4,750 rpm) [11].

### 15.3.2  PARALLEL CONTROL

The parallel mode control algorithm delivers power to wheels through both the electric machine and the engine to meet the driver demand. The torque from the two devices may be blended before being delivered to a set of wheels or could be separately delivered to the front and rear wheels. In either case, the control algorithm must additionally ensure that the energy storage SoC is maintained within a band and a compromise operating point between fuel efficiency and tailpipe emissions is selected for the IC engine.

**FIGURE 15.10**   IC engine usage and battery SoC.

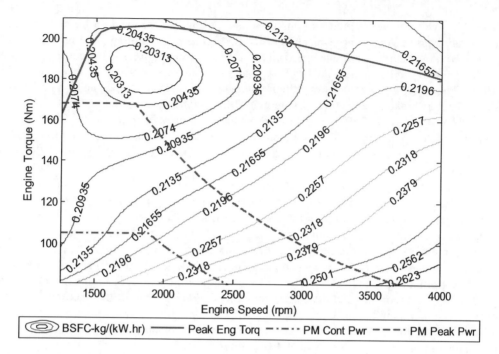

**FIGURE 15.11** BSFCs for 1.9 L diesel engine [11].

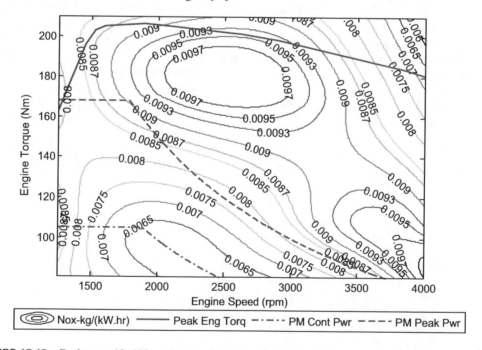

**FIGURE 15.12** Brake-specific $NO_x$ emissions for 1.9 L diesel engine [11].

The IC engine operating speed is matched with the vehicle speed through the transmission gear ratio. The transmission gear shifting strategy is an essential component in the parallel control strategy. Following the gear selection, the control strategy determines the torque commands for the engine and the electric motor to meet the driver demand and manage the energy storage. The goal of the shifting strategy is to match the vehicle speed with the IC engine speed at its best operating

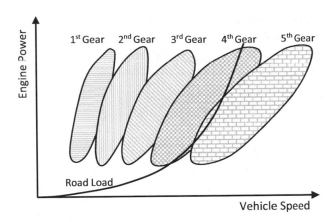

**FIGURE 15.13** Regions of higher IC engine efficiency reflected through each gear ratio.

region. There must also be sufficient hysteresis built into the strategy to prevent frequent shifting for an acceptable drivability.

In an IC engine powertrain, the regions of higher IC engine efficiency in the engine power-vehicle speed plane are smaller for lower gears than it is for higher gears. A qualitative plot showing regions of higher engine efficiency operation reflected through each gear ratio as a function of vehicle speed is shown in Figure 15.13[12]. The plot shows that the overlap regions decrease significantly for lower gears, which makes it more difficult to prevent frequent shifting at lower vehicle speeds. A sufficiently large hysteresis band even at the cost of sacrificing efficiency is needed at lower speeds to prevent frequent shifting for acceptable drivability. At higher vehicle speeds, the larger hysteresis band poses much less of a problem since there is a lot of overlap. The road-load characteristic for a zero percent grade roadway is shown in the figure to emphasize that engine efficiency has to be sacrificed at lower speeds.

The IC engine and the electric motor have their own high efficiency operating regions. In a parallel hybrid vehicle, the vehicle will operate in electric only mode for very low speeds and low power. The IC engine alone is used for propulsion above the minimum power demand level in most parallel control strategies. When the power demand exceeds the capacity of the IC engine, the electric motor is called in to assist the IC engine in the pure parallel mode. In the parallel mode, there is not much of an opportunity to optimize the algorithm for fuel efficient operation, since the operating region of the IC engine is set by the vehicle speed and transmission gear, while the electric motor speed is directly related to vehicle speed. In a series-parallel hybrid vehicle, the parallel mode of operation can be used as the boost mode for the vehicle where meeting the high power demand becomes critical.

### 15.3.3 SERIES-PARALLEL CONTROL

The series-parallel architecture has two electric machines and an IC engine; the power flow can be through the series path, the parallel path or the combination of the two, which is known as the power-split path. The various power flow path options available in this architecture makes the control strategy design complicated, but at the same time, it provides the flexibility to choose one or more of the available power flow paths to maximize the vehicle efficiency for the given driving condition.

The series-parallel architecture with a power-split path can be implemented using a mechanical device coupling or through electronic coupling of the powertrain components. The control strategies of the two types are discussed below.

### 15.3.3.1 Mechanical Power-Split IC Engine Control

The fuel flow rate is determined by the power requirement, which corresponds to the accelerator pedal input. The load torque can be controlled by the generator through its torque control. The control equation presented earlier in Equation 15.4 is repeated here for convenience:

$$I_{gen} \rightarrow T_{gen} = T_s = \frac{r_s}{r_r + r_s} T_p, \; (T_p = \text{engine torque})$$

where generator torque $T_{gen}$ is the same as the sun gear torque. It has been assumed that the engine power requirement is constant; also that all power comes from the IC engine, and that there are no transmission losses. The primary input-output variables for the IC engine operation is shown in Figure 15.14. The constant engine power curve is shown in Figure 15.15. The starter/generator command $I_{gen}$ can be manipulated to operate the engine at the best operating point along the curve. When $I_{gen}$ is set at a higher level, the IC engine torque $T_{ICE}$ (which is the same as the planet gear torque $T_p$) is also high; consequently, more power is delivered to the wheels directly, and less power to the starter/generator. The lower $T_{ICE}$ operating point for a smaller $I_{gen}$ command represents more power to the starter/generator and less power to the wheels from the IC engine; the electric motor torque command can be increased to maintain the same power to be delivered to the wheels, if required, but with increased power flow through the electric power transmission path. Therefore, the power-split ratio between the sun gear (starter/generator) and the ring gear (wheels) can be adjusted by varying the $I_{gen}$ command.

A possible criterion to choose the operating point is maximization of engine fuel efficiency, which is given by

$$\eta_{fuel} = \frac{\text{Engine power}}{\text{Fuel flow rate} \times \text{HHV}}$$

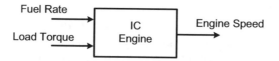

**FIGURE 15.14**   IC engine operation.

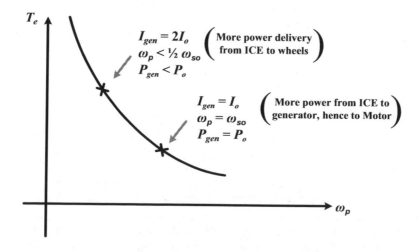

**FIGURE 15.15**   Constant IC engine power curve.

The constant efficiency curves on the engine performance map are shown in Figure 15.16. The best operating point is along a given curve of constant power where that curve is a tangent to a constant efficiency curve. The feedback control system that can be used to keep the IC engine operating along the set of optimal (i.e., the most engine fuel-efficient) points is shown in Figure 15.17. The IC engine speed and torque are maintained at the desired best operating points by controlling the starter/generator current. The power demand translated from the accelerator pedal input is used to control the fuel flow rate. The desired operating point trajectory is shown in Figure 15.18.

### 15.3.3.2 Series-Parallel 2 × 2 Control

In the hybrid architecture shown in Figure 15.9, the electric generator is coupled to the IC engine through a fixed gear-ratio, while the electric motor is coupled to the wheels through another fixed gear ratio. The torque relationships between the powertrain components are derived based on the electric generator and motor speeds reflected to the IC engine side through these fixed gear ratios. The speed relationships when the transmission gear is engaged are

$$\omega_{gen} = \omega_{ICE}$$

$$\omega_{motor} = \omega_{vehicle} = n_{TX} \cdot \omega_{ICE}$$

where $\omega_{gen}$, $\omega_{ICE}$, $\omega_{motor}$ and $\omega_{vehicle}$ are the electric generator, IC engine, electric motor and final drive speeds, respectively, and $n_{TX}$ is the transmission gear ratio. Since the final drive and electric motor speeds are the same when the transmission is engaged, it follows that

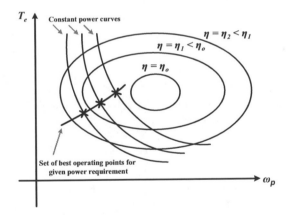

**FIGURE 15.16**  Best IC engine operating points along constant power curves.

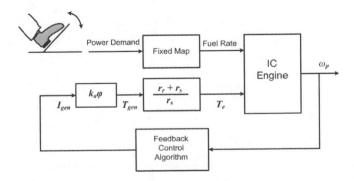

**FIGURE 15.17**  IC engine and starter/generator control system.

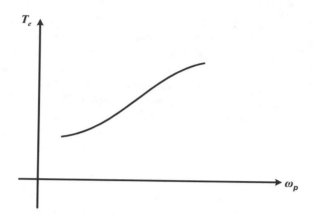

**FIGURE 15.18**   Best IC engine operating points.

$$\omega_{motor} = n_{TX} \cdot \omega_{gen}$$

Also, assume that all of the generator power is transmitted to the wheels through the electric motor using the electric power transmission path. Neglecting all the drivetrain losses, we have

$$T_{motor} = \frac{T_{gen}}{n_{TX}}$$

The traction torque from the hybrid powertrain is

$$T_{TR} = \frac{T_{TX}}{n_{TX}} + T_{motor} = \frac{T_{TX}}{n_{TX}} + \frac{T_{gen}}{n_{TX}}$$

$$\Rightarrow T_{TR} = \frac{1}{n_{TX}} \cdot (T_{TX} + T_{gen}) \tag{15.5}$$

However, the torque produced by the IC engine is delivered to the generator and the transmission giving

$$T_{ICE} = T_{TX} + T_{gen} = n_{TX} \cdot T_{TR} \tag{15.6}$$

Using Equation 15.5, the IC engine torque given by Equation 15.6 is independent of the generator torque. It can be concluded from the analysis that the IC engine set point is determined by the vehicle speed $\omega_{vehicle}$ and the transmission gear ratio $n_{TX}$. The control strategy is shown graphically in Figure 15.19. The proportions of torque delivered to the wheels in the power-split mode through the mechanical and electrical power transmission path may be arbitrarily determined by the generator loading. The proportions for power split and torque split are equal. In the extreme cases of power-split mode, the vehicle operation reverts to using only the mechanical power transmission path or the electrical power transmission path. When the generator torque command is zero, i.e., $T_{gen} = 0$, the IC engine alone delivers traction power to the wheels; when the IC engine is loading only the generator, i.e. $T_{gen} = T_{ICE}$, the vehicle is in the series operation mode, and the transmission can be disengaged.

### 15.3.4   Energy Storage System Control

The energy storage SoC is maintained by recharging the batteries through either a generator coupled to the engine or running the electric motor in the generating mode if the vehicle has only one electric machine. For a series or series-parallel hybrid architecture, the IC engine power demand has to be

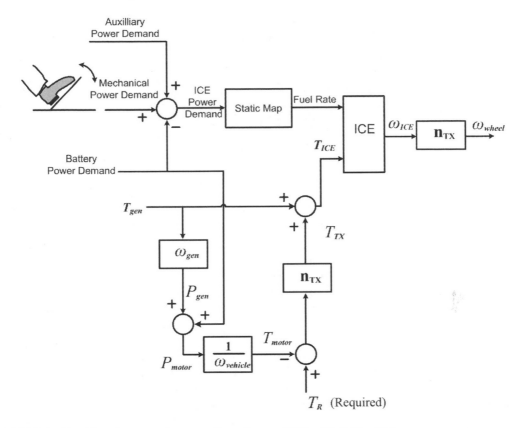

**FIGURE 15.19**   IC engine control strategy for series-parallel 2 × 2 hybrid vehicle.

increased by the amount of electrical power needed to recharge the energy storage. These vehicles have at least two electric machines in the powertrain; the energy storage devices can be recharged while delivering propulsion power through both the IC engine and the electric motor simultaneously. For a parallel vehicle, the parallel mode of operation must be ceased before the energy storage device can be recharged if there is no separate generator present in the hybrid powertrain.

The above discussion leads to the fact that the power demand from the IC engine in a hybrid vehicle depends not only on the driver demand for vehicle propulsion, but also on the ESS charge control algorithm. The thermostat control of the IC engine for a series vehicle, discussed earlier in Section 15.3.1, is a method of ESS charge control where the vehicle powertrain alternates between series mode and electric only mode for the 'on' operating point and 'off' condition of the IC engine, respectively, depending on the SoC limits set in the control algorithm. With wider SoC limits, the battery pack reaches a lower SoC level before the IC engine restarts for the battery recharging using the starter/generator. A narrower band results in lighter use of the battery pack and more frequent on/off operation of the IC engine. The cycling period of the IC engine also depends on the driver power demand. A variable set of SoC limits depending on the driver power demand can be used to attain a compromise between the cycling of IC engine and the use of the battery pack.

Let us now discuss possible variations in power demand that can be used in a series-parallel vehicle for better IC engine efficiency by energy buffering the ESS while delivering the same traction power at the wheels. We will consider the series-parallel 2 × 2 hybrid architecture, shown in Figure 15.9, for this discussion. The thermostat control of the IC engine can be applied for mode selection between series and electric only for lower driver demands. For driver demands below the maximum generator power, the SoC limits essentially determine the vehicle mode. This is the region shown in the lower left section of Figure 15.2. For higher driver demand levels, the power-split strategy in the series-parallel 2 × 2

**FIGURE 15.20**  Power-split strategy for a given speed when ESS is within limits.

hybrid can be designed to operate the IC engine at an optimum operating point given the speed of the IC engine and the SoC of the ESS. In the power-split mode, both the electric machines are available for operation to assist in satisfying the driver demand and maintaining the energy storage SoC within the acceptable limits. The best operating power level for the IC engine is first selected based on the vehicle speed, the transmission gear ratio and the driver demand. If the driver power demand matches the best IC engine operating power level, then the IC engine alone can be used to meet the driver demand and zero torque commands are dispatched to the electric generator and the electric motor. If the driver power demand is larger than the best power level for the IC engine, then the electric motor can be called in to provide additional power to the wheels. If the drive demand is less than the best IC engine power level, then the electric generator can be used to recharge the energy storage thereby providing additional load to the IC engine. This example of power-split control strategy for following the best IC engine operating power level is shown graphically in Figure 15.20.

### 15.3.5  REGENERATION CONTROL

The regeneration control algorithm allows the recovery of a part of the propulsion energy converted into kinetic energy through the electric machine instead of being wasted in the friction brakes of the vehicle. The electric machine runs as a generator in this mode following a negative torque request command from the supervisory controller converting mechanical energy into electrical energy and storing it in the energy storage device.

The regenerative control algorithm can be designed based on three components: the maximum amount of regeneration torque, the rate of change of torque command, and the relationship of the pedal position to the torque command [12]. The maximum amount of regenerative torque which is typically interpreted as negative torque is limited by the capacity of electric machine and its power electronic drive. The maximum allowed regenerative torque can be made a function of the vehicle speed to meet the drivability requirements. A rate limit on the torque command change can be imposed for driver comfort and acceptable drivability. A limit on the jerk is necessary for driver comfort during changes in negative torque command. The pedal position input has to be mapped to a driver request curve based on the maximum torque and the maximum jerk.

In a hybrid vehicle, the regenerative algorithm could implement full regenerative braking where driver inputs from both the acceleration pedal as well as the brake pedal are utilized in determining the negative torque request for the electric machine. For safety concerns, the vehicle must be fitted with friction brakes even though the electric machines are capable of providing braking action. The regenerative braking causes drivability concerns at very low vehicle speeds, and is not capable of braking action at zero vehicle speed. The travel of the brake pedal is mapped into a braking command which is distributed between the mechanical friction brakes and the regenerative brakes. If the electric motor is connected to the front wheels of the hybrid, then applying regenerative braking

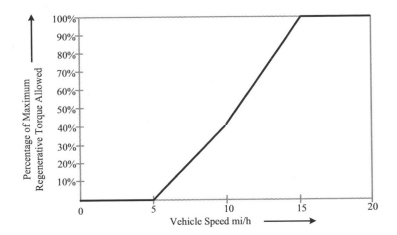

**FIGURE 15.21** Derating of regeneration torque as a function of speed to eliminate driveline shudder.

to the front wheels would assist the friction brakes and still maintain an acceptable bias between front and rear wheel braking. If the electric machine is connected to the rear wheels, then most of the rear wheel braking can be accomplished through regenerative braking, since only about a quarter of total braking action is executed in the rear wheels. The full regenerative braking scheme would contribute to improved fuel economy at the expense of complicating the vehicle braking system. In hybrids converted from conventional vehicles, this entails modifying hydraulic pressures on the brakes to reduce the friction brake command by the amount compensated by the regenerative braking. The control algorithm must ensure that vehicle braking safety is not compromised under any circumstances.

The driver comfort may be compromised by use of excessive regeneration at low vehicle speeds; therefore, the regeneration command should be disabled for those speeds. As the vehicle speed increases, the percentage of maximum allowable regeneration power or torque can be gradually increased. A piecewise linear increase of allowed regeneration torque between 5 and 15 mph is shown in Figure 15.21 for the Akron hybrid vehicle [12]. The absolute value of vehicle speed has been used to account for vehicle driving in reverse. Regeneration strategy following a profile of constant power, constant torque or a combination of the two is possible, but test drivers felt the most comfortable with a constant torque regeneration profile as shown in the figure.

The acceleration pedal input must also be mapped into a regeneration request; a piecewise linear mapping used in the Akron hybrid vehicle is shown in Figure 15.22 [12]. The regeneration strategy affects the drivability of the vehicle during both acceleration and deceleration. The drivers of hybrid vehicles feel comfortable with a constant negative torque when letting up the accelerator pedal. The dotted line in Figure 15.22 indicates the division between requests for propulsion and regeneration. Pedal positions less than 10% of the total pedal travel correspond to regeneration request or negative torque command for the electric machine. The linear mapping inversely translates 0% pedal position to the maximum regeneration torque request $T_{regen,max}$ and 10% pedal position to zero regeneration torque request. $T_{regen,max}$ request also has to be a function of the energy storage SoC. If the SoC is at its upper limit at $SoC_{max}$, then $T_{regen,max}$ has to be reduced to zero; in contrast, if the SoC is at its lower limit at $SoC_{min}$, then $T_{regen,max}$ can be set to the maximum regeneration torque capability of the electric machine. The segment of the curve in Figure 15.22 representing the pedal position for propulsion has been shifted and scaled using piecewise-linear mapping from the range [10%, 100% of modified pedal position] to [0, 100% of available power]. The driver power demand can be converted to torque demand through dividing the power demand by the vehicle speed.

The propulsion torque request from the electric machine should also be limited by the energy storage SoC condition. The torque request corresponds to the driver demand related to the accelerator pedal position and vehicle hybrid operating mode less a bias that depends on the SoC. The

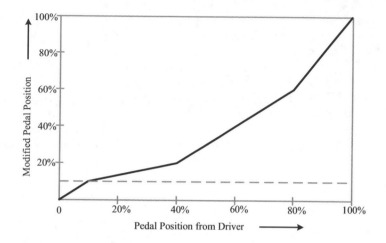

**FIGURE 15.22** Piecewise linear mapping of pedal position from driver input.

regeneration or negative torque request from the electric machine can be directly linked to this bias. The less the energy storage SoC, the less the electric motor should assist propulsion, and the higher should be the magnitude for $T_{regen,max}$. The energy storage SoC would have to be elevated from $SoC_{min}$ with regeneration even when the accelerator pedal is not depressed at all, especially in the case of parallel hybrid vehicles. The bias to be subtracted from the propulsion torque request for the electric machine can be configured as

$$B = \frac{SoC_{max} - SoC}{SoC_{max} - SoC_{min}} \times 100\%$$

According the above relation, if $SoC \geq SoC_{max}$, then no bias is subtracted and full propulsion or positive torque request is passed through to the electric machine. If $SoC < SoC_{min}$, then 100% bias is subtracted, and transmitted torque request for the electric machine is always negative to recharge the energy storage.

## PROBLEMS

### 15.1

The supervisory control module (SCM) of a series-parallel $2 \times 2$ hybrid vehicle has the inputs and outputs as shown in Figure P15.1.

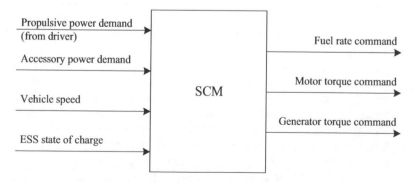

**FIGURE P15.1**

The vehicle is cruising at constant speed on a level road in power-split mode. The stored energy in the ESS is constant. Answer the following questions qualitatively.

a. The accessory power demand increases suddenly because the cabin air conditioner (powered by an electric motor) turns on. How should the SCM adjust its outputs to accommodate this increase while maintaining the vehicle propulsive power level and the ESS conditions?

b. The overall power demand remains constant, but the SCM decides that the ESS stored energy needs to be increased. How should the SCM adjust its outputs to cause the ESS to be charged while maintaining the vehicle propulsive and accessory power levels?

c. The driver increases the propulsive power demand slightly while ascending a grade. How should the SCM adjust its outputs to accommodate this increase while maintaining the accessory power level and the ESS conditions?

d. The driver demands maximum propulsive power to accelerate and pass another vehicle. How should the SCM adjust its outputs to draw maximum power from the ESS and accommodate this demand?

## 15.2

A planetary gear set is used in the powertrain of mechanical power-split series-parallel hybrid electric vehicle. The ring of the gear set is connected to the motor/differential, the planet carrier is connected to the IC engine and the sun is connected to the starter/generator. In this hybrid vehicle, the ring to sun gear radii ratio is given as $\frac{r_r}{r_s} = 2.8$.

In one vehicle operating condition, the ring power demand is $P_{ring} = 32\,kW$ corresponding to the ring speed of $\omega_r = 180\,rad/s$. The ring speed is directly related to the vehicle speed, since it is connected to the electric motor and wheels. The IC engine speed is controlled at 2,100 rpm.

Calculate the (a) ring torque, (b) ICE torque and (c) generator speed.

## REFERENCES

1. F.R. Salmasi, "Control strategies for hybrid electric vehicles: Evolution, classification, comparison and future trends," *IEEE Transactions on Vehicular Technology*, 56(5), 2393–2404, September 2007.
2. V.H. Johnson, K.B. Wipke and D.J. Rausen, "HEV control strategy for realtime optimization off fuel economy and emissions," SAE Paper 2000-01-1543, 2000.
3. A.M. Phillips, M. Jankovic and K. Bailey, "Vehicle system controller design for a hybrid electric vehicle," *Proceedings of IEEE International Conference on Control Applications*, Anchorage, AK, pp. 297–302, September 25–27, Anchorage, AK, 2000.
4. H.-D. Lee and S.-K. Sul, "Fuzzy-logic-based torque control strategy for parallel-type hybrid electric vehicle," *IEEE Transactions on Industrial Electronics*, 45(4), 625–632, August 1998.
5. J.-S. Won and R. Langari, "Fuzzy torque distribution control for a parallel hybrid vehicle," *Expert Systems: International Journal Knowledge Engineering and Neural Networks*, 19(1), 4–10, February 2002.
6. B.M. Baumann, G. Washington, B.C. Glenn and G. Rizzoni, "Mechatronic design and control of hybrid electric vehicles," *IEEE/ASME Transactions on Mechatronics*, 5(1), 58–71, March 2000.
7. J.M. Miller, *Propulsions Systems for Hybrid Vehicles*, Institute of Electrical Engineers, London, 2004.
8. G.H. Gelb, N.A. Richardson, T.C. Wang and B. Berman, "An electromechanical transmission for hybrid vehicle powertrains – design, and dynamometer testing," SAE Congress Paper No. 710235, Detroit, MI, January 1971.
9. G. Paganelli, G. Ercole, A. Brahma, Y. Guezennec and G. Rizzoni, "General supervisory control policy for the energy optimization of charge sustaining hybrid electric vehicles," *Journal of Society of Automotive Engineers of Japan*, 22(4), 511–518, October 2001.

10. A. Sciarretta, M. Back and L. Guzzella, "Optimal control of parallel hybrid electric vehicles," *IEEE Transactions on Control Systems Technology*, 12(3), 352–363, May 2004.
11. S.M.N. Hasan, I. Husain, R.J. Veillette and J.E. Carletta, "A PM brushless DC starter/generator system for a series/parallel 2×2 hybrid electric vehicle," *IEEE Transactions on Industry Applications*, 16(2), 12–21, March–April 2010.
12. N. Picot, *A Strategy to Blend Series and Parallel Modes of Operation in a Series-Parallel 2x2 Hybrid Diesel/Electric Vehicle*, MS Thesis, Electrical Engineering, The University of Akron, December 2007.

# Index